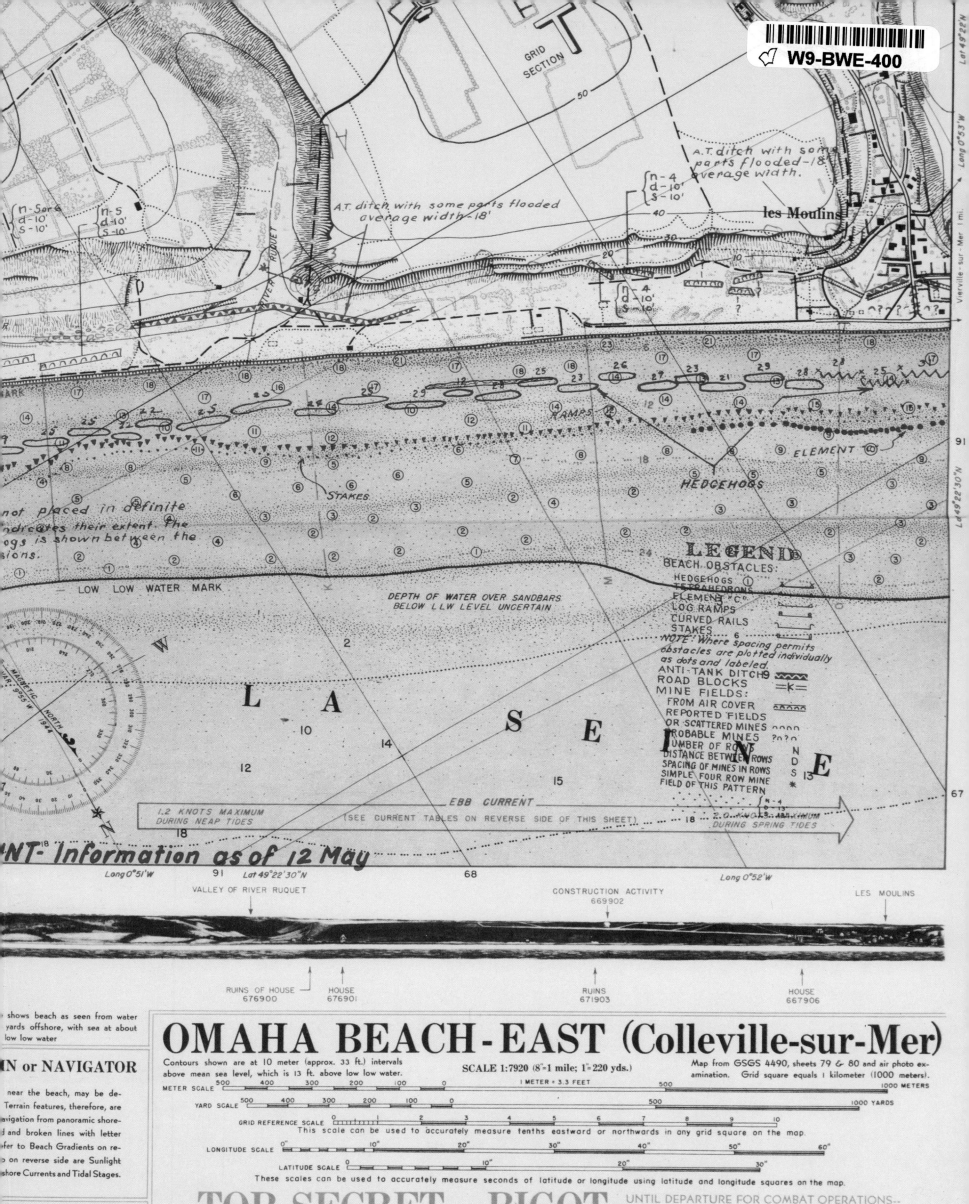

ATLAS OF WORLD WAR II

HISTORY'S GREATEST CONFLICT REVEALED THROUGH RARE WARTIME MAPS AND NEW CARTOGRAPHY

NEIL KAGAN | STEPHEN G. HYSLOP | FOREWORD BY KENNETH W. RENDELL

NATIONAL GEOGRAPHIC

WASHINGTON, D.C.

CONTRIBUTORS

NEIL KAGAN

Neil Kagan, editor, heads Kagan & Associates, Inc., a firm specializing in designing and producing innovative illustrated books. Formerly publisher/managing editor and director of new product development for Time-Life Books, he created numerous book series, including the award-winning *Voices of the Civil War*, *Our American Century*, and *What Life Was Like*. Recently, he edited *Great Photographs of World War II*, *Smithsonian Civil War*, and for National Geographic, the best-selling *Concise History of the World*, *Eyewitness to the Civil War*, *Atlas of the Civil War*, *The Untold Civil War*, *Eyewitness to World War II*, and *The Secret History of World War II*.

STEPHEN G. HYSLOP

Stephen G. Hyslop, author, has written several books on American and world history, including National Geographic's *The Secret History of World War II*, *Eyewitness to World War II*, *Eyewitness to the Civil War*, *Atlas of the Civil War*, and *The Old West*. A former writer and editor at Time-Life Books, he contributed to many volumes on the Second World War, including *Great Photographs of World War II* and *Lightning War*. His articles have appeared in *American History*, *World War II*, and the *History Channel Magazine*.

HARRIS J. ANDREWS

Harris J. Andrews, historian and consultant, specializes in American and world military history and material culture. He is a historian and artifact consultant for the National Museum of the United States Army Project, spanning four centuries of American military life and history. He was a consultant and contributing writer for National Geographic's *The Secret History of World War II*, *Eyewitness to World War II*, *Eyewitness to the Civil War*, and *Atlas of the Civil War*. He long served as a writer, editor, and consultant on military maps, arms, and equipment for Time-Life Books, contributing to its landmark series World War II and to numerous volumes on the Civil War.

KENNETH W. RENDELL

Kenneth W. Rendell, consultant, is the founder and director of The International Museum of World War II, which houses the world's most comprehensive collection of original artifacts and documents relating to the causes, events, and consequences of World War II. He began the collection in 1959 when no similar private or public collections were being formed. He opened the present building as a private museum in 2000 and opened it to the public in 2013 as a nonprofit museum, with unique exhibits and archives that tell the human story of the war, on home fronts and battlefronts. He is the author of *With Weapons and Wits: Propaganda and Psychological Warfare in World War II*; *World War II: Saving the Reality*; *Politics, War, and Personality: Fifty Iconic World War II Documents That Changed the World*; *The Power of Anti-Semitism, 1919–1939: The March to the Holocaust*; and two reference works on historical documents, *Forging History: The Detection of Fake Letters and Documents* and *History Comes to Life*. He was also a major contributor to National Geographic's *The Secret History of World War II*.

GREGORY UGIANSKY

Gregory Ugiansky, cartographer, researches and produces maps for National Geographic, specializing in historical cartography. Since 2000, his work has appeared in hundreds of titles, including travel guides, reference works, and atlases. He has been the lead cartographer for such National Geographic books as *The British World: An Illustrated Atlas*, *Pristine Seas: Journeys to the Ocean's Last Wild Places*, and *The Secret History of World War II*, and he has been a key member of the National Geographic cartographic team for *Family Reference Atlas of the World*, *Visual Atlas of the World*, and *Compact Atlas of the World*.

Allied invasion map of Sicily, July 1943

CONTENTS

CONTRIBUTORS 4

FOREWORD:
UNDERSTANDING WARTIME MAPS 8

ACKNOWLEDGMENTS 252

ADDITIONAL READING 252

ILLUSTRATION CREDITS 253

INDEX 254

ENDPAPERS Top secret reconnaissance maps of Omaha Beach East and Omaha Beach West on the coast of Normandy, prepared for the Allied invasion of occupied France on D-Day, June 6, 1944, showing in red German beach obstacles, mines, and other defenses.

PAGE 1 Soldiers of the U.S. 37th Infantry Division firing from behind a Sherman tank at Japanese troops on the Pacific island of Bougainville in early 1944.

PAGES 2-3 American B-24 Liberators of the U.S. 15th Air Force bombing oil refineries at Ploesti, Romania—a major source of fuel for the German war effort—on August 1, 1943.

PAGES 4-5 Map prepared for the Allied invasion of Sicily in July 1943, with handwritten notes designating landing zones and objectives.

CHAPTER ONE

PRELUDE TO WAR–1941
BLITZKRIEG
16

THE WAR AT A GLANCE 18

PRELUDE TO WAR 20
RISE OF THE DICTATORS 22

CLOSE-UP
THE NAZI DEATH CULT:
GLORIFYING HATRED AND DESTRUCTION 24
AGGRESSION AND APPEASEMENT 26

WAR IN THE EAST 28
THE WINTER WAR 30

WAR IN THE WEST 32
BLITZKRIEG IN THE LOWLANDS 34
ADVANCE TO THE ATLANTIC 36
DELIVERANCE AT DUNKIRK 38
FALL OF FRANCE 40

BATTLE OF BRITAIN 42
DOGFIGHTS FOR HIGH STAKES 44
A PUNISHING BLITZ 46

CLOSE-UP
OPERATION SEA LION 48
STRATEGIC BOMBING OF GERMANY 50

WAR IN THE BALKANS 52
STORMING CRETE 54

CLOSE-UP
SECRET PREPARATIONS
TO INVADE RUSSIA 56

OPERATION BARBAROSSA 58
CLOSE-UP
HOLOCAUST BY BULLETS 60
THE BATTLE FOR MOSCOW 62
CARNAGE IN THE "MEAT-GRINDER" 64

CHAPTER TWO

PRELUDE TO WAR–1943
WAR IN THE PACIFIC
66

THE WAR AT A GLANCE 68

PRELUDE TO WAR 70
CLOSE-UP
PLOTTING THE JAPANESE EMPIRE 72
THE INVASION OF CHINA 74
IMPERIAL RIVALRY IN THE FAR EAST 76

JAPAN'S STUNNING OFFENSIVE 78
THE PATH TO WAR 80
ASSAULT ON PEARL HARBOR 82

CLOSE-UP
SALVAGED FROM THE RUINS 84
DOMINATING THE FAR EAST 86
THE BATAAN DEATH MARCH 88

CARRIER WARFARE 90
CLOSE-UP
"I AM AN AMERICAN" 92
BATTLE OF THE CORAL SEA 94
TURNING POINT AT MIDWAY 96

CLOSE-UP
SECRET REPORT ON MIDWAY 98

ISLAND FIGHTING 100
CLOSE-UP
RELICS OF WAR 102
NAVAL BATTLES OFF THE SOLOMONS 104

CLOSE-UP
NATIONAL GEOGRAPHIC'S
WARTIME MAPS 106
BATTLES FOR PAPUA 108
DOWNING YAMAMOTO 110

CHAPTER THREE

1942–1944
BREAKING HITLER'S GRIP
112

THE WAR AT A GLANCE 114

RESISTING GERMAN DOMINATION 116
ESCAPE LINES TO FREEDOM 118
THE DIEPPE RAID 120

BATTLE OF THE ATLANTIC 122
CLOSE-UP
U-BOAT CHARTS AND INSTRUMENTS 124
THE AMERICAN SHOOTING SEASON 126
SOLVING THE ENIGMA 128

WAR IN THE DESERT 130
ROMMEL'S BIG PUSH 132
BATTLE LINES DRAWN IN EGYPT 134
BREAKTHROUGH AT EL ALAMEIN 136
OPERATION TORCH 138

THE ITALIAN CAMPAIGN 140
BRITISH LANDINGS 142
CLOSE-UP
PATTON'S RACE 144
ALLIED ADVANCES
IN SOUTHERN ITALY 146
COLLISION AT CASSINO 148
FROM ANZIO TO ROME 150

AIR WAR OVER EUROPE 152
TARGETING THE ENEMY 154
CLOSE-UP
ESCAPE MAPS FOR DOWNED AIRMEN 156
TUSKEGEE AIRMEN 158
BOMBING GERMAN CITIES 160
CLOSE-UP
THE OSS: DRAFTING INTELLIGENCE MAPS
162

RUSSIA RESURGENT 164
BRUTAL STRUGGLE AT KHARKOV 166
TURNING POINT AT STALINGRAD 168
A CLASH OF TITANS 170

THE FINAL SOLUTION 172

CHAPTER FOUR

1944–1945
VICTORY OVER GERMANY
174

THE WAR AT A GLANCE 176

THE INVASION OF NORMANDY 178
CLOSE-UP
OVERLORD AND BODYGUARD 180
D-DAY 182
EXPANDING THE BEACHHEAD 184
CLOSE-UP
FUELING FRENCH RESISTANCE 186

THE ALLIED BREAKOUT 188
OPERATION DRAGOON 190
THE LIBERATION OF PARIS 192
CLOSE-UP
VENGEANCE WEAPONS 194
PURSUIT TO THE WEST WALL 196
BATTLE OF THE BULGE 198
ACROSS THE RHINE 200
CLOSE-UP
LONG HAUL IN ITALY 202

DESTRUCTION OF NAZI GERMANY 204
DIVIDED AND CONQUERED 206
THE FALL OF BERLIN 208
CLOSE-UP
EXPOSING THE DEATH FACTORIES 210

CHAPTER FIVE

1943–1945
DEFEATING JAPAN
212

THE WAR AT A GLANCE 214

TWO PATHS TO TOKYO 216
CLOSE-UP
LESSONS IN ATOLL WARFARE 218
MACARTHUR'S ROAD BACK 220
CLOSE-UP
SURVIVAL OFF THE NEW GUINEA COAST 222
WAR UNDER THE PACIFIC 224
TAKING THE MARIANAS 226
BATTLE OF THE PHILIPPINE SEA 228

CHINA-BURMA-INDIA 230
CLOSE-UP
DETACHMENT 101:
BEHIND ENEMY LINES 232
FIGHT TO RECLAIM BURMA 234

RETURN TO THE PHILIPPINES 236
LAST HURRAH FOR JAPAN'S NAVY 238
ADVANCING TO LUZON AND MANILA 240

CLOSING IN ON JAPAN 242
CLOSE-UP
MAPPING IWO JIMA 244
OKINAWA: ORDEAL BY LAND AND SEA 246
SECRET PLANS TO DEFEAT JAPAN 248
HIROSHIMA AND NAGASAKI 250

PLOTTING THE BLITZ The Royal Air Force table map below and clock above, on display at The International Museum of World War II, are like those in the photo at right, taken during the war at an RAF Fighter Command operations room in London, where members of the Women's Auxiliary Air Force plotted incoming German warplanes on the map.

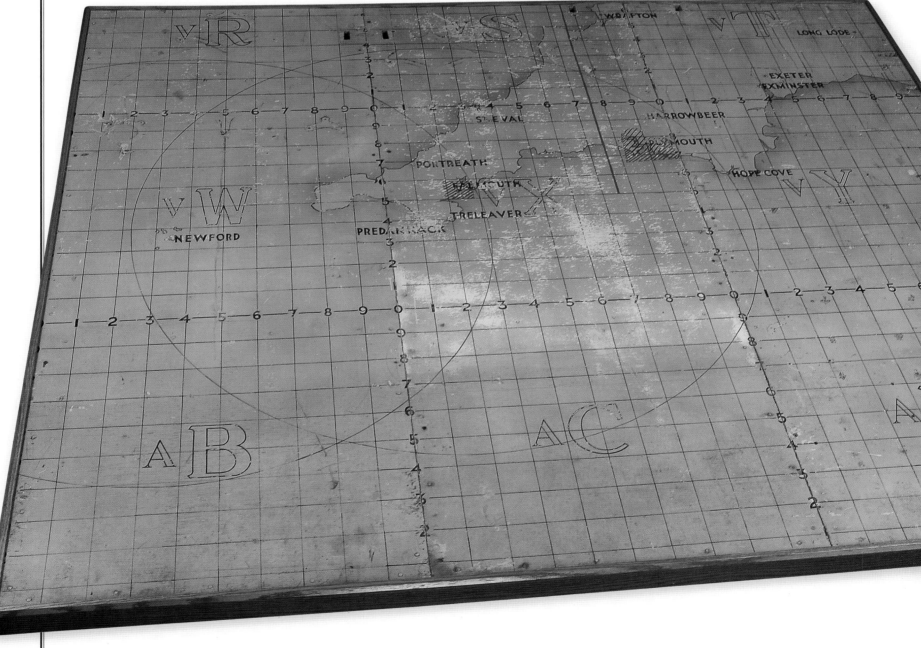

UNDERSTANDING WARTIME MAPS

Napoleon said that an army marches on its stomach, but armies wouldn't know where they were or where to march without maps. Napoleon's box of campaign maps was always at his side.

Maps are the core of military intelligence. They are secret because they show what commanders know and how they are planning to confront the enemy. If the Allies had obtained a map of German invasion plans in May 1940, they wouldn't have been trapped at Dunkirk. If the Germans had secured a map of the D-Day landing sites in Normandy, the Allies would have been driven back from those beaches into the sea.

This National Geographic *Atlas of World War II* may contain more military intelligence than ever gathered in one book. The rare wartime maps in this book, many of them published here for the first time, show what military leaders knew at the moment. Their handwritten annotations, tracing developments day by day, place readers alongside those commanders and planners, who could not be sure how their maps would change as the action unfolded. Such wartime maps offer us a window into a time when critical, life-or-death decisions were made. We look at them today and know how accurate or faulty their information about the enemy was, and how the commanders' troops actually performed. We see history from the perspective of the people using these maps, but we know their future and how their plans turned out. That knowledge is reflected in the National Geographic maps that accompany the wartime maps in this volume and portray crucial battles and campaigns as they actually unfolded. This is the only atlas that combines authoritative new maps and rare wartime maps to give readers a comprehensive view of World War II.

I began collecting maps in the 1960s. That collection, now numbering in the thousands, is exhibited at The International Museum of World War II, Boston, of which I am the founder and director. Located near Boston, the museum has the world's largest and most comprehensive collection of World War II artifacts, including 7,500 on exhibit and more than 500,000 artifacts and documents in its archives. Its exhibits explore the causes and consequences of the war and events on home fronts and battlefronts around the world—everything that made up the mosaic of life and death during the most momentous period in modern history. Without the maps on display at the museum, visitors could not understand the challenges commanders faced. Nearly 150 of the maps and artifacts in National Geographic's *Atlas of World War II* are from collections in the museum. They range in size from the eight-by-seven-foot Royal Air Force (RAF) operations-room table map used to plot the defense of southwest England against the Luftwaffe (left) to razor-thin tissue maps that could be rolled up and put in a pipe or cigarettes or between the front and back of playing cards (right) to help prisoners of war escape.

The RAF table was literally saved from the wrecking ball by a worker who offered it to a dealer, who then called me. I managed to get it shipped, and it eventually became part of the museum's map collection.

Some of the most important maps in that collection—those with handwritten notes

CARD TRICK The front of these playing cards could be peeled off to reveal an escape map printed on tissue paper. Such cards were issued to Allied servicemen to help them evade or escape capture by the Germans, who were alert to such tricks.

AERIAL MAPPING At left, Germans prepare to install a reconnaissance camera on a Luftwaffe Messerschmitt Me-110 in May 1941 during Gen. Erwin Rommel's North African campaign, aimed at seizing control of Egypt from the British. One such reconnaissance flight produced the negative image below of Alexandria, Egypt, on which German officers inscribed notes, identifying possible bombing targets. That aerial mapping allowed for more precise targeting than the 1940 Luftwaffe map of Alexandria at bottom.

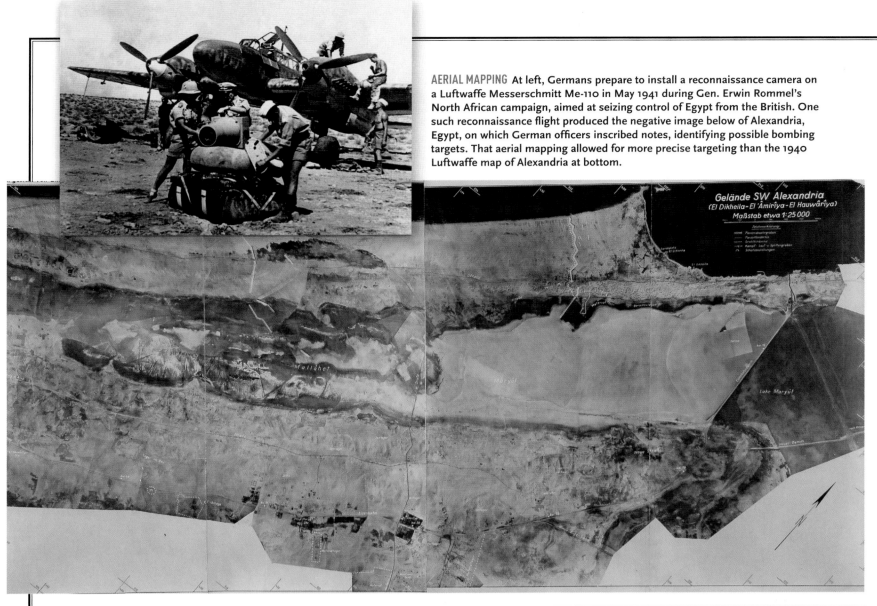

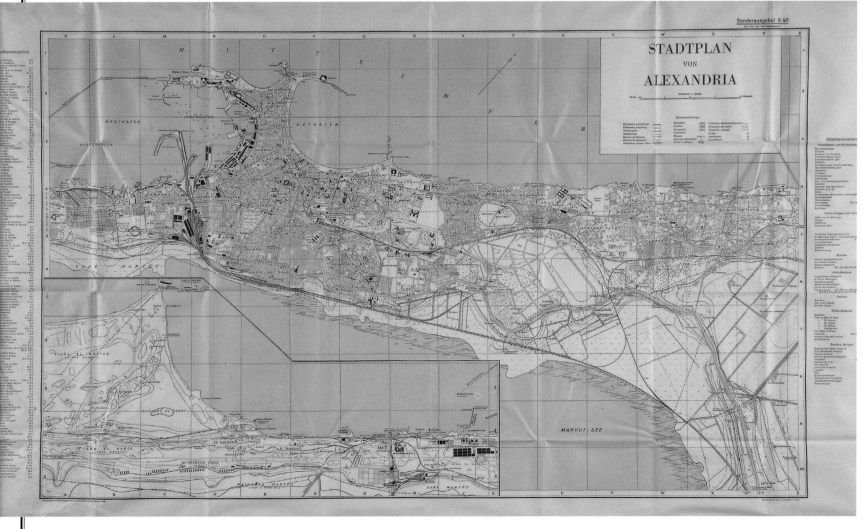

and markings—were acquired from aides who received them as souvenirs from top commanders or held on to the maps when the action moved forward and they were no longer needed. On the map below, handwritten notations in red show enemy positions—intelligence obtained from German prisoners and American patrols as the U.S. Army's VII Corps advanced through the Hurtgen Forest against the fortified West Wall or Siegfried Line on Germany's western frontier in late 1944. Notations on wartime maps were also based on intelligence acquired through aerial reconnaissance, as shown by a negative photograph taken over Alexandria, Egypt, a strategic port held by the British and targeted by the Germans (opposite top). Notes on that negative identifying British defensive positions could be used to refine basic maps like one used by the Luftwaffe to plan air raids on Alexandria (opposite bottom).

A German map of London on which bombing targets were outlined in red (pages 46-47) brought the war home to me in a very personal way. I obtained it from a Luftwaffe veteran who came to see me in my apartment in London's West End. That building was targeted on the map. It was chilling to view my apartment from the perspective of a German bomber intent on destruction. A large German U-boat map of the coast of New England (page 125) on display at the museum has a similar impact on visitors there. Students are struck by the fact that the war was waged right outside Boston Harbor (and other harbors on the East Coast). For a dramatic educational lesson, that map is hard to surpass. I was offered it along with other U-boat maps and a cylindrical computer used to determine a boat's position (page 124). I was so focused on the Boston Harbor map that I paid little attention to that device. I learned later that it was a milestone in navigational computers.

Some maps were produced during the war as propaganda, like one on a German leaflet dropped by air on British and French troops trapped between enemy forces and the sea at Dunkirk in June 1941 (page 38). The message it conveyed was calculated to instill a sense of doom in those stranded soldiers: "Look at this map! It gives your true situation. Your troops are entirely surrounded." Other wartime maps were hand-drawn by men in uniform, including a sketch of hostile terrain on the Pacific island of Guadalcanal (page 103), where U.S. Marines landed in August 1942. They were fighting the jungle as well as the Japanese, and that chart helped them overcome both. Another hand-drawn

BORDER WAR A map drawn up at U.S. VII Corps headquarters on October 31, 1944, traces in blue the line held by its troops—running through Stolberg, Germany, near the Belgian border—and designates opposing German units in red, based on intelligence acquired in part by interrogating prisoners like those shown surrendering below. American troops struggled to advance under fire through the dense Hurtgen Forest around Stolberg and did not drive deep into enemy territory until after the Germans counterattacked in December and were defeated in the ensuing Battle of the Bulge.

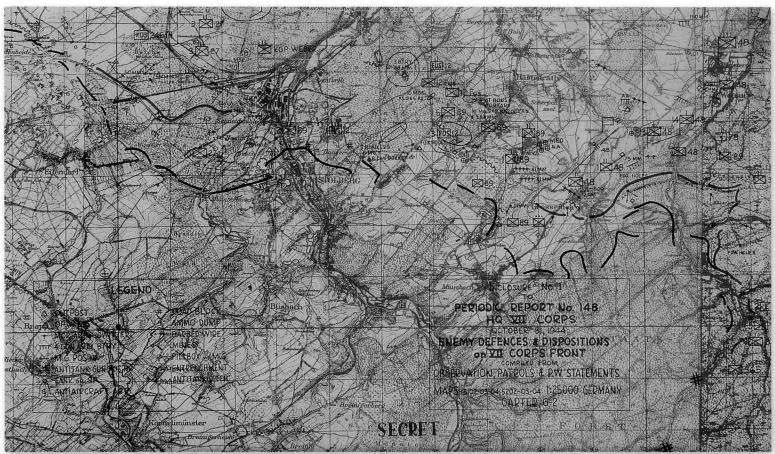

map displayed in the museum's collection, contained in the journal of Capt. Thomas Lanphier (page 111), shows the path he and other American fighter pilots followed from Guadalcanal in April 1943 when they downed the plane carrying Adm. Isoroku Yamamoto and killed that brilliant Japanese strategist, who planned the surprise attack on Pearl Harbor.

A Japanese map of Hawaii and Pearl Harbor is a great rarity. When I read in a Hawaii newspaper that an exhibition on Maui would include one, I assumed it was a reproduction, but I went to the exhibit out of curiosity. It turned out to be genuine, and that map (pages 80-81) and other extraordinary items offered by a Japanese collector who vacationed on Maui were soon on their way to the museum.

GLOBAL REACH The oil company Esso expanded its offerings from road maps to war maps like those above as people on the home front sought to keep track of distant campaigns and far-flung Americans in uniform, who by 1943 were stationed on nearly every continent and many Pacific islands.

INVASION MAPS

Every invasion starts with a map, and throughout this book the reader can examine maps for every major invasion that was conducted or planned during the war. A German map with handwritten details for the planned invasion of England (page 49), known as Operation Sea Lion, proved to be more hopeful than realistic. That operation was scrubbed in late 1940 when the Luftwaffe failed to neutralize the Royal Air Force. Secret German plans for the invasion of Russia included maps of Moscow (page 57), which Hitler hoped to seize within a matter of months. But German troops were stopped short of that city in late 1941 and met with disaster at Stalingrad the following winter. Few of the soldiers in German units designated on a rare Russian map of the fateful battle there (pages 168-69) survived. Stalingrad was the turning point of the war in Europe.

The original planning map for the invasion of Iwo Jima (opposite), conducted in February 1945 as American forces closed in on Japan, shows sketches in colored pencil for landings on both sides of the island (a landing zone on the southern coast was later chosen). Tissue overlays were used to sketch those different invasion possibilities, and dashed lines indicated the rapid progress toward the northern end of the island that the Marines were hoping for. Those projections turned out to be unrealistic because the Japanese had changed tactics. Instead of defending the island on the beaches, they dug in throughout the island, hoping to make an American victory as costly as possible. Preliminary air and naval bombardments had little effect on those Japanese troops.

IWO JIMA U.S. Marines of the 28th Regiment lay low under fire on the beach at Iwo Jima soon after the invasion of that Japanese-occupied island began on February 19, 1945. Mount Suribachi, pictured in the background, is charted at the southwestern tip of Iwo Jima on the original planning map for the invasion (opposite). Although plans called for Marines who landed on the island's south coast near Suribachi to advance rapidly to the east coast, it took them four days to silence enemy guns on that mountain and raise their flag atop it—and more than a month to crush resistance by Japanese troops holed up in bunkers and caves on Iwo Jima.

A relief table map of Iwo Jima displayed at the museum and pictured in this book (page 244) traces the painful yard-by-yard progress of the Marines on that embattled island. The map was on a command ship off the coast, and white chalk lines marked the slowly advancing American lines day by day. Not until 28 days after landing did the Marines reach the Japanese command post at the northern end of the island. Securing Iwo Jima and annihilating its 20,000 Japanese defenders, few of whom surrendered, cost the lives of more than 5,000 Marines. On a personal note, I carried a planning map for that invasion on a Marine Corps trip to Iwo Jima and used it while exploring the island's wartime bunkers and caves. Following that map took me back to 1945 and gave me a direct connection to the horrific battle.

Many invasion maps involved close reconnaissance by pilots, seamen, and frogmen who risked their lives to scout coastlines and chart paths for armed forces landing in enemy territory. Such efforts yielded extraordinarily detailed maps of landing zones, like those prepared for Allied troops who invaded Sicily (pages 142-43) or Normandy (pages 182-83 and the book's endpapers). The D-Day landings in Normandy were the greatest invasion of all and required hundreds of charts to which thousands of people

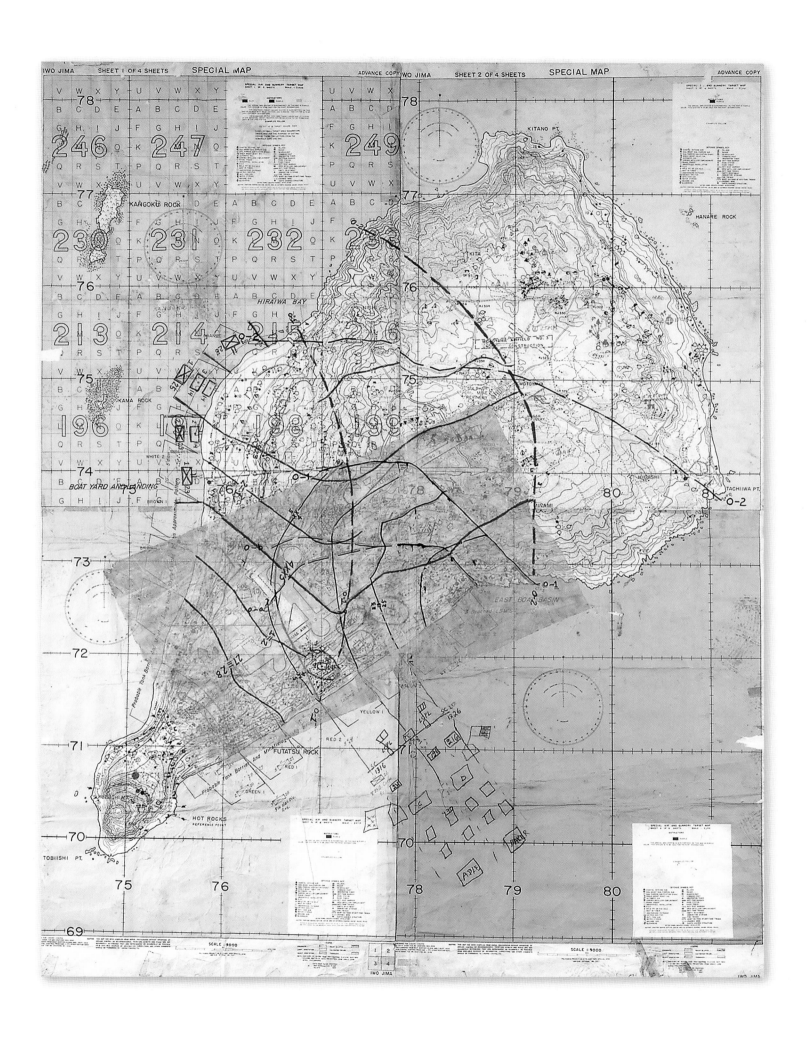

contributed. Some of those maps were forecasts based on intelligence estimates, showing what Allied forces were expected to achieve by D+1—one day after landing—D+2 (page 181), and subsequent days up to D+90, all of which are in the collection at the museum. Others were situation maps, showing the actual positions of forces on any given day (page 192). Commanders used such maps to make momentous decisions such as where and when to attack as Allied troops in occupied France advanced toward Germany.

ESCAPE MAPS

Maps designed by Allied authorities to help prisoners of war escape (pages 156-57) were printed on tissue paper or silk—silk was favored because it is waterproof and doesn't make noise when handled—and smuggled into prisons in various ways. Some were hidden along with tiny compasses in charity parcels sent to prisoners of war (POWs). Others were sewn into the lining of jackets worn by pilots flying over enemy territory. (Compasses were concealed inside their buttons and cap badges.) The son of one of the men involved in creating tissue maps offered me those his father had saved—after being ordered at the end of the war to burn every trace of that clandestine operation.

The Germans knew the Allies were smuggling maps into prisoner camps and intercepted most of them. Many POWs who hoped to reach freedom relied on maps drawn from memory by prisoners, including those who escaped and were captured and brought back. Once they were out of solitary confinement, they added what they had learned to maps composed earlier by prisoners and captured escapees. The results were copied by hand for future escapees. Shown opposite are a few of the hand-drawn maps displayed in the museum, all of which are from Colditz Castle in Germany, a POW camp for defiant officers who might try to escape or had already done so. It was Germany's Alcatraz, an imposing prison from which 130 men nonetheless managed to escape, most of whom were caught sooner or later. In one case, four inmates escaped from the prisoners' theater at Colditz by climbing down a rope made of checkered blankets into a room that offered them a way out (left). Two of them were captured, but the other two reached neutral Switzerland. The commandant at Colditz collected everything used in such escape attempts and placed them in an "escape museum" to train security officers for the camps. At the end of the war, Colditz was in the Soviet zone and the collection was stored in a basement. Years later, when the commandant returned from a Siberian prison, he reclaimed it, and I eventually acquired most of his collection.

Other maps in this book take you to the table where commanders studied them. You are at their side, examining the intelligence. You can almost see them annotating the maps and marking them up for action—where to attack, when to attack, which units should move first. But for me, nothing can rival the haunting feeling of reading a hand-drawn escape map from Colditz and realizing how difficult it was for those who contributed to the map to get away when they had little idea of what lay ahead. They would know from the stars the direction to Switzerland, but exactly how far they had to travel and what stood between them and freedom remained unknown. And everything they did know, all the information on their map, had been learned at great cost and repeated failure. You can feel the anxiety as they passed beyond the map's boundaries into the unknown. They couldn't ask for directions.

—Kenneth W. Rendell
Founder and Director
The International Museum of World War II

TOWERING PRISON Colditz Castle, perched on a hilltop above the Mulde River in Germany, was considered escape-proof by some authorities. But many resourceful Allied prisoners of war held there managed to break out of the castle—including four men who descended through a hole in the floor of a theater where prisoners staged shows (right) and walked out the gate dressed as German officers. Many escapees from Colditz carried hand-drawn maps like those pictured opposite.

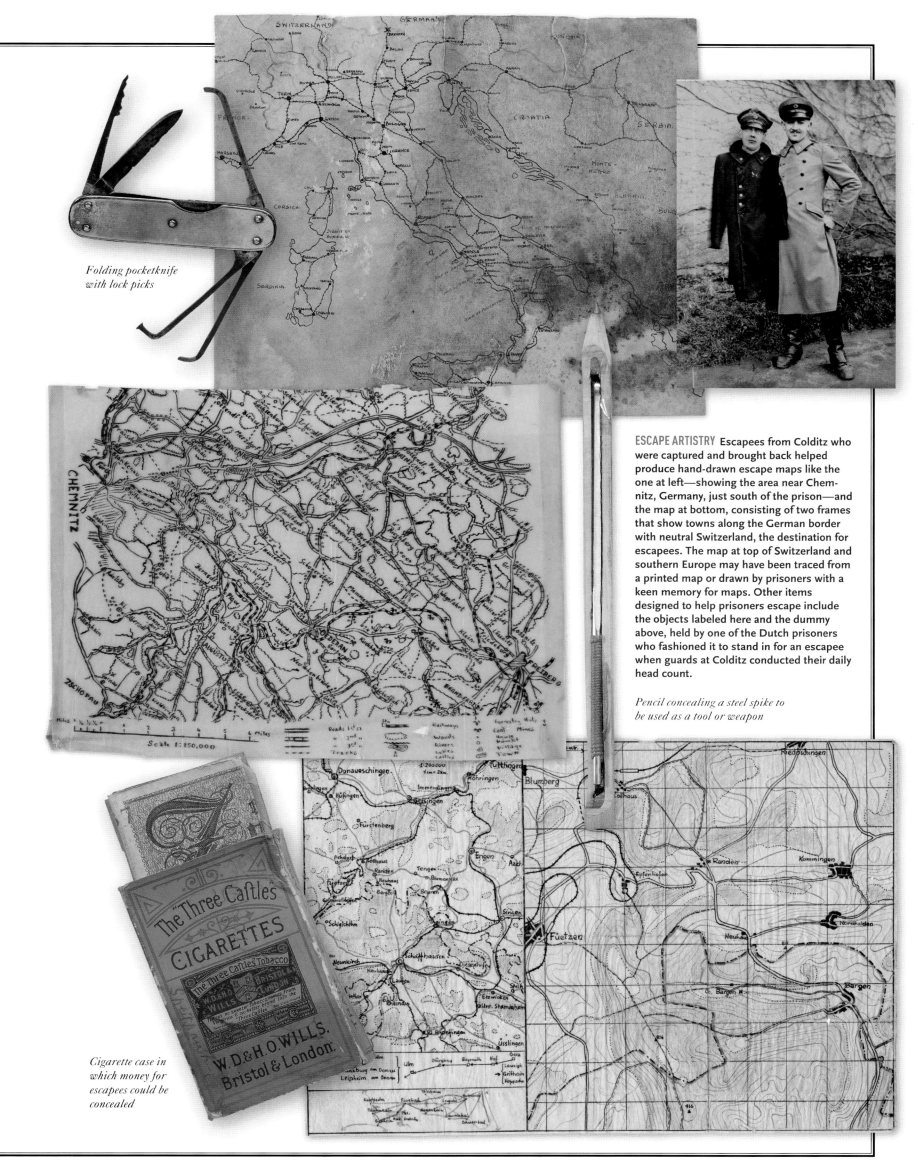

Folding pocketknife with lock picks

ESCAPE ARTISTRY Escapees from Colditz who were captured and brought back helped produce hand-drawn escape maps like the one at left—showing the area near Chemnitz, Germany, just south of the prison—and the map at bottom, consisting of two frames that show towns along the German border with neutral Switzerland, the destination for escapees. The map at top of Switzerland and southern Europe may have been traced from a printed map or drawn by prisoners with a keen memory for maps. Other items designed to help prisoners escape include the objects labeled here and the dummy above, held by one of the Dutch prisoners who fashioned it to stand in for an escapee when guards at Colditz conducted their daily head count.

Pencil concealing a steel spike to be used as a tool or weapon

Cigarette case in which money for escapees could be concealed

CHAPTER 1

"Further successes
are impossible without
the shedding of blood."

ADOLF HITLER, MAY 1939

FIREFIGHT German soldiers race through a blazing Norwegian village in April 1940. The rapid
invasion of Norway was the precursor to a stunning blitzkrieg (lightning war) in which German
troops and tanks overran the Low Countries and
conquered France in just six weeks.

HITLER'S ONSLAUGHT
SETTING EUROPE ABLAZE

In November 1938, Adolf Hitler observed the 15th anniversary of his Munich "Beer Hall" Putsch—a revolt that failed but set him on the path to power—by reminding fellow Nazis that it was also the 20th anniversary of the armistice that ended the Great War in which he served, a ruinous conflict that left Germany shattered. "Had Fate put me at the helm back then," he claimed, "this collapse would never have come about." He traced defeat in 1918 not to the might of the opposing Allies but to the "blindness" of the German people, among them revolutionaries who undermined a crumbling war effort that Hitler refused to admit was already doomed. He himself was blinded by that defeat, which warped his worldview. He demonized those he blamed for subverting the imperial German Reich, notably communists and Jews, for whom his hatred was pathological. And he lashed out at German leaders who accepted Allied peace terms. Hitler's Munich revolt, inspired by Benito Mussolini's coup in Rome, landed him in prison, where he composed his manifesto, *Mein Kampf* (My Struggle). He went on to become chancellor of Germany in 1933 before seizing power as the nation's dictatorial Führer (leader) and forging a menacing new Reich.

By mid-1939, Hitler had annexed Austria and occupied Czechoslovakia. After failing to halt his aggression by appeasing him, British and French leaders pledged to fight if Poland was attacked, as Hitler intended to give Germans *lebensraum* (living space). He was ready to take up where he left off in 1918 by waging war, not just against his old Allied foes but against the Reich's supposed internal enemies, whom Nazis had recently targeted by assailing Jews on November 9–10, 1938, known as Kristallnacht—the Night of Broken Glass.

To avoid the long struggle that exhausted Germans in the last war, commanders prepared for blitzkrieg, led by armored units supported by the Luftwaffe, the Reich's formidable air force. Such tactics helped German troops crush Poland in September 1939 and conquer France with staggering speed in June 1940. Yet Great Britain (United Kingdom), with its powerful navy and stout air defenses, defied invasion and withstood the Luftwaffe's punishing Blitz. In June 1941, Hitler turned against Soviet dictator Joseph Stalin and invaded Russia, striking like lightning before his forces bogged down and were driven back from Moscow. Convinced that Germans were racially superior and would soon triumph, Hitler instead faced a prolonged war of the sort that had brought down the Reich in 1918.

July 28–August 4, 1914 World War I begins between the Central Powers of Germany, Austria-Hungary, and the Ottoman Empire and the Allied Powers of France, Great Britain, and Russia.

November 7, 1917 Bolsheviks seize power in the Russian imperial capital Petrograd (known later as Leningrad and today as St. Petersburg). Their leader Vladimir Lenin will soon act on his pledge to withdraw Russia from the war.

November 11, 1918 World War I ends as Germany, the last of the Central Powers still engaged in combat, yields to the Allies and agrees to an armistice.

June 28, 1919 Treaty of Versailles signed, imposing stringent peace terms on Germany, redrawing the map of Europe, and establishing the League of Nations.

October 28–31, 1922 Fascists march on Rome in support of Benito Mussolini, Italy's emerging dictator.

November 8–9, 1923 Hitler's failed Munich "Beer Hall" Putsch brings him notoriety.

January 21, 1924 Soviet leader Vladimir Lenin dies in Moscow. Joseph Stalin begins maneuvering to succeed him.

Hitler portrayed as a Teutonic Knight

September 1, 1939 World War II begins as German forces invade Poland, leading France and Britain to declare war on Germany.

September, 27, 1939 Polish capital Warsaw falls to the Germans.

November 30, 1939 Soviet troops invade Finland, where they will face strong opposition in the ensuing Winter War.

March 13, 1940 Finland comes to terms with Russia by ceding territory demanded by Stalin.

April 9, 1940 German forces conquer Denmark and invade Norway.

May 10, 1940 Germans invade the Low Countries of Belgium, Luxembourg, and the Netherlands with the ultimate objective of conquering France.

June 4, 1940 Dunkirk falls to the Germans after more than 330,000 Allied soldiers are evacuated from that French port to England.

June 5, 1940 German forces in northern France advance southward toward Paris.

June 14, 1940 Paris falls to the invaders.

June 15–16, 1940 Soviet troops occupy the Baltic states of Latvia, Lithuania, and Estonia.

June 22, 1940 France surrenders to Germany and is divided into a German-occupied zone in the north and a German-dependent zone in the south, administered at Vichy by the compliant Marshal Philippe Pétain.

July 10, 1940 German warplanes of the Luftwaffe launch initial attacks on British ports and convoys.

August 1, 1940 Hitler orders the Luftwaffe to neutralize the Royal Air Force (RAF) as a prerequisite for Operation Sea Lion (planned invasion of Britain).

Stuka dive-bomber in action during the German invasion of Poland

May 21, 1927 First solo flight across the Atlantic is completed in Paris by American Charles Lindbergh, who will later emerge as a prominent isolationist, urging the United States to avoid war with Nazi Germany.

October 24, 1929 Stock market crash begins in the United States, triggering the Great Depression, which will cause economic and political turmoil in Europe and elsewhere around the world.

January 30, 1933 Hitler becomes chancellor of Germany before assuming absolute power as the nation's Führer.

March 4, 1933 Franklin D. Roosevelt is sworn in as president of the United States and pledges that America will act internationally as a good neighbor, respecting "the rights of others."

May 21, 1935 Hitler renounces the Treaty of Versailles and proceeds with rearmament of Germany.

October 3, 1935 Italian forces invade Ethiopia in defiance of the League of Nations.

Propaganda Minister Joseph Goebbels and a "People's Receiver," with limited reception for German radio broadcasts

July 18, 1936 Gen. Francisco Franco launches the Spanish Civil War against the Republican government in Madrid. German and Italian military aid will help Franco win the war three years later.

March 12, 1938 Hitler annexes Austria.

September 30, 1938 British and French leaders yield to Hitler at Munich, allowing him to seize the Sudetenland in Czechoslovakia.

November 9–10, 1938 Propaganda Minister Joseph Goebbels incites attacks by Nazis on Jewish homes, businesses, and synagogues on Kristallnacht (the Night of Broken Glass), leading to the internment of 30,000 German Jews in concentration camps.

March 15, 1939 German troops occupy the remainder of Czechoslovakia.

August 23, 1939 Germany and the Soviet Union conclude a nonaggression pact, including a secret protocol that allows Hitler to seize most of Poland and Stalin to occupy the rest and to threaten the Baltic states and Finland.

Star of David emblem that Nazi authorities required Jews to wear

---

August 13, 1940 Luftwaffe campaign against the RAF begins in earnest.

September 7, 1940 At Hitler's order, the Luftwaffe shifts focus of attacks from the RAF to London and other cities.

September 15, 1940 The RAF inflicts heavy losses on German warplanes attacking London and other targets in what will be remembered as the decisive Battle of Britain Day.

September 17, 1940 Hitler postpones Operation Sea Lion until further notice. Luftwaffe "Blitz" of London and other cities will continue until May 1941, causing extensive damage and casualties but leaving the British war effort intact.

September 27, 1940 Tripartite Pact, signed by Germany, Italy, and Japan, commits those Axis nations to defend one another against attack but does not require them to act in unison offensively.

October 28, 1940 Italian troops in occupied Albania invade Greece, leading the Greek government to ally with Britain against the Axis.

December 18, 1940 Hitler issues Führer Directive 21, ordering his forces to prepare for Operation Barbarossa (invasion of the Soviet Union) within five months.

March 25, 1941 Yugoslavia commits to the Axis, joining Romania, Hungary, and Bulgaria as Hitler prepares to seize Greece and secure the Balkans prior to Operation Barbarossa.

March 27, 1941 Yugoslav officers take power in Belgrade and break with the Axis, prompting Hitler to invade Yugoslavia as well as Greece.

April 6, 1941 Invasion of Yugoslavia and Greece begins.

April 12–13, 1941 Yugoslav capital Belgrade falls to the Germans.

April 27, 1941 Greek capital Athens falls to the Germans as British forces in Greece prepare to evacuate to Crete.

May 20, 1941 German airborne invasion of Crete begins.

Air-raid warden comforting a bombing victim during the Battle of Britain

June 1, 1941 Last Allied troops holding out on Crete are evacuated.

June 22, 1941 More than three million German troops, divided among Army Groups North, Center, and South, launch invasion of the Soviet Union with allied Axis forces.

June 28, 1941 German panzer divisions (armored units) converge at Minsk in a massive encirclement of Russian forces.

July 27, 1941 Army Group Center completes encirclement of Russians at Smolensk, within 200 miles of Moscow.

August 21, 1941 Hitler delays the advance on Moscow by ordering panzers of Army Group Center to help Army Group South take Kiev.

September 8, 1941 Leningrad is cut off and besieged by Army Group North.

September 19, 1941 Russians lose the battle for Kiev after suffering nearly one million casualties.

September 30, 1941 German armored advance on Moscow resumes.

December 5–6, 1941 Soviet troops around Moscow launch a counterattack and drive Germans back from the capital.

December 11, 1941 Following the attack on Pearl Harbor by Germany's Axis partner Japan, Hitler declares war on the United States.

December 16, 1941 Hitler issues stand-fast order to troops under attack in Russia, but many German units will continue to retreat from Moscow and others will struggle to stave off encirclement before the Soviet winter offensive ends.

ОТСТОИМ МОСКВУ!

Red Army poster exhorting Russians to "Fight for Moscow!"

PRELUDE TO WAR

FROM THE GREAT WAR TO AN EVEN GREATER CONFLICT

CHRONOLOGY

NOVEMBER 11, 1918 World War I ends as Germany yields and agrees to an armistice.

JUNE 28, 1919 Treaty of Versailles signed.

OCTOBER 28–31, 1922 Fascists march on Rome in support of Benito Mussolini.

JANUARY 21, 1924 Soviet leader Vladimir Lenin dies. Joseph Stalin maneuvers to succeed him.

JANUARY 30, 1933 Hitler becomes chancellor of Germany before assuming absolute power as the nation's Führer.

OCTOBER 3, 1935 Italian forces invade Ethiopia in defiance of the League of Nations.

JULY 18, 1936 Gen. Francisco Franco launches revolt in Spain.

MARCH 12, 1938 Hitler annexes Austria.

SEPTEMBER 30, 1938 Britain and France yield to Hitler at Munich, allowing him to seize the Sudetenland in Czechoslovakia.

MARCH 15, 1939 German troops occupy the rest of Czechoslovakia.

TRENCH WARFARE Perilous assaults like this one during World War I devastated regiments, whose casualties were compounded by chemical warfare—which led the cavalryman at top to don a gas mask—and awful conditions in trenches, where rats spread disease and gnawed at corpses (opposite). Fighter pilots avoided those horrors, but few served more than a month before being killed or wounded in a crash (opposite top).

Some called it the "war to end all wars," but the ruinous conflict that concluded in 1918 was in fact a tragic precursor to the global catastrophe that erupted in 1939. World War I began in 1914 as a struggle between the Central Powers of Germany, Austria-Hungary, and the Ottoman Empire and the Allied Powers of Britain, France, and Russia, joined by Italy in 1915 and the United States in 1917. Because the original antagonists were all empires, the war extended to some of their colonies in Africa and Asia, but it was waged largely in Europe, where the casualties were appalling. After German forces invaded France through Belgium and were stopped short of Paris, the opposing sides dug in and engaged in trench warfare, resulting in horrendous losses when troops tried to advance under murderous artillery and machine-gun fire. Aerial duels in rudimentary warplanes were dramatic but had little impact on campaigns, and tanks figured significantly only late in the war as the Allies pushed the Germans back and the Central Powers collapsed.

The peace treaty signed at Versailles in 1919 established the League of Nations to resolve disputes but failed to stabilize a continent convulsed when empires fractured. Russia, which withdrew from the war in 1917 during the Bolshevik Revolution and reemerged as the Soviet Union, was not invited to the peace conference and hoped to recover lost ground. Germany had to accept blame for the war and pay reparations and was allowed only a skeletal army of 100,000 men and no air force—terms that swelled the resentments of Hitler and other embittered German veterans. British prime minister David Lloyd George proved prophetic when he warned that if Germany felt unjustly treated at Versailles, "she would find means of exacting retribution from her conquerors." Italy felt slighted as well after gaining little at Versailles to satisfy its imperial ambitions. Postwar economic chaos left millions susceptible to the appeals of fascist strongmen like Mussolini and Hitler, the latter of whom exploited turmoil caused by hyperinflation in the early 1920s and the Great Depression a decade later. By the late 1930s, Hitler and Mussolini had defied the Treaty of Versailles and the League of Nations—which lacked power to punish aggressors—and were backing fellow dictator Francisco Franco in the Spanish Civil War, which foreshadowed a second world war that would far surpass the dreadful toll of the first. ■

REALIGNMENT The defeat of the Central Powers in 1918 shattered the German, Austro-Hungarian, and Ottoman empires, whose prewar borders are shown at right, and reshaped Europe (below). New nations such as Czechoslovakia and Yugoslavia emerged that were internally divided and vulnerable to foreign aggression. Poland was reconstituted and waged war to avoid being reabsorbed by Russia under Lenin, whose Soviet forces crushed Ukraine's bid for independence. By the 1930s, Poland was in a precarious position between the Soviet Union under Stalin and Germany under Hitler, who hoped to annex ethnically German lands such as Austria and the Polish Corridor, separating East Prussia from the rest of Germany. Hitler also intended to reoccupy the Rhineland and had designs on Alsace-Lorraine, which France reacquired from Germany in 1919. France sought insurance against German aggression by maintaining its alliance with Britain and forging an alliance with Poland that proved fateful in 1939.

CENTRAL EUROPE IN 1914

0 mi 200
0 km 200

EUROPE AFTER THE 1919 PEACE CONFERENCE
Unresolved Strife and the Roots of Future Conflicts

June 1920

— Determined or ratified political boundary
- - - Undetermined or unratified political boundary
····· Limit of occupation
— 1914 political boundary

▨ Territory lost by Germany
▨ Territory of the dissolved Austro-Hungarian Empire
▨ Territory of the dissolved Ottoman Empire
▨ Territory lost by Russia

Labels in red indicate new entities or entities that experienced significant boundary and/or political system changes between 1914 and 1920.

0 mi 200
0 km 200

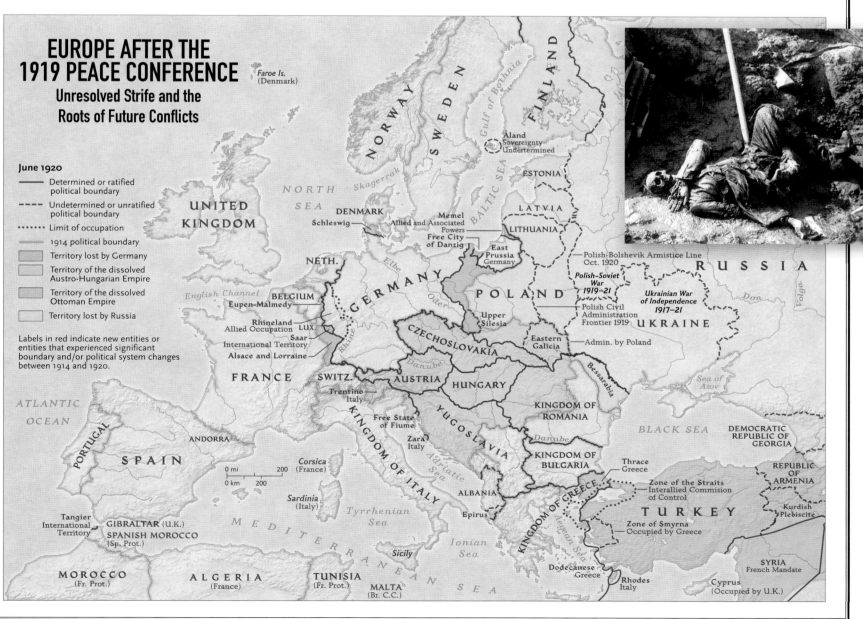

RISE OF THE DICTATORS

I n the chaotic aftermath of World War I, dictators filled the void left when European empires collapsed by forging aggressive new imperial regimes. Fascist demagogue Mussolini (shown gesturing at right) was saluted like an ancient Roman emperor by followers with right arm raised. As Italy's new Caesar, he yearned for conquest and used existing Italian colonies in Africa as staging grounds for his brutal invasion of Ethiopia in 1935. Fascist salutes and strong-arm tactics were also employed by Nazis to help Hitler establish his Third Reich, which followed the first German empire in the Middle Ages and the second that collapsed when Kaiser Wilhelm II abdicated in 1918. Like the Kaiser (German for "Caesar"), Hitler was the Reich's supreme commander, to whom officers swore loyalty. Civilians also signaled their devotion to the Führer and his emerging empire with the greeting "Heil Hitler," the Nazi equivalent of "Hail Caesar."

As right-wing dictators intent on crushing communism, Hitler and Mussolini became allies and backed General Franco's rebellion against Spain's left-wing Republican government (opposite). The Republicans, whose ranks included Marxists and anarchists, were aided by Stalin, who reconstituted the Russian empire by expanding on the ruthless measures of former tsars (Russian "Caesars") and the Bolsheviks who seized power in 1917. Soviet troops joined volunteers from the United States, Britain, and other countries on the Republican side, but the Western democracies remained officially neutral and failed to stop German bombers from blasting Madrid, Guernica, and other Republican strongholds and helping Franco achieve victory in early 1939. The lesson of the Spanish Civil War was that neutrality was no defense against fascist dictators using modern weapons to fulfill age-old dreams of imperial dominance. ■

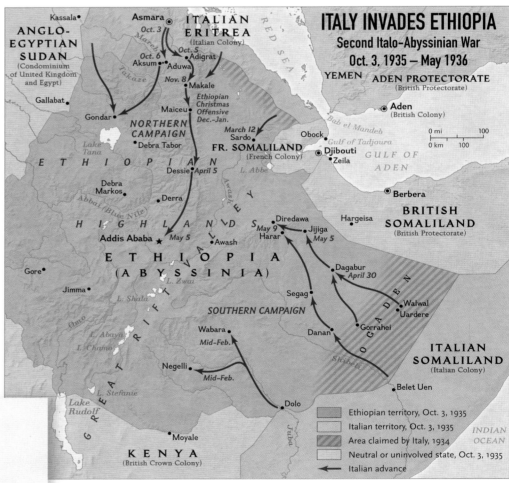

ITALY INVADES ETHIOPIA
Second Italo-Abyssinian War
Oct. 3, 1935 – May 1936

ETHIOPIA BESIEGED In late 1935, Mussolini's forces invaded Ethiopia (also known as Abyssinia) from Italian Somaliland and Eritrea (map above). Emperor Haile Selassie called up all Ethiopian men, but many were armed only with spears or outmoded rifles like the warriors at left. The main Italian thrust descended from Eritrea, bolstered by warplanes and artillery that launched poison-gas attacks. In May 1936, the capital of Addis Ababa fell, and Haile Selassie fled to London. "It was us today," he told Western leaders who appeased Mussolini in a futile effort to keep him from backing Hitler. "It will be you tomorrow."

GENERALISSIMO Shown here in uniform offering a Spanish version of the fascist salute, Gen. Francisco Franco rebelled against the Republican government in Madrid in July 1936 with troops from Spanish Morocco. As mapped below, his Nationalist forces captured Badajoz in Extremadura, bordering Portugal, then besieged Madrid with support from the German Condor Legion, whose air raids were denounced on a Republican poster showing a young bombing victim (inset right). Republicans clung to Madrid and much of eastern Spain but fought among themselves in Barcelona in May 1937 and gradually lost ground. By October 1937, Nationalists had seized the Basque region extending along the Bay of Biscay from San Sebastián in Gipuzkoa. In 1938, they advanced eastward into Aragon and reached the Mediterranean, cutting off Barcelona and the rest of defiant Catalonia, which fell in February 1939. Madrid fell in late March, and the Republicans surrendered on April 1. Franco emerged as Spain's dictator, owing much to Hitler and Mussolini, but he resisted joining the Axis.

MADRID
THE "MILITARY" PRACTICE OF THE REBELS

IF YOU TOLERATE THIS YOUR CHILDREN WILL BE NEXT

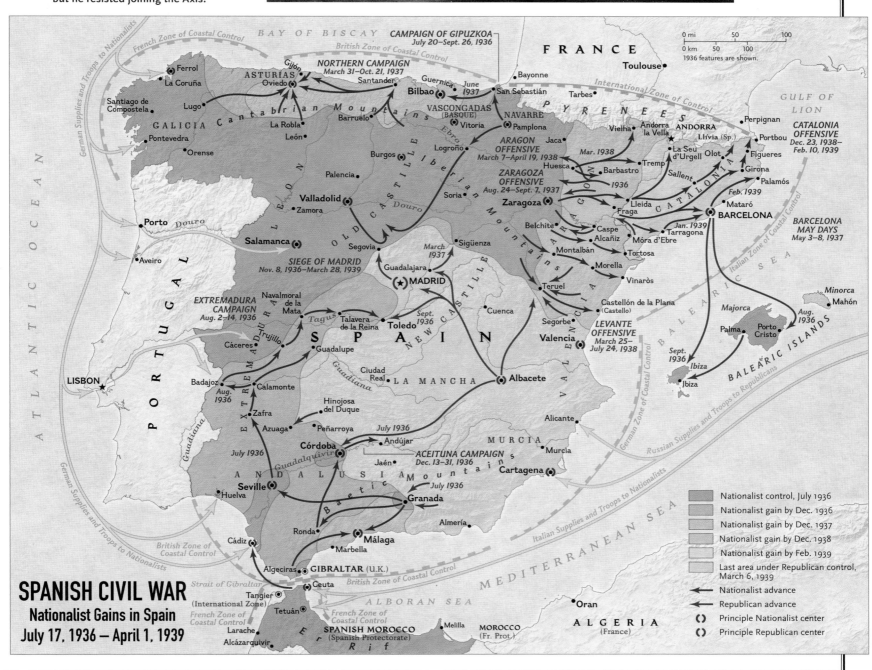

SPANISH CIVIL WAR
Nationalist Gains in Spain
July 17, 1936 – April 1, 1939

Nationalist control, July 1936
Nationalist gain by Dec. 1936
Nationalist gain by Dec. 1937
Nationalist gain by Dec. 1938
Nationalist gain by Feb. 1939
Last area under Republican control, March 6, 1939
Nationalist advance
Republican advance
Principle Nationalist center
Principle Republican center

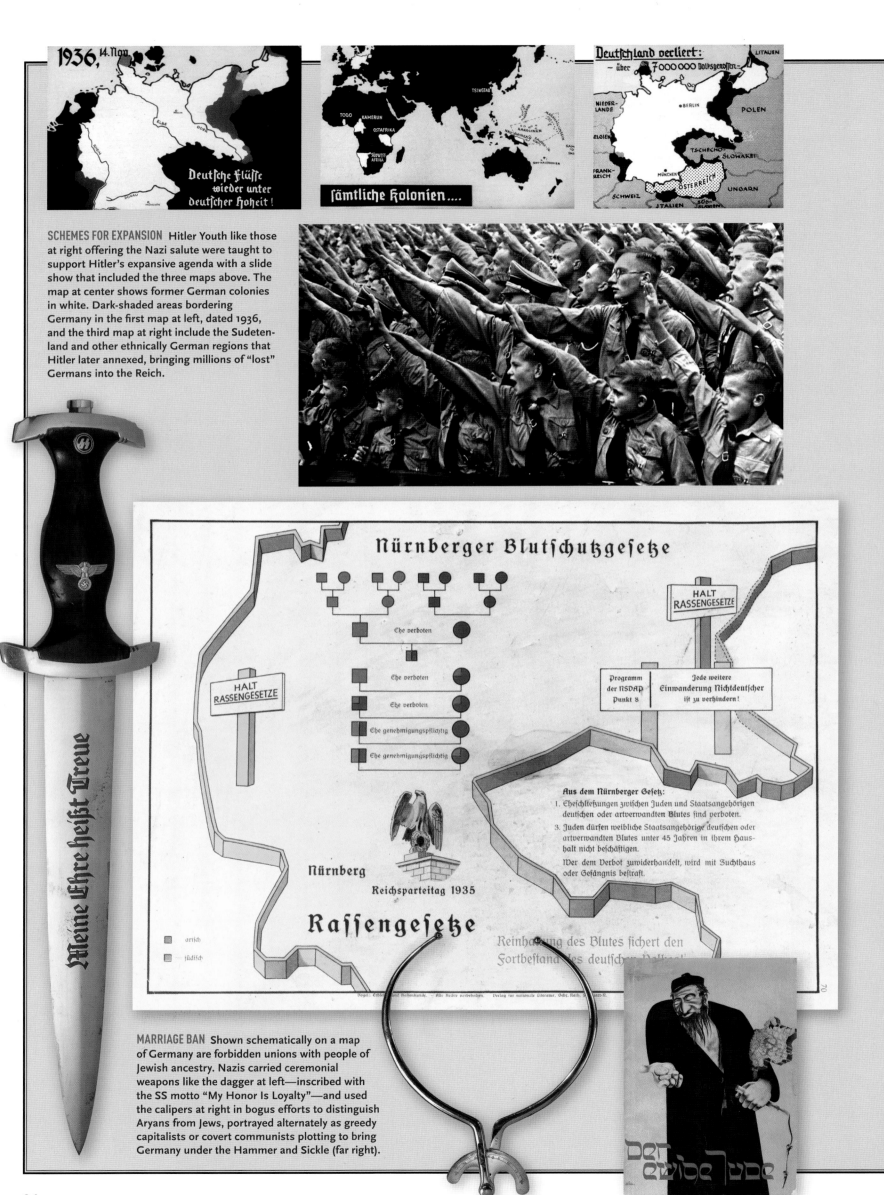

1936, 14. Nov. Deutsche Flüsse wieder unter deutscher Hoheit!

sämtliche Kolonien....

Deutschland verliert: — über 7 000 000 Volksgenossen —

SCHEMES FOR EXPANSION Hitler Youth like those at right offering the Nazi salute were taught to support Hitler's expansive agenda with a slide show that included the three maps above. The map at center shows former German colonies in white. Dark-shaded areas bordering Germany in the first map at left, dated 1936, and the third map at right include the Sudetenland and other ethnically German regions that Hitler later annexed, bringing millions of "lost" Germans into the Reich.

Meine Ehre heißt Treue

Nürnberger Blutschutzgesetze

HALT RASSENGESETZE

Ehe verboten

Ehe verboten

Ehe verboten

Ehe genehmigungspflichtig

Ehe genehmigungspflichtig

HALT RASSENGESETZE

Programm der NSDAP Punkt 8

Jede weitere Einwanderung Nichtdeutscher ist zu verhindern!

Aus dem Nürnberger Gesetz:

1. Eheschließungen zwischen Juden und Staatsangehörigen deutschen oder artverwandten Blutes sind verboten.

3. Juden dürfen weibliche Staatsangehörige deutschen oder artverwandten Blutes unter 45 Jahren in ihrem Haushalt nicht beschäftigen.

Wer dem Verbot zuwiderhandelt, wird mit Zuchthaus oder Gefängnis bestraft.

Nürnberg

Reichsparteitag 1935

Rassengesetze

Reinhaltung des Blutes sichert den Fortbestand des deutschen Volkes

artisch
jüdisch

MARRIAGE BAN Shown schematically on a map of Germany are forbidden unions with people of Jewish ancestry. Nazis carried ceremonial weapons like the dagger at left—inscribed with the SS motto "My Honor Is Loyalty"—and used the calipers at right in bogus efforts to distinguish Aryans from Jews, portrayed alternately as greedy capitalists or covert communists plotting to bring Germany under the Hammer and Sickle (far right).

THE NAZI DEATH CULT: GLORIFYING HATRED AND DESTRUCTION

As Hitler rose to prominence, Nazis fostered a malignant cult that demanded unquestioning loyalty to the Führer and taught his followers to fulfill their destiny as a master race by dominating and displacing supposedly inferior races. Hundreds of thousands of people attended hypnotic rallies where Hitler's hateful rhetoric held them spellbound. Boys inducted into the Hitler Youth underwent rigorous physical and military training and imbibed Nazi propaganda. "From childhood onward," one of them recalled, "we were drilled in toughness and blind obedience." The Nazi League of German Girls also stressed physical fitness, but the imperative for young women was to bear healthy children to bolster Hitler's expansive Reich. Those who gave birth to deformed or mentally impaired children, however, risked having them removed to institutions, where beginning in 1939 "defective" youngsters and adults were killed. Some perished in gas chambers, a method later used to annihilate millions at Nazi killing centers.

The death cult at the heart of Hitler's regime was embraced and enforced by the SS, which originated as his Schutzstaffel (protection squad) and evolved into a sprawling organization whose recruits were expected to carry out lethal tasks without flinching. SS chief Heinrich Himmler was a leading exponent of Nazi racial dogma, which divided society into superhumans of the so-called Aryan master race, subhumans like the Slavs who inhabited much of Eastern Europe, and antihumans, a label applied to Jews as a pretext for ostracizing and ultimately eliminating them. Nazi laws barred marriage and sexual relations between "pure" Germans and Jews, including some Christians with Jewish ancestors. Racial obsessions reinforced Hitler's determination to invade Poland and Russia, where Slavs would be displaced to make room for Germans; Jews and Roma (Gypsies) would be exterminated; and the international communist movement that Hitler called "Jewish Bolshevism" would be attacked at its root. ■

CULT LEADER Flanked by Nazi storm troopers, Hitler ascends to the lectern to address a massive crowd at Bückeburg, Germany, in October 1934, during a harvest festival promoted as part of a new Nazi calendar to replace Christian observances. The bronze statue above—erected at Nuremberg, site of a huge Nazi rally held annually—combines the swastika with the eagle, an old symbol of German might.

AGGRESSION AND APPEASEMENT

Before waging war in 1939, Hitler greatly expanded the Reich by conducting bloodless military takeovers of lands bordering Germany while British and French leaders remained passive. In March 1936, he gambled by sending some 30,000 troops into the Rhineland, an important German industrial area that was demilitarized under the Treaty of Versailles to protect neighboring France and Belgium from another invasion like that launched by Germany in 1914. Hitler's armed forces were not yet formidable, and he was prepared to withdraw from the Rhineland if the French and British intervened militarily. But when they failed to call his bluff and instead sought to appease him, he was emboldened to proceed with his aggressive agenda. In March 1938, he seized Austria after bullying its chancellor into yielding without a fight. Entering Vienna in triumph, the Austrian-born Hitler was welcomed by rapturous crowds, shouting in German, *"Ein Volk, Ein Reich, Ein Führer"* (One People, One Empire, One Leader).

Having annexed Austria with impunity, Hitler then insisted on his right to seize another ethnically German territory, the Sudetenland, which was part of Czechoslovakia. France had pledged to defend Czechoslovakia but would not do so without support from London, where Prime Minister Neville Chamberlain thought that he could reason with the Führer and avoid a conflict for which Britain and its allies were ill-prepared. Meeting with Hitler and Mussolini at Munich in September, Chamberlain and French premier Édouard Daladier gave up the Sudetenland in return for Hitler's empty promise to keep the peace. Chamberlain's notorious claim that this represented "peace with honor" and "peace for our time" was refuted when Germany took over the rest of Czechoslovakia in March 1939. France and Britain then pledged to back Poland if it was attacked, but Hitler doubted their resolve and proceeded with his plans to provide Germans with living space in Eastern Europe through conquest. "Our enemies are little worms," he remarked. "I got to know them at Munich." Their failed effort to appease him led to a war they dreaded and held back from until he forced their hand. ∎

HOSTILE TAKEOVER Angry Czechs shake their fists as German troops enter Prague on March 15, 1939. The response here stood in stark contrast to the enthusiastic welcome Hitler's forces received from many German-speakers when they annexed Austria in March 1938 and occupied the Sudetenland later that year.

GERMAN AGGRESSION IN EUROPE
June 1936 – August 1939

Germany, March 1936
Rhineland, remilitarized March 1936
Territory of the Saar Basin, June 1936
Austria, March 1938
Sudetenland as delineated by the Sept. 1938 Munich Agreement
Protectorate of Bohemia and Moravia, March 1939
Memel Territory, March 1939

0 mi 100 200
0 km 100 200
1939 features are shown.
Present-day city names are in parentheses.

THE TIMES
WEEKLY EDITION
No. 3,221   LONDON THURSDAY OCTOBER 6 1938   PAGE 1
MR. CHAMBERLAIN WELCOMED HOME FROM MUNICH

Cabinet Ministers, Foreign Ambassadors, and High Commissioners of the Dominions, with thousands of the general public, gathered to welcome Mr. Chamberlain

AN EXPANDING REICH As charted above, Hitler began flexing his muscle in 1936 by taking military control of the Rhineland and reattaching it to the Reich along with the Saar, whose inhabitants had voted to rejoin Germany. In 1938, Hitler annexed Austria and then silenced British and French objections to his planned occupation of the Sudetenland, situated along Czechoslovakia's border with Germany, with a cynical peace offering that Neville Chamberlain mistakenly touted as genuine after returning from Munich to London (left). When German troops entered the Sudetenland, some civilians like the distraught woman at upper right saluted tearfully, either because they welcomed annexation or because they felt compelled to hail the armed intruders, who went on to divide what remained of Czechoslovakia into the occupied Protectorate of Bohemia and Moravia and the dependent state of Slovakia, which yielded to the Reich and had to do its bidding.

WAR IN THE EAST

FROM THE INVASION OF POLAND TO THE RUSSO-FINNISH WAR

GERMAN AND RUSSIAN SPHERES OF INFLUENCE 1939–1940

Germany

German sphere of influence

Soviet Union

Soviet sphere of influence

FINLAND

North Sea

ESTONIA

LATVIA

LITHUANIA

★ Moscow

SOVIET UNION (RUSSIA)

Berlin ★

GERMANY

POLAND

Molotov-Ribbentrop Line August 1939

SLOVAKIA

HUNGARY

Bessarabia

ROMANIA

0 mi   400
0 km   400
1939 features are shown.

SPHERES OF INFLUENCE As mapped above, a secret protocol to the 1939 nonaggression pact left eastern Poland at Stalin's mercy along with Finland, the Baltic states, and Bessarabia. The deal freed Hitler to seize the rest of Poland, using as a staging ground Slovakia, which was dependent on Germany. He later maneuvered Romania and Hungary, a nation that was not covered in the protocol, into joining the Axis and backing the Reich.

CHRONOLOGY

AUGUST 23, 1939 Germany and the Soviet Union conclude a nonaggression pact, including a secret protocol that allows Hitler to seize most of Poland and Stalin to occupy the remainder and threaten the Baltic states and Finland.

SEPTEMBER 1, 1939 German forces invade Poland.

SEPTEMBER 17, 1939 Russian troops begin occupying eastern Poland.

SEPTEMBER 27, 1939 Polish capital Warsaw falls to the Germans.

NOVEMBER 30, 1939 Soviet troops invade Finland, where they will face strong opposition in the ensuing Winter War.

MARCH 13, 1940 Finland comes to terms with Russia by ceding territory demanded by Stalin.

The stage was set for the opening act of World War II in late August 1939, when Hitler and Stalin concluded a nonaggression pact containing a secret protocol that divided Eastern Europe into German and Soviet spheres of influence (left). That enabled Hitler to seize most of Poland without Russian opposition and allowed Stalin to occupy eastern Poland and target Finland and the Baltic states. The pact came as a bitter blow to French and British leaders, who had entered into negotiations with Russia for an alliance against Germany but were unable to overcome their distrust of Stalin, notorious for murderous purges he conducted to eliminate opposition to his drastic plans to revolutionize Russia. Hitler had no such qualms about reaching a temporary truce with the Soviet dictator, whose regime he fully intended to destroy in due time. Stalin, Hitler said privately, was "half beast, half giant," who had to be toppled before he ran rampant like Genghis Khan.

Meanwhile, Hitler made good on his vow to wipe Poland off the map by invading that country on September 1. The Luftwaffe soon achieved air supremacy by destroying many Polish warplanes on the ground and downing others manned by pilots who resisted stoutly. German tanks and motorized infantry punched through Polish forces, whose cavalry offered no defense against armored units. German Army Group North advanced from either side of the Polish Corridor, which separated East Prussia from the rest of the Reich. Army Group South invaded along a broad front extending from lower Germany to Slovakia. Within a week, German armored units were approaching Warsaw. By mid-month, the invaders were pounding that city, whose defenders surrendered on September 27. Much of Poland was exposed to a brutal German occupation while the remainder came under Soviet domination.

Britain and France declared war on Germany soon after the invasion began. But French troops did little more than probe German defenses along their shared border, and the British Expeditionary Force was just beginning to assemble in France to meet the German threat when Polish resistance collapsed. The "Phoney War" in the West continued through the winter of 1939–1940 while heavy fighting erupted in the East between Russia and defiant Finland. ∎

FLASHBACK In a scene reminiscent of World War I and earlier conflicts, ill-fated Polish cavalrymen train for battle before the German invasion of their country in 1939, when they fought valiantly but were crushed.

GERMAN INVASION OF POLAND
Phase 1: Sept. 1–14, 1939

0 mi 50 100
0 km 50 100
Present-day city names are in parentheses.

German territory, Aug. 31, 1939
German satellite or puppet state
Polish territory, Aug. 31, 1939
Neutral state, Aug. 31, 1939
Polish position, Aug. 31, 1939
German position, Aug. 31, 1939
German advance, Sept. 1–14, 1939

PIERCING POLAND Closely supported by Stuka dive-bombers (above), German troops invaded Poland on several fronts (map at right). Army Group North, led by Gen. Fedor von Bock, delivered twin blows by Gen. Georg von Küchler's Third Army, which advanced south from East Prussia, and Gen. Günther von Kluge's Fourth Army, which pushed east across the Polish Corridor to seize Danzig before pivoting toward Warsaw. Army Group South, under Gen. Gerd von Rundstedt, applied further pressure as Gen. Johannes Blaskowitz's Eighth Army and Gen. Walter von Reichenau's 10th Army advanced from southeastern Germany while Gen. Wilhelm List's 14th Army invaded from Germany and Slovakia and took Krakow.

GERMAN INVASION OF POLAND
Phase 2: Sept. 15 – Oct. 6, 1939

0 mi 50 100
0 km 50 100
Present-day city names are in parentheses.

German territory, Aug. 31, 1939
German satellite or puppet state
Polish territory, Aug. 31, 1939
Neutral state, Aug. 31, 1939
Polish position, late-Sept. 1939
German position, Sept. 14–Oct. 6, 1939
German advance, Sept. 14–Oct. 6, 1939
German-Russian demarcation line

FALL OF WARSAW In mid-September, as mapped at left, Army Group North enveloped Warsaw's eastern flank while the Eighth Army closed in from the west. Bruising assaults by German infantrymen like those pictured above, combined with air raids and artillery bombardments, forced the surrender of Warsaw on the 27th and sealed Poland's fate.

THE WINTER WAR

RED TSAR Stalin, shown above driving home a point, was so devious and domineering that even his ruthless predecessor, Vladimir Lenin, warned against entrusting him with "absolute authority." His grim reputation strengthened the resolve of Finns to reject his demands and wage a war in which their ski troops (below) often outmaneuvered and outfought the Russian invaders.

Known as the Red Tsar, Joseph Stalin (left) was as much an imperialist as he was a communist, and he exploited his secret protocol with Hitler to reassert authority over countries bordering Russia that had broken free after the last tsar, Nicholas II, abdicated in 1917. Having weakened the Red Army by purging thousands of its senior officers, Stalin used threats to impose on neighboring countries before resorting to armed force. In October 1939, he pressured Latvia, Estonia, and Lithuania into accepting Soviet military bases, which soon enabled Russia to reabsorb those Baltic states without waging war. Stalin then targeted Finland, insisting that it accept a Soviet naval base and cede territory between the Gulf of Finland and Lake Ladoga to provide a buffer zone for Leningrad, Russia's second most important city after Moscow. Finnish leaders in Helsinki refused.

On November 30, 1939, the Red Army invaded Finland, committing over 600,000 troops against fewer than 200,000 defenders. Expecting a quick victory, the Soviets were instead confounded by agile Finnish soldiers, many of them on skis, who knew the terrain far better than their bewildered foes. As one Russian soldier recalled, "There were no roads, no settlements—just forests and lakes. Nothing to get your bearings from." Disoriented and poorly commanded, the invaders blundered into traps and took heavy losses. They performed "like a badly led orchestra," remarked the Finnish chief, Field Marshal Carl Gustaf Mannerheim, who counterattacked in December and pushed Soviets back from his Mannerheim Line above Leningrad. Not until Stalin dispatched more troops in January under Gen. Semyon Timoshenko did the Russians rebound. In March 1940, after Timoshenko pierced the Mannerheim Line, the Finns came to terms. They avoided conquest but yielded to Stalin's demands and ceded substantial territory.

The Red Army's poor showing in the Winter War reinforced Hitler's conviction that when the time came for him to challenge Stalin, his forces would crush the Soviets. But he overlooked another lesson of the conflict—Stalin's capacity to recover from bitter setbacks by drawing on deep reserves of Russian manpower. ■

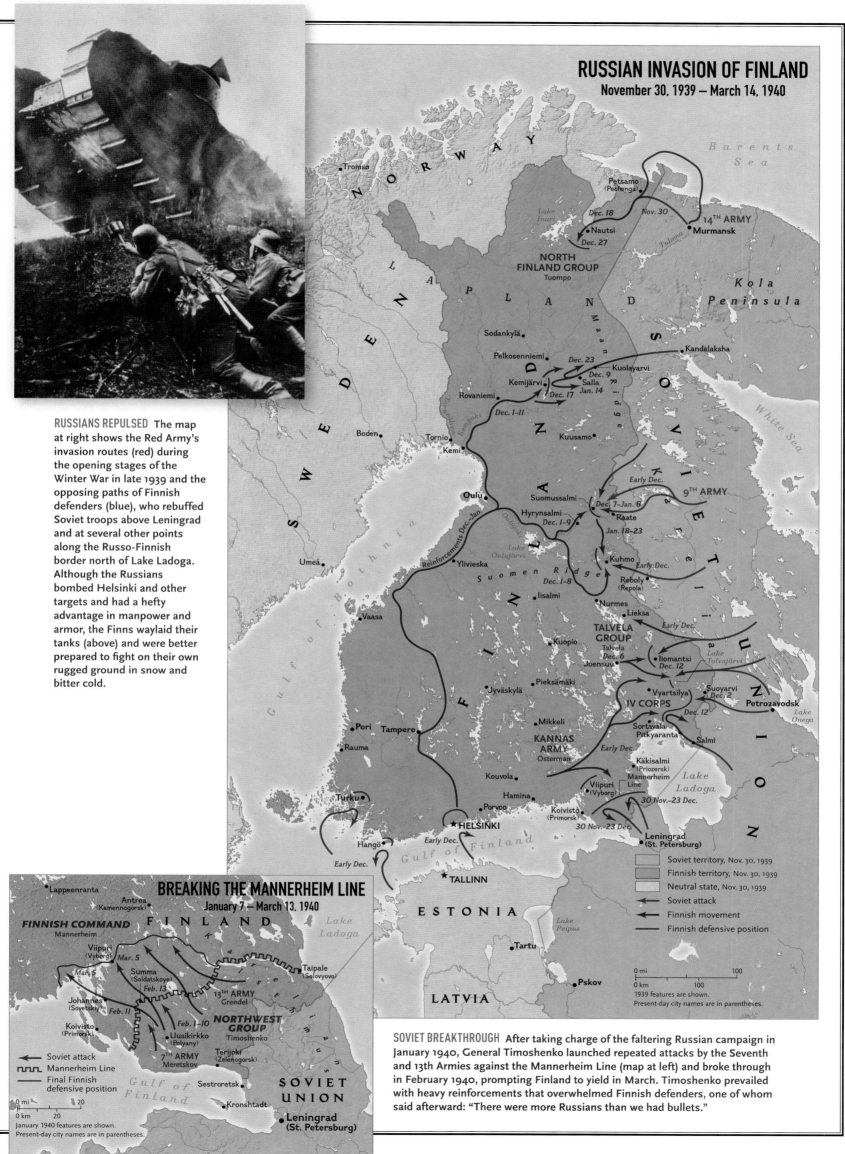

RUSSIAN INVASION OF FINLAND
November 30, 1939 – March 14, 1940

RUSSIANS REPULSED The map at right shows the Red Army's invasion routes (red) during the opening stages of the Winter War in late 1939 and the opposing paths of Finnish defenders (blue), who rebuffed Soviet troops above Leningrad and at several other points along the Russo-Finnish border north of Lake Ladoga. Although the Russians bombed Helsinki and other targets and had a hefty advantage in manpower and armor, the Finns waylaid their tanks (above) and were better prepared to fight on their own rugged ground in snow and bitter cold.

NORWAY
SWEDEN
FINLAND
SOVIET UNION
ESTONIA
LATVIA

Barents Sea
Kola Peninsula
White Sea
Lake Onega
Lake Ladoga
Gulf of Bothnia
Gulf of Finland
Lake Peipus
Lake Inari
Lake Oulujärvi
Lake Tolvajärvi

Tromsø
Petsamo (Pechenga)
Nov. 30
Dec. 18
Nautsi
Dec. 27
Murmansk
14TH ARMY
NORTH FINLAND GROUP
Tuompo
Sodankylä
Pelkosenniemi
Kuolayarvi
Kandalaksha
Dec. 23
Dec. 9
Kemijärvi
Salla
Dec. 17
Jan. 14
Rovaniemi
Dec. 1–11
Boden
Tornio
Kemi
Kuusamo
Oulu
Suomussalmi
9TH ARMY
Early Dec.
Dec. 7–Jan. 8
Hyrynsalmi
Raate
Dec. 1–9
Jan. 18–23
Reinforcements Dec.–Jan.
Ylivieska
Kuhmo
Early Dec.
Suomen Ridge
Dec. 1–8
Reboly (Repola)
Umeå
Iisalmi
Nurmes
Lieksa
Vaasa
Early Dec.
Kuopio
TALVELA GROUP
Talvela
Dec. 6
Ilomantsi
Dec. 12
Joensuu
Jyväskylä
Pieksämäki
Vyartsilya
Suoyarvi
Dec. 2
Petrozavodsk
IV CORPS
Dec. 12
Mikkeli
KANNAS ARMY
Österman
Sortavala
Pitkyaranta
Salmi
Pori
Tampere
Kouvola
Käkisalmi (Priozersk)
Mannerheim Line
Rauma
Viipuri (Vyborg)
Early Dec.
30 Nov.–23 Dec.
Hamina
Koivisto (Primorsk)
30 Nov.–23 Dec.
Turku
Porvoo
Leningrad (St. Petersburg)
★HELSINKI
Hangö
Early Dec.
Early Dec.
★TALLINN
Tartu
Pskov

	Soviet territory, Nov. 30, 1939
	Finnish territory, Nov. 30, 1939
	Neutral state, Nov. 30, 1939
←	Soviet attack
←	Finnish movement
—	Finnish defensive position

0 mi 100
0 km 100
1939 features are shown.
Present-day city names are in parentheses.

BREAKING THE MANNERHEIM LINE
January 7 – March 13, 1940

FINNISH COMMAND
Mannerheim
FINLAND
Lake Ladoga
Lappeenranta
Antrea (Kamennogorsk)
Viipuri (Vyborg)
Mar. 5
Summa (Soldatskoye)
Feb. 13
Taipale (Solovyovo)
Johannes (Sovetskiy)
Feb. 11
Mar. 5
13TH ARMY
Grendel
Feb. 1–10
NORTHWEST GROUP
Timoshenko
Koivisto (Primorsk)
Uusikirkko (Polyany)
Terijoki (Zelenogorsk)
7TH ARMY
Meretskov
SOVIET UNION
Sestroretsk
Gulf of Finland
Kronshtadt
Leningrad (St. Petersburg)

←	Soviet attack
⌐⌐⌐	Mannerheim Line
—	Final Finnish defensive position

0 mi 20
0 km 20
January 1940 features are shown.
Present-day city names are in parentheses.

SOVIET BREAKTHROUGH After taking charge of the faltering Russian campaign in January 1940, General Timoshenko launched repeated attacks by the Seventh and 13th Armies against the Mannerheim Line (map at left) and broke through in February 1940, prompting Finland to yield in March. Timoshenko prevailed with heavy reinforcements that overwhelmed Finnish defenders, one of whom said afterward: "There were more Russians than we had bullets."

WAR IN THE WEST

FROM THE INVASION OF NORWAY TO THE FALL OF FRANCE

CHRONOLOGY

APRIL 9, 1940 German forces conquer Denmark and invade Norway.

MAY 10, 1940 Germans invade the Low Countries of Belgium, Luxembourg, and the Netherlands with the ultimate objective of conquering France.

JUNE 4, 1940 Dunkirk falls to the Germans after more than 330,000 Allied soldiers are evacuated from that French port to England.

JUNE 5, 1940 German troops in northern France advance southward toward Paris.

JUNE 14, 1940 Paris falls to the invaders.

JUNE 22, 1940 France surrenders to Germany and is divided into a German-occupied zone in the north and a German-dependent zone in the south, administered at Vichy by the compliant Marshal Philippe Pétain.

Hitler was surprised when Britain and France, after yielding to him at Munich, responded to the invasion of Poland by declaring war, but he was not dismayed. He looked forward to ending the Reich's long-standing dispute with France, which had regained the border province of Alsace-Lorraine from Germany under the Treaty of Versailles, by defeating the French once and for all. And he hoped that the British, whose Anglo-Saxon heritage and imperial prowess he admired, would then come to terms and accept German domination of continental Europe. While his generals planned a blitzkrieg that would slash through the Low Countries to Paris, Hitler decided to precede that offensive by invading neutral Norway and establishing naval bases there. That would secure the Reich's northern flank against Allied intervention in Norway, which Hitler anticipated, and protect vital shipments of Swedish iron ore to Germany from the Norwegian port of Narvik. Neutral Denmark would also be invaded, leaving Sweden little choice but to accommodate Germany if it hoped to preserve its own neutrality.

On April 9, combined German air, naval, and ground assaults overwhelmed Denmark, which fell within hours. Yet conquering Norway with its long, jagged coastline and mountainous interior was a tougher task. The capital of Oslo and other Norwegian ports were captured by German troops delivered by sea, but those naval operations proved costly. Britain's Royal Navy and Norwegian coastal batteries sank 15 troop transports, and the German fleet lost roughly half its warships, including the heavy cruiser Blücher, which went down in Oslo Fjord, and 10 destroyers wrecked in a fierce battle with the Royal Navy for Narvik.

A clumsy effort by pro-German collaborator Vidkun Quisling to proclaim himself head of state in occupied Oslo backfired when Norwegians spurned him and kept up the fight, aided by Allied forces that had landed on the west coast in April. Consisting of British troops, French Foreign Legionnaires, and Polish soldiers in exile, they fought hard alongside Norwegians and reclaimed Narvik in late May. By then, however, the Germans had invaded France, leading Allied commanders to withdraw forces from Narvik to save them for more pressing engagements. The last Norwegian forces capitulated in June. ■

ROUGH GOING During the invasion of Norway, German mountain troops ascend a trail far too rugged for the soldier up front to make use of his bicycle. Many of the invaders landed near Oslo or elsewhere on Norway's southern coast and advanced inland, supported by paratroopers, and others landed along the west coast. Most Norwegian ports were firmly in German hands by early May with the notable exception of Narvik, linked by rail to Swedish iron mines.

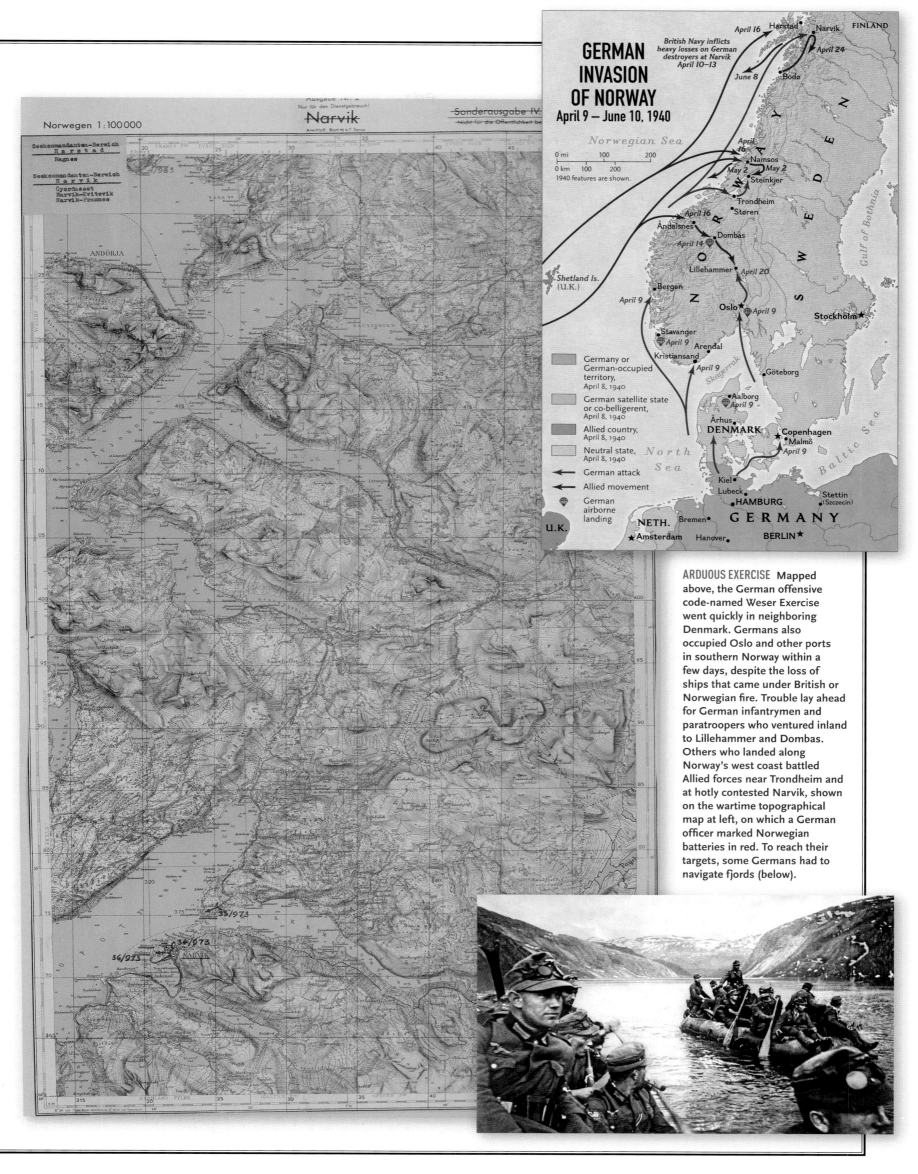

GERMAN INVASION OF NORWAY
April 9 – June 10, 1940

British Navy inflicts heavy losses on German destroyers at Narvik April 10–13

Norwegian Sea

0 mi   100   200
0 km   100   200
1940 features are shown.

Harstad   Narvik   FINLAND
April 16
April 24
June 8   Bodø

April 16   Namsos
May 2   May 2   Steinkjer
Trondheim
Støren
April 16
Åndalsnes   Dombas
April 14
Lillehammer   April 20
Bergen
April 9
Oslo   April 9
Stavanger   April 9   Stockholm
Arendal
Kristiansand   April 9
Göteborg
Skagerrak

Shetland Is. (U.K.)

SWEDEN
NORWAY
Gulf of Bothnia

Aalborg
April 9
Århus
DENMARK   Copenhagen
Malmö
April 9
North Sea   Baltic Sea

Kiel
Lubeck   Stettin (Szczecin)
HAMBURG
Bremen   GERMANY
U.K.   NETH.   BERLIN
Amsterdam   Hanover

Germany or German-occupied territory, April 8, 1940

German satellite state or co-belligerent, April 8, 1940

Allied country, April 8, 1940

Neutral state, April 8, 1940

→ German attack

→ Allied movement

⊕ German airborne landing

Narvik

Norwegen 1:100 000

Ausgabe Nr. 2
Nur für den Dienstgebrauch!

Sonderausgabe IV.
Nicht für die Öffentlichkeit be...

Seekommandanten-Bereich
Harstad
Hagnes

Seekommandanten-Bereich
Narvik
Gyordnesst
Narvik-Kvitevik
Narvik-Framnes

ANDÖRJA

NARVIK

ARDUOUS EXERCISE Mapped above, the German offensive code-named Weser Exercise went quickly in neighboring Denmark. Germans also occupied Oslo and other ports in southern Norway within a few days, despite the loss of ships that came under British or Norwegian fire. Trouble lay ahead for German infantrymen and paratroopers who ventured inland to Lillehammer and Dombas. Others who landed along Norway's west coast battled Allied forces near Trondheim and at hotly contested Narvik, shown on the wartime topographical map at left, on which a German officer marked Norwegian batteries in red. To reach their targets, some Germans had to navigate fjords (below).

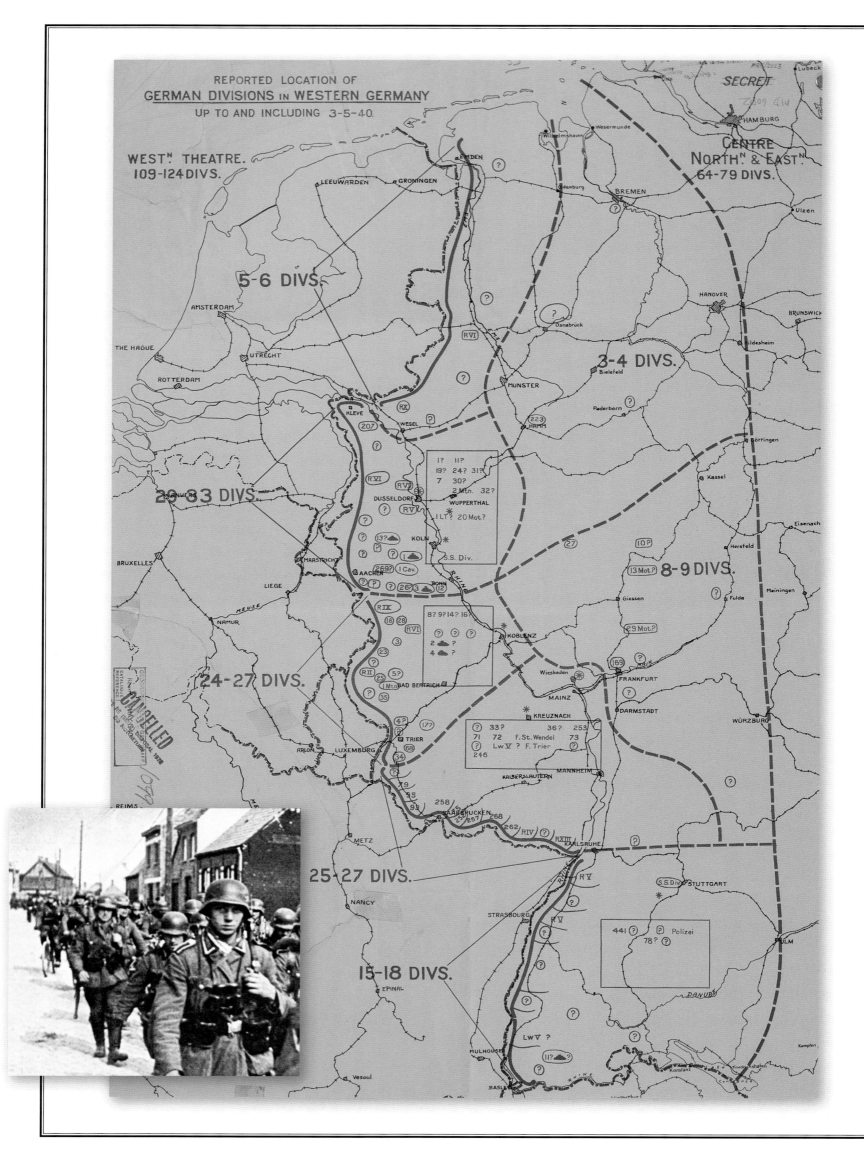

REPORTED LOCATION OF
GERMAN DIVISIONS IN WESTERN GERMANY
UP TO AND INCLUDING 3-5-40.

SECRET

WEST.ᴺ THEATRE.
109-124 DIVS.

CENTRE
NORTH.ᴺ & EAST.ᴺ
64-79 DIVS.

5-6 DIVS.

3-4 DIVS.

29-33 DIVS.

8-9 DIVS.

24-27 DIVS.

25-27 DIVS.

15-18 DIVS.

CANCELLED

BLITZKRIEG IN THE LOWLANDS

The massive German offensive aimed at France that began on May 10, 1940, was long anticipated by the Allies but unfolded in a manner they did not foresee. As shown on the situation map opposite, British intelligence officers estimated that as many as 124 German divisions were positioned in western Germany by May 3. The bulk of those forces were poised near the German border with the Low Countries—Belgium, Luxembourg, and the Netherlands. Allied commanders expected their foes to skirt Germany's border with France, where the fortified French Maginot Line was strongest, and instead descend on Paris through Belgium, as they did in 1914. Although Belgium remained neutral before it was invaded and excluded French and British forces, they planned to enter the country en masse as soon as German troops crossed the border.

The German plan of attack, involving three army groups, was shrewdly designed to exploit that Allied response. Army Group C, led by Gen. Wilhelm Ritter von Leeb, remained opposite the Maginot Line along the French border to keep defenders tied down there. General Bock's Army Group B invaded Holland and northern Belgium on May 10, drawing three French armies and the British Expeditionary Force (BEF) northward in reaction. Those troops soon found themselves in a trap, sprung by panzers (armored units) at the forefront of General Rundstedt's Army Group A that advanced through the Ardennes—a forest extending from Luxembourg into southern Belgium that was mistakenly considered impassable by tanks. A German officer worried that his tanks would be detected as they churned through the Ardennes, but he did not spot "a single French reconnaissance aircraft."

By May 14, hard-driving panzers had emerged from the Ardennes, crossed into northern France, and smashed enemy lines around Sedan with help from the Luftwaffe's fearsome Stukas, which swooped down on French troops in their bunkers. Armored corps were soon pouring through breaches in weak sectors of the Maginot Line along the French border with Belgium and racing toward the sea, a thrust that would cut off nearly one million Allied troops to the north. As one German officer boasted, "The rapid movements and flexible handling of our panzers bewildered the enemy." ∎

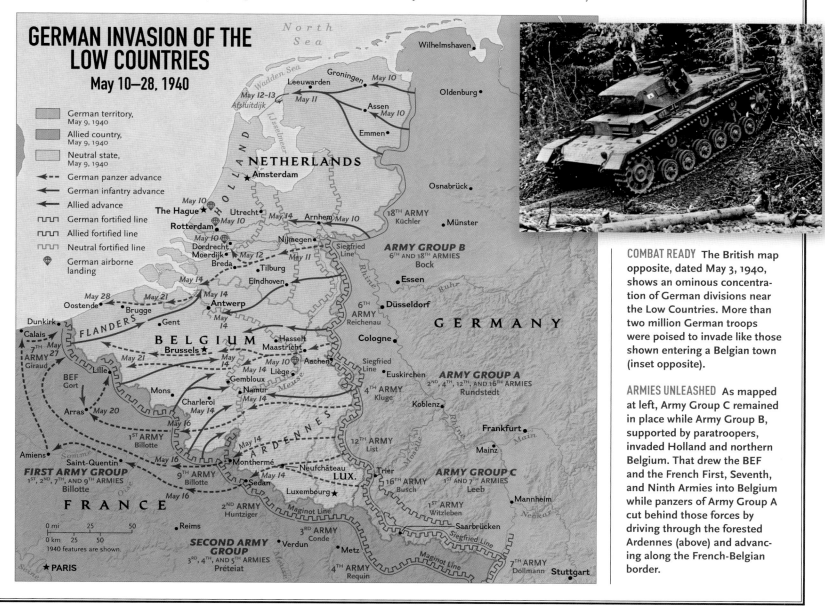

GERMAN INVASION OF THE LOW COUNTRIES
May 10–28, 1940

- German territory, May 9, 1940
- Allied country, May 9, 1940
- Neutral state, May 9, 1940
- German panzer advance
- German infantry advance
- Allied advance
- German fortified line
- Allied fortified line
- Neutral fortified line
- German airborne landing

0 mi 25 50
0 km 25 50
1940 features are shown.

COMBAT READY The British map opposite, dated May 3, 1940, shows an ominous concentration of German divisions near the Low Countries. More than two million German troops were poised to invade like those shown entering a Belgian town (inset opposite).

ARMIES UNLEASHED As mapped at left, Army Group C remained in place while Army Group B, supported by paratroopers, invaded Holland and northern Belgium. That drew the BEF and the French First, Seventh, and Ninth Armies into Belgium while panzers of Army Group A cut behind those forces by driving through the forested Ardennes (above) and advancing along the French-Belgian border.

ADVANCE TO THE ATLANTIC

For Gen. Heinz Guderian, commander of XIX Panzer Corps in Army Group A, the breakthrough his armored forces achieved at Sedan in mid-May 1940 was especially gratifying because it confirmed a doctrine that he and other innovative German officers embraced as they prepared for blitzkrieg. Their goal was to avoid a bloody stalemate by coordinating armored assaults with air strikes to deliver a crushing blow at what they called the *schwerpunkt*—the focal point of the attack, where their forces would break through opposing lines. But that alone did not ensure success if the enemy was agile enough to rally and seal the breach with flank attacks. The key to achieving victory after piercing enemy defenses, Guderian wrote, was to "thrust the arrowhead so deep" that one's opponent was disabled. That meant pressing to the hilt the advantage that armored divisions gave attackers. "Once armored formations are out on the loose," he argued, "they must be given the green light to the very end of the road."

On May 15, Guderian persuaded his immediate superior, Gen. Ewald von Kleist, to give him the green light temporarily. General Rundstedt, commander of Army Group A, worried that overeager panzers would get too far ahead of the supporting infan-

try and fall prey to Allied counterattacks. But as shown on the German situation map below, once Guderian's forces began pushing west to the sea along with Gen. Hermann Hoth's XV Panzer Corps and Gen. Georg Hans Reinhardt's XLI Panzer Corps, they were hard to stop. Rapid gains were made by an officer new to tank warfare who would soon be legendary for his daring armored thrusts, Erwin Rommel, commanding the Seventh Panzer Division in Hoth's corps. His forces raced headlong in pursuit of the retreating French Ninth Army and captured 10,000 of its demoralized troops. Some French commanders struck back, including Col. Charles de Gaulle, whose Fourth Armored Division attacked part of Guderian's corps near Montcornet, France, on May 17 but was outgunned and withdrew the next day.

By late May, the only hope for beleaguered Allied forces was to fall back to the port of Dunkirk, from which they might be evacuated to England if they could hold out long enough for a fleet to extricate them. Hitler gave them time—and exasperated some German commanders—by confirming Rundstedt's order on May 24 to halt his panzers within 20 miles of Dunkirk and allow infantry to catch up. The order was rescinded a few days later, but by then evacuations from Dunkirk were under way. ∎

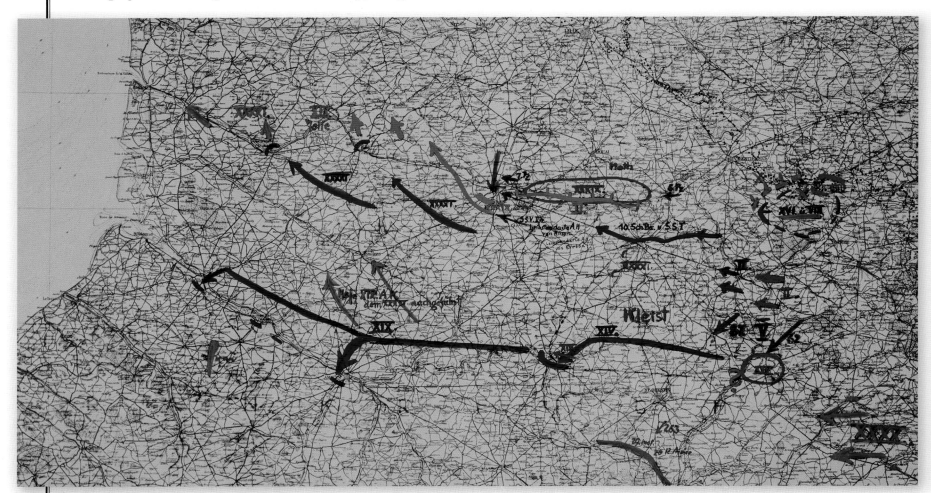

PANZERS' PROGRESS German notations in red on a map of northern France (covering the area within dotted white lines opposite) show Guderian's XIX Panzer Corps advancing to the Somme River estuary (left) by May 20 and Reinhardt's XLI Panzer Corps (designated XXXXI on this map) advancing on a parallel path to the north. Shown at center is Rommel's Seventh Panzer Division (7 Pz) of XV Panzer Corps near Arras, where Rommel repulsed British armor on May 21.

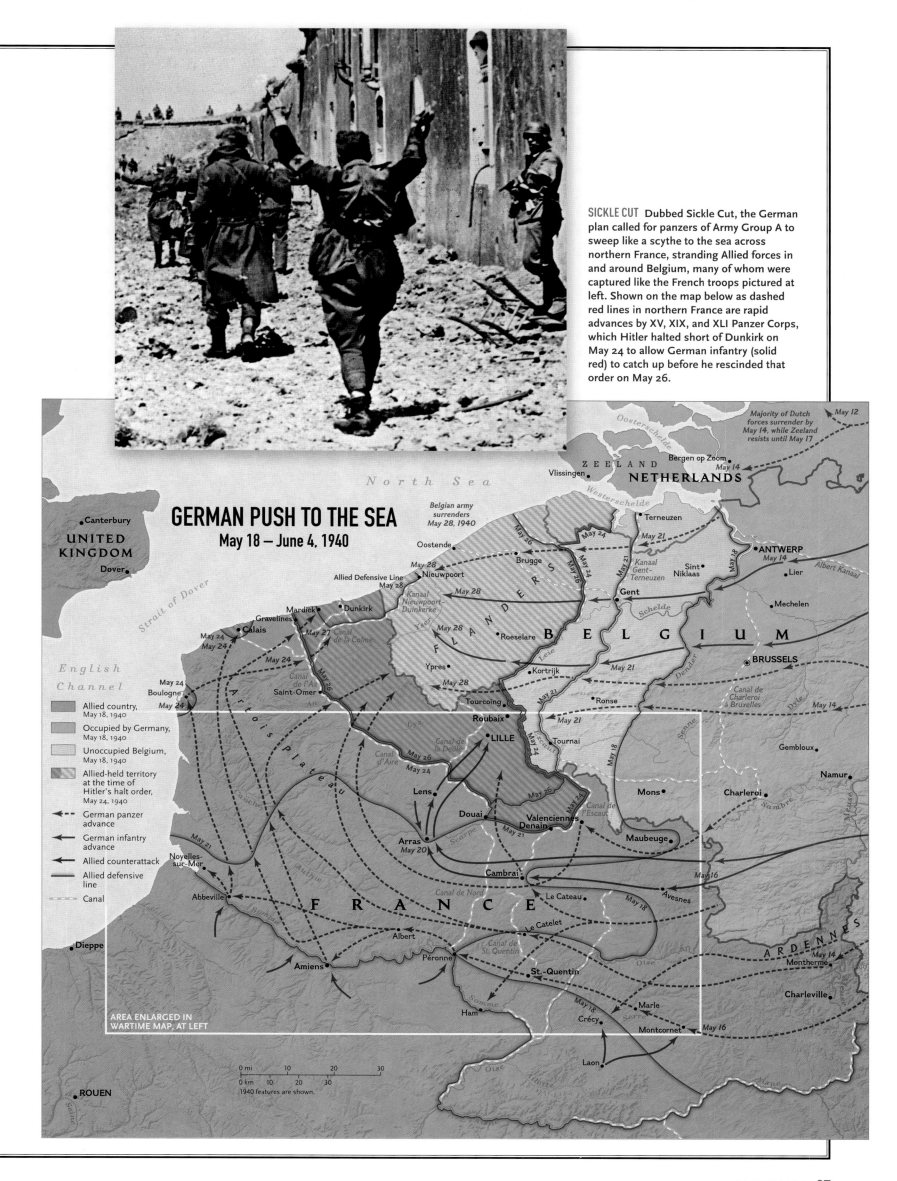

SICKLE CUT Dubbed Sickle Cut, the German plan called for panzers of Army Group A to sweep like a scythe to the sea across northern France, stranding Allied forces in and around Belgium, many of whom were captured like the French troops pictured at left. Shown on the map below as dashed red lines in northern France are rapid advances by XV, XIX, and XLI Panzer Corps, which Hitler halted short of Dunkirk on May 24 to allow German infantry (solid red) to catch up before he rescinded that order on May 26.

GERMAN PUSH TO THE SEA
May 18 – June 4, 1940

Majority of Dutch forces surrender by May 14, while Zeeland resists until May 17

Belgian army surrenders May 28, 1940

NORTH SEA

UNITED KINGDOM

Canterbury
Dover

NETHERLANDS
ZEELAND
Bergen op Zoom
Vlissingen
Terneuzen
ANTWERP
Sint Niklaas
Lier
Mechelen

BELGIUM
Oostende
Brugge
Gent
Roeselare
Kortrijk
BRUSSELS
Gembloux
Namur
Charleroi
Mons
Maubeuge

Strait of Dover
Mardick
Dunkirk
Nieuwpoort
Allied Defensive Line May 28
Ypres
Tourcoing
Roubaix
LILLE
Tournai
Ronse

Gravelines
Calais
Saint-Omer
Lens
Douai
Valenciennes
Denain
Arras
Cambrai
Le Cateau
Avesnes

Boulogne

English Channel

Noyelles-sur-Mer

Abbeville

FRANCE

Dieppe

Albert
Amiens
Péronne
Le Catelet
St.-Quentin
Ham
Marle
Crécy
Montcornet
Laon

ARDENNES
Monthermé
Charleville

Legend
- Allied country, May 18, 1940
- Occupied by Germany, May 18, 1940
- Unoccupied Belgium, May 18, 1940
- Allied-held territory at the time of Hitler's halt order, May 24, 1940
- --→ German panzer advance
- → German infantry advance
- ← Allied counterattack
- — Allied defensive line
- ---- Canal

0 mi 10 20 30
0 km 10 20 30
1940 features are shown.

AREA ENLARGED IN WARTIME MAP, AT LEFT

ROUEN

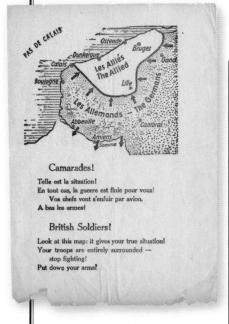

INVITATION TO SURRENDER A map on a bilingual German propaganda leaflet aimed at French and British soldiers shows German forces poised to overrun Allied troops trapped around Dunkirk. *"La guerre est finie pour vous!* (The war is over for you!)" the leaflet states, and concludes: *"A bas les armes!* (Put down your arms!)"

DELIVERANCE AT DUNKIRK

When evacuations from Dunkirk began in earnest on May 26, 1940, British commanders figured that no more than 45,000 of the nearly 400,000 Allied troops holed up there—including more than 250,000 members of the British Expeditionary Force (BEF)—could be rescued before Germans captured the port. That evening, Hitler canceled the order that halted panzers short of Dunkirk and set tanks in motion. Marshy ground and mechanical breakdowns slowed them, but infantry assaults overwhelmed Belgian troops helping to defend the port. On May 28, Belgium surrendered. By then, German warplanes had blasted the docks in Dunkirk and strafed soldiers huddled on the beach, a grim task that one pilot called "unadulterated killing." Cloudy skies and dense smoke over Dunkirk often obscured targets there in the days ahead, however, and lethal attacks on German bombers by British fighter pilots helped negate Field Marshal Hermann Göring's boast to Hitler that the Luftwaffe alone could halt the evacuations.

On the ground, heroic rear-guard actions by French troops enabled a motley fleet of some 1,000 vessels, ranging from tugboats to Royal Navy destroyers, to extract an astonishing 338,000 Allied soldiers before Dunkirk fell on June 4. The rescue of nearly 225,000 BEF troops in that daring Operation Dynamo encouraged the British to keep fighting. More than 100,000 French soldiers were saved as well, but France had lost roughly one-third of its forces since May 10 and now faced catastrophe.

As the last evacuees returned from Dunkirk, Britain's combative new prime minister, Winston Churchill, warned the public "not to assign to this deliverance the attributes of a victory. Wars are not won by evacuations." ∎

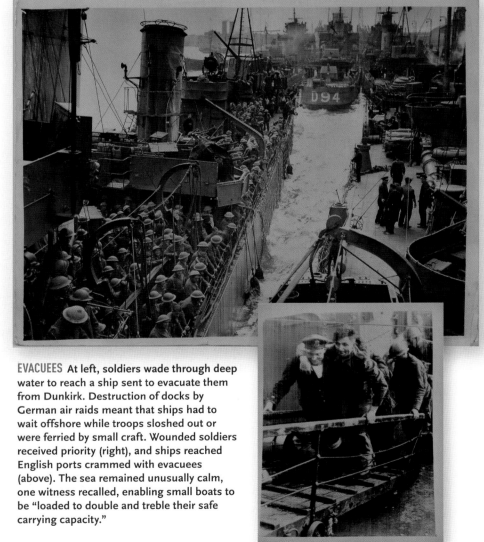

EVACUEES At left, soldiers wade through deep water to reach a ship sent to evacuate them from Dunkirk. Destruction of docks by German air raids meant that ships had to wait offshore while troops sloshed out or were ferried by small craft. Wounded soldiers received priority (right), and ships reached English ports crammed with evacuees (above). The sea remained unusually calm, one witness recalled, enabling small boats to be "loaded to double and treble their safe carrying capacity."

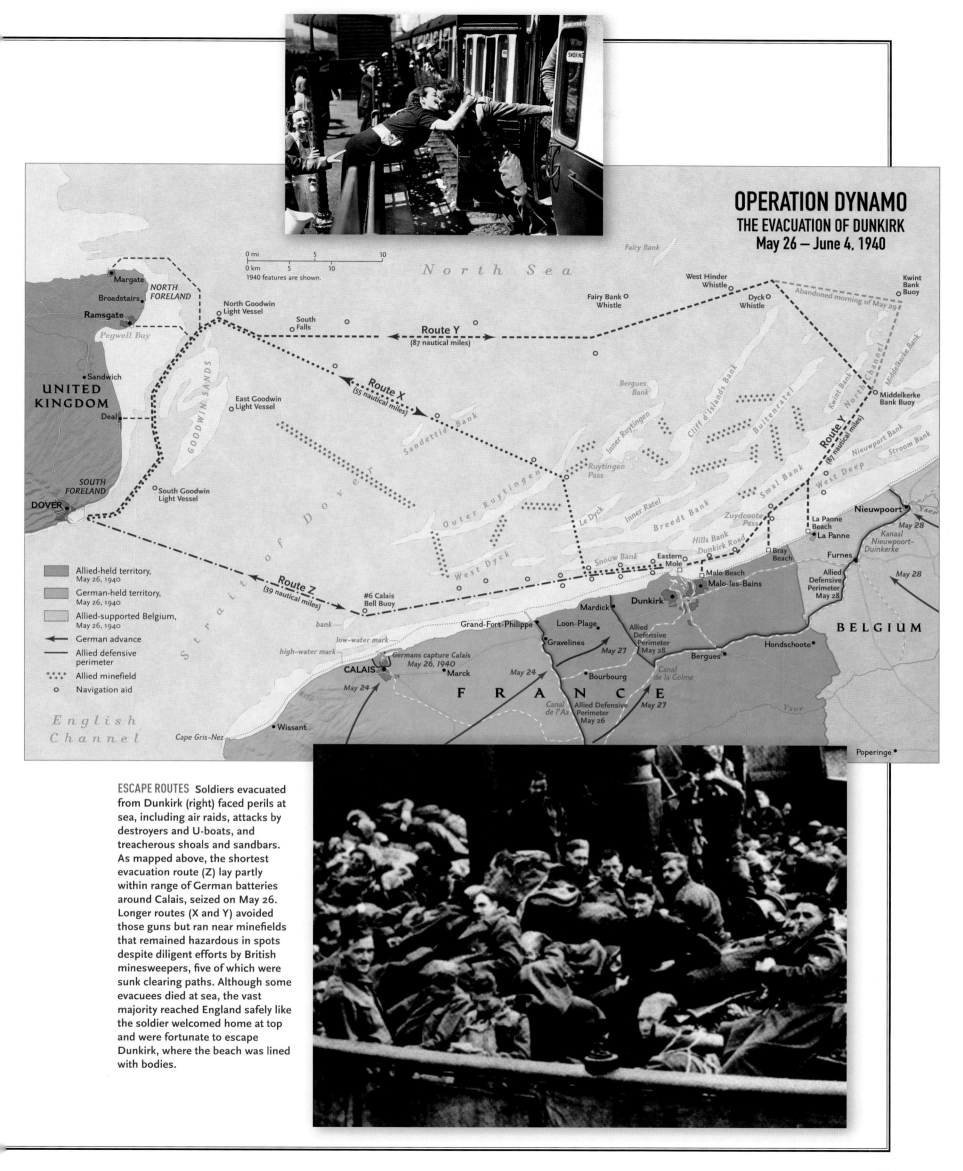

OPERATION DYNAMO
THE EVACUATION OF DUNKIRK
May 26 – June 4, 1940

0 mi — 5 — 10
0 km — 5 — 10
1940 features are shown.

North Sea

Fairy Bank

West Hinder Whistle

Kwint Bank Buoy

Abandoned morning of May 29

Fairy Bank Whistle

Dyck Whistle

Middelkerke Bank Buoy

Margate

NORTH FORELAND

Broadstairs

Ramsgate

Pegwell Bay

North Goodwin Light Vessel

South Falls

Route Y
(87 nautical miles)

Middelkerke Bank

Sandwich

UNITED KINGDOM

East Goodwin Light Vessel

Route X
(55 nautical miles)

Deal

GOODWIN SANDS

Sandettié Bank

Bergues Bank

Cliff d'Islands Bank

Buitenratel

Kwint Bank

North Channel

Route Y
(87 nautical miles)

Nieuwport Bank

Stroom Bank

SOUTH FORELAND

South Goodwin Light Vessel

Strait of Dover

Outer Ruytingen

Ruytingen Pass

Inner Ruytingen

Smal Bank

West Deep

DOVER

Le Dyck

Inner Ratel

Breedt Bank

Zuydcoote Pass

La Panne Beach

Nieuwpoort

Yser

La Panne

Kanaal Nieuwpoort-Duinkerke

Furnes

Hills Bank

Dunkirk Road

Bray Beach

Allied Defensive Perimeter May 28

May 28

West Dyck

Snouw Bank

Eastern Mole

Malo Beach

Malo-les-Bains

BELGIUM

Allied-held territory, May 26, 1940

Allied-supported Belgium, May 26, 1940

German-held territory, May 26, 1940

Route Z
(39 nautical miles)

#6 Calais Bell Buoy

Mardick

Dunkirk

Hondschoote

German advance

Allied defensive perimeter

Allied minefield

Navigation aid

bank

low-water mark

Grand-Fort-Philippe

Loon-Plage

Allied Defensive Perimeter May 28

Bergues

F R A N C E

high-water mark

Gravelines

May 27

Canal de la Colme

Yser

English Channel

CALAIS

Germans capture Calais May 26, 1940

Marck

May 24

Bourbourg

May 24

Canal de l'Aa

Allied Defensive Perimeter May 26

May 27

Poperinge

Cape Gris-Nez

Wissant

BLITZKRIEG **39**

ESCAPE ROUTES
Soldiers evacuated from Dunkirk (right) faced perils at sea, including air raids, attacks by destroyers and U-boats, and treacherous shoals and sandbars. As mapped above, the shortest evacuation route (Z) lay partly within range of German batteries around Calais, seized on May 26. Longer routes (X and Y) avoided those guns but ran near minefields that remained hazardous in spots despite diligent efforts by British minesweepers, five of which were sunk clearing paths. Although some evacuees died at sea, the vast majority reached England safely like the soldier welcomed home at top and were fortunate to escape Dunkirk, where the beach was lined with bodies.

FALL OF FRANCE

Gen. Maxime Weygand, the 73-year-old commander charged with defending France in June 1940, was an old hand at fighting Germans. During World War I, he had served as chief of staff for Ferdinand Foch, a general who rose to become Marshal of France after winning renown in a battle called the "Miracle of the Marne," which halted the German advance on Paris in 1914. It would take a miracle of far greater proportions for Weygand to save the capital now. Ruinous losses that began before he took command on May 19 left him with barely 70 divisions to face nearly 130 German divisions. And blistering attacks by panzers and the Luftwaffe had woefully reduced his armored and air forces. Hoping to avert swift German breakthroughs like those achieved along the Belgian border in mid-May, Weygand wanted to defend in depth below the Somme and Aisne Rivers in northern France. Unable to cover all that ground, he settled on a "checkerboard" defense in which open spaces alternated with dense clusters of troops in villages or woods. He ordered them to cling to those positions "without thought of withdrawal" and added that all officers "must be filled with the grim desire to stand and fight to the death."

No amount of French determination, however, could long prevent the Germans from using their superior numbers and mobility to capture or bypass the static checkers on Weygand's board. Army Group B, aligned to the west along the Somme River, opened the battle on June 5. Adding punch to that drive were seasoned armored units transferred from Group A, including Rommel's Seventh Panzer Division, under the overall command of General Hoth. Rommel's tanks blasted French defenders holding one town then swept around them and forged ahead. "All quiet forward," Rommel reported that night, "enemy in shreds." By June 8, his panzers had reached the Seine River west of Paris. A day later, Army Group A joined the attack and crossed the Aisne River, bolstered by two panzer corps under Guderian that reached the Marne River east of Paris on the 13th. By then, French officials had fled the capital and declared it an open city, which Germans entered unopposed on June 14. Following that disaster, Premier Paul Reynaud resigned in favor of Marshal Philippe Pétain, who agreed to an armistice that divided France into a German-occupied zone in the north and the west coast and a Vichy zone in the south administered by Pétain, who collaborated with the Germans. Hitler accepted the surrender of French forces on June 22 in the same railway carriage outside Paris where German generals had yielded to the Allies in 1918. ∎

HITLER IN PARIS Flanked by architect and administrator Albert Speer (left), Hitler stands before the Eiffel Tower in occupied Paris soon after France surrendered. Under terms he imposed, French troops in German custody remained prisoners of war, to be exchanged gradually for French workers induced to labor for Germany, whose war industries were overseen by Speer.

BURNED OUT A German soldier uses a flamethrower to blast a bunker along the Maginot Line in northeastern France, which was overwhelmed in mid-June after many of its defenders went to fight the invaders elsewhere.

CHANNEL ISLANDS
(U.K. territory occupied by Germany June 1940–May 1945)

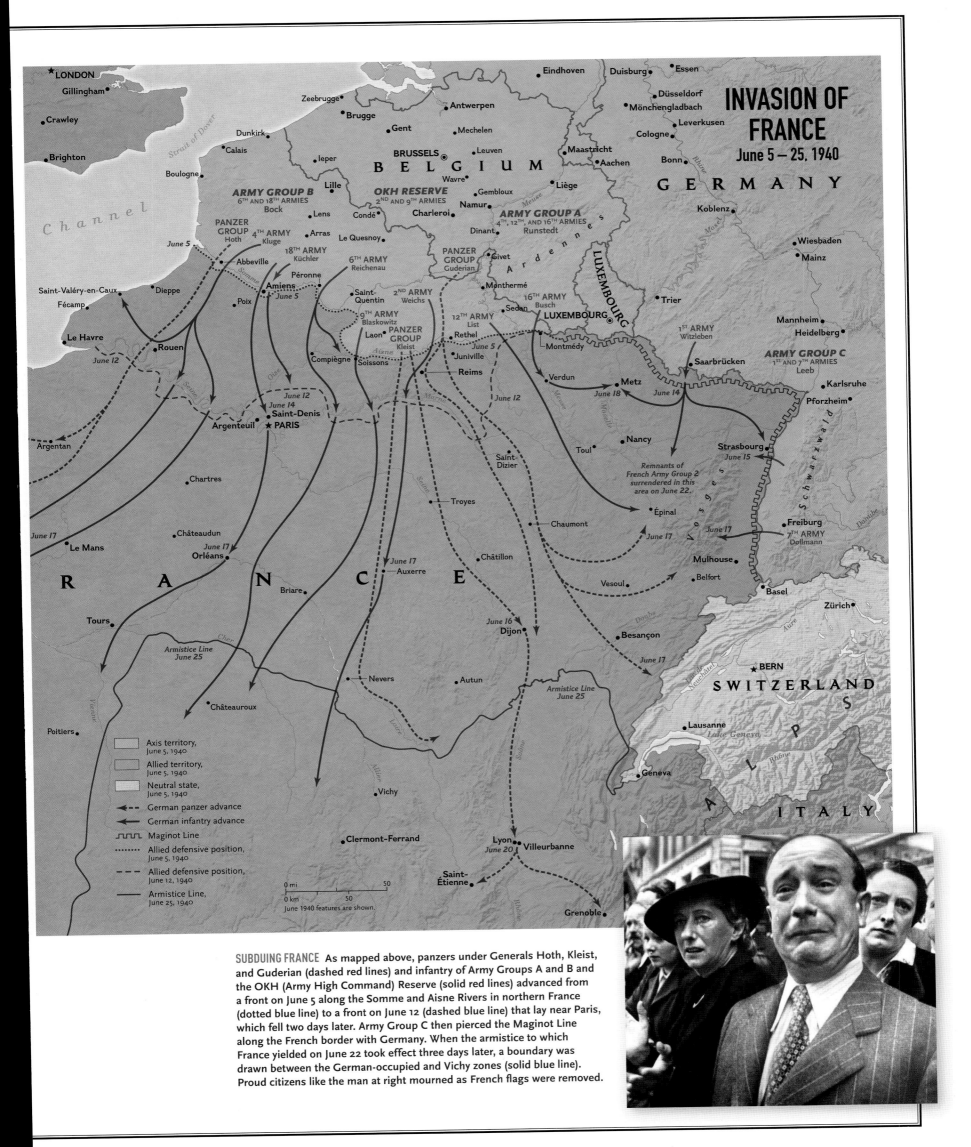

INVASION OF FRANCE
June 5 – 25, 1940

LONDON
Gillingham
Crawley
Brighton

Zeebrugge
Brugge
Gent
Antwerpen
Mechelen
Leuven

Eindhoven
Duisburg
Essen
Düsseldorf
Mönchengladbach
Leverkusen
Cologne

Dunkirk
Calais
Boulogne

Strait of Dover

B E L G I U M
Ieper
Wavre
Gembloux
Namur
Maastricht
Aachen
Bonn

BRUSSELS

Channel

ARMY GROUP B
6TH AND 18TH ARMIES
Bock

OKH RESERVE
2ND AND 9TH ARMIES

Lille
Lens
Condé
Charleroi
Liège

ARMY GROUP A
4TH, 12TH, AND 16TH ARMIES
Runstedt

Koblenz

PANZER GROUP
Hoth

4TH ARMY
Kluge

Arras
Le Quesnoy
Dinant

LUXEMBOURG

Wiesbaden
Mainz

June 5
Abbeville

18TH ARMY
Küchler

6TH ARMY
Reichenau
Péronne
Saint-Quentin

PANZER GROUP
Guderian
Givet
Monthermé

16TH ARMY
Busch

LUXEMBOURG

Trier

Saint-Valéry-en-Caux
Dieppe
Fécamp

Amiens
June 5
Poix

9TH ARMY
Blaskowitz
Laon
PANZER GROUP
Kleist

2ND ARMY
Weichs

Sedan

12TH ARMY
List
Rethel
June 5
Juniville

Montmédy
Verdun
Metz
June 18
June 14

1ST ARMY
Witzleben
Saarbrücken

ARMY GROUP C
1ST AND 7TH ARMIES
Leeb

Mannheim
Heidelberg

Le Havre
Rouen
June 12

Compiègne
Soissons
Reims
June 12

Karlsruhe
Pforzheim

Argenteuil
June 12
June 14
Saint-Denis
★ **PARIS**

Saint-Dizier
Toul
Nancy

Strasbourg
June 15

Argentan

Chartres
Châteaudun

Troyes
Chaumont

Remnants of French Army Group 2 surrendered in this area on June 22.
Épinal
June 17
June 17
June 17

Freiburg
7TH ARMY
Dollmann

June 17
Le Mans
Orléans
June 17

Châtillon
Auxerre
June 17

Mulhouse
Belfort
Basel

Briare

Vesoul

Zürich

F R A N C E

Tours

June 16
Dijon
Besançon
June 17

Châteauroux

Nevers
Autun

Armistice Line June 25

BERN

Poitiers

S W I T Z E R L A N D

Vichy

Lausanne
Lake Geneva

A L P S

Clermont-Ferrand

Lyon
June 20
Villeurbanne

Saint-Étienne

Geneva

I T A L Y

Grenoble

Legend

- Axis territory, June 5, 1940
- Allied territory, June 5, 1940
- Neutral state, June 5, 1940
- ◄---- German panzer advance
- ◄—— German infantry advance
- ⌐⌐⌐⌐ Maginot Line
- ········ Allied defensive position, June 5, 1940
- – – – Allied defensive position, June 12, 1940
- —— Armistice Line, June 25, 1940

0 mi 50
0 km 50
June 1940 features are shown.

SUBDUING FRANCE As mapped above, panzers under Generals Hoth, Kleist, and Guderian (dashed red lines) and infantry of Army Groups A and B and the OKH (Army High Command) Reserve (solid red lines) advanced from a front on June 5 along the Somme and Aisne Rivers in northern France (dotted blue line) to a front on June 12 (dashed blue line) that lay near Paris, which fell two days later. Army Group C then pierced the Maginot Line along the French border with Germany. When the armistice to which France yielded on June 22 took effect three days later, a boundary was drawn between the German-occupied and Vichy zones (solid blue line). Proud citizens like the man at right mourned as French flags were removed.

BATTLE OF BRITAIN

FROM THE LUFTWAFFE'S BLITZ TO THE STRATEGIC BOMBING OF GERMANY

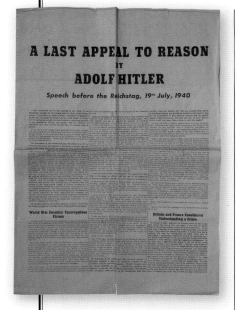

CHRONOLOGY

JULY 10, 1940 The Luftwaffe launches initial attacks on British ports and convoys.

AUGUST 1, 1940 Hitler orders the Luftwaffe to neutralize the RAF as a prerequisite for Operation Sea Lion (planned invasion of Britain).

AUGUST 13, 1940 Luftwaffe campaign against the RAF begins in earnest.

SEPTEMBER 7, 1940 At Hitler's order, the Luftwaffe shifts focus of attacks from the RAF to London and other cities.

SEPTEMBER 15, 1940 The RAF inflicts heavy losses on Luftwaffe warplanes attacking London and other targets in what will be known as the decisive Battle of Britain Day.

SEPTEMBER 17, 1940 Hitler postpones Operation Sea Lion indefinitely. The "Blitz" of London and other cities will continue until May 1941, causing carnage but leaving the British defiant.

AIR DEFENSE RAF pilots-in-training wearing parachute packs scramble to their fighters during an alert. Britain was guarded by a coastal network of radar stations and observers that often gave RAF pilots enough warning to intercept Luftwaffe squadrons before they reached their targets.

Hitler's hopes that London might come to terms once Paris fell faded when Winston Churchill (shown opposite wearing an air-raid helmet) succeeded Neville Chamberlain as British prime minister on May 10, 1940, the same day German troops invaded the Low Countries. On May 13, as Allied forces there were driven back, Churchill vowed to bring the struggle against Germany "to a victorious conclusion," while promising Parliament and the public nothing in the interim "but blood, toil, tears and sweat." He blasted the Nazis by pledging that the British would wage war with all their might "against a monstrous tyranny, never surpassed in the dark, lamentable catalogue of human crime."

Churchill remained defiant after France fell and dismissed Hitler's "Last Appeal to Reason" (left), a propaganda leaflet dropped on Britain that blamed the conflict on Churchill's intransigence. Hitler planned an invasion of England, which would first require an all-out assault by the Luftwaffe on the Royal Air Force (RAF). Only by achieving air supremacy could Germans counter the British advantage at sea, where the Royal Navy remained formidable, and hope to shield the invasion forces.

Before that air war began in earnest, the Luftwaffe launched attacks in July on English ports and convoys that cost the Germans twice as many aircraft as the RAF lost opposing those strikes. Luftwaffe bombers proved vulnerable to swift, maneuverable Supermarine Spitfires and Hawker Hurricanes, but those British fighter planes had to contend with German fighters, notably the powerful Messerschmitt Me-109. The lesson drawn from early losses suffered by the numerically superior Luftwaffe was to focus attacks on RAF fighters and fighter bases until they no longer posed a threat.

On August 1, Hitler ordered the Luftwaffe to overpower the RAF "with all the forces at its command and in the shortest possible time." British fighter bases and aircraft factories would be targeted by German bombers escorted mainly by Me-109s, whose pilots would engage in lethal dogfights with foes flying Spitfires and Hurricanes. Unlike aerial combat in World War I, which was spirited but strategically insignificant, the Battle of Britain between the Luftwaffe and the RAF would determine whether the nation that Churchill committed to war against "monstrous tyranny" could continue to seek victory or might soon be vanquished. ■

BATTLE STATIONS As mapped below, most German fighter bases were situated close to England because those fast fighters guzzled fuel and had shorter range than German bombers, whose bases were located farther from England to reduce the risk of attack. The map shows only RAF fighter bases because the battle was largely defensive for the British, who relied on their fighters and on radar, including high-level stations that detected high-flying aircraft at long range and low-level stations that detected low-flying planes at short range.

BATTLE OF BRITAIN
July 10 – October 31, 1940

Luftwaffe
Luftlotte 5
(from Norway and
Denmark)

ATLANTIC OCEAN

SCOTLAND

Hillhead
School Hill
Aberdeen

Dundee
Douglas Wood
Firth of Tay

Firth of Forth

Drone Hill

Glasgow
Edinburgh

Ayr

RAF Fighter Command 13 Group

Ottercops Moss

Newcastle upon Tyne

Carlisle
Newcastle
Sunderland

NORTHERN IRELAND
Belfast

Middlesbrough
Danby Beacon

Scarborough

Isle of Man

Staxton Wold
York

Irish Sea

Blackpool
Leeds
Bradford
Kingston upon Hull

Liverpool
Manchester
Sheffield
Stenigot

IRELAND
Dublin ★

Anglesey

Wrexham

UNITED

RAF Fighter Command 12 Group
Nottingham
Watnall

West Beckham

AMSTERDAM

KINGDOM
Shrewsbury
ENGLAND

Norwich
Stoke Holy Cross

NETHERLANDS
(Occupied by Germany May 1940–May 1945)
Rotterdam

WALES
Birmingham
Coventry

Cambridge
High Street
Ipswich
Bawdsey

North Sea

North Channel

St. George's Channel

Haycastle
Warren

Gloucester
Oxford
Stanmore
Uxbridge
Reading
LONDON ★
R. Thames

Colchester
Bromley
Canewdon

Celtic Sea

Swansea
Cardiff
Bristol
Rudloe
Bath

Dunkirk
Dover
Dover
Rye
Str. of Dover

BELGIUM
(Occupied by Germany May 1940–Feb. 1945)

Antwerp

BRUSSELS

RAF Fighter Command 11 Group

Dunkirk
Calais

Lille

Bristol Channel

RAF Fighter Command 10 Group
Southampton
Bournemouth

Brighton
Pevensey

Luftwaffe Luftlotte 2

Exeter

Lyme Bay
Bill of Portland

Portsmouth
Ventnor
Isle of Wight

Arras

Penzance

Hawks Tor

Plymouth

Prawle Pt.

Land's End

RAF Fighter Command
- ■ Command headquarters
- — Group boundary
- ● Group headquarters
- ⊥ Fighter base
- ♯ High-level radar station
- ⊤ Low-level radar station

Luftwaffe Command
- — Air fleet boundary
- ■ Air fleet headquarters
- ⊕ Bomber base
- ⊥ Fighter base

English Channel

Dieppe

Range of low-level radar
(aircraft detection at 500 feet)

Range of high-level radar
(aircraft detection at 15,000 feet)

Amiens

Reims

Cherbourg
Le Havre
Rouen

CHANNEL ISLANDS
(Occupied by Germany June 1940–May 1945)

Baie de la Seine

Caen

Seine

Marne

PARIS

Allied country, July 10, 1940
Axis-occupied territory July 10, 1940
Neutral state, July 10, 1940

NORMANDY

Luftwaffe Luftlotte 3

Melun

Troyes

Golfe de St.-Malo

St.-Malo

0 mi   50   100
0 km 50 100
August 1939 features are shown.

St.-Brieuc

Brest

BRITTANY

Rennes

Le Mans

FRANCE
(Occupied by Germany May 1940–Sept. 1944)

Orléans

Auxerre

Lorient

DOGFIGHTS FOR HIGH STAKES

Elevated by Hitler from the rank of field marshal in July 1940, Reich Marshal Hermann Göring (holding a ceremonial sword below) believed that his Luftwaffe alone could defeat the British, precluding the planned invasion of England, dubbed Operation Sea Lion. "The Führer has ordered me to crush Britain with my Luftwaffe," he declared proudly. Despite his lofty title, Göring was an erratic, insecure figure addicted to morphine, which he began taking after he was shot during Hitler's abortive Munich Putsch in 1923. Anxious to impress Hitler after the Luftwaffe failed to halt Allied evacuations at Dunkirk, he launched massive attacks in mid-August aimed at reducing the RAF to impotence. But in the ensuing dogfights, the British often downed more German aircraft than they lost, aided by radar and the superb agility of Spitfires and Hurricanes. "The bastards make infernally tight turns," a German pilot said. "There seems no way of nailing them." German Me-109s were formidable, but they were often short of fuel by the time they entered combat and could not fight long before turning back. Alarmed by steep bomber losses to the British, Göring ordered all bombing missions closely escorted by fighters, which kept pilots from prowling and pouncing on RAF fighters. It was hard to win dogfights, one German ace complained, when you put the "dog on a chain."

Despite such disadvantages, the sheer weight of the Luftwaffe offensive wore down RAF Fighter Command. By late August, many of its bases were badly damaged, with bomb-cratered runways, and it was running short of pilots. Britain might have lost the battle if not for its large complement of foreign fighter pilots, including 145 from Poland and over 200 from New Zealand and Canada combined. In early September, Hitler gave Fighter Command a reprieve when he retaliated for British air raids on Berlin, which were more demoralizing than destructive, by shifting attacks away from RAF bases to London. Göring overestimated enemy losses in fighter planes and thought the city would be lightly defended. On September 15, Fighter Command—which had used the respite to repair airfields and rush newly trained pilots into action—attacked in swarms and downed nearly 60 incoming warplanes. Two days later, Hitler postponed Operation Sea Lion indefinitely. For the first time, an opponent had matched him blow for blow and refused to give way. ∎

AIR CHIEFS Luftwaffe commanders accompany Reich Marshal Hermann Göring (second from right in the foreground) during a tour of air bases established in occupied France, from which German warplanes began launching attacks on British targets in July 1940.

NOSEDIVE At near right, a Luftwaffe Me-110 fighter-bomber—slower and more vulnerable than the Me-109 fighter—goes down during the Battle of Britain. At far right, an RAF Hawker Hurricane loses its wing in a dogfight photographed from a German cockpit.

NAVIGATION MAP This Luftwaffe map for the Battle of Britain was printed on cloth so that it could be easily carried by airmen and might be concealed if they were captured. It combines a rectilinear Mercator projection with lines representing Earth's curvature.

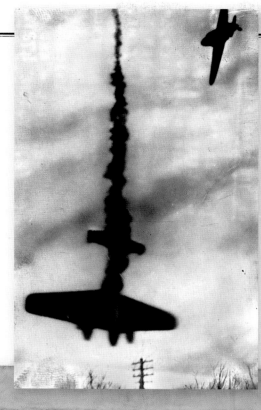

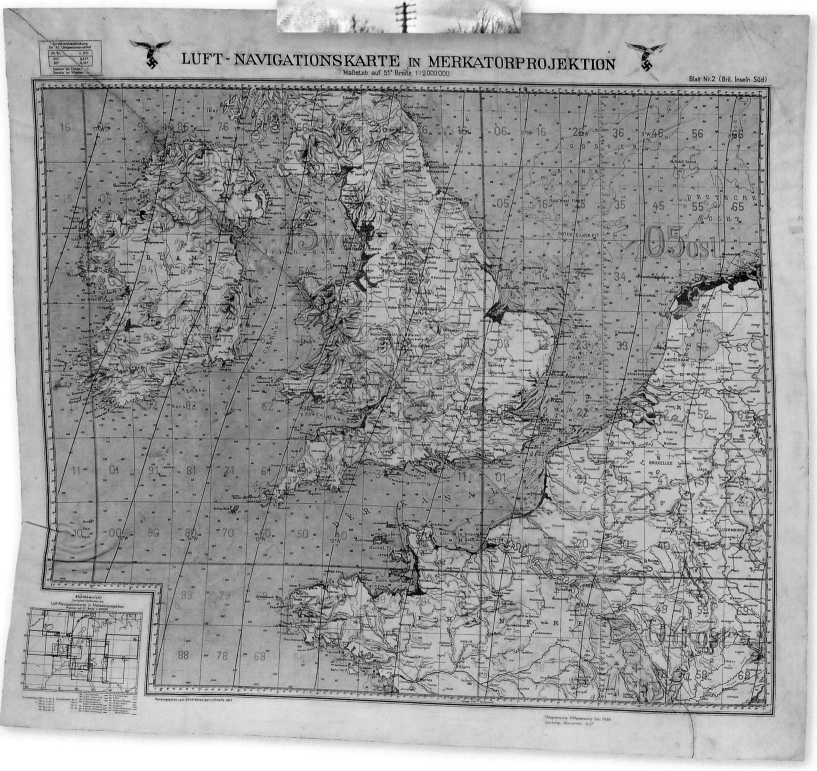

LUFT - NAVIGATIONSKARTE IN MERKATORPROJEKTION

Maßstab auf 51° Breite 1:2 000 000

Blatt Nr. 2 (Brit. Inseln Süd)

A PUNISHING BLITZ

German plans to expose Britain to invasion and defeat with an aerial blitzkrieg were thwarted when the Luftwaffe failed to crush the RAF in September 1940 and Operation Sea Lion was shelved. But the fiery ordeal that the British called the Blitz was just beginning. Punishing German air raids on London and other cities continued into the spring of 1941, most of them conducted at night, when RAF fighters and antiaircraft batteries were less effective at downing incoming warplanes. Darkness also made it harder for bombers to hit prime targets such as docks and power stations that were designated on Luftwaffe maps like that opposite. German efforts to guide pilots to targets at night using radio beams were countered when the British jammed those signals, but precision bombing was not required to wreak havoc among civilians. Many children were evacuated from London to safer homes in the countryside, and thousands of people sought shelter overnight in stations of the London Underground (below).

Hermann Göring envisioned using incendiaries to kindle a great fire that would result in the "total destruction of London." Luftwaffe fire-bombings never engulfed an entire city in flames, but they consumed large parts of London, Coventry, Southampton, and other population centers. By May 1941, the Blitz had killed over 40,000 people and injured many more. Yet the pounding did little to demoralize civilians or fulfill Hitler's strategic objective when he launched the Battle of Britain—to eliminate that nation "as a base from which the war against Germany can be continued." ■

TARGETING LONDON As the Blitz wore on in late 1940, daylight raids on London like the one pictured in this aerial view of a German Heinkel He-111 bomber above the winding Thames River gave way to nighttime attacks, which were harder to defend against and more agonizing for civilians. Londoners could risk destruction by sleeping in their own beds at night or retreat to crowded Underground stations (below) where sleep was fitful.

CHARTING THE BLITZ Red notations on the German operational map of London below indicate areas containing significant targets for the Luftwaffe during the Blitz, including the Royal Docks along the Thames River (I), which were heavily damaged, and the Battersea Power Station (III), which emerged almost unscathed. Residential areas in London were hit when bombers missed such targets or when large areas were deliberately fire-bombed, causing infernos that firefighters struggled to put out (left). Londoners withstood the Blitz, however, and took as their motto: "Keep Calm and Carry On."

Genst. 5. Abt.   Oktober 1940

Übersichtskarte der Zielgebiete I bis IV London
mit den wichtigsten Versorgungsbetrieben

Maßstab 1 : 50 000

OPERATION SEA LION

Hitler's order in September 1940 putting off Operation Sea Lion came as a relief for German commanders assigned to carry out the proposed invasion. German Navy chief Grand Adm. Erich Raeder had nixed a plan by the Army to land some 30 divisions totaling more than 500,000 troops at several places along a 200-mile front on England's south coast. At Raeder's urging, the landing zone was narrowed to about 35 miles along the Strait of Dover (see map at right), where nine German divisions would land initially, followed by two more waves of troops. That gave Raeder some hope of preventing the Royal Navy from shredding an invasion fleet as it crossed to England. But German Army chief of staff Gen. Franz Halder worried that invading on a narrow front would allow the British Army to concentrate its forces. "I might just as well put the troops straight through a sausage machine!" he complained.

Hitler's decision to side with Raeder in that dispute did not solve another problem faced by the Navy, which possessed no landing craft and had to hastily assemble and convert more than 1,000 river barges, many of which lacked engines and would have to be towed to landing zones by tugboats. Meanwhile, the Army rushed to convert tanks so that they could be unloaded off the coast rather than on shore, which would be too difficult and dangerous for heavily loaded barges. By late August, 200 tanks had been converted into watertight submersibles with air-intake tubes that could operate at depths up to 15 feet. Tank crews when submerged could see above water through periscopes but could not spot obstructions placed underwater off beaches where the British anticipated invasions.

Operation Sea Lion was so fraught with risks that Raeder, Halder, and other commanders feared it might falter even if the Luftwaffe succeeded in neutralizing the RAF. When the Luftwaffe failed in that attempt, they viewed their prospects in much the same light as did Churchill, who suggested in a radio address that any Germans who landed would be driven back into the sea and devoured. "We are waiting for the long-promised invasion," he declared. "So are the fishes." ∎

INVASION PLAN A German planning map for Operation Sea Lion shows forces embarking on the French coast between Calais and Dunkirk and landing on the English coast between Hastings and Dover, a port that could be used to reinforce the invasion. The British feared gas attacks, which never materialized, and issued gas masks (opposite top) to the home guards pictured here in training. Despite official opposition to allowing women to take up arms, some received weapons training to defend against a German invasion (opposite bottom).

FOREWARNED An intelligence report issued by the War Office in London in April 1941—when the British remained under the Blitz and could not rule out a German invasion—describes various tactics and techniques planned for Operation Sea Lion such as deploying submersible tanks and dropping paratroopers behind British lines on the coast.

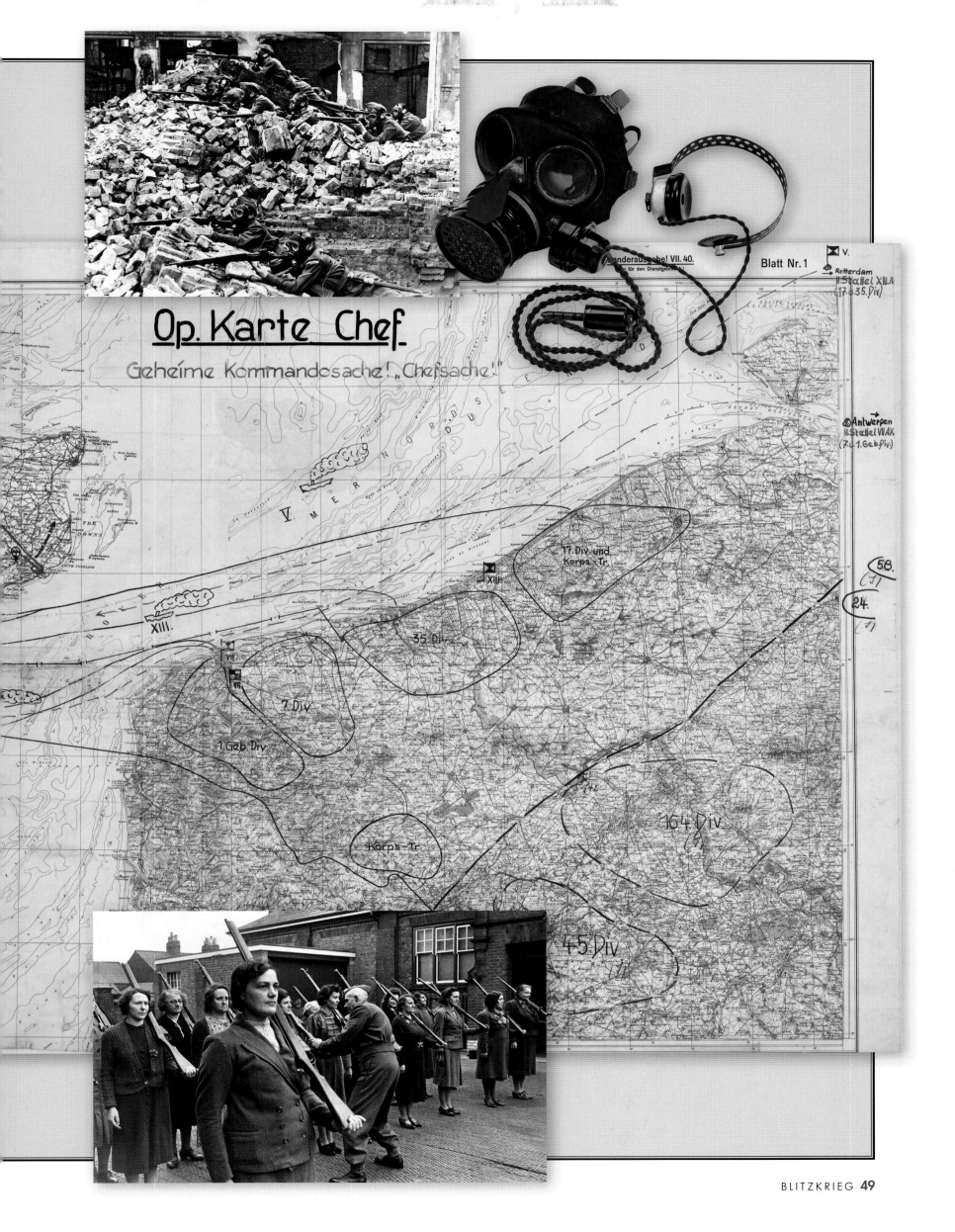

Op. Karte Chef.

Geheime Kommandosache! „Chefsache!"

HARD START Twin-engine Vickers Wellington medium bombers (left) were involved in some of the earliest RAF raids against Germany. The morale-boosting poster opposite, which highlights air raids on Berlin (white circle) and the industrialized Ruhr (detailed on the map at lower right), suggests that Germany had been hard-hit by January 1941, just five months after the attacks began. In fact, many RAF bombers missed their targets during those months or were shot down by German fighters or antiaircraft batteries like the one pictured below (inset), guarding factories in the Ruhr.

STRATEGIC BOMBING OF GERMANY

Britain entered the war far better prepared to defend its airspace than to bomb distant targets. RAF fighters were among the world's best in 1940, but its bombers could not carry large enough payloads to do much damage to German cities or industries and were highly vulnerable to attack unless they flew at night, in which case they seldom hit targets precisely. Early British bombing raids on Germany were often retaliatory and had more of a psychological than strategic impact. Nuisance raids on Berlin in late August 1940, after a stray Luftwaffe bomber mistakenly hit London, succeeded in enraging Hitler, who vowed that if the British targeted "our cities, then we will raze their cities to the ground." The ensuing Blitz was fearful for civilians but enabled the RAF to rehabilitate its hard-pressed Fighter Command and bolster its Bomber Command.

To boost British morale during the Blitz and goad Hitler, the RAF bombed Munich on the night of November 8, 1940, while the Führer was addressing so-called Old Fighters of the Nazi Party on the anniversary of his Munich Putsch. Hitler was unharmed, but the Luftwaffe made good on his vow to retaliate mercilessly by fire-bombing Coventry on the night of November 14, gutting the city center and leaving more than 1,000 people

dead or wounded and tens of thousands homeless. A retaliatory raid by the RAF in December on the German city of Mannheim was far less devastating, causing slightly more than 100 casualties.

The British poster opposite, showing much of Germany under bombardment, offered the public an optimistic view of RAF attacks that was not shared by British commanders. A confidential report issued in 1941 revealed that only one in three RAF aircraft delivered bombs within five miles of their intended targets—and only one in ten did so in the heavily defended Ruhr, Germany's industrial core. At Churchill's urging, the RAF began amassing a force of heavy bombers, many of them four-engine aircraft as opposed to the twin-engine light and medium RAF bombers that entered the air war against Germany. Technological advances in guiding aircraft at night and delivering bombs on target would increase the accuracy of those heavy hitters, but their main task would be to saturate industrial areas and population centers with blockbuster bombs and incendiaries, far surpassing the destruction wrought by the Luftwaffe on British cities. In Churchill's opinion, the only thing that could bring down Hitler was "an absolutely devastating exterminating attack by very heavy bombers from this country upon the Nazi homeland." ∎

Allied Air Offensive against Germany

UP TO JANUARY 1ST 1941

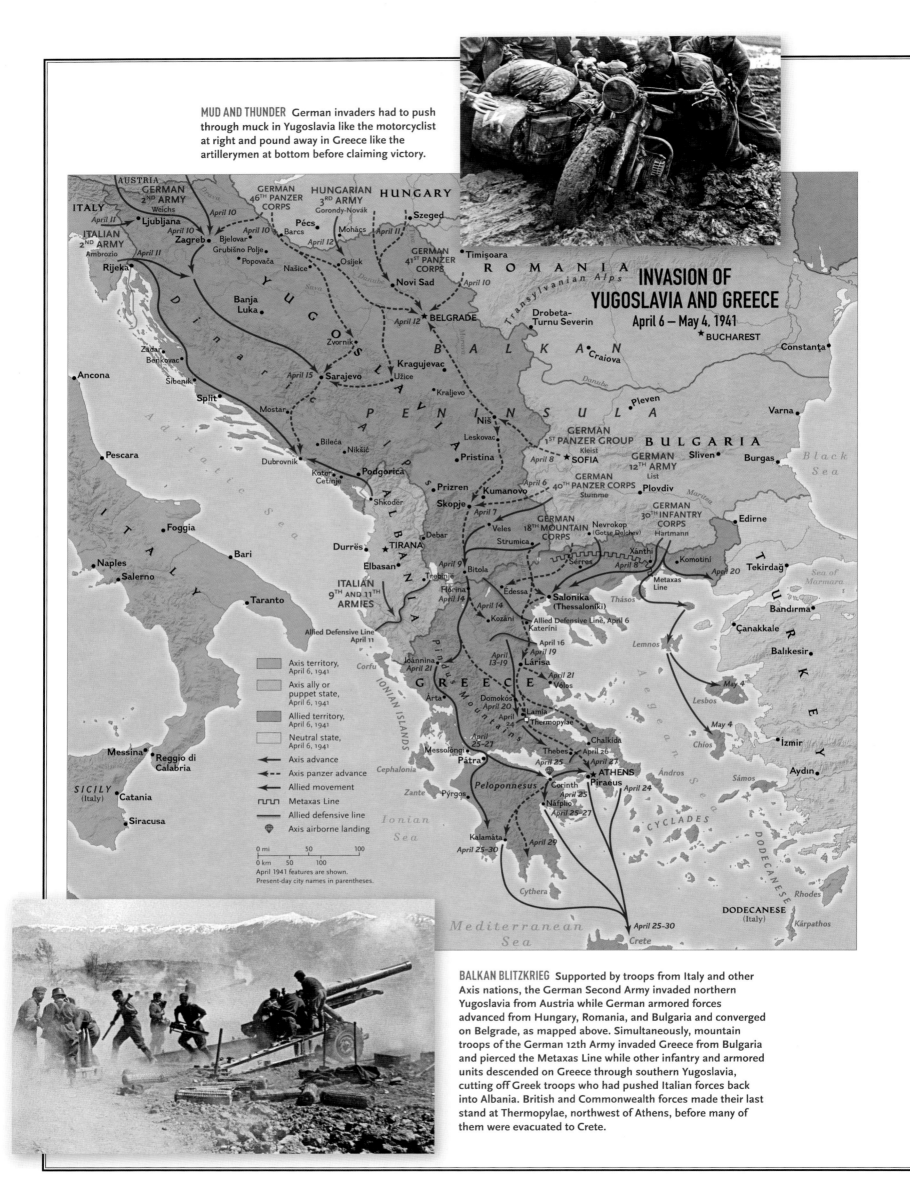

MUD AND THUNDER German invaders had to push through muck in Yugoslavia like the motorcyclist at right and pound away in Greece like the artillerymen at bottom before claiming victory.

INVASION OF YUGOSLAVIA AND GREECE
April 6 – May 4, 1941

▨	Axis territory, April 6, 1941
▨	Axis ally or puppet state, April 6, 1941
▨	Allied territory, April 6, 1941
☐	Neutral state, April 6, 1941
←	Axis advance
◄---	Axis panzer advance
←	Allied movement
⊓⊔⊓⊔	Metaxas Line
——	Allied defensive line
⊕	Axis airborne landing

0 mi — 50 — 100
0 km — 50 — 100

April 1941 features are shown.
Present-day city names in parentheses.

BALKAN BLITZKRIEG Supported by troops from Italy and other Axis nations, the German Second Army invaded northern Yugoslavia from Austria while German armored forces advanced from Hungary, Romania, and Bulgaria and converged on Belgrade, as mapped above. Simultaneously, mountain troops of the German 12th Army invaded Greece from Bulgaria and pierced the Metaxas Line while other infantry and armored units descended on Greece through southern Yugoslavia, cutting off Greek troops who had pushed Italian forces back into Albania. British and Commonwealth forces made their last stand at Thermopylae, northwest of Athens, before many of them were evacuated to Crete.

WAR IN THE BALKANS

THE INVASIONS OF YUGOSLAVIA, GREECE, AND CRETE

The German offensive in the Balkans in April 1941 followed a fateful step taken by Hitler the previous December when he ordered his forces to be ready by May 15, 1941, to "crush Soviet Russia in a quick campaign," designated Operation Barbarossa. Hitler had long intended to invade Russia, but events in 1940 spurred him on. He was alarmed in June when Stalin pressured Romania—whose oil helped fuel the German war machine—into ceding the province of Bessarabia. That did not violate Stalin's secret deal with Hitler, but he feared Stalin might scrap the pact and grab all of Romania. Determined to strike first, Hitler set out to secure Germany's southern flank for Operation Barbarossa by invading Greece, which had sided with Britain after Italian forces occupying Albania crossed the Greek border in October 1940. To isolate Greece, Hitler expanded his Axis alliance with Italy and Japan to include Romania and its Balkan neighbors Hungary, Bulgaria, and Yugoslavia, which bowed to Germany on March 25, 1941. Two days later, Yugoslav officers staged a coup in Belgrade and spurned the Axis. Hitler then called for a "light-ning invasion" of Yugoslavia as well as Greece.

German troops advanced into both countries from Bulgaria on April 6, while additional Axis forces invaded Yugoslavia from Romania, Hungary, Austria, and Italy. Intent on punishing Belgrade for defying him, Hitler unleashed a murderous Luftwaffe air raid on the capital that killed as many as 17,000 people. Yugoslav resistance soon crumbled as Croats broke with Serb leaders in Belgrade, which fell on April 13, and formed a separate Croatian state beholden to Germany.

In Greece, German mountain troops descending from Bulgaria broke through the fortified Metaxas Line while other infantry and armored units crossed the porous Greek border with Yugoslavia and pressed southward. British troops who had arrived in early March with a large complement of Australians and New Zealanders fought hard to stem the German tide at Thermopylae but gave way on April 24. Athens fell three days later. Some 40,000 British soldiers escaped, many of whom were evacuated to the Greek island of Crete, where they would soon be attacked by German paratroopers. ∎

CHRONOLOGY

SEPTEMBER 27, 1940 Tripartite Pact, signed by Axis Powers Germany, Italy, and Japan, commits them to defend one another against attack.

OCTOBER 28, 1940 Italian troops in occupied Albania invade Greece, leading that nation to ally with Britain against the Axis.

DECEMBER 18, 1940 Hitler issues Führer Directive 21, ordering his forces to prepare for Operation Barbarossa (invasion of the Soviet Union) within five months.

MARCH 25, 1941 Yugoslavia commits to the Axis, joining Romania, Hungary, and Bulgaria as Hitler prepares to invade Greece and secure the Balkans prior to Operation Barbarossa.

MARCH 27, 1941 Yugoslav officers seize power in Belgrade and break with the Axis, prompting Hitler to invade Yugoslavia as well as Greece.

APRIL 6, 1941 Invasion of Yugoslavia and Greece begins.

APRIL 12–13, 1941 Yugoslav capital Belgrade falls to the Germans.

APRIL 27, 1941 Greek capital Athens falls to the Germans as British forces in Greece prepare to evacuate to Crete.

MAY 20, 1941 German airborne invasion of Crete begins.

JUNE 1, 1941 Last Allied troops holding out on Crete are evacuated.

GRIM RECKONING The swift conquest of the Balkans was followed by years of guerrilla warfare as partisans lashed out at Axis occupation forces. Partisans responsible for attacks—or hostages seized in retaliation—were often summarily executed like the four victims at left, hanged in Yugoslavia.

STORMING CRETE

At dawn on May 20, 1941, the largest airborne operation yet attempted unfolded on Crete. Thousands of German paratroopers dispatched by Gen. Kurt Student, commander of the Luftwaffe's 11th Air Corps, descended near an airstrip at Maleme that Student planned to use to reinforce the invasion. Gen. Bernard Freyberg, the Allied commander on Crete, had been warned of the attack when Luftwaffe radio signals were intercepted and deciphered. He assigned a division of his fellow New Zealanders, supported by Greek troops, to defend Maleme and the nearby Allied command center at Canea (Chania). Those alert forces killed many vulnerable paratroopers as they landed. Other invaders died when their planes were shot down or their gliders crashed on landing. Enough men of the Seventh Paratroop Division went into battle, however, to place the outcome at Maleme in doubt. Attacks on two other targets on Crete—Retimo (Rethymno) and Heraklion (Irakleio)—involved fewer paratroopers and were repulsed, but Student stepped up the pressure on Maleme. His men seized the airstrip on May 21 and began landing reinforcements, who helped repulse a counterattack on the 22nd and overwhelmed Crete's defenders in the days ahead. Over 17,000 Allied troops were captured, and the remainder were evacuated at month's end from Heraklion and Sfakia by the Royal Navy, which lost nine warships to Luftwaffe attacks.

Victory proved costly for the Germans, who had 4,000 men killed and lost over 200 aircraft on Crete. The two-month Balkan campaign did not delay Operation Barbarossa, which was postponed until late June largely because of spring floods along the Russian frontier. But German occupiers would now have to defend a large area from Yugoslavia to Crete against attacks by partisans or enemy troops, including Soviets if Hitler did not crush them in the "quick campaign" he anticipated. ∎

SHOT DOWN At left, one of many Junkers Ju-52 transports that delivered German paratroopers to drop zones on Crete plummets after being hit by flak. Despite heavy losses inflicted on the invaders by Allied defenders, surviving paratroopers formed assault groups and went into action (above).

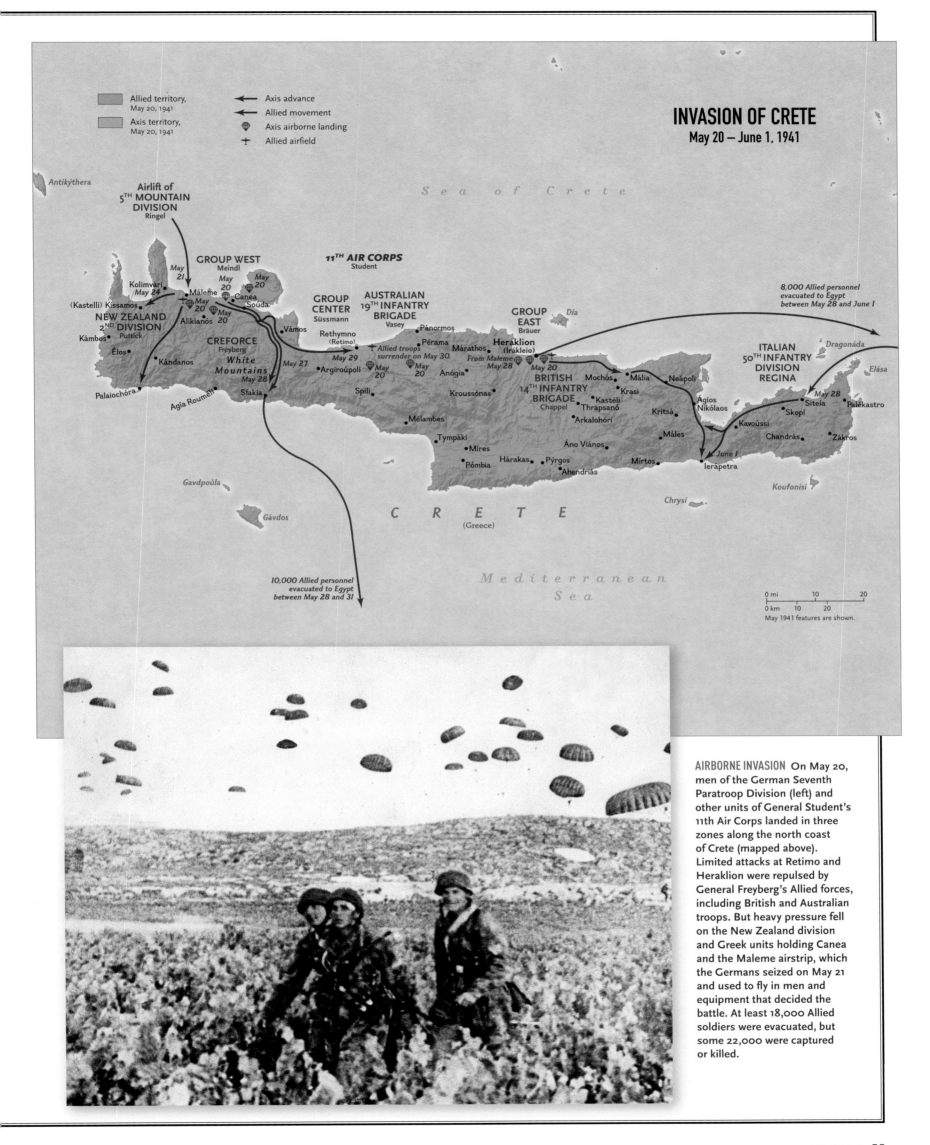

INVASION OF CRETE
May 20 – June 1, 1941

Legend:
- Allied territory, May 20, 1941
- Axis territory, May 20, 1941
- Axis advance
- Allied movement
- Axis airborne landing
- Allied airfield

Antikýthera

Sea of Crete

Airlift of 5TH MOUNTAIN DIVISION — Ringel

GROUP WEST — Meindl

11TH AIR CORPS — Student

May 21
May 20
May 20

Kolimvári
May 24
(Kastelli) Kissamos
Máleme
Canea
Soúda

NEW ZEALAND 2ND DIVISION — Puttick
Alikianós
Kámbos
Élos
Kándanos

CREFORCE — Freyberg
White Mountains May 28

GROUP CENTER — Süssmann

AUSTRALIAN 19TH INFANTRY BRIGADE — Vasey

Rethymno (Retimo)
Vámos
May 27
May 29
Argiroúpoli
Allied troops surrender on May 30
May 20
May 20

Pánormos
Pérama
Márathos
Anógia
Spíli
Kroussónas

GROUP EAST — Bräuer
Día

Heraklion (Irákleio)
From Maleme May 28
BRITISH 14TH INFANTRY BRIGADE — Chappel

Mochós
Kastéli
Thrapsanó
Arkalohóri

Mália
Krasi
Neápoli
Kritsá
Ágios Nikólaos

8,000 Allied personnel evacuated to Egypt between May 28 and June 1

ITALIAN 50TH INFANTRY DIVISION REGINA

Dragonáda
Elása

May 28
Siteía
Skopí
Palékastro
Zákros
Chandrás

Palaiochóra
Agia Rouméli
Sfakia
Mélambes
Tympáki
Míres
Pómbia
Hárakas
Pýrgos
Ahendriás
Áno Viános
Máles
Mirtos
Ierápetra
June 1
Kavoússi

Gavdpoúla
Gávdos

C R E T E
(Greece)

Chrysí
Koufonísi

Mediterranean Sea

10,000 Allied personnel evacuated to Egypt between May 28 and 31

0 mi 10 20
0 km 10 20
May 1941 features are shown.

AIRBORNE INVASION On May 20, men of the German Seventh Paratroop Division (left) and other units of General Student's 11th Air Corps landed in three zones along the north coast of Crete (mapped above). Limited attacks at Retimo and Heraklion were repulsed by General Freyberg's Allied forces, including British and Australian troops. But heavy pressure fell on the New Zealand division and Greek units holding Canea and the Maleme airstrip, which the Germans seized on May 21 and used to fly in men and equipment that decided the battle. At least 18,000 Allied soldiers were evacuated, but some 22,000 were captured or killed.

SECRET PREPARATIONS TO INVADE RUSSIA

Operation Barbarossa called for German soldiers to invade an immense country about which they knew relatively little. Various German intelligence agencies prepared the armed forces for that monumental task by secretly compiling meticulous reports, guides, maps, and atlases for officers who might soon be targeting major cities like Moscow and Leningrad or vital regions like Ukraine, Russia's fertile "breadbasket," which had ports on the Black Sea offering access to the Mediterranean. Some of that guidance came from published sources, which were not always reliable. Highways shown on Russian maps, for example, might turn out to be dirt paths. Stalin's secretive regime often concealed information about strategic port facilities, industrial areas, and transportation networks. To help chart likely targets for the invasion, the Luftwaffe conducted high-altitude photo-reconnaissance missions over Russia.

Atlases and guides like those pictured here were distributed confidentially to trusted commanders, but preparations for Operation Barbarossa involved so many agencies and officials that secrecy was compromised. Germans who spied for the Soviets such as Richard Sorge—a journalist who learned of the invasion from the German ambassador in Tokyo—warned Moscow of the forthcoming attack. But Stalin dismissed those reports as Allied fabrications meant to prod him into a war with Hitler for which the Red Army was not ready. "Have you gone mad?" Stalin said when Soviet generals suggested a preemptive strike against German troops along the Russian border in May 1941. "If you provoke the Germans," he warned, "heads will roll." ■

GUIDES FOR CONQUEST
Among the classified documents produced for Operation Barbarossa were military atlases of Leningrad (above), Ukraine (top), and an area east of Moscow between the towns of Vologda and Arkhangelsk (far right). Some atlases or reports contained foldouts like the map of Leningrad at near right or graphs like the one at upper right, showing precipitation patterns around Leningrad.

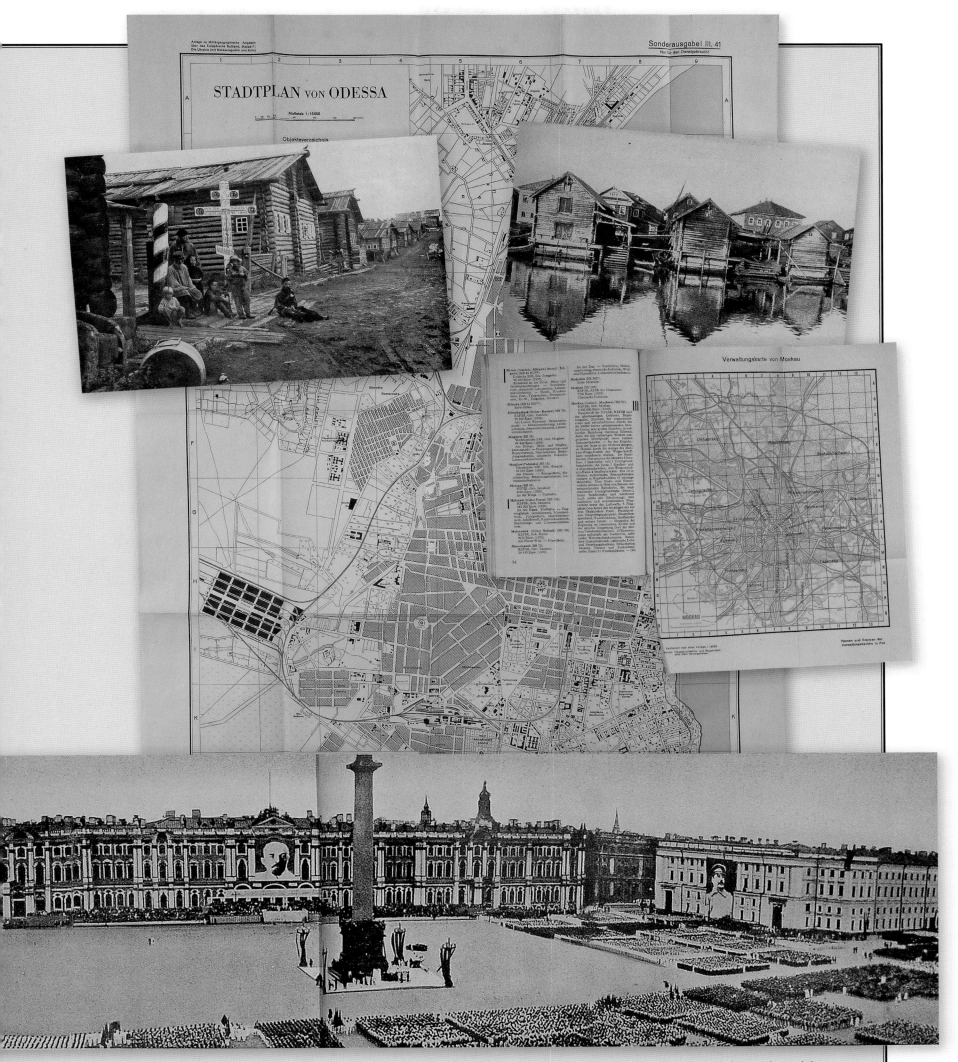

TARGETED CITIES In addition to maps of cities that figured prominently in German invasion plans like Moscow (above right) and the Ukrainian port of Odessa (above left), many atlases and reports prepared for Operation Barbarossa contained photographs, ranging from this panoramic view of a huge Soviet military parade in Leningrad Square beneath large portraits of Lenin and Stalin to pictures of forlorn Russian towns (top). Despite ample evidence that the Soviet Union was industrializing, Hitler viewed the nation as hopelessly backward and planned to cleanse fertile areas like Ukraine of Russian peasants to make room for German colonists, whom he envisioned living in "handsome villages connected by the best roads."

OPERATION
BARBAROSSA

GERMANY'S SURPRISE INVASION OF RUSSIA

CHRONOLOGY

JUNE 22, 1941 German and allied Axis troops invade the Soviet Union.

JUNE 28, 1941 Panzers of Army Group Center converge at Minsk in a major encirclement of Russian forces.

JULY 27, 1941 Army Group Center completes encirclement of Russians at Smolensk.

AUGUST 21, 1941 Hitler delays the advance on Moscow by ordering panzers of Army Group Center to help Army Group South take Kiev.

SEPTEMBER 8, 1941 Leningrad is cut off and besieged by Army Group North.

SEPTEMBER 19, 1941 Russians lose the battle for Kiev after suffering nearly one million casualties.

SEPTEMBER 30, 1941 German armored advance on Moscow resumes.

DECEMBER 5–6, 1941 Soviet troops around Moscow counterattack and drive Germans back.

DECEMBER 16, 1941 Hitler issues stand-fast order, but many German units will continue to retreat from Moscow and others will struggle to stave off encirclement before the Soviet winter offensive ends.

FIGHTING A COLOSSUS In 1941, six million Soviet troops were killed or captured by German invaders like the soldier hurling a grenade at top and the motorized infantrymen at right—panzer grenadiers clearing out Russian sharpshooters near Smolensk. The Red Army endured such losses by enlisting 34 million men and women during the war.

Beginning at dawn on June 22, 1941, more than three million German troops invaded Soviet territory, including the recently annexed Baltic states, eastern Poland, and Bessarabia, where troops from neighboring Romania and other Axis countries joined the offensive. By dismissing warnings of that massive attack, Stalin left his forces woefully vulnerable. On the first day, the Luftwaffe destroyed over 1,200 Russian aircraft, many of them on the ground. Within a week, the invaders were pouring through yawning gaps in the Stalin Line along the prewar Soviet border and taking prisoners in droves.

Like previous campaigns, Operation Barbarossa (see maps opposite) was planned as a blitzkrieg led by armored units. While Field Marshal Leeb's Army Group North targeted Leningrad and Field Marshal Rundstedt's Army Group South invaded southern Ukraine, Field Marshal Bock's Army Group Center pressed toward Moscow—an advance spearheaded by General Guderian's Second Panzer Group and General Hoth's Third Panzer Group, which converged at Minsk in late June and cut off a half million enemy troops.

In July, panzers enveloped Smolensk, within 200 miles of Moscow, but Hitler then halted the advance and ordered Guderian to help Army Group South encircle Kiev. German Army chief of staff Halder objected and urged Hitler to keep tanks and motorized infantry of the panzer groups driving toward Moscow. Privately, Halder feared even that might not bring victory. "We have underestimated the Russian colossus," he wrote. When the Russians lost a dozen divisions, he added, they would "put up another dozen," whereas the Germans were losing more men and vehicles fighting their way across Russia's "endless spaces" than they could readily replace.

In late September, the advance on Moscow resumed, but autumn rains and muddy ground soon slowed Army Group Center to a crawl while Army Group North laid siege to Leningrad and Army Group South entered the Crimean Peninsula. In late November, panzers churned forward on frozen terrain to within a dozen miles of Moscow before stalling in drifting snow and subzero temperatures. Meanwhile, Soviet forces around the capital had been reinforced and were poised to push the invaders back. ■

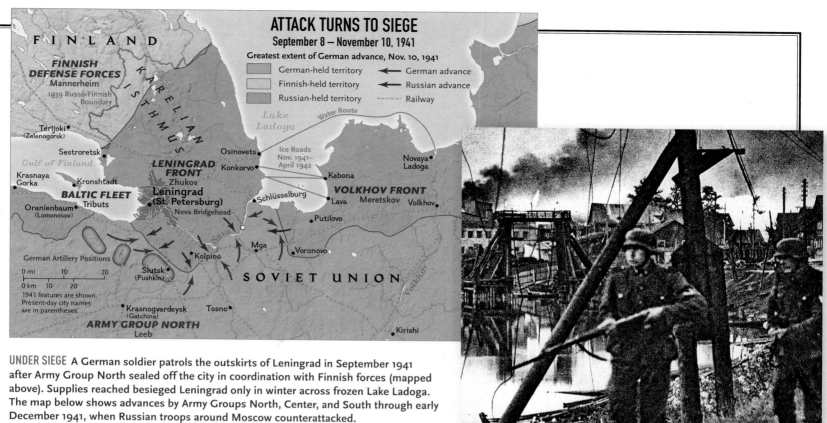

ATTACK TURNS TO SIEGE
September 8 – November 10, 1941
Greatest extent of German advance, Nov. 10, 1941

- German-held territory
- Finnish-held territory
- Russian-held territory
- ← German advance
- ← Russian advance
- --- Railway

FINLAND

FINNISH DEFENSE FORCES Mannerheim
1939 Russo-Finnish Boundary

Terijoki (Zelenogorsk)

KARELIAN ISTHMUS

Sestroretsk

Gulf of Finland

Krasnaya Gorka

Kronshtadt

BALTIC FLEET Tributs

Oranienbaum (Lomonosov)

LENINGRAD FRONT Zhukov
Leningrad (St. Petersburg)
Neva Bridgehead

Lake Ladoga

Osinovets Water Route

Konkorvo

Ice Roads Nov. 1941 – April 1942

Kabona

Schlüsselburg

Lava

Novaya Ladoga

VOLKHOV FRONT Meretskov

Volkhov

Putilovo

Mga

Voronovo

German Artillery Positions

Kolpino

0 mi 10 20
0 km 10 20
1941 features are shown. Present-day city names are in parentheses.

Slutsk (Pushkin)

SOVIET UNION

Krasnogvardeysk (Gatchina)

Tosno

ARMY GROUP NORTH Leeb

Kirishi

UNDER SIEGE A German soldier patrols the outskirts of Leningrad in September 1941 after Army Group North sealed off the city in coordination with Finnish forces (mapped above). Supplies reached besieged Leningrad only in winter across frozen Lake Ladoga. The map below shows advances by Army Groups North, Center, and South through early December 1941, when Russian troops around Moscow counterattacked.

GERMAN INVASION OF THE SOVIET UNION
June 22 – December 5, 1941

- German territory, June 21, 1941
- German ally or puppet state
- Soviet territory, June 21, 1941
- Neutral state, June 21, 1941
- Encircled pocket of Soviet forces
- ← Axis advance

Eastern Front
- ······ July 9, 1941
- ─·─· Sept. 1, 1941
- ─ ─ Oct. 1, 1941
- ─── Nov. 1, 1941
- ─── Dec. 5, 1941

NORWAY

SWEDEN

FINLAND

Helsinki ★

U.S.S.R.

LENINGRAD FRONT Popov, then Voroshilov, then Zhukov, then Fedyuninski, then Khozin

Leningrad (St. Petersburg)

Tikhvin

VOLKHOV FRONT Meretskov

Tallinn

ESTONIAN S.S.R.

Narva

18TH ARMY

Luga Aug. 18

Aug. 10

Novgorod

Staraya Russa

NORTHWESTERN FRONT Kuznetsov, then Sabennikov

Ventspils

LATVIAN S.S.R.

July 1 Riga

Pskov

16TH ARMY Aug. 12

Kalinin (Tver')

KALININ FRONT Konev

9TH ARMY Rzhev

3RD Pzgrp

4TH Pzgrp

★ MOSCOW

Baltic Sea

LITHUANIAN S.S.R.

Dvinsk (Daugavpils)

Vitsyebsk

Mozhaysk

WESTERN FRONT Yeryomenko, then Zhukov

Königsberg (Kaliningrad)

Danzig (Gdańsk)

18TH ARMY

16TH ARMY 4TH Pzgrp

Kaunas

Wilno (Vilnius)

June 27

Minsk

Vyaz'ma July 16

4TH ARMY

Kaluga

Tula

U N I O N   O F   S O V I E T   S O C I A L I S T   R E P U B L I C S   (SOVIET UNION)

Stettin (Szczecin)

ARMY GROUP NORTH 9TH, 16TH, AND 18TH ARMIES Leeb

9TH ARMY 3RD Pzgrp

Bydgoszcz

Smolensk

2ND Pzgrp

GERMANY

Poznań

Mogilev (Mahilyow)

Bryansk Oct. 23

Orel

BRYANSK FRONT Yeryomenko, then Zakharov

Białystok

Volkovysk

BELORUSSIAN S.S.R.

Gomel (Homyel')

2ND ARMY

Warsaw

Breslau (Wrocław)

ARMY GROUP CENTER 2ND, 4TH, 6TH, AND 17TH ARMIES Bock

4TH ARMY 2ND Pzgrp

2ND Pzgrp

2ND ARMY

Brest-Litovsk (Brest)

Pinsk

Kursk

RUSSIAN SOVIET FEDERATIVE SOCIALIST REPUBLIC

Łódź

Częstochowa

Katowice

Kraków

GENERAL GOVERNMENT

Lublin

6TH ARMY 1ST Pzgrp

Chełm

Kowel

Pripet Marshes

Belgorod

6TH ARMY Oct. 24

SOUTHWESTERN FRONT Kirponos, then Timoshenko

Luts'k

17TH ARMY

Przemyśl

PROT. OF BOHEMIA AND MORAVIA

Lwów (L'viv)

Ternopol (Ternopil')

Zhytomyr

Sept. 19

U K R A I N I A N   S. S. R.

Kiev Sept. 15

Kharkov

SLOVAKIA

VIENNA ★

GER.

Bratislava ★

ARMY GROUP SOUTH 11TH, ROM. 3RD, AND ROM. 4TH ARMIES Rundstedt

Vinnytsya

Uman' Aug. 2

Kremenchuk

17TH ARMY

Voroshilovgrad (Luhans'k)

SOUTHERN FRONT Tiulenev, then Ryabyshev, then Cherevichenko

BUDAPEST ★

Debrecen

Pervomays'k

Dnipropetrovs'k

Zaporizhzhya

1ST Pzgrp

Rostov

HUNGARY

MOLDAVIAN S.S.R.

11TH ARMY

Kishinev (Chisinau)

Kherson

Sept. 27

Perekop

TRANSCAUCASUS FRONT Kozlov

Sea of Azov

Odessa

ROMANIAN 3RD ARMY

ROMANIAN 4TH ARMY

CROATIA

Belgrade ●

R O M A N I A

TERRITORY OF THE MILITARY COMMANDER IN SERBIA

Bucharest ★

BULGARIA

Danube

Crimea

Kerch

17TH ARMY

Sevastopol'

Black Sea

0 mi 100 200
0 km 100 200
June 1941 features are shown. Present-day city names are in parentheses.

ORGANIZED TERROR At left, a Jewish woman flees attackers during a pogrom incited by the SS in Lviv, a Polish-Ukrainian border town seized by the Germans on June 30, 1941. Jews were often stripped before they were shot, like the boy and men above and the women below, murdered in October 1942. Such massacres continued after the SS began systematically killing Jews, Roma, and others in gas chambers in 1942.

HOLOCAUST BY BULLETS

ntent on waging a war of annihilation in Russia, Hitler set in motion dreadful atrocities. Over three million Soviet prisoners of war died in captivity, many of them left to starve in filthy holding pens. The Nazi regime's lethal Hunger Plan took food from Ukraine and elsewhere to sustain Germans, famish Russians, and gradually depopulate areas that Hitler envisioned as German colonies. But SS security forces did not wait for targeted groups to waste away from malnutrition before killing them. The invasion in June 1941 marked the onset of the Holocaust—the Nazi campaign to exterminate Jews.

Four SS *einsatzgruppen* (task forces) followed German armies into areas with large Jewish populations such as eastern Poland and Ukraine. SS officers incited pogroms: riots by local people who beat Jews to death or forced them into buildings that were then torched. But most of the killing was done by SS task forces—aided by German police and soldiers, in some cases—and by armed collaborators who helped round up Jews and shoot

them. Communist commissars were also targeted, but they were elusive, whereas many Jews lived together in villages where thousands were seized. Heinrich Himmler and SS security chief Reinhard Heydrich urged on task forces as they went from killing men to shooting women and children as well. Some German officers enabled the massacres, including Field Marshal Walter von Reichenau, who denied efforts by a subordinate to save 90 infants in Ukraine and had them shot to death.

Evidence of the atrocities included photos taken by participants and SS reports signed by Hitler, who stated that "annihilation of the Jews must be the necessary consequence" of the war he started. Some victims survived to tell of the mass executions, including a woman who feigned death in a large burial pit from which she later escaped. "I walked and walked over corpses," she said. "There seemed to be no end to it." A chilling map of operations by Task Force A (opposite) documented the murder of nearly 220,000 Jews in its sector by late 1941. ■

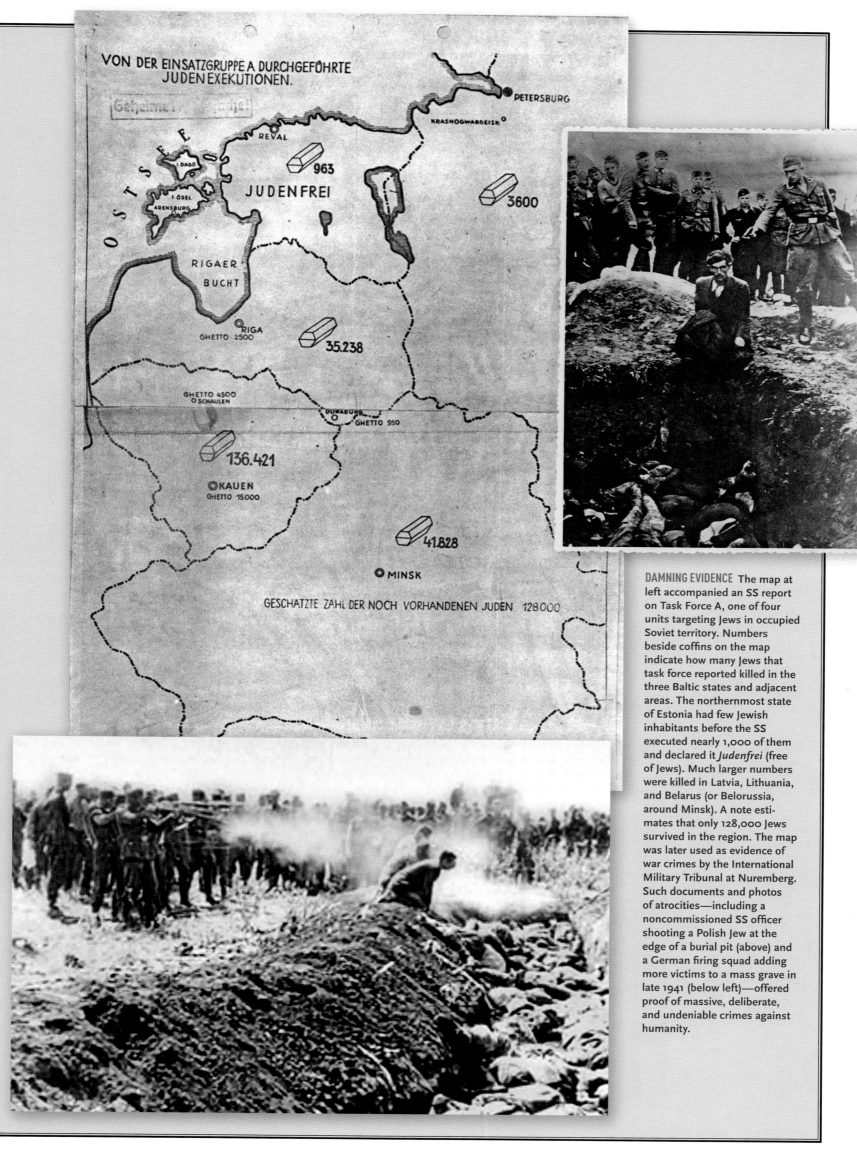

VON DER EINSATZGRUPPE A DURCHGEFÜHRTE
JUDENEXEKUTIONEN.

Geheime Reichssache!

PETERSBURG

KRASNOGWARDEISK

OSTSEE

REVAL

I. DAGÖ

I. ÖSEL
ARENSBURG

JUDENFREI

963

3600

RIGAER
BUCHT

RIGA
GHETTO 2500

35.238

GHETTO 4500
SCHAULEN

DUNABURG
GHETTO 950

136.421

KAUEN
GHETTO 15000

41.828

MINSK

GESCHÄTZTE ZAHL DER NOCH VORHANDENEN JUDEN 128000

DAMNING EVIDENCE The map at left accompanied an SS report on Task Force A, one of four units targeting Jews in occupied Soviet territory. Numbers beside coffins on the map indicate how many Jews that task force reported killed in the three Baltic states and adjacent areas. The northernmost state of Estonia had few Jewish inhabitants before the SS executed nearly 1,000 of them and declared it *Judenfrei* (free of Jews). Much larger numbers were killed in Latvia, Lithuania, and Belarus (or Belorussia, around Minsk). A note estimates that only 128,000 Jews survived in the region. The map was later used as evidence of war crimes by the International Military Tribunal at Nuremberg. Such documents and photos of atrocities—including a noncommissioned SS officer shooting a Polish Jew at the edge of a burial pit (above) and a German firing squad adding more victims to a mass grave in late 1941 (below left)—offered proof of massive, deliberate, and undeniable crimes against humanity.

THE BATTLE FOR MOSCOW

Staggered by the invasion and the swift German advances, Stalin ordered Russian soldiers who retreated without authorization shot and insisted that commanders stand fast. That stance set him at odds with Gen. Georgi Zhukov, who was ousted as the Red Army's chief of general staff after protesting Stalin's disastrous refusal to withdraw beleaguered troops from Kiev. Stalin then relented and summoned Zhukov in October to defend Moscow, which was being fortified against attack (see map opposite). As Russians prepared to commemorate the Bolshevik Revolution in Red Square on November 7 (below), Stalin turned from threatening his own troops to blasting the enemy. "If they want a war of extermination, they shall have it," he declared. Heavy reinforcements were arriving from Siberia, summoned when spy Richard Sorge, whose warnings Stalin had earlier dismissed, reported from Tokyo that Japan would not invade the Soviet Far East. With those seasoned troops, Zhukov planned to take the offensive.

The Soviet counterattack began north of Moscow on December 5 and intensified the next day as Zhukov's forces pushed west from the capital and troops led by Gen. Semyon Timoshenko advanced to the south. Ski troops and Siberian cavalry threaded gaps in German lines, and Russian crews attacked in tanks that started promptly in deep freezes while their foes had to light fires under vehicles to get them going. Many German troops suffered severe frostbite. Belated efforts to supply them with winter clothing forced some to take coats and scarves from Russians. One Soviet officer who fought against them remarked that Germans who had seemed so strong and confident in the summer were now "miserable, snotty guys wrapped in woolen kerchiefs stolen from old women in villages."

On December 16, Hitler ordered forces reeling under the Russian onslaught to stand fast. Some hard-pressed commanders refused to comply and were relieved by Hitler, including General Guderian and another panzer leader, Gen. Erich Hoepner, who did not share the Führer's belief that sheer willpower could overcome this crisis. "The will is there," Hoepner stated. "The strength is lacking." Others heeded Hitler, hunkered down, and prayed that their foes would lose strength as winter wore on. ■

MARCHING TO WAR
Snow blankets Red Square and the Kremlin in 1941 as Russian troops pass in review on November 7, a national holiday celebrating the anniversary of the Bolshevik coup in 1917. Many of these soldiers would soon enter battle against the oncoming Germans as winter tightened its grip on Russia.

FORT MOSCOW The map below, dated August 4, 1941, shows Moscow divided into five defensive sectors with outer and inner rings of barricades, tank traps, and gun emplacements. General Zhukov—pictured here second from left, examining a map—went over to the offensive in December with troops well-suited for winter, like the men in snow camouflage at bottom, entering a town left in flames by retreating Germans.

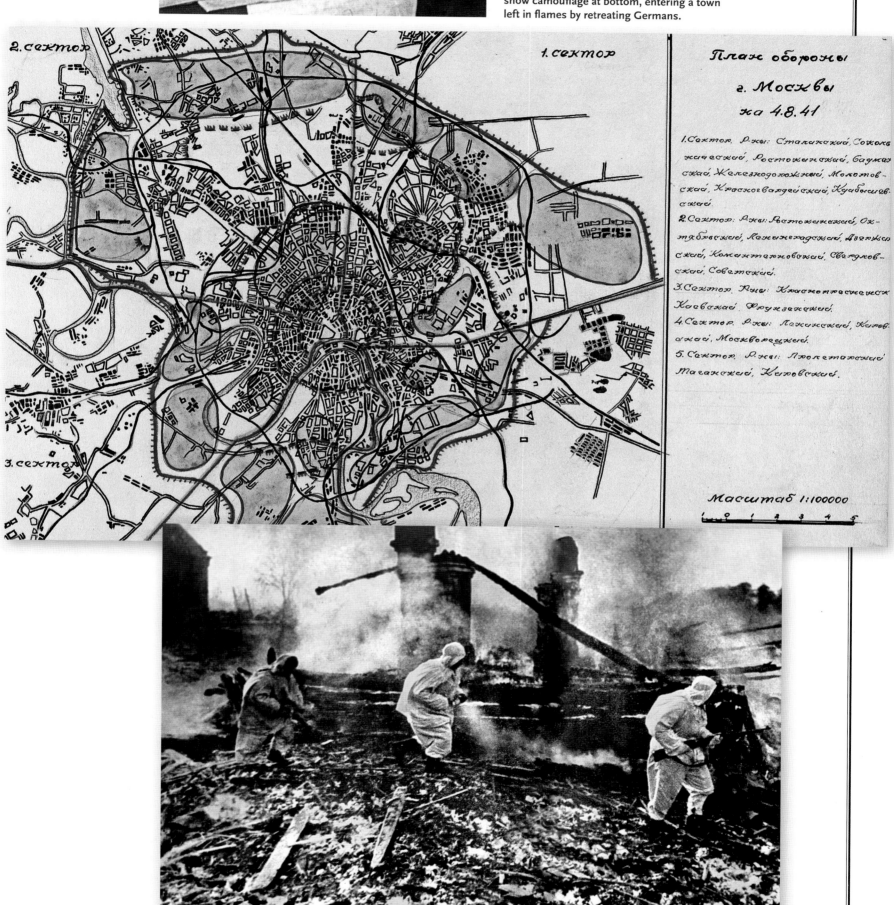

CARNAGE IN THE "MEAT-GRINDER"

Buoyed by the successful Soviet counterattack that began in December, Stalin called on the Red Army to encircle and destroy large elements of Army Group Center that were holding out west of Moscow in response to Hitler's stand-fast order. General Zhukov intended to close the trap at Vyazma, nearly 120 miles from Moscow, but the German Ninth Army and other units clung to a salient between Vyazma and Rzhev that resembled a peninsula (see map below), against which wave after wave of Soviet troops crashed. To hold that salient, Hitler placed the endangered Ninth Army under a confident new commander, Gen. Walther Model. When Hitler opposed Model's plan to send a panzer corps to reinforce Rzhev, the general posed a question that few other German officers would have dared ask: "Who commands the Ninth Army, my Führer, you or I?"

Model won the argument and held the salient against fierce attacks by Soviet tanks and troops, who suffered such heavy losses around Rzhev that they dubbed it the "meat-grinder." Among their toughest foes were soldiers of the Waffen-SS (the military wing of that Nazi organization), who were fully committed to Hitler's war of annihilation. Col. Otto Kumm, commander of the SS "Der Führer" Regiment in "Das Reich" Division, described the carnage at Rzhev that winter: "Every attack is broken at the cost of fearful casualties, often in close combat with grenades and side arms. Mounds of enemy dead pile up in front of the company positions."

Come spring, Rzhev remained under control of the Germans, who held a convoluted line west of Moscow that roughly approximated where they stood the previous October. They had averted disaster, but they now faced a drawn-out conflict that worried German officers with long memories. The Rzhev area, mapped at far right by the Soviets before they attacked there again that summer, came to resemble the dreaded battlefields of World War I, drenched in the blood of both sides time and again until the losers were bled dry. ■

EMBATTLED SALIENT Russian forces came close to pinching off the German salient that extended from Vyazma to Rzhev but were stymied by Model's Ninth Army, supported by armored units. Fighting raged at Rzhev as Soviet forces from the Kalinin Front under Gen. Ivan Konev and the Western Front under General Zhukov pressed in on Model's troops from the north and east. After the Soviets failed to achieve their objective, Zhukov remarked that the salient "proved a much harder nut to crack than we had supposed."

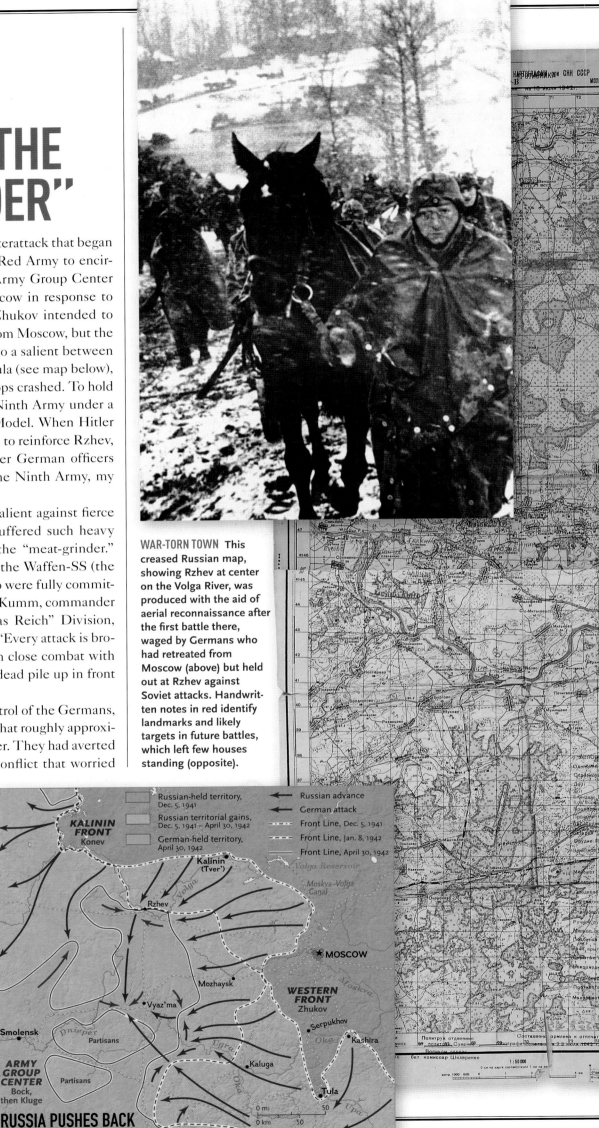

WAR-TORN TOWN This creased Russian map, showing Rzhev at center on the Volga River, was produced with the aid of aerial reconnaissance after the first battle there, waged by Germans who had retreated from Moscow (above) but held out at Rzhev against Soviet attacks. Handwritten notes in red identify landmarks and likely targets in future battles, which left few houses standing (opposite).

RUSSIA PUSHES BACK
Dec. 5, 1941 – April 30, 1942

Russian-held territory, Dec. 5, 1941
Russian territorial gains, Dec. 5, 1941 – April 30, 1942
German-held territory, April 30, 1942
Russian advance
German attack
Front Line, Dec. 5, 1941
Front Line, Jan. 8, 1942
Front Line, April 30, 1942

KALININ FRONT
Konev

Kalinin (Tver')

Rzhev

Volga Reservoir

Moskva-Volga Canal

★ MOSCOW

Mozhaysk

WESTERN FRONT
Zhukov

Serpukhov

Smolensk

Dnieper

Partisans

Vyaz'ma

Kaluga

Oka

Kashira

ARMY GROUP CENTER
Bock, then Kluge

Partisans

Tula

0 mi   50
0 km   50

1941 features are shown.
Present-day city names are in parentheses.

CHAPTER 2

WAR IN THE PACIFIC | PRELUDE TO WAR | 1943

"Before we're through with them, the Japanese language will be spoken only in hell."

VICE ADM. WILLIAM "BULL" HALSEY

DAY OF INFAMY A sailor standing amid wreckage at Ford Island Naval Air Station in Pearl Harbor watches a massive explosion caused when a bomb struck the destroyer U.S.S. *Shaw* on Sunday morning, December 7, 1941. In a single day, the Japanese attacked here and elsewhere across a 6,000-mile span of the Pacific Ocean and Southeast Asia, targeting American bases on Wake Island, Guam, and the Philippines, and the British colonies of Hong Kong and Malaya.

JAPAN TAKES ON AMERICA

CONFLICT ON A GLOBAL SCALE

When Japanese foreign minister Yosuke Matsuoka concluded the Tripartite Pact with Germany and Italy in September 1940, he had America in mind. Educated in the United States, he thought allying his nation with the aggressive Axis would make Americans more cautious and willing to compromise with Japan, which had invaded China in 1937. As he put it, "If you stand firm and start hitting back, the American will know he's talking to a man" and will negotiate "man to man." Like most Americans, however, President Franklin D. Roosevelt believed that when push came to shove, actions spoke louder than words. The appeasement of Hitler at Munich told him that yielding to an aggressor in talks was perilous and that only firm opposition to Japan's brutal occupation of China and its designs on other countries might cause it to back down.

Japanese leaders resented American efforts to deter them from subjugating China and seizing vulnerable European colonies such as French Indochina, British-ruled Burma and Malaya, and the oil-rich Dutch East Indies—a prime objective after the U.S. halted oil shipments to Japan in July 1941. Why, they asked, should Japan abandon imperial expansion at the insistence of Americans who had colonized Hawaii and taken the Philippines from Spain? Defying the United States, with its vast population and productivity, was risky. But if the price for peace was to kowtow to America and withdraw from China, then Japan would fight, and its targets would include the Philippines and the U.S. Pacific Fleet at Pearl Harbor.

Adm. Isoroku Yamamoto, commander of Japan's Combined Fleet, had spent several years in America and knew its strengths. "To fight the United States is like fighting the whole world," he remarked. Yet he hoped to smash the Pacific Fleet with warplanes launched from his formidable aircraft carriers before the American war effort geared up. His surprise attack on Pearl Harbor in December 1941 marked the start of a stunning Japanese offensive that stretched from Hawaii to Burma. The Pacific Fleet was battered but soon revived under Adm. Chester Nimitz, whose forces prevailed at Midway in June 1942 and fought other battles that enabled American and British Commonwealth troops to defeat Japanese forces on Guadalcanal, Papua, and New Guinea. By April 1943, when U.S. fighter pilots went gunning for Yamamoto and shot him down, Japan was in a world of trouble, fighting an American colossus that was bringing its full weight to bear.

March 31, 1854 Commodore Matthew Perry pressures Japan to end its isolation and agree to a treaty allowing American ships access to Japanese ports.

January 3, 1868 Imperial rule is restored in Japan under Emperor Meiji, the grandfather of Emperor Hirohito. During Meiji's reign, which lasts until his death in 1912, Japan becomes a modern industrial and military power.

January 17, 1893 American colonists overthrow the Hawaiian monarchy and establish their own government, leading to the annexation of Hawaii by the United States in 1898.

April 17, 1895 China admits defeat in the First Sino-Japanese War by ceding Taiwan and other territory to Japan.

May 1, 1898 U.S. fleet commanded by Commodore George

Dewey defeats Spanish fleet in Manila Bay during the Spanish-American War, leading to American occupation of the Philippines.

February 8, 1904 Japan instigates the Russo-Japanese War with a surprise attack on a Russian fleet at Port Arthur on the coast of Manchuria.

September 5, 1905 In the Treaty of Portsmouth, negotiated by President Theodore Roosevelt, Russia admits defeat by relinquishing South Sakhalin Island and its naval base at Port Arthur to Japan.

Japanese soldiers taunting Chinese prisoners before their execution in 1938

January 11, 1942 Japanese invade the Dutch East Indies.

January 19, 1942 President Roosevelt authorizes the Manhattan Project, a top secret effort to produce atomic bombs.

January 23, 1942 Japanese seize Rabaul on New Britain, which will serve as their base as they advance on the Solomon Islands and New Guinea.

February 1, 1942 First attacks launched by American aircraft carriers in the Pacific, including

a strike by warplanes from the U.S.S. *Enterprise* that kills the Japanese commander on Kwajalein in the Marshall Islands.

February 15, 1942 British surrender Singapore, yielding Malaya to Japan.

February 19, 1942 President Roosevelt authorizes internment of Japanese Americans.

February 27, 1942 Japanese forces win the Battle of the Java Sea and tighten their hold on the Dutch East Indies.

Aircraft carrier U.S.S. Yorktown *struck by torpedoes during the Battle of Midway on June 4, 1942*

August 22, 1910 Japan annexes Korea.

December 17, 1920 The League of Nations designates the Caroline, Marshall, and Mariana Islands (except for American-ruled Guam) as Japanese mandates, giving Japan official authority over islands it seized from Germany during World War I.

February 6, 1922 Japan agrees to the Washington Naval Treaty, which sets the ratio of battleships allowed to the United States, Great Britain, and Japan at a ratio of 5:5:3 and prohibits the construction of battleships exceeding 35,000 pounds. At the same time, Japan agrees to the Nine-Power Treaty, guaranteeing the sovereignty of China.

December 25, 1926 Hirohito becomes emperor of Japan following the death of his father, Emperor Yoshihito.

September 18–19, 1931 Japanese officers provoke a war with Chinese troops in Manchuria, reconstituted as the Japanese puppet state of Manchukuo in 1932.

THE NEW ORDER
BY ARTHUR SZYK

January 28–May 5, 1932 Japanese forces attack Shanghai and clash with Chinese troops before an uneasy cease-fire is brokered by the League of Nations.

February 24, 1933 Japan withdraws from the League of Nations.

December 29, 1934 Japan renounces naval treaties with the United States and Britain.

July 7–9, 1937 Clashes between Japanese and Chinese troops at the Marco Polo Bridge in Peking (Beijing) lead to a full-scale Japanese invasion of China by month's end.

Illustration by Polish-born artist Arthur Szyk lampooning 1940 Tripartite Pact between Nazi Germany, Fascist Italy, and imperial Japan

December 13, 1937 Japanese troops take Nanking (Nanjing), the Chinese Nationalist capital, and proceed to commit massive atrocities, remembered as the "Rape of Nanking."

July 19, 1940 President Franklin D. Roosevelt signs the Two-Ocean Navy Act, authorizing the construction of 18 aircraft carriers and nearly 200 battleships, cruisers, destroyers, and submarines.

September 22, 1940 Japanese forces advance from China into northern Indochina, left vulnerable by the German conquest of France.

Car plate produced after surprise Japanese attack on December 7, 1941

September 27, 1940 Japan joins the Axis alliance by signing the Tripartite Pact with Germany and Italy.

July 26, 1941 President Roosevelt freezes Japanese assets in the United States, resulting in an oil embargo on Japan as it prepares to occupy all of Indochina.

December 1, 1941 Following the collapse of peace talks in Washington, D.C., Emperor Hirohito authorizes Japanese forces to wage war.

December 7–8, 1941 Japanese offensive begins with attacks on U.S. forces at Pearl Harbor, the Philippines (invaded December 10), Guam (captured December 10), and Wake Island (captured December 23) and invasions of neutral Thailand and British Hong Kong and Malaya.

March 8, 1942 Japanese troops in Burma seize the capital Rangoon.

March 11, 1942 On orders from Washington, Gen. Douglas MacArthur is evacuated from the Philippines to Australia, where he will take command of Allied forces.

April 18, 1942 Bombers commanded by Lt. Col. James Doolittle take off from the carrier U.S.S. *Hornet* and strike Tokyo and other targets in Japan.

May 3, 1942 Japanese occupy Tulagi, near Guadalcanal in the Solomon Islands.

May 4–8, 1942 American and Japanese naval task forces engage in the first contest between opposing aircraft carriers and their warplanes in the closely fought Battle of the Coral Sea.

May 6, 1942 American resistance to Japan's invasion of the Philippines ends with the surrender of U.S. forces on Corregidor off the Bataan Peninsula.

May 26, 1942 Last Allied forces in Burma retreat to India.

British official and islanders on Guadalcanal who served as coastwatchers, spying on Japanese forces there in 1942

June 4–7, 1942 U.S. Pacific Fleet wins the pivotal Battle of Midway, losing one aircraft carrier, the U.S.S. *Yorktown*, while sinking four Japanese carriers.

June 6–7, 1942 Japanese invade the Aleutian Islands of Kiska and Attu.

July 21, 1942 Japanese troops land near Buna on Papua and prepare to advance overland toward Port Moresby.

August 7, 1942 U.S. Marines land on Guadalcanal.

August 8–9, 1942 Japanese

sink several Allied ships off Guadalcanal in the Battle of Savo Island.

August 21, 1942 Marines defeat Japanese troops along the Ilu River near Henderson Field in the first significant battle on Guadalcanal.

August 24–25, 1942 American warplanes launched from aircraft carriers and Henderson Field block the first Japanese attempt to reinforce Guadalcanal in the Battle of the Eastern Solomons.

September 11, 1942 General MacArthur orders U.S. troops in Australia to join Australian forces fighting Japanese invaders on Papua.

September 12–14, 1942 Marines defending Henderson Field on Guadalcanal repulse Japanese assaults on Bloody Ridge.

October 25–27, 1942 Aircraft carrier U.S.S. *Hornet* lost in the Battle of the Santa Cruz Islands in the Solomons, which also proves costly for the Japanese.

November 13–15, 1942 U.S. Navy forces win the Naval Battle of Guadalcanal, shattering a convoy carrying 12,000 Japanese troops to that island.

January 2, 1943 Allied forces win the Battle of Buna on Papua.

February 1–7, 1943 Japanese troops are evacuated from Guadalcanal.

March 2–4, 1943 U.S. and Australian air forces inflict heavy losses on a convoy carrying Japanese troops to Lae, New Guinea, in the Battle of the Bismarck Sea.

April 7, 1943 Admiral Yamamoto launches naval air strikes against Allied bases on Guadalcanal and New Guinea.

April 18, 1943 Admiral Yamamoto killed when U.S. fighter pilots down his plane off Bougainville.

Severed head of a Japanese soldier placed on a burned-out Japanese tank by U.S. Marines on Guadalcanal

PRELUDE TO
== WAR ==

FROM HIROHITO'S ASCENT TO THE AXIS ALLIANCE

CHRONOLOGY

DECEMBER 17, 1920 The League of Nations designates the Caroline, Marshall, and Mariana Islands (except for American-ruled Guam) as Japanese mandates.

DECEMBER 25, 1926 Hirohito succeeds his father, Yoshihito, as emperor of Japan.

SEPTEMBER 18–19, 1931 Japanese officers provoke a war with Chinese troops in Manchuria, reconstituted as the Japanese puppet state of Manchukuo in 1932.

JANUARY 28–MAY 5, 1932 Japanese forces attack Shanghai and clash with Chinese troops until an uneasy cease-fire is brokered by the League of Nations.

FEBRUARY 24, 1933 Japan withdraws from the League of Nations.

JULY 7–9, 1937 Clashes between Japanese and Chinese troops at the Marco Polo Bridge in Peking lead to a full-scale Japanese invasion of China by month's end.

DECEMBER 13, 1937 Japanese troops take Nanking (Nanjing), the Chinese Nationalist capital, and proceed to commit massive atrocities, remembered as the "Rape of Nanking."

SEPTEMBER 22, 1940 Japanese forces advance from China into northern Indochina, left vulnerable by the German conquest of France.

SEPTEMBER 27, 1940 Japan joins the Axis alliance by signing the Tripartite Pact with Germany and Italy.

DIVINE RULER Dressed in court regalia at his enthronement ceremony, Emperor Hirohito was hailed as a "living god," although he later remarked that "it disturbs me to be called that because I have the same bodily structure as an ordinary human being." His sacred status and his role as Japan's commander in chief made him a national icon, for whom men fought and died.

When 24-year-old Hirohito (below) became emperor of Japan on December 25, 1926, his reign was designated *Showa*, meaning "Illustrious Peace." Before long, however, Japan became mired in infamous conflicts, which Hirohito oversaw as commander in chief, a position he held under a constitution enacted in 1889 when his grandfather Meiji was emperor. Meiji and his heirs had to deal carefully with their commanders, who gained clout as Japan became a modern military power and acquired territory overseas, including Taiwan and Korea—acquired from China as its empire crumbled—and Pacific islands confiscated from Germany during World War I. The onset of the Great Depression during Hirohito's reign increased pressure for Japan to revive its economy by enlarging its armed forces, expanding its empire, and acquiring raw materials abroad and captive markets for its products. Several Japanese leaders who opposed that expansion were assassinated, including Prime Minister Osachi Hamaguchi, shot in 1930 after backing a treaty with the United States and Britain that limited the size of the Imperial Japanese Navy. Fearing dissension, Hirohito was reluctant to restrain commanders who acted aggressively.

In September 1931, officers of the Kwantung Army, assigned to protect Japanese residents and property in Manchuria, set out to wrest control of that country from China by sabotaging the Japanese-owned South Manchurian Railway, blaming the incident on Chinese troops and attacking them. Those officers had no authority to start a war in Manchuria, and Hirohito could have reined them in. Instead, he remained passive as Japanese commanders in Korea sent more troops into Manchuria. When Japan prevailed there, Hirohito commended the officers who ignited the conflict for acting in "self-defense," signaling that he would back further military efforts to expand the empire as long as they succeeded.

Condemned for aggression in Manchuria and for invading Shanghai in 1932, Japan withdrew from the League of Nations in 1933 and from international naval treaties in 1934 and moved toward an all-out war in China that would set Tokyo sharply at odds with Washington. Hirohito worried that his commanders were overreaching but shared their belief that it would be shameful to back down once troops were committed abroad. ∎

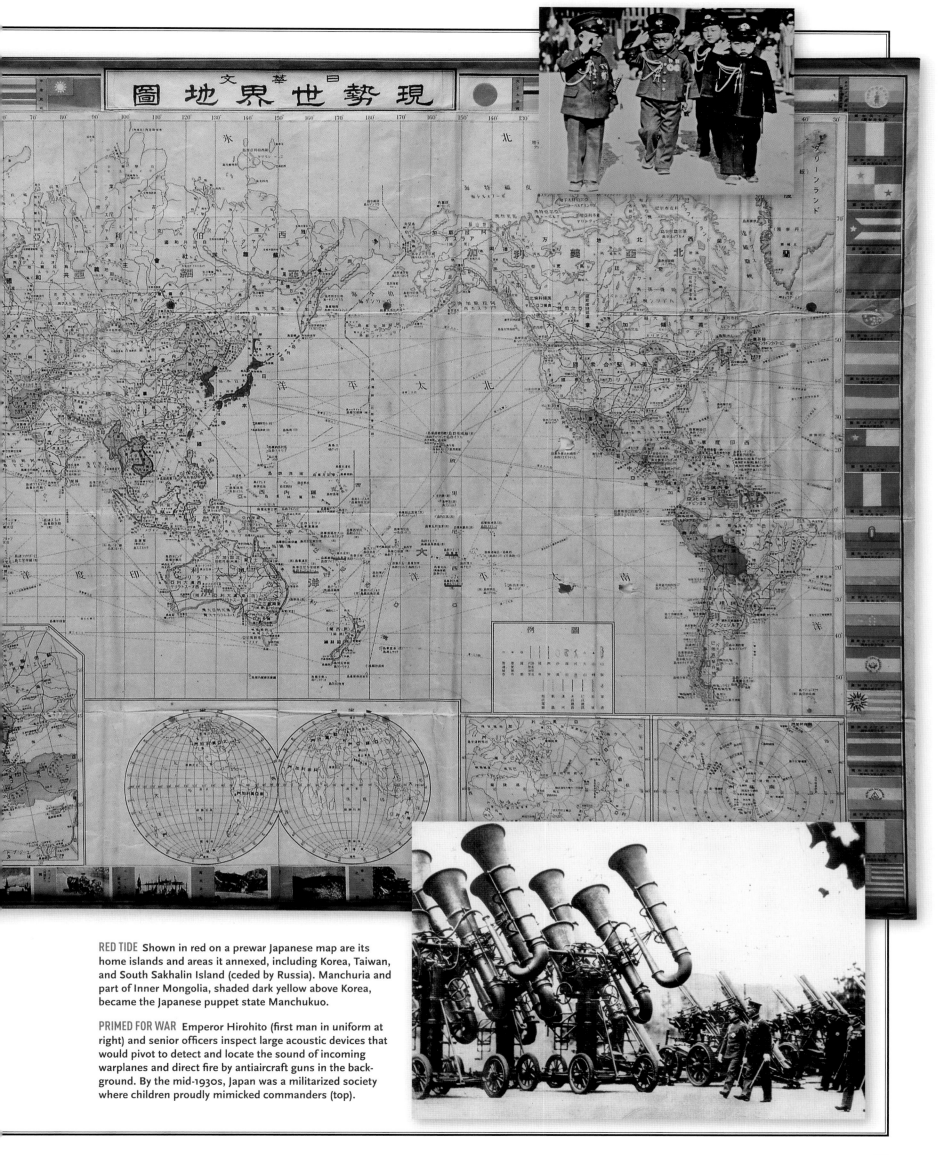

RED TIDE Shown in red on a prewar Japanese map are its home islands and areas it annexed, including Korea, Taiwan, and South Sakhalin Island (ceded by Russia). Manchuria and part of Inner Mongolia, shaded dark yellow above Korea, became the Japanese puppet state Manchukuo.

PRIMED FOR WAR Emperor Hirohito (first man in uniform at right) and senior officers inspect large acoustic devices that would pivot to detect and locate the sound of incoming warplanes and direct fire by antiaircraft guns in the background. By the mid-1930s, Japan was a militarized society where children proudly mimicked commanders (top).

PLOTTING THE JAPANESE EMPIRE

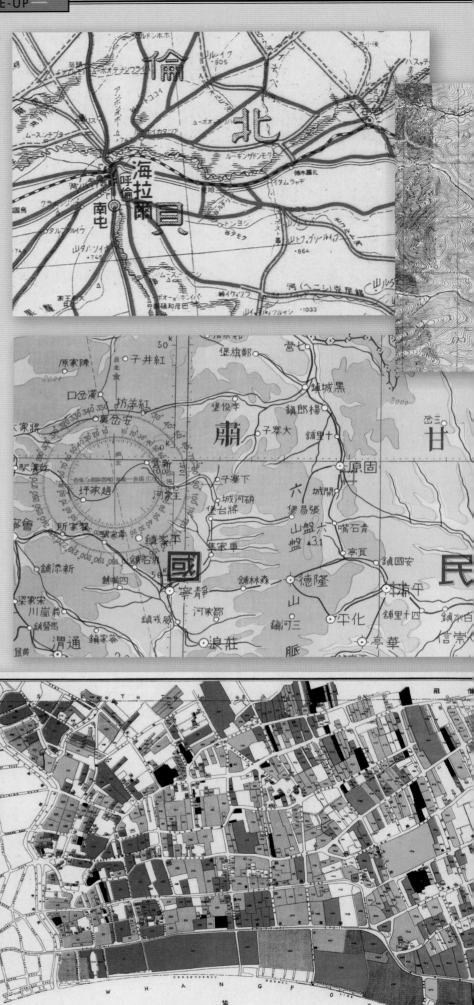

Long before Japanese troops invaded Manchuria in 1931 (below) and renamed it Manchukuo, military cartographers began charting paths for imperial expansion by producing *gaihozu*—maps of "outer lands" that might be colonized or occupied by Japan. Starting around 1870, cartographers copied foreign maps, to which they often added notes and details based on reports from Japanese civilians or officers. For example, Japanese notes in red on a Russian base map of Vladivostok (far right, top) offered commanders intelligence on that strategic port on the Sea of Japan involved in the Russo-Japanese War of 1904-05.

Other Japanese military maps were produced from scratch, including a chart of the Shanghai International Settlement (near right, bottom), showing Japanese districts in green. Tensions between Japan and China led to intense fighting in Shanghai in 1932 and a second battle for the city in 1937. By then, maps of China and surrounding areas, often made by Japanese surveyors disguised as traveling merchants, were of vital interest to military commanders. Among the places Japanese forces occupied was Hulunbuir in Inner Mongolia (mapped near right, top), which became part of Manchukuo. ■

CALCULATED MOVE Japanese troops invade Manchuria, seized from China after it was infiltrated and surveyed by Japan.

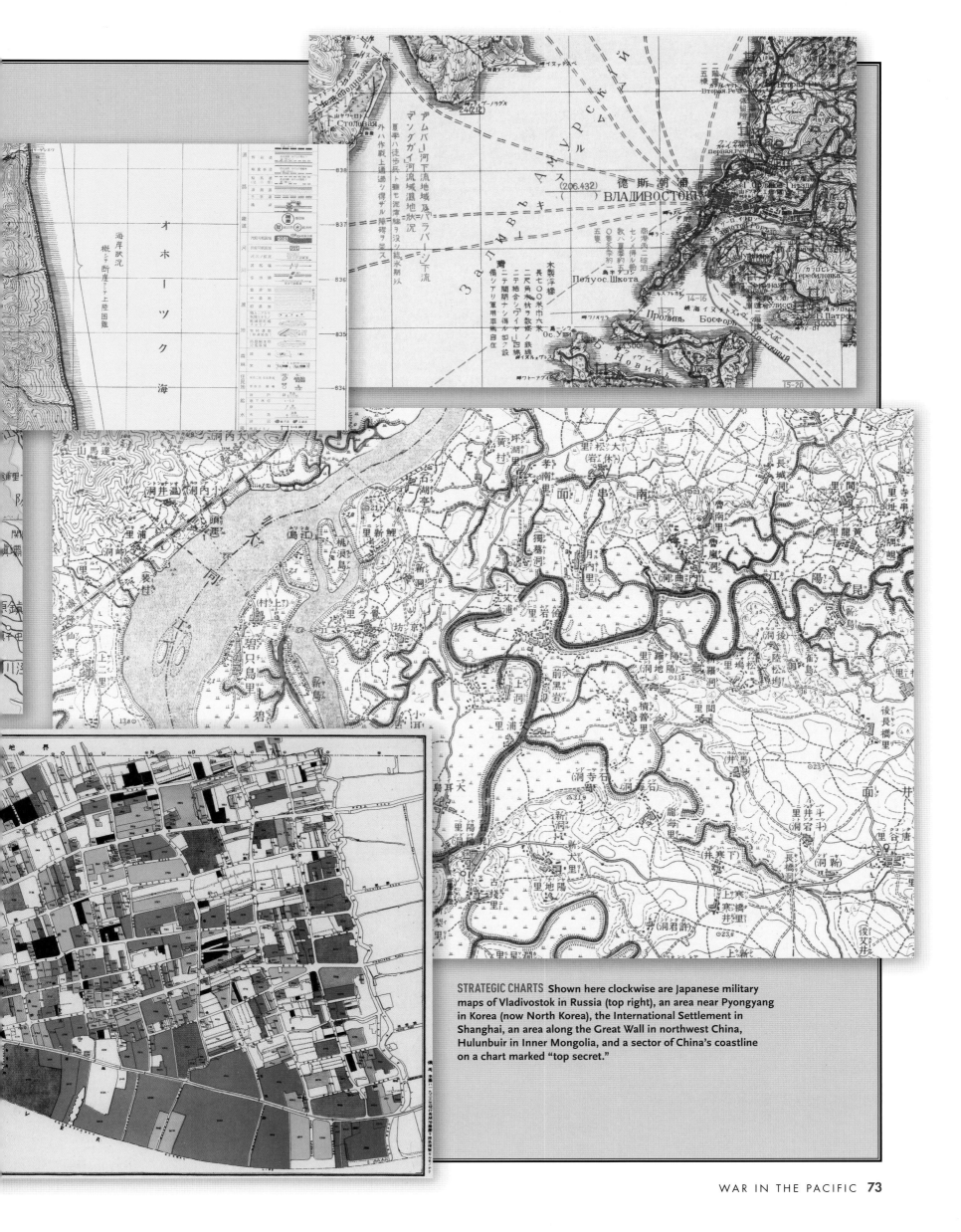

STRATEGIC CHARTS Shown here clockwise are Japanese military maps of Vladivostok in Russia (top right), an area near Pyongyang in Korea (now North Korea), the International Settlement in Shanghai, an area along the Great Wall in northwest China, Hulunbuir in Inner Mongolia, and a sector of China's coastline on a chart marked "top secret."

THE INVASION OF CHINA

I n July 1937, Chinese soldiers clashed with Japanese forces at the Marco Polo Bridge in Peking, where foreign powers stationed troops to protect their residents. As tensions rose, Emperor Hirohito authorized an invasion to "chastise the Chinese Army," having been assured by his commanders that the war would be wrapped up in a few months. Japanese soldiers soon secured Peking, but the conflict then escalated. In August, Chinese Nationalist leader Chiang Kai-shek drew the invaders into a punishing battle for Shanghai, where many foreigners resided. Japanese troops took Shanghai and proceeded to devastate Nanking, the Nationalist capital. Told to take no prisoners, they went from shooting soldiers to targeting civilians in an orgy of violence. Thousands of women were raped, and at least 200,000 people were killed.

The notorious "Rape of Nanking" turned American public opinion firmly against Japan and failed to subdue the Nationalists, who withdrew up the Yangtze River to Chungking (Chongqing). Meanwhile, Chinese Communists led by Mao Zedong were waging guerrilla warfare against the invaders. A conflict that was supposed to last months dragged on for years and left Japan facing a crucial decision—whether to pull back, as the United States urged, or expand its offensive to include Indochina and other European colonies in the Far East. ■

INFAMOUS INVASION Below, Japanese troops cheer after seizing the railroad station in Shanghai in 1937. A photo of a bloodied infant crying amid the wreckage there (opposite bottom) was emblematic of the invasion, which was widely condemned. Other shocking images reinforced the impression that Japan was an outlaw nation, including a severed head in Nanking (opposite top), where Japanese troops ran amok, and civilians who died in a stampede to an air-raid shelter when Chungking was bombed (above).

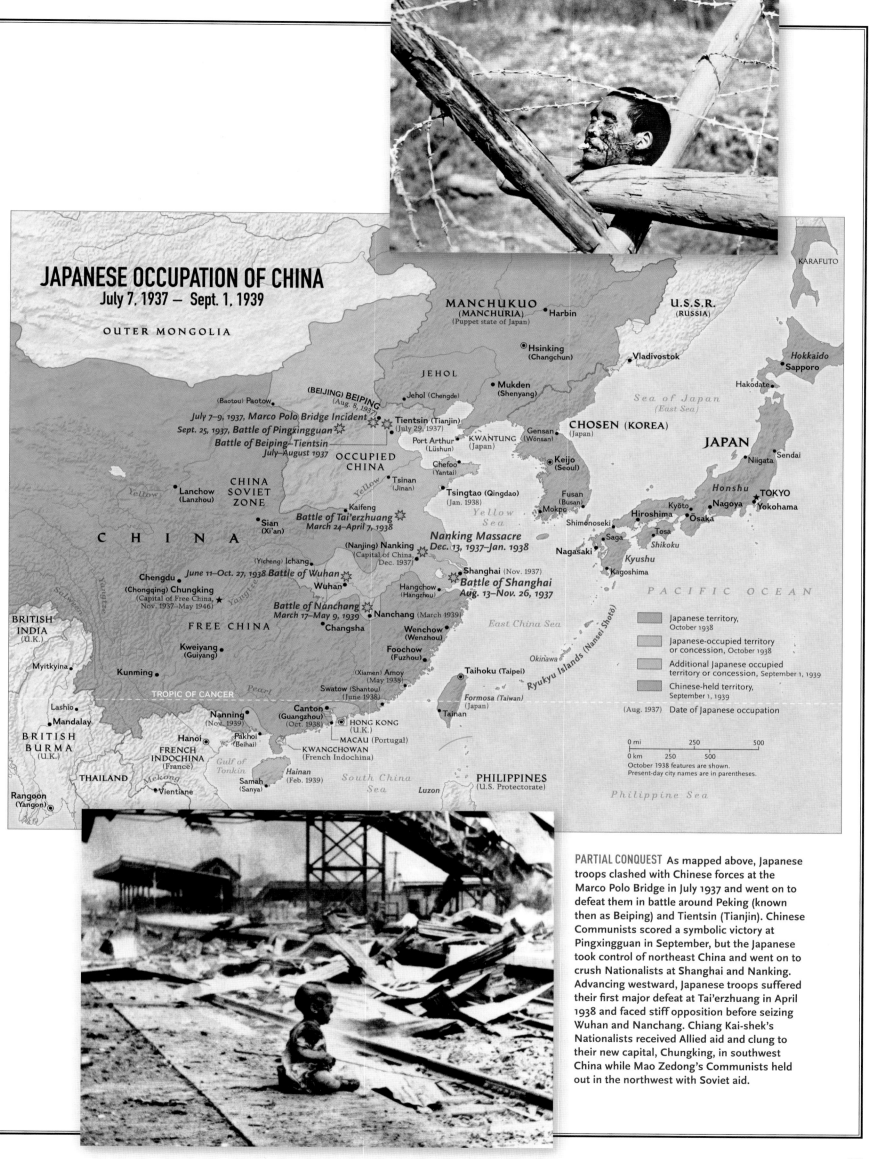

JAPANESE OCCUPATION OF CHINA
July 7, 1937 — Sept. 1, 1939

OUTER MONGOLIA

KARAFUTO

MANCHUKUO
(MANCHURIA)
(Puppet state of Japan)
• Harbin

U.S.S.R.
(RUSSIA)

JEHOL

⊙ Hsinking
(Changchun)

• Vladivostok

Hokkaido
Sapporo

• Mukden
(Shenyang)

Hakodate

*Sea of Japan
(East Sea)*

(Baotou) Paotow •

(BEIJING) BEIPING
(Aug. 8, 1937)

• Jehol (Chengde)

July 7–9, 1937, Marco Polo Bridge Incident
Sept. 25, 1937, Battle of Pingxingguan ✧
Battle of Beiping–Tientsin
July–August 1937

✧ Tientsin (Tianjin)
(July 29, 1937)

Port Arthur
(Lüshun)

KWANTUNG
(Japan)

Gensan
(Wŏnsan)

CHOSEN (KOREA)
(Japan)

JAPAN

Honshu

• Niigata

Sendai

OCCUPIED
CHINA

Chefoo
(Yantai)

⊙ Keijo
(Seoul)

Kyōto

Nagoya

TOKYO
Yokohama

CHINA
SOVIET
ZONE

• Tsinan
(Jinan)

Fusan
(Busan)

Hiroshima

Ōsaka

• Lanchow
(Lanzhou)

Yellow

Tsingtao (Qingdao)
(Jan. 1938)

Mokpo •

Shimonoseki

Saga

Tosa

Shikoku

Kaifeng •

• Sian
(Xi'an)

Battle of Tai'erzhuang
March 24–April 7, 1938 ✧

*Yellow
Sea*

Nagasaki

Kyushu

Kagoshima

Nanking Massacre
Dec. 13, 1937–Jan. 1938

C H I N A

(Yicheng) Ichang •

(Nanjing) Nanking
(Capital of China,
Dec. 1937)

Shanghai (Nov. 1937)

Battle of Shanghai
Aug. 13–Nov. 26, 1937

PACIFIC OCEAN

Chengdu •

June 11–Oct. 27, 1938 Battle of Wuhan ✧

(Chongqing) Chungking
(Capital of Free China,
Nov. 1937–May 1946) ★

• Wuhan

Hangchow
(Hangzhou)

Battle of Nanchang
March 17–May 9, 1939 ✧

Nanchang (March 1939)

FREE CHINA

Changsha •

Wenchow
(Wenzhou)

East China Sea

Salween

BRITISH
INDIA
(U.K.)

Kweiyang
(Guiyang) •

Foochow
(Fuzhou)

Okinawa

Ryukyu Islands (Nansei Shoto)

Myitkyina •

Kunming •

(Xiamen) Amoy
(May 1938) •

Taihoku (Taipei) •

TROPIC OF CANCER

Pearl

Swatow (Shantou)
(June 1938)

Lashio •

• Mandalay

Nanning
(Nov. 1939) •

Canton
(Guangzhou)
(Oct. 1938) •

⊙ HONG KONG
(U.K.)

Formosa (Taiwan)
(Japan)

• Tainan

Philippine Sea

BRITISH
BURMA
(U.K.)

Hanoi •

Pakhoi
(Beihai) •

MACAU (Portugal)

KWANGCHOWAN
(French Indochina)

THAILAND

FRENCH
INDOCHINA
(France)

*Gulf of
Tonkin*

Hainan
(Feb. 1939)

Mekong

*South China
Sea*

PHILIPPINES
(U.S. Protectorate)

Luzon

Rangoon
(Yangon) ⊙

Samah
(Sanya) •

• Vientiane

Legend:
- Japanese territory, October 1938
- Japanese-occupied territory or concession, October 1938
- Additional Japanese occupied territory or concession, September 1, 1939
- Chinese-held territory, September 1, 1939

(Aug. 1937) Date of Japanese occupation

0 mi — 250 — 500
0 km — 250 — 500

October 1938 features are shown.
Present-day city names are in parentheses.

PARTIAL CONQUEST As mapped above, Japanese troops clashed with Chinese forces at the Marco Polo Bridge in July 1937 and went on to defeat them in battle around Peking (known then as Beiping) and Tientsin (Tianjin). Chinese Communists scored a symbolic victory at Pingxingguan in September, but the Japanese took control of northeast China and went on to crush Nationalists at Shanghai and Nanking. Advancing westward, Japanese troops suffered their first major defeat at Tai'erzhuang in April 1938 and faced stiff opposition before seizing Wuhan and Nanchang. Chiang Kai-shek's Nationalists received Allied aid and clung to their new capital, Chungking, in southwest China while Mao Zedong's Communists held out in the northwest with Soviet aid.

IMPERIAL RIVALRY IN THE FAR EAST

Japanese imperialists believed they were destined to dominate the Far East and supplant Westerners who had long colonized the region. Beginning in the 17th century, European trading companies with royal charters and their own armed forces had cleared the way for the Netherlands to acquire the Dutch East Indies (from which Indonesia emerged) and Britain to colonize India, Burma, and Malaya (including Singapore). By the late 1800s, France ruled most of Indochina (Vietnam, Laos, and Cambodia), and once-mighty China was subject to humiliating foreign incursions and a debilitating opium trade, which the British enforced by waging war. U.S. forces entered the imperial fray when they occupied the Philippines during the Spanish-American War in 1898 and went on to crush an insurgency by Filipinos seeking independence. Westerners extracted precious raw materials such as oil and rubber from their colonies and exploited cheap labor, including servants who bowed to them and bore their burdens.

Japanese imperialists vowed to free the Far East from Western interference and unite the region under Asian rule. Whether they would long be viewed as liberators by Asians they colonized was doubtful considering the hostility Japanese troops and officials aroused in China. But leaders in Tokyo had more compelling reasons for targeting European colonies, which became vulnerable to attack in 1940 when German forces overran Holland, defeated France, and menaced Britain. Bogged down in China, Japan now had a chance for quick conquests that would provide labor, fuel, and other assets to boost its imperial war effort. "Seize this golden opportunity!" urged Army Minister Shunroku Hata in June. "Don't let anything stand in the way!"

Japanese forces seized that opportunity in September 1940 by crossing from China into northern Indochina, which Vichy French authorities soon surrendered to Japan. That set the stage for further advances to the south, aimed at British Malaya and the Dutch East Indies. One large obstacle that stood in the way was the Philippines. If bypassed, that would leave potentially hostile U.S. forces in the heart of the region Japan intended to dominate. If attacked, that meant war with America and its Pacific Fleet, based at Pearl Harbor. After joining the Axis on September 27, 1940, Japan moved toward an all-out attack on the European colonies—and war with the United States. ■

RESISTANCE Burmese demonstrators block a road in 1939 to protest British colonial rule of their country. When war broke out, many indigenous people in colonies such as Burma and the Dutch East Indies—where white guests like those dining opposite had numerous attendants at their beck and call—viewed Japanese intervention as preferable to Western domination before Japan imposed its own brand of imperialism on those countries.

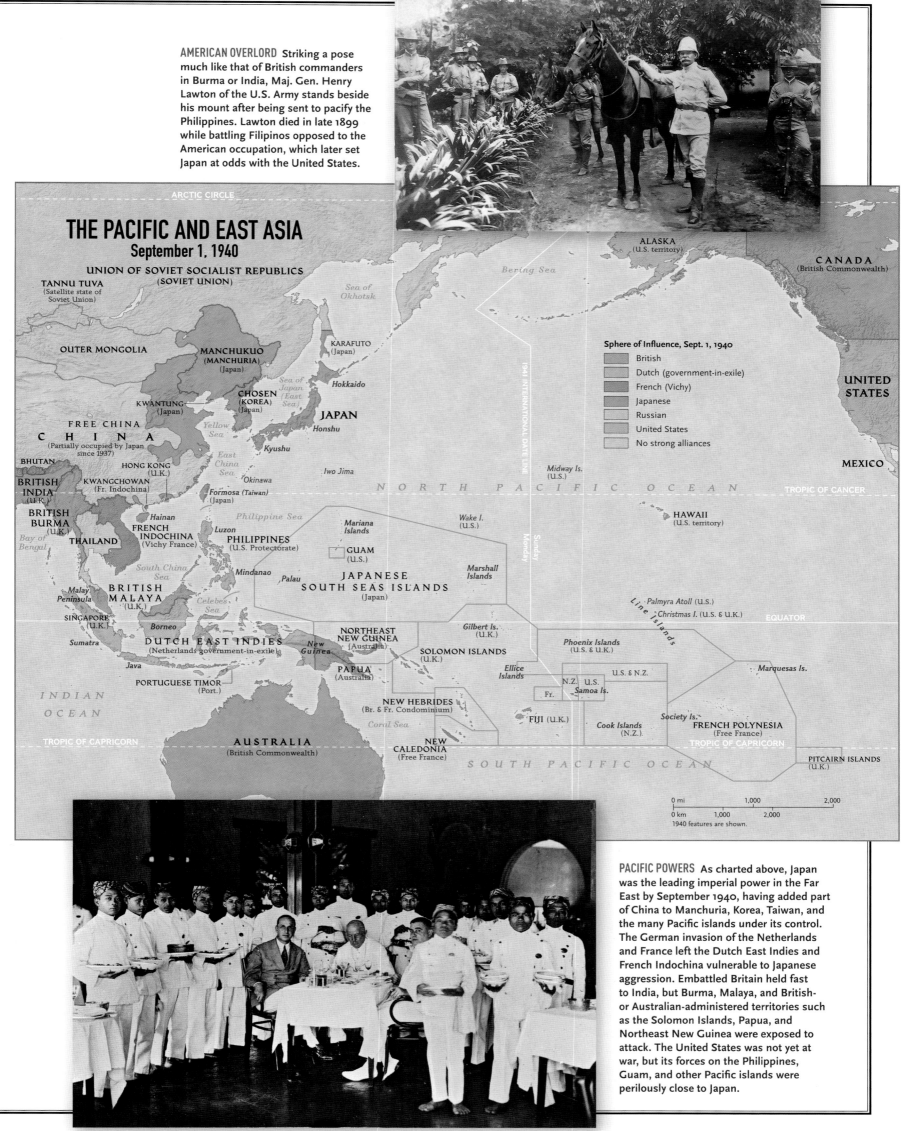

AMERICAN OVERLORD Striking a pose much like that of British commanders in Burma or India, Maj. Gen. Henry Lawton of the U.S. Army stands beside his mount after being sent to pacify the Philippines. Lawton died in late 1899 while battling Filipinos opposed to the American occupation, which later set Japan at odds with the United States.

THE PACIFIC AND EAST ASIA
September 1, 1940

ARCTIC CIRCLE

UNION OF SOVIET SOCIALIST REPUBLICS
(SOVIET UNION)

TANNU TUVA
(Satellite state of Soviet Union)

OUTER MONGOLIA

MANCHUKUO
(MANCHURIA)
(Japan)

KARAFUTO
(Japan)

Sea of Okhotsk

Bering Sea

ALASKA
(U.S. territory)

CANADA
(British Commonwealth)

KWANTUNG
(Japan)

CHOSEN
(KOREA)
(Japan)

Hokkaido

Sea of Japan (East Sea)

1941 INTERNATIONAL DATE LINE

UNITED STATES

FREE CHINA

C H I N A
(Partially occupied by Japan since 1937)

JAPAN

Honshu

Yellow Sea

Kyushu

East China Sea

Okinawa

Iwo Jima

NORTH PACIFIC OCEAN

Midway Is. (U.S.)

Sphere of Influence, Sept. 1, 1940
- British
- Dutch (government-in-exile)
- French (Vichy)
- Japanese
- Russian
- United States
- No strong alliances

MEXICO

BHUTAN

BRITISH INDIA
(U.K.)

HONG KONG (U.K.)

KWANGCHOWAN
(Fr. Indochina)

Formosa (Taiwan)
(Japan)

Philippine Sea

TROPIC OF CANCER

HAWAII
(U.S. territory)

BRITISH BURMA
(U.K.)

Hainan

FRENCH INDOCHINA
(Vichy France)

Luzon

PHILIPPINES
(U.S. Protectorate)

Mariana Islands

Wake I. (U.S.)

Bay of Bengal

THAILAND

South China Sea

Mindanao

Palau

GUAM (U.S.)

JAPANESE SOUTH SEAS ISLANDS
(Japan)

Marshall Islands

Malay Peninsula

BRITISH MALAYA
(U.K.)

Celebes Sea

Palmyra Atoll (U.S.)
Christmas I. (U.S. & U.K.)

Line Islands

EQUATOR

SINGAPORE (U.K.)

Borneo

DUTCH EAST INDIES
(Netherlands government-in-exile)

Sumatra

New Guinea

NORTHEAST NEW GUINEA
(Australia)

Gilbert Is. (U.K.)

SOLOMON ISLANDS
(U.K.)

Phoenix Islands
(U.S. & U.K.)

Marquesas Is.

Java

PORTUGUESE TIMOR
(Port.)

PAPUA
(Australia)

Ellice Islands

U.S. & N.Z.

INDIAN OCEAN

N.Z. U.S.
Fr. Samoa Is.

Society Is.

FRENCH POLYNESIA
(Free France)

TROPIC OF CAPRICORN

AUSTRALIA
(British Commonwealth)

NEW HEBRIDES
(Br. & Fr. Condominium)

FIJI (U.K.)

Cook Islands (N.Z.)

TROPIC OF CAPRICORN

NEW CALEDONIA
(Free France)

Coral Sea

SOUTH PACIFIC OCEAN

PITCAIRN ISLANDS
(U.K.)

Sunday Monday

0 mi   1,000   2,000
0 km   1,000   2,000
1940 features are shown.

PACIFIC POWERS As charted above, Japan was the leading imperial power in the Far East by September 1940, having added part of China to Manchuria, Korea, Taiwan, and the many Pacific islands under its control. The German invasion of the Netherlands and France left the Dutch East Indies and French Indochina vulnerable to Japanese aggression. Embattled Britain held fast to India, but Burma, Malaya, and British- or Australian-administered territories such as the Solomon Islands, Papua, and Northeast New Guinea were exposed to attack. The United States was not yet at war, but its forces on the Philippines, Guam, and other Pacific islands were perilously close to Japan.

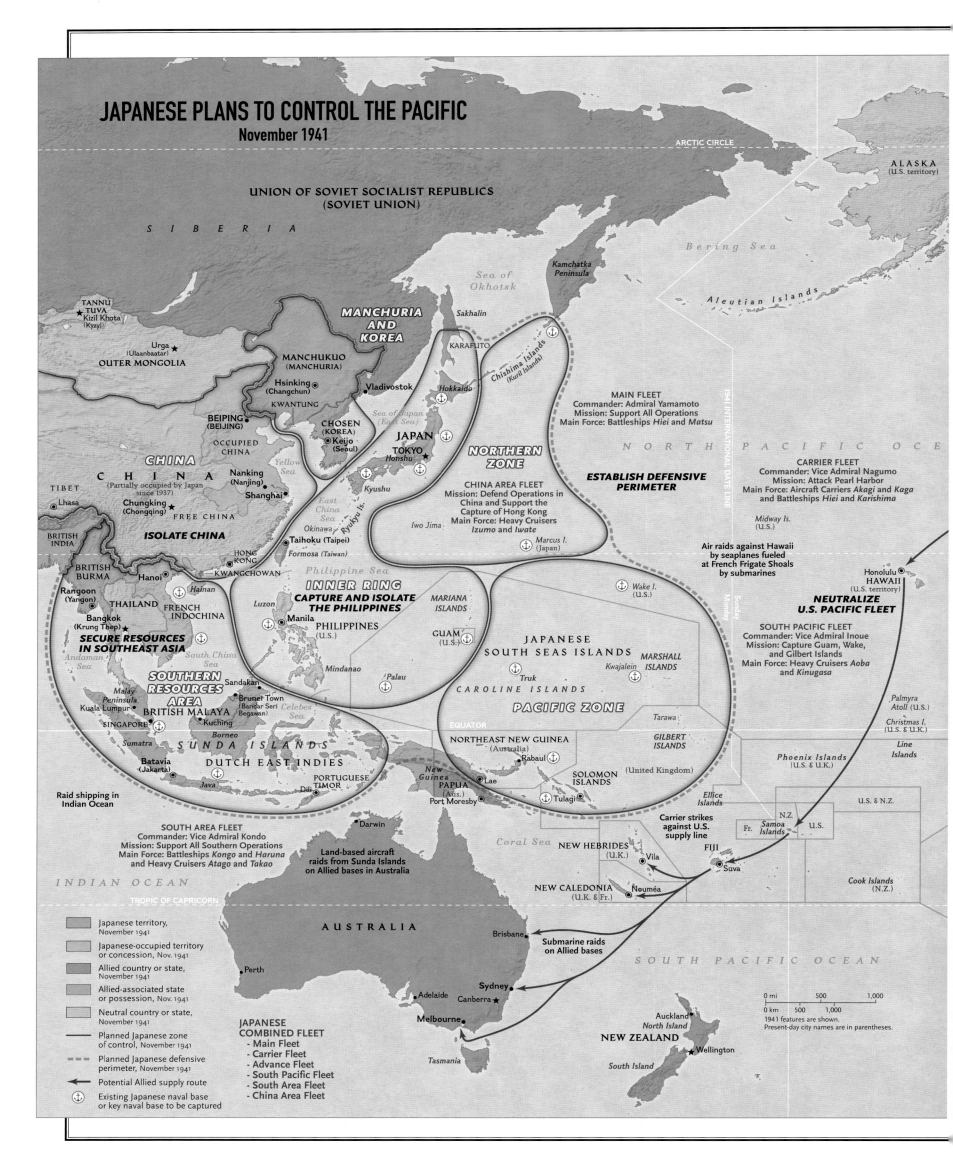

JAPANESE PLANS TO CONTROL THE PACIFIC
November 1941

ARCTIC CIRCLE

ALASKA (U.S. territory)

UNION OF SOVIET SOCIALIST REPUBLICS (SOVIET UNION)

SIBERIA

Bering Sea

Aleutian Islands

Sea of Okhotsk

Kamchatka Peninsula

TANNU TUVA
★ Kizil Khota (Kyzyl)

Urga ★ (Ulaanbaatar)

OUTER MONGOLIA

MANCHURIA AND KOREA

Sakhalin

KARAFUTO

Chishima Islands (Kuril Islands)

MAIN FLEET
Commander: Admiral Yamamoto
Mission: Support All Operations
Main Force: Battleships *Hiei* and *Matsu*

MANCHUKUO (MANCHURIA)

Hsinking (Changchun)

Vladivostok

KWANTUNG

Hokkaido

Sea of Japan (East Sea)

NORTHERN ZONE

NORTH PACIFIC OCE

BEIPING (BEIJING)

CHOSEN (KOREA)

Keijo (Seoul)

JAPAN

TOKYO
Honshu

CARRIER FLEET
Commander: Vice Admiral Nagumo
Mission: Attack Pearl Harbor
Main Force: Aircraft Carriers *Akagi* and *Kaga*
and Battleships *Hiei* and *Karishima*

CHINA

OCCUPIED CHINA

Nanking (Nanjing)

Yellow Sea

Shanghai

Kyushu

ESTABLISH DEFENSIVE PERIMETER

CHINA AREA FLEET
Mission: Defend Operations in China and Support the Capture of Hong Kong
Main Force: Heavy Cruisers *Izumo* and *Iwate*

East China Sea

CHINA (Partially occupied by Japan since 1937)

TIBET
Lhasa

Chungking (Chongqing) ★

FREE CHINA

ISOLATE CHINA

Okinawa

Ryukyu Is.

Iwo Jima

Marcus I. (Japan)

Midway Is. (U.S.)

Air raids against Hawaii by seaplanes fueled at French Frigate Shoals by submarines

Honolulu
HAWAII (U.S. territory)

BRITISH INDIA

BRITISH BURMA

HONG KONG

Taihoku (Taipei)

Formosa (Taiwan)

Philippine Sea

INNER RING

Wake I. (U.S.)

NEUTRALIZE U.S. PACIFIC FLEET

Hanoi

KWANGCHOWAN

Rangoon (Yangon)

Hainan

THAILAND

FRENCH INDOCHINA

Luzon

Manila

PHILIPPINES (U.S.)

CAPTURE AND ISOLATE THE PHILIPPINES

MARIANA ISLANDS

GUAM (U.S.)

SOUTH PACIFIC FLEET
Commander: Vice Admiral Inoue
Mission: Capture Guam, Wake, and Gilbert Islands
Main Force: Heavy Cruisers *Aoba* and *Kinugasa*

Bangkok (Krung Thep) ★

SECURE RESOURCES IN SOUTHEAST ASIA

South China Sea

Andaman Sea

JAPANESE SOUTH SEAS ISLANDS

MARSHALL ISLANDS

Kwajalein

Mindanao

Palau

Truk

Palmyra Atoll (U.S.)

Christmas I. (U.S. & U.K.)

Line Islands

SOUTHERN RESOURCES AREA

Malay Peninsula
Kuala Lumpur

Sandakan

Brunei Town (Bandar Seri Begawan)

Celebes Sea

CAROLINE ISLANDS

PACIFIC ZONE

Tarawa

SINGAPORE

Kuching

BRITISH MALAYA

Borneo

Sumatra

SUNDA ISLANDS

DUTCH EAST INDIES

EQUATOR

NORTHEAST NEW GUINEA (Australia)

GILBERT ISLANDS

Phoenix Islands (U.S. & U.K.)

Batavia (Jakarta)

Java

PORTUGUESE TIMOR

Dili

New Guinea

PAPUA (Aus.)

Port Moresby

Rabaul

SOLOMON ISLANDS

Lae

(United Kingdom)

Tulagi

Ellice Islands

U.S. & N.Z.

N.Z.

Fr.

Samoa Islands

U.S.

Cook Islands (N.Z.)

Raid shipping in Indian Ocean

SOUTH AREA FLEET
Commander: Vice Admiral Kondo
Mission: Support All Southern Operations
Main Force: Battleships *Kongo* and *Haruna* and Heavy Cruisers *Atago* and *Takao*

Darwin

Carrier strikes against U.S. supply line

Coral Sea

NEW HEBRIDES (U.K.)

Vila

FIJI

Suva

Land-based aircraft raids from Sunda Islands on Allied bases in Australia

NEW CALEDONIA (U.K. & Fr.)

Nouméa

INDIAN OCEAN

TROPIC OF CAPRICORN

AUSTRALIA

Brisbane

Submarine raids on Allied bases

SOUTH PACIFIC OCEAN

Perth

Sydney

Adelaide

Canberra ★

Melbourne

Auckland
North Island

0 mi   500   1,000
0 km   500   1,000

1941 features are shown.
Present-day city names are in parentheses.

JAPANESE COMBINED FLEET
- Main Fleet
- Carrier Fleet
- Advance Fleet
- South Pacific Fleet
- South Area Fleet
- China Area Fleet

NEW ZEALAND

Tasmania

South Island

Wellington ★

Japanese territory, November 1941

Japanese-occupied territory or concession, Nov. 1941

Allied country or state, November 1941

Allied-associated state or possession, Nov. 1941

Neutral country or state, November 1941

Planned Japanese zone of control, November 1941

Planned Japanese defensive perimeter, November 1941

Potential Allied supply route

Existing Japanese naval base or key naval base to be captured

1941 INTERNATIONAL DATE LINE

Sunday | Monday

JAPAN'S STUNNING OFFENSIVE

FROM PEARL HARBOR TO THE BATAAN DEATH MARCH

Map labels:
- ARCTIC CIRCLE
- CANADA
- Juneau
- Vancouver
- Seattle
- UNITED STATES
- San Francisco
- Los Angeles
- San Diego
- MEXICO
- Submarine raids against supply and communication routes
- TROPIC OF CANCER
- From Panama Canal
- **ADVANCE FLEET**
  Commander: Vice Admiral Shimizu
  Mission: Observe U.S. Fleets in Hawaii
  Main Force: Submarine Support
  Yasukunimaru and Submarines *I-9* and *I-15*
- EQUATOR
- Marquesas Is.
- Society Is.
  Tahiti
  FRENCH POLYNESIA

When Germany invaded Russia in late June 1941, Japanese leaders debated whether to join their Axis ally and attack the Soviets—who had defeated Japanese troops along the northern border of Manchukuo in 1939—or proceed with plans to target European colonies in the Far East. They did not rule out invading Russia if the German advance on Moscow succeeded, but they saw more to be gained by seizing those Asian colonies and their resources, which they hoped to use to subdue China and sustain a vast empire they called the Greater East Asia Co-Prosperity Sphere. French Indochina and the Dutch East Indies were fairly easy targets, but the British would not yield Malaya and Burma without a fight, and their American allies would have to be dealt with as well. On July 2, Tokyo authorized "preparations for war with Great Britain and the United States."

After Japan took all of Indochina in late July and was subjected to an American oil embargo, Emperor Hirohito asked Prime Minister Hideki Tojo—a general committed to imperial expansion—to make one last effort to avert war. Talks in Washington faltered after deciphered cables from Tokyo indicated that Japan would attack if a deal was not reached by November 30. President Roosevelt declined to make concessions under the gun. On December 1, Admiral Yamamoto gave aircraft carriers the go-ahead to bomb Pearl Harbor—one of several blows delivered simultaneously in a vast Japanese offensive that expanded World War II enormously. ■

CHRONOLOGY

JULY 26, 1941 President Roosevelt freezes Japanese assets in the United States, resulting in an oil embargo on Japan.

DECEMBER 1, 1941 Emperor Hirohito authorizes Japanese forces to wage war.

DECEMBER 7–8, 1941 Japanese offensive begins with attacks on U.S. forces at Pearl Harbor, the Philippines, Guam, and Wake Island and invasions of neutral Thailand and British Hong Kong and Malaya.

FEBRUARY 15, 1942 British surrender Singapore, yielding Malaya to Japan.

FEBRUARY 27, 1942 Japanese forces win the Battle of the Java Sea and tighten their hold on the Dutch East Indies.

MARCH 8, 1942 Japanese troops in Burma seize the capital Rangoon.

MAY 6, 1942 American resistance to Japan's invasion of the Philippines ends as U.S. forces surrender on Corregidor.

WAR PLANS Japan's primary objective was to seize oil, rubber, and other strategic assets in the Southern Resources Area, mapped opposite. That meant invading the Dutch East Indies as well as British-ruled Malaya and Burma, which would set Japan at odds with the United States. Anticipating American opposition, Japanese commanders planned to invade the Philippines, within their inner ring of defense, as well as more distant Allied possessions that lay within their defensive perimeter. Admiral Yamamoto—seated at left (front row, center) with officers of his Combined Fleet, which embraced various Japanese fleets—set out to sever Allied supply lines and stifle American retaliation by smashing the U.S. Pacific Fleet at Pearl Harbor.

THE PATH TO WAR

No nation invested more in naval air power before World War II than Japan. Admiral Yamamoto drew heavily on that investment when he assigned six big aircraft carriers of Vice Adm. Chuichi Nagumo's Mobile Force to launch more than 400 warplanes of the First Air Fleet against Pearl Harbor. Shielded by battleships, cruisers, destroyers, and submarines, the carriers were dispatched by Yamamoto on November 26 as peace talks in Washington were breaking down. Five days later, Emperor Hirohito authorized war on the United States and Yamamoto sent Nagumo a coded message to proceed with the attack: "Climb Mount Niitaka."

To avoid detection, the carrier task force observed radio silence and followed a northerly path to Hawaii (see map below), a route that was little traveled and subject to winter storms, which thwarted aerial reconnaissance. As indicated by the Japanese map at right, showing Pearl Harbor in detail at lower left, that target was well charted by 1941. Intelligence on ships in the harbor and nearby air bases was provided by spies, notably Takeo Yoshikawa, a naval officer attached to the Japanese consulate in Honolulu who spied on the Pacific Fleet.

At dawn on Sunday, December 7, the carriers turned into the wind to launch their planes amid heavy swells. "The carriers were rolling considerably, pitching and yawing," remarked Tokuji Iizuka, the pilot of an Aichi 99 dive-bomber on the I.J.N. *Akagi*, Nagumo's flagship. When planes left the flight deck, he added, they "would sink out of sight" before bobbing up and ascending through the clouds. Iizuka took off with the second wave of attackers around 7 A.M. Not until he reached Oahu two hours later did the clouds break and allow him a breathtaking view of Pearl Harbor in the distance, wreathed in smoke as bombs dropped by the first wave shattered the peace. ∎

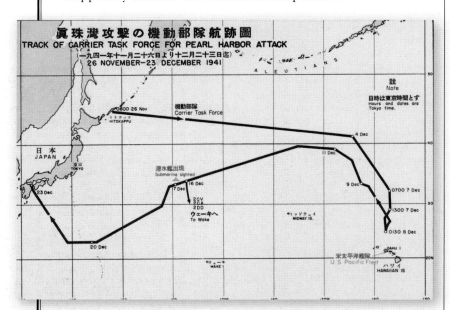

LINE OF ATTACK Based on a Japanese chart using Tokyo time, this map shows the path of the carrier task force that set out on November 26 (November 25 in the United States) and bombed Pearl Harbor on December 7 (December 8 in Japan). Part of the task force later attacked American-held Wake Island.

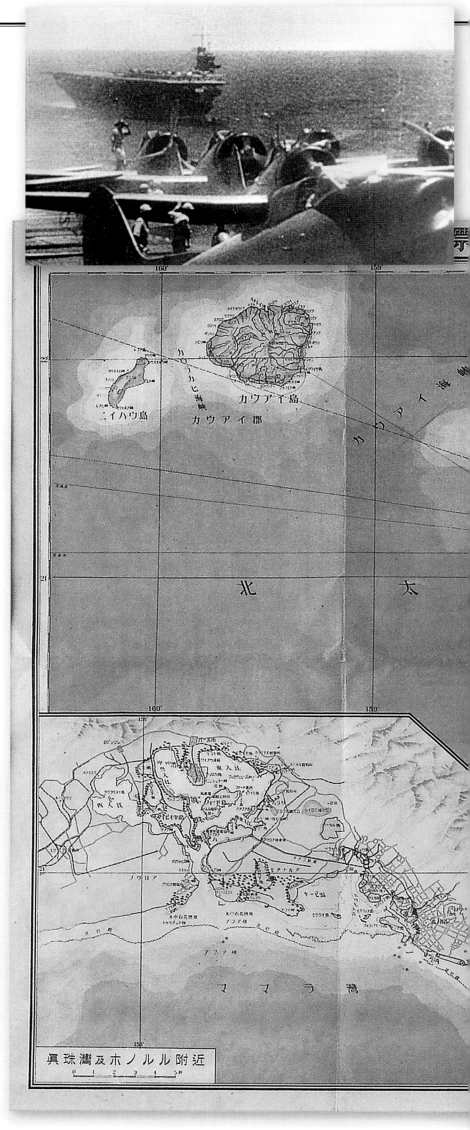

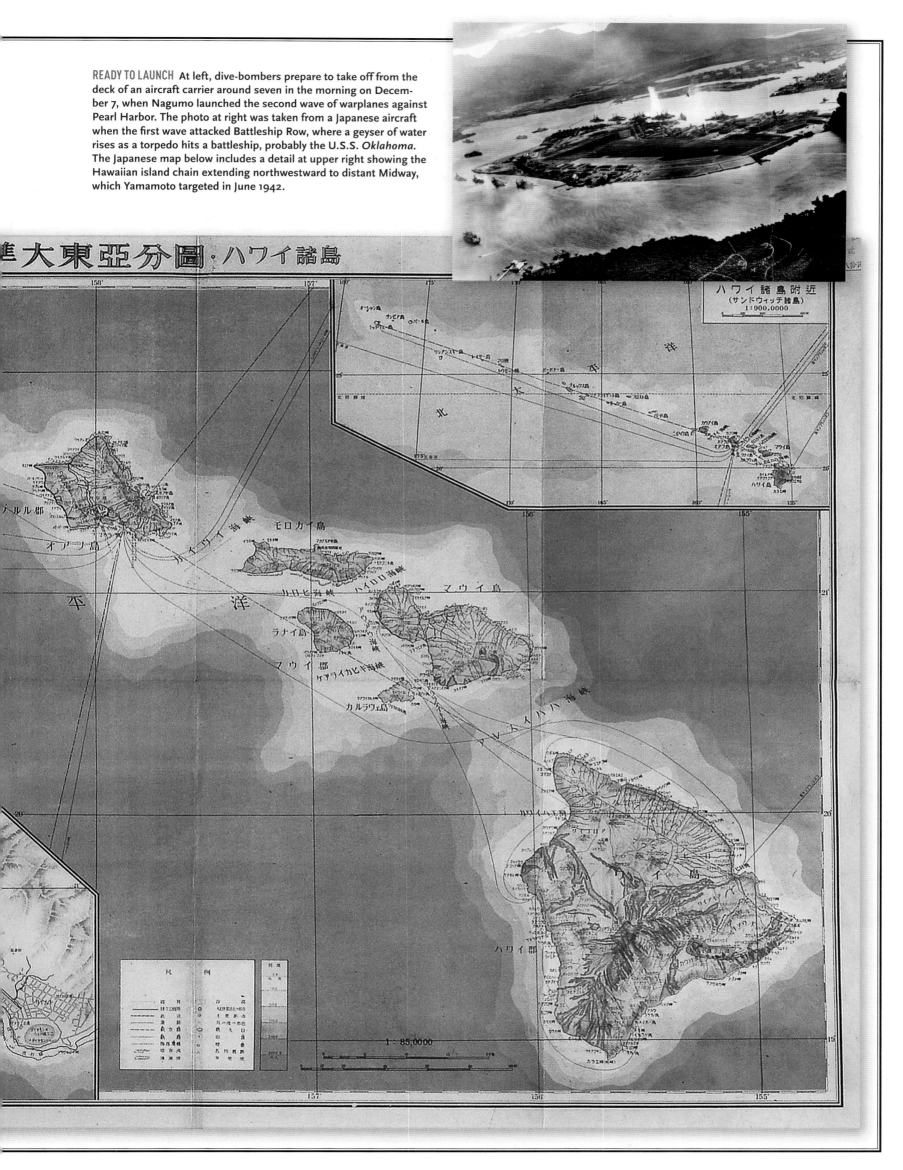

READY TO LAUNCH At left, dive-bombers prepare to take off from the deck of an aircraft carrier around seven in the morning on December 7, when Nagumo launched the second wave of warplanes against Pearl Harbor. The photo at right was taken from a Japanese aircraft when the first wave attacked Battleship Row, where a geyser of water rises as a torpedo hits a battleship, probably the U.S.S. *Oklahoma*. The Japanese map below includes a detail at upper right showing the Hawaiian island chain extending northwestward to distant Midway, which Yamamoto targeted in June 1942.

進大東亞分圖・ハワイ諸島

ASSAULT ON PEARL HARBOR

The surprise attack on December 7 was not entirely unforeseen. Chiefs in Washington knew that Japan would soon wage war, and commanders at Pearl Harbor and elsewhere in the Pacific were warned that hostile action was "possible at any moment." But officers informed of the threat doubted that an attack would occur as far from Japan as Pearl Harbor. They knew the Philippine islands were vulnerable to assault but thought the outer limits of any Japanese offensive would be U.S. bases on Guam, Wake Island, or Midway, situated 1,300 miles closer to Japan than Oahu. Two aircraft carriers that Yamamoto hoped to attack at Pearl Harbor, U.S.S. *Enterprise* and U.S.S. *Lexington*, were away on the 7th because they had been sent to deliver warplanes to Midway and Wake Island. Pearl Harbor was not on high alert.

As shown below in a map retracing the assault in Tokyo time, the first wave of Japanese fighters and bombers came in from the north and were ordered to attack by Cmdr. Mitsuo Fuchida at 7:49 A.M. Hawaii time. Their objectives included airfields on Oahu, including Hickam Field near Pearl Harbor and Ford Island amid that harbor (see map opposite). But their prime targets were the warships moored there. Some planes came in low and released torpedoes, one of which struck the battleship U.S.S. *Oklahoma* and caused it to capsize. A bomb dropped at high level on the battleship U.S.S. *Arizona* penetrated its magazine and triggered a catastrophic explosion. Around 9 A.M., the second wave of warplanes came in and added to the carnage. Within a few hours, the attackers sank or badly damaged all eight battleships at Pearl Harbor and 11 other warships, destroyed 170 aircraft, and killed or wounded more than 3,500 Americans.

As shocking as this assault was, the enormity of the offensive was even more stunning. On that same day, Guam, Wake Island, and the Philippines came under attack, and Japanese troops invaded neutral Thailand and British-ruled Hong Kong and Malaya. The Pacific Fleet dodged a bullet, however, when the fuel depots and repair yards it relied on emerged largely intact. Winston Churchill had no doubt that America would rebound from the attack and cheered its entry into the war on December 8. "Today we are all in the same boat with you," Roosevelt cabled Churchill, who trusted that Britain's alliance with the U.S. and the Soviet Union would ultimately sink the Axis. ∎

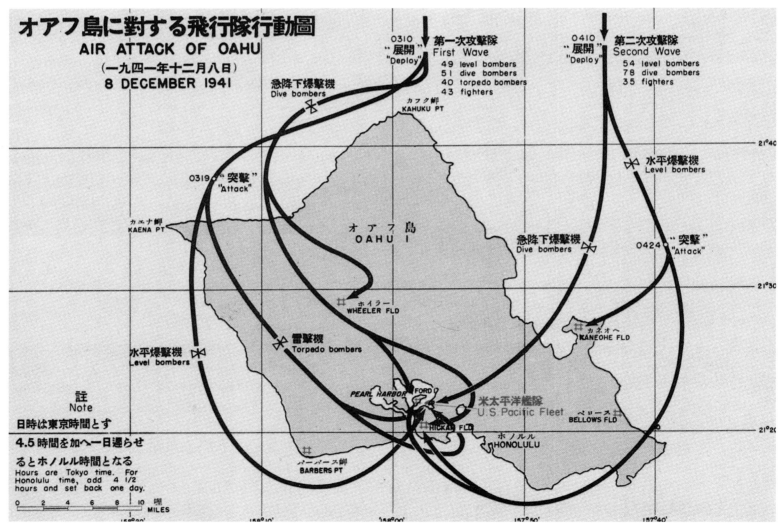

ZEROING IN A map derived from a Japanese original using Tokyo time (19 and a half hours later than Hawaii time) delineates the two waves of warplanes that descended on Oahu and Pearl Harbor. The second wave faced alert defenders and lost 20 aircraft, compared with 9 losses for the first wave.

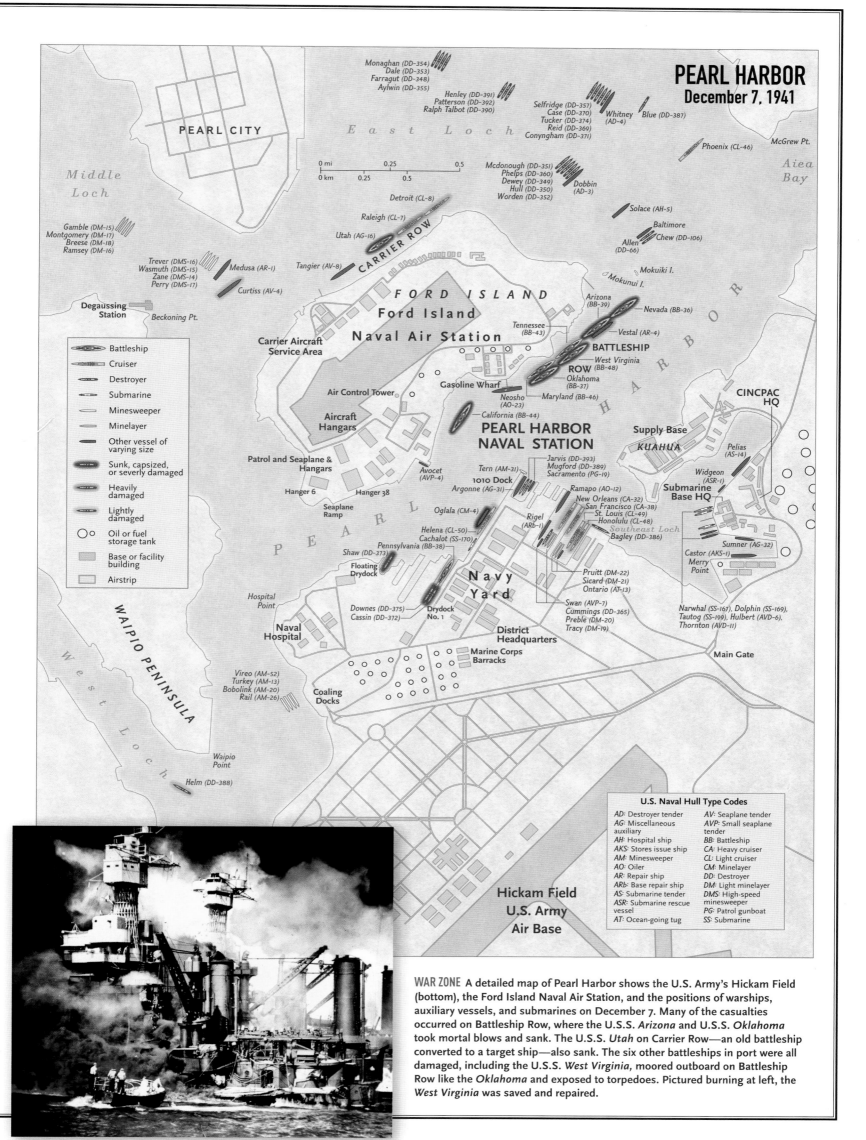

PEARL HARBOR
December 7, 1941

WAR ZONE A detailed map of Pearl Harbor shows the U.S. Army's Hickam Field (bottom), the Ford Island Naval Air Station, and the positions of warships, auxiliary vessels, and submarines on December 7. Many of the casualties occurred on Battleship Row, where the U.S.S. *Arizona* and U.S.S. *Oklahoma* took mortal blows and sank. The U.S.S. *Utah* on Carrier Row—an old battleship converted to a target ship—also sank. The six other battleships in port were all damaged, including the U.S.S. *West Virginia,* moored outboard on Battleship Row like the *Oklahoma* and exposed to torpedoes. Pictured burning at left, the *West Virginia* was saved and repaired.

SALVAGED FROM THE RUINS

Unlike some strategic bombing raids during World War II that obliterated their targets, the tactical assault on Pearl Harbor left haunting relics of the historic battle that drew America into the conflict, including the blasted hulk of the *Arizona* (opposite), which went down in a harbor too shallow to immerse it completely. Other vestiges of the attack had symbolic importance for those who were targeted at Pearl Harbor but emerged defiant, including the tattered flag of the U.S.S. *California* (below right), one of several stricken battleships that were salvaged and returned to service.

Also recovered was the Japanese mini-submarine *HA-19* (bottom right). The only one of five such vessels assigned to the attack that was captured afterward, it served as an attraction in rallies promoting the sale of U.S. war bonds. Found on the *HA-19* was a map of Pearl Harbor (bottom left) with handwritten locations for U.S. warships as determined through espionage, which also contributed to another Japanese map indicating the position of ships on Carrier Row and Battleship Row (opposite top). A third chart retrieved after the battle detailed an anchorage off the Hawaiian island of Maui where the Japanese thought part of the Pacific Fleet might be moored (opposite bottom). Such evidence of the carefully planned attack told American officers that they were dealing with determined foes who would not easily be defeated. ∎

ARTIFACTS OF BATTLE The bloodstained U.S. Navy dress jumper at left was worn by a man who tended the wounded on December 7. Like the battle-torn flag above, it signals that what President Roosevelt called "a date which will live in infamy" would also be remembered as a day of heroic effort and endurance.

MINI-SUB As indicated by the map of Pearl Harbor they carried (above), the mission of the two-man crew on mini-sub *HA-19*—shown at right after it was captured—was to slip into the shallow harbor and launch their single torpedo.

敵礁泊隊恥報告用紙 A

（真珠港）

LOST AND FOUND The life preserver at left was recovered after the *Arizona* went down in flames and smoke (below) at a cost of 1,177 lives.

TACTICAL MAPS Espionage and other forms of intelligence gathering went into the making of the Japanese charts of Pearl Harbor above and Lahaina Roads below, an anchorage off the Hawaiian island of Maui where it was thought U.S. warships might be harbored.

MEMENTOS OF WAR Among the items found at Pearl Harbor after the attack were a sailor's cap from the *Arizona* (above), large range-finding binoculars (above right) from that battleship, goggles worn by a Japanese pilot (right), and a navigational instrument (below) from a plane that was shot down.

敵礁泊隊恥報告用紙 B

DOMINATING THE FAR EAST

U nlike the surprise assault on Pearl Harbor, Japanese attacks on European colonies in the Far East were anticipated by some commanders, but the war in Europe left those outposts short of military resources. The British High Command knew by November 1941 that Japan might soon launch an offensive directed at populous Singapore on the southern tip of the Malay Peninsula and dispatched a naval force including the battleship H.M.S. *Prince of Wales* and the heavy cruiser H.M.S. *Repulse,* which arrived in Singapore minus an aircraft carrier that was supposed to accompany them but required repairs. Sent out with no fighter cover when the Japanese invasion of Malaya began on December 8, the *Prince of Wales* and *Repulse* came under attack by bombers two days later and went down. To make matters worse, the British commander in Malaya, Lt. Gen. Arthur Percival, had almost no tanks to combat those rumbling through the jungle toward Singapore. Percival's troops far outnumbered the oncoming Japanese 25th Army, but many of them were demoralized soldiers from India who, when captured, agreed to serve in the Indian National Army, which backed Japan in the hope of freeing India from British rule. On February 15, 1942, after Japanese forces cut off water supplies to bomb-ravaged Singapore, Percival surrendered, capping the worst British defeat of the war.

By then, much of the Dutch East Indies had been occupied by Japanese troops. Dutch colonists were too few to put up much of a fight, and not many Indonesians on the islands were inclined to aid them. The one significant military asset left to the East Indies after the Netherlands fell to Germany in May 1940 was a small Dutch navy under Adm. Karel Doorman. That was combined with the U.S. Asiatic Fleet and warships of other Allied nations to form a fleet designated ABDA (American, British, Dutch, and Australian), which Doorman led in late February against an invasion fleet destined for Java, one of the last East Indian islands targeted by the Japanese. Defeated in the Battle of the Java Sea, Doorman went down with his ship, and Java fell to Japan on March 12.

Around the same time, Japanese troops who had invaded Burma to cut off supplies to their foes in China captured the Burmese capital, Rangoon, and used that port to bring in reinforcements. Overwhelmed, Allied forces consisting of British, Burmese, Indian, and Chinese Nationalist troops—including two divisions led by Chiang Kai-shek's American chief of staff, Lt. Gen. Joseph Stilwell—retreated northward to India. Many were killed or captured before the remnant crossed the Indian border in May. Stilwell led a contingent to safety but was in no mood to celebrate. "We got run out of Burma," he said, "and it is humiliating as hell." Such were the sentiments of many Allied commanders caught up in Japan's relentless offensive. ∎

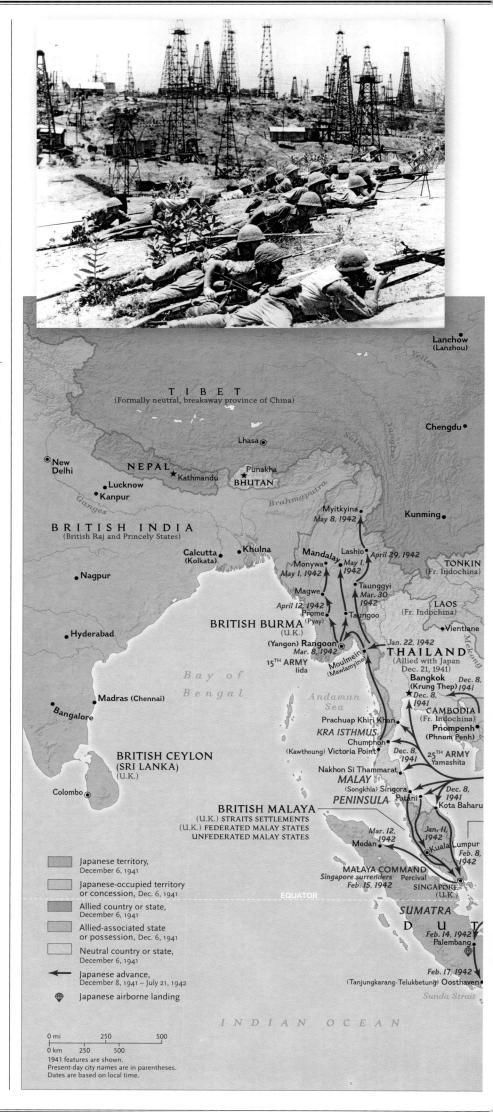

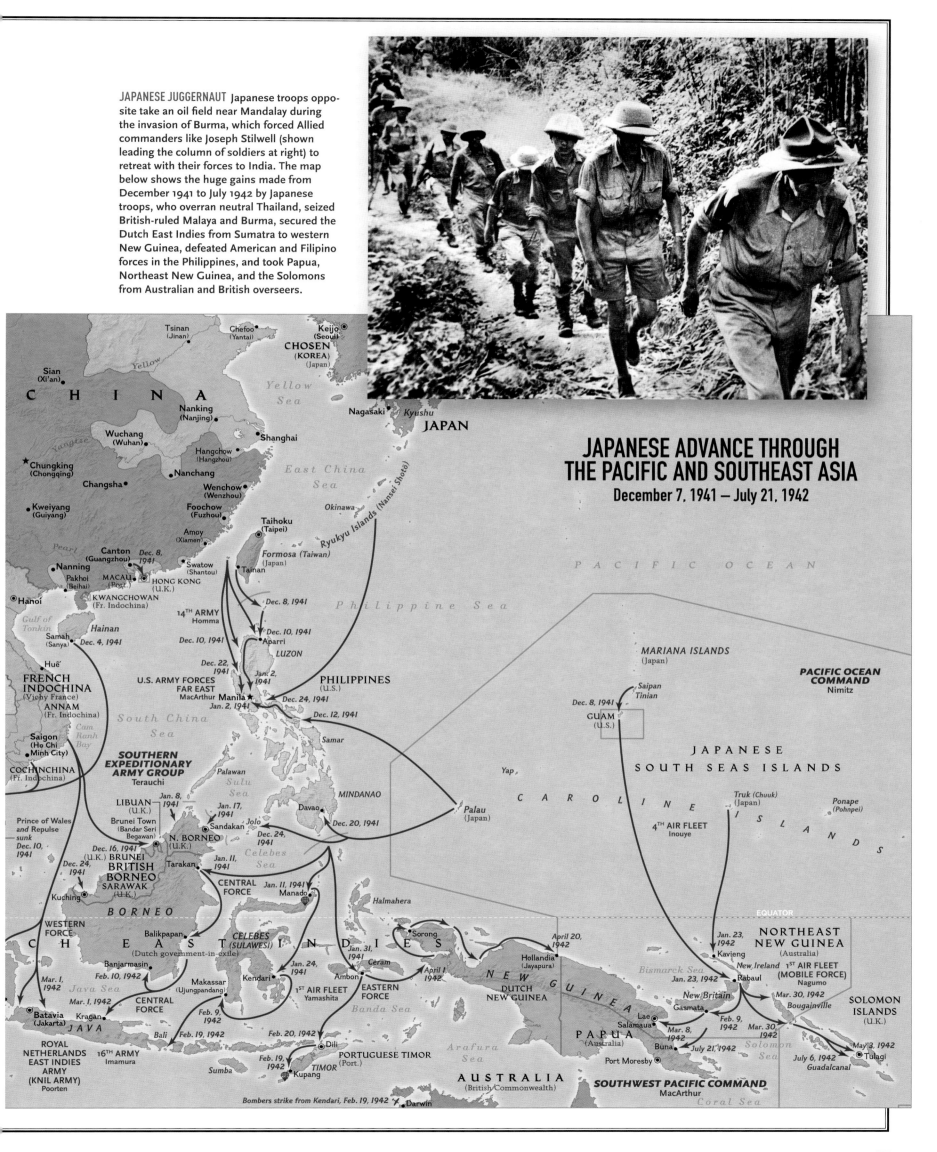

JAPANESE JUGGERNAUT Japanese troops opposite take an oil field near Mandalay during the invasion of Burma, which forced Allied commanders like Joseph Stilwell (shown leading the column of soldiers at right) to retreat with their forces to India. The map below shows the huge gains made from December 1941 to July 1942 by Japanese troops, who overran neutral Thailand, seized British-ruled Malaya and Burma, secured the Dutch East Indies from Sumatra to western New Guinea, defeated American and Filipino forces in the Philippines, and took Papua, Northeast New Guinea, and the Solomons from Australian and British overseers.

JAPANESE ADVANCE THROUGH THE PACIFIC AND SOUTHEAST ASIA
December 7, 1941 – July 21, 1942

CHINA

Sian (Xi'an)
Chungking (Chongqing)
Kweiyang (Guiyang)
Changsha
Wuchang (Wuhan)
Hangchow (Hangzhou)
Nanchang
Nanking (Nanjing)
Shanghai
Wenchow (Wenzhou)
Foochow (Fuzhou)
Amoy (Xiamen)
Canton (Guangzhou)
Nanning
Pakhoi (Beihai)
MACAU (Port.)
HONG KONG (U.K.)
KWANGCHOWAN (Fr. Indochina)
Hanoi
Hainan
Samah (Sanya)
Huế
FRENCH INDOCHINA (Vichy France)
ANNAM (Fr. Indochina)
Saigon (Ho Chi Minh City)
COCHINCHINA (Fr. Indochina)

Tsinan (Jinan)
Chefoo (Yantai)
Keijo (Seoul)
CHOSEN (KOREA) (Japan)

Nagasaki
Kyushu
JAPAN

Okinawa
Ryukyu Islands (Nansei Shoto)
Taihoku (Taipei)
Formosa (Taiwan) (Japan)
Tainan
Swatow (Shantou)

Dec. 8, 1941
Dec. 4, 1941
Dec. 8, 1941
14TH ARMY Homma
Dec. 10, 1941
Dec. 10, 1941
Aparri
LUZON
U.S. ARMY FORCES FAR EAST
MacArthur Manila ★
Jan. 2, 1941
Dec. 22, 1941
Jan. 2, 1941
Dec. 24, 1941
Dec. 12, 1941
PHILIPPINES (U.S.)
Samar

Prince of Wales and Repulse sunk Dec. 10, 1941
SOUTHERN EXPEDITIONARY ARMY GROUP Terauchi
Palawan
Dec. 24, 1941
LIBUAN (U.K.)
Jan. 8, 1941
Brunei Town (Bandar Seri Begawan)
Dec. 16, 1941 (U.K.) BRUNEI
N. BORNEO (U.K.)
Jan. 17, 1941
Sandakan
Jolo
MINDANAO
Davao
Dec. 20, 1941
Jan. 24, 1941
BRITISH BORNEO SARAWAK (U.K.)
Tarakan
Jan. 11, 1941
Kuching
BORNEO
Celebes Sea
CENTRAL FORCE
Jan. 11, 1941
Manado

WESTERN FORCE
Balikpapan
CELEBES (SULAWESI) (Dutch government-in-exile)
Jan. 31, 1941
Ceram
DUTCH EAST INDIES
Sorong
April 20, 1942
Hollandia (Jayapura)
DUTCH NEW GUINEA
Banjarmasin
Feb. 10, 1942
Makassar (Ujungpandang)
Kendari
Ambon
April 1, 1942
1ST AIR FLEET Yamashita
EASTERN FORCE
Mar. 1, 1942
Mar. 1, 1942
CENTRAL FORCE
Feb. 9, 1942
Batavia (Jakarta)
Kragan
JAVA
Bali
Feb. 19, 1942
Feb. 20, 1942
Dili
PORTUGUESE TIMOR (Port.)
ROYAL NETHERLANDS EAST INDIES ARMY (KNIL ARMY) Poorten
16TH ARMY Imamura
Sumba
Feb. 19, 1942
Kupang
TIMOR
Bombers strike from Kendari, Feb. 19, 1942
Darwin
AUSTRALIA (British Commonwealth)

PACIFIC OCEAN

MARIANA ISLANDS (Japan)
Saipan
Tinian
Dec. 8, 1941
GUAM (U.S.)
PACIFIC OCEAN COMMAND Nimitz

JAPANESE SOUTH SEAS ISLANDS

Yap
Palau (Japan)
CAROLINE ISLANDS
Truk (Chuuk) (Japan)
Ponape (Pohnpei)
4TH AIR FLEET Inouye

Halmahera

NEW GUINEA
NORTHEAST NEW GUINEA (Australia)
Jan. 23, 1942
Kavieng
New Ireland
1ST AIR FLEET (MOBILE FORCE) Nagumo
Jan. 23, 1942
Rabaul
Bismarck Sea
New Britain
Mar. 30, 1942
Bougainville
SOLOMON ISLANDS (U.K.)
Gasmata
Feb. 9, 1942
Lae
Salamaua
Mar. 8, 1942
Buna
PAPUA (Australia)
July 21, 1942
Mar. 30, 1942
Port Moresby
SOUTHWEST PACIFIC COMMAND MacArthur
Coral Sea
Solomon Sea
July 6, 1942
Guadalcanal
May 3, 1942
Tulagi

EQUATOR

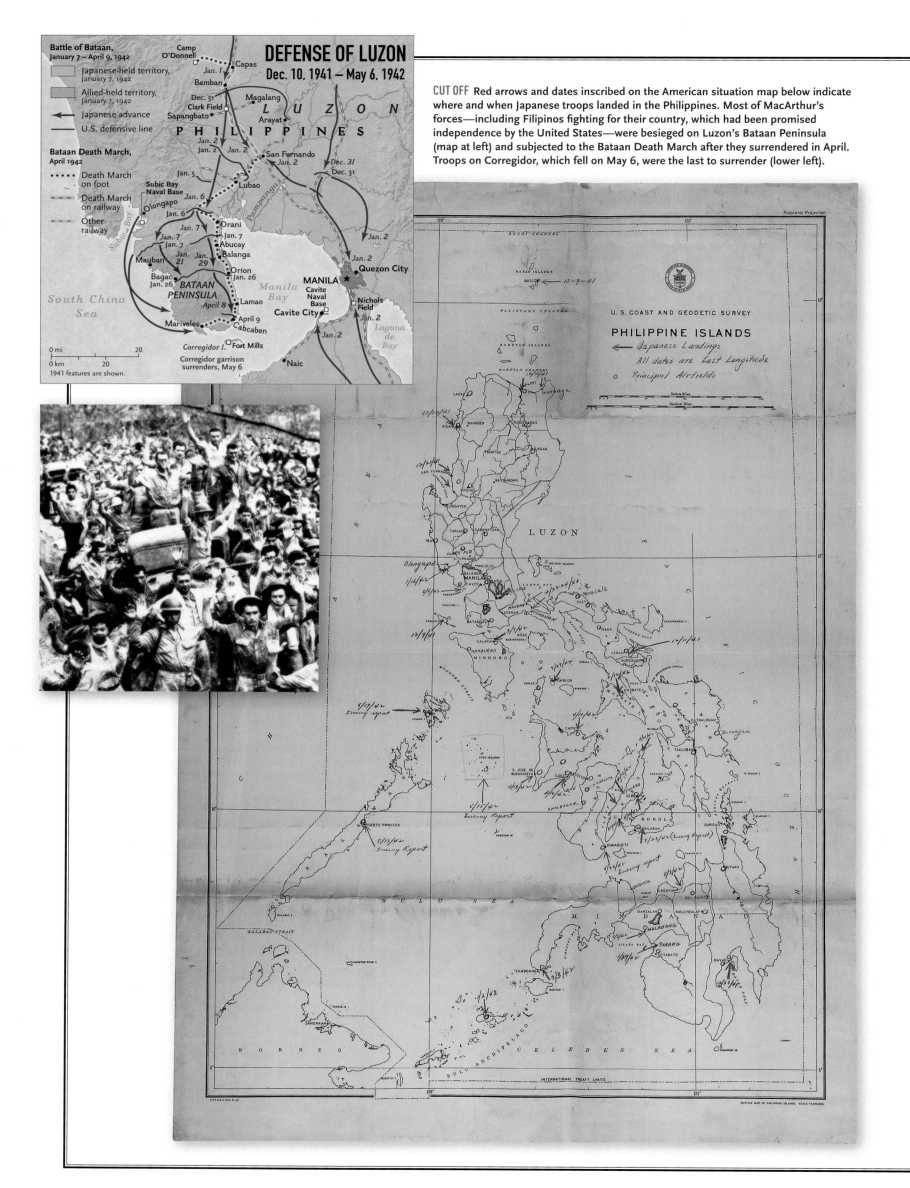

DEFENSE OF LUZON
Dec. 10, 1941 – May 6, 1942

Battle of Bataan,
January 7 – April 9, 1942

Japanese-held territory,
January 7, 1942

Allied-held territory,
January 7, 1942

← Japanese advance

U.S. defensive line

Bataan Death March,
April 1942

• • • • Death March
on foot

Death March
on railway

Other
railway

Camp
O'Donnell
Capas
Jan. 1
Bamban
Dec. 31
Magalang
Clark Field
Sapangbato
Arayat
LUZON
PHILIPPINES
Jan. 2
Jan. 2
Jan. 2
San Fernando
Jan. 2
Dec. 31
Dec. 31
Jan. 5
Lubao
Subic Bay
Naval Base
Olongapo
Jan. 6
Jan. 6
Orani
Jan. 7
Jan. 7
Abucay
Jan. 7
Balanga
Mauban
Jan. 21
Jan. 29
Orion
Jan. 26
Bagac
Jan. 26
BATAAN
PENINSULA
Lamao
April 8
Mariveles
April 9
Cabcaben
Corregidor I.
Fort Mills
Corregidor garrison
surrenders, May 6
Naic
Jan. 2
MANILA
Cavite
Naval
Base
Cavite City
Quezon City
Nichols
Field
Jan. 2
Jan. 2
South China
Sea
Manila
Bay
Laguna
de Bay

0 mi   20
0 km   20
1941 features are shown.

CUT OFF Red arrows and dates inscribed on the American situation map below indicate where and when Japanese troops landed in the Philippines. Most of MacArthur's forces—including Filipinos fighting for their country, which had been promised independence by the United States—were besieged on Luzon's Bataan Peninsula (map at left) and subjected to the Bataan Death March after they surrendered in April. Troops on Corregidor, which fell on May 6, were the last to surrender (lower left).

U. S. COAST AND GEODETIC SURVEY

PHILIPPINE ISLANDS

← Japanese Landings
All dates are East Longitude
○ Principal Airfields

THE BATAAN DEATH MARCH

On December 23, 1941, Gen. Douglas MacArthur ordered American and Filipino troops under his command to abandon Manila, the capital of the Philippines, and withdraw to the Bataan Peninsula on the far side of Manila Bay (see map opposite). Japanese air strikes at Clark Field, northwest of Manila, on December 8 had destroyed many American warplanes on the ground and cleared the way for the invasion that began two days later. By January 1942, 22,000 U.S. soldiers and nearly 60,000 Filipino recruits were besieged at Bataan by 200,000 Japanese troops. MacArthur's men fought hard and gave ground grudgingly as the invaders forced them back toward the tip of the peninsula, where the island of Corregidor served as their headquarters. Casualties, tropical diseases, and relentless enemy pressure left them in desperate straits. In March, on orders from Washington, MacArthur was evacuated by PT (patrol torpedo) boat to an airfield on the island of Mindanao, which was not fully occupied by the Japanese, and flown to Australia, where he vowed to return to the Philippines. Left behind were some 70,000 American and Filipino troops, whose ordeal grew worse when they were captured.

Unprepared to handle so many prisoners and contemptuous of men who surrendered rather than fight to the death, Japanese soldiers marched their captives nearly 70 miles north to a railroad station at San Fernando, where they would be transported to Capas, near Camp O'Donnell, a captured Allied base that would serve as their prison. Already weary and hungry when the march began, they had little to drink and went without food for days. Many who could not keep up and fell by the wayside were killed by their guards or left to die. An American officer, Maj. Alva Fitch, helped a faltering chaplain keep going until he collapsed. "I then commended him to his maker," Fitch related, "and left him to the gentle mercies of the Japanese." Those who survived the march were then packed into sweltering boxcars for the trip to Capas. "Some collapsed, the weakest died," recalled one captive who endured that journey. "Even the Japanese guards suffered." More than 7,000 prisoners who set out on the Bataan Death March perished before reaching Camp O'Donnell, and only about half of the men held there in wretched conditions survived confinement. ∎

LETHAL JOURNEY At upper right, exhausted American prisoners of war sit with their hands bound during the Bataan Death March. Thousands died during the trek. Many who reached Camp O'Donnell later perished there and were carried by surviving prisoners to the prison's burial ground (above).

CARRIER WARFARE

STRIKING BACK AT JAPAN

CHRONOLOGY

DECEMBER 25, 1941 Adm. Chester Nimitz arrives at Pearl Harbor to take charge of the U.S. Pacific Fleet and sets out to restore morale and take offensive action.

APRIL 18, 1942 Bombers commanded by Lt. Col. James Doolittle take off from the carrier U.S.S. *Hornet* and strike Tokyo and other targets in Japan.

MAY 4–8, 1942 American and Japanese naval task forces engage in the first contest between opposing aircraft carriers and their warplanes in the closely fought Battle of the Coral Sea.

JUNE 3, 1942 Japanese invasion force heading for Midway is spotted and targeted unsuccessfully by B-17 bombers based there, launching the Battle of Midway.

JUNE 4–7, 1942 U.S. Pacific Fleet wins the Battle of Midway, losing the aircraft carrier U.S.S. *Yorktown* but sinking four Japanese carriers.

Before war erupted in the Pacific, battleships "still ruled the waves," wrote Lt. Cmdr. Edwin Layton, chief intelligence officer for the Pacific Fleet. But the attack on Pearl Harbor confirmed that warplanes launched by aircraft carriers could sink warships situated far beyond the firing range of any battleship. When Adm. Chester Nimitz took charge of the Pacific Fleet in late December 1941, he knew that the intact aircraft carriers *Enterprise* and *Lexington* mattered more when it came to striking back at Japan than the battleships the fleet lost. The return of the U.S.S. *Yorktown* from the Atlantic in January 1942 gave him a third carrier to replace the recently arrived U.S.S. *Saratoga*, torpedoed that month by a Japanese sub. Admiral Nimitz was willing to risk his few carriers in battle because he received good intelligence on Admiral Yamamoto's larger fleet from Layton and Lt. Cmdr. Joseph Rochefort, whose team of cryptanalysts were cracking the Japanese naval code. Nimitz also had tough skippers eager to avenge Pearl Harbor like Vice Adm. William "Bull" Halsey, commander of the *Enterprise*, who said of his foes: "Before we're done with them, the Japanese language will be spoken only in hell."

After raiding Japanese-occupied Kwajalein in the Marshall Islands, Halsey escorted the fleet's newest carrier, U.S.S. *Hornet*, on a daring raid against Tokyo. They could not get close enough to well-defended Japan for conventional carrier-based warplanes, which had a range of about 300 miles, to hit Tokyo and return. Instead, 16 longer-range B-25 bombers commanded by Lt. Col. James Doolittle of the U.S. Army Air Forces (USAAF) were launched from the *Hornet* on April 18 at a distance of 670 miles. Too heavy to land on the carrier, they dropped their bombs and continued on. Most of the crews landed in friendly Chinese territory, but nine airmen were captured by the Japanese and three were executed. Publicly, Japanese officials derided the modest attack as the "do-little" raid. But it troubled Yamamoto, who resolved to extend Japan's defensive perimeter far across the Pacific to American-occupied Midway, leading to a pivotal battle there. ■

DOOLITTLE'S RAIDERS Above, Lt. Col. James Doolittle stands at left beside Capt. Marc Mitscher, commanding officer of the U.S.S. *Hornet*, surrounded by pilots and crewmen who would soon raid Tokyo, delivering 500-pound bombs like the one in the foreground. At right, sailors look on as one of the 16 B-25B Mitchell bombers involved in the Doolittle Raid lifts off from the deck of the *Hornet* on the morning of April 18, 1942.

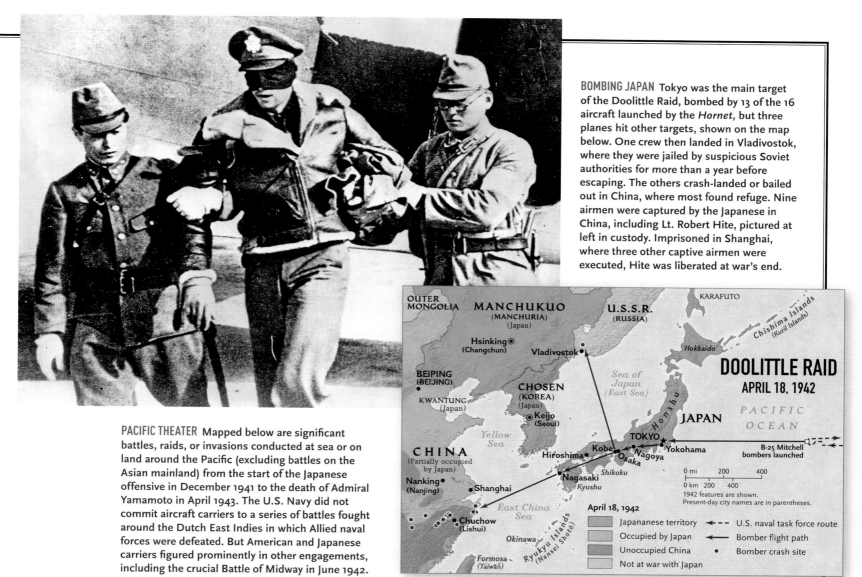

BOMBING JAPAN Tokyo was the main target of the Doolittle Raid, bombed by 13 of the 16 aircraft launched by the *Hornet*, but three planes hit other targets, shown on the map below. One crew then landed in Vladivostok, where they were jailed by suspicious Soviet authorities for more than a year before escaping. The others crash-landed or bailed out in China, where most found refuge. Nine airmen were captured by the Japanese in China, including Lt. Robert Hite, pictured at left in custody. Imprisoned in Shanghai, where three other captive airmen were executed, Hite was liberated at war's end.

PACIFIC THEATER Mapped below are significant battles, raids, or invasions conducted at sea or on land around the Pacific (excluding battles on the Asian mainland) from the start of the Japanese offensive in December 1941 to the death of Admiral Yamamoto in April 1943. The U.S. Navy did not commit aircraft carriers to a series of battles fought around the Dutch East Indies in which Allied naval forces were defeated. But American and Japanese carriers figured prominently in other engagements, including the crucial Battle of Midway in June 1942.

DOOLITTLE RAID
APRIL 18, 1942

OUTER MONGOLIA
MANCHUKUO (MANCHURIA) (Japan)
U.S.S.R. (RUSSIA)
KARAFUTO
Chishima Islands (Kuril Islands)
Hsinking (Changchun)
Vladivostok
Hokkaido
BEIPING (BEIJING)
KWANTUNG (Japan)
CHOSEN (KOREA) (Japan)
Sea of Japan (East Sea)
Keijo (Seoul)
Yellow Sea
JAPAN
Honshu
CHINA (Partially occupied by Japan)
Hiroshima
Kobe
Osaka
Nagoya
TOKYO
Yokohama
PACIFIC OCEAN
B-25 Mitchell bombers launched
Nanking (Nanjing)
Shanghai
Nagasaki
Shikoku
Kyushu
East China Sea
0 mi 200 400
0 km 200 400
1942 features are shown.
Present-day city names are in parentheses.
Chuchow (Lishui)
Okinawa
Ryukyu Islands (Nansei Shoto)
April 18, 1942
Formosa (Taiwan)

Japananese territory — ← U.S. naval task force route
Occupied by Japan — ← Bomber flight path
Unoccupied China — • Bomber crash site
Not at war with Japan

PACIFIC THEATER
Dec. 1941 – April 1943

✦ Major battle or raid

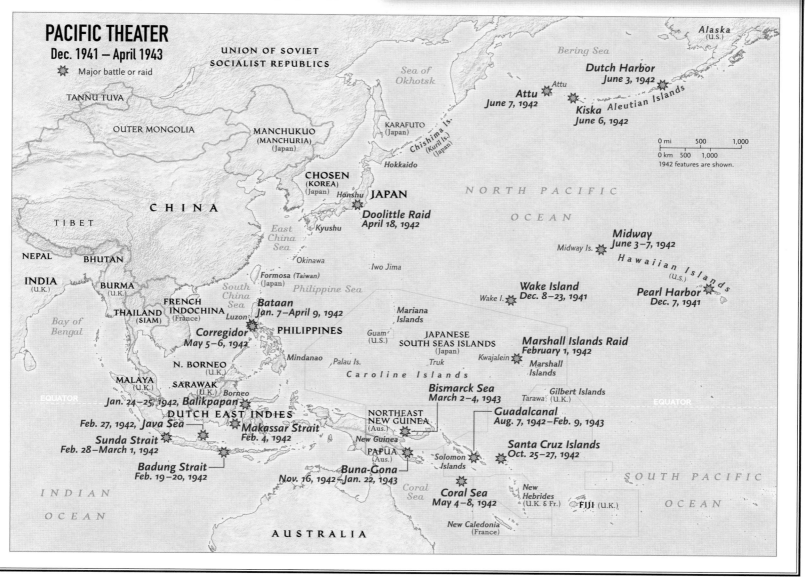

UNION OF SOVIET SOCIALIST REPUBLICS
TANNU TUVA
OUTER MONGOLIA
MANCHUKUO (MANCHURIA) (Japan)
Sea of Okhotsk
Bering Sea
Alaska (U.S.)
Dutch Harbor June 3, 1942
Attu June 7, 1942
Attu
Kiska June 6, 1942
Aleutian Islands
KARAFUTO (Japan)
Chishima Is. (Kuril Is.) (Japan)
Hokkaido
CHINA
TIBET
CHOSEN (KOREA) (Japan)
Honshu JAPAN
Doolittle Raid April 18, 1942
Kyushu
East China Sea
NORTH PACIFIC OCEAN
Midway June 3–7, 1942
Midway Is.
NEPAL BHUTAN
Okinawa
Iwo Jima
Hawaiian Islands (U.S.)
INDIA (U.K.)
BURMA (U.K.)
Formosa (Taiwan) (Japan)
South China Sea
Philippine Sea
Pearl Harbor Dec. 7, 1941
THAILAND (SIAM)
FRENCH INDOCHINA (France)
Bataan Jan. 7–April 9, 1942
Luzon
Wake Island Dec. 8–23, 1941
Wake I.
Bay of Bengal
Corregidor May 5–6, 1942
PHILIPPINES
Mariana Islands
Guam (U.S.)
JAPANESE SOUTH SEAS ISLANDS (Japan)
Marshall Islands Raid February 1, 1942
N. BORNEO (U.K.)
Mindanao
Palau Is.
Truk
Kwajalein
Marshall Islands
MALAYA (U.K.)
SARAWAK (U.K.)
Borneo
Caroline Islands
EQUATOR
Jan. 24–25, 1942, Balikpapan
DUTCH EAST INDIES
Bismarck Sea March 2–4, 1943
Gilbert Islands
Tarawa (U.K.)
EQUATOR
Feb. 27, 1942, Java Sea
Makassar Strait Feb. 4, 1942
NORTHEAST NEW GUINEA (Aus.)
New Guinea
Guadalcanal Aug. 7, 1942–Feb. 9, 1943
Sunda Strait Feb. 28–March 1, 1942
PAPUA (Aus.)
Solomon Islands
Santa Cruz Islands Oct. 25–27, 1942
SOUTH PACIFIC OCEAN
Badung Strait Feb. 19–20, 1942
Buna-Gona Nov. 16, 1942–Jan. 22, 1943
Coral Sea
Coral Sea May 4–8, 1942
New Hebrides (U.K. & Fr.)
FIJI (U.K.)
INDIAN OCEAN
New Caledonia (France)
AUSTRALIA

0 mi 500 1,000
0 km 500 1,000
1942 features are shown.

"I AM AN AMERICAN"

In February 1942, Lt. Gen. John DeWitt, in charge of the Western Defense Command, recommended removing all Japanese Americans from the West Coast. "The Japanese race is an enemy race," he wrote, adding that those who were "Americanized" had the same "racial strains" as those in Japan at war with the United States. There was no evidence, however, that Japanese Americans were a security threat. As FBI director J. Edgar Hoover stated, their proposed removal was "based primarily on public and political pressure rather than on factual data." In Hawaii, home to nearly 160,000 Japanese Americans, they were too important to the economy to be quarantined. On the West Coast, by contrast, they were a small minority, subject to racial prejudice and animosity that increased after the attack on Pearl Harbor. President Roosevelt accepted DeWitt's recommendation and ordered the removal of nearly 120,000 Japanese Americans to camps surrounded by barbed wire and watched by armed guards.

As shown on the wartime map below, Japanese American men, women, and children were first taken to dismal assembly centers. Some were housed in the stables at Santa Anita Racetrack. They were then transferred to one of ten relocation camps, known more accurately today as internment camps. As the war progressed and fears of Japanese subversion receded, authorities began to release and resettle internees. Those who pledged loyalty to the United States were eligible for military service, a path chosen by 20,000 Japanese Americans. Some who declined to pledge loyalty—including American citizens who refused to do so on principle—were sent to Tule Lake, the most crowded and closely guarded camp. On the assumption that internees would be better assimilated if they settled in places with few other Japanese Americans, relocation cities were designated in the East and Midwest. Despite the mistreatment that caused more than 5,000 former internees to leave the United States for Japan at war's end, most continued to affirm what one store owner in San Francisco stated in bold letters (inset) before he was detained: "I am an American." ∎

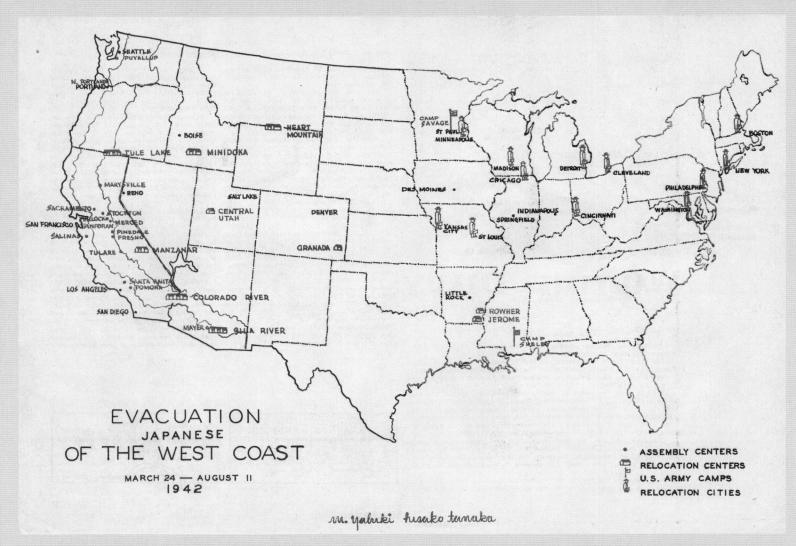

EVACUATION
JAPANESE
OF THE WEST COAST

MARCH 24 — AUGUST II
1942

• ASSEMBLY CENTERS
▫ RELOCATION CENTERS
⚑ U.S. ARMY CAMPS
▢ RELOCATION CITIES

FORCED RELOCATION Signed at bottom by the Japanese American who produced it, this map published in 1944 documents the government's drastic internment program. Although some internees moved to relocation cities in the East and Midwest after being released, many others returned to the West Coast.

TRUE CITIZENS Japanese Americans Tom and Ruth Kasai appear in a family album containing his U.S. Army dog tag and medals he received, including the Purple Heart, awarded after he was wounded in action in France. A telegram stating that he had been wounded (top left) reached his wife at an internment camp. Conditions were bleak at camps like Manzanar in California, cloaked in dust kicked up by hot winds (bottom) and surrounded by barbed wire (lower left). But some internees preserved ancestral traditions such as crafting the Senninbari vest below, based on a Japanese sash thought to bring the wearer good fortune.

BATTLE OF THE CORAL SEA

Before Admiral Yamamoto launched his Midway offensive, he lent naval support to the planned invasions of Port Moresby—situated within striking distance of Australia (see map below)—and Tulagi, a small island in the lower Solomons that would serve as a naval base while the Japanese built an airfield on nearby Guadalcanal. Two heavy carriers, I.J.N. *Shokaku* and I.J.N. *Zuikaku*, would be deployed as a striking force if U.S. warships opposed the invasions, and the light carrier I.J.N. *Shoho* would lead a covering force assigned to shield Japanese troopships. Analysis of coded Japanese radio signals informed Admiral Nimitz of those deployments, and he dispatched the carriers *Yorktown* and *Lexington*, each with a task force of cruisers and destroyers. Rear Adm. Frank Fletcher on the *Yorktown* had overall command of his own Task Force 17 as well as Task Force 11, led by Rear Adm. Aubrey Fitch on the *Lexington*. As they entered the Coral Sea, the stage was set for the first battle ever fought between opposing aircraft carriers and their warplanes.

On May 4, 1942, bombers from the *Yorktown* attacked Japanese invasion forces at Tulagi. Alerted by that strike, the *Shokaku* and *Zuikaku* approached from the north and sent out scout planes, as did Fletcher's carriers, but cloud cover kept ships on either side from being spotted until May 7. That morning, Japanese planes sank the destroyer U.S.S. *Sims* and wrecked an oiler that fueled Task Force 17, U.S.S. *Neosho*. A short time later, American planes blasted a more significant target, the carrier *Shoho*. "Scratch one flattop!" radioed a jubilant squadron leader as the ship went down. On May 8, the Battle of the Coral Sea reached a searing conclusion as the two big carriers on each side launched strikes that damaged the *Shokaku* and *Yorktown* and sank the *Lexington* after most of its crew was rescued. The Pacific Fleet could ill afford to lose a carrier, but the battle proved even costlier for Japan. The *Zuikaku* lost so many planes and pilots that it soon returned to port with the stricken *Shokaku*. The invasion of Port Moresby was scrubbed, and neither carrier would be available for Yamamoto's assault on Midway. ■

FATAL BLAST Bombed on May 8, 1942, the doomed carrier *Lexington* is rocked by a massive explosion that hurled the plane at left off the flight deck. The map inset provides an overview of the Battle of the Coral Sea (detailed opposite), with American task force movements in blue and Japanese movements in red.

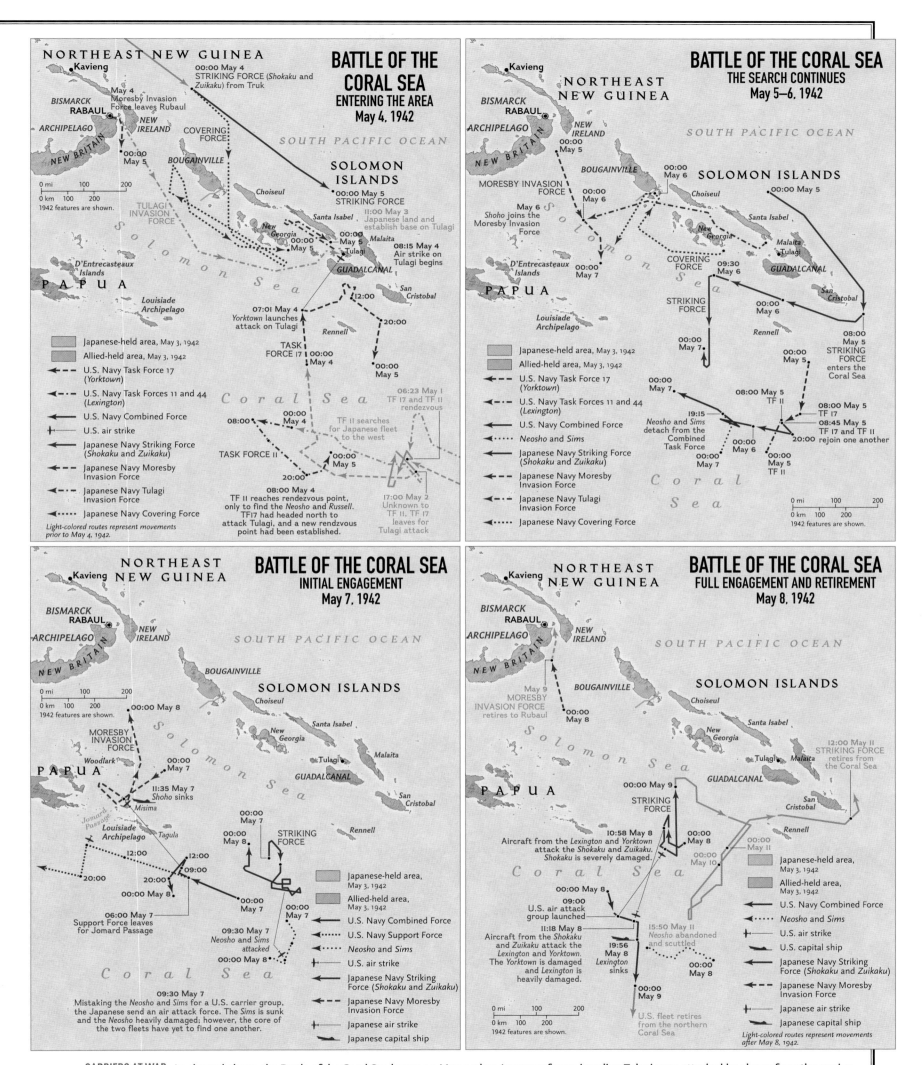

CARRIERS AT WAR As charted above, the Battle of the Coral Sea began on May 4 when Japanese forces invading Tulagi were attacked by planes from the carrier *Yorktown* (Task Force 17). A striking force comprising the carriers *Shokaku* and *Zuikaku* then bore down on the *Yorktown* and *Lexington* (Task Force 11). Neither side spotted the other until May 7, when Americans lost the destroyer *Sims* but sank the carrier *Shoho*, covering troopships bound for Port Moresby. That invasion was called off after fierce attacks on May 8 sank the *Lexington*, badly damaged the *Shokaku*, and depleted the *Zuikaku*'s air power.

TURNING POINT AT MIDWAY

Confident of victory, Admiral Yamamoto divided his forces for his sprawling Midway offensive. He sent a task force as a diversion to blast a U.S. base in the Aleutians, where Japanese troops would soon land, and assigned Vice Admiral Nagumo's First Air Fleet (Mobile Force), which had attacked Pearl Harbor, to bomb Midway before Japanese troops landed there. Two of Nagumo's six aircraft carriers were unavailable following the Battle of the Coral Sea, but Yamamoto planned to bring up reinforcements following the initial attack and hoped to shatter the U.S. Pacific Fleet as it came to Midway's defense. He thought his foes had lost both the *Lexington* and the *Yorktown* in the Coral Sea, but the *Yorktown* made it back to Pearl Harbor and was quickly repaired. That gave Admiral Nimitz three carriers to foil Yamamoto's plans, which code-breakers revealed to him in advance. He sent Task Force 16 under Rear Adm. Raymond Spruance, in charge of the *Enterprise* and *Hornet*, out with Task Force 17 under Rear Admiral Fletcher, who had overall command on the *Yorktown*. Nimitz figured they had a fighting chance if they got the jump on Nagumo.

U.S. Navy scout planes spotted the Japanese invasion force 700 miles west of Midway on June 3, 1942, and spotted Nagumo's carriers approaching Midway from the northwest around 5:30 A.M. on June 4 (see map opposite). Fletcher ordered Spruance to pursue those carriers and prepared to commit the *Yorktown* to battle as well. Around 8:30, after withstanding attacks by bombers from Midway, Nagumo learned that one of his own scouts had sighted an enemy carrier. By then, warplanes he had launched earlier against Midway were returning. Nagumo cleared the flight decks for them by ordering planes armed with bombs for a second raid on Midway lowered to the hangar decks and rearmed with torpedoes to target carriers. That arduous process was under way when torpedo planes sent by Spruance attacked. Coming in low without fighter escorts, most were downed by enemy fire, but the attack delayed the launch of Nagumo's planes. They were about to take off when dive-bombers from the *Enterprise* and *Yorktown* swooped down at 10:25. Within minutes, Nagumo's flagship, I.J.N. *Akagi*, and two other carriers, I.J.N. *Soryu* and I.J.N. *Kaga*, were engulfed in flames, fed when planes loaded with fuel and explosives ignited. I.J.N. *Hiryu* was the only carrier to survive the attack. It too was bombed later that day after launching strikes on the *Yorktown*, which eventually sank, as did the *Hiryu*. Devastated by the outcome, Yamamoto withdrew. As Nimitz later stated, "Midway was the most crucial battle of the Pacific War, the engagement that made everything else possible." ∎

OFF-KILTER CREWMEN prepare to abandon the *Yorktown*, listing after it was torpedoed by planes from the Japanese carrier *Hiryu* on June 4.
The abandoned *Yorktown* did not go down until June 7, one day after it was torpedoed by a Japanese submarine, which also sank the destroyer
U.S.S. *Hammann* as its crew tried to salvage the carrier.

DECISIVE BATTLE On June 4, one day after the Japanese invasion fleet was spotted and targeted unsuccessfully by Midway-based B-17s, warplanes from Nagumo's Mobile Force attacked Midway at 6:30 A.M. Bombers that had taken off earlier from the U.S. base there (at bottom on the map below) then made ineffective attacks on Nagumo's four carriers. At 9:25, torpedo planes from the *Enterprise* and *Hornet* approached Nagumo's fleet and took heavy losses before Douglas Dauntless dive-bombers from the *Enterprise* and *Yorktown* scored lethal hits on the *Akagi*, *Soryu*, and *Kaga* at 10:25. The *Hiryu* escaped and launched strikes that disabled the *Yorktown*. Dauntlesses then bombed the *Hiryu*, which sank early on June 5. On June 6, Dauntlesses struck again (inset photo upper right), blasting the heavy cruiser I.J.N. *Mikuma* (right), which went down. The loss of the *Yorktown* on the 7th did little to diminish a great American victory.

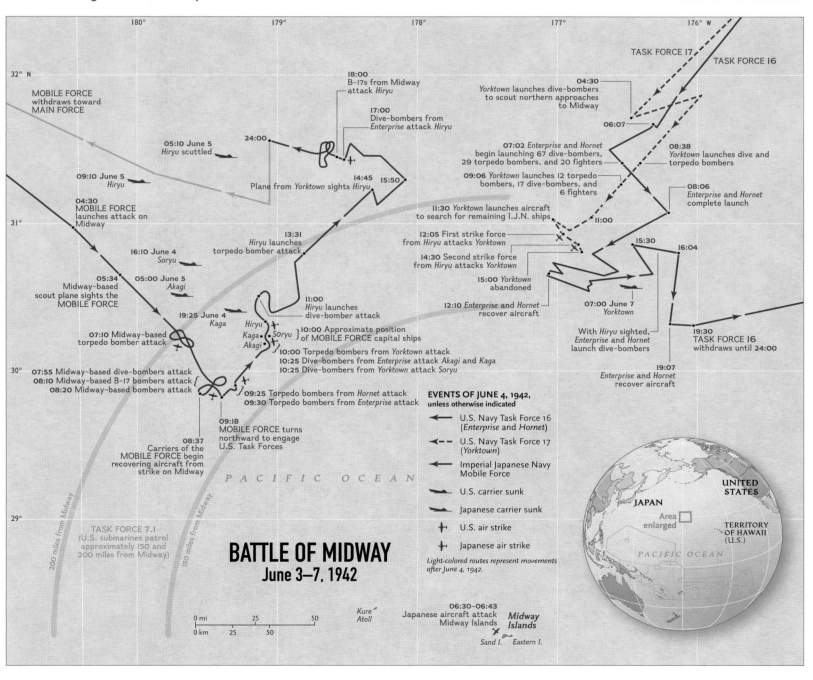

MOBILE FORCE withdraws toward MAIN FORCE

05:10 June 5 *Hiryu* scuttled

09:10 June 5 *Hiryu*

04:30 MOBILE FORCE launches attack on Midway

16:10 June 4 *Soryu*

05:34 Midway-based scout plane sights the MOBILE FORCE

05:00 June 5 *Akagi*

19:25 June 4 *Kaga*

07:10 Midway-based torpedo bomber attack

Hiryu *Kaga* *Soryu* *Akagi*

07:55 Midway-based dive-bombers attack
08:10 Midway-based B-17 bombers attack
08:20 Midway-based bombers attack

08:37 Carriers of the MOBILE FORCE begin recovering aircraft from strike on Midway

09:18 MOBILE FORCE turns northward to engage U.S. Task Forces

09:25 Torpedo bombers from *Hornet* attack
09:30 Torpedo bombers from *Enterprise* attack

24:00

18:00 B-17s from Midway attack *Hiryu*

17:00 Dive-bombers from *Enterprise* attack *Hiryu*

14:45 15:50

Plane from *Yorktown* sights *Hiryu*

13:31 *Hiryu* launches torpedo bomber attack

11:00 *Hiryu* launches dive-bomber attack

10:00 Approximate position of MOBILE FORCE capital ships

10:00 Torpedo bombers from *Yorktown* attack
10:25 Dive-bombers from *Enterprise* attack *Akagi* and *Kaga*
10:25 Dive-bombers from *Yorktown* attack *Soryu*

TASK FORCE 17   TASK FORCE 16

Yorktown launches dive-bombers to scout northern approaches to Midway

04:30

06:07

07:02 *Enterprise* and *Hornet* begin launching 67 dive-bombers, 29 torpedo bombers, and 20 fighters

09:06 *Yorktown* launches 12 torpedo bombers, 17 dive-bombers, and 6 fighters

08:38 *Yorktown* launches dive and torpedo bombers

08:06 *Enterprise* and *Hornet* complete launch

11:30 *Yorktown* launches aircraft to search for remaining I.J.N. ships

11:00

12:05 First strike force from *Hiryu* attacks *Yorktown*

14:30 Second strike force from *Hiryu* attacks *Yorktown*

15:00 *Yorktown* abandoned

12:10 *Enterprise* and *Hornet* recover aircraft

15:30   16:04

07:00 June 7 *Yorktown*

With *Hiryu* sighted, *Enterprise* and *Hornet* launch dive-bombers

19:30 TASK FORCE 16 withdraws until 24:00

19:07 *Enterprise* and *Hornet* recover aircraft

PACIFIC OCEAN

TASK FORCE 7.1 (U.S. submarines patrol approximately 150 and 200 miles from Midway)

200 miles from Midway

150 miles from Midway

EVENTS OF JUNE 4, 1942, unless otherwise indicated

⟵ U.S. Navy Task Force 16 (*Enterprise* and *Hornet*)

⟵-- U.S. Navy Task Force 17 (*Yorktown*)

⟵ Imperial Japanese Navy Mobile Force

⬩ U.S. carrier sunk

⬩ Japanese carrier sunk

✛ U.S. air strike

✛ Japanese air strike

Light-colored routes represent movements after June 4, 1942.

BATTLE OF MIDWAY
June 3–7, 1942

0 mi   25   50
0 km   25   50

Kure Atoll

06:30–06:43 Japanese aircraft attack Midway Islands

Midway Islands

✕

Sand I.   *Eastern I.*

JAPAN   Area enlarged

UNITED STATES

TERRITORY OF HAWAII (U.S.)

PACIFIC OCEAN

MAPPING MIDWAY Traced here are crucial events in the Battle of Midway until early on June 6, by which time the *Hiryu* (shown evading bombs at right) and three other Japanese carriers had gone down but the stricken *Yorktown* remained afloat. Abbreviations include CV (fleet carrier), BB (battleship), CA (heavy cruiser), CL (light cruiser), DD (destroyer), TBD (Douglas Devastator torpedo bomber), SBD (Douglas Dauntless dive-bomber), VSB (scout bomber), PBY (Catalina scout plane), and SS (submarine).

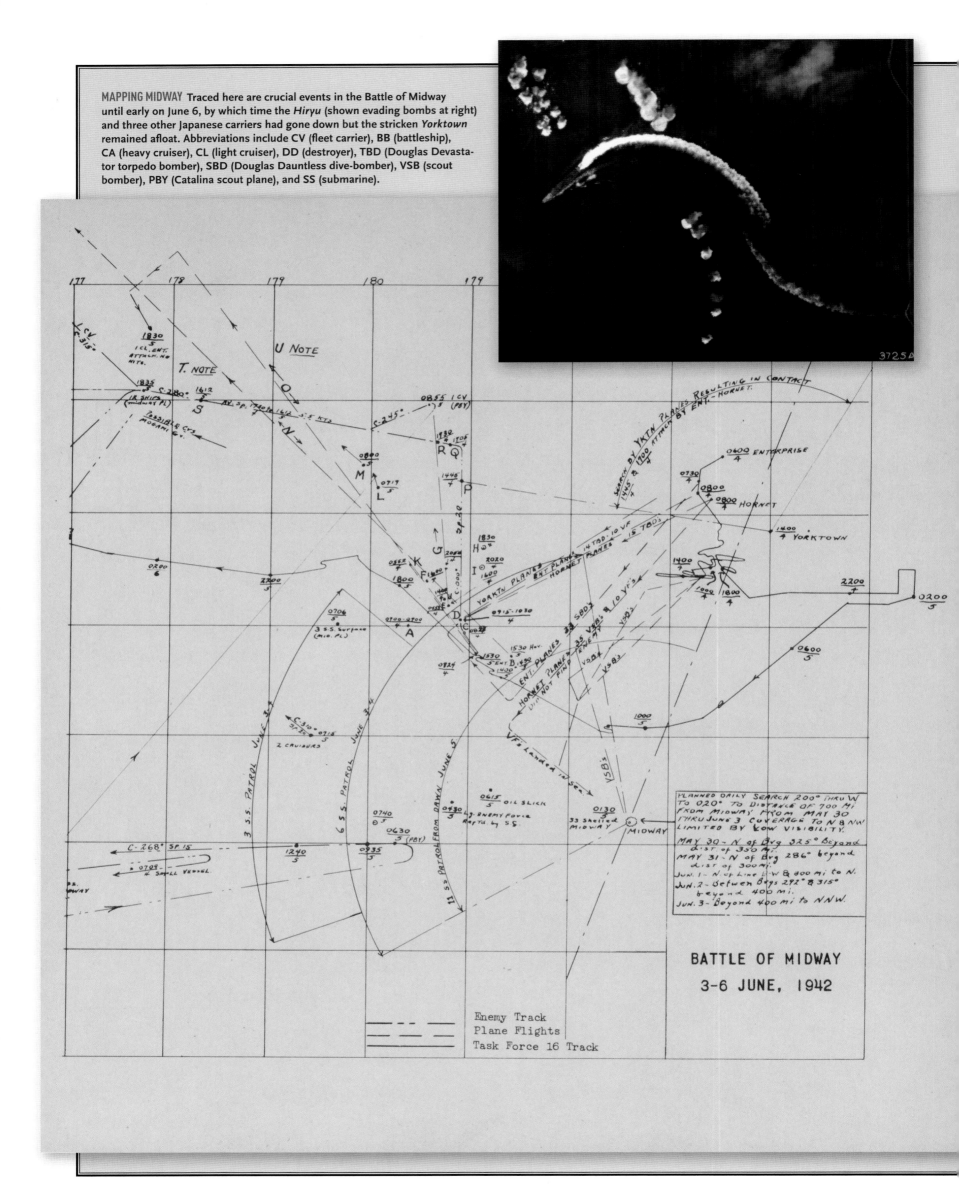

BATTLE OF MIDWAY
3-6 JUNE, 1942

Enemy Track
Plane Flights
Task Force 16 Track

SECRET

LEGEND

A. 6 TBD, 4 B-26, Midway. Torpedo Attack results not observed. Midway SBD's dive bombing attack on CV's and BB, 2 hits on CV, 1 hit on BB, fires started on both. B-17's high level attack on CV's, 1 CV damaged, 1 DD damaged.

B. "Large friendly force" (Midway planes).

C. 0857-4. Attack. Midway planes - 1 BB damaged, 1 CV damaged.

D. Attack. ENTERPRISE, HORNET, YORKTOWN. 4 CV, 3 disabled (KAGA, AKAGI, SORYU), 2 BB - 1 damaged, 4-6 cruisers - 1 damaged. 6 DD.

E. Contact. Enemy planes headed toward Midway (PBY).

F. 3 burning CV, 2 cruisers, 4 DD (Midway planes). Same position 1745-4 Bombed by B-17's.

G. Midway planes 1800-4 reported battle bearing 355°. (Corrected position planes).

H. B-17's Midway attacked CA and set afire. Did not contact CV's.

I. B-17's from Oahu reported 2 hits on burning CV.

J. NAUTILUS torpedoed burning CV.

K. Contact. 2 CV's, BB (PBY).

L. Course 338°, speed 25. 5 ships (PBY). Probably cruisers and Dp's, that had stood by 3 burning CV's rejoining striking force.

M. Course 310°, speed 12. 1 CV on fire, 2 BB, 3-4 CA (PBY).

N. HORNET search 5th based on Midway contact 0800-5 1 damaged CV, 2 BB, 3 CA, DD's. Search started 1525-5. 26 VSB.

O. ENTERPRISE search 5th based on Midway contact 0800-5 1 damaged CV, 2 BB, 3 CA, DD's. Search started 1528-5. 32 SBD.

P. Contact. YORKTOWN planes. 1 CV, 2 BB, 3 CA-CL, 4 DD.

Q. Attack. ENTERPRISE 1 CV - HIRYU, 6 hits, 2 BB, 2 hits, on 1 BB, 3 CA-CL, 4 DD.

R. Attack. HORNET 1 CV burning badly (HIRYU), 1 or 2 BB, 3 hits, CA's 2 hits on 1 CA, DD's. CV not attacked as considered of no value as target.

S. Midway planes. 1 CV, 2 BB, 3 CA, 5 DD. Course 280°, speed 10.

T. NOTE: Damaged CV probably sunk during 5th.

U. NOTE: 1 CV probably joined this group during forenoon of 5 June. Probably detached from group evening of 5th and escaped to NW.

V. 1 CV retiring 177° into front. 9 VF at 10,000 feet.

W. NOTE: Plane reported distance CV from Midway 425 miles, bearing 313°. Distance probably too great based on flight between 1835 and 1852 positions.

X. Cruiser planes. 2 CL, 2 DD "from scene of first attack."

Y. Attack. HORNET, 1 BB, 1 CA, 1 CL, 3 DD or 2 CA, 1 CL, 3 DD. 1 BB disabled, 1 CA damaged, 1 DD sunk or 1 CA sunk (TAKAO?), 1 CA damaged, 1 DD sunk.

0200
5

8-36b

SECRET REPORT ON MIDWAY

During the war, the U.S. Pacific Fleet issued secret bulletins (below) that analyzed engagements in which the fleet took part and proposed ways of improving its tactics and battle-readiness. The detailed map at left accompanied a lengthy analysis of the Battle of Midway, a great victory that nonetheless revealed to Admiral Nimitz and his staff serious flaws in the way their forces conducted carrier warfare—a new form of naval combat involving much trial and error. The crux of the battle occurred northwest of Midway at position D on the map, where warplanes launched northeast of Midway by Task Forces 16 (*Enterprise* and *Hornet*) and 17 (*Yorktown*) attacked four Japanese carriers on the morning of June 4. The report noted that one squadron of planes from the *Hornet* could not find those carriers, ran out of fuel, and ditched in the sea, which could have been avoided with better reconnaissance and communications. Heavy losses of torpedo bombers during the attacks demonstrated the "absolute necessity of fighter support" for those vulnerable planes, according to the report, which also pointed out that high-level bombers such as B-17s had little success targeting ships that were intact and capable of maneuvering. The results, as shown in the photograph opposite of the carrier *Hiryu* dodging bombs on June 4, were described as "mostly 'near misses,' and not near enough." Attacks later that day by dive-bombers from the *Enterprise* (Q) and *Hornet* (R) doomed the *Hiryu* and damaged several Japanese warships escorting that carrier. ■

SECRET

12

SECRET INFORMATION BULLETIN NO. 1

BATTLE EXPERIENCE

FROM

PEARL HARBOR TO MIDWAY

DECEMBER 1941 TO JUNE 1942

INCLUDING

MAKIN ISLAND RAID 17-18 AUGUST

UNITED STATES FLEET
HEADQUARTERS OF THE COMMANDER IN CHIEF

13

SECRET

SECRET INFORMATION BULLETIN NO.11

BATTLE EXPERIENCE

NAVAL OPERATIONS
SOLOMON ISLANDS AREA
12 JULY - 10 AUGUST 1943

CAUTION
THIS BULLETIN AND THE INFORMATION CONTAINED HEREIN MUST NOT FALL INTO THE HANDS OF THE ENEMY

UNITED STATES FLEET
HEADQUARTERS OF THE COMMANDER IN CHIEF

RESTRICTED ACCESS U.S. Navy bulletins like the two above were distributed confidentially to officers on a "need to know" basis. Secrecy was essential because the reports revealed what the Pacific Fleet knew about Japanese plans and tactics and how it intended to conduct future battles.

ISLAND FIGHTING
FROM GUADALCANAL TO PAPUA AND NEW GUINEA

CHRONOLOGY

AUGUST 7, 1942 U.S. Marines land on Guadalcanal.

SEPTEMBER 11, 1942 Gen. Douglas MacArthur orders U.S. troops to join Australians fighting Japanese forces on Papua.

NOVEMBER 13–15, 1942 U.S. Navy forces win the Naval Battle of Guadalcanal.

JANUARY 2, 1943 Allied forces win the Battle of Buna on Papua.

FEBRUARY 1–7, 1943 Japanese troops are evacuated from Guadalcanal.

APRIL 7, 1943 Admiral Yamamoto launches naval air strikes against Allied bases on Guadalcanal and New Guinea.

APRIL 18, 1943 Admiral Yamamoto killed when U.S. fighter pilots down his plane off Bougainville.

Victory at Midway enabled U.S. forces to challenge Japanese troops for control of islands off the east coast of Australia, including Guadalcanal in the Solomons. The immediate objective was to protect supply lines between the United States and Australia, where General MacArthur was preparing for offensive action on Papua and New Guinea (see top map opposite). In June 1942, Allied coastwatchers spying on Japanese forces who had occupied Tulagi in May reported that they were building an airstrip on nearby Guadalcanal from which bombers could strike ships bound for Australia.

Beginning on August 7, nearly 20,000 U.S. Marines landed on Guadalcanal, Tulagi, and other islands in the vicinity. Supported by ships of the Pacific Fleet and Army forces, they launched the first of many bitter struggles to reclaim territory from Japanese troops,

who seldom surrendered. Of the 800 or so occupying Tulagi and other small islands, all but a few dozen died fighting after killing or wounding more than 300 Marines. There was little resistance initially on Guadalcanal, where Navy construction crews called Seabees transformed the airstrip begun by their foes into a U.S. air base, Henderson Field. But Japanese troops delivered by convoy from Rabaul in New Britain launched a furious attack in September at Bloody Ridge, overlooking Henderson Field, where they were stopped by machine-gunners. "When one wave was mowed down," an American officer recalled, "another wave followed it into death." In October, Marines defending Henderson Field withstood another attack, and Nimitz sent his toughest commander, "Bull" Halsey, to battle Japanese naval forces and cut off enemy reinforcements. ∎

FIRST WAVE Troops of the First Marine Division (upper right) rush ashore on Guadalcanal on August 7, 1942. Marines seized an unfinished Japanese airstrip there (above) that became Henderson Field, named for Maj. Lofton Henderson, who died leading an attack by torpedo planes at Midway.

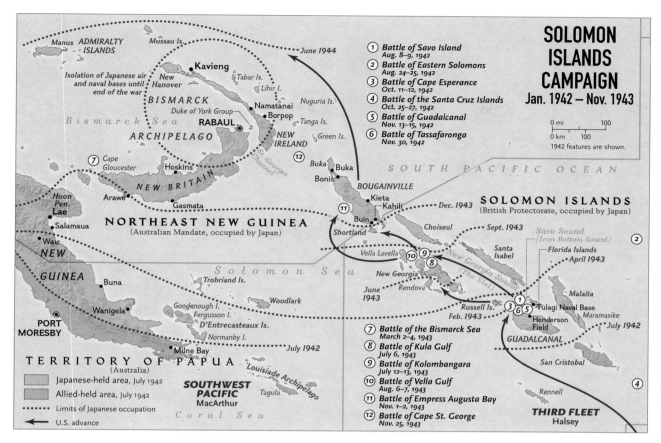

SOLOMON ISLANDS CAMPAIGN
Jan. 1942 – Nov. 1943

1. **Battle of Savo Island** Aug. 8–9, 1942
2. **Battle of Eastern Solomons** Aug. 24–25, 1942
3. **Battle of Cape Esperance** Oct. 11–12, 1942
4. **Battle of the Santa Cruz Islands** Oct. 25–27, 1942
5. **Battle of Guadalcanal** Nov. 13–15, 1942
6. **Battle of Tassafaronga** Nov. 30, 1942

7. **Battle of the Bismarck Sea** March 2–4, 1943
8. **Battle of Kula Gulf** July 6, 1943
9. **Battle of Kolombangara** July 12–13, 1943
10. **Battle of Vella Gulf** Aug. 6–7, 1943
11. **Battle of Empress Augusta Bay** Nov. 1–2, 1943
12. **Battle of Cape St. George** Nov. 25, 1943

0 mi 100
0 km 100
1942 features are shown.

Manus ADMIRALTY ISLANDS
Mussau Is.
Kavieng
New Hanover
Tabar Is.
Lihir I.
BISMARCK ARCHIPELAGO
Duke of York Group
RABAUL
Namatanai
Borpop
Tanga Is.
Nuguria Is.
Isolation of Japanese air and naval bases until end of the war
June 1944
Bismarck Sea
Green Is.
SOUTH PACIFIC OCEAN
NEW IRELAND
Cape Gloucester
Hoskins
NEW BRITAIN
St. Georges Channel
Buka
Buka
Bonis
Kieta
Kahili
Buin
BOUGAINVILLE
SOLOMON ISLANDS
(British Protectorate, occupied by Japan)
Dec. 1943
Shortland
Choiseul
Sept. 1943
Huon Pen.
Lae
Arawe
Gasmata
Salamaua
NORTHEAST NEW GUINEA
(Australian Mandate, occupied by Japan)
Wau
NEW GUINEA
Buna
Wanigela
PORT MORESBY
Solomon Sea
Trobriand Is.
Woodlark
Goodenough I.
Fergusson I.
D'Entrecasteaux Is.
Normanby I.
Milne Bay
July 1942
TERRITORY OF PAPUA (Australia)
Louisiade Archipelago
Tagula
SOUTHWEST PACIFIC
MacArthur
Coral Sea
Vella Lavella
New Georgia Sound (The Slot)
Santa Isabel
Florida Islands
April 1943
Savo Sound (Iron Bottom Sound)
New Georgia
June 1943
Rendova
Russell Is.
Feb. 1943
Tulagi Naval Base
Henderson Field
GUADALCANAL
Malaita
Maramasike
July 1942
San Cristobal
Rennell
THIRD FLEET
Halsey

Japanese-held area, July 1942
Allied-held area, July 1942
Limits of Japanese occupation
U.S. advance

AMERICAN ADVANCES Maps below chart the invasion of Guadalcanal and the seizure of the airstrip that became Henderson Field, the Battle of Bloody Ridge in September on the outskirts of Henderson, and a subsequent battle in October that left Americans in control of that airfield. As detailed on the map at left, clashes between warships offshore culminated in the Naval Battle of Guadalcanal in November, which led the Japanese to withdraw in early 1943. U.S. forces then invaded New Georgia in July and Bougainville in November, while General MacArthur's forces advanced beyond Papua on New Guinea and subjected the Japanese base at Rabaul to air strikes.

GUADALCANAL
AND THE FLORIDA ISLANDS
August 7, 1942

Buena Vista Island
Gavutu Seaplane Base (Tulagi Seaplane Base)
Olevugha
Florida Island (Nggela Sule)
Tulagi I.
Gavutu and Tanambogo Islands
FLORIDA ISLANDS
MALAITA
AMPHIBIOUS INVASION FORCE
Savo Island
C. Esperance
Savo Sound (Iron Bottom Sd.)
2nd and 5th Marines
Nggela Pile
Nggella Channel
Sealark Channel
Indispensable Strait
Verahue
Lunga Point
1st, 5th, and 11th Marines
Kakambona
Tenaru
Lengo Channel
Koli Pt.
Taivu Point
Tasimbako
Area enlarged in adjacent maps
Aola Bay
Beaufort Bay
GUADALCANAL
PACIFIC OCEAN
0 mi 10 20
0 km 10 20
1942 features are shown.

INITIAL LANDINGS
AND CAPTURE OF THE AIRFIELD
August 7–8, 1942

Japanese-held territory, August 6, 1942
U.S. advance, August 7–8, 1942
U.S. position, evening of August 7, 1942
U.S. position, evening of August 8, 1942
Japanese bivouac position, August 7–8, 1942

Lunga Point
5th Marines Aug. 8
Lunga
Kukum
Savo Sound (Iron Bottom Sd.)
1ST MARINE DIVISION
1st, 5th, and 11th Marines
Vandegrift
1st Bn. 5th Marine Regiment
Aug. 8
Aug. 7
Red Beach extension
Red Beach
1st Marine Regiment
RXI airfield (renamed after capture)
16:00 Aug. 8
Lunga
Tenaru
Aug. 7
Unopposed landings begin on Red Beach 09:00 Aug. 7
Bloody Ridge (unnamed at the time)
Aug. 7
Aug. 8
1st Marine Regiment
GUADALCANAL
0 mi 1 2
0 km 1 2
1942 features are shown.

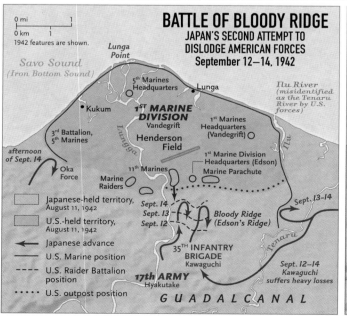

BATTLE OF BLOODY RIDGE
JAPAN'S SECOND ATTEMPT TO DISLODGE AMERICAN FORCES
September 12–14, 1942

0 mi 1
0 km 1
1942 features are shown.

Lunga Point
Savo Sound (Iron Bottom Sound)
5th Marines Headquarters
Lunga
Ilu River (misidentified as the Tenaru River by U.S. forces)
Kukum
1ST MARINE DIVISION
Vandegrift
Henderson Field
1st Marines Headquarters (Vandegrift)
1st Marine Division Headquarters (Edson)
Marine Parachute
3rd Battalion, 5th Marines
afternoon of Sept. 14
Oka Force
Marine Raiders
11th Marines
Sept. 14
Sept. 13
Sept. 12
Bloody Ridge (Edson's Ridge)
Sept. 13–14
Sept. 12–14 Kawaguchi suffers heavy losses
35TH INFANTRY BRIGADE
Kawaguchi
17TH ARMY
Hyakutake
GUADALCANAL

Japanese-held territory, August 11, 1942
U.S.-held territory, August 11, 1942
Japanese advance
U.S. Marine position
U.S. Raider Battalion position
U.S. outpost position

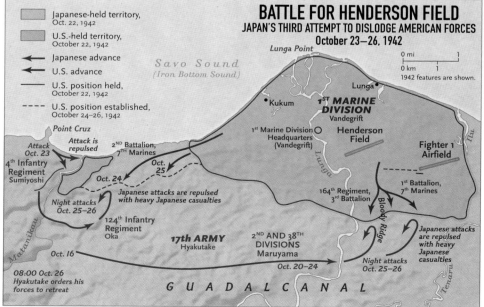

BATTLE FOR HENDERSON FIELD
JAPAN'S THIRD ATTEMPT TO DISLODGE AMERICAN FORCES
October 23–26, 1942

Japanese-held territory, Oct. 22, 1942
U.S.-held territory, October 22, 1942
Japanese advance
U.S. advance
U.S. position held, October 22, 1942
U.S. position established, October 24–26, 1942

Lunga Point
Savo Sound (Iron Bottom Sound)
Point Cruz
Attack Oct. 23
Attack is repulsed
2ND Battalion, 7TH Marines
Oct. 25
Oct. 24
Kukum
Lunga
1ST MARINE DIVISION
Vandegrift
Henderson Field
1st Marine Division Headquarters (Vandegrift)
Fighter 1 Airfield
1st Battalion, 7TH Marines
4th Infantry Regiment Sumiyoshi
Japanese attacks are repulsed with heavy Japanese casualties
Night attacks Oct. 25–26
124th Infantry Regiment Oka
17TH ARMY Hyakutake
Oct. 16
164th Regiment, 3rd Battalion
2ND AND 38TH DIVISIONS Maruyama
Bloody Ridge
Japanese attacks are repulsed with heavy Japanese casualties
Night attacks Oct. 25–26
Oct. 20–24
08:00 Oct. 26 Hyakutake orders his forces to retreat
GUADALCANAL
0 mi 1
0 km 1
1942 features are shown.

RELICS OF WAR

Some vestiges of the fighting on Guadalcanal, like the Japanese helmet at lower right, could have been found on any contested island in the Pacific. But the map displayed here—the front of which appears below and the back opposite—is unique to Guadalcanal and sheds light on the first significant battle there. Bearing the name of Second Lt. R. R. Binder of the U.S. Marine Corps, it consists of a printed map of the island, with a hand-drawn chart on the back portraying a crucial area near Lunga Point and the emerging Henderson Field on Guadalcanal's north coast. The airfield was the main reason that Marines seized the island—and that Japanese troops fought to regain control there.

Despite maps like this one, Guadalcanal was unfamiliar territory for Marines, who devised some peculiar place-names and confused some existing place-names. The stream they labeled Alligator Creek was in fact inhabited by crocodiles. And on Binder's map and others issued to Marines, the Ilu River was mislabeled the Tenaru River. For that reason, the so-called Battle of the Tenaru on August 21, 1942, is sometimes referred to as the Battle of the Ilu. By whatever name, it was a harrowing start to the bloody struggle for Guadalcanal, which continued for several months and claimed thousands of lives on both sides.

The battle was instigated by Col. Kiyono Ichiki, who landed uncontested before dawn on August 19 with some 900 men of his 28th Infantry Regiment on Taivu Point, east of Lunga Point, where Marines were defending the airfield. Ichiki was supposed to wait for more troops to arrive before attacking, but he thought there were only about 2,000 Marines on Guadalcanal—the actual number was then nearly 10,000—and figured his troops could handle them. Ichiki's forces were soon detected. When they crossed the sandbar at the mouth of the shallow Ilu River around 1 A.M. on the 21st, Marines awaited them with rifles, machine guns, and a 37-mm gun loaded with canister that sprayed deadly shrapnel. Desperate Japanese charges inflicted more than 100 casualties on the Marines, but their commander, Maj. Gen. Alexander Vandegrift, sent a battalion across the river that pinned down the surviving attackers. Tanks then crossed the sandbar with guns blazing and crushed dead and wounded Japanese soldiers under their tracks, which looked "like meat grinders" when the battle ended, one Marine observed. Ichiki's forces were all but annihilated, and he reportedly died by his own hand rather than be captured. ∎

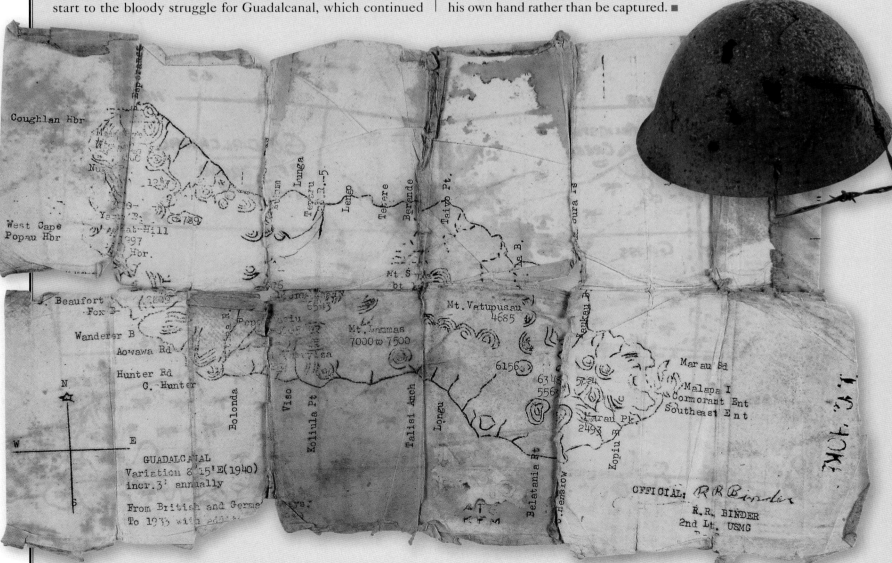

CONTESTED ISLAND Worn and torn, this official Marine Corps map of Guadalcanal, based on earlier British and German charts, shows the island's mountainous interior and landmarks on the north coast that figured in battles between U.S. and Japanese forces, including Lunga Point to the west, near Henderson Field.

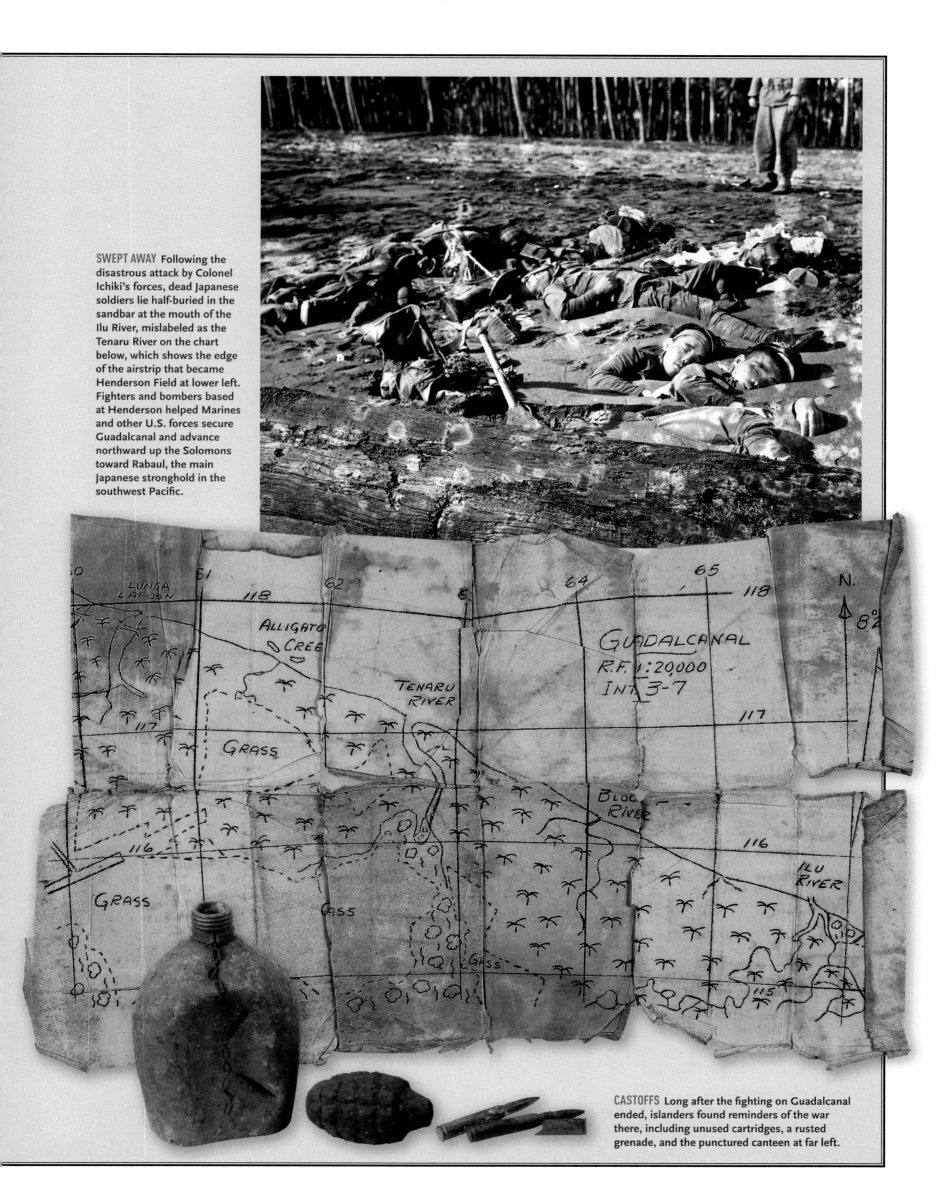

SWEPT AWAY Following the disastrous attack by Colonel Ichiki's forces, dead Japanese soldiers lie half-buried in the sandbar at the mouth of the Ilu River, mislabeled as the Tenaru River on the chart below, which shows the edge of the airstrip that became Henderson Field at lower left. Fighters and bombers based at Henderson helped Marines and other U.S. forces secure Guadalcanal and advance northward up the Solomons toward Rabaul, the main Japanese stronghold in the southwest Pacific.

CASTOFFS Long after the fighting on Guadalcanal ended, islanders found reminders of the war there, including unused cartridges, a rusted grenade, and the punctured canteen at far left.

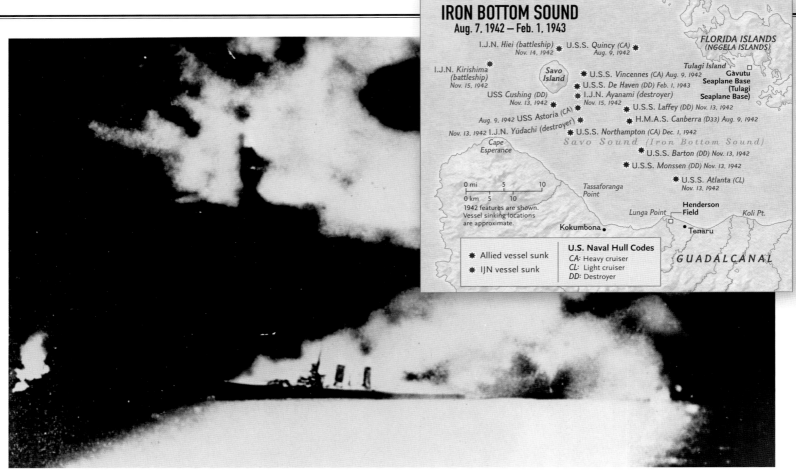

IRON BOTTOM SOUND
Aug. 7, 1942 – Feb. 1, 1943

FLORIDA ISLANDS
(NGGELA ISLANDS)

I.J.N. *Hiei* (battleship)
Nov. 14, 1942

U.S.S. Quincy (CA)
Aug. 9, 1942

I.J.N. *Kirishima*
(battleship)
Nov. 15, 1942

Savo
Island

U.S.S. Vincennes (CA) Aug. 9, 1942

Tulagi Island   Gavutu
Seaplane Base
(Tulagi
Seaplane Base)

U.S.S. De Haven (DD) Feb. 1, 1943

USS Cushing (DD)
Nov. 13, 1942

I.J.N. Ayanami (destroyer)
Nov. 15, 1942

U.S.S. Laffey (DD) Nov. 13, 1942

Aug. 9, 1942 USS Astoria (CA)

Nov. 13, 1942 I.J.N. Yūdachi (destroyer)

H.M.A.S. Canberra (D33) Aug. 9, 1942

U.S.S. Northampton (CA) Dec. 1, 1942

Cape
Esperance

Savo Sound (Iron Bottom Sound)

U.S.S. Barton (DD) Nov. 13, 1942

U.S.S. Monssen (DD) Nov. 13, 1942

U.S.S. Atlanta (CL)
Nov. 13, 1942

0 mi   5   10

0 km   5   10

1942 features are shown.
Vessel sinking locations
are approximate.

Tassaforanga
Point

Henderson
Field

Lunga Point

Koli Pt.

Kokumbona

Tenaru

GUADALCANAL

✳ Allied vessel sunk

✳ IJN vessel sunk

U.S. Naval Hull Codes
CA: Heavy cruiser
CL: Light cruiser
DD: Destroyer

DEADLY WATERS Iron Bottom Sound earned that title during the Battle of Savo Island on August 8–9, 1942, when four cruisers went down—U.S.S. *Quincy* (above), U.S.S. *Astoria*, U.S.S. *Vincennes*, and H.M.A.S. *Canberra*. Several other ships on the map at top sank later during the Naval Battle of Guadalcanal.

ISLAND FIGHTING

NAVAL BATTLES OFF THE SOLOMONS

When Admiral Halsey took command of U.S. naval forces in the South Pacific in October 1942, he said it was "the hottest potato" ever handed him. His urgent task was to gain control of the sea-lanes on which troops and supplies reached Guadalcanal. Both sides had suffered heavy losses in those waters since early August, when four Allied cruisers went down off Savo Island in Iron Bottom Sound—so called for the many ships sunk there (see map above). Later that month, in the Battle of the Eastern Solomons, Japanese dive-bombers targeted the carrier *Enterprise* (opposite top), knocking it out of action for two months. Shortly after Halsey took charge of the Guadalcanal campaign, he lost the carrier *Hornet* and the services of the refitted *Enterprise*, damaged in a bruising contest with Japanese carriers off Santa Cruz Island. Halsey rushed repairs on the *Enterprise* and spared no effort to halt the delivery of Japanese troops to Guadalcanal by Rear Adm. Raizo Tanaka's fast convoys, known as the Tokyo Express.

In early November, a convoy of two dozen transports and destroyers under Tanaka prepared to advance down the Slot (see map opposite) and land 12,000 troops on Guadalcanal. Tanaka's convoy was preceded by a bombardment force led by Vice Adm. Hiroaki Abe aboard the battleship I.J.N. *Hiei*, assigned to blast Henderson Field. Around 1:30 A.M. on November 13, Abe's warships came up against a smaller task force led by Rear Adm. Daniel Callaghan in Iron Bottom Sound. Engaged by Callaghan at close range, Abe's gunners crippled five opposing warships, including the cruiser U.S.S. *Juneau*, which was later torpedoed by a Japanese submarine and blew up, killing 700 men—among them all five Sullivan brothers (inset). Callaghan's forces disabled the *Hiei*, which was sunk by dive-bombers from the *Enterprise* after it was abandoned. Spared bombardment by Abe, Henderson Field was targeted the following night by cruisers led by Vice Adm. Gunichi Mikawa. That did not stop bombers there from joining planes from the *Enterprise* in blasting Tanaka's convoy on the 14th and sinking six transports. The Japanese offensive concluded that night when a task force led by Rear Adm. Willis Lee beat back an attack in the Slot by Vice Adm. Nobutake Kondo, who lost the battleship I.J.N. *Kirishima* in a duel with the battleships U.S.S. *Washington* and U.S.S. *South Dakota*. Defeat in the Naval Battle of Guadalcanal led the Japanese to withdraw their troops from that island in early 1943. ∎

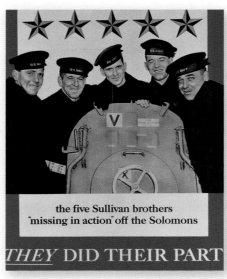

the five Sullivan brothers
'missing in action' off the Solomons

THEY DID THEIR PART

FIVE STARS The five Sullivan brothers in this wartime poster—Joseph, Francis, Albert, Madison, and George—perished when the U.S.S. *Juneau* went down.

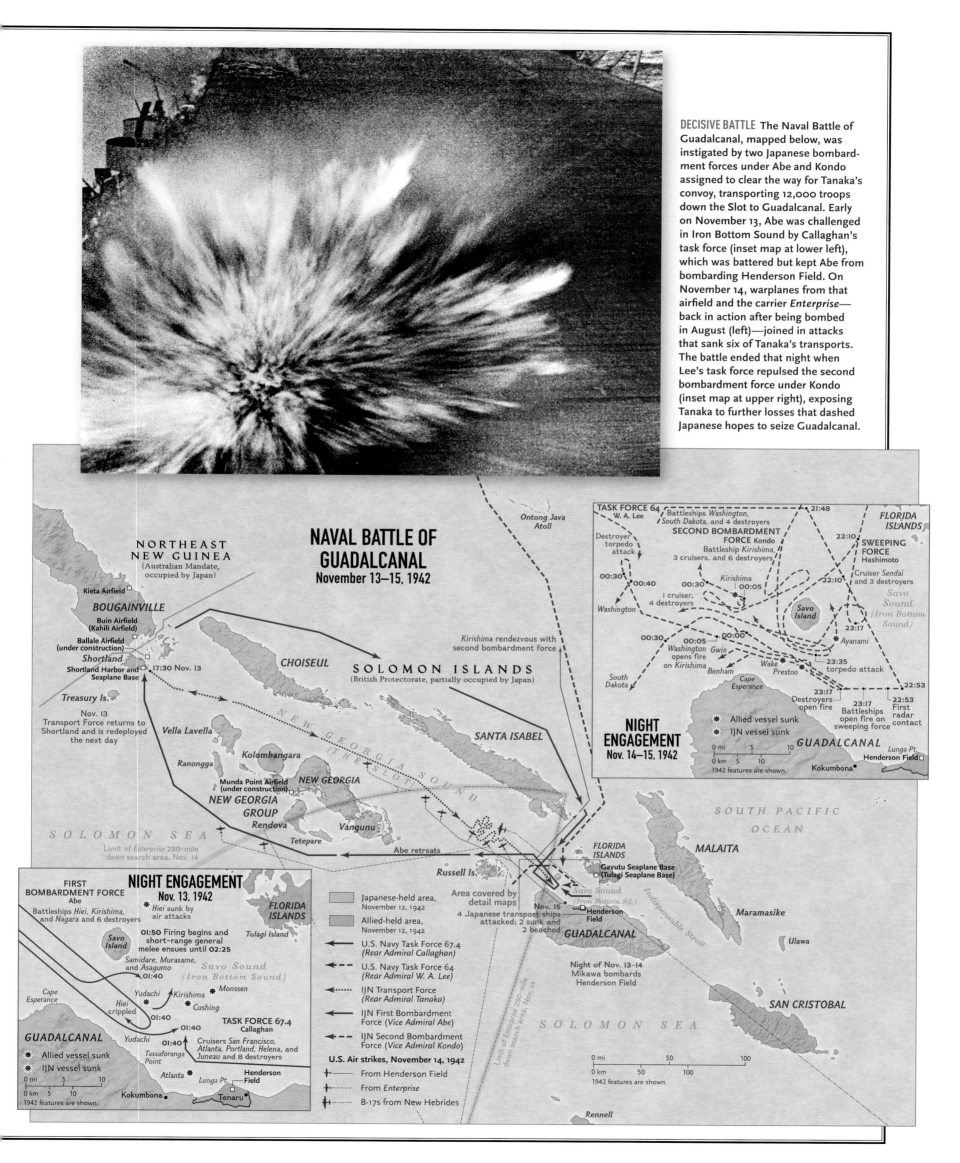

DECISIVE BATTLE The Naval Battle of Guadalcanal, mapped below, was instigated by two Japanese bombardment forces under Abe and Kondo assigned to clear the way for Tanaka's convoy, transporting 12,000 troops down the Slot to Guadalcanal. Early on November 13, Abe was challenged in Iron Bottom Sound by Callaghan's task force (inset map at lower left), which was battered but kept Abe from bombarding Henderson Field. On November 14, warplanes from that airfield and the carrier *Enterprise*— back in action after being bombed in August (left)—joined in attacks that sank six of Tanaka's transports. The battle ended that night when Lee's task force repulsed the second bombardment force under Kondo (inset map at upper right), exposing Tanaka to further losses that dashed Japanese hopes to seize Guadalcanal.

NAVAL BATTLE OF GUADALCANAL
November 13–15, 1942

NORTHEAST NEW GUINEA
(Australian Mandate, occupied by Japan)

Kieta Airfield

BOUGAINVILLE

Buin Airfield (Kahili Airfield)

Ballale Airfield (under construction)
Shortland
Shortland Harbor and Seaplane Base — 17:30 Nov. 13

Treasury Is.

Nov. 13 Transport Force returns to Shortland and is redeployed the next day

CHOISEUL

SOLOMON ISLANDS
(British Protectorate, partially occupied by Japan)

Kirishima rendezvous with second bombardment force

Vella Lavella

Ranongga

Kolombangara

NEW GEORGIA SOUND (THE SLOT)

Munda Point Airfield (under construction)
NEW GEORGIA

SANTA ISABEL

NEW GEORGIA GROUP

Rendova

Vangunu

Tetepare

SOLOMON SEA

Limit of *Enterprise* 250-mile dawn search area, Nov. 14

Abe retreats

Russell Is.

Area covered by detail maps
4 Japanese transport ships attacked; 2 sunk and 2 beached

FLORIDA ISLANDS

Gavutu Seaplane Base (Tulagi Seaplane Base)

Savo Sound (Iron Bottom Sd.)

Nov. 15
Henderson Field

GUADALCANAL

Kokumbona

Night of Nov. 13-14
Mikawa bombards Henderson Field

MALAITA

Maramasike

Ulawa

SOUTH PACIFIC OCEAN

Indispensable Strait

SAN CRISTOBAL

SOLOMON SEA

Limit of *Enterprise* 250-mile dawn search area, Nov. 14

Rennell

Ontong Java Atoll

Legend:
Japanese-held area, November 12, 1942
Allied-held area, November 12, 1942
U.S. Navy Task Force 67.4 (Rear Admiral Callaghan)
U.S. Navy Task Force 64 (Rear Admiral W. A. Lee)
IJN Transport Force (Rear Admiral Tanaka)
IJN First Bombardment Force (Vice Admiral Abe)
IJN Second Bombardment Force (Vice Admiral Kondo)

U.S. Air strikes, November 14, 1942
From Henderson Field
From *Enterprise*
B-17s from New Hebrides

Upper right inset
TASK FORCE 64
W. A. Lee

Battleships *Washington, South Dakota,* and 4 destroyers

SECOND BOMBARDMENT FORCE Kondo
Battleship *Kirishima,* 3 cruisers, and 6 destroyers

Destroyer torpedo attack

FLORIDA ISLANDS

SWEEPING FORCE Hashimoto
Cruiser *Sendai* and 3 destroyers

Savo Sound (Iron Bottom Sound.)

21:48
22:10
22:10

00:30 00:40 00:30 *Kirishima* 00:05
Washington 1 cruiser, 4 destroyers

Savo Island

23:17

Ayanami

00:30 00:05 00:00
Washington opens fire on *Kirishima*
Gwin *Wake* *Benham* *Preston* 23:35 torpedo attack

South Dakota

Cape Esperance

23:17 Destroyers open fire
23:17 Battleships open fire on sweeping force
22:53 First radar contact

22:53

* Allied vessel sunk
* IJN vessel sunk

GUADALCANAL

Lunga Pt.
Henderson Field

Kokumbona

NIGHT ENGAGEMENT
November 14–15, 1942

0 mi 5 10
0 km 5 10
1942 features are shown.

Lower left inset
FIRST BOMBARDMENT FORCE Abe

Battleships *Hiei, Kirishima,* and *Nagara* and 6 destroyers

NIGHT ENGAGEMENT
Nov. 13, 1942

Hiei sunk by air attacks

FLORIDA ISLANDS

01:50 Firing begins and short-range general melee ensues until 02:25

Savo Island

Tulagi Island

Samidare, Murasame, and *Asagumo*
01:40

Hiei crippled

Cape Esperance

Yudachi *Kirishima* *Monssen*

01:40 *Cushing*

Savo Sound (Iron Bottom Sound)

GUADALCANAL

01:40
Yudachi 01:40
Tassaforanga Point

TASK FORCE 67.4 Callaghan
Cruisers *San Francisco, Atlanta, Portland, Helena,* and *Juneau* and 8 destroyers

* Allied vessel sunk
* IJN vessel sunk

0 mi 5 10
0 km 5 10
1942 features are shown.

Atlanta *Lunga Pt.* Henderson Field

Kokumbona *Tenaru*

NATIONAL GEOGRAPHIC'S WARTIME MAPS

W hen America entered the war, the heavy demand for accurate charts of battle zones was filled not only by government and military agencies but also by the National Geographic Society, whose maps proved useful to many officers, including the commander of the Pacific Fleet. In September 1942, Admiral Nimitz was flying with staff officers to confer with General Vandegrift on Guadalcanal when the pilot of their B-17 lost his way in bad weather. For guidance, the pilot relied on a small-scale chart of the Solomons that showed only the larger islands, none of which was spotted. At that point, Nimitz related, "it was our good fortune that the Marine officer on my staff followed the practice of always carrying a National Geographic map in his briefcase." Shown at right reduced in size, it included "an inset of the Solomons showing the smaller as well as the larger islands." Flying low and consulting the map, they recognized small islands off San Cristóbal, south of Guadalcanal, and made it to Henderson Field, where Nimitz met with Vandegrift and conferred a medal on Lt. Col. Evans Carlson (below), commander of the Second Marine Raider Battalion. In a postwar letter to Gilbert Grosvenor, president of the National Geographic Society, Nimitz stated that his flight to Guadalcanal was one of many occasions "when your maps proved invaluable to the forces in the Pacific. Your charts were in wide service in planning work, particularly for areas which were not adequately covered by the official maps available." ■

COMMAND PERFORMANCE General Vandegrift stands in the background at left as Admiral Nimitz decorates Lt. Col. Evans Carlson for his service on Guadalcanal. National Geographic maps (right) and publications (above) kept the public and the military well informed as the war progressed.

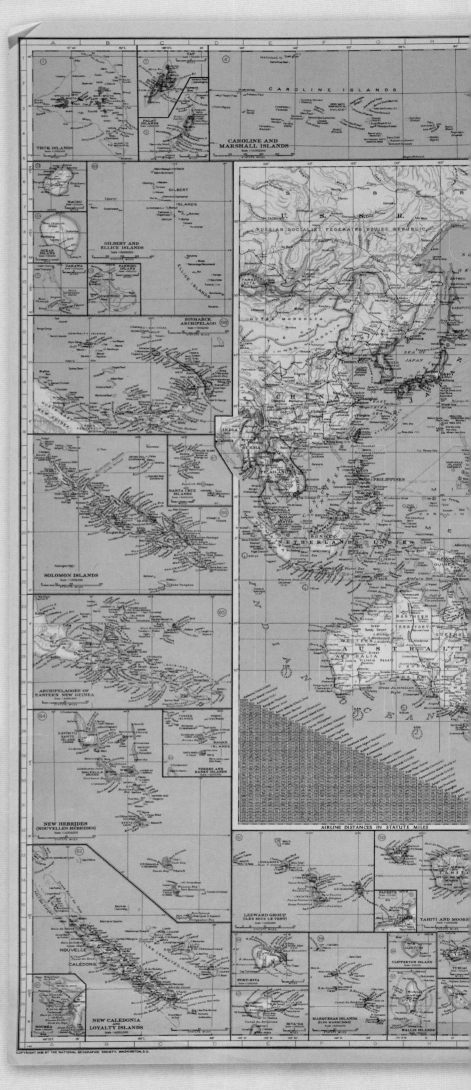

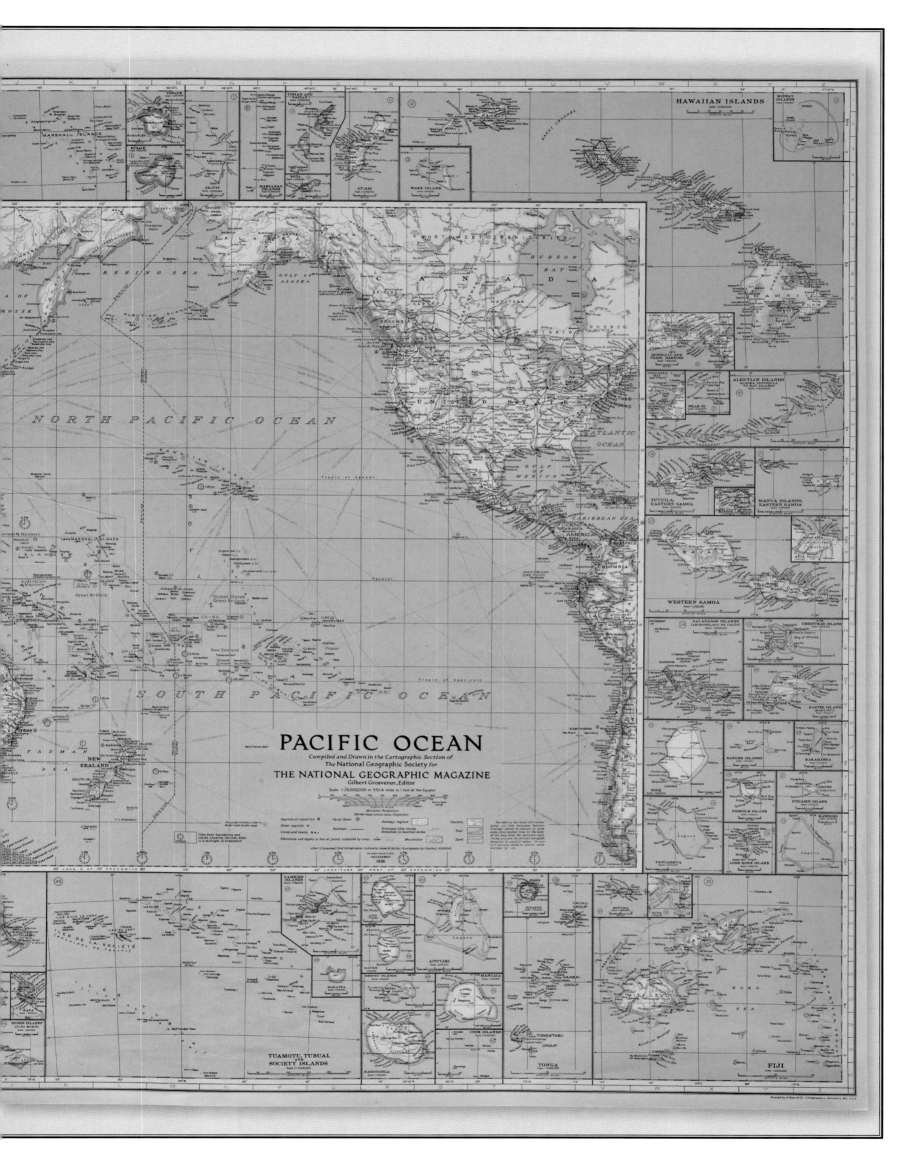

PACIFIC OCEAN

Compiled and Drawn in the Cartographic Section of
The National Geographic Society for
THE NATIONAL GEOGRAPHIC MAGAZINE
Gilbert Grosvenor, Editor

BATTLES FOR PAPUA

In mid-1942, Japanese commanders targeted Papua, an Australian-held territory at the eastern end of New Guinea (see map at top right opposite). Their main objective was Port Moresby, an Allied stronghold that they could use to threaten nearby Australia and keep General MacArthur's forces there on the defensive. After plans to invade Port Moresby were disrupted by the U.S. Navy during the Battle of the Coral Sea in May, Japanese troops landed in July around lightly defended Buna on the far side of Papua and advanced toward Port Moresby on a grueling trail called the Kokoda Track over the steep Owen Stanley Range. To bolster Australian troops defending Papua, MacArthur sent reinforcements, including men of the U.S. 32nd Infantry Division. Some of those raw American troops advanced overland as the Japanese fell back to Buna and nearby Gona, where they dug in and resisted fiercely. Other Americans were airlifted over the Owen Stanley Range and rushed into battle at Buna under inexperienced leaders. Many who were not killed or wounded fell ill with malaria or other tropical diseases, and morale plummeted as the men ran short of food and other supplies.

In late November, MacArthur sent Lt. Gen. Robert Eichelberger to Papua with orders to rally the troops and sack officers who were not up to the fight. "Bob," MacArthur said to him in parting, "I want you to take Buna, or not come back alive." Eichelberger understood that he and his men would have to be as relentless in battle as Japanese troops who were ready to die for their cause. After ensuring that his soldiers were well led and well fed, he launched a determined assault on enemy lines at Buna while Australians attacked at Gona and at nearby Sanananda with some American support. By late December, Japanese defenses were crumbling. "Rotting bodies, sometimes weeks old," formed part of their fortifications, a journalist noted. "The living fired over the bodies of the dead." In early January 1943, American and Australian troops took Buna. By month's end, the battle for Papua was over—a costly Allied victory that left much fighting to be done before MacArthur secured New Guinea and could return to the Philippines. ∎

ACT OF MERCY A Papuan leads an Australian soldier he found blinded in a thicket to safety at an Allied camp. Papuans frequently aided Australians and Americans during the war and were suspicious of Japanese invaders, who had conscripted native people in New Britain to serve as bearers for them.

BATTLE LINES ON PAPUA Letters on the map of Papua at top right opposite indicate locations of the six battle maps labeled A through F. From late July to late September, Japanese forces consisting largely of Maj. Gen. Tomitaro Horii's Nankai Shitai (South Seas Detachment) advanced on the Kokoda Track over the Owen Stanley Range to within 30 miles of Port Moresby (map A). Bolstered by reinforcements, troops of the AIF (Australian Imperial Force) pushed the Japanese back toward Buna and Gona (B) while one regiment of the U.S. 32nd Division advanced on a parallel track and other Allied units were airlifted over the mountains (C). Australians then advanced toward Japanese strongholds at Gona and Sanananda (D) while Americans targeted Buna (E). Fierce Japanese resistance at Buna was overcome after MacArthur sent Eichelberger to revive the American assault, which penetrated enemy lines in December (F). After capturing Buna in early 1943, U.S. troops joined Australians in seizing Sanananda and securing Papua.

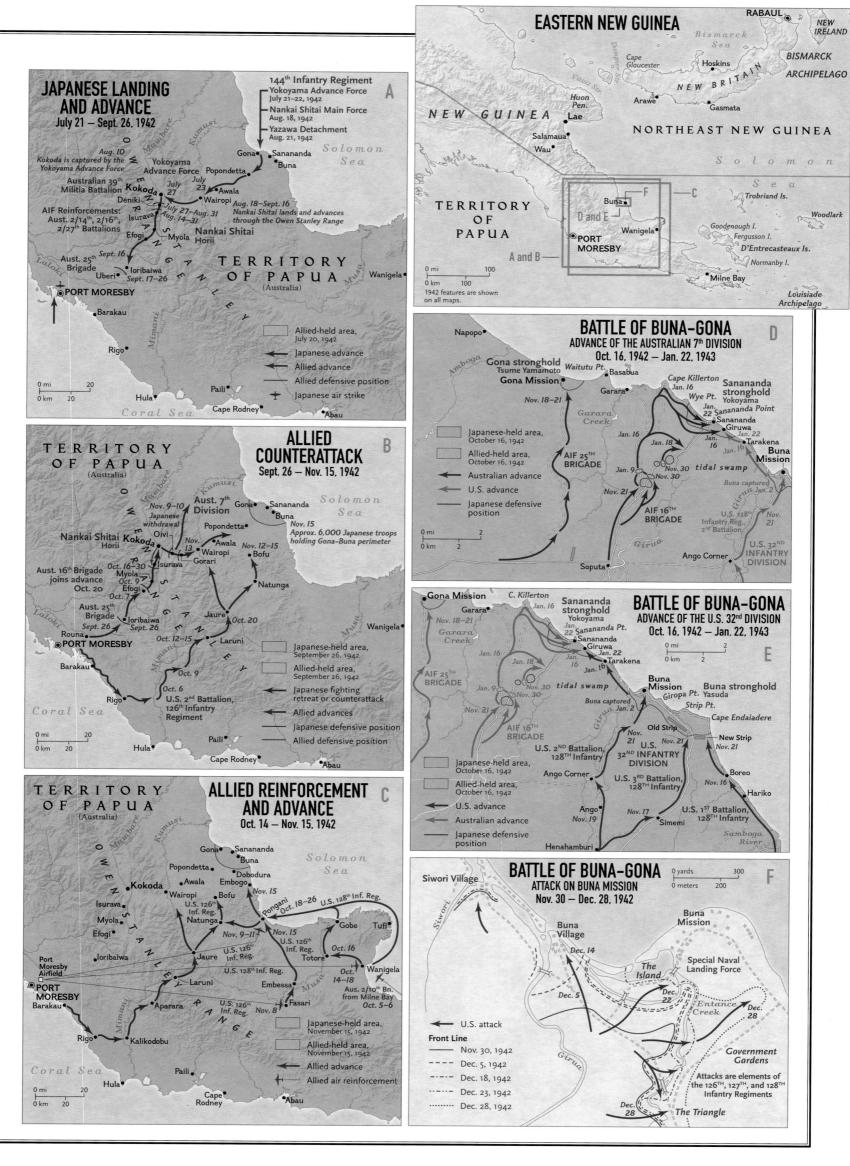

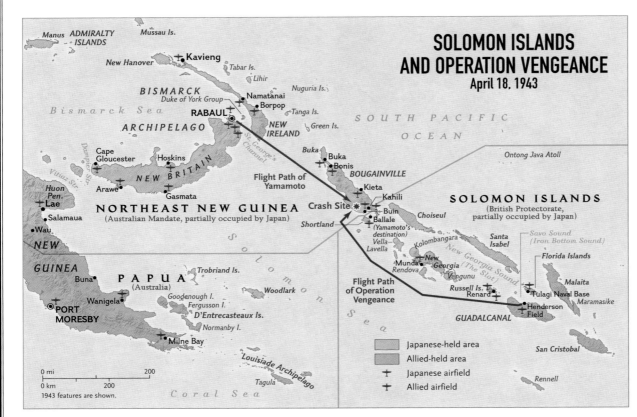

SOLOMON ISLANDS AND OPERATION VENGEANCE
April 18, 1943

Manus ADMIRALTY ISLANDS
Mussau Is.
New Hanover
Kavieng
Tabar Is.
Lihir
Nuguria Is.
BISMARCK
Duke of York Group
Namatanai
Borpop
Tanga Is.
Bismarck Sea
RABAUL
Green Is.
ARCHIPELAGO
NEW IRELAND
SOUTH PACIFIC OCEAN
Cape Gloucester
Hoskins
Buka
Buka
Ontong Java Atoll
NEW BRITAIN
Buka
Bonis
BOUGAINVILLE
Flight Path of Yamamoto
Huon Pen.
Arawe
Gasmata
Kieta
Kahili
SOLOMON ISLANDS
Lae
Vitiaz Str.
NORTHEAST NEW GUINEA
(Australian Mandate, partially occupied by Japan)
Crash Site
Buin
Ballale
Choiseul
(British Protectorate, partially occupied by Japan)
Salamaua
Shortland
(Yamamoto's destination)
Santa Isabel
Saxo Sound (Iron Bottom Sound)
Wau
NEW GUINEA
Vella-Lavella
Kolombangara
New Georgia Sound (The Slot)
Florida Islands
Buna
PAPUA
(Australia)
Trobriand Is.
Munda
New Georgia
Rendova
Vangunu
Malaita
Maramasike
Wanigela
Goodenough I.
Woodlark
Flight Path of Operation Vengeance
Russell Is.
Renard
Tulagi Naval Base
PORT MORESBY
Fergusson I.
D'Entrecasteaux Is.
Normanby I.
Henderson Field
Milne Bay
GUADALCANAL
San Cristobal
0 mi   200
Louisiade Archipelago
Tagula
0 km   200
Rennell
1943 features are shown.
Coral Sea

Japanese-held area
Allied-held area
✝ Japanese airfield
✝ Allied airfield

PRIME TARGET Below, Admiral Yamamoto, in dress white uniform, speaks to Japanese naval pilots at Rabaul, where he launched his I-Go offensive on April 7, 1943. On April 18, as mapped at left, Yamamoto flew from Rabaul to Japanese bases around Bougainville. Alerted by his deciphered itinerary, fighter pilots took off from Henderson Field and followed the path traced here to Bougainville, where they downed Yamamoto's plane and ended his life, accomplishing a mission dubbed Operation Vengeance.

DOWNING YAMAMOTO

Before the war began, Admiral Yamamoto said that if Japan took on the United States, his fleet would "run wild for six months or a year, but I have utterly no confidence for the second or third year." By 1943, that conflict was in its second year and the Pacific Fleet was growing at a pace Yamamoto's fleet could not match. Hoping to thwart enemy advances in the southwest Pacific, he flew on April 3 to the Japanese base at Rabaul on New Britain to launch Operation I-Go, involving naval air strikes against Allied bases on Guadalcanal and Papua. Those attacks did not catch his opponents by surprise. Since Pearl Harbor, American forces had greatly enhanced their ability to anticipate assaults, using techniques known to the Japanese such as radar and other methods that even Yamamoto, well aware of American technological prowess, did not envision. U.S. Navy code-breakers, aided by machines that were forerunners of digital computers, could now decipher Japanese radio messages fast enough to wreck enemy plans.

On April 13, Yamamoto's enciphered itinerary for his flight on the 18th to visit three Japanese bases around Bougainville in the Solomons was broadcast to officers there. Within 36 hours, cryptanalysts at Pearl Harbor had deciphered most of that itinerary. Admiral Nimitz agreed with Commander Layton's intelligence assessment that "shooting down Yamamoto would be a vital and serious blow to the Japanese," and received permission from Washington to order an attack carried out by pilots at Henderson Field on Guadalcanal. Led by Maj. John Mitchell of the USAAF, they took off at 7:10 A.M. on April 18 in P-38 Lightnings, swift fighters equipped with drop tanks to extend their range, and flew low over the Coral Sea to avoid detection by Japanese radar (see map opposite). Capt. Thomas Lanphier, Jr.—assigned to lead the "killer flight" of four P-38s that would target Yamamoto's bomber while other pilots dueled with fighters escorting the admiral—charted their course in his journal (below). At 9:45, they intercepted Yamamoto's flight off Bougainville and sent his plane crashing into the jungle, where a Japanese search party later found his body amid the wreckage. Yamamoto's death was a bitter blow for Japan, which had lost the initiative and now faced an agonizing struggle to stave off defeat. ■

KILLER FLIGHT Capt. Thomas Lanphier, Jr.—pictured standing at right beside Lt. Rex Barber, with whom he shared credit for downing Yamamoto—sketched the path they followed on April 18 on the right page of this journal entry. After swinging west of the Solomons to avoid detection, they returned directly to Henderson Field.

CHAPTER 3

BREAKING HITLER'S GRIP | 1942-1944

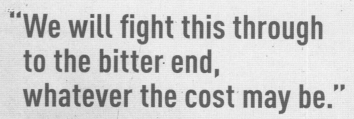

"We will fight this through
to the bitter end,
whatever the cost may be."

FRANKLIN D. ROOSEVELT TO WINSTON CHURCHILL,
JANUARY 1942

HARD LANDING Wounded Canadian troops lie near
a disabled tank following a failed Allied amphibious raid on the German-occupied port of Dieppe,
France, on August 19, 1942. After this setback,
Anglo-American commanders decided to delay an
invasion of France and concentrate on defeating
Axis forces in the Mediterranean and the Atlantic
while bombers targeted Germany and Soviet
troops fought to break Hitler's grip on Russia.

AN EPIC STRUGGLE

BATTLES IN EUROPE, NORTH AFRICA, AND THE ATLANTIC

By 1942, Hitler's forces controlled much of Europe, which Germans labeled Festung Europa (Fortress Europe) to signal that they would hold it against all opposition. That did not sit well with Winston Churchill. As leader of the defiant British and ally of the resilient Russians and the oncoming Americans, he bristled at any suggestion that Hitler was Europe's unchallenged master. "Never use that term again," he snapped when a British commander referred to "Hitler's European Fortress." Churchill considered such language defeatist, but he was keenly aware of how hard it would be to penetrate occupied Europe and open a second front to relieve pressure on Soviet troops fighting on the Eastern Front. Unwilling to risk an invasion of Europe in 1942, Churchill encouraged President Roosevelt to commit American soldiers to North Africa, where the British faced armored forces led by Erwin Rommel. U.S. Army chief George Marshall feared that Churchill's Mediterranean strategy would postpone a decisive advance into Germany through France. But prospects for that frontal assault on Fortress Europe would not be promising until the Allies achieved air superiority and won the Battle of the Atlantic, where U-boats menaced vital supply lines between America and Britain.

In mid-1942, German forces regained momentum in Russia and advanced in North Africa toward Cairo. But later that year, the tide turned. British and Commonwealth troops won the Battle of El Alamein, Anglo-American forces seized French North Africa from Vichy authorities beholden to the Nazis, and the Soviets trapped a German army at Stalingrad and annihilated it in early 1943. The Red Army went on to win a massive tank battle against the Germans at Kursk that July while Allied troops crossed from Tunisia to Sicily, causing Mussolini to fall from power. The grueling Italian campaign that followed did not lead directly to an invasion of Germany. But it tied down German troops while Allied forces prepared to invade France, and it provided new bases for warplanes that blasted Axis cities and industries and degraded the Luftwaffe, which was much diminished by early 1944. A British propaganda leaflet dropped on the Reich, where civilian casualties were mounting under fearsome air raids, declared in German: "Fortress Europe Has No Roof." Before long, the walls of that fortress would be breached as Russians advanced in the east and D-Day approached in the west.

1942

January 1, 1942 Representatives of the United States, Great Britain, the Soviet Union, and 23 other Allied countries and governments in exile sign the Declaration of the United Nations, pledging to employ their full resources against the Axis Powers and make no separate peace with those enemies.

January 2, 1942 Jean Moulin returns covertly to France from Britain to unify French resistance groups under Gen. Charles de Gaulle, leader of the Free French government in exile in London.

January 11, 1942 First attack launched in Operation Drumbeat, a German U-boat offensive against Allied merchant ships off the Atlantic coast of North America.

January 20, 1942 SS security chief Reinhard Heydrich convenes the Wannsee Conference outside Berlin to coordinate the "Final Solution of the Jewish Question," a plan to exterminate European Jews.

January 21, 1942 Gen. Erwin Rommel launches his second offensive in North Africa, advancing with armored forces from El Agheila, Libya, toward British-ruled Egypt.

March 28–29, 1942 The RAF carries out its first major incendiary bombing raid, destroying shipyards and the historic German city of Lübeck on the Baltic Sea.

May 12–28, 1942 Soviet troops are soundly defeated in the

Depth charge dropped on a submerged U-boat by the U.S. Coast Guard cutter Spencer

JANUARY 1943–MAY 1944

January 15, 1943 Andrée "Dédée" de Jongh, who organized the Comet Line to help downed Allied airmen escape, is arrested in France and imprisoned but spared execution.

January 21, 1943 Allied chiefs authorize a combined strategic bomber offensive in which the RAF will blast German cities at night and the U.S. Eighth Air Force will conduct daylight raids on military and industrial targets.

January 24, 1943 President Roosevelt calls for the unconditional surrender of Axis forces.

January 31, 1943 Gen. Friedrich Paulus, commander of the German Sixth Army, surrenders at Stalingrad, ending

a battle that marks a turning point in Russia's struggle to defend its territory and repulse the invaders.

February 19–25, 1943 American forces in Tunisia suffer heavy casualties and fall back but avert defeat in the Battle of Kasserine Pass.

March 14, 1943 German troops in Russia recapture Kharkov, setting the stage for a German offensive aimed at cutting off a Soviet salient around Kursk.

April 19, 1943 Warsaw Ghetto Uprising begins as Jews confined there resist deportation and extermination.

May 7, 1943 Allied troops secure North Africa by capturing Tunis, the last Axis bastion in Tunisia.

May 16, 1943 Warsaw Ghetto Uprising ends with the destruction by SS troops of the Great Synagogue of Warsaw.

May 24, 1943 As U-boat losses mount, due to Allied code-breaking and enhanced anti-submarine warfare, Grand Adm. Karl Dönitz withdraws German submarines from the North Atlantic.

An American P-51 fighter pilot with briefing notes on the back of his hand

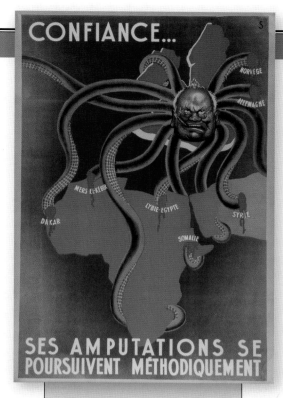

CONFIANCE...

SES AMPUTATIONS SE POURSUIVENT MÉTHODIQUEMENT

Second Battle of Kharkov, a city captured by the Germans the previous October.

May 27, 1942 SS security chief Heydrich is mortally wounded in Prague by Czech commandos trained in Britain by the SOE (Special Operations Executive).

June 13, 1942 President Roosevelt authorizes the OSS (Office of Strategic Services), which will join the SOE in promoting resistance to the Nazis in occupied countries.

June 21, 1942 Rommel seizes Tobruk, Libya, which will serve as a supply base as he invades Egypt.

July 3–4, 1942 Sevastopol, the last remaining Russian stronghold in Crimea, falls to the Germans.

July 3–15, 1942 Four U-boats are sunk in American waters as coastal convoys and other defensive measures against attacks by German submarines take hold.

July 23, 1942 Hitler confirms plans to attack Stalingrad in southern Russia in conjunction with an advance on Baku in the Caucasus. The deportation of Jews from the Warsaw Ghetto to Treblinka extermination camp begins under a plan dubbed Operation Heydrich for the assassinated SS overseer of the Final Solution.

1942 Vichy French poster portraying Churchill as an imperialist monster whose tentacles are being severed by Axis forces

August 19, 1942 Allied raid on Dieppe fails, contributing to the Allied decision to postpone the invasion of occupied France until 1944.

October 23, 1942 Lt. Gen. Bernard Montgomery, commanding the British Eighth Army, launches the decisive Second Battle of El Alamein in Egypt by attacking Rommel's army.

October 30, 1942 British crewmen board the disabled sub *U-559* in the Mediterranean and recover documents that help cryptanalysts solve the German naval Enigma, used to encode U-boat messages.

November 4, 1942 Rommel concedes defeat at El Alamein and withdraws.

November 8, 1942 Allied forces consisting largely of American troops invade Vichy French Morocco and Algeria.

November 11, 1942 Germans occupy Vichy France, increasing pressure on resistance fighters and leaders there.

November 19, 1942 The Red Army launches a counteroffensive against German troops at Stalingrad.

December 24, 1942 Adm. Jean Darlan, the former Vichy commander in French North Africa who surrendered to the Allies in November, is assassinated in Algiers.

Sign for U.S. Army forces, which remained segregated throughout the war

Soviet artillerymen firing on German troops in Crimea, reclaimed by the Russians in early May 1944

July 5–August 23, 1943 Soviet forces repulse enemy armored forces in the Battle of Kursk, leaving German troops on the defensive in Russia.

July 9–10, 1943 Allied forces invade Sicily.

July 25, 1943 Mussolini is ousted as Italy's leader and arrested.

July 27–28, 1943 RAF bombers ignite a firestorm in Hamburg, Germany, where more than 40,000 people are killed.

August 17, 1943 U.S. Eighth Air Force loses 60 B-17 bombers in daylight raids conducted without fighter escorts on strategic German factories at Schweinfurt and Regensburg.

September 3, 1943 Montgomery's Eighth Army lands unopposed at Reggio di Calabria on the Italian mainland.

September 8, 1943 Italy surrenders to the Allies, and German forces take control there.

September 9, 1943 Lt. Gen. Mark Wayne Clark's Fifth Army lands at Salerno, Italy, and encounters heavy German resistance.

September 12, 1943 Mussolini is freed by German commandos sent by Hitler, who then installs him in northern Italy as a Fascist figurehead.

November 5–6, 1943 Soviet troops retake the Ukrainian capital Kiev.

November 17, 1943 Treblinka extermination camp closes following the execution of more than 780,000 people there. Killings continue at Auschwitz and other Nazi camps.

November 22–23, 1943 RAF Bomber Command blasts Berlin, causing extensive damage.

November 28–December 1, 1943 Roosevelt, Churchill, and Stalin

meet in the Iranian capital Tehran and agree that an Allied invasion of German-occupied France will take place in the spring of 1944.

December 11, 1943 Long-range P-51 Mustangs flown by pilots of the 354th Fighter Group begin escorting American bombers to targets in Germany.

January 22, 1944 Allied troops land at Anzio, near Rome, in an effort to skirt the well-defended German Gustav Line to the south, but their beachhead at Anzio will be contained by German troops for the next four months.

January 27, 1944 Soviet troops break the siege of Leningrad after more than one million Russians perished there of famine and other war-related causes.

February 15, 1944 Bombers of the U.S. 15th Air Force in Italy destroy the historic Benedictine monastery atop Monte Cassino in an unsuccessful bid to achieve a breakthrough in the Gustav Line.

April 5, 1944 The 15th Air Force launches attacks on Ploesti, Romania, a major source of refined oil for Germany.

May 9, 1944 Soviets retake Sevastopol and oust German troops from Crimea.

May 18, 1944 Allied forces capture Monte Cassino and break through German defenses elsewhere along the Gustav Line.

May 23, 1944 Allied troops break out of their beachhead at Anzio and force German troops to abandon Rome, which Clark's Fifth Army will enter on June 5, one day before the Allied invasion of Normandy.

Label for Zyklon-B, used to kill people in gas chambers at Nazi concentration and extermination camps

RESISTING GERMAN
DOMINATION
DEFIANCE AND REPRESSION

CHRONOLOGY

JANUARY 2, 1942 Jean Moulin returns covertly to France from Britain to unify French resistance groups under Free French leader Gen. Charles de Gaulle.

MAY 27, 1942 SS security chief Reinhard Heydrich is mortally wounded in Prague by Czech commandos trained by the SOE (Special Operations Executive).

JUNE 13, 1942 President Roosevelt authorizes the OSS (Office of Strategic Services), which will join the SOE in promoting resistance to the Nazis.

AUGUST 19, 1942 Allied raid on Dieppe fails, contributing to the Allied decision to postpone the invasion of occupied France until 1944.

NOVEMBER 11, 1942 Germans occupy Vichy France, increasing pressure on resistance fighters and leaders.

JANUARY 15, 1943 Andrée "Dédée" de Jongh, who organized the Comet Line to help downed Allied airmen escape, is arrested in France and imprisoned but spared execution.

JUNE 21, 1943 Jean Moulin is arrested in France and subsequently tortured to death.

It took German forces only a few months in 1940 to overrun Norway, Denmark, Holland, Belgium, and France. But harsh terms imposed by the invaders led to years of strife as civilians resisted occupation and risked execution (below). In France, 600,000 men were forced to labor in Germany or build the Atlantic Wall—coastal fortifications intended to prevent Allied troops from liberating Western Europe. Vichy authorities in southern France went along with that, and French police helped SS officers round up Jews and track down Communists and others who fought as partisans. In August 1942, Communists hurled grenades at Luftwaffe airmen attending a soccer match in Paris, killing at least three and wounding others. Germans retaliated by executing 88 hostages, including 14 people arrested for issuing the resistance newspaper *L'Humanité*.

Repression was even fiercer in some countries that Germany annexed and brought directly under the swastika (inset). In Poland, the SS set out to kill all officers and influential figures who might oppose annexation, but a large underground resistance movement called the Polish Home Army took shape. In the Protectorate of Bohemia and Moravia, formerly part of Czechoslovakia (see map opposite), several thousand people were executed in retaliation for the death of SS security chief Reinhard Heydrich, who was mortally wounded in May 1942 by Czech commandos trained in Britain by the SOE (Special Operations Executive), authorized by Churchill to "set Europe ablaze." Allied agencies also supported networks that helped downed pilots in occupied Europe escape. The cities of Marseille and Lyon in Vichy France were hotbeds of resistance where those wanted by the Nazis found refuge. But after German troops occupied the Vichy zone in November 1942, few places other than remote rural areas were safe for resistance leaders like Jean Moulin—arrested in Lyon in June 1943 and tortured to death—or resistance fighters like the Maquis, who were supplied with Allied weapons and attacked Germans and their French collaborators. ■

FIRING LINE German troops stage a mock execution of French resistance agent Georges Blind in an effort to make him talk. He refused to betray any secrets and died in a concentration camp.

ARMED RESISTANCE French partisans known as Maquis or Maquisards receive instruction in handling a Sten submachine gun, many of which were dropped by parachute to resistance fighters supported by the Allies.

GERMAN DOMINATION OF EUROPE
December 1941

German Reich and organized territories

German allies or dependent states

Under German military administration

Under military administration of German allies or dependent states

Allied states

Allied-held areas

Neutral states

REICHSKOMMISSARIAT NORWAY

FINLAND

EASTERN KARELIA (Finnish military admin.)

0 mi 400
0 km 400
1942 features are shown.
Present-day city names are in parentheses.

Oslo

Stockholm ★

Helsinki ★

Leningrad (St. Petersburg)

Reval (Tallinn)

SWEDEN

MOSCOW ★

SOVIET UNION

North Sea

DENMARK

Copenhagen ★

Riga ⊙

REICHSKOMMISSARIAT OSTLAND

Smolensk ·

Eastern Front Dec. 5, 1941

IRELAND

UNITED KINGDOM

Dublin ★

Hamburg ·

Danzig (Gdańsk)

Kaunas ⊙

Minsk ·

Gomel (Homyel') ·

Baltic Sea

Amsterdam ⊙

REICHSKOMMISSARIAT NETHERLANDS

BERLIN ★

Warsaw ·

Stalingrad (Volgograd)

LONDON ★

REICHSKOMMISSARIAT BELGIUM AND N. FRANCE

Brussels ⊙

GERMAN REICH

Leipzig ·

Dresden ·

Breslau (Wrocław) ·

GENERAL GOVERNMENT

Rowno (Rivne) ·

Kiev ·

Kharkov ·

Frankfurt ·

Prague ⊙

Kraków ⊙

REICHSKOMMISSARIAT UKRAINE

Rostov ·

PARIS ⊙

PROTECTORATE OF BOHEMIA AND MORAVIA

Munich ·

SLOVAKIA

Vienna ★

Bratislava ★

Eastern Front Nov. 24, 1942

FRANCE

Bern ★ LIECH.

SWITZ.

Budapest ★

Odessa ·

Sea of Azov

Vichy ★

Lyon ·

HUNGARY

Crimea

Bordeaux ·

VICHY FRANCE

Milan ·

Zagreb ★

ROMANIA

Sevastopol' ·

Black Sea

Toulouse ·

CROATIA

Belgrade ⊙

Bucharest ·

MONACO

SAN MARINO

Marseille ·

ANDORRA

MONTENEGRO (It. Governate)

TERRITORY OF THE MILITARY COMMANDER IN SERBIA

Sofia ·

BULGARIA

Istanbul ·

PORTUGAL

MADRID ★

Barcelona ·

Corsica (Vichy France)

ITALY

DALMATIA (It. Governate)

Cetinje ·

Ankara ★

Lisbon ★

SPAIN

ROME ★

Naples ·

Tirana ·

ALBANIA (It. Prot.)

Salonika (Thessaloniki) ·

TURKEY

Sardinia (Italy)

Mediterranean Sea

GREECE (German and Italian military administration, Bulgarian annexation)

SYRIA (Free France)

(Tanger) Tangier (International Zone)

GIBRALTAR (U.K.)

SPANISH MOROCCO (Spanish Prot.)

Algiers ⊙

Sicily (Italy)

Athens ·

DODECANESE (Italy)

CYPRUS (British C.C.)

Tetuán (Tétouan)

ALGERIA (Vichy France)

Tunis ⊙

TUNISIA (Vichy France)

FRENCH MOROCCO (Vichy France)

CONTINENTAL DOMINANCE As detailed above, by December 1941 much of Europe had been occupied, absorbed, or drawn into the Axis by Germany, which kept a tight hold on France and other nations along the Atlantic to prevent Allied forces from invading there. Francisco Franco resisted pressure from Hitler to enter the war on Germany's side, but neither Spain nor other neutral countries threatened the Reich's continental dominance.

SECRET SIGNALS Clandestine radio sets enabled French resistance cells like this one to arrange for the delivery of weapons by the SOE and OSS.

MAJOR ESCAPE ROUTES
FROM OCCUPIED FRANCE
June 25, 1940 – Nov. 8, 1942

Axis territory, Nov. 8, 1942

Axis ally or dependent state, Nov. 8, 1942

Occupied France, Nov. 8, 1942

Allied state, Nov. 8, 1942

Neutral state, Nov. 8, 1942

→ O'Leary Line

--→ Comet Line

····→ Shelburne Line (established late 1943)

0 mi   100   200
0 km   100   200
November 1942 features are shown.

DELIVERANCE Mapped above are escape lines that enabled downed Allied airmen to return to bases in Britain. The Comet Line, organized by Andrée "Dédée" de Jongh (top), was among the most durable of those operations, in part because it employed cutoffs, where a conductor left escapees who were later picked up by another guide unknown to his or her predecessor, reducing the risk that one arrest would lead to others. Like the Comet Line, the O'Leary Line—led by Albert-Marie Guérisse (left), alias Patrick O'Leary—routed escapees to British-held Gibraltar to be shipped home. The Shelburne Line, organized later by MI9, evacuated downed airmen from the coast of Brittany.

ESCAPE LINES TO FREEDOM

Allied airmen on bombing missions to Germany ran great risks. More than 55,000 of the 120,000 men who served in the RAF Bomber Command during the war were killed, and nearly 10,000 were captured. But some 5,000 Allied airmen shot down in occupied Europe escaped, many of them aided by people who risked their own lives to save them. Most escape lines originated in Belgium or northern France (see map opposite) along the flight paths of Allied bombers. The Comet Line was organized by Andrée "Dédée" de Jongh of Belgium, aided by her father and others who arranged safe houses for airmen and furnished them with civilian clothing and counterfeit documents that could pass inspection. Like many resistance operations, this network relied on skilled forgers who kept up with frequent changes made in German documents and stamps to hinder forgery. Conductors guided the airmen to neutral Spain, where British officials with diplomatic immunity quietly arranged for them to return to Britain by way of Gibraltar.

MI9, a British agency established to help servicemen stranded or captured in enemy territory escape, funded the Comet Line and sustained the O'Leary Line, led by Albert-Marie Guérisse, a Belgian who had been evacuated from Dunkirk to England, where he took the name Patrick O'Leary before embarking on a covert mission to France. In mid-1942, O'Leary and MI9 opened a new route that avoided the perilous trek over the Pyrenees into Spain by evacuating escapees by ship at night from a safe house on the Mediterranean coast of Vichy France. The German occupation of the Vichy zone in November ended that operation and imperiled resistance efforts in Marseille, where O'Leary and his confederates were based. An informant betrayed them to the Gestapo, and O'Leary was arrested in March 1943. He survived confinement in a concentration camp, as did Dédée de Jongh, seized in January 1943 but spared execution because the Germans wrongly considered her a mere accessory to her father, who was put to death.

The Comet Line continued under new leadership, and additional escape lines formed, including the Shelburne Line, established by MI9 in late 1943 to help downed airmen escape from northwest France to Britain across the English Channel. Hundreds of people operating escape lines in occupied Europe lost their lives during the war so that stranded airmen could reach freedom and carry on the fight against Nazi Germany. ■

DECEPTIVE DOCUMENTS Above, a forger working for a Dutch resistance network produces convincing replicas of identity cards and other official documents for fugitives or foes of German occupation forces. Papers like the forged identity card for a French resistance fighter (right) were examined at frequent checkpoints by German agents or local police collaborating with them.

THE DIEPPE RAID

Under pressure from their allies to commit to opening a second front in Europe, British chiefs in mid-1942 authorized a raid on Dieppe, a German-held port on the northwest coast of France. Some 6,000 troops, most of them Canadians, were assigned to storm Dieppe and destroy port facilities before withdrawing. The raid was a trial run for capturing a port where ships could land troops and supplies during a full-scale invasion of occupied France, but the British did not bring their full resources to bear. To avoid civilian casualties, they refrained from bombing Dieppe in advance. The Royal Navy sent destroyers to target German coastal batteries but would not risk deploying a battleship for that purpose. Intelligence gathering was limited to aerial reconnaissance, which pinpointed some German defenses, as detailed on the map at right, but failed to detect machine-gun nests in cliffs overlooking the pebble beach, on which tanks could not gain traction. The results when the raid unfolded at dawn on August 19, 1942, were disastrous. Landings were poorly coordinated, troops were pinned down, and tanks were stranded and blasted. Few units advanced beyond the beaches before the operation was cut short and men were evacuated at midday. More than 4,000 Allied servicemen were killed, wounded, or captured in the debacle at Dieppe, which discouraged an Allied invasion of France in 1943 and prompted those planning for D-Day in 1944 to avoid an amphibious assault on a French port.

A few soldiers captured at Dieppe later managed to escape, notably Sgt. Maj. Lucien Dumais, a French Canadian who made it back to Britain with the help of Patrick O'Leary. In late 1943, after the O'Leary Line collapsed, Dumais infiltrated France for MI9 and helped other Allied escapees reach Britain by organizing the Shelburne Line. ∎

BITTER SETBACK Dead bodies on the beach (above) and the dazed expression of a survivor (upper right) testify to the costly Allied defeat at Dieppe. Red dots on the map at right between the casino and tobacco factory in Dieppe show where some Canadian forces landed and were stopped short, including the 7th Field Company of Royal Canadian Engineers (RCE), the Royal Hamilton Light Infantry (R.H.L.I.), and the Essex Scottish Regiment.

BATTLE OF THE ATLANTIC

COMBATING THE U-BOAT PERIL

CHRONOLOGY

JANUARY 11, 1942 First attack launched in Operation Drumbeat, a German U-boat offensive against Allied merchant ships off the Atlantic coast of North America.

JULY 3–15, 1942 Four U-boats are sunk in American waters as coastal convoys and other defensive measures take hold.

OCTOBER 30, 1942 British crewmen board the disabled sub *U-559* in the Mediterranean and recover documents that help cryptanalysts solve the advanced German naval Enigma, used to encode U-boat messages.

MAY 24, 1943 As German losses mount owing to code-breaking and enhanced anti-submarine warfare, Grand Adm. Karl Dönitz withdraws U-boats from the North Atlantic.

For Vice Adm. Karl Dönitz, commander in chief of the German U-boat fleet, America's entry into the war offered an opportunity to regain the initiative in the crucial battle for control of the Atlantic and the maritime supply lines on which Allied hopes rested. The British had reduced losses in the North Atlantic by neutralizing Germany's surface fleet—which pulled back after the vaunted battleship *Bismarck* was sunk in May 1941—and by organizing convoys that shielded merchant ships against U-boats. Ships in American coastal waters, however, went unescorted and were highly vulnerable to attack. Beginning in January 1942, when Dönitz launched Operation Drumbeat, U-boats wreaked havoc off American shores. U-boat captains called it their "Second Happy Time," the first having ended when transatlantic convoys were instituted.

Defenses along the American coast soon improved. But Allied shipping losses in the mid-Atlantic increased alarmingly in the spring of 1942 after the German Navy enhanced the Enigma machine used to encipher its signals, including those sent from headquarters to coordinate the movements of U-boats that hunted in wolf packs. Messages revealing the whereabouts of those packs and enabling convoys to evade them could no longer be promptly deciphered at Bletchley Park, Britain's top secret code-breaking facility. Those were tense times for Winston Churchill, who wrote later that the "only thing that ever really frightened me during the war was the U-boat peril." By year's end, however, wizards at Bletchley had solved the enhanced naval Enigma with the help of a "pinch"—the recovery of coding documents from a U-boat that was attacked and boarded. That breakthrough, combined with technological advances in anti-submarine warfare, shifted the Battle of the Atlantic firmly in favor of the Allies. U-boat crews would continue to launch attacks sporadically until war's end, but their happy times were over. ∎

ON TARGET Above, a U-boat captain gives orders while tracking a ship through the submarine's attack periscope. Long-range Type IX U-boats carried 16 torpedoes like those on which crewmen are performing maintenance at upper right. Convoys like the one at right—pictured off the British coast in 1942—included warships, but the merchant ships they guarded remained vulnerable to U-boats hunting in wolf packs.

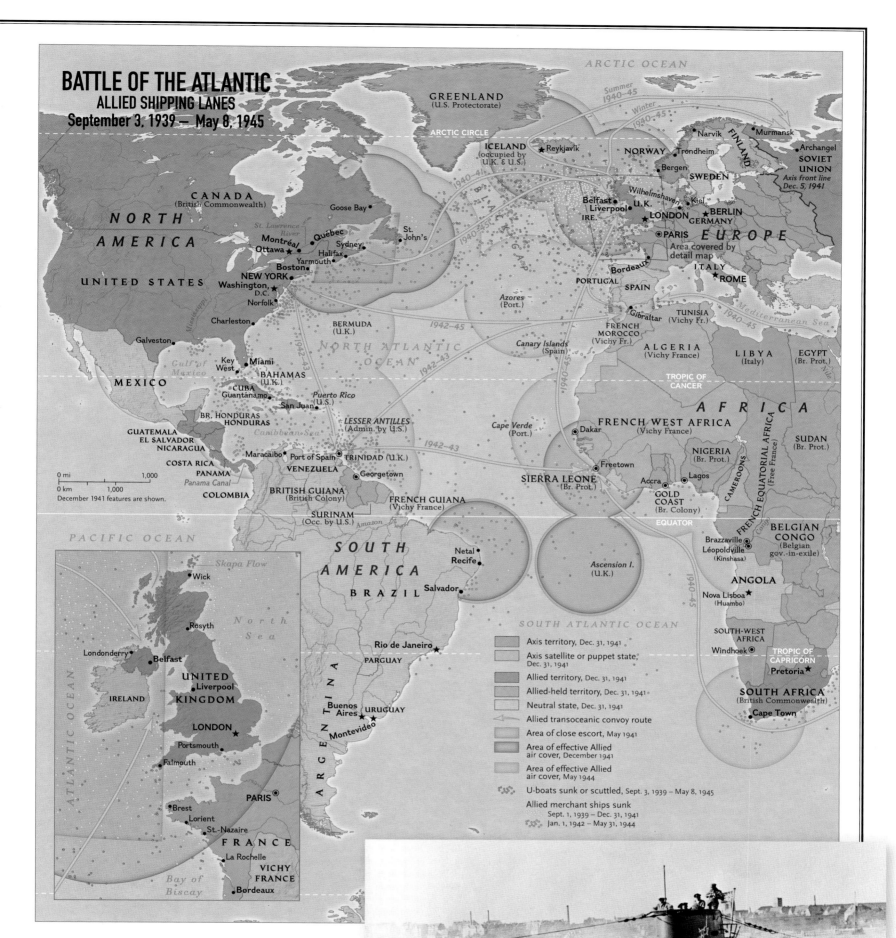

BATTLE OF THE ATLANTIC
ALLIED SHIPPING LANES
September 3, 1939 — May 8, 1945

ARCTIC OCEAN

GREENLAND
(U.S. Protectorate)

ARCTIC CIRCLE

ICELAND
(occupied by
U.K. & U.S.)

★ Reykjavik

NORWAY   Trondheim   Narvik   FINLAND   Murmansk
Bergen   Archangel
                SWEDEN   SOVIET
Belfast U.K. Wilhelmshaven Kiel   UNION
Liverpool   Axis front line
IRE. ★ LONDON ★ BERLIN   Dec. 5, 1941
        ◉ PARIS GERMANY
        Area covered by
        detail map   ITALY
PORTUGAL SPAIN   ★ ROME

CANADA
(British Commonwealth)

NORTH
AMERICA

St. Lawrence
River
Montréal • Québec
Ottawa ★   Sydney
       Halifax
UNITED STATES Yarmouth
NEW YORK •
Washington, ★
        D.C.
Norfolk •

St. John's

Goose Bay

Bordeaux

Charleston •

BERMUDA
(U.K.)

NORTH ATLANTIC
OCEAN

Azores
(Port.)

Gibraltar
FRENCH
MOROCCO
(Vichy Fr.)

TUNISIA
(Vichy Fr.)

ALGERIA
(Vichy France)

LIBYA
(Italy)

EGYPT
(Br. Prot.)

Galveston •

Gulf of
Mexico

Key • • Miami
West

MEXICO   BAHAMAS
                (U.K.)
        CUBA
Guantanamo •   Puerto Rico
        San Juan • (U.S.)

BR. HONDURAS
HONDURAS
GUATEMALA
EL SALVADOR
NICARAGUA

Caribbean Sea

LESSER ANTILLES
(Admin. by U.S.)

Canary Islands
(Spain)

TROPIC OF
CANCER

A F R I C A

Cape Verde
(Port.)

Dakar ◉

FRENCH WEST AFRICA
(Vichy France)

SUDAN
(Br. Prot.)

COSTA RICA
PANAMA
Panama Canal

Maracaibo • Port of Spain •
VENEZUELA   TRINIDAD (U.K.)

COLOMBIA

Georgetown ◉

BRITISH GUIANA
(British Colony)

SURINAM
(Occ. by U.S.)

FRENCH GUIANA
(Vichy France)

Amazon

Freetown ◉
SIERRA LEONE
(Br. Prot.)

Accra ◉
GOLD
COAST
(Br. Colony)

NIGERIA
(Br. Prot.)
        Lagos •

CAMEROONS

FRENCH EQUATORIAL AFRICA
(Free France)

EQUATOR

BELGIAN
CONGO
(Belgian
gov.-in-exile)

Brazzaville •
Léopoldville •
(Kinshasa)

PACIFIC OCEAN

0 mi   1,000
0 km   1,000
December 1941 features are shown.

SOUTH
AMERICA

BRAZIL

Natal •
Recife •

Salvador •

Ascension I.
(U.K.)

SOUTH ATLANTIC OCEAN

ANGOLA
Nova Lisboa ★
(Huambo)

SOUTH-WEST
AFRICA

Windhoek ◉

TROPIC OF
CAPRICORN

Pretoria ★

Rio de Janeiro ★

PARAGUAY

Legend

Axis territory, Dec. 31, 1941

Axis satellite or puppet state,
Dec. 31, 1941

Allied territory, Dec. 31, 1941

Allied-held territory, Dec. 31, 1941

Neutral state, Dec. 31, 1941

Allied transoceanic convoy route

Area of close escort, May 1941

Area of effective Allied
air cover, December 1941

Area of effective Allied
air cover, May 1944

U-boats sunk or scuttled, Sept. 3, 1939 – May 8, 1945

Allied merchant ships sunk
Sept. 1, 1939 – Dec. 31, 1941
Jan. 1, 1942 – May 31, 1944

SOUTH AFRICA
(British Commonwealth)
Cape Town •

A R G E N T I N A

Buenos
Aires
Montevideo ★

URUGUAY

Detail map (British Isles / France)

Skapa Flow

Wick •

North
Sea

Rosyth •

Londonderry • • Belfast

UNITED
KINGDOM

IRELAND   • Liverpool

LONDON ★

Portsmouth •

Falmouth •

ATLANTIC OCEAN

PARIS ◉

• Brest
Lorient •
St.-Nazaire •

F R A N C E

La Rochelle •

VICHY
FRANCE

Bordeaux •

Bay of
Biscay

FRAGILE SUPPLY LINES At right, crewmen stand on deck as a U-boat returns to base on the west coast of occupied France. Such bases enabled U-boats to be launched closer to Allied shipping lanes (mapped above), including those carrying supplies from America to Britain and the Mediterranean. Allied merchant ship losses prior to 1942 (yellow dots) were concentrated around the British Isles (detailed above left). Merchant ship losses thereafter (green dots) spread far across the Atlantic as U-boats expanded their range. In 1943, Allied air patrols (shaded areas) and other defensive measures caused steep U-boat losses (red dots) in the North Atlantic, ending the critical threat to supply lines there.

U-BOAT CHARTS AND INSTRUMENTS

Capt. Reinhard Hardegan, one of the first U-boat commanders sent by Admiral Dönitz (right) to sink ships off the North American coast, departed so soon after Germany declared war on the U.S. that he lacked charts of the waters in which he would operate. Hardegan relied instead on an "old student tourist guide," he recalled, and "used it to navigate along the coast." Captains who followed in his aggressive path were aided by official maps, including tidal and depth charts (below)—vital information for U-boats that often operated close to shore, sometimes entering waters too shallow to allow them to submerge if they came under attack. They were also aided by instruments like those shown here, which helped them chart their position at night by the stars and target ships. ■

LOCATION German naval quadrant charts like that for the U.S. East Coast at right enabled U-boat commanders to signal their position by radio using the code number assigned to each quadrant on the chart—a more secure system for locating navy vessels in wartime than if they communicated using degrees of latitude and longitude.

GUIDANCE The German Navy issued atlases like the one inset above containing tidal and depth charts for operational areas, including waters off the Canadian Maritimes (above). The navigational slide computer at right was used to determine a U-boat's position based on the stars, which could be charted using a star globe (opposite).

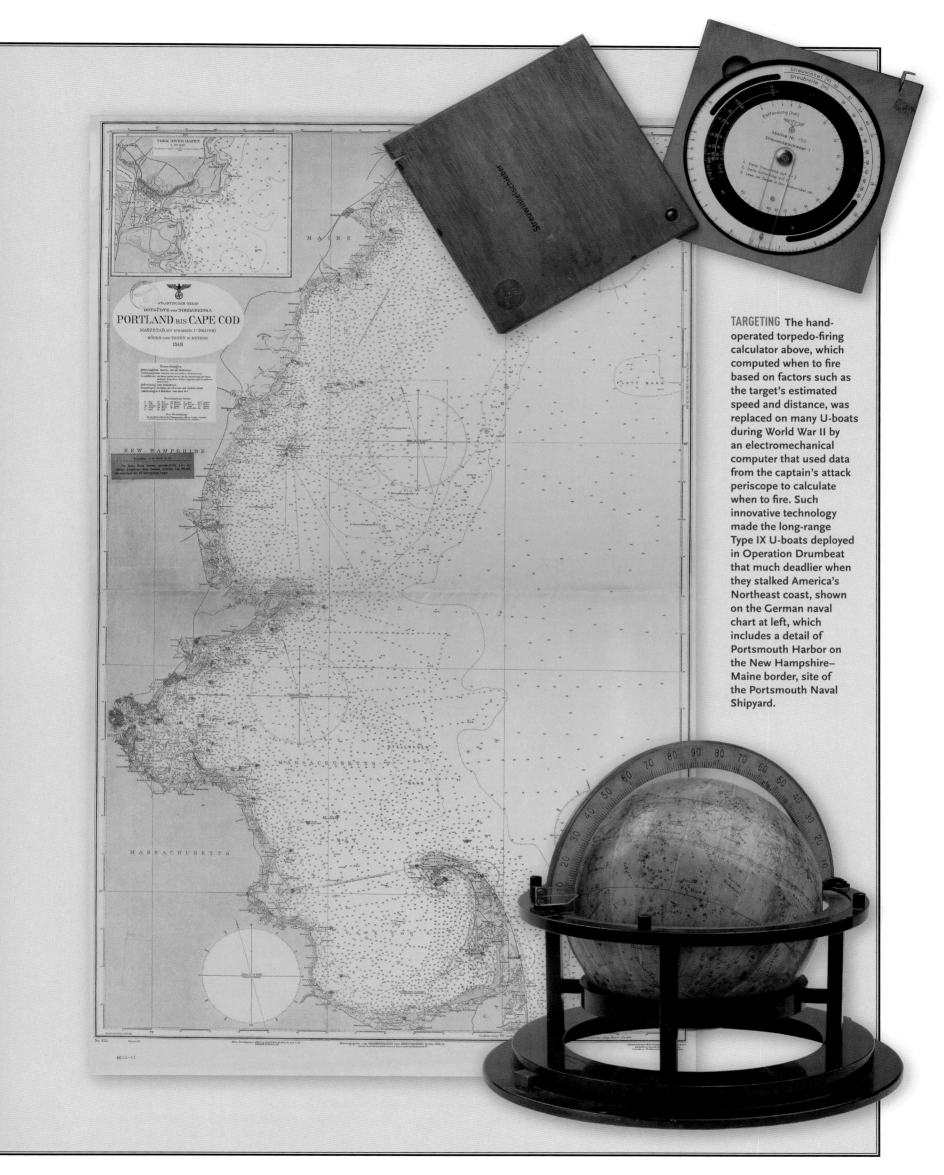

TARGETING The hand-operated torpedo-firing calculator above, which computed when to fire based on factors such as the target's estimated speed and distance, was replaced on many U-boats during World War II by an electromechanical computer that used data from the captain's attack periscope to calculate when to fire. Such innovative technology made the long-range Type IX U-boats deployed in Operation Drumbeat that much deadlier when they stalked America's Northeast coast, shown on the German naval chart at left, which includes a detail of Portsmouth Harbor on the New Hampshire–Maine border, site of the Portsmouth Naval Shipyard.

THE AMERICAN SHOOTING SEASON

On January 11, 1942, Captain Hardegan struck the first blow in Operation Drumbeat when his *U-123* sank the British freighter *Cyclops* off the coast of Nova Scotia, resulting in the death of 87 crewmen. Hardegan's Type IX was one of five such U-boats that Dönitz committed to the operation, which ranged from the Canadian Maritimes to Cape Hatteras. Collectively, the five commanders and their crews sank merchant ships at an alarming rate of roughly one a day before returning to base in early February. Hunting mainly at night, they exploited the fact that blackouts had not yet been imposed in the United States, enabling them to spot the silhouettes of freighters backlit by the glow of New York and other coastal cities. Many ships went down within sight of shore.

Dönitz followed up Operation Drumbeat by sending several additional waves of U-boats across the Atlantic to prowl in American waters, including shorter-range Type VIIs that were refueled in mid-ocean by supply boats called "milk cows." With more forces deployed, he extended their range southward from Cape Hatteras to the Caribbean and the Gulf of Mexico (see chart below). Among their prime targets were oil tankers—floating tinderboxes that when struck by torpedoes erupted in smoke and flames with deadly consequences. During the first six months of 1942, nearly 400 ships were sunk at a cost of some 5,000 lives. U-boat officers called it the "American Shooting Season." By July 1942, however, their depredations were diminishing as blackouts took effect along the coast, aerial surveillance increased, and convoys were organized. Dönitz began withdrawing U-boats from American waters to step up attacks on Allied supply lines in mid-ocean, where the Battle of the Atlantic was approaching its climax. ∎

SOUTHERN CAMPAIGN At upper right, officers examine a torpedo fired by the German submarine *U-67* that missed an oil tanker and ran ashore on the Dutch island of Curaçao in February 1942. By then, Admiral Dönitz had expanded his U-boat offensive southward into the Caribbean and the Gulf of Mexico, shown above on a German naval quadrant chart. The stopwatch atop the chart was used to measure the running time of a torpedo.

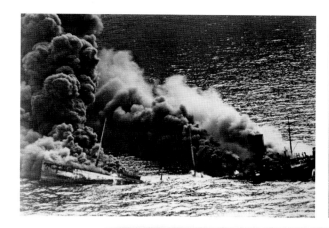

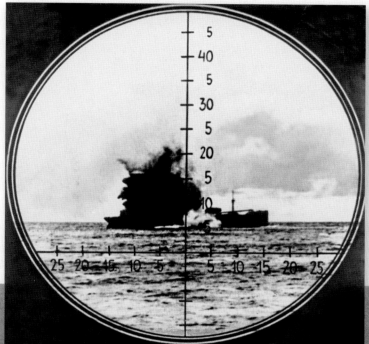

TANKERS TARGETED Torpedo strikes such as that photographed at left through a U-boat attack periscope triggered fierce explosions on loaded oil tankers like the three pictured above. The *Dixie Arrow* (top left) and *Byron D. Benson* (center) were sunk off Cape Hatteras in the spring of 1942. The *Pennsylvania Sun* (right), targeted in the Gulf of Mexico that July while carrying fuel for the U.S. Navy, remained afloat and was repaired.

TRANSATLANTIC FORAY Below, two long-range Type IX U-boats cruise on the surface on their way to America during Operation Drumbeat in early 1942. U-boats could move faster on the surface, using powerful diesel engines that recharged the electric motors they relied on when they submerged to avoid detection.

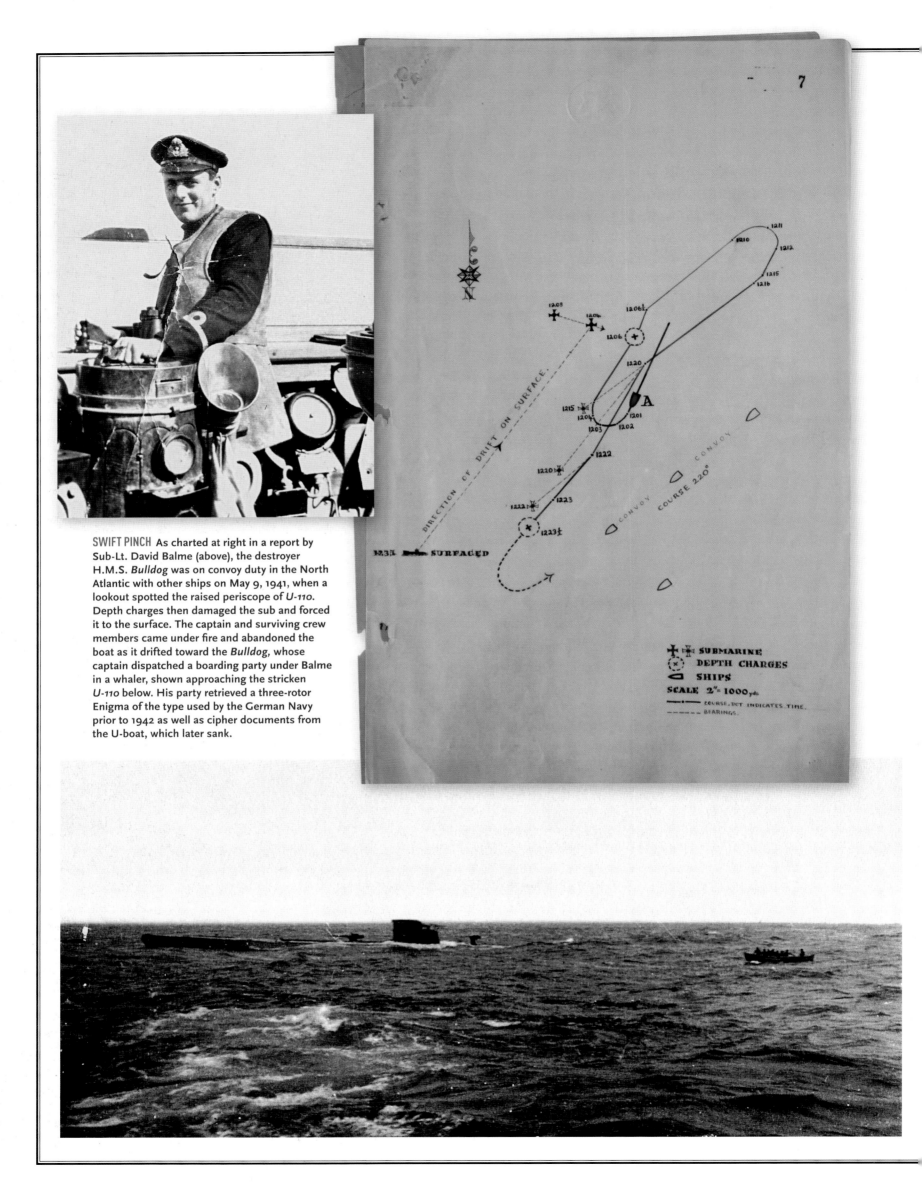

SWIFT PINCH As charted at right in a report by Sub-Lt. David Balme (above), the destroyer H.M.S. *Bulldog* was on convoy duty in the North Atlantic with other ships on May 9, 1941, when a lookout spotted the raised periscope of *U-110*. Depth charges then damaged the sub and forced it to the surface. The captain and surviving crew members came under fire and abandoned the boat as it drifted toward the *Bulldog*, whose captain dispatched a boarding party under Balme in a whaler, shown approaching the stricken *U-110* below. His party retrieved a three-rotor Enigma of the type used by the German Navy prior to 1942 as well as cipher documents from the U-boat, which later sank.

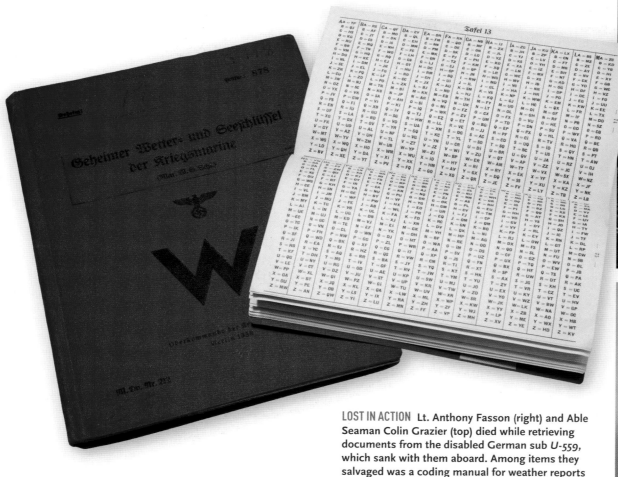

LOST IN ACTION Lt. Anthony Fasson (right) and Able Seaman Colin Grazier (top) died while retrieving documents from the disabled German sub *U-559*, which sank with them aboard. Among items they salvaged was a coding manual for weather reports (similar to that above), which helped cryptanalysts solve the four-rotor naval Enigma (below).

BATTLE OF THE ATLANTIC

SOLVING THE ENIGMA

Between May and November 1942, U-boats sank more than 900 ships, nearly three times the number they sank during the same period a year earlier. The alarming increase occurred after U-boats were equipped with Enigma cipher machines containing four rotors, like the one shown here, rather than three. That multiplied exponentially the number of possible Enigma settings and stumped cryptanalysts at Bletchley Park, who had solved the three-rotor Enigma in 1941 with the help of pinches, including the daring recovery of an Enigma from the disabled *U-110* (opposite bottom) by a boarding party from the British destroyer H.M.S. *Bulldog*. "Speed was essential owing to the possibility of U-boat sinking," wrote Sub-Lt. David Balme (opposite top) in a report including a map of the operation. One man in his party pressed the keys of an odd machine resembling a typewriter in the U-boat's W/T (wireless transmitter) office, Balme noted, "and finding the results peculiar passed it up the hatch."

When the four-rotor Enigma entered service and code-breakers could no longer protect convoys by deciphering U-boat messages, they were desperate for another pinch. It occurred in the Mediterranean on October 30, 1942, when three men from the destroyer H.M.S. *Petard* swam to the battered *U-559*, forced to the surface by depth charges. Abandoned by its crew, it was taking on water when Lt. Anthony Fasson (above) and Able Seaman Colin Grazier (top) entered, grabbed documents, and passed them to Tommy Brown, the *Petard*'s young canteen assistant, who escaped as the U-boat sank with the two men aboard. The documents they died for included a manual used to encode weather reports before they were enciphered on the Enigma, a precaution taken because weather reports were repetitive and provided cribs: common phrases used to decipher messages. With the weather code in hand, cryptanalysts broke the Enigma cipher and could again read U-boat signals. That intelligence combined with innovations like Huff Duff—high-frequency radio direction finders that fixed on signals from subs—led to the sinking of so many U-boats that Dönitz withdrew the remainder from the North Atlantic in late May 1943. Some would later return there, but the Allies had won the Battle of the Atlantic. ■

AFRICAN CAULDRON Above, Italians captured by the British march toward a detention area in Libya in January 1941. Rommel set out in March 1941 to regain ground lost by Italy but was forced back to El Agheila, where he launched his second offensive in January 1942. Although he seized the port of Tobruk in June and invaded Egypt, his maritime supply lines from Italy and Greece (mapped below) were menaced by attacks from British bases on Malta. Defeated at El Alamein, he withdrew to Tunisia, where Axis forces were defeated following the Allied invasion of French North Africa in November.

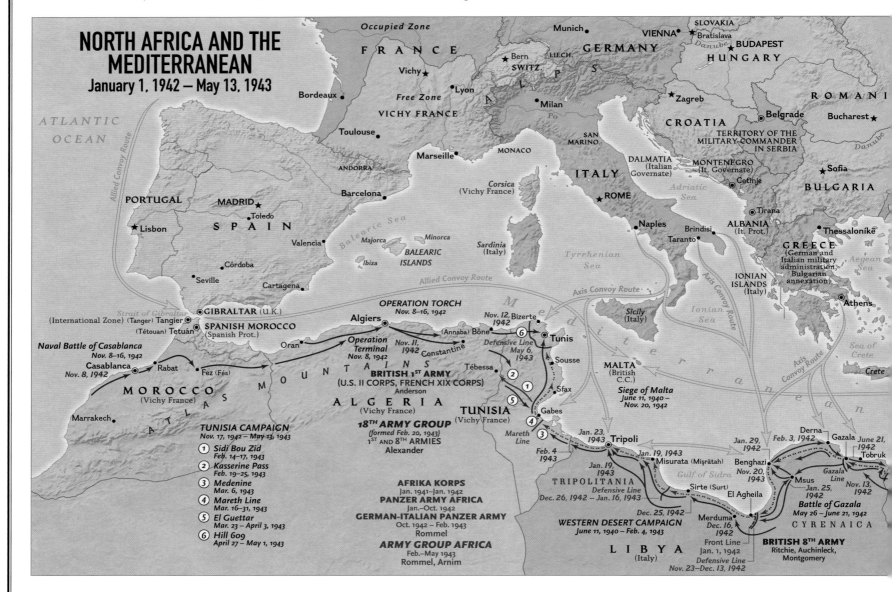

NORTH AFRICA AND THE MEDITERRANEAN
January 1, 1942 – May 13, 1943

WAR IN THE DESERT

THE STRUGGLE FOR NORTH AFRICA

By January 1942, Gen. Erwin Rommel was back at El Agheila in Libya (see map below), where he had launched his North African campaign the previous March. He had been repulsed, but he remained confident. His outstanding trait, wrote a British officer who opposed him, was "resilience . . . no sooner was he knocked down than he was on his feet again." Rommel understood the ebb and flow of war in the desert, where those who made dramatic advances were subject to dramatic reversals. Such had been the pattern in North Africa since September 1940, when troops from Italian-held Libya invaded British-ruled Egypt and made rapid gains before they were outflanked and outfought. Some

200,000 Italian soldiers then retreated in disarray, many of whom became prisoners of war (opposite) before Hitler dispatched Rommel to Libya to repair the damage. Known as the "Desert Fox" for cunning maneuvers and swift attacks that had sent British and Commonwealth troops reeling in 1941, he advanced across Libya to the Egyptian border with the armored forces of his Afrika Korps. But his opponents clung to Tobruk—denying Rommel the use of that port to maintain his supply line and prolong his offensive—and pushed him back to El Agheila.

Furnished with additional tanks and troops for his newly designated panzer army, Rommel recognized that the British were overextended and set out to achieve in 1942 what had eluded him in 1941—the conquest of Egypt and the Suez Canal, which would bring North Africa and potentially the Middle East under Axis forces or compliant Vichy authorities in French Morocco, Algeria, and Tunisia. U.S. troops would invade Morocco and Algeria in November 1942, however, and Rommel's army would ultimately be caught between the oncoming Yanks and their resurgent British allies. ∎

CHRONOLOGY

JANUARY 21, 1942 Gen. Erwin Rommel launches his second offensive in North Africa, advancing with his armored forces from El Agheila, Libya, toward British-ruled Egypt.

JUNE 21, 1942 Rommel seizes Tobruk, Libya, a port that will serve as a supply base as he invades Egypt.

OCTOBER 23, 1942 Lt. Gen. Bernard Montgomery, commanding the British Eighth Army, launches the decisive Second Battle of El Alamein in Egypt by attacking Rommel's army.

NOVEMBER 4, 1942 Rommel concedes defeat at El Alamein and withdraws.

NOVEMBER 8, 1942 Allied forces consisting largely of American troops invade Vichy French Morocco and Algeria in Operation Torch.

MAY 7, 1943 Allied troops secure North Africa by capturing Tunis, the last Axis bastion in Tunisia.

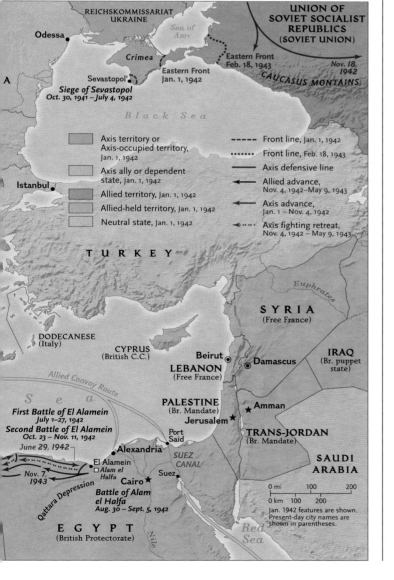

DESERT RAIDERS British commandos of the Special Air Service, which originally consisted of paratroopers, carry Vickers aircraft machine guns for a raid behind Axis lines in North Africa.

ROMMEL'S BIG PUSH

O n January 21, 1942, Rommel advanced from El Agheila against the British Eighth Army, led by Maj. Gen. Neil Ritchie and overseen by Gen. Claude Auchinleck, British commander in chief in the Middle East. Auchinleck's strength had been reduced as troops, warplanes, and other assets were shifted from his theater to combat the Japanese offensive in the Far East. To make matters worse, German U-boats had entered the Mediterranean and were preying on convoys that supplied the Eighth Army, which was ill-equipped to defend the ground it had gained in Libya in late 1941. As shown at right on a German situation map dated February 11, Rommel's army—including Italian units (purple) as well as the German Afrika Korps (shown in blue and designated D.A.K.)—had by then seized Benghazi and forced Ritchie's forces (red) to withdraw to a fortified line that extended southward from the Mediterranean coast near Gazala.

After pausing to consolidate and resupply his forces, Rommel attacked the Gazala Line in late May, aided by the Luftwaffe, which pounded the southernmost stronghold on the line, stoutly defended by French forces who had spurned Vichy authorities and gone over to the British. When they finally gave way, Ritchie's forces were outflanked and had to claw their way out to avoid annihilation. Following that defeat, Auchinleck proposed to withdraw his forces from Libya, which meant abandoning Tobruk (designated on the German map by the headquarters flag of the Eighth Army). But Churchill insisted that the port be defended. "Tobruk was the symbol of British resistance," Rommel later wrote, "and we were now going to finish with it for good." Blasted from the air on June 20, Tobruk fell a day later to Rommel, who captured more than 30,000 troops and 2,000 vehicles and gained a supply base for his advance into Egypt. Promoted to the rank of field marshal by Hitler, he knew that hard fighting lay ahead and wrote his wife: "I would much rather that he had given me one more division." ■

DESERT FOX Renowned for leading from the front, Rommel crosses the desert in Libya, equipped with captured British goggles to keep dust out of his eyes. In a few weeks in early 1942, his forces drove the British back nearly 300 miles, as shown here on a German map.

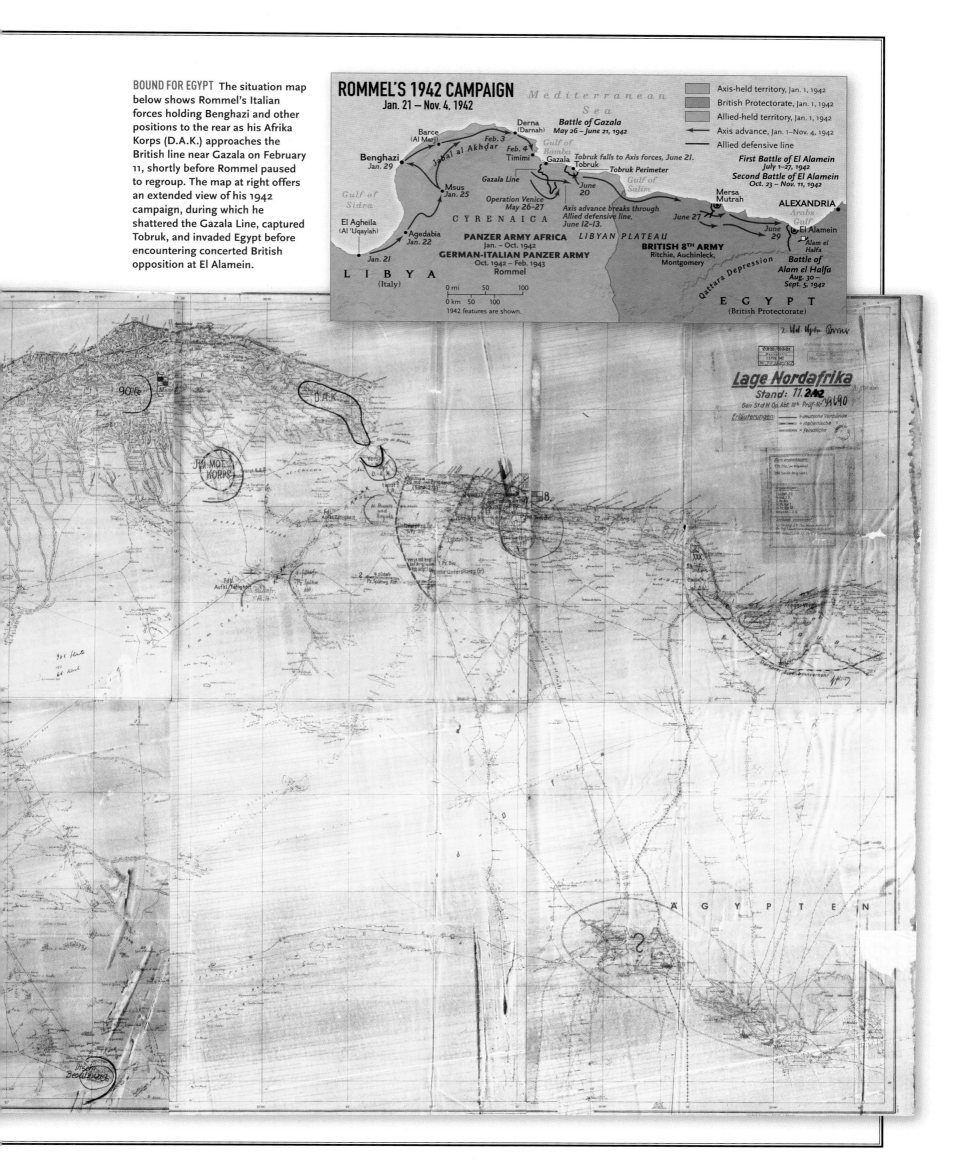

BOUND FOR EGYPT The situation map below shows Rommel's Italian forces holding Benghazi and other positions to the rear as his Afrika Korps (D.A.K.) approaches the British line near Gazala on February 11, shortly before Rommel paused to regroup. The map at right offers an extended view of his 1942 campaign, during which he shattered the Gazala Line, captured Tobruk, and invaded Egypt before encountering concerted British opposition at El Alamein.

ROMMEL'S 1942 CAMPAIGN
Jan. 21 – Nov. 4, 1942

Mediterranean Sea

Axis-held territory, Jan. 1, 1942
British Protectorate, Jan. 1, 1942
Allied-held territory, Jan. 1, 1942
Axis advance, Jan. 1–Nov. 4, 1942
Allied defensive line

Battle of Gazala
May 26 – June 21, 1942

Derna (Darnah)
Feb. 3
Barce (Al Marj)
Benghazi
Jan. 29
Jabal al Akhdar
Feb. 4
Timimi
Gulf of Bomba
Gazala
Tobruk
Tobruk falls to Axis forces, June 21.
Tobruk Perimeter

First Battle of El Alamein
July 1–27, 1942
Second Battle of El Alamein
Oct. 23 – Nov. 11, 1942

Gazala Line
Msus
Jan. 25
Operation Venice
May 26–27
June 20
Gulf of Salim
Mersa Mutrah
ALEXANDRIA
Arabs Gulf

CYRENAICA
Axis advance breaks through Allied defensive line, June 12–13.
June 27
June 29
El Alamein
Alam el Halfa

El Agheila (Al 'Uqaylah)
Agedabia
Jan. 22
PANZER ARMY AFRICA
Jan. – Oct. 1942
GERMAN-ITALIAN PANZER ARMY
Oct. 1942 – Feb. 1943
Rommel
LIBYAN PLATEAU
BRITISH 8TH ARMY
Ritchie, Auchinleck, Montgomery
Battle of Alam el Halfa
Aug. 30 – Sept. 5, 1942

Jan. 21
LIBYA
(Italy)
Qattara Depression
EGYPT
(British Protectorate)

0 mi   50   100
0 km   50   100
1942 features are shown.

Lage Nordafrika
Stand: 11. 2.42

ÄGYPTEN

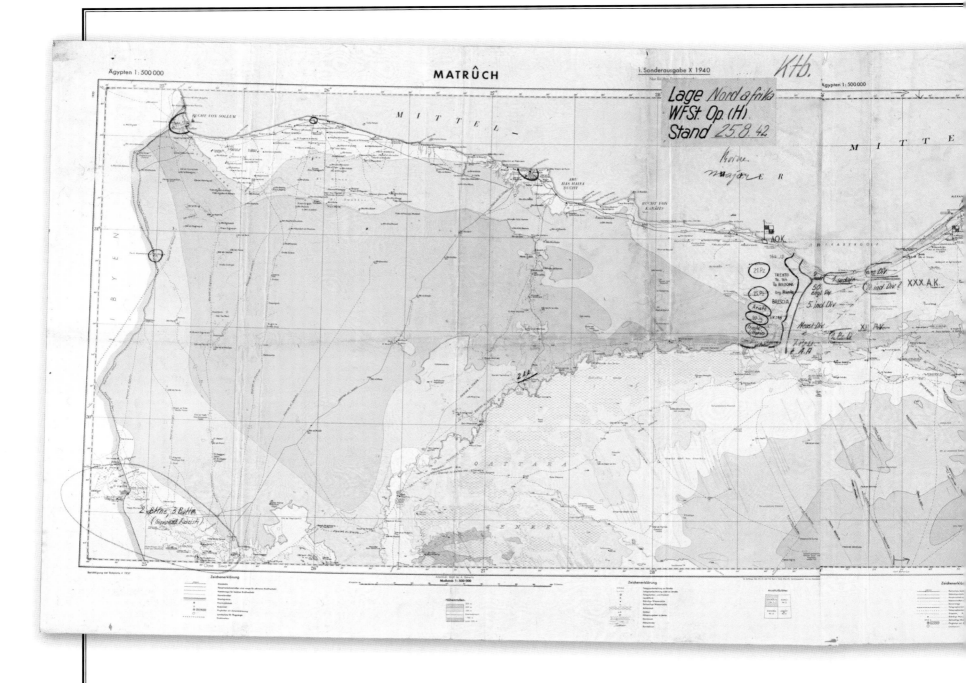

BATTLE LINES DRAWN IN EGYPT

The loss of Tobruk was a bitter blow for the British. "Defeat is one thing," Churchill wrote afterward; "disgrace is another." Under mounting pressure from his superiors in London, Auchinleck relieved Ritchie and took personal command of the Eighth Army, which he withdrew to a defensive line in Egypt between El Alamein on the Mediterranean coast and the Qattara Depression, whose sand dunes, marshes, and soft salt flats were impenetrable by tanks, leaving Rommel little room to maneuver (see the topographical map above). During the First Battle of El Alamein in July 1942, Auchinleck held his ground. But he lost the support of Churchill, who ousted him as Middle East commander in favor of Lt. Gen. Harold Alexander and placed the Eighth Army under the confident and combative Lt. Gen. Bernard "Monty" Montgomery. Alexander met with Monty in Cairo and gave him a succinct order: "Go down to the desert and defeat Rommel."

Rommel did not have time on his side. The British were now close to their supply base at Alexandria, whereas Rommel's supply lines were elongated and subject to attack. Although cryptanalysts at Bletchley Park had not yet solved the advanced German naval Enigma, they were deciphering Enigma messages sent by other German and Italian armed forces and providing intelligence known as Ultra that helped the British sink 100 Axis ships in the Mediterranean between January and August 1942, many of them carrying oil and armaments for Rommel's forces. Supplies that reached ports in Libya were targeted by the Allied Desert Air Force as they were transported overland to El Alamein. Eager to attack while his panzers were still well fueled, Rommel attempted to break through at the southern end of the British line in late August. Informed of that plan by Ultra, Monty allowed some of Rommel's panzers to penetrate as far as Alam el Halfa, where they ground to a halt under blistering fire. When that battle ended on September 5 with Rommel's diminished forces back where they started, he knew he could not outflank his foes and went over to the defensive while Montgomery planned a bruising, head-on attack at El Alamein. ■

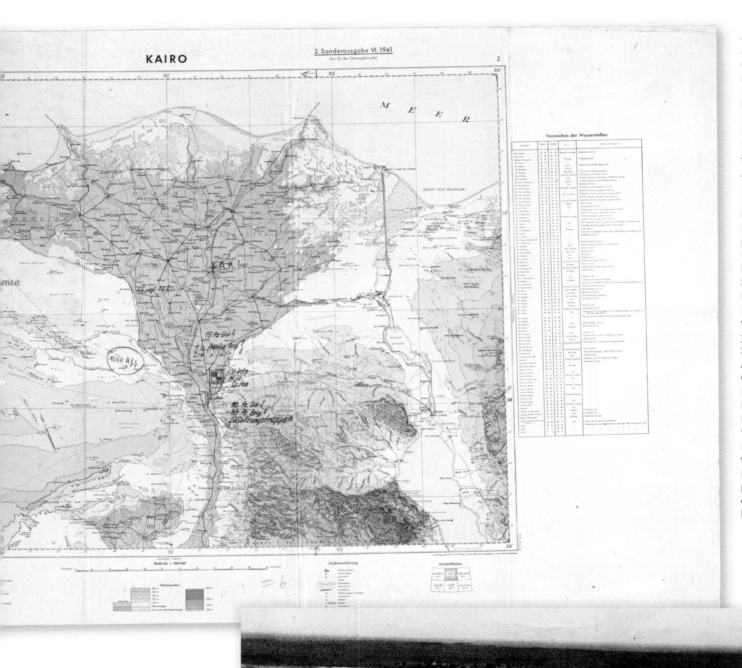

ARRAYED IN EGYPT
A German situation map dated August 25, 1942, shows the opposing Axis (blue) and British (red) lines between the Mediterranean and the impassable Qattara Depression (coded gray for land below sea level). A blue flag denotes Rommel's headquarters (upper left), and red flags indicate Montgomery's headquarters near the port of Alexandria and British Middle East headquarters in Cairo. Several units labeled here fought in both the Battle of Alam el Halfa, which began on August 30, and the decisive Second Battle of El Alamein, including the German 15th and 21st Panzer Divisions and the British Seventh Armored Division (labeled in red "7 Pz D"). The Australian Ninth Division, shown at the north end of the British line, figured prominently in the climactic El Alamein battle.

TROOPS ADRIFT German soldiers struggle over windblown sand dunes near El Alamein in 1942. Other terrain around El Alamein was level and firm enough to allow troops as well as tanks to advance steadily, but the two sides laid millions of mines that made this one of the war's most treacherous battlefields.

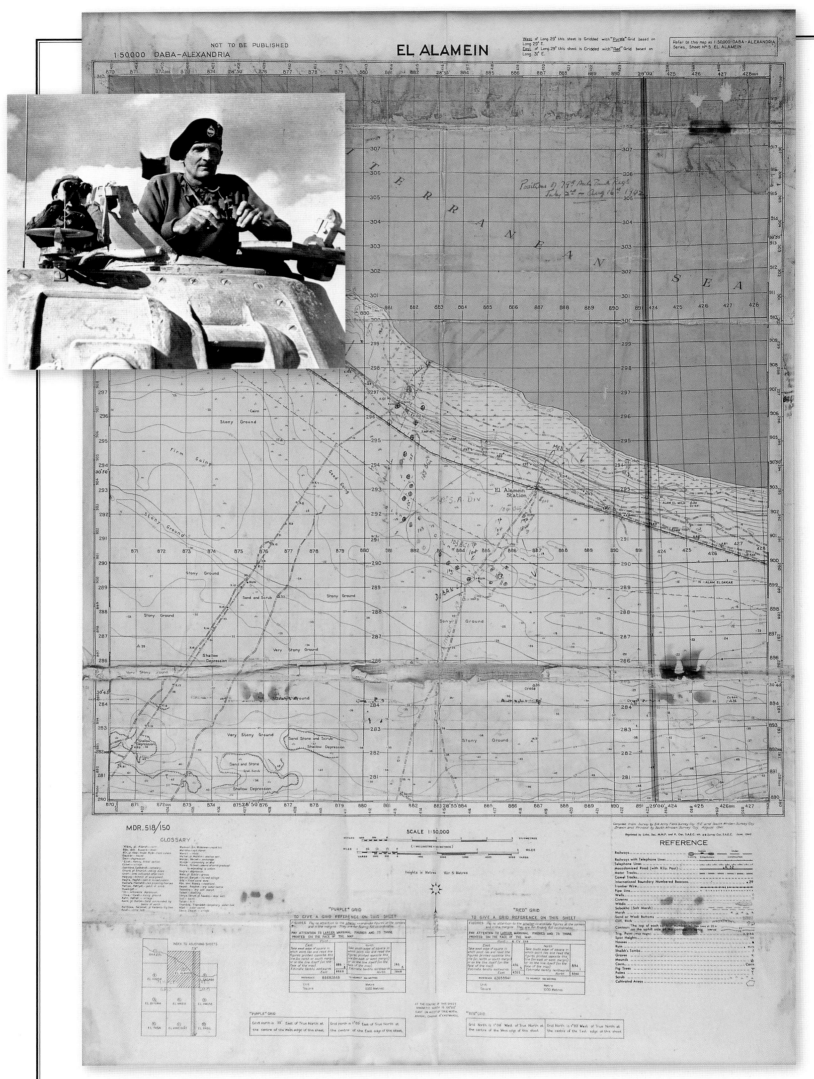

GOOD GOING Notations in blue near El Alamein Station on this British map show units of the First South African Division, one of several British Commonwealth forces that attacked at the north end of the German line during the Second Battle of El Alamein. Montgomery, pictured in an American-made Grant tank, began by sending sappers to clear mines from promising avenues of attack like those marked "Good Going" and "Firm Going" on this map, allowing infantry and armor to advance.

BREAKTHROUGH AT EL ALAMEIN

As battle loomed at El Alamein in October 1942, Montgomery exuded confidence that was based in part on intelligence he received on the dwindling supplies and ill health of Rommel, who flew to Germany for treatment in late September. Command passed temporarily to Gen. Georg Stumme, who was not well either and was taken in by elaborate British deceptions indicating that Monty would attack at the southern end of the line in November. When the battle opened with a thunderous artillery barrage on the night of October 23 and British sappers began clearing mines for an attack at the northern end near El Alamein Station (see map opposite), Stumme suffered a fatal heart attack.

Rommel returned on October 25 to find Montgomery's forces, led by the hard-charging Ninth Australian Division, on the verge of a breakthrough in the north. By throwing the 21st Panzer Division into that fight along with the 15th Panzer Division, Rommel averted disaster on that flank. But he was left with too few resources to overcome Operation Supercharge, a furious assault at the center of the line launched by Monty on November 2. Infantry led the way—including New Zealanders who had been pushed out of Crete by the Germans and were now turning the tables on them—followed by British armored divisions, which were hit hard but pressed Rommel's depleted panzers to the breaking point. Defying an order from Hitler to stand fast and seek "victory or death," Rommel withdrew on November 4, having lost most of his tanks and with more than 30,000 men killed, wounded, or captured. ∎

TANK KILLERS Above, British infantrymen capture a German crewman in an immobilized Panzer III tank during the decisive Battle of El Alamein. Tanks were often disabled by artillery like the British 25-pounder shown firing during that battle (top left). Gunners of the Fourth Indian Division at El Alamein used landmarks and targets plotted on an artillery board sheet with a 360-degree compass (top right) to direct fire by 25-pounders that could turn full circle.

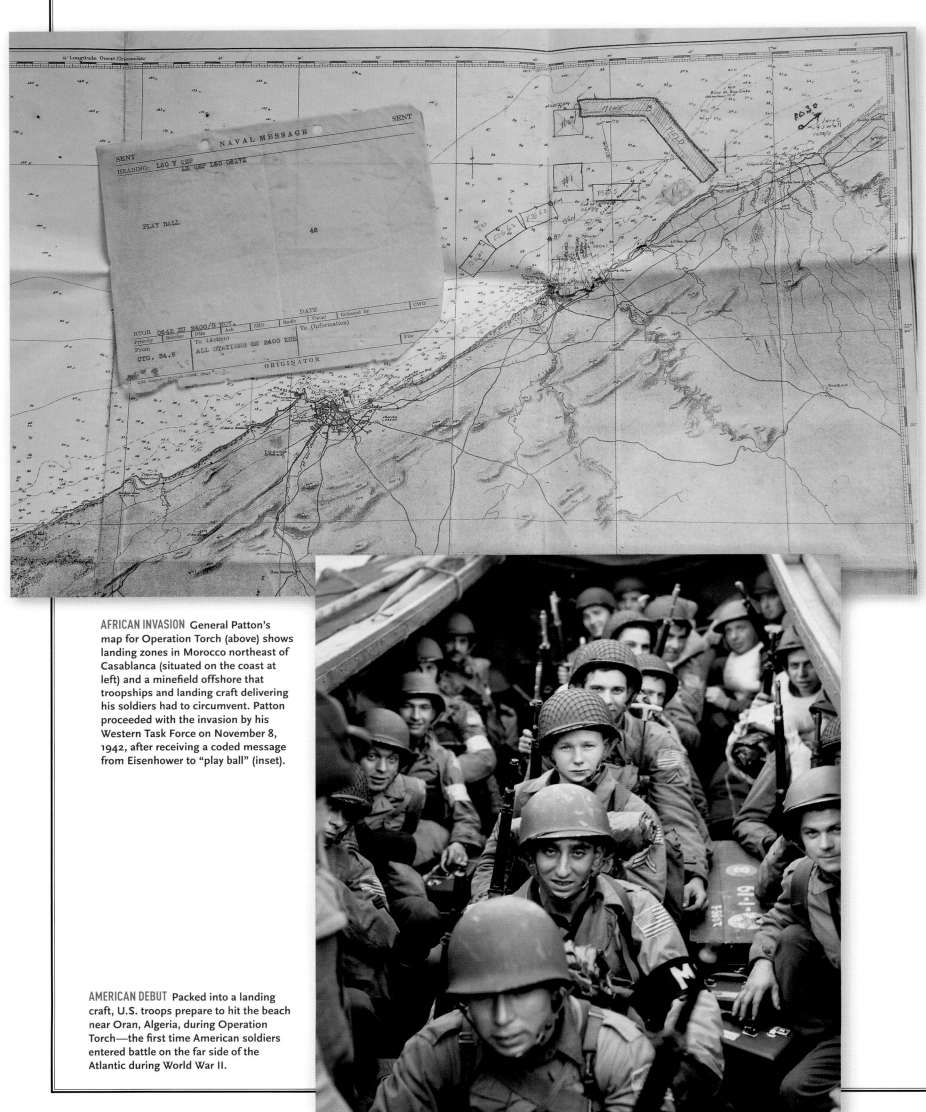

AFRICAN INVASION General Patton's map for Operation Torch (above) shows landing zones in Morocco northeast of Casablanca (situated on the coast at left) and a minefield offshore that troopships and landing craft delivering his soldiers had to circumvent. Patton proceeded with the invasion by his Western Task Force on November 8, 1942, after receiving a coded message from Eisenhower to "play ball" (inset).

AMERICAN DEBUT Packed into a landing craft, U.S. troops prepare to hit the beach near Oran, Algeria, during Operation Torch—the first time American soldiers entered battle on the far side of the Atlantic during World War II.

OPERATION TORCH

The Allied invasion of French North Africa, designated Operation Torch, was led by an American commander, Lt. Gen. Dwight D. Eisenhower, and carried out largely by American troops, supported by British forces. "This is an American enterprise in which we are your help mates," Churchill told Roosevelt. FDR wanted the United States to take the lead not just to boost the nation's morale but because Americans were less likely to be opposed by Vichy French forces than the British, who had attacked the French fleet in July 1940 to keep it out of German hands. French resistance was sporadic when Allied troops landed in Morocco and Algeria beginning on November 8, 1942 (see map below). The Vichy commander in North Africa, Adm. Jean Darlan, soon agreed to a cease-fire. Maj. Gen George Patton, pictured to the right of Eisenhower (inset), knew that green American troops landing in Morocco were fortunate not to face determined opposition. Had they been "opposed by Germans," he stated, "we never would have gotten ashore."

The real test came a few months later in Tunisia when Amer-

ican armored forces faced Rommel's panzers—who were being pursued by Montgomery's Eighth Army after withdrawing from Egypt—and Gen. Hans-Jürgen von Arnim's Fifth Panzer Army, which landed at Tunis to reinforce Rommel. Fortified with two of Arnim's panzer divisions, Rommel scorched the U.S. II Corps at Kasserine Pass in late February 1943 before determined resistance from British infantry backed by artillery and anti-tank units of the U.S. Ninth Division induced him to pull back. Following that battle, which cost the Americans nearly 200 tanks and 6,000 casualties, Eisenhower sent the hard-driving Patton to whip II Corps into shape while Montgomery's army drove Axis forces into a trap around Tunis. Hitler refused to evacuate them and had more troops air-lifted there. In early May, the revived II Corps descended on Bizerte, north of Tunis, while other Allied troops closed in from the south. By then, the ailing Rommel had returned to Germany, leaving Arnim in charge. On May 7, he surrendered to the Allies, who captured nearly 250,000 Axis troops, bringing the long struggle for control of North Africa to a close. ∎

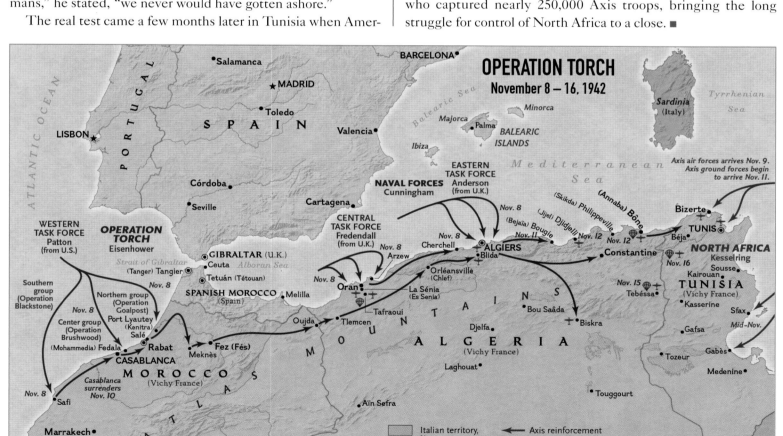

TORCHED On November 8, Allied task forces landed in Morocco and Algeria (above). Vichy French commanders soon yielded to Operation Torch. Axis troops were then caught in Tunisia between Montgomery's army advancing from Egypt and Eisenhower's forces advancing from Algeria.

THE ITALIAN CAMPAIGN
BRUTAL FIGHTING OVER RUGGED TERRAIN

CHRONOLOGY

JULY 9–10, 1943 Allied forces invade Sicily.

JULY 25, 1943 Mussolini is ousted as Italy's leader and arrested.

SEPTEMBER 8, 1943 Italy surrenders to the Allies, and German forces take control there.

SEPTEMBER 9, 1943 Lt. Gen. Mark Wayne Clark's Fifth Army lands under German fire at Salerno, Italy.

SEPTEMBER 12, 1943 Mussolini is freed by German commandos sent by Hitler.

JANUARY 22, 1944 Allied troops land at Anzio, near Rome, skirting the German Gustav Line (Winter Line) to the south, but they will soon meet with heavy German resistance.

MAY 18, 1944 Monte Cassino falls to Allied forces as they break through along the Gustav Line.

MAY 23, 1944 Allies break out of their beachhead at Anzio, prompting German troops to abandon Rome before Clark's troops enter the city on June 5.

SALVO The British battleship H.M.S. *Warspite* fires at Axis targets on shore at Catania, Sicily, on July 17, 1943, in support of Montgomery's Eighth Army.

The Anglo-American alliance was tested in 1943 when the British proposed advancing from North Africa to Sicily and from there to mainland Italy. Speaking for the U.S. Army, Gen. George Marshall argued for invading occupied France as soon as possible and opposed invading Italy, which he viewed not as Hitler's "soft underbelly," in Churchill's words, but as a hard target. Its steep terrain would impede Allied forces and prevent them from reaching Germany, shielded from Italy by neutral Switzerland and the towering Alps. After much debate, however, Marshall joined President Roosevelt and General Eisenhower in approving a campaign designed to knock Italy out of the war and tie down German divisions there prior to the invasion of France, which the Americans insisted must take place in 1944.

For the invasion of Sicily, code-named Operation Husky, a fleet of more than 3,000 ships and landing craft assembled on the coast of Tunisia to convey some 80,000 troops to the island and shield them with naval firepower (below). Before the first troops came ashore at dawn on July 10, 1943, airborne forces landed behind Axis lines to seize roads, bridges, and other targets. Anglo-American coordination made for successful landings, but that did not stop General Patton from engaging in a "horse race" to Messina—the gateway to mainland Italy—between his Seventh Army and the British Eighth Army. Patton claimed a narrow victory but not before many Axis troops had escaped to the mainland, where the Allies faced a long and grueling struggle. ■

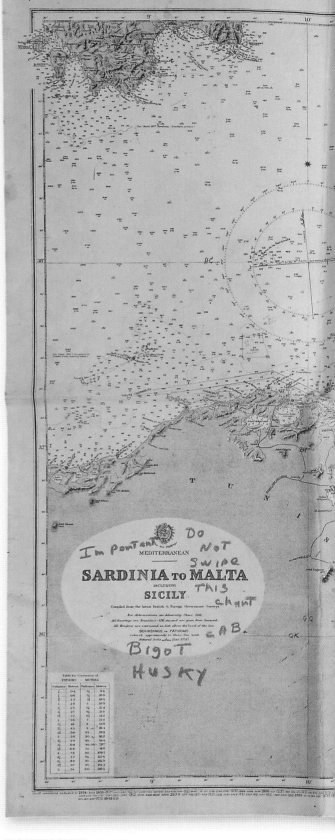

TARGETING SICILY Labeled "Bigot" (Secret), this chart was used by Cmdr. Charles Buchanan of the U.S. Navy to direct an amphibious task force from Tunisia (lower left) to Sicily (upper right). Allied deceptions hinting that Sardinia (upper left) or Greece might be targeted kept Hitler from reinforcing his troops on Sicily.

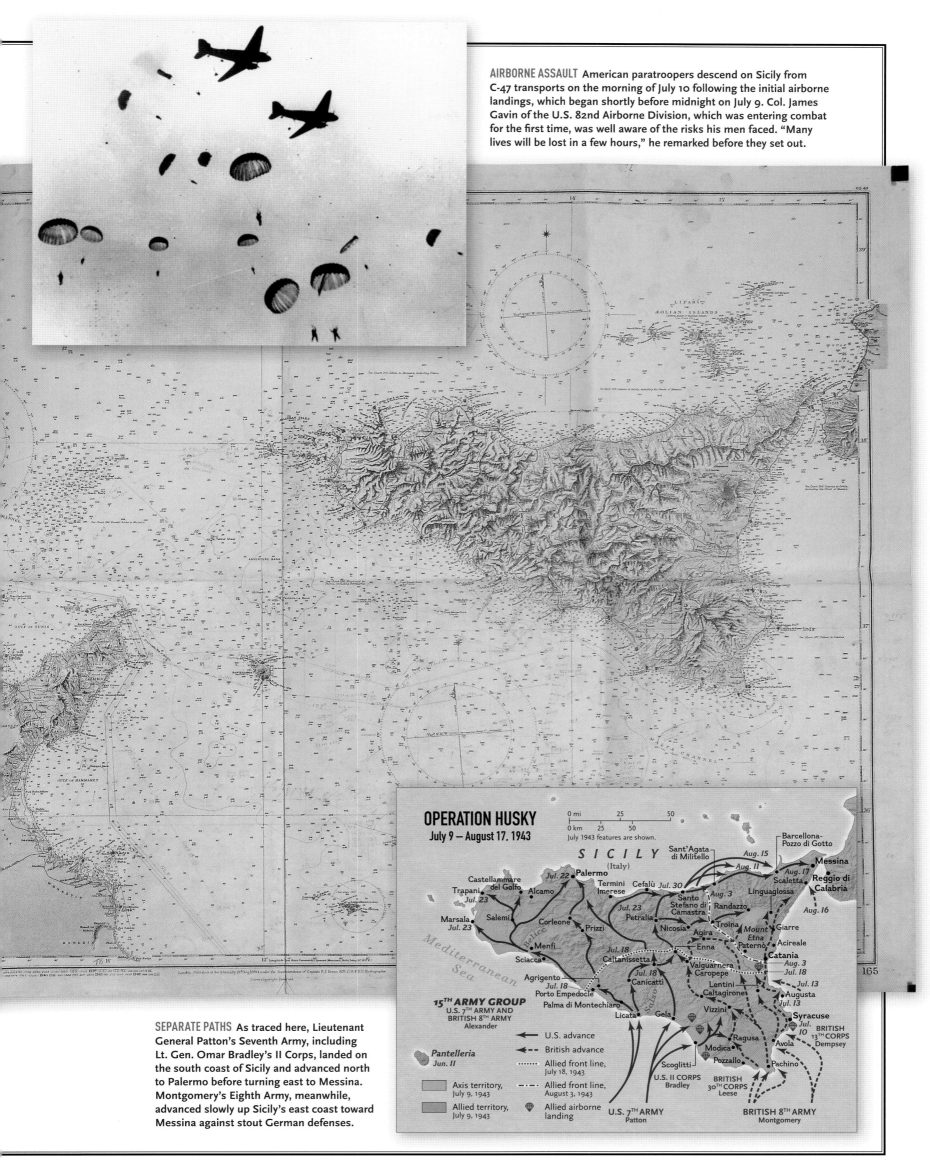

AIRBORNE ASSAULT American paratroopers descend on Sicily from C-47 transports on the morning of July 10 following the initial airborne landings, which began shortly before midnight on July 9. Col. James Gavin of the U.S. 82nd Airborne Division, which was entering combat for the first time, was well aware of the risks his men faced. "Many lives will be lost in a few hours," he remarked before they set out.

SEPARATE PATHS As traced here, Lieutenant General Patton's Seventh Army, including Lt. Gen. Omar Bradley's II Corps, landed on the south coast of Sicily and advanced north to Palermo before turning east to Messina. Montgomery's Eighth Army, meanwhile, advanced slowly up Sicily's east coast toward Messina against stout German defenses.

OPERATION HUSKY
July 9 – August 17, 1943

July 1943 features are shown.

0 mi 25 50
0 km 25 50

SICILY (Italy)

Mediterranean Sea

15TH ARMY GROUP
U.S. 7TH ARMY AND
BRITISH 8TH ARMY
Alexander

→ U.S. advance
⇢ British advance
···· Allied front line, July 18, 1943
—·— Allied front line, August 3, 1943

Axis territory, July 9, 1943
Allied territory, July 9, 1943
Allied airborne landing

Pantelleria Jun. 11

U.S. II CORPS Bradley

U.S. 7TH ARMY Patton

BRITISH 30TH CORPS Leese

BRITISH 13TH CORPS Dempsey

BRITISH 8TH ARMY Montgomery

Barcellona-Pozzo di Gotto · Messina · Scaletta · Reggio di Calabria · Sant'Agata di Militello · Aug. 15 · Aug. 11 · Aug. 17 · Aug. 16 · Linguaglossa · Santo Stefano di Camastra · Randazzo · Aug. 3 · Jul. 30 · Cefalù · Termini Imerese · Palermo · Jul. 22 · Castellammare del Golfo · Trapani Jul. 23 · Alcamo · Salemi · Marsala Jul. 23 · Corleone · Prizzi · Menfi · Sciacca · Agrigento Jul. 18 · Porto Empedocle Jul. 18 · Palma di Montechiaro · Licata · Gela · Jul. 23 · Petralia · Nicosia · Enna · Caltanissetta · Jul. 18 · Canicatti · Jul. 18 · Agira · Troina · Valguarnera Caropepe · Lentini · Caltagirone · Jul. 18 · Vizzini · Modica · Ragusa · Scoglitti · Pozzallo · Pachino · Avola · Augusta Jul. 13 · Syracuse Jul. 10 · Giarre · Acireale · Catania Aug. 3 · Jul. 18 · Jul. 13 · Mount Etna · Paternò

BREAKING HITLER'S GRIP **141**

BRITISH LANDINGS

Operation Husky was an enormous amphibious operation that would rival the complexity of the Allied landings on the coast of France a year later. In fact, more Allied divisions landed in Sicily on July 10, 1943, than came ashore at Normandy on D-Day. Meticulous planning and daring reconnaissance went into the production of Husky invasion maps like the one at right, showing landing zones for the British Eighth Army on Sicily's east coast. Months before the invasion, parties designated COPP (Combined Operations Pilotage Parties) were launched secretly at night from submarines off the coast of Sicily and paddled ashore in folding boats to reconnoiter beaches at great risk. One party lost two-thirds of its men conducting those forays in March 1943. Such efforts enabled planners to chart landing sites in remarkable detail. Beach 47 on the map at right, for example, is described as "Soft sandy beach . . . Water offshore fairly shallow with some irregularities of under-water contour. Probably suitable for all LC [landing craft]." Among the first British forces to come ashore on July 10 were Royal Navy Beach Commandos, who secured each site, directed incoming landing craft, and kept the huge operation moving.

Good planning and good luck in the form of light resistance by Italian troops—many of whom were demoralized and poorly equipped—enabled Montgomery's Eighth Army to land in Sicily with minimal casualties. He needed all the strength he could muster. After taking the city of Syracuse and advancing up the coast road toward Messina, his troops met with mounting German resistance as they approached Mount Etna. That imposing barrier left the army little room to maneuver on the coast. Monty sent part of his forces around the western flank of the volcano, but the Germans extended their Etna Line across the island and blocked that end run. Not until mid-August did the Eighth Army break through the Etna Line. By then, Field Marshal Albert Kesselring, the German commander in Italy, had decided to withdraw troops to the mainland from Messina before Montgomery or Patton could reach that port. ■

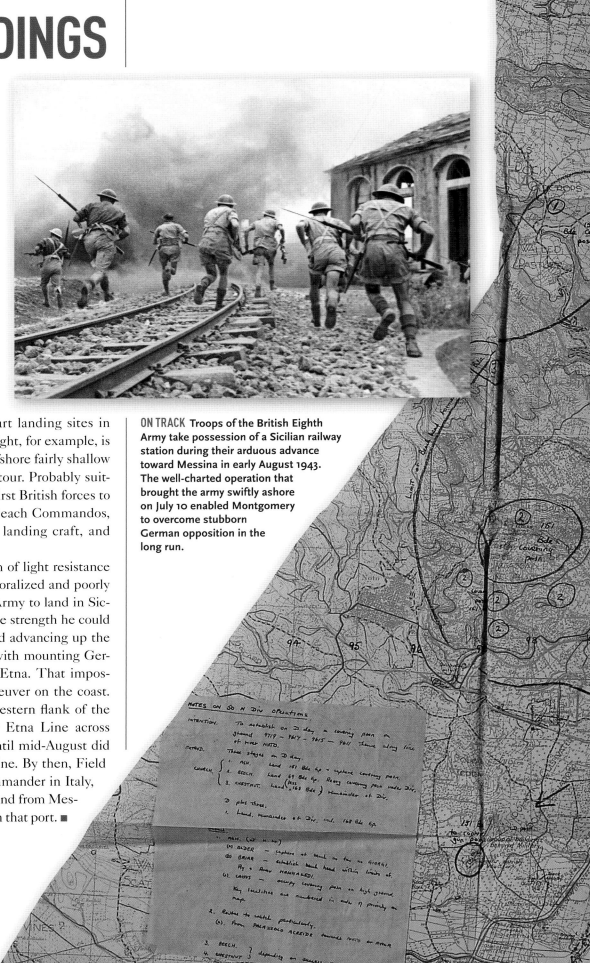

ON TRACK Troops of the British Eighth Army take possession of a Sicilian railway station during their arduous advance toward Messina in early August 1943. The well-charted operation that brought the army swiftly ashore on July 10 enabled Montgomery to overcome stubborn German opposition in the long run.

INVASION MAP A densely annotated chart shows Eighth Army landing sites within three sectors, designated Jig, How, and George. Notes in blue describe conditions at various beaches, where soft, deep sand often made it difficult to haul vehicles onto firm ground (opposite). Other notes attached to the map indicate objectives for brigades, one of which was assigned to enter Syracuse by "nightfall D-Day" (July 10).

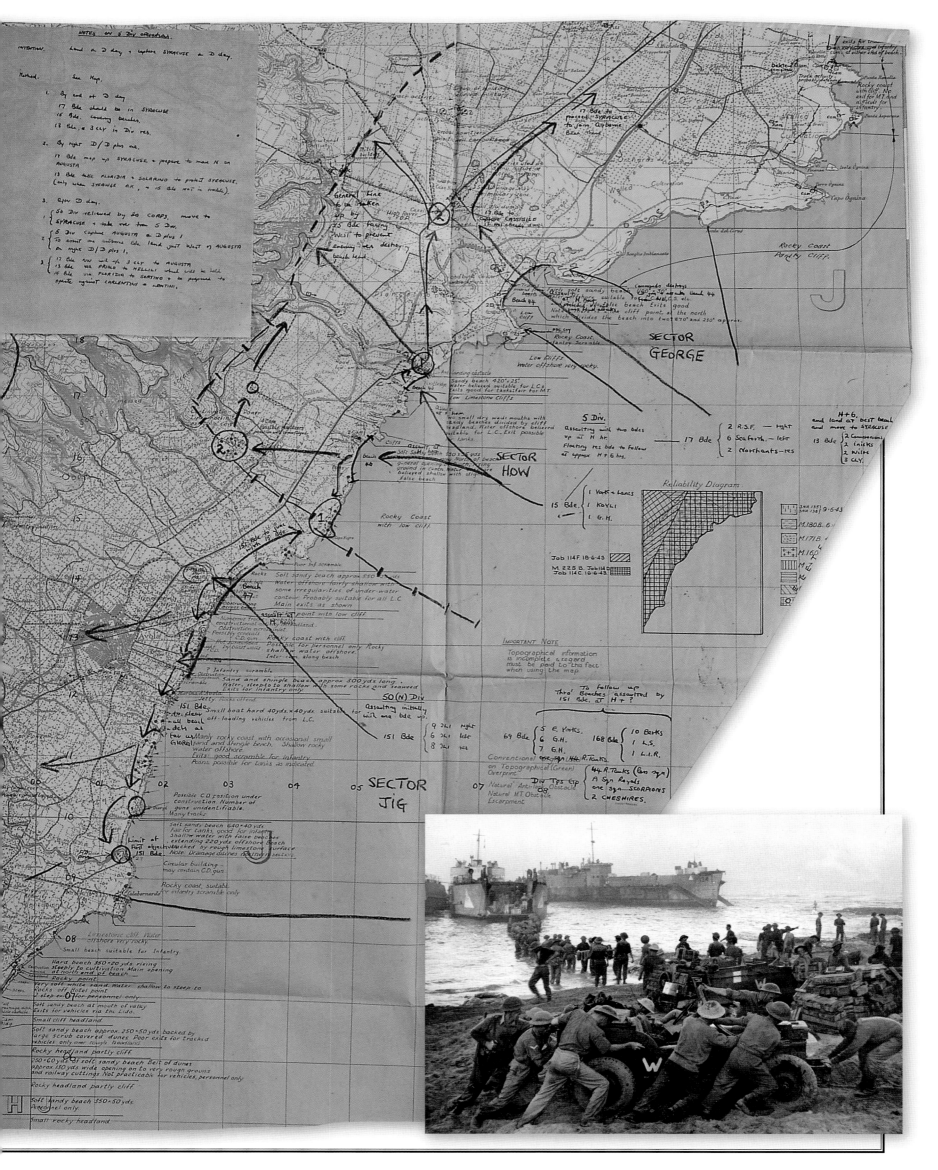

PATTON'S RACE

No commander on Sicily covered more ground with his troops than George Patton, who made good use of his map of the island (right). Marked "secret" and dated "18 July 1943," it designates with a flag his Seventh Army headquarters at Gela on the south coast, where his forces landed on July 10. Their initial assignment was to protect the flank of Montgomery's Eighth Army on the east coast. But after repulsing an attack by the Hermann Göring Panzer Division near Gela, Patton received permission on July 17 to take Sicily's capital, Palermo. A blue line between his headquarters and Palermo shows the path followed by Omar Bradley's II Corps. Italian resistance was collapsing, and Bradley saw "no glory in the capture of hills, docile peasants, and spiritless soldiers."

After entering Palermo unopposed on July 23, Patton turned east toward Messina and tried to outdo Monty. "This is a horse race in which the prestige of the U.S. Army is at stake," he said. "We must take Messina before the British." Like the British, however, the Americans found the going harder as they neared the Etna Line. Part of Patton's army edged along Highway 113 on the north coast, which the Germans had obstructed (below), while other units moved inland and blasted through the Etna Line at Troina. Patton's vanguard entered Messina on August 17 a few hours ahead of Montgomery's lead troops. But Kesselring eluded them by evacuating more than 100,000 Axis soldiers and 10,000 vehicles to the Italian mainland. ∎

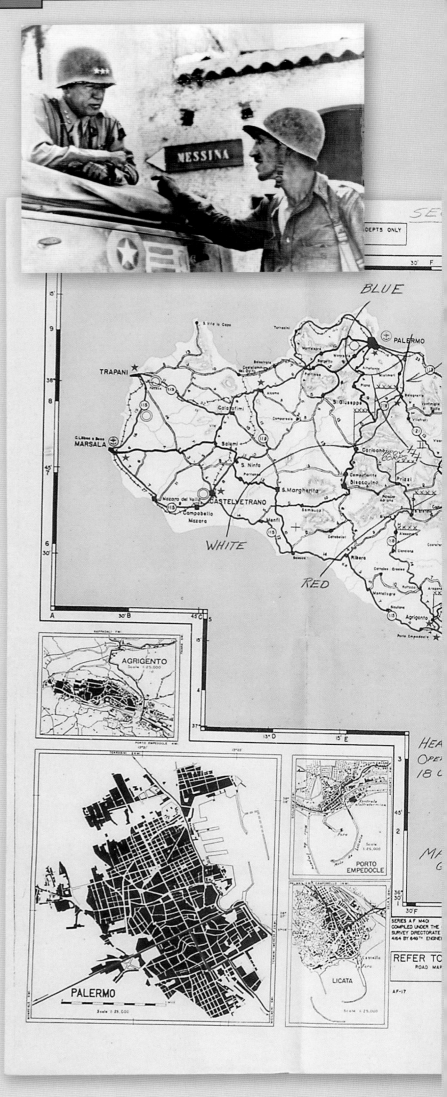

SIDETRACKED Men of Patton's Third Infantry Division descend a steep cliff after German engineers blew up the road on Sicily's north coast.

ROAD TO MESSINA Wearing three stars on his helmet as a lieutenant general, Patton confers with Lt. Col. Lyle Bernard, commander of the U.S. 30th Infantry Regiment, on the way to Messina (opposite). Patton's map below shows his headquarters at Gela on the south coast and the dividing line between his Seventh Army in the west and Montgomery's Eighth Army in the east as of July 18. After taking Palermo (detailed bottom left), he was authorized to advance east to Messina (detailed below right) in conjunction with Montgomery's army. Many Sicilians had lost faith in Mussolini, and some sympathized with Americans like the wounded soldier at right, receiving blood plasma from a medic.

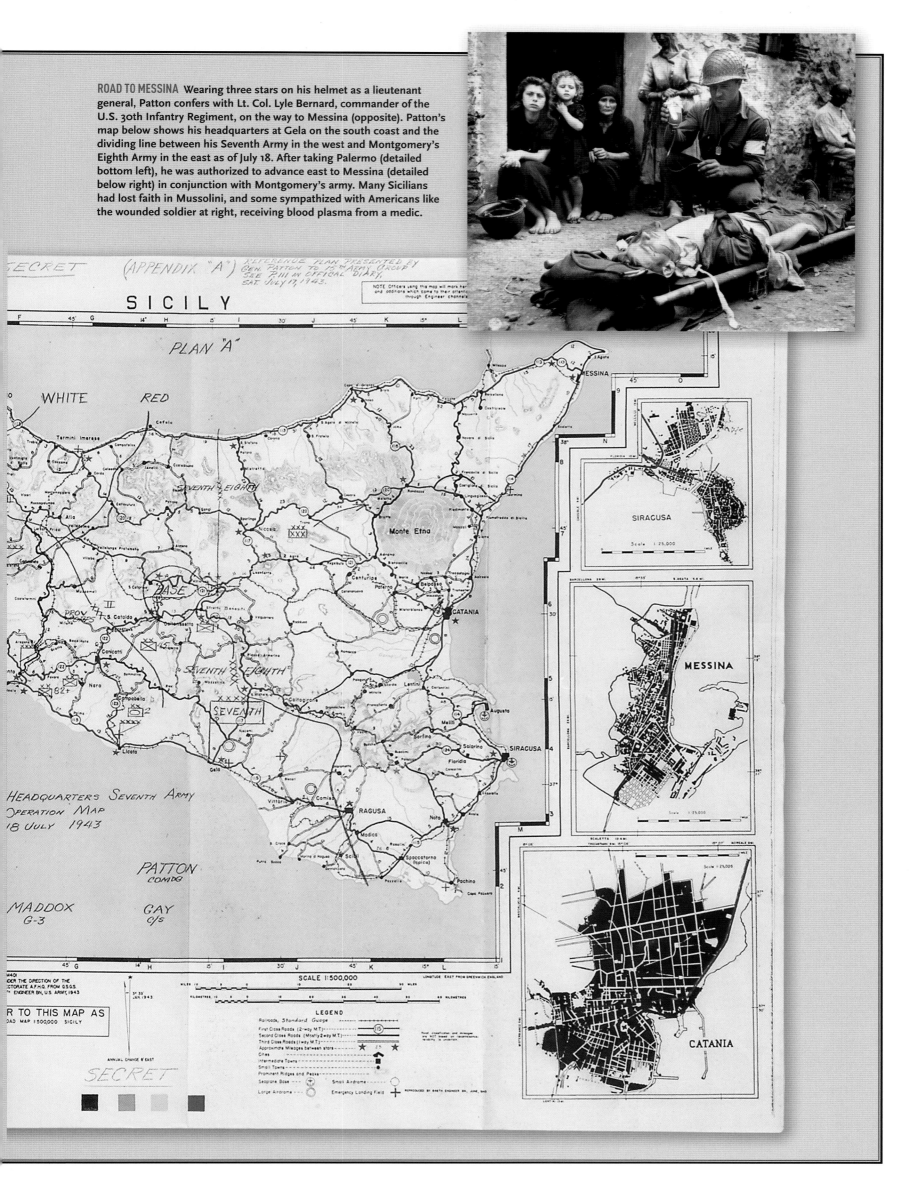

ALLIED ADVANCES IN SOUTHERN ITALY

Disgraced by the collapse of Italian resistance on Sicily, Mussolini was deposed and arrested on July 25, 1943. His successor, Field Marshal Pietro Badoglio, declared that Italy would remain in the Axis but entered into secret talks with the Allies. Suspecting that Badoglio would soon capitulate, Hitler sent seven German divisions to hold northern Italy and authorized a commando operation to free Mussolini (below), who would serve as Hitler's puppet in the north. In late August, Kesselring's troops withdrew from the boot of Italy toward Salerno, a likely landing zone for an Allied advance on Naples and Rome (see map opposite). That withdrawal spared Montgomery's Eighth Army, which crossed from Messina and landed with ease at Reggio di Calabria on September 3. But it spelled trouble for Lt. Gen. Mark Wayne Clark and his recently formed U.S. Fifth Army, which included the British X Corps. The Seventh Army was reserved for future operations in France, which had priority over Italy, and its commander, Patton, was reprimanded and reassigned after assailing two shell-shocked soldiers he deemed cowards.

Word that Badoglio had surrendered to the Allies cheered Clark's forces as they neared Salerno. But Germans were ready for them when they landed on September 9 and came under fire from planes, tanks, and artillery. Allied warships offshore helped suppress German defenses as time went on, but Clark's decision to land British and American troops on opposite sides of a river entering the Gulf of Salerno left him in a bind when German armored forces attacked the American sector on the 13th. Reinforced by paratroopers of the 82nd Airborne and troops of the U.S. 45th Infantry Division and aided by Allied air strikes, Clark's troops hit back and held on until the Eighth Army arrived from the south and threatened to outflank the Germans, who withdrew north of Naples. The Allies entered that city on October 1 to find the docks wrecked, the water and sewage systems destroyed, and the ruins mined by their foes. Since landing, the Fifth Army had suffered 10,000 casualties. Hard fighting lay ahead as the Allies entered the Apennine Mountains and confronted the formidable German Gustav Line (Winter Line), which barred their way to Rome. ∎

DICTATOR'S FLIGHT After being freed by German commandos from a mountaintop lodge, where he was held captive, Mussolini prepares to board a plane for Germany, where Hitler would then send him back to Italy to serve as a Fascist figurehead in the north. The rescue took place on September 12, 1943, three days after Allied troops landed at Salerno, supported by warships that provided antiaircraft fire day and night (right) and also targeted German tanks and artillery.

ITALIAN CAMPAIGN
July 9, 1943 – May 7, 1945

GERMANY

HUNGARY

SWITZERLAND

FRANCE

Mulhouse
Basel
Besançon
Zürich
Bern
Vaduz ★ **LIECHTENSTEIN**
Innsbruck
Salzburg
Graz
Lausanne
Geneva
Como
Bergamo
Brescia
Trento May 3, 1945
Vicenza
Verona Apr. 26, 1945
Treviso
Udine
May 2, 1945
Ljubljana
Trieste
May 7, 1945
Zagreb
Pécs
Novi Sad

CROATIA

Monza
Novara
MILAN Apr. 27, 1945
Reggio nell'Emilia
Padua Apr. 29, 1945
VENICE
Rijeka
Turin May 2, 1945
Piacenza Apr. 29, 1945
Parma
U.S. 5TH ARMY
Ferrara Apr. 23, 1945
Banja Luka
Genoa
Modena
Bologna
Jan. 15–Apr. 8, 1945
Ravenna
DALMATIA (Italian Governorate)
Sarajevo

Nice
MONACO
Apr. 23, 1945 Gothic Line
Aug. 4–26, 1944
Pisa
Livorno
Poggibonsi
Prato
Florence
Forlì
Rimini Sept. 25, 1944
SAN MARINO
Pesaro
Aug. 4–26, 1944
Ancona
Split

Ligurian Sea

Cecina
Arezzo
ITALY
June 17, 1944
BRITISH 8TH ARMY
MONTENEGRO

German forces evacuate Oct. 5, 1944
CORSICA
Ajaccio
U.S. 5TH ARMY
Perugia
June 17, 1944
Orvieto
Terni
Pescara
Gustav Line Jan. 15 – May 11, 1944
DALMATIA (Italian Governorate)
Cetinje

June 9, 1944
ROME ★ June 4, 1944
Oct. 8, 1943
Sept. 28, 1943
June 5, 1944
Feb. 19, 1944
Latina
Anzio Nettuno
Terracina
Cassino
Foggia
Durrës
Gaeta
Giugliano in Campania
NAPLES
Sept. 25, 1943
Bari
Sept. 14, 1943

German forces evacuate Sept. 19, 1944
SARDINIA
U.S. VI CORPS
Auletta
Brindisi
OPERATION SHINGLE January 22, 1944
Salerno
U.S. 5TH ARMY Clark
Sept. 14, 1943
Taranto
BRITISH 1ST AIRBORNE DIVISION

Sassari
Tyrrhenian Sea
OPERATION AVALANCHE September 9, 1943
Sept. 14, 1943
Corigliano Calabro
OPERATION SLAPSTICK September 9, 1943

Cagliari
15TH ARMY GROUP
U.S. 5TH ARMY, U.S. 7TH ARMY AND BRITISH 8TH ARMY
Alexander
Sept. 9, 1943

Mediterranean Sea
SICILY
Messina
Palermo
Trapani
Reggio di Calabria
BRITISH 8TH ARMY
OPERATION BAYTOWN September 3, 1943

Axis territory, July 9, 1943
Axis satellite or puppet state, July 9, 1943
Allied territory, July 9, 1943
Allied-occupied territory, July 9, 1943
Neutral state, July 9, 1943

Bizerte
Enna
Catania July 23, 1943
Licata
Gela
Syracuse
Avola

→ U.S. 5TH Army advance
--▶ British 8TH Army advance
······ Allied front line
∿∿∿ Axis defensive line

ALGERIA
Tunis
'Aïn Beïda
TUNISIA
Sousse
Pantelleria
Linosa
U.S. 7TH ARMY Patton
OPERATION HUSKY July 9 – August 17, 1943
Valletta
MALTA (British Crown Colony)
BRITISH 8TH ARMY Montgomery

Qairouan

0 mi 50 100
0 km 50 100
July 1943 features are shown.

LONG HAUL As detailed above, the Eighth Army landed at Reggio di Calabria on September 3, 1943, six days before the Fifth Army landed at Salerno and the British First Airborne Division—transported by ship for lack of aircraft—landed at Taranto. Determined German resistance along the Gustav Line south of Rome during the winter of 1943–44 and along the Gothic Line in late 1944 prolonged the war in Italy until Germany surrendered in 1945.

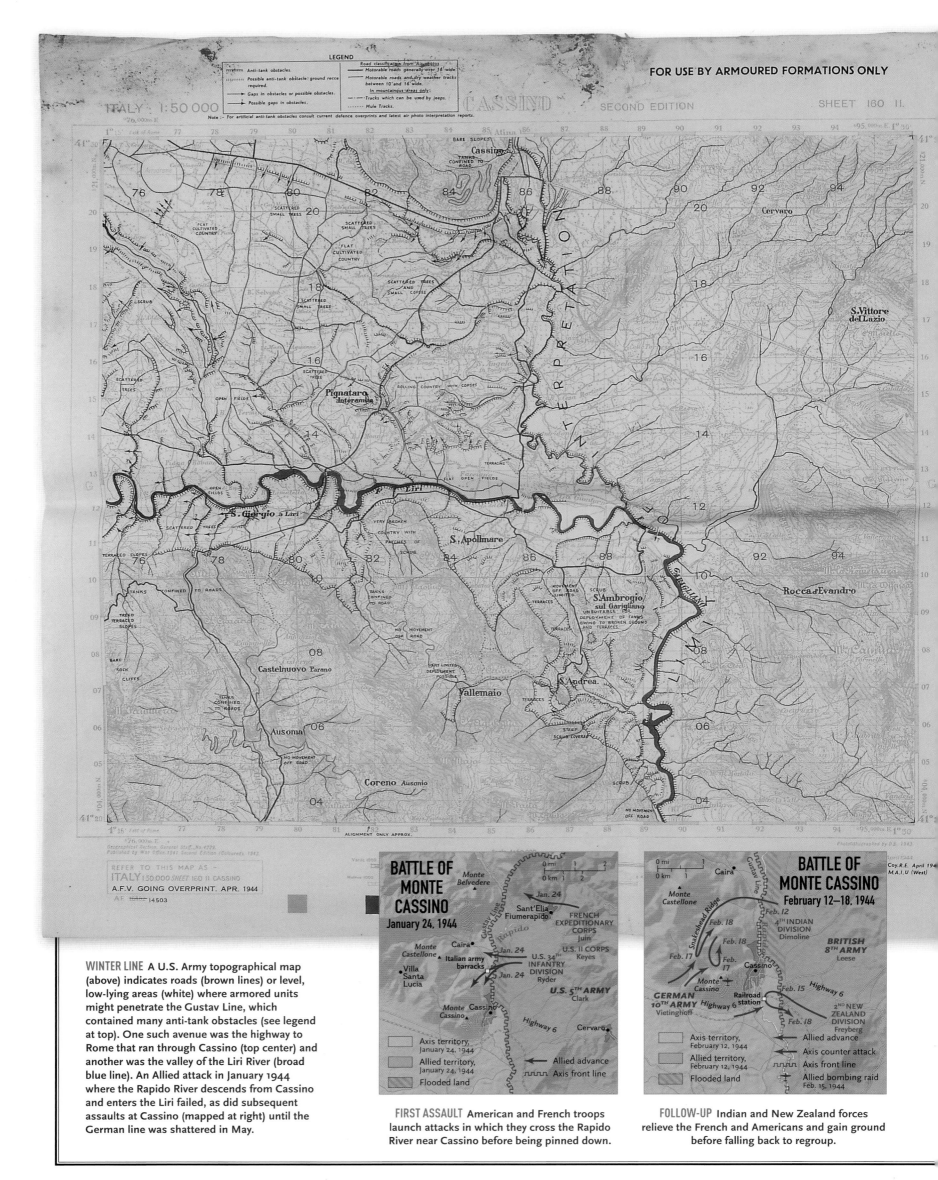

BATTLE OF MONTE CASSINO
January 24, 1944

Monte Belvedere

Jan. 24

Sant'Elia Fiumerapido

FRENCH EXPEDITIONARY CORPS
Juin

Monte Castellone

Caira

Italian army barracks

Jan. 24

Villa Santa Lucia

U.S. II CORPS
Keyes

U.S. 34TH INFANTRY DIVISION
Ryder

Jan. 24

U.S. 5TH ARMY
Clark

Monte Cassino

Monte Cassino

Highway 6

Cervaro

Axis territory, January 24, 1944
Allied territory, January 24, 1944
Flooded land
→ Allied advance
Axis front line

FIRST ASSAULT American and French troops launch attacks in which they cross the Rapido River near Cassino before being pinned down.

BATTLE OF MONTE CASSINO
February 12–18, 1944

Caira

Monte Castellone

Snakeshead Ridge

Feb. 18

Feb. 18

Feb. 17

Feb. 12

4TH INDIAN DIVISION
Dimoline

BRITISH 8TH ARMY
Leese

Feb. 17

Feb. 17

Cassino

Monte Cassino

Railroad station

Feb. 15

Highway 6

GERMAN 10TH ARMY
Vietinghoff

Highway 6

Feb. 18

2ND NEW ZEALAND DIVISION
Freyberg

Axis territory, February 12, 1944
Allied territory, February 12, 1944
Flooded land
→ Allied advance
← Axis counter attack
Axis front line
→ Allied bombing raid Feb. 15, 1944

FOLLOW-UP Indian and New Zealand forces relieve the French and Americans and gain ground before falling back to regroup.

WINTER LINE A U.S. Army topographical map (above) indicates roads (brown lines) or level, low-lying areas (white) where armored units might penetrate the Gustav Line, which contained many anti-tank obstacles (see legend at top). One such avenue was the highway to Rome that ran through Cassino (top center) and another was the valley of the Liri River (broad blue line). An Allied attack in January 1944 where the Rapido River descends from Cassino and enters the Liri failed, as did subsequent assaults at Cassino (mapped at right) until the German line was shattered in May.

BLASTED BATTLEGROUND An aerial view shows the town of Cassino in ruins following Allied bombing raids in mid-March 1944, one month after the Monte Cassino monastery above the town was blasted in similar fashion. The bombing failed to crush resistance by German troops, who found cover amid the rubble and kept up the fight.

THE ITALIAN CAMPAIGN

COLLISION AT CASSINO

Perched high above the town of Cassino, the historic Benedictine monastery on Monte Cassino was caught in the crosshairs when Clark's Fifth Army targeted the formidable Gustav Line, known to the Allies as the Winter Line, in early 1944. That German defensive barrier included fortified artillery and machine-gun posts on high ground overlooking rivers that Clark's troops had to cross and passes they had to secure to reach Rome, 80 miles to the northwest. Big guns on Monte Cassino and other peaks and minefields in the valleys made advances so perilous that the Allies sought to skirt that line by landing at Anzio, situated on Italy's west coast, just 30 miles from Rome. With the invasion of France approaching, however, not enough troops or landing craft were available to ensure success at Anzio. Costly assaults on the Gustav Line would continue, which if repulsed would at least keep German defenders tied down while the risky Anzio operation unfolded. Shortly before troops landed there on January 22, Clark launched a disastrous attack south of Cassino where the Rapido River enters the Liri River. "We had the feeling we were being sacrificed," recalled a sergeant in the U.S. 36th Infantry Division, which lost nearly 1,700 men there.

More sacrifices lay ahead as fighting intensified at Cassino, linked to Rome by a highway and railroad. American and Allied forces of various nationalities tried repeatedly to take that town (see battle maps at left), reduced to rubble by Allied bombers, which also pulverized the Monte Cassino monastery. Dubbed "Little Stalingrad" for the brutal fighting that occurred amid the ruins there and in the town below, Monte Cassino remained in enemy hands until it was seized in May by Polish soldiers, who had been released from Soviet prison camps to fight the Germans. Their attack formed part of a massive assault on the Gustav Line, which collapsed shortly before troops at Anzio broke out of the beachhead where they long been confined and advanced on Rome. ∎

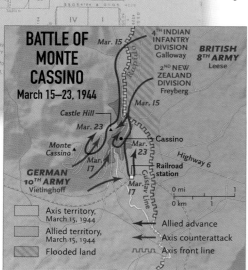

QUAGMIRE Germans repulse New Zealanders in Cassino's ruins, and Indian forces are stopped short of Monte Cassino.

BREAKTHROUGH Poles capture Monte Cassino while other Allied forces shatter the Gustav Line to the south and advance on Rome.

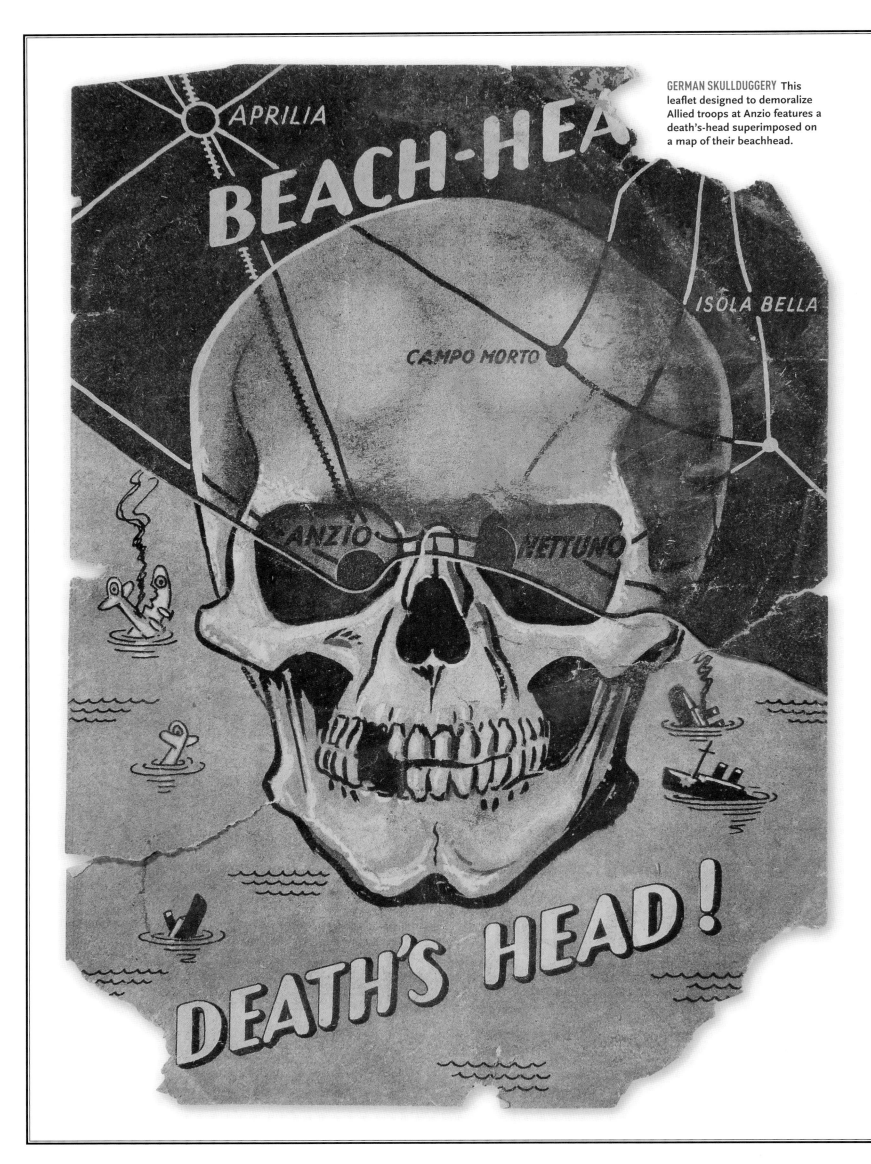

GERMAN SKULLDUGGERY This leaflet designed to demoralize Allied troops at Anzio features a death's-head superimposed on a map of their beachhead.

APRILIA

BEACH-HEA

ISOLA BELLA

CAMPO MORTO

ANZIO NETTUNO

DEATH'S HEAD!

FROM ANZIO TO ROME

Conceived as a shortcut to Rome, Anzio nearly became a dead end for tens of thousands of Allied troops. Two divisions landed there unopposed in January 1944, but those forces were not sufficient to induce their cautious commander, Maj. Gen. John Lucas, to move out before Germans boxed them in. A German propaganda leaflet (opposite) warning troops at Anzio that their beachhead would become a death trap was not an idle threat. In February, panzers and infantry penetrated that beachhead and wreaked havoc before the attack faltered under intense artillery fire and air strikes.

Maj. Gen. Lucian Truscott, the keen commander of the U.S. Third Infantry Division, then replaced Lucas and held Anzio while reinforcements arrived. In May, he was instructed to break out of the beachhead and cut off the German 10th Army as it retreated from the crumbling Gustav Line. Advancing on May 23, his forces pushed toward Valmontone to block

Highway 6 (see map at left), the main German avenue of retreat. But Fifth Army commander Clark was itching to take Rome and ordered Truscott to divert forces from Valmontone to the Italian capital. "I was dumbfounded," recalled Truscott, whose effort to stop the 10th Army from escaping to fight again in northern Italy fizzled while Clark rushed to the capital. "To be first in Rome was poor compensation for this lost opportunity," concluded Truscott. Clark's capture of Rome, from which Germans withdrew before his troops arrived on June 5, 1944, was overshadowed by the Allied invasion of Normandy the following day—and by the grueling campaign to liberate northern Italy that continued until the war in Europe ended. ■

BREAKOUT FROM ANZIO
May 23 – June 4, 1944

★ ROME
June 4
Colonna
Palestrina
Frascati
Highway 6
June 2
Rocca di Papa
Labico
Marino
Valmontone
Lake Albano
Albano Laziale
Ariccia
May 30
Artena
Velletri
Lanuvio
May 26
Cori
Pratica di Mare
Ardea
Cisterna di Roma
May 23
May 25
U.S. VI CORPS Truscott
May 23
Littoria
Nettuno
Anzio

0 mi 5 10
0 km 5 10
May 1944 features are shown.

Contact with U.S. II Corps May 25

Axis territory, May 23, 1944
Allied front line, May 23, 1944
Allied territory, May 23, 1944
Allied front line, May 25, 1944
Allied advance
Allied front line, May 26, 1944

BREAKOUT Above, Allied reinforcements disembark at Anzio following fighting in early 1944 that left buildings in ruins. As mapped at upper left, Truscott's troops broke out of the Anzio beachhead on May 23 and advanced toward Highway 6 at Valmontone to cut off Germans retreating from the Gustav Line. But Clark then shifted many of Truscott's forces toward Rome, where Italian civilians welcomed Americans by displaying the Stars and Stripes (upper right). Truscott and others thought Clark should have given priority to capturing German troops, who did not stop fighting when Rome fell.

AERIAL ARMADA American B-17s head out from England to bomb German war industries in August 1943, escorted partway by fighters leaving contrails. The map below shows the range of Allied bombers based in England and Italy and designates targets, including German cities and launchpads for missiles deployed late in the war. Unlike the strategic Eighth Air Force, the tactical Ninth Air Force provided close support for Allied troops.

ALLIED BOMBING RAIDS
August – November, 1943

Legend:

- Axis territory, Oct. 7, 1943
- Axis satellite or puppet state, Oct. 7, 1943
- Allied territory, Oct. 7, 1943
- Allied-held territory, Oct. 7, 1943
- Neutral state, Oct. 7, 1943
- Allied front line
- 8th Air Force
- 9th Air Force
- 15th Air Force
- Royal Air Force (RAF)
- Airfield and aircraft construction
- Densely populated area
- Nazi Party center
- Oil refinery
- Railway center
- Secret weapons site
- Shipbuilding center
- U-boat installation
- War industry facility

United States 15th Air Force begins operations from Foggia Nov. 2, 1943

Allied front line Oct. 7, 1943

AIR WAR OVER EUROPE

BOMBING AROUND THE CLOCK

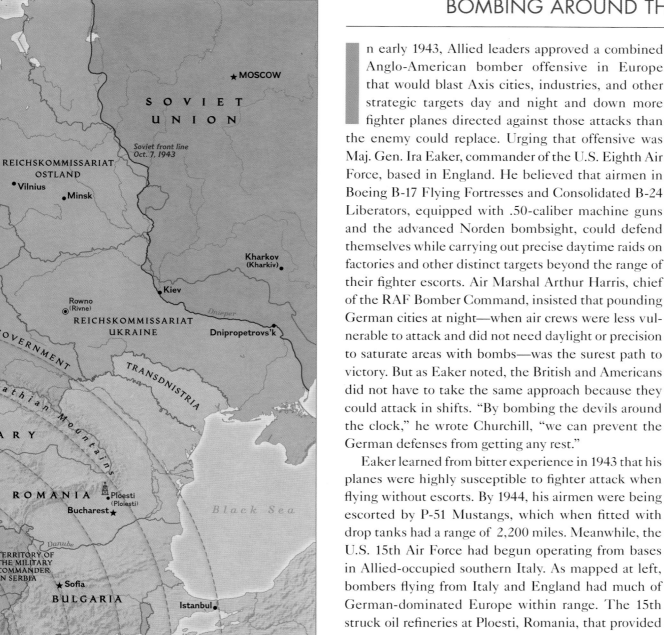

In early 1943, Allied leaders approved a combined Anglo-American bomber offensive in Europe that would blast Axis cities, industries, and other strategic targets day and night and down more fighter planes directed against those attacks than the enemy could replace. Urging that offensive was Maj. Gen. Ira Eaker, commander of the U.S. Eighth Air Force, based in England. He believed that airmen in Boeing B-17 Flying Fortresses and Consolidated B-24 Liberators, equipped with .50-caliber machine guns and the advanced Norden bombsight, could defend themselves while carrying out precise daytime raids on factories and other distinct targets beyond the range of their fighter escorts. Air Marshal Arthur Harris, chief of the RAF Bomber Command, insisted that pounding German cities at night—when air crews were less vulnerable to attack and did not need daylight or precision to saturate areas with bombs—was the surest path to victory. But as Eaker noted, the British and Americans did not have to take the same approach because they could attack in shifts. "By bombing the devils around the clock," he wrote Churchill, "we can prevent the German defenses from getting any rest."

Eaker learned from bitter experience in 1943 that his planes were highly susceptible to fighter attack when flying without escorts. By 1944, his airmen were being escorted by P-51 Mustangs, which when fitted with drop tanks had a range of 2,200 miles. Meanwhile, the U.S. 15th Air Force had begun operating from bases in Allied-occupied southern Italy. As mapped at left, bombers flying from Italy and England had much of German-dominated Europe within range. The 15th struck oil refineries at Ploesti, Romania, that provided the Reich with nearly a third of its petrol, and the Eighth targeted German plants that were deriving oil from coal.

Like the British, American crews sometimes bombed cities at night, using incendiaries to kindle firestorms. More than a million Germans were killed or wounded in such attacks, which also cost the lives of many airmen targeted by night fighters and antiaircraft batteries (right). More effective militarily were air raids on targets like the French railroad network, which was blasted in early 1944 to slow the German response to the looming Allied invasion. By then, the Luftwaffe had lost so many fighters defending against bombers that the Allies were advancing from air superiority to air supremacy. ■

CHRONOLOGY

JANUARY 21, 1943 Allied chiefs authorize a combined bomber offensive in which the RAF will blast German cities at night and the U.S. Eighth Air Force will conduct daylight raids on strategic targets.

JULY 27–28, 1943 RAF bombers ignite a firestorm in Hamburg, Germany, where more than 40,000 people are killed.

AUGUST 17, 1943 U.S. Eighth Air Force loses 60 B-17 bombers in daylight raids on German arms factories conducted without fighter escorts.

DECEMBER 11, 1943 Long-range P-51 Mustangs of the 354th Fighter Group begin escorting American bombers to Germany.

APRIL 5, 1944 The U.S. 15th Air Force based in Italy launches air raids on Ploesti, Romania, a major source of refined oil for Germany.

FEARSOME FLAK Whether operating day or night, Allied airmen on bombing missions had to contend not just with Luftwaffe fighters but with radar-coordinated antiaircraft batteries like the one below, firing its powerful 88-mm guns in unison. Even high-flying B-17s at altitudes approaching 30,000 feet were vulnerable to such batteries.

TARGETING THE ENEMY

Aerial reconnaissance, used to gather intelligence on enemy assets and map bombing targets, evolved rapidly during World War II. Cameras like the F24—shown below being operated from a Blenheim bomber early in the war—were surpassed by cameras with lenses that had a longer focal length and higher resolution for use in advanced reconnaissance aircraft operating above the limit of antiaircraft batteries and most fighters. Reconnaissance versions of the Supermarine Spitfire could reach altitudes above 40,000 feet. De Havilland Mosquito reconnaissance planes flew nearly as high, had a range of more than 2,000 miles, and carried up to four fixed cameras, which operated automatically and could produce stereoscopic images for a three-dimensional view of target areas.

Transforming reconnaissance photographs into targeting maps involved careful research and analysis. Intelligence reports and existing maps could help identify specific targets within a photo like that of the district in Rome outlined below, taken by an Allied reconnaissance plane in April 1943 when the city was still an Axis stronghold. The map derived from that photograph (opposite bottom) pinpoints several places of strategic value to the Axis, including the San Lorenzo freight depot. Bombing such targets with precision, however, was a greater technological challenge than mapping them accurately. Air raids on that freight depot and other transportation facilities in Rome on July 19, 1943, caused widespread damage and killed 3,000 people. ∎

TARGET-SPOTTER An RAF reconnaissance photographer peers through a bulky F24 camera from the open observation port of a bomber in 1940—a technique improved on as reconnaissance aircraft with fixed cameras of higher resolution entered service. The technology available when the area outlined at right was photographed from high above Rome in 1943 yielded a revealing close-up (opposite left), from which a targeting map of the San Lorenzo freight depot and nearby facilities was drawn (opposite right).

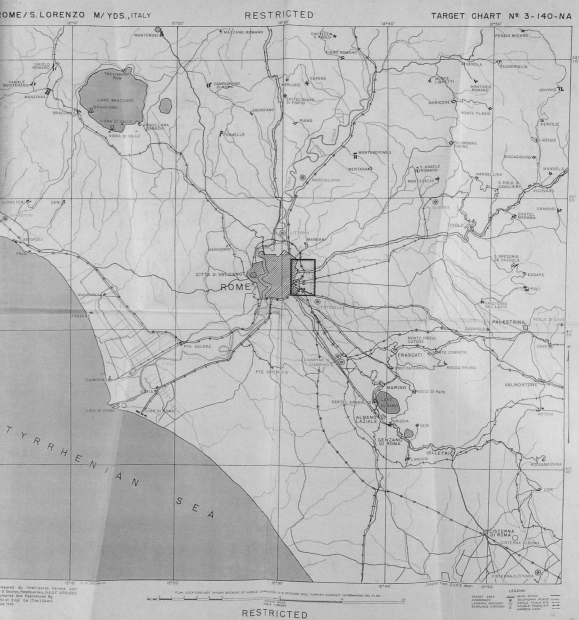

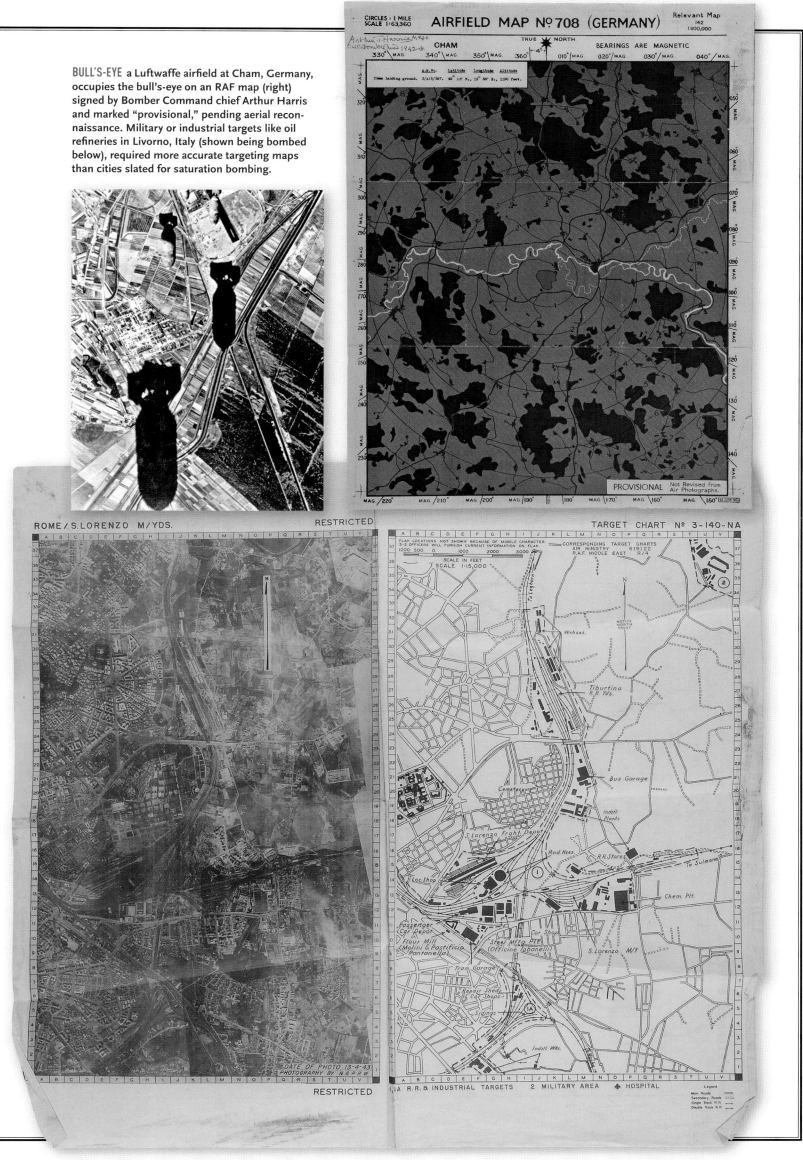

BULL'S-EYE a Luftwaffe airfield at Cham, Germany, occupies the bull's-eye on an RAF map (right) signed by Bomber Command chief Arthur Harris and marked "provisional," pending aerial reconnaissance. Military or industrial targets like oil refineries in Livorno, Italy (shown being bombed below), required more accurate targeting maps than cities slated for saturation bombing.

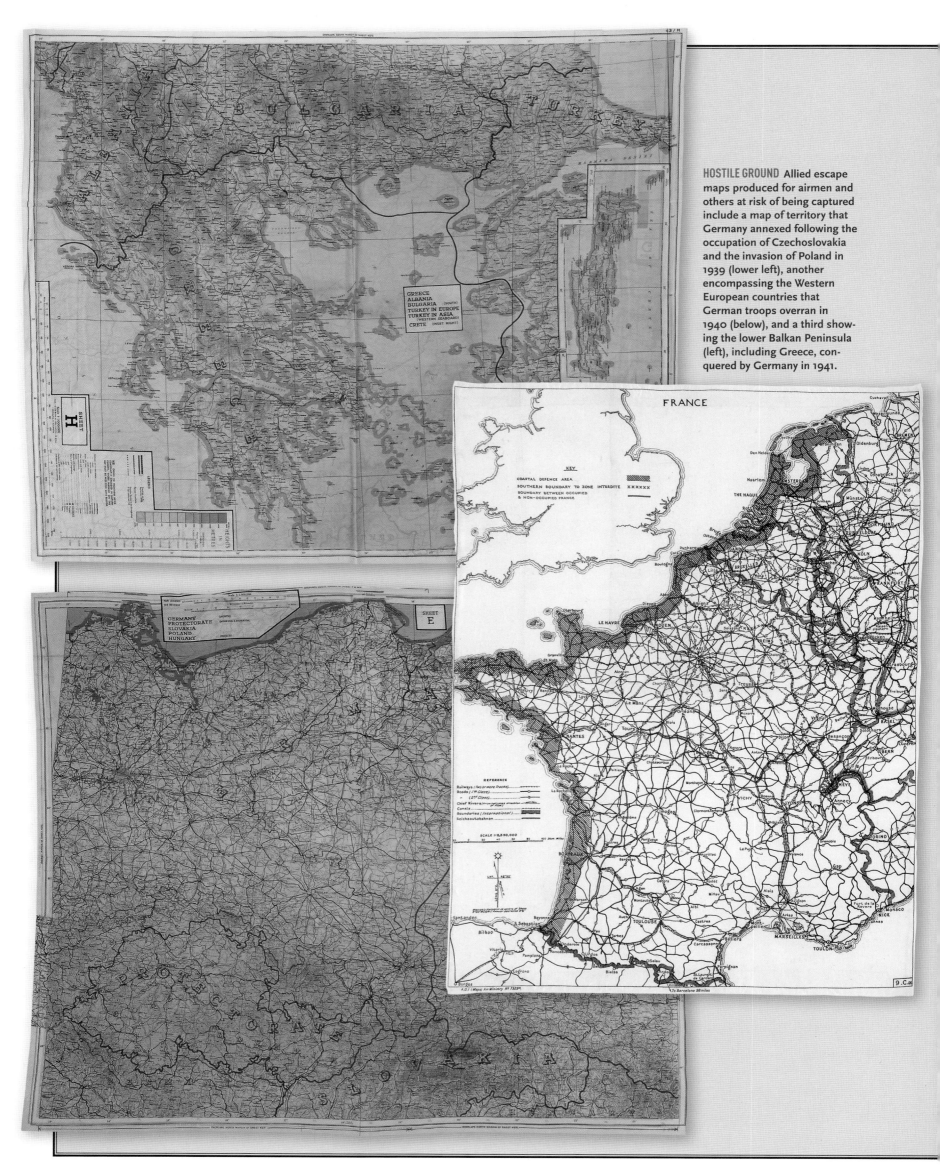

HOSTILE GROUND Allied escape maps produced for airmen and others at risk of being captured include a map of territory that Germany annexed following the occupation of Czechoslovakia and the invasion of Poland in 1939 (lower left), another encompassing the Western European countries that German troops overran in 1940 (below), and a third showing the lower Balkan Peninsula (left), including Greece, conquered by Germany in 1941.

ESCAPE MAPS FOR DOWNED AIRMEN

Some Allied airmen downed over enemy territory were sheltered by people at odds with the Germans and their Axis allies. The Americans shown resting in a hayloft in Yugoslavia (below right), for example, were among hundreds taken in by partisans who resisted the Axis occupation there, including Chetniks who harbored the servicemen until the OSS arranged for them to be flown back to 15th Air Force bases in Italy. Most downed airmen, however, would end up spending the rest of the war in prison camps unless they managed to evade capture or escape confinement. Allied agencies such as the OSS and Britain's MI9 equipped departing airmen and other servicemen for escape and evasion by issuing them special maps and other gear. Operating on the principle that prisoners of war (POWs)—particularly those with special training and skills like airmen—should try to break out and return to duty, MI9 spared no effort to design maps and compasses like those below, which servicemen could conceal from their captors.

Escape maps like those shown here were based on the best available prewar maps of European countries, to which significant wartime details were added for escapees such as the thick red line on the map of France, Belgium, and Holland opposite, indicating German coastal defenses of the Atlantic Wall. Many maps were printed on silk or other soft fabric that was waterproof, easily concealed, and silent when handled, and that did not crease or tear when compressed. Although most escape attempts failed, such maps helped some POWs make successful "home runs" to Allied territory and reminded others that "Fortress Europe" was neither impregnable nor inescapable. ■

POINTERS Displayed below on a 1944 escape map of central Germany are mini-compasses that could be concealed by prisoners inside buttons, badges, or pipe stems (bottom left) as well as strips of magnetized steel that pointed north when balanced on a belt buckle (bottom center) or spike (bottom right).

TUSKEGEE AIRMEN

Before they flew as fighters over Europe, black pilots known as the Tuskegee Airmen for their Alabama training ground faced flak from their fellow Americans. Their commander, Lt. Col. Benjamin Davis, Jr.—shown briefing pilots with his hand on a map (below) and standing in flight gear beside his P-47 Thunderbolt (opposite)—had been shunned at West Point by his white classmates. "What they did not realize," Davis wrote, "was that I was stubborn enough to put up with their treatment to reach the goal I had come to obtain." After he and his pilots began flying combat missions in North Africa, their performance was criticized by a superior officer, whose claims were investigated and refuted.

Tuskegee Airmen proved their mettle in Italy, downing a dozen German fighters in two days in late January 1944. Ira Eaker, the newly appointed chief of the Mediterranean Allied Air Forces, then assigned Davis's 332nd Fighter Group to close escort duty, which meant clinging to 15th Air Force bombers flying from bases in Italy and fighting only when those bombers were attacked. That offered fewer chances for the kills aces compiled when they were free to roam and pounce on their foes. But as shown on the cover of an album in which these photographs were preserved (left), Tuskegee Airmen took pride in their role as "protectors" and excelled at shielding the bombers they escorted. By war's end, they had won 95 Distinguished Flying Crosses and helped clear the way for the desegregation of U.S. military forces in 1948. ■

PROTECTORS Among those pictured in this album is Lt. Louis Hill (below left) of the 477th Bombardment Group, which trained for bombing missions but did not enter combat. Also shown here are pilots of the 332nd Fighter Group beside a P-51 Mustang (bottom), three of the fighter group's P-47s in flight (opposite top), and Tuskegee Airmen posing before a bomber (opposite bottom).

FAR-RANGING FIGHTERS As mapped below, Tuskegee Airmen began serving as fighter pilots in North Africa in 1943 and supported the invasion of Sicily. By early 1944, they were based in southern Italy and flying missions to Monte Cassino and Anzio. Late in the war, Lt. Earl Lane (left) and other Tuskegee Airmen escorted bombers deep into Germany. On one such mission, Lane and two others in the 332nd each downed a Messerschmitt Me-262, the first operational jet fighter, introduced in mid-1944.

TUSKEGEE AIRMEN IN EUROPE
April 1943 – May 1945

April 1, 1943

- Axis territory
- Axis satellite or puppet state
- Allied territory
- Neutral state
- Allied front line, April 1, 1943

By April 9, 1945

- Allied front line, April 9, 1945
- Tuskegee mission
- Allied airfield

0 mi 200
0 km 200
April 1943 features are shown.

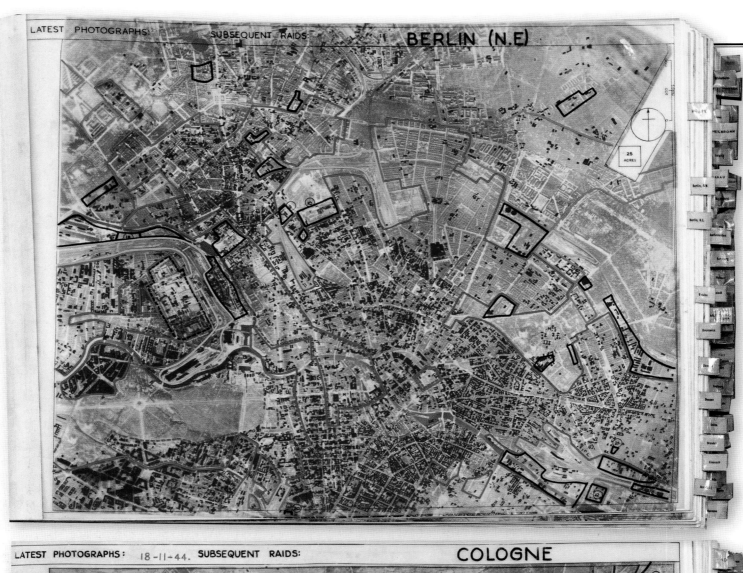

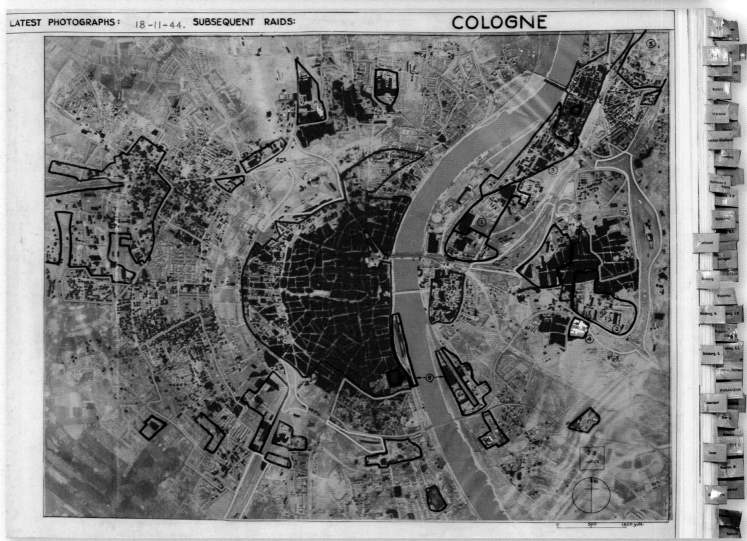

BOMBED OUT These bomb-damage assessment maps show the cumulative impact of multiple air raids on Cologne as of November 1944 (top) and on Berlin as of March 1945 (bottom). Based on aerial reconnaissance photos taken before and after air raids, they show urban areas that were badly damaged or destroyed in blue. Sectors that were fully built-up before they were bombed are outlined in red. Less-dense residential areas are outlined in green, and industrial areas are outlined in black.

BOMBING GERMAN CITIES

Beginning in March 1942, the RAF sent heavy bombers to blast German population centers with explosives and incendiaries, causing devastation that far exceeded the punishment inflicted on British cities by the Luftwaffe. The first targets chosen by Air Marshal Harris to test incendiary bombing tactics were Lübeck and Rostock, historic port cities on the Baltic whose wooden buildings erupted in flames. Then in late May 1942, Harris launched the first of many "thousand-bomber" raids on major cities by targeting Cologne. Like Berlin, Cologne had wide avenues that helped firemen contain blazes and avert a firestorm. In a single night, however, nearly 500 people were killed, 5,000 injured, and 45,000 left homeless. By late 1944, after numerous air raids, a bomb-damage assessment map based on photo-reconnaissance (opposite top) showed much of Cologne reduced to ruins (coded blue).

The morality and effectiveness of bombing cities would long be questioned. Targeting industrial centers such as Hamburg—where more than 40,000 people died in air raids that ignited a firestorm in July 1943—disrupted German war production, which was shifted away from cities as the bombing intensified but failed to meet the needs of German armed forces in the long run. Predictions that strategic bombing would turn horrified civilians against the war were not fulfilled, however. Germans gradually lost faith in Hitler, but support for the troops, whose losses far surpassed civilian casualties, remained firm. Despite repeated bombings of Berlin between August 1943 and March 1944 that caused widespread damage (see map, opposite bottom), the capital's civil defenses were so sturdy that fewer than 10,000 people were killed there in attacks that cost the RAF more than 2,500 casualties. Blistering assaults on German cities such as Dresden (below) would continue, but the Reich would be defeated not by bombers aloft but by soldiers on the ground. ■

DEADLY DEVASTATION A blackened statue overlooks charred ruins after Allied warplanes fire-bombed Dresden in February 1945, killing nearly 25,000 people. Although Churchill advocated bombing German cities, he later described strategic attacks aimed at civilians like the dazed survivors of bombed-out Mannheim (above left) as "acts of terror and wanton destruction."

THE OSS: DRAFTING INTELLIGENCE MAPS

Authorized by President Roosevelt in June 1942, the Office of Strategic Services (OSS) did much more than engage in espionage and covert operations. True to its title, it provided strategic services to a wide array of officers and officials, ranging from commanders in the field to the commander in chief in Washington. Maps produced by the OSS Cartography Department packed a wealth of information and intelligence into a visual frame that could be grasped quickly and clearly. The OSS map below, for example, sums up the territorial gains and losses of the opposing forces in Russia from late 1941, when the Germans appeared close to victory, to December 1942, when the tide began to turn in Russia's favor. For busy officials in Washington, such pictures could be worth more a thousand words by encapsulating campaigns that might take up an entire chapter in a written report.

During the war, a few dozen OSS cartographers—many of them geographers by training—produced more than 800 maps, a considerable accomplishment in an era when much of the work had to be done by hand. The tools of their trade included basic drafting instruments as well as specialized devices. An Austin Photo Interpretometer (opposite), for example, provided in-depth views of stereoscopic aerial reconnaissance photos, used to create conventional topographical maps as well as three-dimensional models of terrain that Allied forces would assault or invade. Existing maps in the agency's vast collection provided OSS cartographers with a framework, but filling in the picture involved meticulous research, analysis, and artistry. ■

Graphic lettering pen

Staedtler Mars Lumograph drawing leads

RUSSIAN REBOUND The OSS map above conveys Soviet counterattacks in late 1941 (left) and late 1942 (right) as black lines penetrating the red ground previously gained by their German foes. The intelligence conveyed by the map was that the Russians were remarkably resilient, capable of enduring staggering losses and striking back.

Dietzgen Champion drawing instruments (in box), including compasses, ruling pens, and other tools

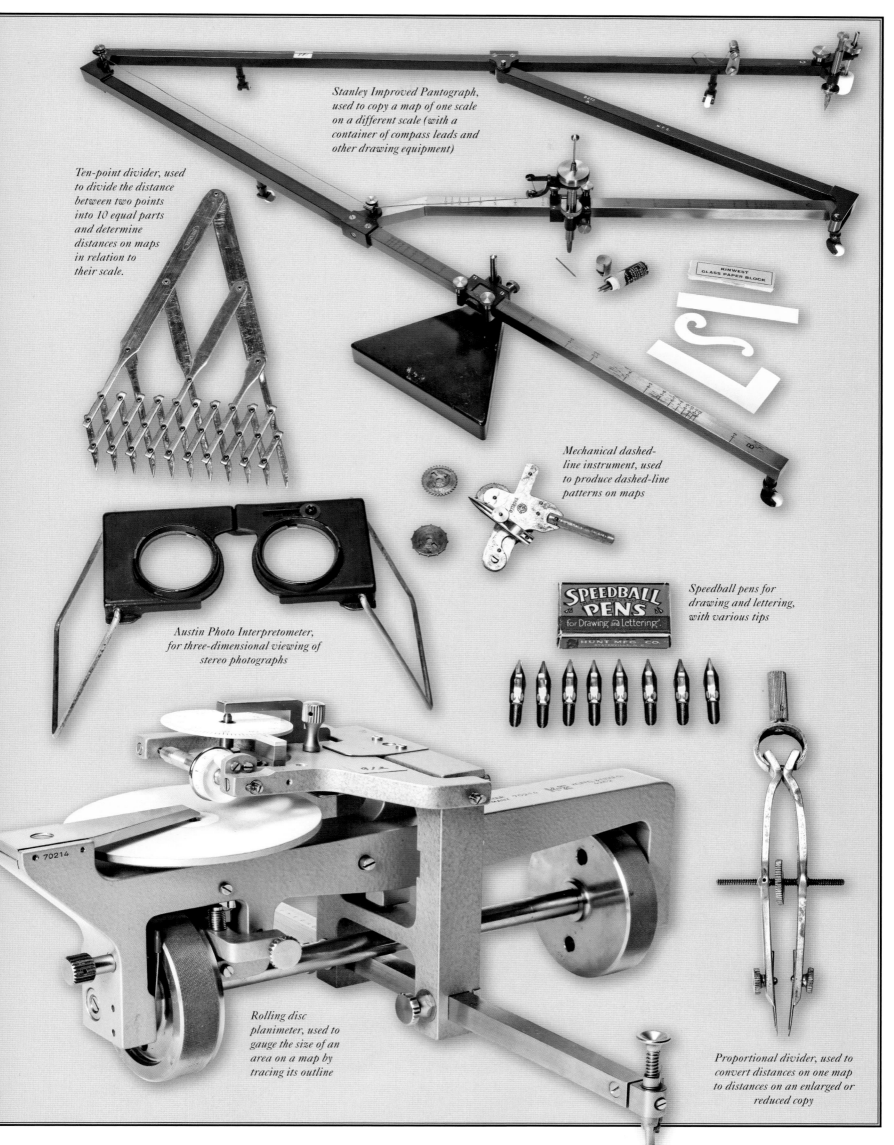

Stanley Improved Pantograph, used to copy a map of one scale on a different scale (with a container of compass leads and other drawing equipment)

Ten-point divider, used to divide the distance between two points into 10 equal parts and determine distances on maps in relation to their scale.

Mechanical dashed-line instrument, used to produce dashed-line patterns on maps

Speedball pens for drawing and lettering, with various tips

Austin Photo Interpretometer, for three-dimensional viewing of stereo photographs

Rolling disc planimeter, used to gauge the size of an area on a map by tracing its outline

Proportional divider, used to convert distances on one map to distances on an enlarged or reduced copy

RUSSIA
RESURGENT
BATTLES TO RECLAIM THE SOVIET UNION

CHRONOLOGY

MAY 12–28, 1942 Soviet troops are soundly defeated in the Second Battle of Kharkov.

JULY 3–4, 1942 Sevastopol, the last Russian stronghold in Crimea, falls to the Germans.

JULY 23, 1942 Hitler confirms plans to attack Stalingrad in conjunction with an advance on Baku in the Caucasus.

NOVEMBER 19, 1942 Red Army troops launch a counteroffensive at Stalingrad.

JANUARY 31, 1943 Gen. Friedrich Paulus surrenders the German Sixth Army at Stalingrad.

JULY 5–AUGUST 23, 1943 Soviets repulse German armored forces in the Battle of Kursk.

JANUARY 27, 1944 Russians break the siege of Leningrad.

Hitler spent long hours poring over maps of Russia, but he never fully grasped the enormity of that country or the challenges it posed to advancing armies. After his forces failed to reach Moscow before winter closed in and were driven back from the capital, he sent armies in pursuit of another distant objective in 1942—oil-rich Baku in the Caucasus, a tempting target in a contest that was as much about seizing fuel, food, and other vital resources as it was about seizing Russian territory. The campaign would be carried out by Army Group South, while Army Group Center held firm west of Moscow and Army Group North maintained its grip on Leningrad.

In May 1942, German troops crushed a bid by the Red Army to liberate the city of Kharkov and made gains in Crimea, where they would soon take Sevastopol. As Army Group South advanced, however, Soviet commanders conserved strength by pulling back. They hoped to contain and exhaust the Germans within an area bounded in the south by the Caucasus Mountains and in the east by a line extending from Voronezh on the Don River to Stalingrad on the Volga River (see map opposite). In July, Hitler divided Army Group South in two for an offensive code-named Operation Blue. Group A was assigned to cross the mountains and take Baku, while Group B shielded that advance by neutralizing the Voronezh-Stalingrad line. After Voronezh fell to the Germans, Hitler ordered the Sixth Army and Fourth Panzer Army to advance on Stalingrad and smash enemy forces there. He was stretching his troops too thin. The drive to Baku faltered in the rugged Caucasus, and Stalingrad became a death trap for Germans caught amid blasted ruins. The surrender of the Sixth Army there in early 1943 was ominous for the invaders, who lost a huge tank battle at Kursk in July and were pushed back toward their own border. The question was no longer whether the Soviet Union would survive but whether Nazi Germany could avoid destruction. ■

WELL ARMORED Pictured near Moscow in 1942, Russian crewmen meet with farmworkers whose contributions helped pay for their sturdy T-34 tanks, more than 50,000 of which were made during the war. The Russians lost more tanks than the Germans did but made up for it by outproducing their foes.

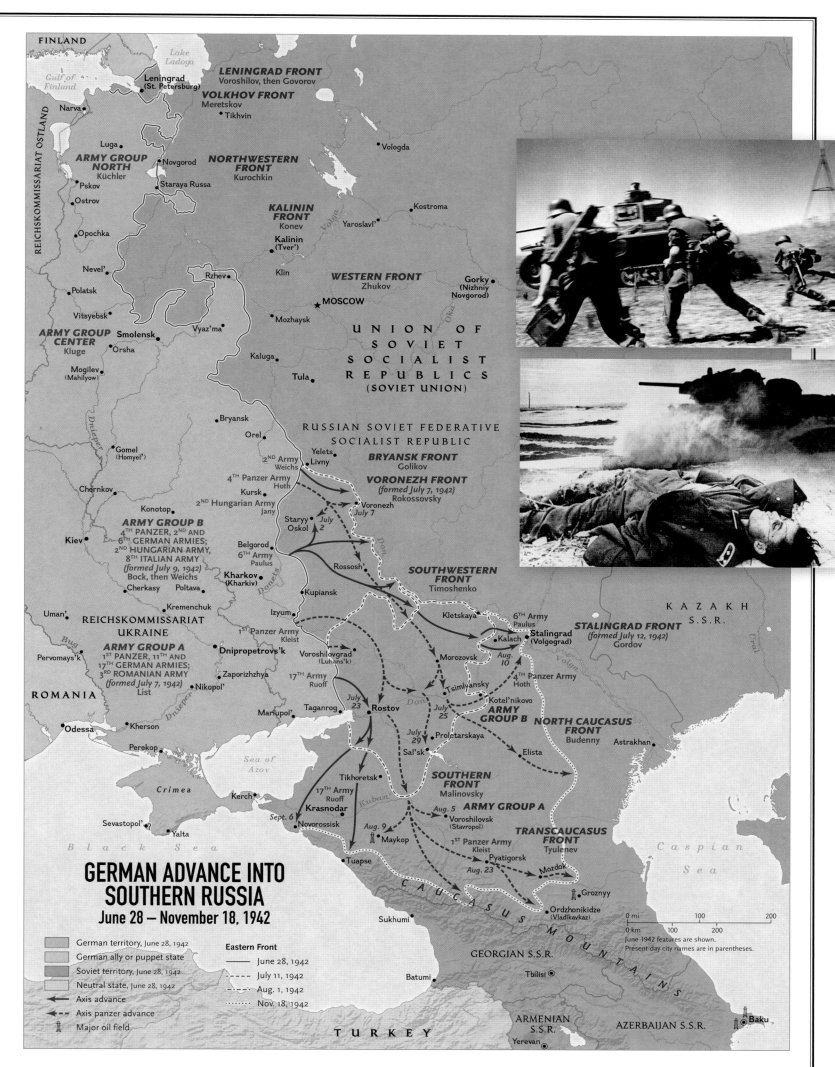

FINLAND

Gulf of Finland

Lake Ladoga

• Narva

• Leningrad (St. Petersburg)

LENINGRAD FRONT
Voroshilov, then Govorov

VOLKHOV FRONT
Meretskov

• Tikhvin

• Luga

ARMY GROUP NORTH
Küchler

• Novgorod

• Pskov

• Staraya Russa

• Ostrov

NORTHWESTERN FRONT
Kurochkin

• Vologda

• Opochka

• Kostroma

• Nevel'

KALININ FRONT
Konev

• Yaroslavl'

• Polatsk

• Rzhev

Kalinin (Tver')

• Klin

• Vitsyebsk

WESTERN FRONT
Zhukov

• Gorky (Nizhniy Novgorod)

ARMY GROUP CENTER
Kluge

Smolensk

• Vyaz'ma

• Mozhaysk

★ MOSCOW

• Orsha

• Mogilev (Mahilyow)

• Kaluga

U N I O N   O F   S O V I E T   S O C I A L I S T   R E P U B L I C S   (SOVIET UNION)

• Tula

• Bryansk

REICHSKOMMISSARIAT OSTLAND

• Gomel (Homyel')

• Orel

RUSSIAN SOVIET FEDERATIVE SOCIALIST REPUBLIC

• Chernkov

• Konotop

• Yelets

• Livny

2ND Army Weichs

BRYANSK FRONT
Golikov

4TH Panzer Army Hoth

• Kursk

VORONEZH FRONT
(formed July 7, 1942)
Rokossovsky

2ND Hungarian Army Jany

• Voronezh July 7

ARMY GROUP B
4TH PANZER, 2ND AND 6TH GERMAN ARMIES; 2ND HUNGARIAN ARMY, 8TH ITALIAN ARMY
(formed July 9, 1942)
Bock, then Weichs

Staryy Oskol *July 2*

• Kiev

Belgorod

6TH Army Paulus

Kharkov (Kharkiv)

• Cherkasy

• Poltava

• Kupiansk

• Rossosh'

SOUTHWESTERN FRONT
Timoshenko

• Kremenchuk

Izyum

• Kletskaya

6TH Army Paulus

KAZAKH S.S.R.

• Uman'

REICHSKOMMISSARIAT UKRAINE

1ST Panzer Army Kleist

• Kalach

Stalingrad (Volgograd)

STALINGRAD FRONT
(formed July 12, 1942)
Gordov

• Pervomays'k

ARMY GROUP A
1ST PANZER, 11TH AND 17TH GERMAN ARMIES; 3RD ROMANIAN ARMY
(formed July 7, 1942)
List

Dnipropetrovs'k

Voroshilovgrad (Luhans'k)

• Morozovsk

Aug. 10

4TH Panzer Army Hoth

• Zaporizhzhya

17TH Army Ruoff

• Nikopol'

ROMANIA

• Tsimlyansky

• Kotel'nikovo

ARMY GROUP B

NORTH CAUCASUS FRONT
Budenny

• Astrakhan

• Mariupol'

Taganrog

July 23 Rostov

July 25

• Odessa

• Kherson

July 29

Sal'sk

• Proletarskaya

• Elista

• Perekop

Sea of Azov

SOUTHERN FRONT
Malinovsky

Crimea

• Kerch

Tikhoretsk

Aug. 5

ARMY GROUP A

Voroshilovsk (Stavropol)

17TH Army Ruoff

Krasnodar

Sept. 6

• Novorossisk

Aug. 9

• Maykop

1ST Panzer Army Kleist

TRANSCAUCASUS FRONT
Tyulenev

• Pyatigorsk

Caspian Sea

• Sevastopol'

• Yalta

• Tuapse

Kuban

Aug. 23

• Mozdok

• Groznyy

Black Sea

• Ordzhonikidze (Vladikavkaz)

• Sukhumi

C A U C A S U S   M O U N T A I N S

GERMAN ADVANCE INTO SOUTHERN RUSSIA
June 28 – November 18, 1942

GEORGIAN S.S.R.

• Tbilisi

German territory, June 28, 1942	
German ally or puppet state	
Soviet territory, June 28, 1942	
Neutral state, June 28, 1942	

Eastern Front

— June 28, 1942
--- July 11, 1942
- - - Aug. 1, 1942
····· Nov. 18, 1942

→ Axis advance
-→ Axis panzer advance
⚑ Major oil field

0 mi   100   200
0 km   100   200

June 1942 features are shown.
Present-day city names are in parentheses.

ARMENIAN S.S.R.

AZERBAIJAN S.S.R.

⚑ Baku

T U R K E Y

• Batumi

• Yerevan

OPERATION BLUE In July 1942, after winning a crushing victory near Kharkov and seizing Crimea and Sevastopol, Army Group South was divided for Operation Blue (mapped above). Group A pushed into the Caucasus and was stopped well short of Baku. Group B was drawn into a desperate battle at Stalingrad. Russian counterattacks that winter (inset top) left many Germans who had advanced rapidly earlier in the year (inset bottom) frozen in their tracks.

BRUTAL STRUGGLE AT KHARKOV

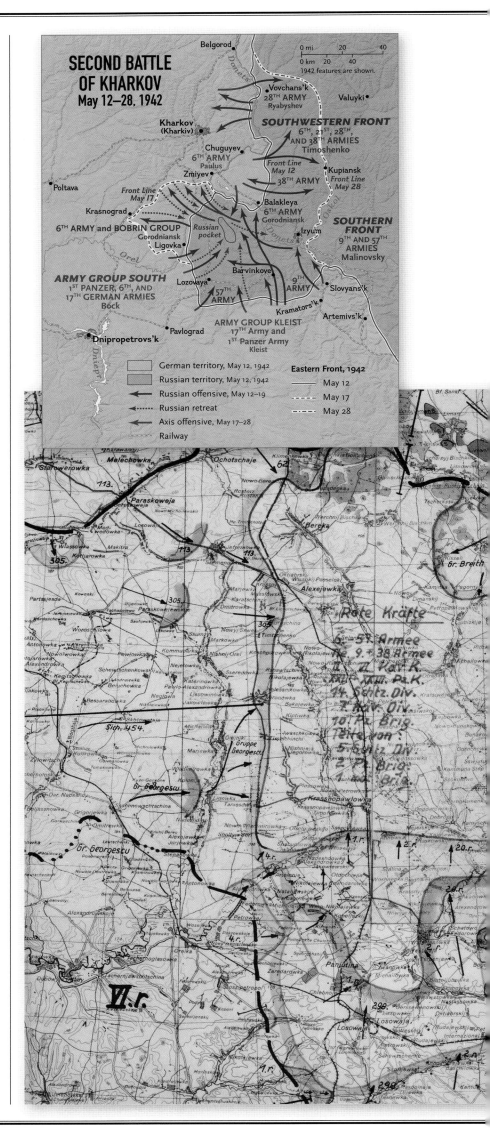

SECOND BATTLE OF KHARKOV
May 12–28, 1942

1942 features are shown.

German territory, May 12, 1942
Russian territory, May 12, 1942
→ Russian offensive, May 12–19
⇢ Russian retreat
➔ Axis offensive, May 17–28
—— Railway

Eastern Front, 1942
—— May 12
---- May 17
—·— May 28

U naware that Army Group South, led by Field Marshal Fedor von Bock, was being reinforced in the spring of 1942 for its upcoming offensive, Soviet marshal Semyon Timoshenko prepared to advance against Bock from two salients, or bulges, in the line separating their forces. Timoshenko's objective was to retake Kharkov, Russia's fourth largest city, in a classic pincer movement (see map inset at right). Attacking on May 12, Red Army troops in the northern salient made little progress and ground to a halt under Luftwaffe air strikes. But Timoshenko's forces to the south achieved a breakthrough against the Sixth Army, led by Gen. Friedrich Paulus, a staff officer new to field command. As the incursion there deepened, Paulus wanted to pull back his forces but heeded Hitler's order to stand fast while Bock prepared to counterattack.

On May 17, the First Panzer Army cut behind Timoshenko's troops and bottled them up. The German situation map at right charts the progress of Bock's forces (black arrows) day by day as they squeezed their foes into an ever tighter bind. On May 20, Timoshenko asked his commissar, future Soviet premier Nikita Khrushchev, to persuade Stalin to cancel the offensive and allow troops to break out. Commissars were appointed by the Kremlin to ensure that officers were loyal to the regime and relentless in battling the enemy. Stalin rebuffed Khrushchev and refused to cancel the Kharkov offensive before Timoshenko's troops were doomed. More than 200,000 were captured and 100,000 killed in a disaster reminiscent of those suffered by the Red Army in 1941. Timoshenko and Khrushchev feared that Stalin might have them executed. Instead, Stalin demoted Timoshenko and emptied his pipe on Khrushchev's head to humiliate him.

After this bitter defeat in the Second Battle of Kharkov—the first occurred when Germans captured the city in October 1941—Stalin allowed commanders to make tactical withdrawals to more defensible positions. Hitler, on the other hand, emerged overconfident, sure that Army Group South could both seize Baku and shatter the Voronezh-Stalingrad line. Bock took Voronezh, but Hitler thought he was too slow and sacked him in July before issuing Führer Directive No. 45, which called for an attack on Stalingrad and an advance down the Volga River to Astrakhan on the Caspian Sea. Hitler's grand scheme looked feasible on a map, but German troops would have to fight for Stalingrad block by block, week after week, until that ruined city became a maze from which there was no escape. ∎

ENCIRCLEMENT The inset map at top shows how Soviet forces (blue) tried to crush Germans (red) around Kharkov by advancing northeast of the city—where the Russians were contained—and to the south, where they made deep incursions before the Germans counterattacked. The color-coded German map at right charts that counterattack from May 17 to May 24, 1942, when Red Army forces listed under the heading "Rote Krafte" were trapped. The Soviet Sixth and 57th Armies were virtually annihilated.

HARD-PRESSED Russian soldiers like those pictured here, holed up in a house with submachine guns in hand, fought desperately against German invaders during the Second Battle of Kharkov in May 1942 and the third battle there in March 1943, which also ended in defeat for the Soviets. Not until late August 1943, after repulsing the German offensive at Kursk, did they win the final battle for Kharkov.

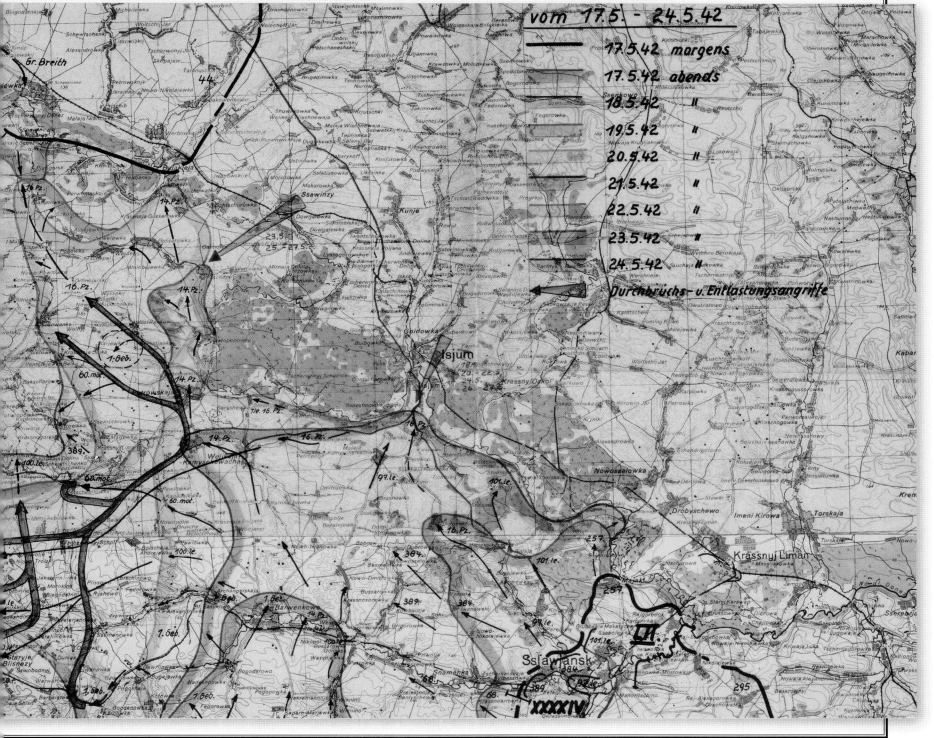

TURNING POINT AT STALINGRAD

In late July 1942, as German forces neared the city bearing his name, Stalin warned that Red Army officers who withdrew from the enemy without permission would be court-martialed and soldiers who retreated in panic would be shot. During the long struggle that followed at Stalingrad, Russian security forces shot to death more than 13,000 Russian soldiers for cowardice and other offenses. Most troops fought not to avoid execution by Soviet overseers, however, but to avoid annihilation by the despised Germans, who left them little room to retreat. Bolstered by the Fourth Panzer Army, General Paulus's 300,000-man-strong Sixth Army pressed the Russians into a tight pocket at Stalingrad, with their backs to the Volga. Supplies and reinforcements were ferried to the city from the east bank of the river under heavy fire. In mid-August, the Luftwaffe bombed Stalingrad, killing thousands of people. The ruins provided Soviet troops and partisans with cover in the rubble as Germans stormed the city. Streets, houses, and factories changed hands repeatedly in vicious combat the Germans called *rattenkrieg* (rat war). Joining in the defense of Stalingrad were Russian women who served as medics, snipers, and pilots of the 588th Night Bomber Regiment, dubbed "Night Witches" by Germans.

On November 11, Paulus's battle-weary troops made one last push to take the city. Savage fighting ensued "for every yard of ground, for every brick and stone," wrote Gen. Vasily Chuikov, commander of the Soviet 62nd Army. Some Germans broke through to the Volga, but it was too little too late. On November 19, the Red Army launched Operation Uranus, a massive counterattack that overwhelmed Romanian forces and other Axis troops guarding the German perimeter. Part of the Fourth Panzer Army escaped capture, but Paulus obeyed Hitler's order to stand fast as Soviet pincers closed around the Sixth Army. A thin red line on the Russian map at right, showing the situation in early January 1943, encircles the area west of Stalingrad in which Axis forces (blue) were surrounded. Trapped in and around the city, Paulus's men were starving and freezing. Promoted to field marshal by Hitler, who urged him to fight "to the last soldier," Paulus instead surrendered his shattered army, reduced to less than 100,000 men, on January 31. A German commander later called this defeat "the turning point of the entire war." ■

STREET FIGHTING Russian soldiers fight amid the rubble of Stalingrad, which favored Soviet defenders over German attackers, who had to leave cover in order to advance. "The snipers don't give us any rest," one German officer at Stalingrad wrote. "They shoot bloody well."

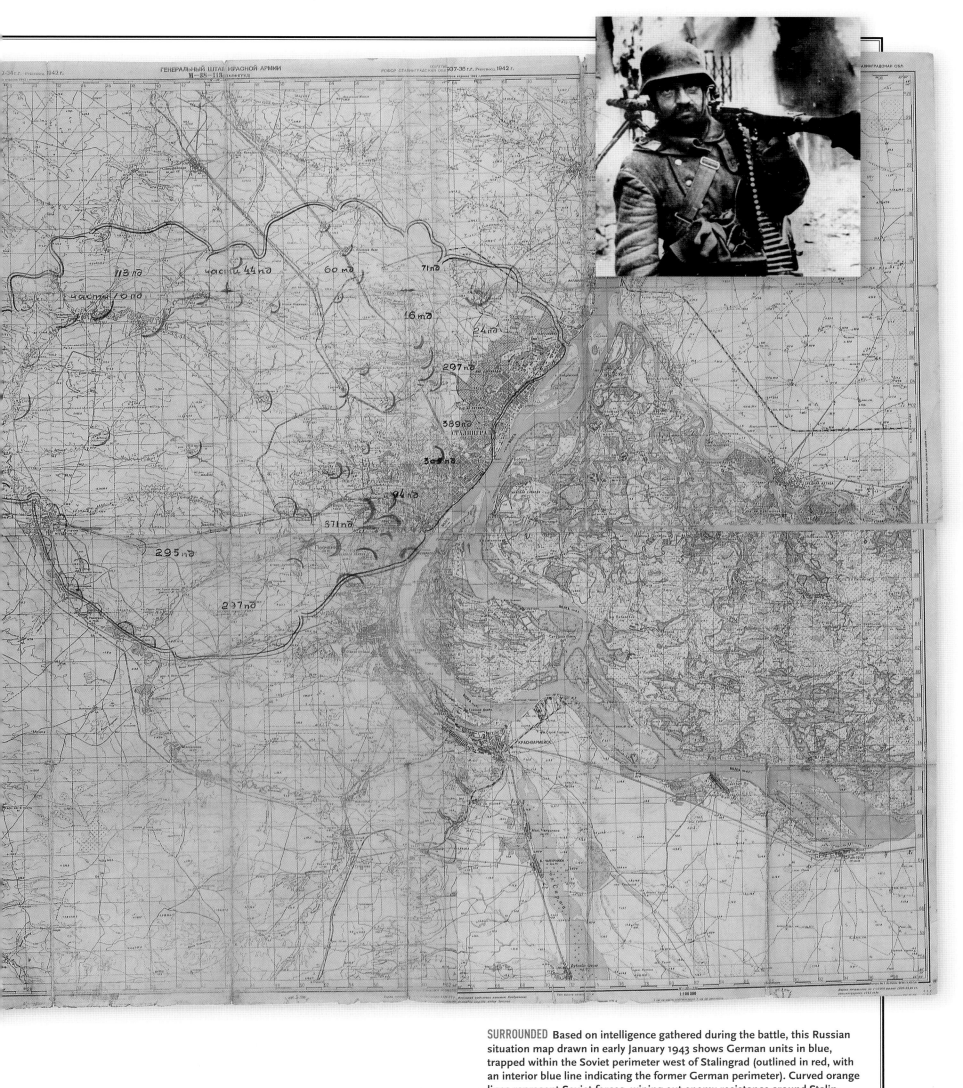

ГЕНЕРАЛЬНЫЙ ШТАБ КРАСНОЙ АРМИИ
М—38—113

113 пд   части 44пд   60 мд   71пд

части 16 пд

16 мд

24 пд

297 пд

389 пд

СТАЛИНГРАД

305 пд

94 пд

371 пд

295 пд   Песчанка

297 пд

КРАСНОАРМЕЙСК

1:100 000

SURROUNDED Based on intelligence gathered during the battle, this Russian situation map drawn in early January 1943 shows German units in blue, trapped within the Soviet perimeter west of Stalingrad (outlined in red, with an interior blue line indicating the former German perimeter). Curved orange lines represent Soviet forces, wiping out enemy resistance around Stalingrad, on the west bank of the Volga River. German troops like the machinegunner pictured at top clung desperately to the city but had no way out.

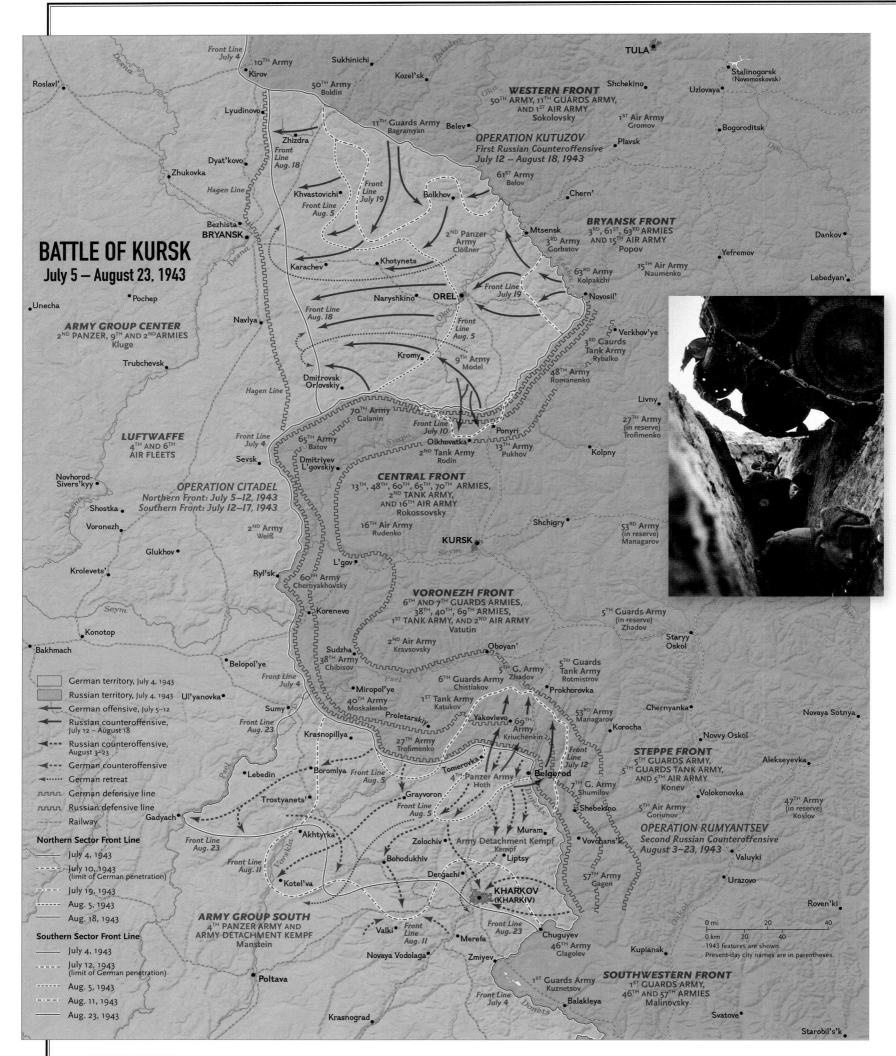

BATTLE OF KURSK
July 5 – August 23, 1943

WESTERN FRONT
50TH ARMY, 11TH GUARDS ARMY, AND 1ST AIR ARMY
Sokolovsky

OPERATION KUTUZOV
First Russian Counteroffensive
July 12 – August 18, 1943

BRYANSK FRONT
3RD, 61ST, 63RD ARMIES AND 15TH AIR ARMY
Popov

ARMY GROUP CENTER
2ND PANZER, 9TH AND 2ND ARMIES
Kluge

LUFTWAFFE
4TH AND 6TH AIR FLEETS

OPERATION CITADEL
Northern Front: July 5–12, 1943
Southern Front: July 12–17, 1943

CENTRAL FRONT
13TH, 48TH, 60TH, 65TH, 70TH ARMIES, 2ND TANK ARMY, AND 16TH AIR ARMY
Rokossovsky

VORONEZH FRONT
6TH AND 7TH GUARDS ARMIES, 38TH, 40TH, 69TH ARMIES, 1ST TANK ARMY, AND 2ND AIR ARMY
Vatutin

STEPPE FRONT
5TH GUARDS ARMY, 5TH GUARDS TANK ARMY, AND 5TH AIR ARMY
Konev

OPERATION RUMYANTSEV
Second Russian Counteroffensive
August 3–23, 1943

ARMY GROUP SOUTH
4TH PANZER ARMY AND ARMY DETACHMENT KEMPF
Manstein

SOUTHWESTERN FRONT
1ST GUARDS ARMY, 46TH AND 57TH ARMIES
Malinovsky

Legend

- German territory, July 4, 1943
- Russian territory, July 4, 1943
- German offensive, July 5–12
- Russian counteroffensive, July 12 – August 18
- Russian counteroffensive, August 3–23
- German counteroffensive
- German retreat
- German defensive line
- Russian defensive line
- Railway

Northern Sector Front Line
- July 4, 1943
- July 10, 1943 (limit of German penetration)
- July 19, 1943
- Aug. 5, 1943
- Aug. 18, 1943

Southern Sector Front Line
- July 4, 1943
- July 12, 1943 (limit of German penetration)
- Aug. 5, 1943
- Aug. 11, 1943
- Aug. 23, 1943

0 mi 20 40
0 km 20 40
1943 features are shown.
Present-day city names are in parentheses.

INVADERS REPULSED As mapped above, German thrusts by Model's Ninth Army north of Kursk and Hoth's Fourth Panzer Army south of Kursk—intended to trap enemy forces within the salient—were contained by the Soviets, who had prepared formidable defenses, including trenches narrow enough to allow their tanks to cross over without harming troops underneath (inset). The Russians then counterattacked and beat back the Germans.

A CLASH OF TITANS

By the time the Battle of Stalingrad ended, Germans had been ousted from the Caucasus and relinquished most of the ground they had gained in the summer of 1942. Russian commanders, emboldened by success, pressed ahead in February 1943 and secured much of eastern Ukraine, including the cities of Kharkov and Kursk. Field Marshal Erich von Manstein, a keen German strategist, recognized that the Russians were overextended and recaptured Kharkov in March, leaving Soviet troops in a salient that encompassed Kursk (see map opposite). Operation Citadel, the German plan to cut off that salient and regain Kursk, took several months to develop. Cautious after the disaster at Stalingrad, Hitler agreed to delay action until heavier German tanks reached the battlefront. Warned of the attack by spies, the Soviets prepared to thwart enemy onslaughts with tank traps, minefields, artillery, Katyusha rockets, and air strikes before committing the bulk of their armor.

At dawn on July 5, Gen. Hermann Hoth's Fourth Panzer Army, heavily reinforced after Stalingrad, pushed into the salient from the south while Gen. Walther Model's Ninth Army, replete with panzer divisions, advanced from the north. Altogether, the Germans threw 900,000 troops and 2,700 tanks into the battle. Awaiting them were more than a million Soviets, 3,600 tanks, and the strongest anti-tank defenses the Germans had ever encountered. In five grueling days, Hoth's panzers advanced just 20 miles and Model's forces managed only eight miles. Prospects that the two armies would meet as planned and bottle up their foes were dim. After a head-on clash near Prokhorovka on July 12 in which Hoth's forces destroyed many more tanks than they lost but gained little ground, Soviets counterattacked and Hitler scrubbed Operation Citadel.

Gen. Ivan Konev, whose tanks and troops helped contain Hoth's panzers, called Kursk the "swan song of the German armored force," which had shredded Russian lines in the past. An invasion Hitler thought would smash the Soviet state in a few months had now consumed two years. In the next twelve months, Russians would break the brutal siege of Leningrad and free their homeland from German invaders, who would leave behind nearly two million men dead or captured. ■

ARMORED ARMAGEDDON During the Battle of Kursk, both sides preceded massive armored assaults with air strikes, as shown above by the warplanes streaking ahead of Russian tanks to bomb German forces. After defeating their foes at Kursk, Soviet troops made rapid gains in Ukraine, recapturing Kiev in November 1943 and reaching the line shown on the Russian map at left, west of Kiev, in December.

THE FINAL SOLUTION

HITLER'S DEATH SENTENCE FOR EUROPEAN JEWS

CHRONOLOGY

JANUARY 20, 1942 SS security chief Reinhard Heydrich convenes the Wannsee Conference to coordinate the "Final Solution of the Jewish Question."

JULY 23, 1942 Deportation of Jews from the Warsaw Ghetto to Treblinka extermination camp begins under Operation Heydrich.

MAY 16, 1943 Warsaw Ghetto Uprising, launched on April 19, ends with the destruction of the ghetto and the Great Synagogue of Warsaw.

NOVEMBER 17, 1943 Treblinka closes following the execution of more than 780,000 people there. Killings continue at Auschwitz and other Nazi camps.

OPERATION HEYDRICH After Reinhard Heydrich—pictured above to the right of SS chief Heinrich Himmler—was attacked in Prague and died in June 1942, the SS launched Operation Heydrich, aimed at exterminating Polish Jews. Among the victims were occupants of the Warsaw Ghetto (right), shown being led away from the smoldering ghetto in 1943. Avraham Neyer, pictured up front in a dark coat, was the only one in his family to survive.

Murderous hatred for Jews was a prime motive for Hitler when he ignited the most destructive conflict in history. "The world war is here," he told Nazi leaders after invading Poland in 1939. "The annihilation of Jews must be the necessary consequence." His fateful decision to invade the Soviet Union was based in part on his desire to eradicate what he called the "Jewish Bolshevik conspiracy," although many Jews targeted by SS task forces and their accomplices in German-occupied Russia were not Bolsheviks or Communists. Nearly one million Jews were massacred there by late 1941. They died too conspicuously to satisfy SS security chief Reinhard Heydrich, tasked with overseeing what Nazis called the "Final Solution of the Jewish Question." That meant extermination, but genocide committed openly could provoke resistance from Jews and those who sympathized with them or feared becoming victims of Nazi persecution.

In January 1942, Heydrich met with German officials and SS officers at Wannsee, outside Berlin, and announced that all Jews in areas under German occupation or control were subject to the Final Solution and would be "deported to the East." Those were code words for extermination, to be carried out in gas chambers. Jews told that they were being deported to the East would in fact be transported in boxcars on existing rail lines to SS extermination camps (see map opposite). The secrecy surrounding the Final Solution was eventually dispelled, and some Jews resisted deportation and execution, including occupants of the Warsaw Ghetto, whose uprising began in April 1943 and ended in May when their ghetto was razed and the survivors were hauled away (below).

Many of the six million Jewish men, women, and children who perished in the Holocaust were killed in extermination camps. But some were sent to concentration camps, where inmates toiled in wretched conditions and often died of disease or mistreatment or were put to death when they were no longer able to work. Others besides Jews ended up in extermination or concentration camps, including Roma, Jehovah's Witnesses, Communists and other political dissidents, prisoners of war, homosexuals, and captured Allied agents. The words of one Jewish survivor applied to them all. The aim of their SS overseers, he said, was "to destroy our human dignity, to fill us with contempt for ourselves and our fellows." Such was the inhuman punishment inflicted on millions by Hitler's contemptible regime. ■

NETWORK OF TERROR
January 20, 1942 — May 8, 1945

0 mi 200
0 km 200

January 1942 features are shown.
Present-day city names are in parentheses.

REICHSKOMMISSARIAT NORWAY
Grini □ Oslo ○ Bredtveit
Berg
★ Stockholm

FINLAND
Vaivara ● Leningrad (St. Petersburg)
Klooga □ Lagedi

SWEDEN

MOSCOW ★

SOVIET UNION

Axis front line
Jan. 20, 1942

Kaiserwald □
Riga ◉

North Sea

REICHSKOMMISSARIAT OSTLAND
Vilnius ●

DENMARK □ Horserød
★ Copenhagen
Stutthof □

● Minsk

Koldichevo ●

Baltic Sea

Kharkiv ●

IRELAND

UNITED KINGDOM
★ LONDON

REICHSKOMMISSARIAT NETHERLANDS Neuengamme □
Westerbork □ Sachsenhausen □ Ravensbrück □
Amsterdam ◉ Bergen- Belsen ★ BERLIN
Vught □ CHEŁMNO □
Dora-Mittelbau □
GERMANY

TREBLINKA □
Warsaw ●
Łódź □ □ Poniatowa
SOBIBÓR
Skarżysko-Kamienna □ □ Trawniki
Starachowice Budzyń MAJDANEK
Gross-Rosen □ □ □ BEŁŻEC
AUSCHWITZ □ □ Płaszów
Kraków ◉ GENERAL GOVERNMENT L'viv
Janowska

REICHSKOMMISSARIAT UKRAINE
Kiev ●
Dnieper

Berdychiv ●

Breendonk □ □ Mechelen
Brussels ◉
REICHSKOMMISSARIAT BELGIUM AND N. FRANCE

Buchenwald □

Vistula

Flossenbürg □
PROT. OF BOHEMIA & MORAVIA

SLOVAKIA

Chernivtsi ●

TRANSDNISTRIA

Carpathian Mountains

Compiègne
PARIS ◉ □ Drancy
Schirmeck- Vorbrück
Pithiviers □

Rhine
Dachau □
Natzweiler- Struthof □
Vittel □

Vienna ●
Mauthausen □

HUNGARY
★ Budapest

Danube

Chisinau ●
Iași ●
Odessa ●

Loire
FRANCE

SWITZ.
LIECH.

A L P S

Bolzano □

Black Sea

Bay of Biscay

VICHY FRANCE

San Sabba □

Rhône

Fossoli di Carpi □

Po
SAN MARINO

CROATIA

Sabac ● ● Sajmište
TERR. OF THE MILITARY COMMANDER IN SERBIA
Niš ●

ROMANIA
Bucharest ★

Danube

MONACO

I T A L Y

MONTENEGRO (It. Governate)

BULGARIA

Gurs □
Pyrenees
ANDORRA □ Rivesaltes
SPAIN
Corsica (Vichy France)

DALMATIA (It. Governate)
ALBANIA (It. Protectorate)
Salonika ●
★ ROME

★ Thessaloníki

TURKEY

☐ Axis territory, Jan. 20, 1942
☐ Axis satellite or puppet state, Jan. 20, 1942
☐ Allied territory, Jan. 20, 1942
☐ Neutral state, Jan. 20, 1942
— Axis front line
— Major railway
□ Extermination camp
□ Concentration camp

MURDER INSTITUTIONALIZED The map above shows extermination camps and concentration camps established by the SS in Germany and German-controlled territory. Many rail lines leading to camps on the map were used to transport victims such as Jews in the Warsaw Ghetto, who were packed into boxcars (top) and killed in gas chambers at Treblinka and other extermination camps. Many concentration camp inmates were killed in gas chambers as well or shot to death. The vast Auschwitz complex included concentration camps and a killing center, where the lethal gas Zyklon-B was first tested on inmates in 1941. Between 1940 and 1945, nearly one million Jews and more than 100,000 other people were murdered at Auschwitz.

CHAPTER 4

VICTORY OVER GERMANY | 1944-1945

"We'll have only one chance to stop the enemy, and that's while he's in the water ... struggling to get ashore."

FIELD MARSHAL ERWIN ROMMEL

D-DAY Men of the U.S. First Infantry Division wade ashore under fire at Omaha Beach on June 6, 1944. The Allied invasion here on the coast of Normandy tightened the screws on Nazi Germany, already under relentless pressure from Soviet troops on the Eastern Front.

ENDGAME EUROPE

FROM D-DAY TO THE FALL OF BERLIN

The Allied invasion of German-occupied France that began in the early hours of June 6, 1944, was long in the making. By gaining supremacy in the Atlantic in 1943, the Allies had cleared the way for a huge build-up of American troops and equipment in Great Britain. Between January and June 1944, nine million tons of supplies and 800,000 soldiers crossed the Atlantic from the United States to bolster the invasion, designated Operation Overlord. Meanwhile, Allied pilots exploited their hard-won superiority over the diminished Luftwaffe by blasting French railways and bridges to keep their foes from rushing reserves to Normandy when troops landed there. Anglo-American commanders battle tested in North Africa and Italy, including Eisenhower, Patton, and Montgomery, prepared to lead invasion troops against their old foe Rommel, assigned to strengthen French coastal defenses while the bulk of the German Army struggled to hold back resurgent Soviets on the Eastern Front.

Although the landings on D-Day were less costly than Allied leaders feared, American forces destined for Omaha Beach paid a dreadful price before securing that sector. Casualties mounted as invasion forces advanced inland and met with fierce resistance. Not until late July did they break out, aided by devastating air raids that gouged holes in enemy lines through which armor advanced, including tanks of Patton's U.S. Third Army. On August 15, a second Allied invasion designated Operation Dragoon unfolded on the French Mediterranean coast. Resistance groups took up arms, and some began liberating Paris before Allied troops entered the city in late August.

The offensive in France and the Low Countries coincided with a massive onslaught by the Red Army, whose troops advanced into German-occupied Poland before invading Germany proper by entering East Prussia. Hitler refused to concede defeat and launched a desperate counterattack at year's end against the Western Allies, whose advance had stalled as they ran short of supplies and came up against the formidable West Wall (Siegfried Line) along the German border. The resulting Battle of the Bulge, won by those Allies in January 1945, delayed their advance across the Rhine until March while vengeful Soviets closed on Berlin. "We may be destroyed," Hitler had remarked earlier, "but if we are, we shall drag a world with us—a world in flames." On April 30, with Berlin in flames and about to fall to the Russians, he committed suicide. A week later, Germany surrendered unconditionally.

JUNE–DECEMBER 1944

June 5, 1944 After postponing the invasion of Normandy for one day because of bad weather, Supreme Allied Commander Dwight Eisenhower gives his forces the go-ahead. Rome falls to Allied troops.

June 6, 1944 Allied troops land in Normandy on D-Day, suffering nearly 10,000 casualties but securing all five beaches assigned to them.

June 9, 1944 German High Command receives an intelligence estimate, based on false reports from double agents under British control, that the Normandy landings are a diversion. German forces will remain in strength around Calais, awaiting an invasion there, until July.

June 10, 1944 Germans of the Second SS Panzer Division, destined for Normandy, retaliate for partisan attacks by massacring French civilians at Oradour-sur-Glane.

June 13, 1944 British armored forces attempting to outflank German troops holding Caen in Normandy are repulsed at Villers-Bocage. The first German V-1 cruise missiles are launched, with London as the target.

June 22, 1944 Soviet troops launch Operation Bagration, a major offensive that will carry them beyond Russia's prewar border to the Vistula River near Warsaw by early August.

June 26–27, 1944 American troops take the port of Cherbourg in Normandy after German demolition teams wreck the harbor there.

July 3–4, 1944 Tens of thousands of German troops are cut off as Soviets capture the city of Minsk in Belarus, a borderland disputed by Russia and Poland before Germans seized it in 1941.

July 18, 1944 British and Canadian forces of Montgomery's 21st Army Group launch Operation Goodwood around Caen in Normandy, tying down German armored divisions as

German propaganda poster in occupied Belgium, portraying a grim reaper awaiting Allied invaders with the words "We are happy to welcome Europe's enemies"

JANUARY–MAY 1945

January 8, 1945 Facing defeat in the Battle of the Bulge, Hitler authorizes withdrawals by German armored divisions.

January 17, 1945 Soviet troops capture Warsaw during a winter offensive that will take them across Poland to the Oder River in Germany by March.

January 27, 1945 Soviets liberate the last prisoners at Auschwitz— a concentration camp complex

Troops of the U.S. First Infantry Division on the march during the Battle of the Bulge

including gas chambers in which more than a million people were killed—after hurried efforts by the SS to evacuate and dismantle the complex.

February 4–11, 1945 Roosevelt, Churchill, and Stalin meet at Yalta in Crimea and agree to divide Germany into occupation zones and partition Berlin.

February 8, 1945 Western Allied forces begin advancing toward the Rhine.

February 13, 1945 Budapest falls to the Soviets, who gain control of Hungary.

American troops prepare to launch Operation Cobra and break out at Saint-Lô.

July 20, 1944 Hitler survives a deadly bomb blast at the Wolf's Lair, his command center in East Prussia, and a plot by German officers to assassinate him and overthrow the Nazi regime collapses.

July 25, 1944 Operation Cobra begins in Normandy as American bombers blast German lines in preparation for advances by the U.S. First and Third Armies.

August 1, 1944 Partisans of the Polish Home Army launch the Warsaw Uprising against German occupation troops, who will crush the insurgency by October. Lt. Gen. Omar Bradley takes charge of the newly formed U.S. 12th Army Group in France.

August 6–11, 1944 Panzer divisions sent by Hitler to cut off the American advance in Normandy are defeated at Mortain, clearing the way for Patton's Third Army and Montgomery's troops around Caen to press forward and encircle German forces at Falaise.

August 15, 1944 Allied troops land along the French Mediterranean Coast in Operation Dragoon.

August 20, 1944 Soviets launch an offensive along the Black Sea

Eisenhower encouraging paratroopers of the U.S. 101st Airborne Division before their departure for Normandy

that will force Romania and Bulgaria to abandon the Axis and yield to Moscow.

August 20–21, 1944 Allied troops in Normandy close the Falaise Pocket, capturing some 50,000 German troops, and advance on Paris.

August 25, 1944 Free French soldiers liberate Paris following a partisan uprising there.

September 3–4, 1944 Montgomery's forces in Belgium seize Brussels and the major port of Antwerp, which will remain closed to Allied ships until the Schelde Estuary leading to Antwerp is cleared of German batteries and mines in November.

September 8, 1944 Germany launches its first V-2 ballistic missile attack on London.

September 12, 1944 Troops of the U.S. Fifth Army attack German defenses along the Gothic Line in northern Italy.

September 17–25, 1944 Allied airborne forces fail to break through German lines near the Rhine in the Netherlands during Operation Market Garden.

September 19, 1944 Finland agrees to an armistice with the Soviet Union, whose troops invaded Finland in June 1944 to end its military collaboration with Germany and enforce concessions that Finland made to Stalin at the end of the Winter War in 1940. Under the agreement, Finland will fight to evict German troops from its territory.

October 12, 1944 Athenians celebrate as German forces leave the city and withdraw from Greece in response to Soviet advances in Romania and Bulgaria.

October 14, 1944 Field Marshal Erwin Rommel commits suicide rather than face execution for the plot against Hitler that culminated on July 20—a conspiracy he knew of in advance and did not oppose or disclose.

British poster evoking the "flame of French Resistance" that Charles de Gaulle said must never be put out

October 16, 1944 Red Army troops enter East Prussia, the first German state threatened by the Soviets, who will follow this incursion with a massive invasion three months later.

October 21, 1944 After crossing from Belgium into Germany, American troops capture the city of Aachen. Their efforts to drive deeper into the Reich in November will falter amid supply problems and stiff German resistance in the Hürtgen Forest.

December 16, 1944 German offensive against American troops in the Ardennes ignites the Battle of the Bulge.

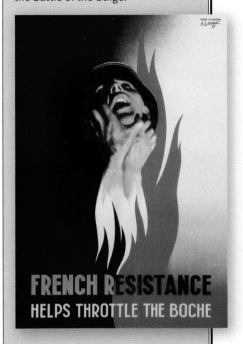

FRENCH RESISTANCE HELPS THROTTLE THE BOCHE

February 13–14, 1945 Allied fire-bombing of Dresden, Germany, destroys much of the city and kills more than 25,000 people.

March 7, 1945 American troops seize a bridge across the Rhine at Remagen.

March 22–23, 1945 Allied ground troops and airborne forces launch a massive advance across the Rhine to capture the Ruhr, Germany's industrial core.

March 31, 1945 Stalin receives a message from Eisenhower that Western Allied forces will not target Berlin.

April 5, 1945 Marshal Tito (born Josip Broz), the Communist leader responsible for reconstituting Yugoslavia, signs an agreement allowing Russian troops there temporarily. As Yugoslavia's postwar premier, Tito will resist alignment with the Soviet Union.

April 12, 1945 Allied strategic bombing ends in Europe.

The dead bodies of Mussolini (center), his mistress Claretta (right), and a Fascist cohort (left) on display in Milan on April 29, 1945

April 13, 1945 Russian troops capture Vienna. Like Berlin, Vienna will be partitioned after the war ends by the major Allied Powers, which will divide Austria as a whole into occupation zones.

April 16, 1945 Red Army troops along the Oder and Neisse Rivers in eastern Germany launch a decisive offensive against Berlin.

April 25, 1945 American and Soviet forces meet along the Elbe River in Germany.

April 28, 1945 Mussolini is executed by partisans in northern Italy.

April 30, 1945 Hitler commits suicide as Soviets seize control of Berlin and raise their flag atop the Reichstag, Germany's historic parliament building.

May 1, 1945 Joseph Goebbels, Hitler's designated successor as Reich chancellor, commits suicide, leaving Grand Admiral Karl Dönitz in sole charge of Germany and its shattered armed forces.

May 2, 1945 German forces in Italy surrender.

May 5, 1945 Uprising against German occupiers is launched by

Czech partisans in Prague. Soviet troops will arrive there four days later, tightening Russia's grip on postwar Czechoslovakia and other Eastern European countries.

May 7–8, 1945 Germany surrenders unconditionally to the Allies.

Headline announcing Hitler's death in Soviet-occupied Berlin on April 30, 1945

THE INVASION OF
NORMANDY
SMASHING INLAND ON A BROAD FRONT

CHRONOLOGY

JUNE 6, 1944 Allied forces land in Normandy on D-Day, suffering nearly 10,000 casualties but securing all five beaches assigned to them.

JUNE 10, 1944 Germans of the Second SS Panzer Division, destined for Normandy, retaliate for partisan attacks by massacring French civilians at Oradour-sur-Glane.

JUNE 26–27, 1944 American troops take the port of Cherbourg in Normandy after German demolition teams wreck the harbor there.

JULY 18, 1944 British and Canadian forces under Montgomery launch Operation Goodwood around Caen, tying down German armored divisions as American troops under Bradley prepare to launch Operation Cobra and break out at Saint-Lô.

BRAIN TRUST Seated before a map of Europe, Supreme Allied Commander Eisenhower (center) meets with top officers in early 1944 after arriving in London to refine the original plan for the invasion of Normandy (top) and implement Operation Overlord. On D-Day, Field Marshal Montgomery (just right of Eisenhower) would command British and Canadian forces of his 21st Army Group as well as American divisions that would later join the 12th Army Group under Lt. Gen. Omar Bradley (far left).

Planning for Operation Overlord began in London more than a year before the invasion took place. Allied staff officers led by Lt. Gen. Frederick Morgan debated where to pierce the Atlantic Wall (see map opposite), German coastal fortifications extending from Norway to the southwest coast of France. The shortest route to Germany lay across the Strait of Dover (Pas-de-Calais), but landing around Calais meant attacking the strongest sector of the Atlantic Wall. Morgan and staff decided instead to land on the coast of Normandy, which lay farther from Germany but was less heavily fortified. Their original plan (left), drawn up in strict secrecy, called for three divisions to come ashore on a narrow front on D-Day. But when Eisenhower and Montgomery arrived in London in early 1944 to serve respectively as supreme commander and field commander of the Allied Expeditionary Force destined for Normandy, they altered the invasion plan based on amphibious operations in Italy. Five divisions would land on D-Day on a broader front, supported by three airborne divisions and followed by an immense influx of men and materiel. The huge commitment of landing craft and other resources to Normandy meant that a second invasion of France along the Mediterranean coast, which was meant to coincide with Overlord to prevent Germans in the south from being shifted to Normandy, would instead take place a few months after Overlord unfolded.

German commanders did not ignore the potential threat to Normandy. Rommel—in charge of Army Group B under Field Marshal Gerd von Rundstedt, German commander in chief in the West—laced beaches there with mines as well as obstructions that would force landing craft to disgorge troops at low tide, leaving them more exposed to enemy fire. Rommel wanted panzer divisions deployed at likely landing sites in Normandy to repulse invaders before they established a beachhead and were reinforced. "Everything we have must be on the coast," he insisted. Rundstedt disagreed, and Hitler decided to hold most German armored forces in reserve under his own control until the invasion took place. Only one panzer division guarded the Normandy coast beforehand. An elaborate Allied deception campaign called Operation Bodyguard—which included simulating phantom divisions and feeding false reports to Berlin from German agents under British control—led Hitler to view landings at Normandy as a diversion, which would be followed by a massive Allied thrust across the Strait of Dover. ∎

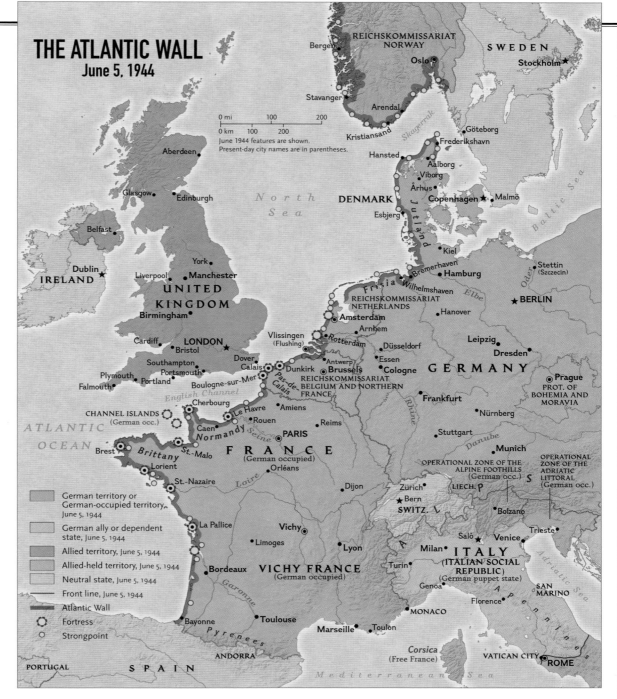

THE ATLANTIC WALL
June 5, 1944

0 mi 100 200
0 km 100 200
June 1944 features are shown.
Present-day city names are in parentheses.

REICHSKOMMISSARIAT NORWAY

SWEDEN

Bergen
Oslo
Stockholm ★
Stavanger
Arendal
Kristiansand
Skagerrak

Göteborg
Frederikshavn
Hansted
Aalborg
Viborg
Århus
Copenhagen ★ • Malmö

DENMARK
Jutland
Esbjerg
North Sea
Baltic Sea

Aberdeen
Glasgow • Edinburgh
Belfast
Dublin ★
IRELAND
York
Liverpool • Manchester
UNITED KINGDOM
Birmingham
Cardiff
LONDON ★
Bristol
Southampton
Portsmouth
Plymouth Portland
Falmouth
Dover
Calais
Boulogne-sur-Mer
English Channel
Cherbourg
CHANNEL ISLANDS (German occ.)
Caen
Normandy
Brest
Brittany
Lorient
St.-Malo
St.-Nazaire
La Pallice

ATLANTIC OCEAN

Kiel
Bremerhaven
Wilhelmshaven
Frisia
Elbe
Hamburg
Stettin (Szczecin)
Oder
★ BERLIN

REICHSKOMMISSARIAT NETHERLANDS
Amsterdam
Arnhem
Hanover
Leipzig
Dresden
Vlissingen (Flushing)
Rotterdam
Antwerp
Düsseldorf
Essen
Cologne
Dunkirk
Brussels
Pas-de-Calais
REICHSKOMMISSARIAT BELGIUM AND NORTHERN FRANCE
Frankfurt
Prague
PROT. OF BOHEMIA AND MORAVIA
Le Havre
Rouen
Amiens
Reims
Seine
PARIS
Rhine
Nürnberg
Stuttgart
FRANCE (German occupied)
Orléans
Loire
Dijon
Zürich
★ Bern
SWITZ.
Munich
Danube
OPERATIONAL ZONE OF THE ALPINE FOOTHILLS (German occ.)
OPERATIONAL ZONE OF THE ADRIATIC LITTORAL (German occ.)
LIECH.
Bolzano
Limoges
Vichy
Lyon
Turin
Salò
Venice
Milan
ITALY (ITALIAN SOCIAL REPUBLIC) (German puppet state)
Trieste
Adriatic Sea
Bordeaux
VICHY FRANCE (German occupied)
Garonne
Genoa
Florence
SAN MARINO
Bayonne
Pyrenees
Toulouse
Marseille
Toulon
MONACO
Apennines
VATICAN CITY ★ ROME
PORTUGAL
SPAIN
ANDORRA
Corsica (Free France)
Mediterranean Sea

Legend:
■ German territory or German-occupied territory, June 5, 1944
■ German ally or dependent state, June 5, 1944
■ Allied territory, June 5, 1944
■ Allied-held territory, June 5, 1944
□ Neutral state, June 5, 1944
— Front line, June 5, 1944
— Atlantic Wall
◌ Fortress
○ Strongpoint

PIERCING THE WALL The German defensive barrier known as the Atlantic Wall included two areas that met the requirements for a massive Allied invasion—beaches that were accessible to landing craft, tanks, and other vehicles and were not too far from British ports or from Germany, the ultimate objective. Suitable beaches around Calais were only 30 miles from the port of Dover and 200 miles from the German border, but their proximity to the Reich meant that they were well defended. The other promising landing site—between the fortified ports of Le Havre and Cherbourg in Normandy—was farther from Germany but was chosen because beaches there were less heavily defended. Rommel, pictured below (front row, third from left) inspecting a beach near Calais in April 1944, made sure that obstacles laid there to snag landing craft and amphibious tanks were also installed on the Normandy coast. But his request to defend that coast with several armored divisions that could meet invaders head-on was denied.

OVERLORD AND BODYGUARD

Operation Overlord was shielded from the Germans by Operation Bodyguard, inspired by Churchill's remark that truth in wartime should always be "attended by a bodyguard of lies." That meant simulating preparations for landings elsewhere than Normandy to keep German forces dispersed. Bodyguard deceptions fed Hitler's fear of invasions across much of occupied Europe, from Norway to Greece. But as indicated by stout defenses around Calais and deciphered enemy radio signals, the Germans viewed an invasion across the Strait of Dover as the most likely outcome—an expectation that Allied intelligence officers helped reinforce.

While planners for Overlord produced detailed maps of the Normandy landing zone for Montgomery's 21st Army Group (below), the masterminds of Bodyguard concocted a fictitious invasion force called FUSAG (First U.S. Army Group), supposedly consisting of 50 divisions preparing to cross the Strait of Dover after Montgomery's diversionary landing at Normandy. Patton played the part of FUSAG's commander by conspicuously reviewing a few real units assigned to him (opposite). Props for the hoax included dummy tanks and warplanes that would look convincing if German reconnaissance pilots managed to penetrate British airspace over Dover, where Patton's legions were reportedly massing.

The FUSAG deception was sustained by cunning double agents like Juan Pujol Garcia, who had enlisted as a German spy with the intention of serving the Allies. He filed false reports that helped keep German troops tied down at Calais awaiting the fictitious army group long after Overlord unfolded. ∎

PLANS AND RUSES A pre-invasion map (top) shows D-Day landing sites for British and Canadian troops (blue) at Gold, Juno, and Sword Beaches and for American troops (green) at Utah and Omaha Beaches. A map of Utah Beach (left), based on aerial photos, was used to plan landings there. To divert German attention from Normandy, dummy tanks and planes like those pictured here were placed across from Calais in the staging area of FUSAG, Patton's fictitious army group.

BODYGUARDS Among the crafty double agents who sold FUSAG to German spymasters were, from left to right, Dusko Popov of Yugoslavia, Spaniard Juan Pujol Garcia, Russian-born Nathalie "Lily" Sergueiew, and Roman Garby-Czerniawski of Poland. Patton posed as FUSAG's chief (right) until he took charge of a real army in France in July 1944.

PREVIEW This Overlord chart forecasts the situation two days after Allied forces landed, aided by tactical deceptions that included dropping dummies by parachute (left) to distract Germans from incursions by real paratroopers. As predicted here, panzer divisions held in reserve would soon join the one panzer division stationed close to the beaches.

U.S.   SECRET
BRITISH.   MOST SECRET
Copy N⁰ __100__

SITUATION D+2 *(First Light)*

1. Five Divs. One Airborne Div & Three Tk Bdes plus overheads landed

2. Estimated number of enemy Divs shown in BLUE
   U.S. FORMATIONS indicated thus   ★
   BRITISH FORMATIONS   "   "   ⊕

3. Air Situation.   No airfields yet available.

One Infantry Division

(2) C.O.R.P.S ★
(Two Divs One Tk Bde)

(1) C.O.R.P.S ⊕
(Three Divs Two Tk Bdes)

Airborne Div.

Up To Four Divisions (Three Panzer & One Infantry)

D-DAY

Like the invasion of Sicily, the invasion of Normandy was preceded by daring coastal and aerial reconnaissance that yielded detailed charts of landing zones, including the map at right showing four sectors on Omaha Beach—Fox Red, Fox Green, Easy Red, and Easy Green. "Easy" did not mean that troops would land easily there. Foul weather forced Eisenhower to postpone Overlord until June 6, after which two weeks would pass before the moon and tides were again favorable for paratroopers landing inland before dawn and soldiers landing on the beaches at daybreak. His decision to proceed on the 6th, during a predicted lull in the storm, caught German commanders by surprise. But some Allied landing craft and amphibious tanks sank in swells, and men who stayed afloat were seasick. Nausea mingled with dread as they disembarked under fire. "Many were hit in the water and drowned," recalled Sgt. Bob Slaughter of the U.S. 29th Infantry Regiment. "There were dead men in the water and live men acting dead, letting the tide take them in."

Nearly 3,000 Americans were killed or wounded on Omaha Beach, most of them in the first few hours. As shellfire from Allied warships began silencing enemy gunners on the cliffs, however, soldiers rallied and pushed inland through ravines toward Colleville-sur-Mer. Americans who landed at Utah Beach faced little resistance, and British and Canadian troops advanced several miles inland from their beaches and withstood a late-day counterattack by the 21st Panzer Division. When Rommel returned that night to Normandy—after celebrating his wife's birthday during a storm he thought would preclude an invasion—his worst fears were realized. He had warned a fellow officer that their only chance was to stop the enemy in the water. Now nearly 160,000 Allied troops had landed. ■

UNDER FIRE An embattled American soldier lays low on Omaha Beach in a picture taken by war photographer Robert Capa on D-Day. Capa landed with men of the U.S. First Infantry Division who were assigned to come ashore in the Easy Red sector but drifted off course to Fox Green. The top secret map at right was carried by Ens. Joseph Vaghi, who served as beachmaster at Easy Red, directing men and equipment.

St. Laurent-sur-Mer

les Moulins

OMAHA BEACH - EAST (Colleville-sur-Mer)

EASY RED

EASY GREEN

DOG RED

DE LA SEINE

NOTE to COXSWAIN or NAVIGATOR

TOP SECRET - BIGOT

EXPANDING THE BEACHHEAD

Following D-Day, the Allies had to transport troops and supplies to Normandy in vast amounts without access to a deepwater port. Germans assumed that their foes would require such a port, which lent credence to Allied deceptions portraying the Normandy landings as a diversion, to be followed by a big push aimed at a deepwater port like Calais. While the German 15th Army remained in place around Calais to defend against that anticipated thrust, the Allies reinforced their Normandy beachhead by constructing artificial harbors called mulberries, using components prefabricated in British ports and towed across the English Channel. Mulberry A, completed off Omaha Beach in mid-June and linked to shore by a pontoon bridge, was wrecked a few days later by one of the worst storms to hit the coast in that season. Mulberry B, constructed off Gold Beach near Arromanches, withstood that storm and helped boost Allied strength in Normandy to one million men by early July.

Reinforcements for the troops who landed on D-Day were essential because expanding the beachhead proved even tougher than establishing it on June 6. Inland from the beaches lay the forbidding *bocage*, consisting of low fields surrounded by dense hedgerows that sheltered German snipers, machine-gunners, and anti-tank units. Not until June 27 did American troops seize the deepwater port of Cherbourg (see map opposite), which German demolition teams rendered useless until later that year. Another important objective, heavily defended Caen, was not taken on D-Day, as Montgomery planned, and held out against repeated attacks. On June 13, the British Seventh Armored Division tried to outflank Caen but was repulsed at Villers-Bocage by elements of the First and Second SS Panzer Divisions. Allied bombers blasted Caen on July 6, killing many French civilians but few Germans, who withdrew south of the city and resisted tenaciously as Montgomery tried to punch through their defenses. Although held in check, his forces kept several German armored divisions tied down while American troops prepared to launch Operation Cobra at Saint-Lô, west of Caen, and break out of the beachhead. ■

SUPPLY LINE Landing craft disgorge tanks and trucks at Omaha Beach on June 8, 1944, under barrage balloons whose mooring cables deterred enemy aircraft. Such landings on Normandy beaches at low tide continued after the artificial harbor Mulberry B entered service, hastening delivery of troops and supplies.

FITFUL PROGRESS The map below shows the slow expansion of the Allied beachhead in Normandy from D-Day to July 24. To the west, troops of the U.S. First Army—led by Omar Bradley and later part of his 12th Army Group—fought their way in June up the Cotentin Peninsula to Cherbourg. To the east, British and Canadian forces of Montgomery's 21st Army Group met with stiff opposition from German panzer divisions around Caen. American soldiers like the gunners firing an M3 105-mm light howitzer at upper left encountered similar resistance as they pushed south from Carentan, below Utah Beach. Impeding their progress were tangled hedgerows like those lining a road in the *bocage* near Saint-Lô (upper right), where Operation Cobra began on July 25.

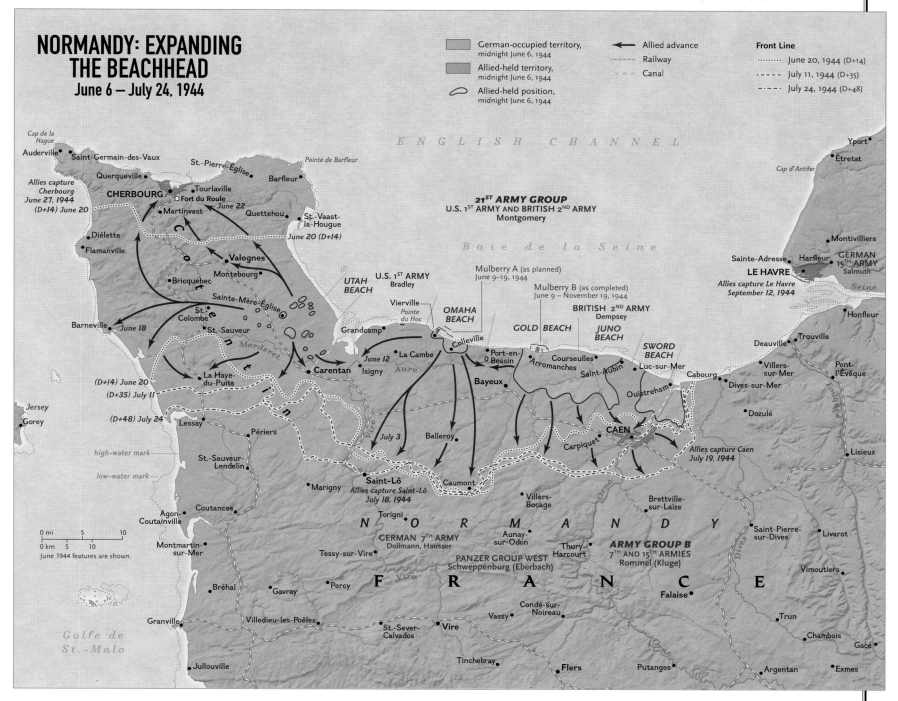

NORMANDY: EXPANDING THE BEACHHEAD
June 6 – July 24, 1944

German-occupied territory, midnight June 6, 1944
Allied-held territory, midnight June 6, 1944
Allied-held position, midnight June 6, 1944

← Allied advance
---- Railway
— ·— Canal

Front Line
·········· June 20, 1944 (D+14)
- - - - - July 11, 1944 (D+35)
— ·— ·— July 24, 1944 (D+48)

FUELING FRENCH RESISTANCE

Before and after D-Day, Allied agents of the OSS, its British counterpart the SOE, and the Free French government in exile armed French resistance groups and organized attacks that hindered German opposition to the invasion of Normandy. Among those agents was American-born Virginia Hall (lower left), who had aided resistance groups in France for the SOE before fleeing to Spain in late 1942 to evade the Gestapo, whose officers knew she had a wooden leg, which made her conspicuous. In early 1944, she transferred to the OSS, dyed her hair gray, and returned furtively to France disguised as a lame old peasant woman to arrange by radio airdrops of weapons to French guerrillas known as the Maquis—a perilous assignment because Germans monitored radio transmissions and could trace them to their source. Although the Gestapo was on the lookout for Hall and considered her "one of the most dangerous Allied agents in France," she avoided arrest and linked up after D-Day with one of the many Jedburgh teams, consisting of OSS, SOE, and Free French operatives who para-

chuted behind enemy lines to coordinate assaults by partisans on German troops and their lines of communication. Trained for combat, Jedburgh teams carried concealed weapons like the Colt pistol in a shoulder holster at lower right and the gouging knife, inset, into which attackers inserted their fingers.

Like the Allied agents who aided them, French partisans defied German forces at great risk. On June 10, troops of the Second SS Panzer Division ("Das Reich"), which was redeployed from southern France to Normandy right after D-Day, retaliated for assaults that slowed them by slaughtering inhabitants of the small town of Oradour-sur-Glane. Among the victims were more than 400 women and children, locked in a church that was set aflame. Expected to reach Normandy within a few days, that SS division did not arrive there for a few weeks, too late to repulse the invasion. ■

IN HARM'S WAY All Allied agents or commandos were at risk of being executed if seized behind German lines, whether they operated in civilian dress like Virginia Hall—pictured below on a driver's license she obtained in Estonia in 1938—or in uniform like the Jedburgh team members at right, about to take off from Harrington Airfield in England in a B-24 that would drop them into France.

WELL ARMED Allied agents provided weapons and expertise to French resistance fighters like the Maquis at right, pictured with their banner near Paris around the time the French capital was liberated in August 1944.

OPERATIONS - FRANCE

SO OPERATIVES IN BEFORE D-DAY	28
SPECIAL FORCE DETACHMENTS	40
O.G.'s (19 SECTIONS)	285
JEDBURGH TEAMS	70
TOTAL OSS OPERATIONAL PERSONNEL	**423**

ABOUT 6000 TONS OF ARMS, AMMO, ETC. SUPPLIED BY AIR

ABOUT 70,000 MAQUIS ORGANIZED & LED

STRATEGIC OPERATIONS
(UNDER SFHQ DIRECTION AND COORDINATED WITH SHAEF PLANS)
DESTROYED ALMOST ALL THE 800 STRATEGIC TARGETS SET BY SHAEF.
DELAYED GERMAN REENFORCEMENTS TO BEACHHEAD.
IMMOBILIZED ENEMY FORCES IN THE INTERIOR, PARTICULARLY IN BRITTANY.
PREVENTED RETREAT AND INSURED CAPTURE OF 20,000 GERMANS SOUTH OF LOIRE.
FORCED GERMAN COMMUNICATIONS INTO THE CLEAR BY CUTTING FIELD TELEPHONES.
PREVENTED GERMAN DEMOLITIONS.
MOPPED UP.
REESTABLISHED ORDER.
SUPPLIED INTELLIGENCE THROUGHOUT TO ALLIED HQ.

TACTICAL OPERATIONS
THE 285 O.G.'S SUFFERED 7 KILLED, 6 WOUNDED, 4 MISSING.

THEY KILLED 461 GERMANS, WOUNDED 467, DESTROYED 33 VEHICLES, 3 LOCOMOTIVES, 2 TRAINS, 32 BRIDGES, 3 AIRCRAFT, MINED 17 ROADS, CUT 11 POWER AND COMMUNICATIONS LINES. MAQUIS LED BY O.G.'S CAPTURED OVER 10,000 PRISONERS.

○ OG SECTION
▲ JEDBURGH TEAM

DECLASSIFIED L-97
CIA - HR 70-2

PATHS OF LIBERATION An OSS chart lists the agency's contributions to the liberation of France, including operations launched before and after the invasion of Normandy and the Allied landings in southern France in August 1944. Many of those operations were conducted by the Maquis with arms furnished by the OSS.

10 DELAY TYPE FIRING DEVICES M-1 ASSORTED

SPY GEAR Among the weapons and gear supplied to Allied agents or resistance groups they supported were the garrote at top right, used to strangle opponents; the time fuses above, which enabled saboteurs to get away before explosives they laid destroyed strategic targets such as the bridge at upper right; the radio set concealed in a suitcase at lower right, used to report on German forces in Normandy before D-Day; and the knife at lower right, whose detachable handle could hold a suicide capsule.

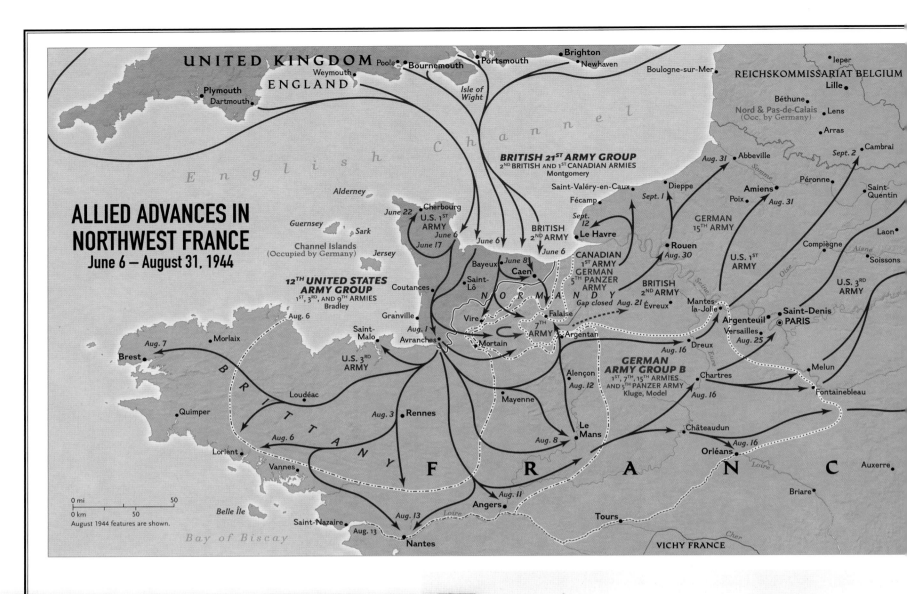

ALLIED ADVANCES IN NORTHWEST FRANCE
June 6 – August 31, 1944

UNITED KINGDOM
ENGLAND

Plymouth
Dartmouth
Weymouth
Poole
Bournemouth
Portsmouth
Brighton
Newhaven
Boulogne-sur-Mer

Isle of Wight

REICHSKOMMISSARIAT BELGIUM
Ieper
Lille
Béthune
Nord & Pas-de-Calais (Occ. by Germany)
Lens
Arras
Cambrai
Sept. 2

English Channel

Alderney
Guernsey
Sark
Jersey
Channel Islands (Occupied by Germany)

Cherbourg
June 22
U.S. 1ST ARMY
June 6
June 17

June 6
BRITISH 2ND ARMY
June 6

BRITISH 21ST ARMY GROUP
2ND BRITISH AND 1ST CANADIAN ARMIES
Montgomery

Saint-Valéry-en-Caux
Fécamp
Le Havre
Sept. 1
Aug. 31
Abbeville
Dieppe
Sept. 12
Poix
Aug. 31
Amiens
Péronne
Saint-Quentin
Laon
Compiègne
Soissons

12TH UNITED STATES ARMY GROUP
1ST, 3RD, AND 9TH ARMIES
Bradley

Bayeux
June 8
Caen

CANADIAN 1ST ARMY
GERMAN 5TH PANZER ARMY

Gap closed Aug. 21

GERMAN 15TH ARMY
Rouen
Aug. 30
U.S. 1ST ARMY

BRITISH 2ND ARMY
Évreux
Mantes-la-Jolie

U.S. 3RD ARMY

Coutances
Saint-Lô
NORMANDY
Granville
Vire
Falaise
7TH ARMY
Argentan

Mortain
Aug. 1

Dreux
Aug. 16

Argenteuil
Versailles
Aug. 25
Saint-Denis
PARIS

Saint-Malo
Avranches
Aug. 6

Morlaix
Aug. 7
Brest

U.S. 3RD ARMY

BRITTANY

Loudéac

Quimper

Lorient
Aug. 6

Vannes

Rennes
Aug. 3

Mayenne

Alençon
Aug. 12

GERMAN ARMY GROUP B
1ST, 7TH, 15TH ARMIES AND 5TH PANZER ARMY
Kluge, Model

Aug. 16

Chartres

Melun
Fontainebleau

Le Mans
Aug. 8

Châteaudun
Aug. 16
Orléans

FRANCE

Angers
Aug. 11

Aug. 13
Saint-Nazaire
Aug. 13
Nantes

Tours

VICHY FRANCE

Briare
Auxerre
Loire
Cher

0 mi   50
0 km   50
August 1944 features are shown.

Belle Île

Bay of Biscay

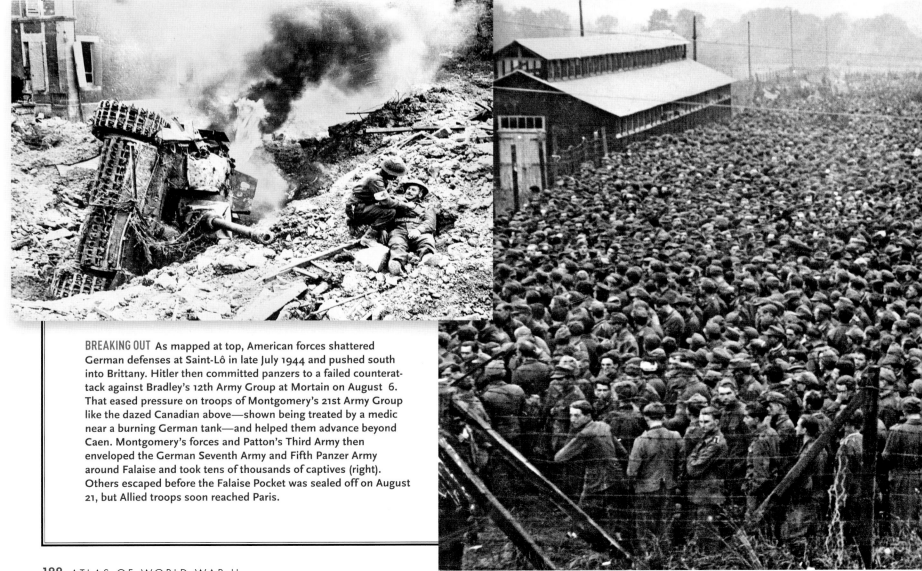

BREAKING OUT As mapped at top, American forces shattered German defenses at Saint-Lô in late July 1944 and pushed south into Brittany. Hitler then committed panzers to a failed counterattack against Bradley's 12th Army Group at Mortain on August 6. That eased pressure on troops of Montgomery's 21st Army Group like the dazed Canadian above—shown being treated by a medic near a burning German tank—and helped them advance beyond Caen. Montgomery's forces and Patton's Third Army then enveloped the German Seventh Army and Fifth Panzer Army around Falaise and took tens of thousands of captives (right). Others escaped before the Falaise Pocket was sealed off on August 21, but Allied troops soon reached Paris.

BRUSSELS AND NORTHERN FRANCE

GERMANY

LUXEMBOURG
(Annexed by
Germany)

GERMAN
1ST ARMY

Alsace & Lorraine
(Annexed by
Germany)

	German territory or German-occupied territory, August 1, 1944
	Allied territory, August 1, 1944
	Neutral state, August 1, 1944
→	Allied advances
→	Mortain counterattack August 7-12, 1944
- - -	Falaise Breakout August 20, 1944
——	Allied front line, August 1, 1944
- - -	Allied front line, August 6, 1944
-·-·-	Allied front line, August 13, 1944
······	Allied front line, August 20, 1944

THE ALLIED
BREAKOUT
FROM NORMANDY TO THE RHINE

O n July 25, 1944, more than 1,500 B-17s and B-24s launched Operation Cobra by carpet bombing German lines near Saint-Lô (see map at left), beyond which the tangled *bocage* gave way to open country allowing for rapid advances. Some bombs went astray, killing American troops, but the attack devastated enemy units like the Panzer Lehr Division, led by Gen. Fritz Bayerlein. "My front lines looked like the face of the moon," he related, "and at least 70 percent of my troops were knocked out—dead, wounded, crazed or numbed." His once dreaded division was left with only 14 tanks: "We could do nothing but retreat."

Among the American forces that poured through gaps forged by the bombers was Patton's newly arrived Third Army. No longer posing as commander of a fictitious army group destined for Calais, Patton served now under Omar Bradley, who on August 1 took charge of the genuine 12th Army Group, including the First Army, which he entrusted to Lt. Gen. Courtney Hodges. As Bradley's forces advanced southward into Brittany, Hitler tried to cut them off by ordering a reckless counterattack by battered divisions of the German Seventh Army at Mortain, where the panzers were blasted by artillery and air strikes. Patton then mounted his own blitzkrieg by sending armored divisions sweeping around the southern flank of the German Seventh Army while Montgomery's forces advanced to the north against the depleted Fifth Panzer Army. Caught in a pocket at Falaise, at least 50,000 Germans were killed, wounded, or captured. But many escaped when Field Marshal Günther von Kluge—who had taken charge of all German forces in France after Rundstedt was relieved and Rommel was wounded—allowed units to retreat without Hitler's permission. Like Rommel, Kluge had not warned Hitler after learning in advance of an assassination plot that culminated on July 20 when a bomb exploded at the Führer's headquarters without killing him. Recalled by Hitler to Germany in August, Kluge took his own life, as Rommel would two months later. In a letter written before he died, Kluge urged Hitler to spare Germans further suffering by ending "a struggle which has become hopeless." But Hitler would not surrender. Allies who had broken out in France would now have to batter their way into Germany. ■

CHRONOLOGY

JULY 25, 1944 American forces launch Operation Cobra in Normandy to break out of their beachhead.

AUGUST 15, 1944 Allied troops land along the French Mediterranean Coast in Operation Dragoon.

AUGUST 20–21, 1944 Germans are defeated in Normandy as the Falaise Pocket closes around those who have not escaped.

AUGUST 25, 1944 Free French soldiers liberate Paris following a partisan uprising there.

SEPTEMBER 17–25, 1944 Allied airborne forces fail to break through German lines near the Rhine in the Netherlands during Operation Market Garden.

DECEMBER 16, 1944 German offensive against American troops in the Ardennes ignites the Battle of the Bulge.

FEBRUARY 8, 1945 Western Allied forces begin advancing toward the Rhine, which they will cross in March.

HARD-WON TROPHY American infantrymen in France display a captured Nazi flag beside a disabled German tank in this photo taken at Chambois, near Falaise, as the pocket closed there in August.

ANOTHER D-DAY At right, Allied paratroopers descend near the French Riviera on August 15, 1944, to join others of the First Airborne Task Force who landed before dawn. The paratroopers helped clear the way for Truscott's VI Corps, which arrived from Italy (see inset map below) and came ashore around Saint-Tropez (main map below). Lt. Gen. Alexander Patch, commanding the U.S. Seventh Army, coordinated American and British operations with those of Free French troops under Gen. Jean de Lattre de Tassigny, whose forces arrived from North Africa and secured Marseille and Toulon on August 28. Around the same time, VI Corps closed the German 19th Army's escape route along the Rhône River.

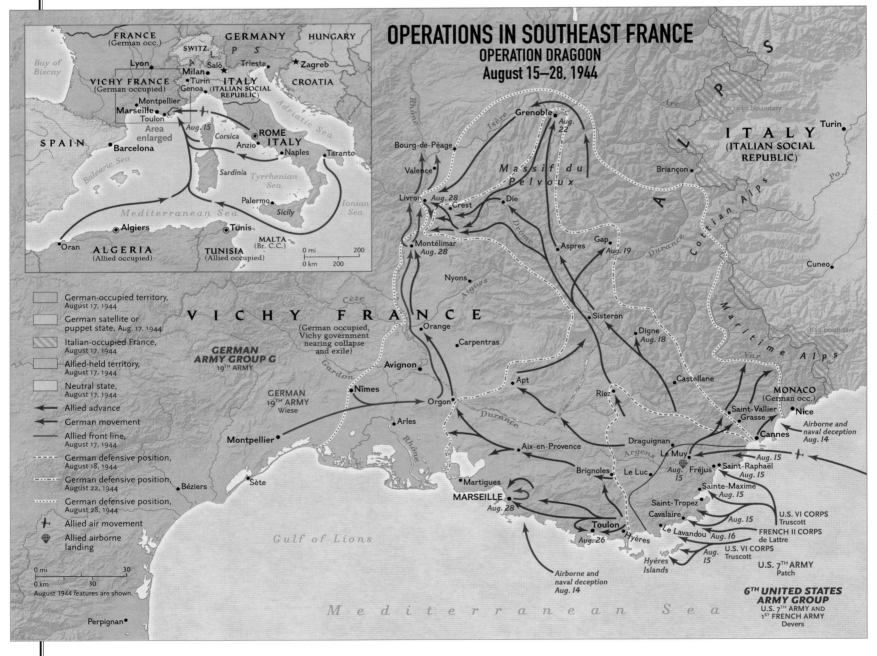

OPERATIONS IN SOUTHEAST FRANCE
OPERATION DRAGOON
August 15–28, 1944

Legend:
- German-occupied territory, August 17, 1944
- German satellite or puppet state, Aug. 17, 1944
- Italian-occupied France, August 17, 1944
- Allied-held territory, August 17, 1944
- Neutral state, August 17, 1944
- Allied advance
- German movement
- Allied front line, August 17, 1944
- German defensive position, August 18, 1944
- German defensive position, August 22, 1944
- German defensive position, August 28, 1944
- Allied air movement
- Allied airborne landing

OPERATION DRAGOON

Originally designated Operation Anvil and planned to coincide with the invasion of Normandy, the Allied invasion of southern France was renamed Operation Dragoon and postponed until August 1944. By then, many German troops in the south had been shifted northward to defend against the onslaught in Normandy. Those who remained behind were vulnerable to attack. Objectives for Allied forces assigned to Dragoon included capturing Marseille and other ports on the Mediterranean where supplies and reinforcements could be delivered, cutting off enemy forces in the south, and linking up with Allied armies in northern France for the decisive invasion of Germany.

Before dawn on August 15, American and British paratroopers of the First Airborne Task Force—who wore crests like the one inset—began landing inland to secure high ground along the French Riviera, where Gen. Lucian Truscott's U.S. VI Corps, transferred from Italy, came ashore at daybreak (see map opposite). Gains by Truscott's men and by Free French troops—who secured the ports of Marseille and Toulon—forced the German 19th Army to withdraw northward along the Rhône River. Truscott's corps then moved to cut off the Germans in the vicinity of Montélimar but met with strong resistance. Although much of the 19th Army escaped, more than 50,000 Germans were captured or killed before they could squeeze through the gap that VI Corps closed in late August. As one witness reported, Allied air strikes on roads clogged with German vehicles left "an inextricable tangle of twisted steel frames and charred corpses," which only bulldozers could clear.

Within three weeks of landing, Allied troops aided by French partisans had liberated much of southern France and linked up with invasion forces advancing eastward from Normandy. Operation Dragoon—undertaken over the objection of Churchill, who argued instead for an advance from Italy into the Balkans—strengthened Eisenhower's bid to invade Germany through France, which he and U.S. Army chief George Marshall had long viewed as the one sure path to victory. ∎

UNBOWED Facing no imminent threat, Allied troops stand upright after landing on the French Mediterranean coast on August 15, following a naval and air bombardment of German defenses that shrouded the beach in smoke. Allied casualties on the 15th were slight compared with losses on D-Day at Normandy.

THE LIBERATION OF PARIS

Parisians did not wait for Allied troops to free their city. On August 19, a loose coalition of resistance fighters known as French Forces of the Interior (FFI), which included Communists as well as followers of Free French leader Charles de Gaulle, rose up against German occupation forces in Paris commanded by Gen. Dietrich von Choltitz, who had orders from Hitler to destroy the city rather than surrender it. "Paris must not fall into the hands of the enemy," Hitler insisted, "except as a field of ruins." Reluctant to take actions that might brand him as a war criminal, Choltitz arranged a truce with the FFI that soon collapsed. "As long as there is a single German left in Paris, we shall fight," declared Henri Rol-Tanguy, a Communist firebrand known as Colonel Rol. Concerned that the uprising might fail and subject Parisians to reprisals—or succeed and leave Communists in control—de Gaulle urged Eisenhower to send in Allied troops, led by the French Second Armored Division.

When those French forces broke through German defenses outside Paris and entered the city on August 25, Choltitz defied orders and surrendered. On August 29, men of the U.S. 28th Infantry Division marched in a victory parade through Paris (opposite bottom). They then went straight to the front north of the city (see map below) to resume the war against Germany, which Hitler would prolong until Berlin lay in ruins. ∎

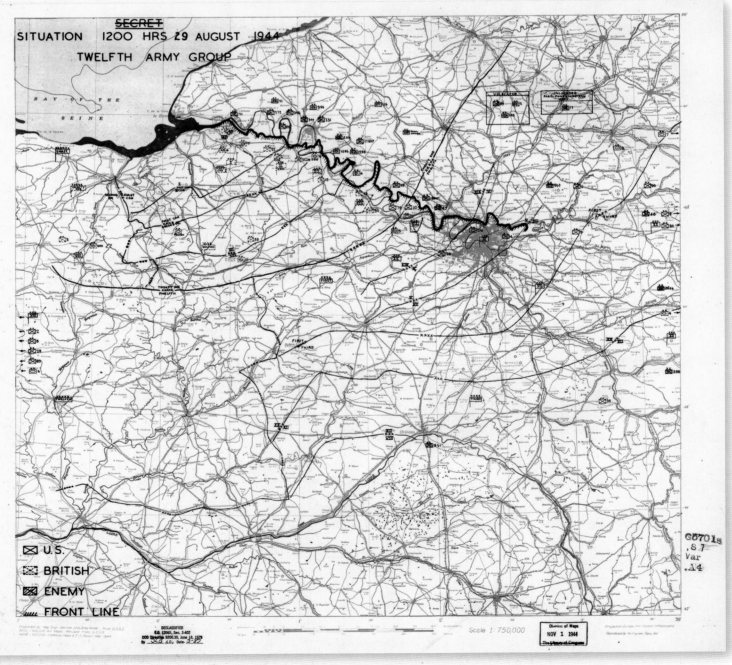

FRONT LINE A 12th Army Group map shows the front between Allied and German forces (thick black line) extending from the mouth of the Seine River (blue line) to just north of Paris on August 29. Shown around Paris are the U.S. Fourth and 28th Infantry Divisions and the French Second Armored Division.

UP IN ARMS Above, French partisans man a barricade in Paris during the uprising that began there on August 19 and ended six days later when French forces entered the city in triumph. Americans who followed the French into Paris were hailed as heroes like troops of the 28th Infantry Division (below), shown marching down the Champs-Élysées on August 29. After liberation, French women who had consorted with Germans had their heads shaved (right), and many French collaborators were executed.

FLYING BOMB Below, crewmen haul a V-1 guided missile into position for launching. RAF fighter pilots downed V-1s in various ways, including disrupting airflow over their wings, as attempted by the Spitfire at right. The map at bottom, published in September 1944, shows where 2,400 V-1s came down in Kent that summer. In the accompanying article, the county's civil defense chairman states that downing V-1s in Kent, where they caused hundreds of deaths, was justified to avoid greater casualties in London.

2,400 FLY BOMBS FELL IN KENT

200 MORE THAN LONDON

Official Story Of County's Ordeal

WHEN the sirens of Kent wailed in the early hours of Tuesday, June 13th, many sleepy-eyed people, clad in dressing gowns and slippers, rushed into their gardens as they heard a plane roaring overhead. It seemed in trouble.

Flames were shooting from its tail. Excitedly they shouted that another enemy bomber had fallen victim to our defences.

In the North Kent area the onlookers saw the plane plunge downward, and as it hit the ground there was a terrific explosion.

The plane fell en route into Invasion.

People dismissed it as an enemy bomber that had been shot down before it could release its bomb. The authorities knew better.

PRELUDE TO BATTLE

And so—two nights later—did the public, for the planes with the flaming tails came over too frequently to be ordinary bombers. Quietly it was realised that the Germans were using their much-vaunted V1 weapon.

The flying bomb menace had begun in earnest, and in all 2,400 of the bombs were to fall in Kent, 150 more than fell in London.

And just west, Alderman E. E. Churchman, C.B.E., chairman of Kent's Civil Defence Committee, reviewed the story of the county's ordeal during those fateful weeks, and we see the typical courage with which they were faced.

MAIDSTONE SHELLED THE SAME NIGHT

This is the story he told to reporters:—

"Much planning and preparation had been made preparatory for D-Day. Local Civil Defence services had been reinforced, the County Home Guard was strengthened, and supported by Regional Reserve personnel and other forces of England, whilst all attendant organisations had been reviewed and the brought to the highest pitch of efficiency.

D-Day came and passed. Our invasion was launched from Southampton and set from the Kent coast such had been prepared to be right out of the picture. Once again, as has happened so often in this war, vast and careful planning would seem to have been wasted.

The night of Monday, June 12th, passed quietly, when, at 03.06 in the early morning of Tuesday, 13th, Folkestone reporting that the town was being heavily shelled. An hour later Maidstone was also heavily shelled. The duel shelling seemed cold.

Towards the end of the Maidstone shelling it was reported that six brilliant falling away in flames was crossing this area heading for London.

THE FIRST OF THE MANY

At 06.26 this machine crashed at Swanscombe. The incident was reported within four minutes, and it was established as the first plutonea enemy to Greater—

Three-quarters of an hour later a second crashed at Cuxton. Meanwhile a than machine was exciting nutrend.

As I read the diddle, the guns on the French coast started Folkestone in order to cloud the machine plan whom was skilling Maidstone in order to divert attention from the spotting 'plane and the flying bottle.

The following night and early morning passed quietly, but shortly before midnight on the Thursday flying bombs were in prevail coming in in considerable numbers, in being shot down over Kent during the four 24 hours. Then the flying bottle had come and was to continue with us for some 80 days.

During the first week 101 were shot down over Kent, and in that then "possible" to visualise what was in store for her people.

KENT SAVED THE CAPITAL

It was obvious that London was the target and that the flying bomb was made to cover, roughly, the distance between the launching site and London. Between, all shooting to be relatively on London.

But it was equally obvious that London could not rely upon all her own defence, and that the fight to save London from the were would take place over that place, over the S.E. region of England, and Kent in particular. A hard, but inevitable decision.

Much has been said about shooting the flying bomb down into "open country."

What is this "open country"? Our coastal towns, pretty countryside dotted with villages, cottages, farms and houses. Here and there some lay down.

A flying bomb exploding in the air, let alone on the ground, will strip the roof, bring down the ceilings, shatter the windows of all beneath. Whether it be a cottage or 800 houses—and whether it be a cottage house, it was somebody's home.

So—to somebody's life, taken to save London. The punishment did not begin and end with the bomb for the county had to take a veritable hail of machine-gun bullets, and even shells as well as, for a long time, the fragments of A.A. gunfire.

I have seen one of them cry as a bomb swiped and sped Londonwards, and to see the typified Kent's attitude to London.

WATERY GRAVE

It was to round the middle of July that the A.A. guns were massed on the coast in a great arc, stretching from Dungeness to Dover, and have come into their own and the coast started pouring with 10 houses demolished. At Dartford news were killed, while Folkestone, Bexley, Maidstone, Beverides, Rokesdon, Watering-bury and others, to name a few, all mourned fatal casualties.

Flying 1,000 flying bombs were shot down within and several of them were destroyed in the air and the other towns down there suffering best.

The fight ended on Friday, September 1st, and Kent launching a sigh of relief—how deep each one of us duly knows in his own heart.

Kent's small 1,386 flying bomb's shot down on Kentish soil, 1,600 or more shot into the sea from her mast, 130 dead and 1,700 injured, and vast material damage.

The figure which I have given refer only to that part of Kent which is known, for our purposes, as S.E. Region, but actually the immense area than the eight areas and only a fraction of the heavier raids which have been and hand her Sidcup, Orpington, Bromley, Beckenham and Penge, while actual within the London boroughs, and statistical journal, must be credited to the administrative county of Kent and lay within its narrowing angle which lead to spot in the centre of London.

Then bombs justify, if justification was needed, the policy of shooting down the bombs over the more open part of Kent far from the S.E. which included on them 318 people and killed 1,700 people if need. A complete re-calculation must be frequently figured.

I think the fight of the flying bomb battle and one one look back on it.

LONDON'S DEBT TO KENT AND SUSSEX

Was the Government right in ordering, to be shot down, shot down amidst the continuous, and for war-time purposes increased London boundary? Yes. Of that there is not the faintest doubt. Every attempt to which you can put the known figures answers that question is the affirmative. London would never have won through come, or if she had her dead would have been numbered in London.

From the 1,000 bombs launched, Kent accounted for some 2, but.

Kent wasn't for behind that total, which means that these bombs, shot there, took the hatefuls of the plenty, destiny, at or to their own heads.

London may well honour Kent and Sussex.

I begin this statement by referring to the work that had been undertaken and prepared before D-Day and expressed the view that "it would seem to have been wasted." Whatever every not, every preparation, met the requirements of the flying bomb. Every service had been stretched to the utmost.

THE PEOPLE WERE GLORIOUS

Maidstone Borough, Tonbridge Rural, Bridge-Blean, Malling, Tunbridge Wells, Dartford Borough, Swanscombe, Maidstone Rural, New Romney, Hythe, Tenterden, and Cranbrook Rural, Sittingbourne, Sevenoaks Rural, Dover Borough, the Southern and the Medway group of towns all suffered severe casualties during August alone, and it would be invidious to praise.

Police, National Fire Service, Civil Defence, Local Government officials, U.S.—all and every service has given of its very best, but over and above all it has been the People themselves—the great and glorious People—whether it was driven a witness of a housewife at home—who beat V.1. It has been indeed a People's war, and bravely have the People waged it, whether they be of London or of Kent.

Where the Doodle Bugs Crashed in Kent.   Summer 1944.

This Map, exclusive to the "Kent Messenger," indicates where each flying bomb crashed in the Kent Section of the South East Region. It vividly portrays how Kent earned the name of "Bomb Alley."

EACH OF THESE SMALL DOTS REPRESENTS A FLYING BOMB BROUGHT DOWN INTO THE SEA

Reprinted from the "Kent Messenger" (the County Paper of Kent) issue of September 15th, 1944.

Editor and Proprietor: H. R. PRATT BOORMAN, Maidstone, Kent, England.

Price 6d.
ALL PROCEEDS TO SERVICE CHARITIES.

VENGEANCE WEAPONS

One week after D-Day in Normandy, Hitler hit back by ordering the first strike by V-1 guided missiles, aimed at London. Labeled "V" for "Vergeltung" (Vengeance), they were secret weapons but came as no surprise to British authorities, who had learned of the V-1 and made plans to defend against the missile, whose top speed of 375 miles an hour left it vulnerable to fighter planes and antiaircraft batteries. Several thousand V-1s were directed at London in the summer of 1944. But as shown on the map opposite, many came down southeast of the city in Kent, where they did less damage than in London because that county was not densely populated. Known as doodlebugs or buzz bombs for the ominous sound they made, V-1s sometimes fell short of London accidentally, but others were downed in Kent deliberately to reduce casualties in a city vital to the Allied war effort.

The V-1 menace diminished as the Allies bombed launch sites and occupied areas in France and Belgium within 150 miles of England, the missile's maximum range. But a new threat emerged that September—the V-2, a supersonic ballistic missile that could not be intercepted. With a range of 220 miles, V-2s could reach London from areas that remained in German hands until 1945. Many were also fired at Antwerp, a major Allied port in Belgium. Air strikes on Peenemünde, where the V-2 was developed, had disrupted production, however, and caused work to be shifted to an underground factory, where concentration camp inmates toiled in dreadful conditions. Far fewer V-2s were launched than V-1s, and far more people died producing V-2s than were killed by them. Meanwhile, Allied bombers devastated German cities, and Soviet troops prepared to wreak vengeance on the Reich for Hitler's ruinous invasion of Russia. ∎

BALLISTIC STRIKE A V-2 rocket like the one pictured at left on its launchpad hit London's Smithfield Market on March 8, 1945, killing more than 100 people and leaving survivors dazed like the man above.

PURSUIT TO THE WEST WALL

n early September 1944, Montgomery's 21st Army Group entered Belgium and seized the great port of Antwerp. Fuel and other essential supplies could not be delivered there, however, until the Allies seized German batteries along the Schelde River estuary and removed mines that menaced ships approaching Antwerp. Instead of focusing on that task, Montgomery proposed to leap ahead by sending paratroopers to seize bridges in Holland that his forces could use to cross the Rhine and invade the Ruhr, Germany's industrial heartland. Designated Market Garden, the risky operation collapsed in late September when German forces prevented airborne and armored forces from linking up at Arnhem and seizing a crucial bridge over the Rhine River (see maps below).

Market Garden delayed efforts to clear the way to Antwerp, which did not begin receiving supplies until late November. That slowed advances by Bradley's 12th Army Group, including Patton's Third Army, which ran short of fuel as it approached the West Wall (Siegfried Line), the defensive barrier along Germany's western frontier. "My men can eat their belts," Patton said, "but my tanks have gotta have gas." The one significant breach in the West Wall that autumn was achieved largely by infantry. In October, the battle-tested U.S. First Infantry Division—which had landed on Omaha Beach on D-Day—combined with the U.S. 30th Infantry Division to seize the heavily defended German city of Aachen, just across the border from Belgium. But Eisenhower lacked resources to exploit that breakthrough, and his forces would have to overcome a furious German counterattack before delving deeper into the Reich. ■

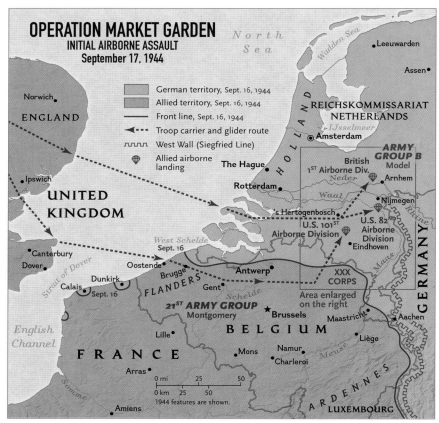

PERILOUS DESCENT Allied paratroopers who descended on Holland during Operation Market Garden (top left) suffered casualties when some came down awry (top center) and others came under fire (top right). The British First Airborne Division and U.S. 82nd and 101st Airborne Divisions flew from England (map at left) and landed in Holland near Arnhem, Nijmegen, and Eindhoven, respectively. U.S. paratroopers seized some bridges intact, but others were blown by Germans who kept tanks of the British XXX Corps from reaching Arnhem, where the First Airborne was crushed by the Ninth and 10th SS Panzer Divisions (map at right).

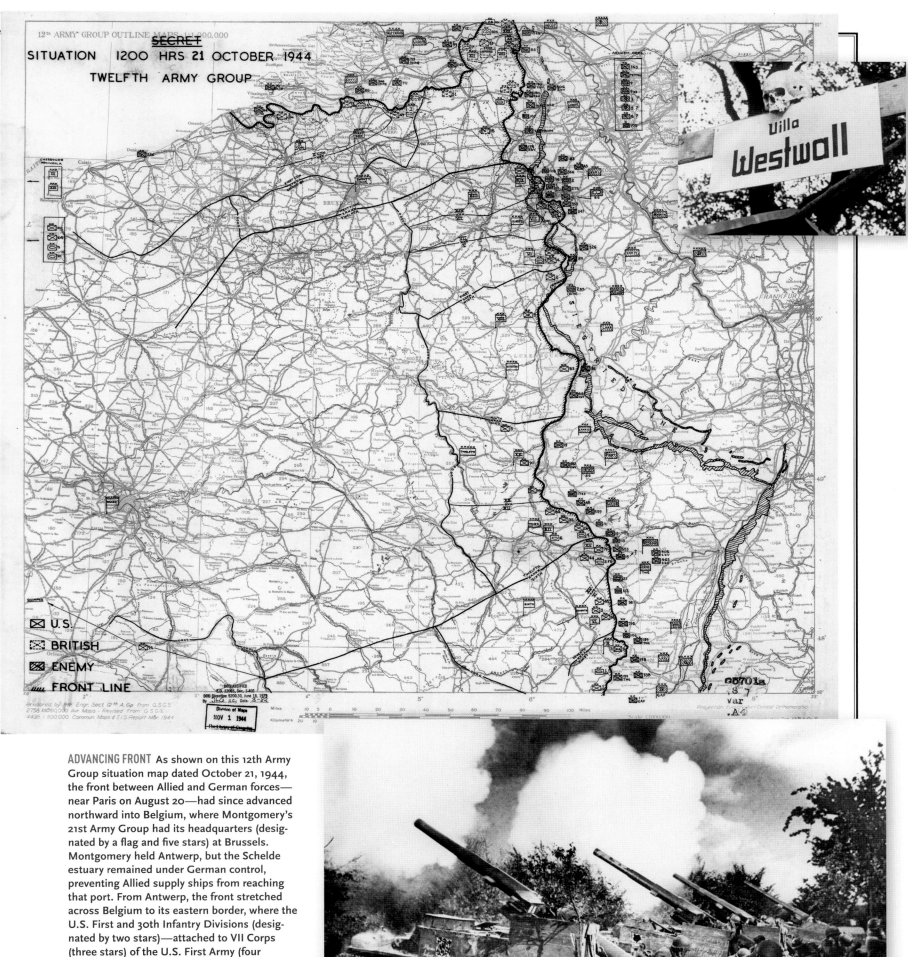

12th ARMY GROUP OUTLINE MAPS 1:1,000,000

SITUATION 1200 HRS 21 OCTOBER 1944

TWELFTH ARMY GROUP

⊠ U.S.
⊡ BRITISH
⊠ ENEMY
〜 FRONT LINE

Villa **Westwall**

ADVANCING FRONT As shown on this 12th Army Group situation map dated October 21, 1944, the front between Allied and German forces—near Paris on August 20—had since advanced northward into Belgium, where Montgomery's 21st Army Group had its headquarters (designated by a flag and five stars) at Brussels. Montgomery held Antwerp, but the Schelde estuary remained under German control, preventing Allied supply ships from reaching that port. From Antwerp, the front stretched across Belgium to its eastern border, where the U.S. First and 30th Infantry Divisions (designated by two stars)—attached to VII Corps (three stars) of the U.S. First Army (four stars)—had crossed into Germany and attacked Aachen, targeted by 155-mm guns mounted on the chassis of Sherman tanks (right). Aachen was captured, but First Army troops took heavy casualties in the dense Hürtgen Forest south of that city and made little progress. In France, Patton's Third Army and other forces of Bradley's 12th Army Group had not yet reached the West Wall on the German border (inset above) and were short of fuel and other supplies.

BATTLE OF THE BULGE

The greatest threat to the Reich in late 1944 came from Soviet troops, who entered the German state of East Prussia, where they assaulted civilians, many of whom fled westward to avoid the rampaging Red Army. Hitler chose to commit German reserves not against the Russians, however, but against Allied troops on the Western Front. By enlisting all able-bodied males between 16 and 60, he created new Volksgrenadier divisions and replenished depleted units for an assault on American lines in the forested Ardennes, which German tanks had crossed on their way to France in 1940. Hitler's objective was to recapture Antwerp and stall Allied armies in the West, enabling his forces to concentrate against Soviets in the East.

Launched on December 16 by infantry and armor, the attack caught Americans in the snow-covered Ardennes by surprise and pushed them back, forming a bulge in the front that would soon be 50 miles deep (see maps opposite). Bad weather prevented the Allies from launching air strikes or landing paratroopers, but Eisenhower sent 11,000 men of the 101st Airborne Division in trucks to hold Bastogne, a vital crossroads amid the bulge. When Germans surrounded them and demanded that their commander, Brig. Gen. Anthony McAuliffe, surrender, he replied "Nuts!" and kept up the fight until tanks of Patton's Fourth Armored Division broke through on December 26 and secured Bastogne. Allied forces then tightened their grip on the bulge, which became a death trap for tens of thousands of Germans, exposed to air strikes as the skies cleared. Hitler's costly decision to commit what remained of the Luftwaffe to the battle on January 1, 1945, failed to avert a bitter German defeat. All he achieved was to delay an Allied invasion of western Germany that would prove relatively merciful for civilians, while vengeful Soviet troops advanced toward Berlin. ■

FIRE AND ICE Searing combat in cold weather was trying for men on both sides, including a German machine-gunner in the Ardennes (top left) and a weary American at Bastogne (top right). Germans like those above, advancing past blasted Allied vehicles in December, were pounded and repulsed in January.

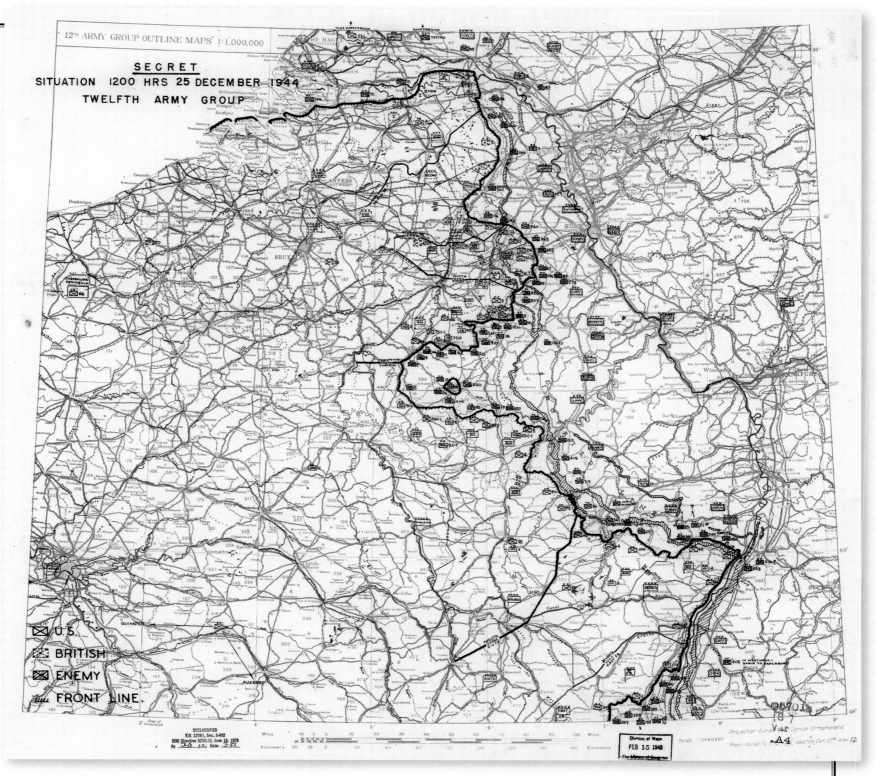

BUSTING THE BULGE Four 12th Army Group situation maps chart the Battle of the Bulge in sequence. On December 25 (above), the 101st Airborne Division was surrounded at Bastogne, amid the bulge, but the Fourth Armored Division was approaching from the south and reached Bastogne the next day. By January 1 (below left), the bulge was deeper because some Germans had advanced west toward the Meuse River. But it was also narrower because the 101st Airborne and other American units had pushed north from Bastogne, placing German units to the west at risk of being pinched off. By January 15 (below center), Hitler had authorized withdrawals and the bulge had receded. By January 31 (below right), Allied troops had closed off the bulge and won the battle.

JANUARY 1

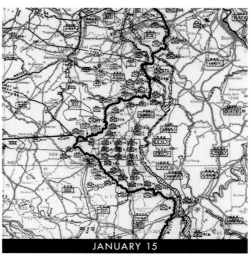

JANUARY 15

JANUARY 31

ACROSS THE RHINE

After winning the Battle of the Bulge, Allied forces under Eisenhower prepared to storm Germany by piercing the West Wall and crossing the broad Rhine River east of that fortified line. Montgomery's Canadian First Army and British Second Army would advance toward the Rhine from central Holland, while the U.S. Ninth Army would cross the Rur River in southern Holland to link up with those troops. Once that northern offensive was well under way, Bradley would unleash other American forces to the south, including Patton's Third Army in the Ardennes.

Montgomery's offensive in Holland began on February 8 near Nijmegen, where his earlier plan to break through German lines had faltered during Operation Market Garden. Once again, his forces met with stiff resistance. To complicate matters, Germans destroyed dams on the Rur River before Americans could secure them, causing floods that stalled the Ninth Army for two weeks and left British and Canadian troops only a narrow corridor in which to press forward. By late February, however, both the Ninth Army and the U.S. First Army to its south—whose troops had earlier breached the West Wall around Aachen—were on the move and pushing the enemy back toward the Rhine. Germans then began withdrawing across that river and destroying bridges behind them. On March 7, however, a railroad bridge at Remagen was seized while demolition was under way. Despite desperate German attempts to bring down the damaged bridge, American engineers kept it open until they could lay pontoon bridges across the river for advancing troops of the First Army.

In late March, the Allies launched a big push across the Rhine that included airborne assaults and amphibious landings on the east bank. By March 30, pincers consisting of Montgomery's forces to the north and Bradley's forces to the south were closing around Field Marshal Walther Model's depleted Army Group B in the Ruhr (see map opposite). Deemed a war criminal by the Soviets for relentless campaigns he waged in Russia that did not spare civilians, Model refused to surrender when his forces were surrounded in April and took his own life. ■

HAZARDOUS CROSSING Crouching to avoid enemy fire, men of the U.S. 89th Infantry Division cross the Rhine in a landing craft on March 26, 1945. After arriving in France in January 1945, the 89th joined Patton's hard-driving Third Army and suffered more than 1,000 casualties during the invasion of Germany.

CONQUEST The map below charts the situation on March 30, 1945, after Allied troops crossed the Rhine—shown as a blue line running along the front through Köln (Cologne)—and enveloped Model's Army Group B in the Ruhr. Advancing to the north are the Canadian First Army, British Second Army, and U.S. Ninth Army, attached to Montgomery's 21st Army Group. Advancing to the south is Bradley's 12th Army Group, including the U.S. First, Third, and Seventh Armies. At right, Seventh Army troops stand atop an abandoned German 274-mm railroad gun.

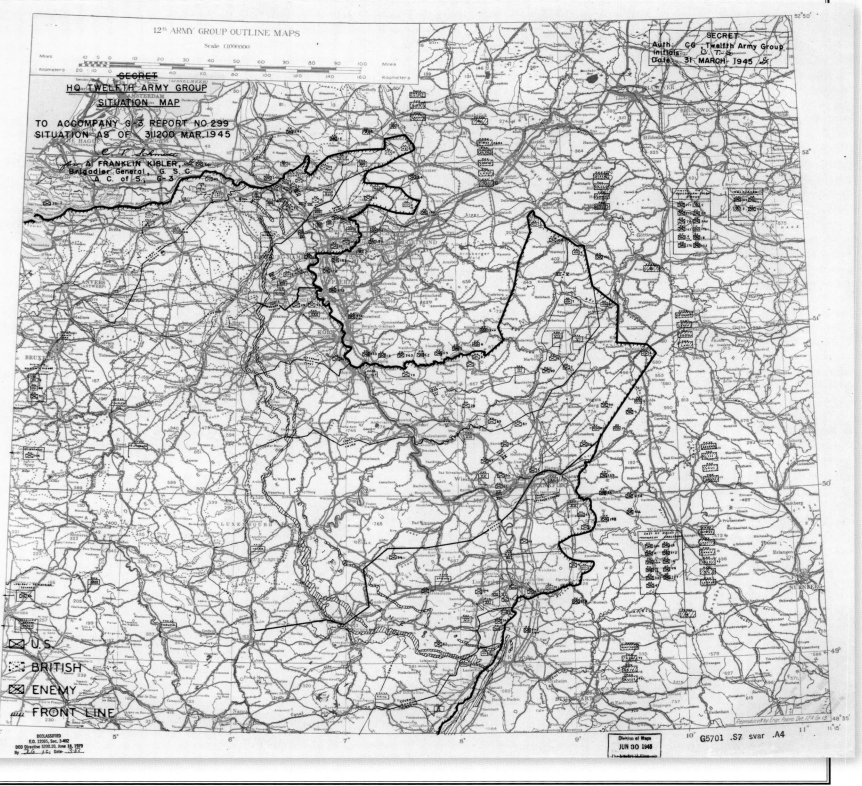

LONG HAUL IN ITALY

Allied troops who remained in Italy after the invasion of occupied France carried on a grueling campaign that brought them little attention or glory. Some Americans back home thought the war there was won when Rome fell to the Allies on June 5, 1944. Sgt. Bill Mauldin, who served with the U.S. 45th Infantry Division in Italy before becoming a cartoonist for the Army newspaper *Stars and Stripes*, wrote that soldiers received letters from misinformed well-wishers that said in effect, "I'm so glad you're in Italy while the fighting is in France." In fact, troops of the American-led Fifth Army and the British-led Eighth Army continued waging war in Italy without the numerical superiority that Allied forces elsewhere in Europe enjoyed. With 20 divisions in all, those two armies kept 26 German divisions tied down in Italy and succeeded in breaking through the fortified Gothic Line in the mountains north of Florence before winter weather halted operations temporarily in December 1944.

OSS mapmakers provided the U.S. Army with a three-dimensional plaster model of northern Italy (opposite), showing the steep terrain that Allied troops traversed in late 1944 and the populous Po River Valley, which those troops entered in the spring of 1945. The OSS also sent agents and officers like those pictured below behind enemy lines on secret missions that included helping Italian partisans attack German occupation forces and Fascist militias. Such covert operations helped undermine Mussolini, who was captured by partisans and executed on April 28, 1945. By then, Gen. Heinrich von Vietinghoff, whose German troops were being routed in the Po Valley by the Fifth and Eighth Armies, was engaged in talks that would lead him to surrender his forces on May 2, completing the liberation of Italy. ∎

ALLIED INFILTRATORS Pictured are officers who operated behind German lines in Italy, including Lt. Richard Kelly (far left), whose OSS Maritime Unit landed Italian marines in German territory to serve as Allied spies and saboteurs.

3-D TOPO MAP Designed to provide officers with an in-depth view of the terrain Allied troops traversed in northern Italy, this OSS plaster model reveals the contrast between the rugged Apennine Mountains north of Florence—which had few roads and favored German defenders—and the accessible Po Valley, which enabled rapid Allied advances in the spring of 1945. Italian partisans seized control of Milan and Turin on April 25, before Allied troops arrived there, and that became Italy's Liberation Day.

NORTHERN ADVANCES The map at right charts Operation Bagration—a huge Russian offensive unleashed in June 1944 that was aimed mainly at Army Group Center in German-occupied Belarus and Poland but also targeted Army Group North in the Baltic states. As Soviets advanced, they were embraced by some civilians like the Polish man below, but many Poles would come to regard them as occupiers.

SOUTHERN INVASIONS As mapped at bottom, an offensive launched in August 1944 brought Romania, Bulgaria, and Hungary under Soviet control. Russians also entered territory that would soon be reconstituted as Yugoslavia by Marshal Tito, a Communist who would resist alignment with Moscow.

RUSSIAN OPERATIONS IN NORTH CENTRAL EUROPE
June 22 – August 19, 1944

	German territory or German-occupied territory, June 22, 1944
	Russian territory, June 22, 1944

Russian advances

Eastern Front
— June 22, 1944
--- July 18, 1944
⋯ Aug. 19, 1944

RUSSIAN OPERATIONS IN SOUTH CENTRAL EUROPE
Aug. 19 – Dec. 26, 1944

	Axis territory or Axis-occupied territory, Aug. 19, 1944		Allied-held territory, Aug. 19, 1944
	Axis ally or dependent state, Aug. 19, 1944		Neutral state, Aug. 19, 1944
	Russian territory, Aug. 19, 1944		Russian advance
			Axis retreat

Eastern Front
— Aug. 19, 1944
--- Sept. 26, 1944
⋯ Dec. 31, 1944

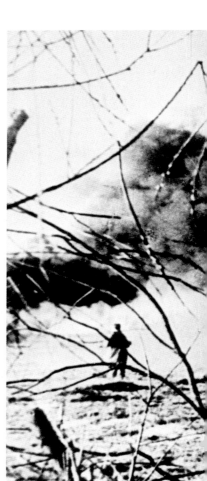

DESTRUCTION OF
NAZI GERMANY
THE RED ARMY'S ASSAULT ON THE REICH

On June 22, 1944, three years to the day after German troops invaded Soviet territory, the Red Army launched Operation Bagration, a massive offensive on the Eastern Front aimed primarily at annihilating Army Group Center, the once mighty force that reached the outskirts of Moscow in 1941. Having since recaptured from the Germans nearly all the ground held by the Soviet Union before the war began, the Red Army now advanced into areas that Stalin had annexed following his ill-fated pact with Hitler in 1939, including the Baltic states and Belarus, a borderland long disputed by Russia and Poland. Deceptions indicating a Russian offensive to the south around the Black Sea left Germans to the north exposed when nearly 1.5 million Soviet troops attacked. Hitler made things worse by not allowing forces caught in that onslaught to withdraw until it was too late. The Fourth and Ninth Armies were decimated as pincers closed around them at Minsk (see top map opposite), and the Third Panzer Army was hard-hit as well.

Russians then advanced into German-annexed Poland before halting to regroup in August at the Vistula River near Warsaw, where a determined uprising by Polish partisans against German occupation forces was eventually crushed.

The Red Army did not renew its offensive in Poland and take Warsaw until January 1945. In the meantime, Russian troops made great strides to the north—where they advanced from the Baltic states into East Prussia—and momentous gains to the south, where they invaded Romania and other nations allied with Germany (bottom map opposite). After Soviets seized the Ploesti oil fields and denied their output to fuel-hungry German forces, King Michael I of Romania ousted that country's pro-Nazi dictator, Ion Antonescu, and yielded to Russia. Bulgaria switched sides as well, but German troops kept Hungary from leaving the Axis until Budapest fell in February 1945. By then, Russians were poised to deliver the deathblow to Hitler's regime in Berlin—and dominate Eastern Europe for decades to come. ■

CHRONOLOGY

JUNE 22, 1944 Soviets launch Operation Bagration, a major offensive that will carry them beyond Russia's prewar border to the Vistula River near Warsaw by early August.

AUGUST 1, 1944 Partisans of the Polish Home Army launch the Warsaw Uprising against German occupation forces, who will crush the insurgency within two months.

AUGUST 20, 1944 Soviets launch an offensive along the Black Sea that will force Romania and Bulgaria to abandon the Axis and yield to Moscow.

OCTOBER 16, 1944 Red Army troops enter East Prussia, the first German state threatened by the Soviets, who will follow this incursion with a massive invasion three months later.

FEBRUARY 4–11, 1945 Stalin, Roosevelt, and Churchill meet at Yalta in Crimea and agree to divide Germany into occupation zones and partition Berlin.

FEBRUARY 13, 1945 Budapest falls to the Soviets, who gain control of Hungary.

APRIL 16, 1945 Red Army troops in eastern Germany launch a decisive offensive against Berlin.

APRIL 25, 1945 American and Soviet forces meet along the Elbe River in Germany.

APRIL 30, 1945 Hitler commits suicide as Soviets overrun Berlin.

MAY 7–8, 1945 Germany surrenders unconditionally to the Allies.

GERMANY BESIEGED Soviet tanks and troops advance in early 1945 toward Königsberg, a port in East Prussia from which Germans were evacuated until that besieged city fell to the Russians in April.

CARVING UP THE REICH
RESULTS OF THE POTSDAM CONFERENCE OF
July 17 – August 2, 1945

Although agreed upon at the Potsdam Conference, boundaries were not fully implemented until 1947.

American Zone
British Zone
French Zone
Polish Zone
Soviet Zone

Allied powers declared that Austria was a victim of Nazi aggression and should be liberated, but the Soviet occupation of eastern Austria was harsh.

0 mi   50   100
0 km 50 100
1947 features are shown.

CARVING UP GERMANY The map at right shows postwar Soviet, American, British, French, and Polish occupation zones in Germany and German-annexed Austria, including the divided cities of Berlin and Vienna. Plans made at Yalta to partition the Reich were not confirmed until Allied leaders met at Potsdam in July 1945. Nothing prohibited Eisenhower's forces from entering the proposed Soviet zone in April 1945 and seizing Berlin, as urged by Churchill. As mapped below, on April 15, Eisenhower decided to halt U.S. troops of the 12th Army Group short of Berlin and concentrate on securing areas in and around western Germany that his forces had not yet occupied.

CLOSING IN ON BERLIN
April 15, 1945

0 mi   50   100
0 km 50 100
1945 features are shown.
Present-day city names are in parentheses.

Many of the post war European boundaries were formalized in the Potsdam Agreement, Aug. 1, 1945

German territory or German-occupied territory, April 15, 1945
German ally or dependent state, April 15, 1945
Allied territory, April 15, 1945
Allied-held territory, April 15, 1945
Neutral state, April 15, 1945
——— Front line, April 15, 1945

DIVIDED AND CONQUERED

Stalin had a strong hand to play when he met with Roosevelt and Churchill at the Crimean city of Yalta in February 1945. Recent advances by the Red Army had positioned Soviets to occupy eastern Germany while American, British, and French troops occupied western Germany. Separate occupation zones for those forces were drawn up at Yalta along with plans to divide Berlin, which was situated in the Soviet zone but would be partitioned among the Allied Powers (see top map opposite).

Left unresolved was who would capture Berlin. After Eisenhower's troops seized the Ruhr in early April, armed opposition wilted in western Germany but persisted in the east, where Russian soldiers enraged by the brutal German occupation of their homeland were raping German women and committing other atrocities. Millions of German civilians in the path of the Red Army were evacuated or fled westward on their own initiative to escape the Soviet occupation zone (below).

American units, advancing up to 50 miles a day, entered that zone and met Soviet forces along the Elbe and Mulde Rivers in late April (bottom map opposite). Yanks and Russians embraced there (inset), but at higher levels the alliance was severely strained.

Churchill, who doubted Stalin's promise at Yalta to hold free elections in Poland, had urged Eisenhower to take Berlin as a way of prodding Stalin to honor his commitment. But there was no assurance that the Soviet dictator and his huge Red Army would yield to such pressure. Eisenhower stuck by his decision to stop short of Berlin with the support of 12th Army Group commander Omar Bradley, who estimated that seizing the capital would cost at least 100,000 casualties and called that a "pretty stiff price to pay for a prestige objective . . . especially when we've got to fall back and let the other fellow take over." Soviet commanders, on the other hand, had suffered more than 10 million casualties fighting the Germans and were eager to storm Berlin and drive a stake through the heart of Hitler's Reich. ∎

SEEKING REFUGE German civilians fleeing assaults by Russian forces cross a damaged railroad bridge over the Elbe River in 1945 with baggage in hand, seeking refuge to the west. One Red Army veteran stated bluntly that Soviet invaders raped German women "on a collective basis."

THE FALL OF BERLIN

The final battle in the savage struggle between Germany and Russia opened before dawn on April 16, 1945, when Soviet artillery along the Oder River unleashed a thunderous bombardment that reverberated 40 miles away on the outskirts of Berlin (see map below). German troops had pulled back to avoid that pounding and held firm initially. But they could not long withstand onslaughts by the First Belorussian Front under Marshal Georgi Zhukov, hailed as the savior of Moscow, whose numerically superior forces now bludgeoned their way toward Berlin. "They keep coming at us in hordes, wave after wave," reported a commander in the depleted German Ninth Army, mauled at Minsk the year before. "My men are fighting until they run out of ammunition," he added. "Then they are wiped out or completely overrun." To the south, Marshal Ivan Konev, commander of the First Ukrainian Front, shredded the Fourth Panzer Army before pivoting toward Berlin to compete with Zhukov for that prize. "Whoever reaches Berlin first," said Stalin, "let him take it." Zhukov had a shorter path to the city and won the race, but Konev's swift advance drew a noose around the capital.

On April 26, a half million Soviets launched a furious assault on central Berlin, site of the Reich Chancellery—under which lay Hitler's bombproof Führerbunker—and the nearby Reichstag, the old German parliament building, abandoned after an arsonist set it ablaze in 1933 and Hitler seized emergency powers. Berlin's last-ditch defenders, including Waffen-SS units and civilians of the Volkssturm, a people's militia made up largely of boys and old men, were outmanned and outgunned. But many fought to the bitter end in subway tunnels and streets as the city became a funeral pyre for the Reich and the leader who drove it to ruin. On April 30, Adolf Hitler committed suicide and was cremated by aides. That evening, Soviet troops fought their way into the Reichstag and raised their red flag over the smoldering capital. A week later, Grand Adm. Karl Dönitz, left in charge of the doomed Reich and its shattered armed forces, conceded defeat, and Germany surrendered unconditionally to the victorious Allies. ■

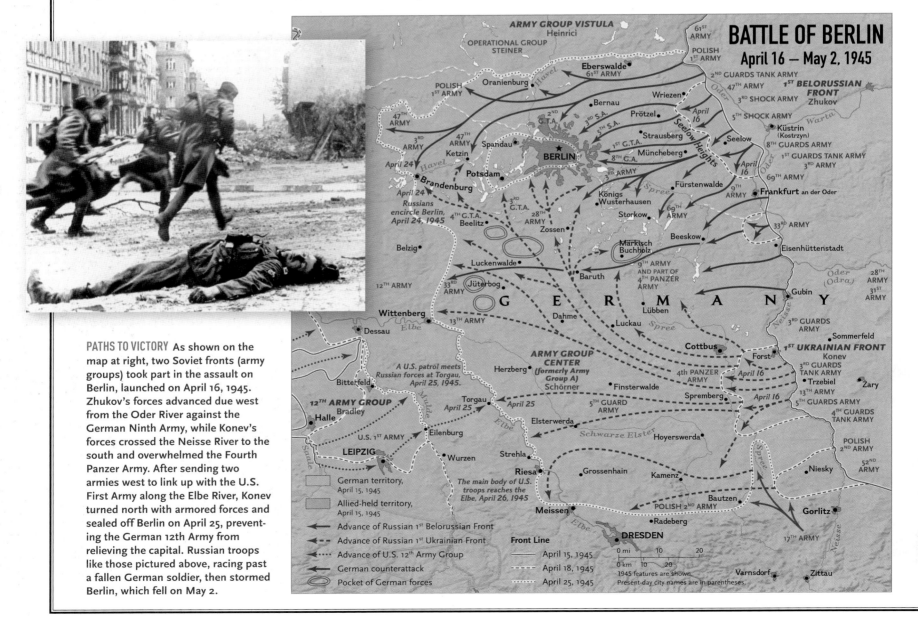

PATHS TO VICTORY As shown on the map at right, two Soviet fronts (army groups) took part in the assault on Berlin, launched on April 16, 1945. Zhukov's forces advanced due west from the Oder River against the German Ninth Army, while Konev's forces crossed the Neisse River to the south and overwhelmed the Fourth Panzer Army. After sending two armies west to link up with the U.S. First Army along the Elbe River, Konev turned north with armored forces and sealed off Berlin on April 25, preventing the German 12th Army from relieving the capital. Russian troops like those pictured above, racing past a fallen German soldier, then stormed Berlin, which fell on May 2.

HEART OF BERLIN
April 1945

Lehrter Bahnhof

Moltke Bridge
Ministry of the Interior

Königsplatz

Kroll Opera House
Reichstag

Victory Column

Brandenburge Gate

TIERGARTEN
Führerbunker

Zoo Flak Tower
Reich Chancellery

Berlin Zoo

Landwehr Canal

0 mi 0.25 0.5
0 km 0.25 0.5

Potsdamer Bridge
Potsdamer Bahnhof

Kaiser Wilhelm Memorial Church

DEATHBLOW As traced below on a Red Army map showing Soviet advances in central Berlin, troops of Gen. Vasily Chuikov's Eighth Guards Army crossed the Landwehr Canal below the Tiergarten, a park adjacent to the Reichstag and Reich Chancellery (see map of the same area at left). Meanwhile, the Third Shock Army crossed the Spree River above the park. That sealed Berlin's fate and led Hitler to commit suicide in his Führerbunker (right) on April 30. Soviets raised their flag over the Reichstag that night—and reenacted the flag-raising for posterity on May 2 (above).

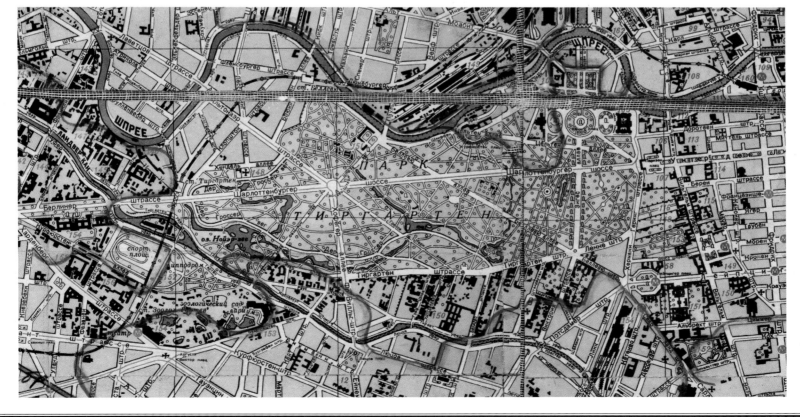

AUSCHWITZ-BIRKENAU COMPLEX
OSWIECIM, POLAND
26 JUNE 1944

BIRKENAU
(AUSCHWITZ II)

SS BARRACKS

BODY ASHES THROWN
INTO MARSHES

AUSCHWITZ I

PRZEMSZA RIVER

SOLA RIVER

VISTULA RIVER

SS WAR INDUSTRIES
(I.G. FARBEN ETC.)

AUSCHWITZ III (BUNA)

ENLARGED FROM THE ORIGINAL NEGATIVE AND
CAPTIONED IN 1978 BY THE CIA

PHOTO MAP In 1978, CIA photoanalysts used World War II reconnaissance photographs of an I.G. Farben plant (right) to zero in on the nearby Auschwitz-Birkenau killing center and expose gas chambers, crematoriums, and prisoner barracks (below). Proposals to curb such atrocities included bombing railroads used to deliver prisoners (above) and bombing camps, which provided slave labor for war work at I.G. Farben and elsewhere.

GUARD TOWERS

WOMEN'S CAMPS

PRISONERS

PRISONERS

CREMATORIUM II

UNDRESSING ROOM

GAS CHAMBER

CREMATORIUM

ENGINE ROOM

PRISONERS

UNDRESSING ROOM

ENGINE ROOM

BOXCARS

PRISONERS ON WAY TO GAS CHAMBERS

ENLARGED FROM THE ORIGINAL NEGATIVE AND
CAPTIONED IN 1978 BY THE CIA

CREMATORIUM III

GAS CHAMBER

EXPOSING THE DEATH FACTORIES

The horrors of the Nazi regime were laid bare in 1945 when Allied troops liberated concentration camps whose guards had fled, leaving behind skeletons in crematoriums (bottom) and skeletal prisoners, many of whom starved to death. Such appalling evidence of genocide raised a troubling question: What could the Allies have done to combat the systematic murder of millions? In mid-1944, the U.S. War Department had considered proposals to bomb Auschwitz, a sprawling camp that included Birkenau, a killing center where as many as 10,000 people a day died in gas chambers. Authorities decided against bombing Auschwitz, mainly to avoid diverting resources from attacks on strategic targets essential to the German war effort. But they also wanted to avoid killing prisoners. It was hard to map targets precisely, and even harder to bomb precise targets like gas chambers without destroying nearby barracks housing tens of thousands of inmates.

In August 1944, American warplanes bombed an I.G. Farben plant that produced synthetic petroleum and rubber for Germany and was located within five miles of Birkenau. Aerial reconnaissance photographs of that plant and its surroundings taken between April 1944 and early 1945 were later examined by two photoanalysts at the Central Intelligence Agency, Dino Brugioni and Robert Poirier, who used techniques unavailable during World War II to produce close-up photographic maps of Birkenau (opposite bottom). Their images also documented the dismantling of that killing center in January 1945 as Soviet troops approached Auschwitz in German-occupied Poland. In a futile effort to eliminate evidence of Nazi atrocities, SS chief Heinrich Himmler ordered Auschwitz and some other camps evacuated and dismantled before Allied forces reached them. That did not stop the carnage. Prisoners were marched to concentration camps farther from Allied lines, and many died along the way. Others were shot by guards or herded into buildings that were set afire. Those who survived the journey were crammed into filthy compounds and left to starve when Allied forces drew near.

Whether SS camps or railroads leading to them should have been bombed to curtail such atrocities would long be debated. But as shown by the murderous treatment of Jews and other prisoners as the Third Reich crumbled, only one thing could end the slaughter—defeat and destruction of the criminal Nazi regime. ∎

OUTRAGE **Horrific scenes in liberated concentration camps—including human remains in ovens at Buchenwald (below) and piles of dead at Dachau (left)—fueled debate over whether bombing could have reduced the death toll and should have been authorized.**

CHAPTER 5

DEFEATING JAPAN | 1943-1945

"Gentlemen, we will not neutralize;
we will not destroy;
we will obliterate the defenses."

REAR ADM. HOWARD KINGMAN,
PREPARING TO BOMBARD TARAWA ATOLL

FIREPOWER Smoke rings billow from a battery of five-inch guns aboard the cruiser U.S.S. *Minneapolis,* firing at Japanese positions on Makin Atoll in the Gilbert Islands on November 20, 1943. Despite intense bombardments here and on nearby Tarawa Atoll, attacked the same day, Japanese troops resisted fiercely before they were annihilated in fighting that foretold a long, bitter struggle to win control of the Pacific and force Japan to surrender.

FIGHT TO THE DEATH

CRUSHING JAPANESE RESISTANCE

President Roosevelt signaled a fundamental shift in the war against Japan during his State of the Union Address in early 1943. "Last year, we stopped them," he said of Japanese forces. "This year, we advance." Allied victories on Guadalcanal and Papua confirmed that Japanese gains in the Pacific had indeed been halted. But there was no consensus on how to advance and win the war. Gen. Douglas MacArthur, having pledged to return to the Philippines, insisted that the road to Tokyo ran through Manila. Adm. Ernest King, chief of the U.S. Navy and Marine Corps, argued for island-hopping across the central Pacific until Japan was within range of strategic bombers and invasion forces. Others urged an Allied offensive in Burma that would aid Chinese troops against Japanese invaders. A nation with limited resources would have had to choose between those options, but America was now fully mobilized. The most productive of the major warring powers— and the only one to avoid sustained attacks on its homeland— the United States could pursue various paths to victory.

In May 1943, the Joint Chiefs of Staff authorized a dual drive against Japan by MacArthur and Adm. Chester Nimitz, the Pacific Fleet commander. Although the two belonged to different military branches and took different approaches, there was close cooperation between services. U.S. naval forces supported MacArthur's soldiers as they took New Guinea and invaded the Philippine island of Leyte in October 1944. Nimitz's sailors, naval airmen, and Marines were joined by Army troops who shared the burden of seizing islands that Japanese troops defended to the death, including bases on Tarawa and Makin Atolls captured by American forces in November 1943. Subsequent landings on Saipan, Tinian, and Guam in the Mariana Islands allowed B-29s to begin blasting Japan in late 1944. But that was not enough to induce surrender. Island fighting intensified in February 1945 with the American invasion of Iwo Jima, where Lt. Gen. Tadamichi Kuribayashi vowed that every man would "resist until the end, making his position his tomb." By then, U.S. submarine attacks had stemmed the flow of oil and other vital supplies to Japan, and it faced dual threats— invasion by way of Okinawa and nuclear Armageddon as the top secret Manhattan Project achieved its explosive objective. Japan's leaders were learning a hard lesson that Kuribayashi had absorbed while serving as a prewar military attaché in Washington. "The United States," he wrote then, "is the last country in the world Japan should fight."

MAY 1943–SEPTEMBER 1944

May 11, 1943 U.S. troops land on Attu in the Aleutian Islands, launching a campaign that will oust Japanese forces from the Aleutians.

May 12–25, 1943 Allied leaders meet at the Trident Conference in Washington, D.C., and authorize an offensive in northern Burma by troops under Lt. Gen. Joseph Stilwell and a bombing campaign by Maj. Gen. Claire Chennault's 14th Air Force in China.

June 21–30, 1943 Operation Cartwheel begins as U.S. Marines under Adm. William Halsey's command land on Japanese-occupied New Georgia in the Solomon Islands and General MacArthur's troops advance on New Guinea.

August 31, 1943 Col. Carl Eifler, head of OSS Detachment 101, sends Capt. Vincent Curl to recruit Kachin warriors to serve as guerrillas behind Japanese lines in Burma.

November 1, 1943 U.S. forces invade Bougainville, the ultimate objective in Halsey's campaign for control of the Solomons.

November 20, 1943 American forces land on Tarawa and Makin Atolls in the Gilbert Islands, the first steps in an advance across the central Pacific directed by Admiral Nimitz and Vice Adm. Raymond Spruance, commander of the U.S. Fifth Fleet.

December 26, 1943 The First Marine Division lands at Cape Gloucester on New Britain as U.S. air strikes on Rabaul intensify, neutralizing that big Japanese base.

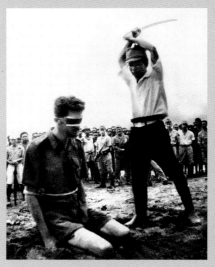

Japanese officer executing a captured Australian commando in New Guinea

OCTOBER 1944–SEPTEMBER 1945

October 20, 1944 MacArthur returns to the Philippines by landing with his troops on Leyte.

October 23–26, 1944 The U.S. Third and Seventh Fleets inflict a crushing defeat on the Japanese Navy in the Battle of Leyte Gulf. Kamikaze attacks by Japanese pilots on U.S. warships begin and will intensify in months to come.

November 24, 1944 B-29 bombers based on Saipan launch the first American air strike on Tokyo from the Marianas, targeting the Nakajima aircraft-engine factory.

Kamikaze pilot with rising-sun headband

Attempted kamikaze attack on aircraft carrier U.S.S. Sangamon off Okinawa

February 1, 1944
American forces land on Japanese-occupied Kwajalein in the Marshall Islands.

February 17–18, 1944
U.S. Navy forces attack the Japanese naval and air base on Truk in the Caroline Islands to cover landings on Eniwetok in the Marshalls.

February 29, 1944
MacArthur's troops invade the Admiralty Islands off New Guinea to secure airfields for Maj. Gen. George Kenney's Fifth Air Force, supporting the New Guinea campaign.

March 8, 1944 Lt. Gen. Renya Mutaguchi launches a costly Japanese advance from Burma into India, where his troops will falter under pressure and withdraw in July.

March 31–April 1, 1944 Adm. Mineichi Koga, successor to Yamamoto as commander of Japan's Combined Fleet, dies in a plane crash in the Philippines,

during which Japanese plans to launch a decisive naval battle in the Pacific are lost and later recovered by the Allies.

April 22, 1944 MacArthur's forces land at Hollandia, New Guinea, continuing a campaign in which they advance along the north coast of New Guinea toward the Philippines with support from the U.S. Seventh Fleet and Australian units.

May 27, 1944 MacArthur's troops land on Biak off New Guinea's north coast.

U.S. Marine hurling a hand grenade at Japanese troops on Tarawa Atoll

June 15, 1944
Marines shielded by Spruance's Fifth Fleet invade Saipan in the Mariana Islands, where air bases will be constructed for bombers targeting Japan.

June 19-20, 1944
Naval airmen of Task Force 58, dispatched by Spruance under the command of Vice Adm. Marc Mitscher, win the Battle of the Philippine Sea west of the Marianas with support from U.S. submarines.

July 21–24, 1944 Marines land on Guam and Tinian in the Marianas.

July 26–27, 1944 President Roosevelt confers with MacArthur and Nimitz in Honolulu and approves MacArthur's plan to retake the Philippines, with support from the U.S. Navy.

August 3, 1944 Stilwell's troops capture Myitkyina in northern Burma, clearing the way for supplies from India to reach the Chinese Nationalist base at Kunming along the Ledo and Burma Roads.

September 15, 1944 Marines land on Peleliu in the Palau Islands. MacArthur's troops land on Morotai, an island west of New Guinea that will serve as a base for invading the Philippines.

Battle-weary Marine smoking a cigarette after landing with American forces on Saipan

---

December 10, 1944
U.S. forces capture the port of Ormoc, on the west coast of Leyte, cutting off Japanese reinforcements to that island and enabling MacArthur to proceed with his planned invasion of the main Philippine island, Luzon.

January 9, 1945
Troops of the U.S. Sixth Army land on Luzon unopposed but will encounter stiff Japanese opposition as they advance toward Clark Field and Manila.

February 3, 1945 U.S. troops enter Manila, where they will battle Japanese forces holding out in the city's walled historic district, Intramuros.

February 19, 1945 Marines land on Iwo Jima, where a bitter, five-week-long battle ensues.

March 3, 1945 MacArthur's forces take Manila, but their efforts to secure Luzon and other Philippine islands will continue into the summer.

March 9–10, 1945 B-29s fire-bomb Tokyo, devastating the Japanese capital.

Col. Paul Tibbets (center) and ground crew at Tinian, standing before the B-29 Enola Gay that would bomb Hiroshima

April 1, 1945 American troops invade Okinawa, incurring desperate Japanese opposition on land and at sea.

April 12, 1945 President Roosevelt dies and is succeeded by Harry S. Truman, who learns for the first time of the top secret American effort to produce atomic bombs.

May 3, 1945 British forces recapture the Burmese capital Rangoon.

June 18, 1945 Truman approves an invasion of Kyushu, one of the

Japanese home islands, in late 1945, but he hopes to defeat Japan before then using atomic bombs, if necessary.

July 16, 1945 An atomic bomb developed at Los Alamos Laboratory is tested successfully at the Trinity Site in New Mexico.

July 24, 1945 Truman informs Stalin at the Potsdam Conference in Germany that the U.S. has perfected a "new weapon of unusual destructive force."

July 26, 1945 Allied leaders issue the Potsdam Declaration, threatening Japan with "prompt and utter destruction" unless it surrenders unconditionally.

August 6, 1945 A B-29 piloted by Col. Paul Tibbets takes off from Tinian and drops an atomic bomb on Hiroshima, Japan, destroying much of the city.

August 9, 1945 Nagasaki becomes the second Japanese city blasted by an atomic bomb. Soviet troops enter the war against Japan by invading Manchuria (Manchukuo).

August 15, 1945 Emperor Hirohito announces that Japan will yield to the Potsdam Declaration.

September 2, 1945 Japanese representatives formally surrender aboard the battleship U.S.S. Missouri in Tokyo Bay.

Chicago Daily Times *cover on August 15, 1945, when Emperor Hirohito announced that Japan was surrendering*

TWO PATHS TO
TOKYO

MACARTHUR AND NIMITZ ON SEPARATE TRACKS

CHRONOLOGY

JUNE 21–30, 1943 Operation Cartwheel begins as U.S. Marines under Halsey's command land on Japanese-occupied New Georgia in the Solomons and MacArthur's troops advance on New Guinea.

NOVEMBER 1, 1943 U.S. troops land on Bougainville, Halsey's ultimate objective in the Solomons.

NOVEMBER 20, 1943 American forces land on Tarawa and Makin Atolls in the Gilbert Islands, the first steps in an advance across the central Pacific directed by Admiral Nimitz.

FEBRUARY 29, 1944 MacArthur's troops invade the Admiralty Islands off New Guinea to secure airfields for Kenney's Fifth Air Force.

JUNE 15, 1944 Marines land on Saipan in the Mariana Islands, where air bases will be constructed for bombers targeting Japan.

JUNE 19–20, 1944 Naval forces of the U.S. Fifth Fleet win the Battle of the Philippine Sea west of the Marianas.

JULY 21–24, 1944 Marines land on Guam and Tinian in the Marianas.

SEPTEMBER 15, 1944 Marines land on Peleliu in the Palau Islands. MacArthur's troops land on Morotai, an island west of New Guinea that will serve as his base for invading the Philippines.

STORMING TARAWA U.S. Marines advance inland under heavy fire on Tarawa Atoll in November 1943. A simultaneous assault on nearby Makin Atoll was undertaken by the troops of the Army's 27th Infantry Division, supported by the escort carrier U.S.S. *Liscome Bay*, which was torpedoed by a Japanese submarine and sank with a loss of more than 600 men.

Officially, General MacArthur and Admiral Nimitz were partners in a dual drive against Japan in the Pacific, but they had their differences. MacArthur resented Nimitz and Navy chief Ernest King for pushing their plan to leapfrog across the Pacific from one island chain to another at the expense of his bid to advance on Japan by way of the Philippines. He needed naval support to pursue that path, however, and received it from Nimitz's commander in the South Pacific, Admiral Halsey. Incensed by the attack on Pearl Harbor, Halsey was eager to kill Japanese forces on either side of the line separating his own operational zone in the South Pacific from MacArthur's zone (see map opposite). MacArthur arranged for Halsey to cross that line above Guadalcanal and advance up the Solomon chain while MacArthur's troops pushed west from Papua along the north coast of New Guinea.

The joint operation, called Cartwheel, began in late June 1943. Marines and soldiers under Halsey's command landed on New Georgia and engaged in harrowing combat under conditions that drove some men new to jungle warfare mad. But by seizing crucial objectives such as the Japanese airstrip at Munda Point on New Georgia and bypassing the enemy elsewhere, Halsey reached Bougainville, the last big link in the chain, in November. By then, MacArthur's American and Australian forces had made similar gains on New Guinea, aided by Maj. Gen. George Kenney's Fifth Air Force, which went on to neutralize the big Japanese base at Rabaul on New Britain in conjunction with Halsey's carrier-based warplanes.

Nimitz's drive across the central Pacific began in the Gilbert Islands on November 20 with landings on Japanese-occupied islands within two atolls—lightly defended Makin and stoutly defended Tarawa (below). Despite a bombardment meant to clear their way, Marines suffered more than 3,000 casualties before securing Tarawa. MacArthur denounced that frontal attack in a memo to the secretary of war as a "tragic and unnecessary" waste of American lives. Similar criticism would be aimed at some of MacArthur's later operations in the Philippines. There was little agreement on which objectives men should die for, but one thing was clear: Victory in the Pacific required the combined effort of America's armed services. ■

ARMY-NAVY MATCH General MacArthur sits at center between President Roosevelt and Admiral Nimitz in Honolulu in July 1944. Although MacArthur and Nimitz continued to disagree over which path was most likely to yield victory over Japan, the Navy closely supported MacArthur's advance toward the Philippines.

DUAL DRIVE Before launching Operation Cartwheel in mid-1943, MacArthur arranged for Halsey to cross the line (designated on the map below) dividing his South Pacific Area from MacArthur's Southwest Pacific Area and advance up the Solomons while MacArthur advanced on New Guinea. Their ultimate objective was to neutralize the menacing Japanese base at Rabaul on New Britain, after which MacArthur would secure New Guinea in 1944 and invade the Philippines. Forces directed by Nimitz began advancing across the central Pacific by storming Tarawa and Makin in November 1943, to be followed in 1944 by landings on Kwajalein and Eniwetok in the Marshall Islands, attacks on Truk in the Caroline Islands, and invasions of Saipan, Tinian, and Guam in the Mariana Islands, which would bring strategic bombers within range of Japan.

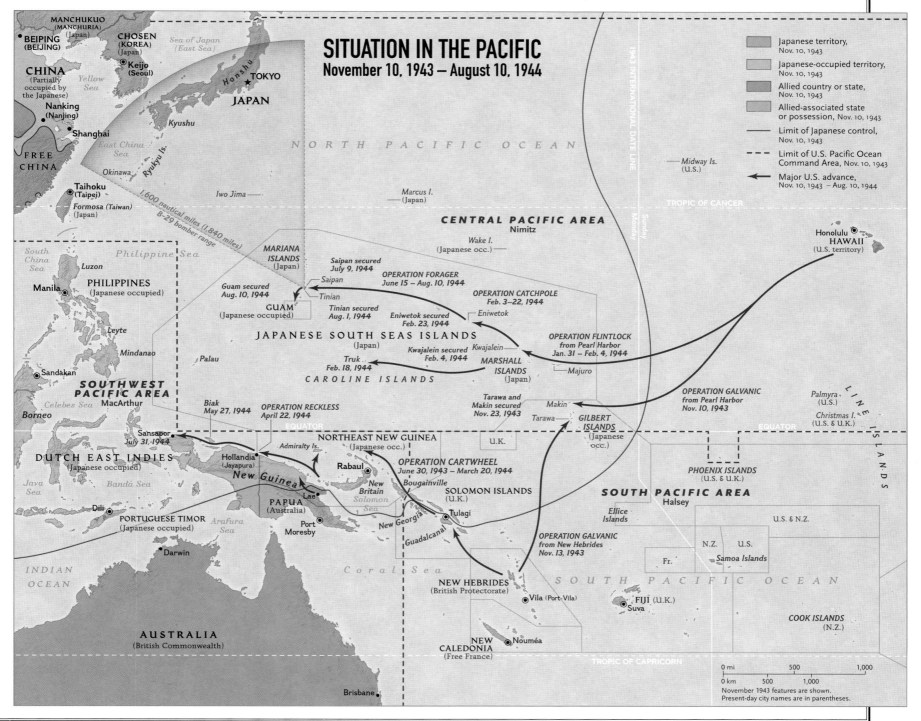

SITUATION IN THE PACIFIC
November 10, 1943 – August 10, 1944

Japanese territory, Nov. 10, 1943
Japanese-occupied territory, Nov. 10, 1943
Allied country or state, Nov. 10, 1943
Allied-associated state or possession, Nov. 10, 1943
Limit of Japanese control, Nov. 10, 1943
Limit of U.S. Pacific Ocean Command Area, Nov. 10, 1943
Major U.S. advance, Nov. 10, 1943 – Aug. 10, 1944

November 1943 features are shown.
Present-day city names are in parentheses.

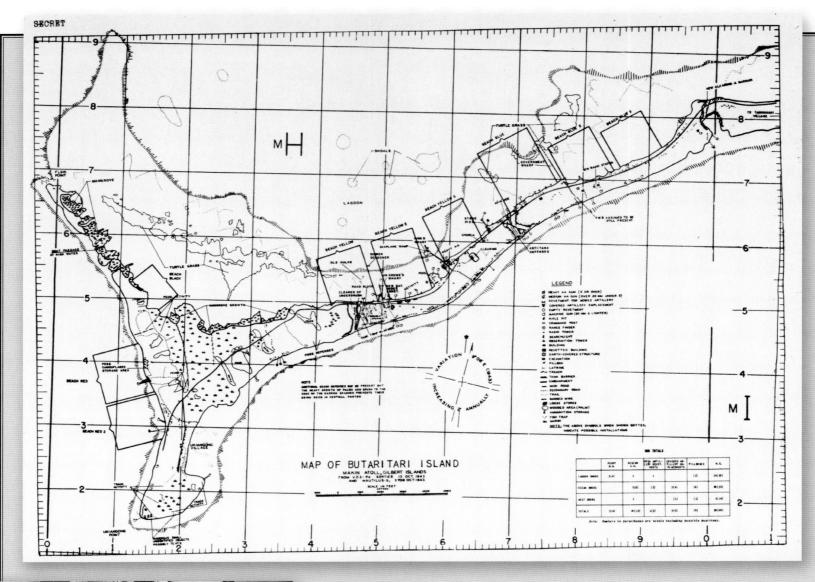

MAP OF BUTARITARI ISLAND
MAKIN ATOLL, GILBERT ISLANDS
FROM VD3-P4 SORTIES 13 OCT. 1943
AND NAUTILUS-3, 1906 OCT. 1943
SCALE IN FEET

POINTERS At left, a Marine intelligence officer instructing platoon leaders destined for Tarawa Atoll places his pointer on the south side of a relief model of Betio. Slips of paper on the far side of the model indicate where Marines would land—the northwest shore of Betio as mapped below, based on reconnaissance by the Seventh Air Force and planes from the carrier U.S.S. *Enterprise* (designated CV 16). The map above of Butaritari in Makin Atoll, based on reconnaissance by the U.S.S. *Nautilus* and Navy airmen of photographic squadron VD-3, shows landing zones for the 27th Infantry Division on the northeast shore.

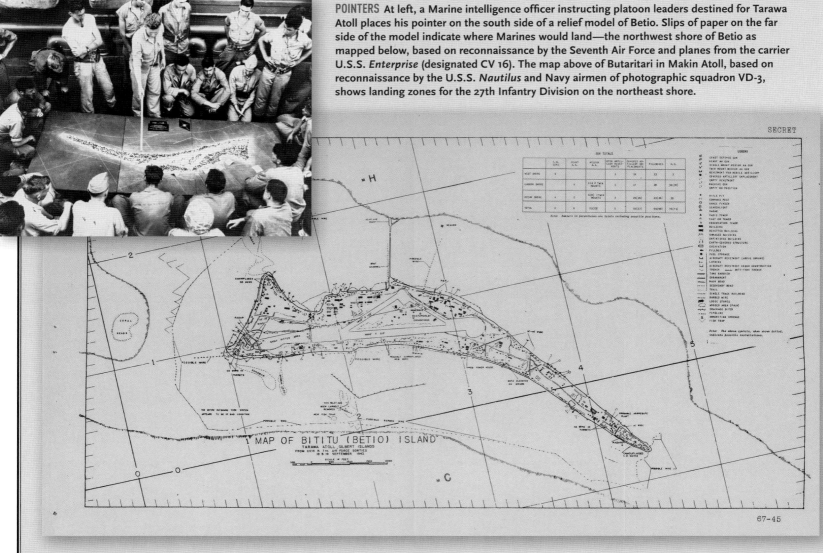

MAP OF BITITU (BETIO) ISLAND
TARAWA ATOLL, GILBERT ISLANDS
FROM CV16 & 7th AIR FORCE SORTIES
15 & 19 SEPTEMBER 1943
SCALE IN FEET

67-45

LESSONS IN ATOLL WARFARE

Americans targeting the Gilbert Islands on November 20, 1943, were aided by aerial and naval surveillance that yielded maps of Japanese defenses on the two tiny islands they invaded—Butaritari in Makin Atoll (opposite top) and Betio in Tarawa Atoll (opposite bottom). Airmen of the Seventh Air Force and a naval carrier task force took reconnaissance photos of Betio, which was bombed repeatedly before the invasion. Flights by Navy scout planes helped map Butaritari, and the submarine U.S.S. *Nautilus* surveyed both islands, using cameras installed in its periscope to record shoreline defenses not visible from above. Further intelligence for mapmakers came from Marines who had raided Butaritari in October 1942 in an effort to draw Japanese forces away from Guadalcanal. No such raid occurred on heavily defended Betio, but civilians from Allied countries who had lived on Tarawa Atoll or sailed there were interviewed by intelligence officers. Some thought the water off Betio might be too shallow to allow landing craft to clear a treacherous coral reef. Navy planners reckoned otherwise but obtained 125 amtracs—amphibious tracked vehicles that could crawl over the reef, if necessary, and land the first battalions on shore.

Nothing went as planned at Betio on November 20. Japanese defenses were even stronger than indicated by reconnaissance. Preliminary bombardments failed to silence fire from pillboxes that were well camouflaged and housed guns that blasted the slow amtracs leading the assault. "They were laying lead to us from a pillbox like holy hell," recalled one Marine, who was one of the few who survived when an amtrac carrying two dozen men stalled under fire. Landing craft following behind the amtracs could not get over the reef and disgorged their occupants, many of whom were shot as they waded ashore over rough coral. More than 1,000 Marines died and twice as many fell wounded before the last Japanese defenders on Betio were killed in their bunkers or committed suicide. Among the painful lessons learned there was the need for precise depth charts for waters off targeted islands. For future landings in the Pacific, the Navy deployed frogmen to reconnoiter shorelines and coral reefs, through which underwater demolition teams cleared channels for landing craft. ∎

HARD-WON Shrouded in dust and smoke, Marine artillerymen take aim at Japanese holdouts on Betio in Tarawa Atoll, where the Second Marine Division achieved a costly victory on November 23, 1943. Of the 2,600 Japanese troops defending the island, only 27 surrendered rather than face death. Butaritari in Makin Atoll was secured on November 24 by Army troops who greatly outnumbered their foes but were new to combat and advanced cautiously.

MACARTHUR'S ROAD BACK

To return to the Philippines, MacArthur first had to break Japan's grip on New Guinea, the Pacific's largest island and one of the war's most forbidding battlegrounds, with dense jungle, swollen rivers, and towering mountain ranges. In January 1944, MacArthur had more than 1,000 miles to go before reaching islands off western New Guinea from which to invade the Philippines. Although he complained in writing that "probably no American commander has ever been so poorly supported," he had many assets at his disposal, including sturdy Australian troops who grappled with the enemy inland while U.S. forces moved along the north coast, often leaping ahead to distant objectives. Those swift advances were supported by Kenney's Fifth Air Force and Vice Adm. Thomas Kinkaid's Seventh Fleet, which unlike Halsey's larger Third Fleet was permanently at MacArthur's disposal, giving him mobility that he used to outmaneuver his foes.

After securing Lae and Finschaffen in late 1943 (see map opposite), MacArthur invaded the Admiralty Islands in late February 1944 (below) to seize Japanese airfields for Kenney's airmen. They went on to blast the next big target on New Guinea, the port of Hollandia, which fell to MacArthur in late April. That leap stranded the Japanese 18th Army at Wewak, east of Hollandia. Troops under Gen. Hatazo Adachi made several attempts to break through American lines at Aitape before they were crushed in battle in early August. Later that month, MacArthur's forces finally secured Biak, a large coral island off northern New Guinea where Japanese defenders had allowed the Americans to land unopposed before fiercely contesting their advance inland—a tactic that some Japanese commanders would employ against future landings.

MacArthur was justly proud of the big strides he took while avoiding heavy losses, but many isolated Japanese units remained on New Guinea to be mopped up. That thankless task was relegated to the Australians, who helped clear MacArthur's path to the Philippines but were left behind in October 1944 as he prepared to reclaim that American protectorate with U.S. troops. ∎

ADMIRALTY LANDING Troops of the U.S. First Cavalry Division invade Los Negros in the Admiralty Islands on February 29, 1944. Here and elsewhere, MacArthur chose landing zones that were lightly defended, enabling troops to establish beachheads, receive reinforcements, and repulse subsequent attacks. Americans took the Admiralties and their airfields at a cost of 326 lives—one-tenth the Japanese death toll there.

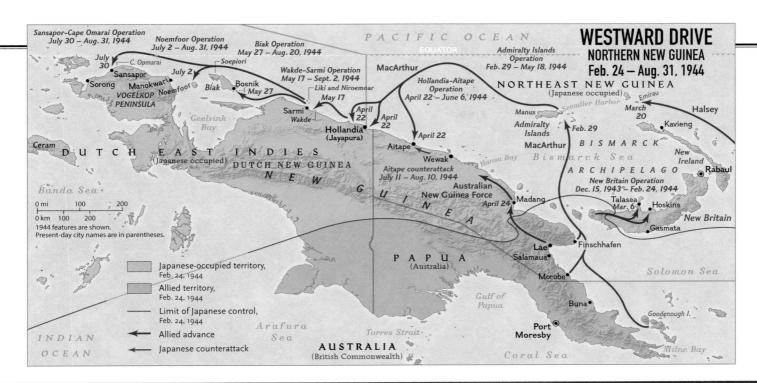

Sansapor–Cape Omarai Operation
July 30 – Aug. 31, 1944

Noemfoor Operation
July 2 – Aug. 31, 1944

Biak Operation
May 27 – Aug. 20, 1944

PACIFIC OCEAN

EQUATOR

Admiralty Islands Operation
Feb. 29 – May 18, 1944

July 30

C. Opmarai

Soepiori

Sorong
Sansapor
Manokwari
July 2
Noemfoor
VOGELKOP PENINSULA
Biak
Bosnik
May 27

Wakde–Sarmi Operation
May 17 – Sept. 2, 1944

Liki and Niroemoar
May 17

Sarmi
Wakde

April 22

Hollandia
(Jayapura)

April 22

Aitape
April 22

Wewak

MacArthur

Hollandia–Aitape Operation
April 22 – June 6, 1944

NORTHEAST NEW GUINEA
(Japanese occupied)

Manus
Seeadler Harbor
Admiralty Islands
Feb. 29
MacArthur

Emirau
March 20

Halsey

Kavieng

New Ireland

BISMARCK
ARCHIPELAGO

Rabaul

New Britain Operation
Dec. 15, 1943 – Feb. 24, 1944

Talasea
Mar. 6
Hoskins
New Britain
Gasmata

Ceram

DUTCH EAST INDIES
(Japanese occupied)

DUTCH NEW GUINEA

NEW

GUINEA

Banda Sea

Geelvink Bay

Hansa Bay

Bismarck Sea

Aitape counterattack
July 11 – Aug. 10, 1944

Australian New Guinea Force
April 24

Madang

Lae
Salamaua

Finschhafen

0 mi   100   200
0 km   100   200
1944 features are shown.
Present-day city names are in parentheses.

PAPUA
(Australia)

Morobe

Solomon Sea

Japanese-occupied territory, Feb. 24, 1944

Allied territory, Feb. 24, 1944

Limit of Japanese control, Feb. 24, 1944

Allied advance

Japanese counterattack

INDIAN
OCEAN

Arafura Sea

Torres Strait

AUSTRALIA
(British Commonwealth)

Gulf of Papua

Buna

Goodenough I.

Port Moresby

Coral Sea

Milne Bay

AMPHIBIOUS ASSAULT Troops, trucks, and antiaircraft guns crowd the deck of a landing craft bound for Sansapor near New Guinea's western tip, where MacArthur's forces landed unopposed in late July 1944. As shown on the map at top, MacArthur's naval resources allowed him to advance by leaps and bounds along New Guinea's north coast and envelop Japanese troops, who received less help from their own ships, which were prey to American bombers.

SKIP-BOMBER At left, a Douglas A-20 Havoc Bomber barely clears a Japanese merchant ship moments after skip-bombing the vessel off Wewak, New Guinea, in March 1944. Many such attacks were launched in support of MacArthur's offensive by the Fifth Air Force at the instigation of its resourceful commander, George Kenney.

SURVIVAL CHARTS Two maps printed on rayon for downed airmen in rafts and rescuers operating between New Guinea (below) and New Ireland (opposite) show the direction, steadiness, and speed of currents—with numbers indicating how many miles per day the current would carry a raft—as well as the direction and speed of prevailing winds, which could also affect the course of rafts. Winds are more variable than currents, and instructions for such maps told airmen to gauge the direction and approximate speed of the wind—mapped here with broad arrows and numbers indicating velocity on the Beaufort scale—and to factor that in when navigating.

SURVIVAL OFF THE NEW GUINEA COAST

Airmen of General Kenney's Fifth Air Force often conducted skip-bombing attacks at low level (pictured opposite) that left them vulnerable if ships they targeted were armed. "Upon passing over the target, the element of surprise is lost," one pilot remarked, "so it is best to pull all the power you can and make a hurried departure." Kenney noted that his bombers often returned to base "holed" by fire from Japanese guns. His pilots were skilled and kept losses to a minimum, but some planes went down. Provisions for the survival of Army or Navy airmen who crash-landed included maps printed on cloth that was water resistant and could be stuffed in a pocket and readily retrieved in an emergency. The two examples shown here—the front and back of a map produced by the U.S. Navy Hydrographic Office—show the direction and velocity of currents and prevailing winds in winter months off the north coast of New Guinea (opposite bottom) and off the Admiralty Islands and New Ireland (below). Downed airmen at sea

equipped with inflatable rafts, paddles, and a compass could use such maps to navigate toward land. The maps also helped search-and-rescue personnel determine where survivors in rafts might be in relation to the crash site.

Rescuers in Navy PBY Catalina flying boats sometimes went to heroic lengths to retrieve survivors. In February 1944, during a Fifth Air Force raid on the Japanese air and naval base at Kavieng on the northern tip of New Ireland, debris from an exploding ammunition dump caused several planes to crash-land in Kavieng Harbor, within range of Japanese guns on shore. In what Kenney called "one of the most striking rescues of the war," Lt. Nathan Green Gordon, a Navy Catalina pilot assigned to the Fifth Air Force, landed under fire, "picked up three men, saw two more clinging to a piece of debris, landed again, kept seeing more survivors, and kept on landing, until he had gone into that hornets' nest seven times." For risking his life to save 15 airmen, Gordon received the Medal of Honor. ■

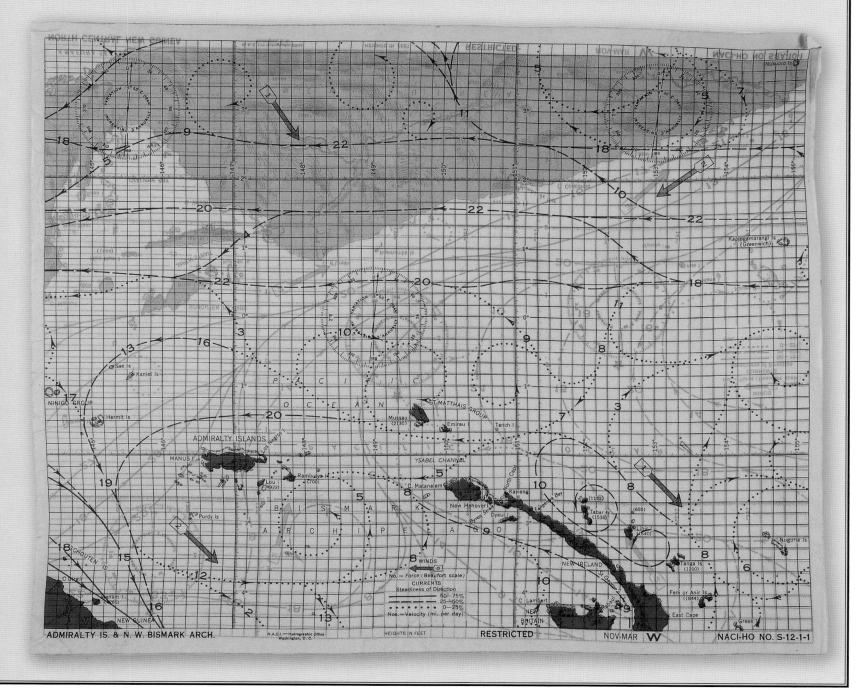

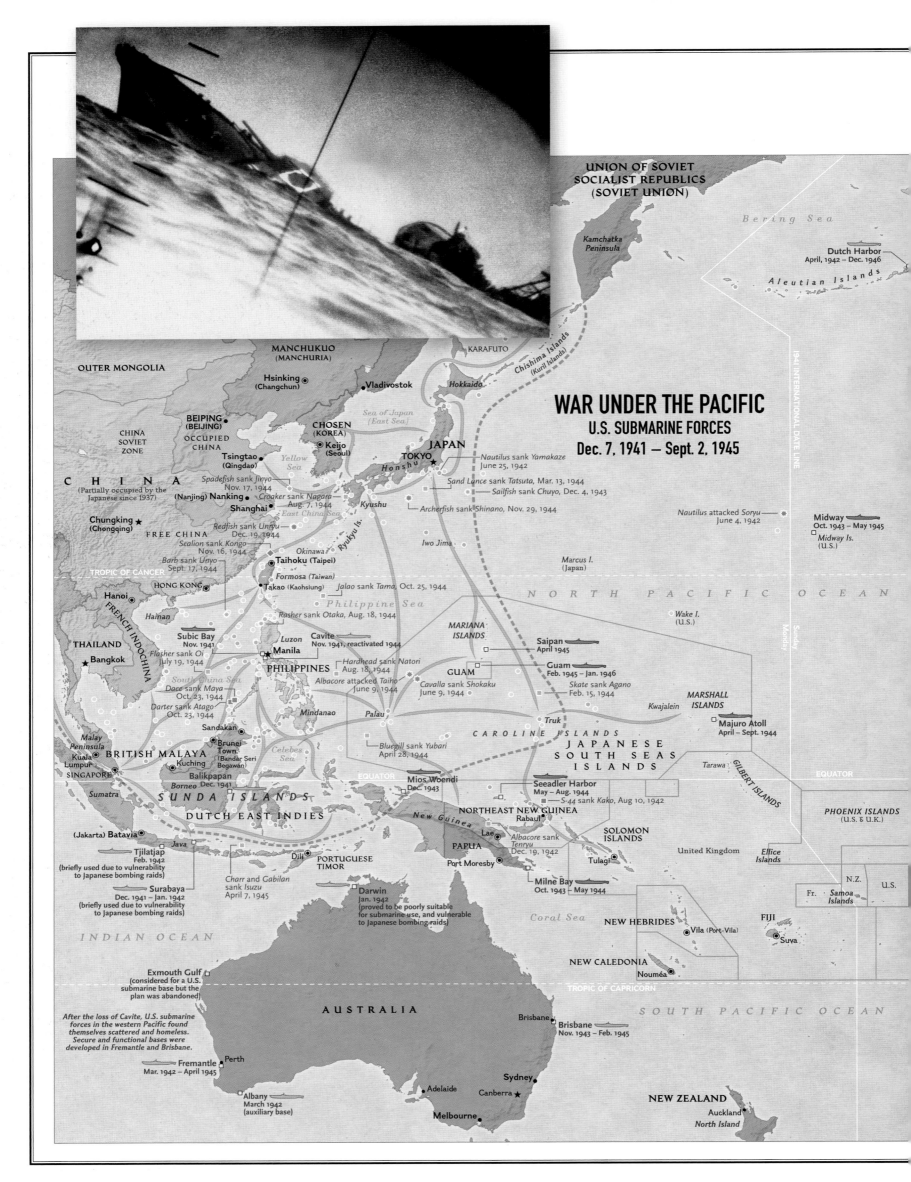

WAR UNDER THE PACIFIC
U.S. SUBMARINE FORCES
Dec. 7, 1941 – Sept. 2, 1945

UNION OF SOVIET
SOCIALIST REPUBLICS
(SOVIET UNION)

Bering Sea

Kamchatka
Peninsula

Aleutian Islands

Dutch Harbor
April, 1942 – Dec. 1946

KARAFUTO

*Chishima Islands
(Kuril Islands)*

MANCHUKUO
(MANCHURIA)

OUTER MONGOLIA

Hsinking
(Changchun)

● Vladivostok

Hokkaido

*Sea of Japan
(East Sea)*

BEIPING
(BEIJING)

CHINA
SOVIET
ZONE

OCCUPIED
CHINA

CHOSEN
(KOREA)

● Keijo
(Seoul)

Honshu

JAPAN
● TOKYO

Nautilus sank *Yamakaze*
June 25, 1942

Tsingtao
(Qingdao)

*Yellow
Sea*

C H I N A
(Partially occupied by the
Japanese since 1937)

Spadefish sank *Jinyo*
Nov. 17, 1944

(Nanjing) Nanking

Shanghai ●

East China Sea

Croaker sank *Nagara*
Aug. 7, 1944

Kyushu

Sand Lance sank *Tatsuta*, Mar. 13, 1944

Sailfish sank *Chuyo*, Dec. 4, 1943

Archerfish sank *Shinano*, Nov. 29, 1944

Nautilus attacked *Soryu*
June 4, 1942

Midway
Oct. 1943 – May 1945

Chungking ★
(Chongqing)

FREE CHINA

Redfish sank *Unryo*
Dec. 19, 1944

Sealion sank *Kongo*
Nov. 16, 1944

Barb sank *Unyo*
Sept. 17, 1944

Okinawa ●

Ryukyu Is.

Taihoku (Taipei)

Iwo Jima

*Marcus I.
(Japan)*

*Midway Is.
(U.S.)*

TROPIC OF CANCER

HONG KONG ●

Formosa (Taiwan)
Takao (Kaohsiung)

Jalao sank *Tama*, Oct. 25, 1944

Philippine Sea

N O R T H   P A C I F I C   O C E A N

Hanoi ●

Hainan

FRENCH INDOCHINA

Rasher sank *Otaka*, Aug. 18, 1944

*Wake I.
(U.S.)*

THAILAND

Bangkok ★

Subic Bay
Nov. 1941

Flasher sank *Oi*
July 19, 1944

Luzon
● Manila

Cavite
Nov. 1941, reactivated 1944

Hardhead sank *Natori*
Aug. 18, 1944

MARIANA
ISLANDS

Saipan
April 1945

Guam
Feb. 1945 – Jan. 1946

PHILIPPINES

GUAM

Skate sank *Agano*
Feb. 15, 1944

MARSHALL
ISLANDS

South China Sea

Dace sank *Maya*
Oct. 23, 1944

Darter sank *Atago*
Oct. 23, 1944

Albacore attacked *Taiho*
June 9, 1944

Cavalla sank *Shokaku*
June 9, 1944

Kwajalein

Majuro Atoll
April – Sept. 1944

Mindanao

Palau

Truk

*Malay
Peninsula*

Sandakan ●

Brunei
Town
(Bandar Seri
Begawan)

Kuching

*Celebes
Sea*

Bluegill sank *Yubari*
April 28, 1944

C A R O L I N E   I S L A N D S

JAPANESE
SOUTH SEAS
ISLANDS

Tarawa

GILBERT ISLANDS

EQUATOR

BRITISH MALAYA

Kuala
Lumpur

SINGAPORE ●

Balikpapan
Dec. 1941

Borneo

S U N D A   I S L A N D S

DUTCH EAST INDIES

Sumatra

EQUATOR

Mios Woendi
Dec. 1943

Seeadler Harbor
May – Aug. 1944

S-44 sank *Kako*, Aug 10, 1942

PHOENIX ISLANDS
(U.S. & U.K.)

Java

(Jakarta) Batavia ●

New Guinea

NORTHEAST NEW GUINEA
Rabaul ●

Lae ●

Albacore sank *Tenryu*
Dec. 19, 1942

SOLOMON
ISLANDS

United Kingdom

*Ellice
Islands*

N.Z.   U.S.

Tjilatjap
Feb. 1942
(briefly used due to vulnerability
to Japanese bombing raids)

Dili ●

PORTUGUESE
TIMOR

PAPUA

Port Moresby ●

Tulagi ●

Fr.   *Samoa
Islands*

Charr and *Gabilan*
sank *Isuzu*
April 7, 1945

Surabaya
Dec. 1941 – Jan. 1942
(briefly used due to vulnerability
to Japanese bombing raids)

Darwin
Jan. 1942
(proved to be poorly suitable
for submarine use, and vulnerable
to Japanese bombing raids)

Milne Bay
Oct. 1943 – May 1944

Coral Sea

NEW HEBRIDES

Vila (Port-Vila) ●

FIJI

Suva ●

I N D I A N   O C E A N

NEW CALEDONIA

Nouméa ●

Exmouth Gulf
(considered for a U.S.
submarine base but the
plan was abandoned)

TROPIC OF CAPRICORN

S O U T H   P A C I F I C   O C E A N

*After the loss of Cavite, U.S. submarine
forces in the western Pacific found
themselves scattered and homeless.
Secure and functional bases were
developed in Fremantle and Brisbane.*

A U S T R A L I A

Brisbane ●

Brisbane
Nov. 1943 – Feb. 1945

Fremantle
Mar. 1942 – April 1945

● Perth

Adelaide ●

Sydney ●

Canberra ★

NEW ZEALAND

Albany
March 1942
(auxiliary base)

Melbourne ●

Auckland ●
North Island

1941 INTERNATIONAL DATE LINE

Sunday

Monday

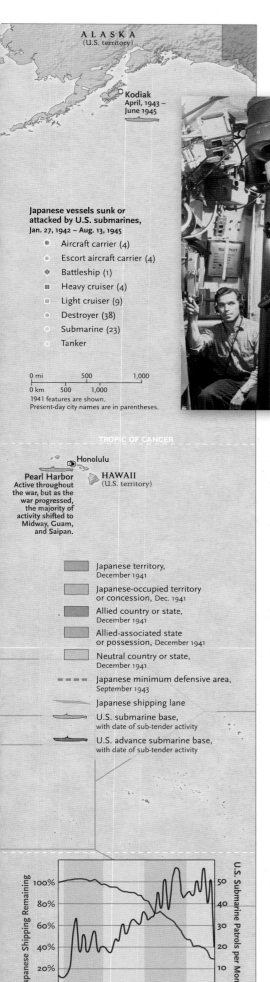

Japanese vessels sunk or attacked by U.S. submarines, Jan. 27, 1942 – Aug. 13, 1945

- ✴ Aircraft carrier (4)
- ✦ Escort aircraft carrier (4)
- ◆ Battleship (1)
- ■ Heavy cruiser (4)
- ▫ Light cruiser (9)
- ◌ Destroyer (38)
- ○ Submarine (23)
- ○ Tanker

0 mi ___ 500 ___ 1,000
0 km ___ 500 ___ 1,000
1941 features are shown.
Present-day city names are in parentheses.

TROPIC OF CANCER

Honolulu

Pearl Harbor
Active throughout the war, but as the war progressed, the majority of activity shifted to Midway, Guam, and Saipan.

HAWAII
(U.S. territory)

- ▬ Japanese territory, December 1941
- ▬ Japanese-occupied territory or concession, Dec. 1941
- ▬ Allied country or state, December 1941
- ▬ Allied-associated state or possession, December 1941
- ▬ Neutral country or state, December 1941
- ▬▬▬ Japanese minimum defensive area, September 1943
- ⚓ Japanese shipping lane
- ⚓ U.S. submarine base, with date of sub-tender activity
- ⚓ U.S. advance submarine base, with date of sub-tender activity

(chart at bottom left: Japanese Shipping Remaining (left axis, 0%–100%) vs. U.S. Submarine Patrols per Month (right axis, 0–50), years 1942–1945)

SEARCH AND DESTROY American submarine captains in the Pacific like the skipper above, peering through a periscope, targeted Japanese merchant ships and warships such as the destroyer I.J.N. *Yamakaze* (opposite), shown sinking in a photo taken in June 1942 through the periscope of the sub that destroyed it, the U.S.S. *Nautilus*.

HUNTING GROUNDS The map at left shows U.S. and Allied submarine bases when Japan went to war with the United States in December 1941, some of which were captured by the Japanese, including Cavite in the Philippines. The map also shows U.S. advance submarine bases established during the war as American forces gained ground. Japanese shipping lanes in the far western Pacific and the South China Sea were prime hunting grounds for submarines conducting a strategic campaign to prevent essential supplies from reaching Japan. American subs also targeted troop and supply ships destined for Japanese-occupied islands and helped U.S. forces seize control of island chains like the Marianas by spying on enemy fleet movements and attacking warships.

WAR UNDER THE PACIFIC

By 1944, U.S. submarines in the Pacific were waging strategic warfare on a scale surpassed only by the German U-boat fleet earlier in the war. What Grand Adm. Karl Dönitz had attempted to do in the Atlantic—throttle Britain by severing its maritime supply lines—was now being done to Japan by Vice Adm. Charles Lockwood's submarine fleet in the southwest Pacific. Lockwood understood that while his submarines could harm the enemy by targeting warships, they could inflict even greater damage at less cost by attacking vulnerable oil tankers and other vessels carrying supplies on which Japan's war effort depended. As he wrote later, "Tankers—those were the ships we most wanted to sink."

As shown on the map at left, U.S. submarine bases proliferated in the Pacific as the war progressed. Subs on patrol from newly established bases such as Milne Bay on New Guinea had sufficient range to enter the South China Sea and attack ships carrying oil and rubber from Burma and the Dutch East Indies and other resources vital to Japan before returning to base. Japanese warships sometimes escorted merchant ships in convoys, but that protection diminished as the Japanese Navy suffered losses and was stretched thin. Prowling the South China Sea aboard the sub U.S.S. *Jack* on February 19, 1944, Cmdr. Thomas Dykers targeted a loosely escorted convoy and sank four tankers carrying aviation fuel without once being depth-charged. "Needless to say," he said of his crew afterward, "morale is soaring."

Unlike Lockwood's fleet, which doubled in size between December 1941 and mid-1944, the Japanese submarine fleet dwindled. Used largely in battle against U.S. warships, its losses increased when commanders adopted predictable tactics like deploying submarines as sentries in picket lines off Japanese-occupied islands. In May 1944, as the U.S. Navy prepared to land troops on the Marianas, destroyers targeted a picket line there and sank six Japanese subs in 12 days.

Lockwood's versatile fleet continued to conduct strategic warfare against enemy supply lines while carrying out other missions, such as targeting troopships and warships, delivering special forces and underwater demolition teams to Pacific islands, rescuing downed Allied airmen, and reporting on enemy fleet movements. Many submarines performed multiple tasks during patrols. Soon after taking charge of the U.S.S. *Redfin* in March 1944, Lt. Cmdr. Marshall Austin sank a tanker, a destroyer, and three Japanese Army supply ships and also landed six partisans on a Philippine island to organize an uprising that would coincide with MacArthur's invasion. Then on June 13, the *Redfin* scored a coup without firing a shot. Austin spotted a powerful Japanese fleet leaving a base in the southern Philippines on its way to the Marianas and provided early warning that helped the U.S. Navy meet that threat and shield American invasion forces. ∎

SEIZING SAIPAN As shown on the inset map below, Saipan was the northern-most of the three Mariana Islands invaded in 1944 and the closest to Tokyo. Home to a sizable Japanese population and defended by 30,000 troops, it was targeted first. On June 15, the Second and Fourth Marine Divisions landed on the southwest coast, followed by soldiers of the 27th Infantry Division. Air, naval, and artillery fire helped those forces drive Japanese troops off Mount Tapotchau and trap them at the northern end of the island. Some civilians there leaped to their death from cliffs despite efforts by Americans to calm their fears (above) and help those in danger, including an infant found near death by a medic (right).

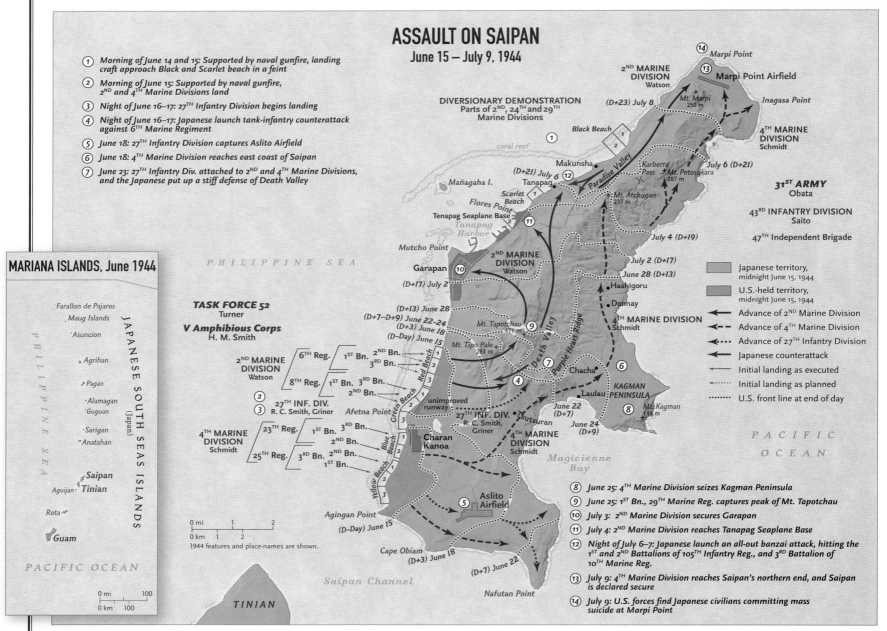

ASSAULT ON SAIPAN
June 15 – July 9, 1944

① Morning of June 14 and 15: Supported by naval gunfire, landing craft approach Black and Scarlet beach in a feint

② Morning of June 15: Supported by naval gunfire, 2ND and 4TH Marine Divisions land

③ Night of June 16–17: 27TH Infantry Division begins landing

④ Night of June 16–17: Japanese launch tank-infantry counterattack against 6TH Marine Regiment

⑤ June 18: 27TH Infantry Division captures Aslito Airfield

⑥ June 18: 4TH Marine Division reaches east coast of Saipan

⑦ June 23: 27TH Infantry Div. attached to 2ND and 4TH Marine Divisions, and the Japanese put up a stiff defense of Death Valley

⑧ June 25: 4TH Marine Division seizes Kagman Peninsula

⑨ June 25: 1ST Bn., 29TH Marine Reg. captures peak of Mt. Tapotchau

⑩ July 3: 2ND Marine Division secures Garapan

⑪ July 4: 2ND Marine Division reaches Tanapag Seaplane Base

⑫ Night of July 6–7: Japanese launch an all-out banzai attack, hitting the 1ST and 2ND Battalions of 105TH Infantry Reg., and 3RD Battalion of 10TH Marine Reg.

⑬ July 9: 4TH Marine Division reaches Saipan's northern end, and Saipan is declared secure

⑭ July 9: U.S. forces find Japanese civilians committing mass suicide at Marpi Point

TASK FORCE 52
Turner

V Amphibious Corps
H. M. Smith

Japanese territory, midnight June 15, 1944
U.S.-held territory, midnight June 15, 1944
→ Advance of 2ND Marine Division
-◄- Advance of 4TH Marine Division
····◄ Advance of 27TH Infantry Division
← Japanese counterattack
— Initial landing as executed
···· Initial landing as planned
···· U.S. front line at end of day

MARIANA ISLANDS, June 1944

Farallon de Pajaros
Maug Islands
Asuncion
Agrihan
Pagan
Alamagan
Guguan
Sarigan
Anatahan
Saipan
Aguijan · Tinian
Rota
Guam

JAPANESE SOUTH SEAS ISLANDS (Japan)

PHILIPPINE SEA

PACIFIC OCEAN

0 mi   100
0 km   100

0 mi   1   2
0 km   1   2
1944 features and place-names are shown.

2ND MARINE DIVISION Watson — 6TH Reg. — 1ST Bn. / 3RD Bn. / 2ND Bn.
8TH Reg. — 1ST Bn. / 3RD Bn. / 2ND Bn.

27TH INF. DIV. R. C. Smith, Griner

4TH MARINE DIVISION Schmidt — 23RD Reg. — 1ST Bn. / 3RD Bn. / 2ND Bn.
25TH Reg. — 3RD Bn. / 2ND Bn. / 1ST Bn.

DIVERSIONARY DEMONSTRATION
Parts of 2ND, 24TH and 29TH Marine Divisions

31ST ARMY Obata
43RD INFANTRY DIVISION Saito
47TH Independent Brigade

Marpi Point
Marpi Point Airfield
(D+23) July 8   Mt. Marpi 250 m
Inagasa Point
2ND MARINE DIVISION Watson
Black Beach
4TH MARINE DIVISION Schmidt
coral reef
(D+21) July 6   Makunsha   Karberra Pass Mt. Petosukara 287 m
July 6 (D+21)
Tanapag Paradise Valley
Mañagaha I.   Scarlet Beach   Mt. Atchugan 237 m
Flores Point
Tenapag Seaplane Base
Tanapag Harbor
Mutcho Point
Garapan
(D+17) July 2
Hashigoru
Donnay
July 4 (D+19)
July 2 (D+17)
June 28 (D+13)
(D+13) June 28
(D+7–D+9) June 22–24
(D+3) June 18
(D-Day) June 15
Mt. Tapotchau 471 m
Mt. Tipo Pale 281 m
Chacha   Laulau
KAGMAN PENINSULA
Mt. Kagman 146 m
June 22 (D+7)
June 24 (D+9)
27TH INF. DIV. R. C. Smith, Griner
Charan Kanoa
Afetna Point
unimproved runway
Aslito Airfield
Agingan Point
(D-Day) June 15
Cape Obiam
(D+3) June 18
Nafutan Point
(D+7) June 22
Saipan Channel
Magicienne Bay
PACIFIC OCEAN
PHILIPPINE SEA
Red Beach / Green Beach / Blue Beach / Yellow Beach

TINIAN

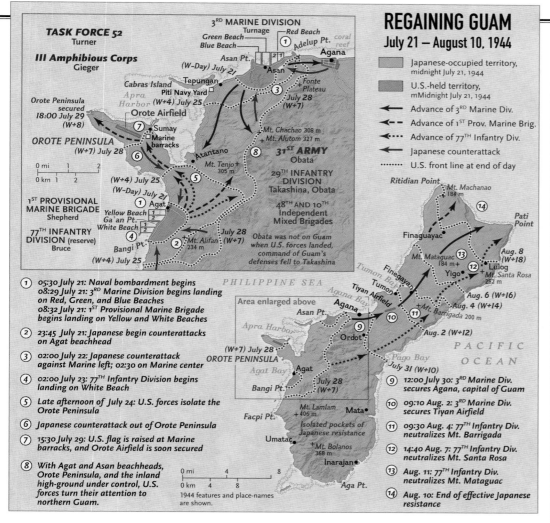

REGAINING GUAM
July 21 – August 10, 1944

TASK FORCE 52 Turner

III Amphibious Corps Gieger

3RD MARINE DIVISION Turnage

![legend] Japanese-occupied territory, midnight July 21, 1944
U.S.-held territory, mMidnight July 21, 1944
← Advance of 3RD Marine Div.
←- Advance of 1ST Prov. Marine Brig.
← Advance of 77TH Infantry Div.
→ Japanese counterattack
···· U.S. front line at end of day

Orote Peninsula secured 18:00 July 29 (W+8)

 OROTE PENINSULA (W+7) July 28

1ST PROVISIONAL MARINE BRIGADE Shepherd

77TH INFANTRY DIVISION (reserve) Bruce

31ST ARMY Obata
29TH INFANTRY DIVISION Takashina, Obata
48TH AND 10TH Independent Mixed Brigades

Obata was not on Guam when U.S. forces landed; command of Guam's defenses fell to Takashina

PHILIPPINE SEA

① 05:30 July 21: Naval bombardment begins 08:29 July 21: 3RD Marine Division begins landing on Red, Green, and Blue Beaches 08:32 July 21: 1ST Provisional Marine Brigade begins landing on Yellow and White Beaches

② 23:45 July 21: Japanese begin counterattacks on Agat beachhead

③ 02:00 July 22: Japanese counterattack against Marine left; 02:30 on Marine center

④ 02:00 July 23: 77TH Infantry Division begins landing on White Beach

⑤ Late afternoon of July 24: U.S. forces isolate the Orote Peninsula

⑥ Japanese counterattack out of Orote Peninsula

⑦ 15:30 July 29: U.S. flag is raised at Marine barracks, and Orote Airfield is soon secured

⑧ With Agat and Asan beachheads, Orote Peninsula, and the inland high-ground under control, U.S. forces turn their attention to northern Guam.

⑨ 12:00 July 30: 3RD Marine Div. secures Agana, capital of Guam

⑩ 09:10 Aug. 2: 3RD Marine Div. secures Tiyan Airfield

⑪ 09:30 Aug. 4: 77TH Infantry Div. neutralizes Mt. Barrigada

⑫ 14:40 Aug. 7: 77TH Infantry Div. neutralizes Mt. Santa Rosa

⑬ Aug. 11: 77TH Infantry Div. neutralizes Mt. Mataguac

⑭ Aug. 10: End of effective Japanese resistance

1944 features and place-names are shown.

BATTLE FOR GUAM On July 21, the Third Marine Division and First Provisional Brigade landed on Guam, followed by the 77th Infantry Division. After repulsing a Japanese counterattack, the American forces advanced northward and overwhelmed their foes, securing Guam in August.

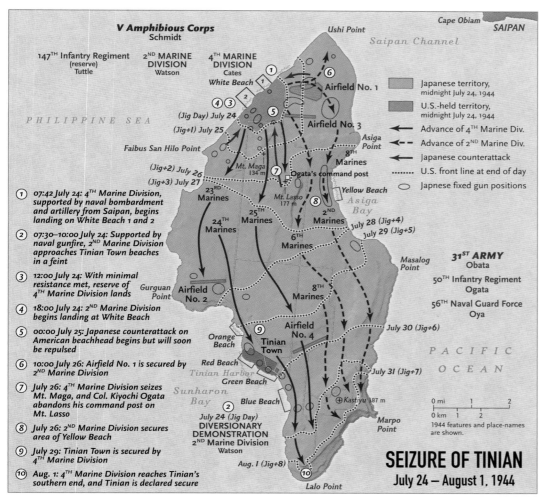

V Amphibious Corps Schmidt

147TH INFANTRY REGIMENT (reserve) Tuttle

2ND MARINE DIVISION Watson

4TH MARINE DIVISION Cates

PHILIPPINE SEA

![legend] Japanese territory, midnight July 24, 1944
U.S.-held territory, midnight July 24, 1944
← Advance of 4TH Marine Div.
←- Advance of 2ND Marine Div.
···· Japanese counterattack
···· U.S. front line at end of day
◯ Japnese fixed gun positions

31ST ARMY Obata
50TH Infantry Regiment Ogata
56TH Naval Guard Force Oya

① 07:42 July 24: 4TH Marine Division, supported by naval bombardment and artillery from Saipan, begins landing on White Beach 1 and 2

② 07:30–10:00 July 24: Supported by naval gunfire, 2ND Marine Division approaches Tinian Town beaches in a feint

③ 12:00 July 24: With minimal resistance met, reserve of 4TH Marine Division lands

④ 18:00 July 24: 2ND Marine Division begins landing at White Beach

⑤ 00:00 July 25: Japanese counterattack on American beachhead begins but will soon be repulsed

⑥ 10:00 July 26: Airfield No. 1 is secured by 2ND Marine Division

⑦ July 26: 4TH Marine Division seizes Mt. Maga, and Col. Kiyochi Ogata abandons his command post on Mt. Lasso

⑧ July 26: 2ND Marine Division secures area of Yellow Beach

⑨ July 29: Tinian Town is secured by 4TH Marine Division

⑩ Aug. 1: 4TH Marine Division reaches Tinian's southern end, and Tinian is declared secure

SEIZURE OF TINIAN
July 24 – August 1, 1944

1944 features and place-names are shown.

FEINT ON TINIAN On July 24, the Second Marine Division feigned a landing at Tinian Town while the Fourth Marine Division landed virtually unopposed to the north, where the Second Marines then came ashore. After overcoming Japanese resistance there, the two divisions swept southward.

TAKING THE MARIANAS

In June 1944, the U.S. Fifth Fleet bore down on the Japanese-occupied islands of Saipan, Tinian, and Guam in the Marianas, which if captured would bring powerful new B-29 bombers within range of Tokyo. Led by Vice Adm. Raymond Spruance, the massive fleet included 15 aircraft carriers and dozens of transports carrying 125,000 Marines and Army troops. Spruance's task was to support their landings with overwhelming naval and air power while guarding against attack by Vice Adm. Jisaburo Ozawa's First Mobile Fleet, which contained most of Japan's warships. "The Japanese are coming after us," Spruance told his officers, based on reconnaissance by submarines and coastwatchers and intelligence that the Japanese Navy was seeking a decisive battle to protect its home islands.

On June 15, Marines stormed Saipan (see map opposite), whose defenders were pounded relentlessly by the Fifth Fleet. Only Ozawa's intervention could save them, but a carrier task force dispatched by Spruance beat back the First Mobile Fleet in the Battle of the Philippine Sea on June 19–20. In early July, desperate Japanese soldiers, hemmed in by American forces at Saipan's northern tip, launched a suicide attack and were scythed down. Many civilians then killed themselves rather than yield to Americans they had been told would slaughter them.

In late July, Marines and infantry invaded the large island of Guam (top map left)—an American possession before the war—and the small island of Tinian (bottom map left), where Marines quickly gained the upper hand by landing where they were not expected. Although Tinian was taken by August 1, die-hard Japanese troops would long hold out there and on Guam, where the defeated Japanese commander committed suicide on August 11 but some of his men were still in hiding when the war ended. Seizing the Marianas cost more than 25,000 American casualties, but the impact on Japan was staggering. Emperor Hirohito had warned that if Saipan fell, "air attacks on Tokyo will follow." His fears would soon be realized. ∎

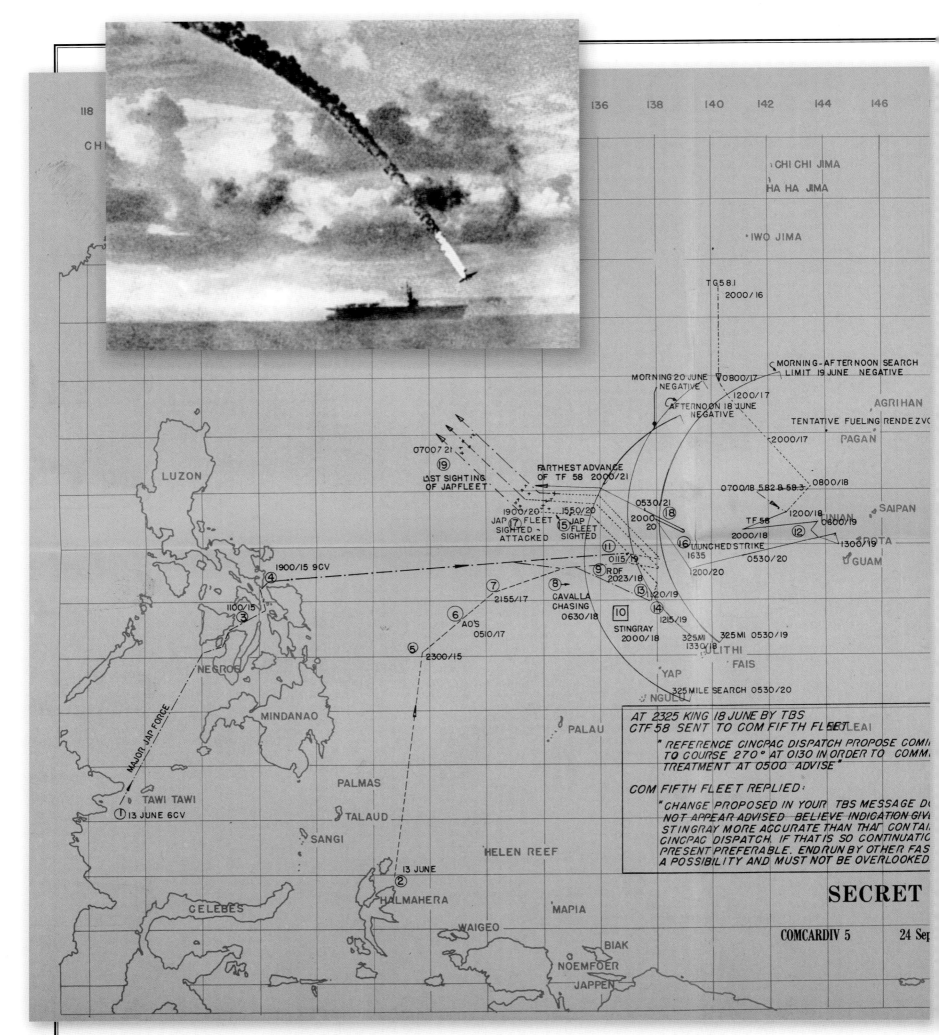

BATTLE CHART A map accompanying a secret U.S. Navy report on the Battle of the Philippine Sea issued in September 1944 charts events in numerical sequence from 1 (the initial sighting of Ozawa's First Mobile Fleet on June 13) to 19 (the last sighting of that fleet as it withdrew on June 21). Acronyms used in the map legend at far right include CV (aircraft carrier), BB (battleship), AO (fleet oiler), DF (direction finding), CINC (commander in chief), PBM (Martin PBM Mariner search plane), TF (task force), SOWESPAC (Southwest Pacific Area), and KING (Greenwich mean time plus 10 hours).

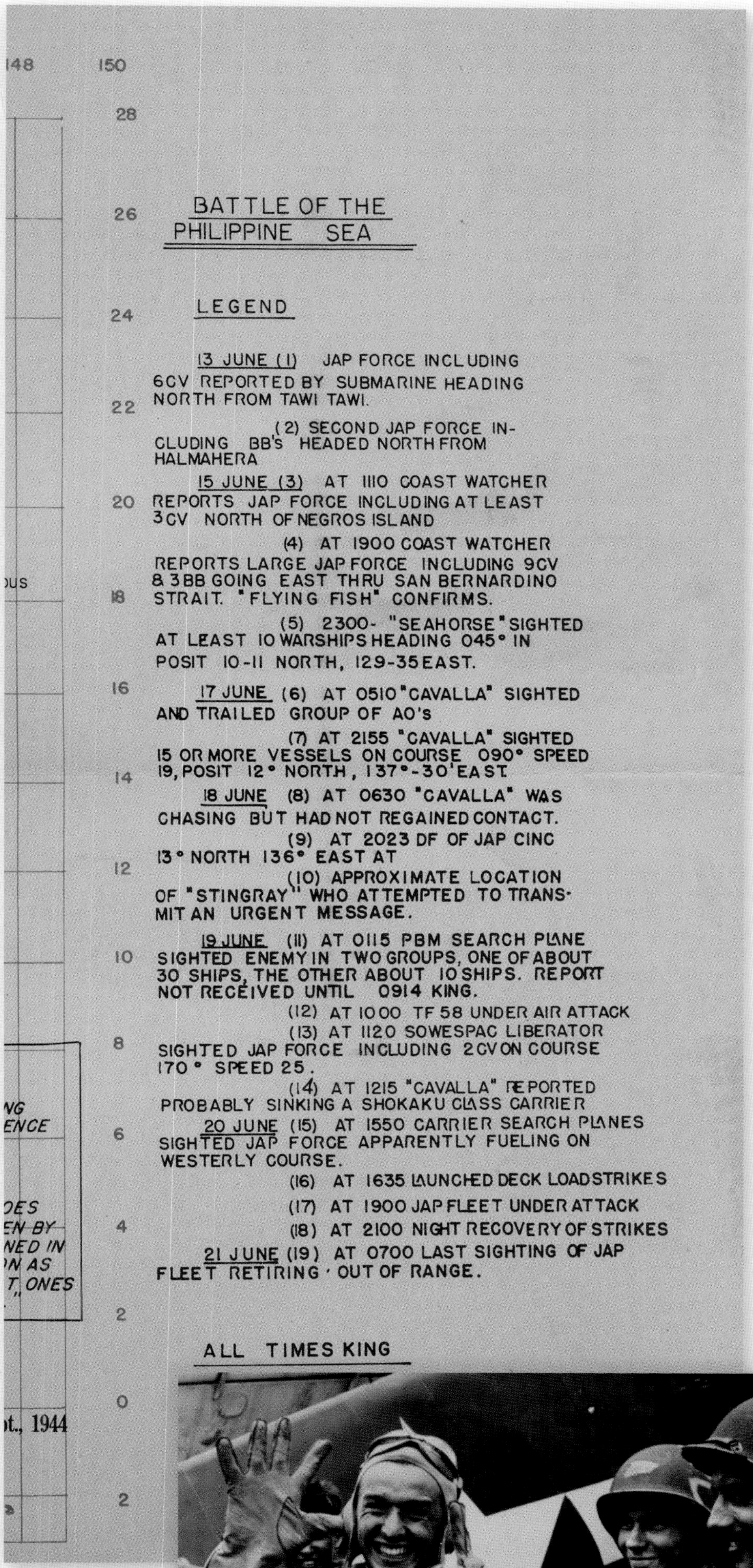
BATTLE OF THE PHILIPPINE SEA
LEGEND
13 JUNE (1) JAP FORCE INCLUDING 6CV REPORTED BY SUBMARINE HEADING NORTH FROM TAWI TAWI.
(2) SECOND JAP FORCE INCLUDING BB'S HEADED NORTH FROM HALMAHERA
15 JUNE (3) AT 1110 COAST WATCHER REPORTS JAP FORCE INCLUDING AT LEAST 3CV NORTH OF NEGROS ISLAND
(4) AT 1900 COAST WATCHER REPORTS LARGE JAP FORCE INCLUDING 9CV & 3BB GOING EAST THRU SAN BERNARDINO STRAIT. "FLYING FISH" CONFIRMS.
(5) 2300- "SEAHORSE" SIGHTED AT LEAST 10 WARSHIPS HEADING 045° IN POSIT 10-11 NORTH, 129-35 EAST.
17 JUNE (6) AT 0510 "CAVALLA" SIGHTED AND TRAILED GROUP OF AO'S
(7) AT 2155 "CAVALLA" SIGHTED 15 OR MORE VESSELS ON COURSE 090° SPEED 19, POSIT 12° NORTH, 137°-30' EAST
18 JUNE (8) AT 0630 "CAVALLA" WAS CHASING BUT HAD NOT REGAINED CONTACT.
(9) AT 2023 DF OF JAP CINC 13° NORTH 136° EAST AT
(10) APPROXIMATE LOCATION OF "STINGRAY" WHO ATTEMPTED TO TRANSMIT AN URGENT MESSAGE.
19 JUNE (11) AT 0115 PBM SEARCH PLANE SIGHTED ENEMY IN TWO GROUPS, ONE OF ABOUT 30 SHIPS, THE OTHER ABOUT 10 SHIPS. REPORT NOT RECEIVED UNTIL 0914 KING.
(12) AT 1000 TF 58 UNDER AIR ATTACK
(13) AT 1120 SOWESPAC LIBERATOR SIGHTED JAP FORCE INCLUDING 2CV ON COURSE 170° SPEED 25.
(14) AT 1215 "CAVALLA" REPORTED PROBABLY SINKING A SHOKAKU CLASS CARRIER
20 JUNE (15) AT 1550 CARRIER SEARCH PLANES SIGHTED JAP FORCE APPARENTLY FUELING ON WESTERLY COURSE.
(16) AT 1635 LAUNCHED DECK LOADSTRIKES
(17) AT 1900 JAP FLEET UNDER ATTACK
(18) AT 2100 NIGHT RECOVERY OF STRIKES
21 JUNE (19) AT 0700 LAST SIGHTING OF JAP FLEET RETIRING - OUT OF RANGE.
ALL TIMES KING

TWO PATHS TO TOKYO

BATTLE OF THE PHILIPPINE SEA

Victory in the Battle of the Philippine Sea was achieved through the combined efforts of U.S. Navy forces in the air, on the surface, and underwater. As charted on the after-battle map at left, Spruance received an early warning of enemy intentions on June 13, 1944, when the submarine U.S.S. *Redfin* spotted Ozawa's First Mobile Fleet heading north from the island of Tawi Tawi (position 1 on the map) on its way to the Marianas. A coastwatcher spying on the fleet as it passed through the Philippines (3) reported at least three aircraft carriers, and another coastwatcher later sighted all nine of Ozawa's carriers (4). Meanwhile, a Japanese task force under Vice Adm. Ryunosuke Kusaka, destined for New Guinea to oppose MacArthur's landing at Biak, was ordered to shift course and link up with Ozawa. Spotted on June 13 near the island of Halmahera (2), it was tracked by the submarines U.S.S. *Seahorse* and U.S.S. *Cavalla* (positions 5 through 8) as it approached Ozawa's flagship, I.J.N. *Taiho,* whose location (9), some 500 miles west of Guam, was determined on June 18 by monitoring its radio signals.

By then, Spruance had sent Vice Adm. Marc Mitscher's Task Force 58, with 15 aircraft carriers, to guard western approaches to the Marianas. Mitscher proposed advancing toward Ozawa overnight on the 18th to launch an attack at dawn. Based in part on a signal from the submarine U.S.S. *Stingray* (10), however, Spruance was concerned that Ozawa's fast carriers might make an "end run" around Task Force 58 and threaten Americans on Saipan. He kept Mitscher close to the Marianas, where warplanes launched by Ozawa approached the task force on June 19 (12). Radar enabled Mitscher's airmen to get the jump on their foes, many of whom had been hastily trained as Japanese casualties soared. Flying Grumman F6F Hellcats that outperformed opposing Mitsubishi Zeroes, U.S. fighter pilots downed nearly 300 Japanese aircraft while losing about 30 planes in the "Great Marianas Turkey Shoot." Submarines added to Japanese losses when the *Cavalla* sank the carrier I.J.N. *Shokaku* (14) and a torpedo fired by the U.S.S. *Albacore* struck the *Taiho,* which later sank after Ozawa escaped. A third carrier, I.J.N. *Hiyo,* went down on June 20 when planes launched by Mitscher (16) attacked Ozawa's fleet (17) and were recovered at night by carriers lit up to guide them home (18). Some aircraft ran out of fuel and crashed, but the battle was a devastating setback for the Japanese Navy. ■

TURKEY SHOOT Standing by a Grumman Hellcat on the new U.S.S. *Lexington,* Lt. Alexander Vraciu holds up six fingers for the planes he downed during the "Great Marianas Turkey Shoot." Another photo taken during that engagement shows a Japanese plane plummeting (opposite top).

CHINA-BURMA-INDIA

FLYING TIGERS AND JUNGLE FIGHTERS

CHRONOLOGY

MAY 12–25, 1943 Allied leaders meeting at the Trident Conference in Washington, D.C., authorize an offensive in northern Burma by troops under Stilwell's command and a bombing campaign by Chennault's 14th Air Force in China.

AUGUST 31, 1943 Col. Carl Eifler, head of OSS Detachment 101, sends Capt. Vincent Curl to recruit Kachin warriors to serve as guerrillas behind Japanese lines in Burma.

MARCH 8, 1944 Japanese Gen. Renya Mutaguchi launches a costly offensive from Burma into India, where his forces will falter under pressure and withdraw in July.

AUGUST 3, 1944 Stilwell's troops capture Myitkyina in northern Burma, clearing the way for supplies from India to reach Chinese Nationalists at Kunming on the Ledo and Burma Roads.

MAY 3, 1945 British forces recapture the Burmese capital Rangoon.

ntent on holding China, Japanese chiefs kept nearly one million troops stationed there while their forces in the Pacific were stretched thin and lost ground. Japanese troops controlled eastern China, but Chiang Kai-shek's Nationalist forces held out at Kunming, not far from Burma (see map opposite). Japan had invaded Burma in early 1942 to cut off supplies to the Nationalists and keep Allied troops at bay, but American airmen continued to operate in China against the Japanese. Flying Tigers of the American Volunteer Group—organized to support Chinese Nationalists before the United States entered the war—formed the nucleus of the 23rd Fighter Group, which in 1943 became part of the 14th Army Air Force, based at Kunming and led by Maj. Gen. Claire Chennault, founder of the Flying Tigers. As he prepared to bomb distant Japanese targets, pilots of the Air Transport Command flew troops and supplies over the mountainous "Hump" between British India and China—perilous flights that claimed the lives of 1,000 airmen by war's end.

Lt. Gen. Joseph Stilwell, U.S. Army commander in the theater designated CBI (China-Burma-India) and Chiang's chief of staff, proposed invading northern Burma and restoring the overland supply line between India and China that was severed when the Japanese closed the Burma Road. Stilwell called on American-trained Chinese units to enter Burma and fight in conjunction with Merrill's Marauders, led by Brig. Gen. Frank Merrill. The Marauders emulated commandos from India called Chindits, organized by British Brig. Gen. Orde Wingate, who pioneered operations behind enemy lines in Burma. Stilwell's forces would be aided by Chindits as well as Kachin warriors, armed and instructed by agents of OSS Detachment 101. His arduous campaign, conducted in dense jungle, would help set the stage for a larger Allied offensive that ultimately broke Japan's grip on Burma. ∎

WINGED TIGERS A Chinese soldier at an airfield near Kunming guards Curtiss P-40K fighters of the U.S. 23rd Fighter Group, painted to resemble grimacing tigers like aircraft flown by the original Flying Tigers of the American Volunteer Group. Some of those pilots joined the 23rd Fighter Group, which was organized in 1942 and later incorporated into Chennault's 14th Air Force, whose members wore a shoulder patch featuring a winged tiger (inset above) and flew fighters and bombers against Japanese targets.

AIR TRANSPORT A Curtiss C-46 Commando transport plane comes in for a landing over the rooftops of a Chinese village. Such missions were conducted by Air Transport Command pilots and crewmen, whose flights "over the Hump" between India and China helped fuel the 14th Air Force and supply the Nationalist Army.

CBI THEATER The map below shows the flight paths followed by pilots of the Air Transport Command from bases situated between Ledo and Dibrugarh in easternmost India to Kunming in southwestern China. Those flights passed over mountains through which no roads ran. Allied plans to forge an overland supply line between India and China involved invading northern Burma and capturing Myitkyina, through which the new Ledo Road (constructed along the rugged Ledo Trail) would connect with the existing Burma Road to Kunming.

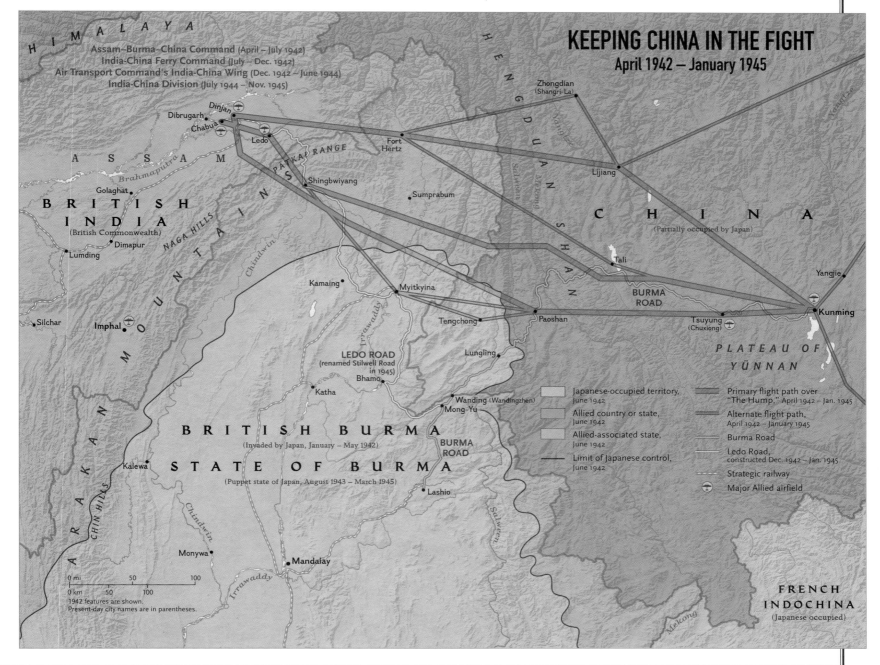

KEEPING CHINA IN THE FIGHT
April 1942 – January 1945

Assam–Burma–China Command (April – July 1942)
India-China Ferry Command (July – Dec. 1942)
Air Transport Command's India-China Wing (Dec. 1942 – June 1944)
India-China Division (July 1944 – Nov. 1945)

HIMALAYA

HENGDUANSHAN

Zhongdian
(Shangri-La)

Dibrugarh
Dinjan
Chabua
Ledo

PATKAI RANGE

Fort
Hertz

Lijiang

ASSAM

Brahmaputra

Shingbwiyang

Sumprabum

C H I N A
(Partially occupied by Japan)

Golaghat

B R I T I S H
I N D I A
(British Commonwealth)

NAGA HILLS

Dimapur

Lumding

Chindwin

Kamaing

Myitkyina

Tali

Yangjie

BURMA
ROAD

Silchar

Imphal

MOUNTAINS

Tengchong

Paoshan

Tsuyung
(Chuxiong)

Kunming

LEDO ROAD
(renamed Stilwell Road
in 1945)

Lungling

PLATEAU OF
YÜNNAN

Bhamo

Katha

Wanding (Wandingzhen)
Mong-Yu

Irrawaddy

B R I T I S H   B U R M A
(Invaded by Japan, January – May 1942)

BURMA
ROAD

S T A T E   O F   B U R M A
(Puppet state of Japan, August 1943 – March 1945)

Kalewa

ARAKAN

CHIN HILLS

Chindwin

Lashio

Salween

	Japanese-occupied territory, June 1942		Primary flight path over "The Hump," April 1942 – Jan. 1945
	Allied country or state, June 1942		Alternate flight path, April 1942 – January 1945
	Allied-associated state, June 1942		Burma Road
	Limit of Japanese control, June 1942		Ledo Road, constructed Dec. 1942 – Jan. 1945
			Strategic railway
			Major Allied airfield

Monywa

Mandalay

0 mi   50   100
0 km   50   100
1942 features are shown.
Present-day city names are in parentheses.

Irrawaddy

Mekong

F R E N C H
I N D O C H I N A
(Japanese occupied)

DETACHMENT 101: BEHIND ENEMY LINES

Organized secretly by the OSS in 1942, Detachment 101 was led by Capt. Carl Eifler (below right), a former U.S. Customs officer who had busted smugglers along the Mexican border. When he reported to work under Stilwell, he was told to begin sabotaging Japanese supply lines in Burma within 90 days. "All I want to hear," Stilwell said, "is booms coming out of the jungle." Eifler and his OSS officers began training agents in India, including Burmese refugees who had fled the Japanese invasion of their country. Recruits who signed on were assured that if they died in action, their next of kin would be compensated.

Impressed by the courage and stamina of Kachin warriors in northern Burma who were aiding the British against the Japanese, Eifler sent OSS Capt. Vincent Curl in late August 1943 to establish a base among them near Myitkyina, the objective of Stilwell's forthcoming offensive. Curl won the confidence of an influential Kachin chief named Zhing Htaw Naw, who was suffering from malaria, by reviving him with quinine. The chief agreed to supply hundreds of men who would be armed, trained, and paid by the OSS. Soon several thousand Kachins were sabotaging bridges and rail lines and ambushing the enemy. Their intimate knowledge of the jungle and their ability to spy on the Japanese undetected enabled OSS officers to draw detailed maps of areas where opposing forces were active (opposite top). As shown on an OSS map made in April 1944 when the Allied assault on Myitkyina was under way (opposite bottom), Detachment 101 had many command posts in that area, directing guerrilla warfare against Japanese troops and reporting on their movements. ∎

WAR ZONE Detachment 101 relied mightily on the Kachin, whose territory in northern Burma (shown in green on this map) encompassed Myitkyina, a vital road and rail junction that Allied troops targeted to secure supply lines from India to American and Chinese Nationalist forces at Kunming.

SNAKE CHARMER Shown handling a poisonous snake, Carl Eifler was known to take risks but rejected any volunteer who was "a hell-raiser or glory-seeker." OSS agents in Asia carried a blood chit (left) identifying them as Americans and seeking help in various languages if wounded.

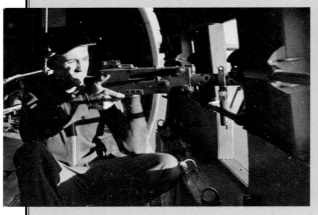

JUNGLE WARFARE Above, Kachin troops enlisted by the OSS wade along a stream, enabling them to move quietly without leaving tracks their foes might detect. At left, a machine-gunner poses in a C-47 transport. Planes of Detachment 101's "Red Ass" squadron were used to conduct surveillance, evacuate wounded men, and deliver weapons to recruits like the Kachin at right, kneeling beside a fallen enemy.

CARTOGRAPHY 101 Close surveillance contributed to the hand-drawn OSS map at right, which notes that "during raids Japs hide in bushes" near a suspension bridge. The Department 101 map at bottom, showing command and subcommand posts around Myitkyina, was contained in a report to OSS chief William Donovan from Lt. Col. William Peers, who succeeded Eifler. Peers gave operational control to commanders in areas with code names such as Tramp, Knothead, and Pat. Each command area had various stations and subunits, which might consist of a few OSS officers and numerous Kachin recruits like those pictured below.

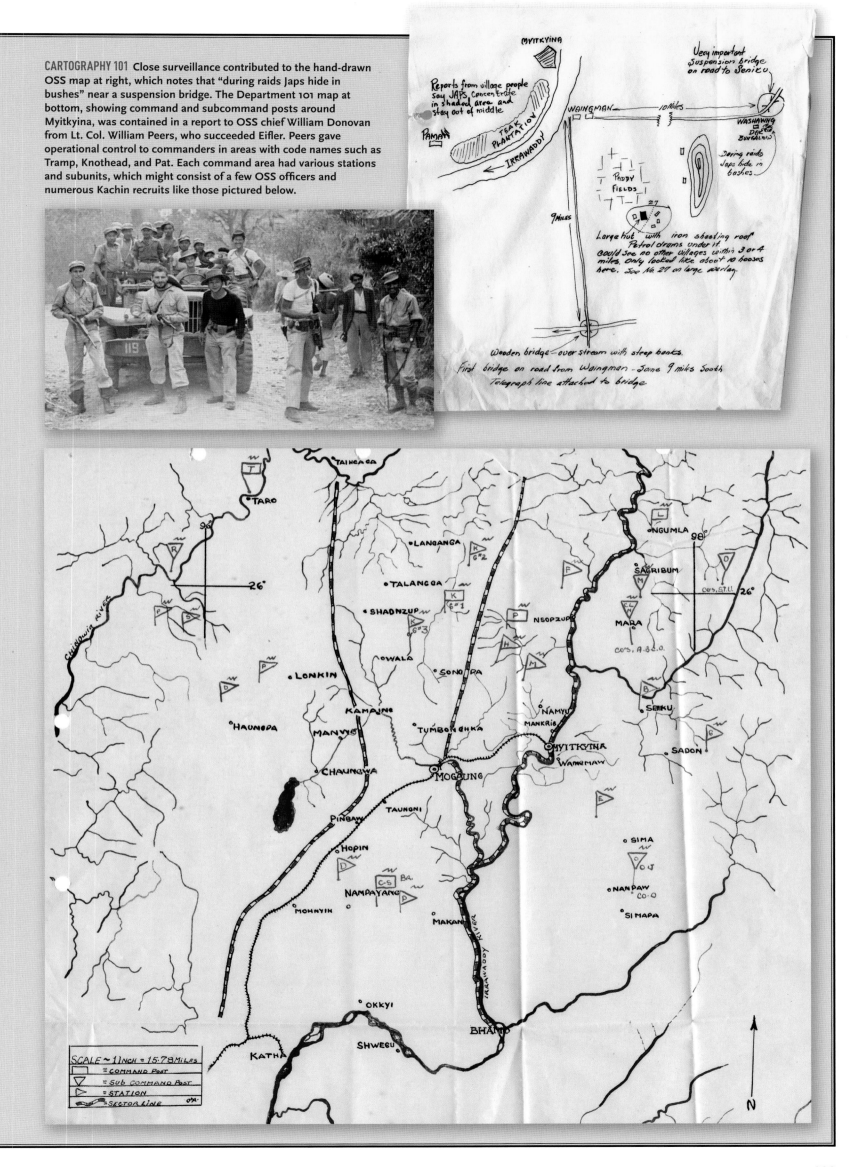

FIGHT TO RECLAIM BURMA

Merrill's Marauders included veterans of Pacific campaigns with a knack for jungle warfare. Orde Wingate, the British Chindit commander, trained them for his upcoming operation behind Japanese lines in central Burma and was livid when Stilwell claimed those Marauders for his own campaign. Stilwell could "take his Americans and stick 'em," Wingate swore. Such disputes were common in CBI because resources were limited. Stilwell resented Chennault's 14th Air Force for hogging supplies flown over the Hump from India. By seizing Myitkyina and its nearby airfield—which Japanese fighter pilots used to attack those flights—Stilwell would boost supply deliveries by road and air to Nationalist troops in China and keep Japanese troops tied down there.

As it turned out, Wingate's operation aided Stilwell's campaign, which began in early 1944. In March, Chindits landed in gliders at a jungle clearing called Broadway and other airstrips (see map below). Joined by Chindits who arrived overland, they tore up tracks and waged guerrilla warfare, preventing Japanese reinforcements from reaching Myitkyina. Wingate died in a plane crash in late March, but Chindits continued to support Stilwell's troops, including his X Force (Chinese troops based in India as opposed to the Y Force in China) and Merrill's Marauders. Advancing toward Myitkyina on parallel tracks with the help of Detachment 101 and its Kachin recruits, they suffered as much from tropical diseases as from battle wounds. Monsoon rains made things worse, but Marauders rallied and seized the Myitkyina airstrip on May 17. That brought Stilwell enough aid to besiege the town and finally take it in early August. "Myitkyina over at last," he wrote. "Thank God."

Meanwhile, Japanese forces led by Lt. Gen. Renya Mutaguchi had invaded India, where he hoped to trigger a rebellion against British rule. But Indian forces under Lt. Gen. William Slim did not greet the Japanese as liberators and withstood sieges alongside British troops at Kohima and Imphal (near map opposite), where Slim flew in fresh units and supplies and forced the invaders to withdraw. Combined with the loss of Myitkyina, Mutaguchi's defeat weakened Japan's hold on Burma, which Allied forces reclaimed in an offensive beginning in late 1944 (far map opposite). The only Japanese gains came in China, where they captured forward bases of the 14th Air Force, reducing its range. That did not stop Americans from launching strategic bombers from Pacific bases closer to Japan, which faced ruin while many of its troops remained bogged down in China. ∎

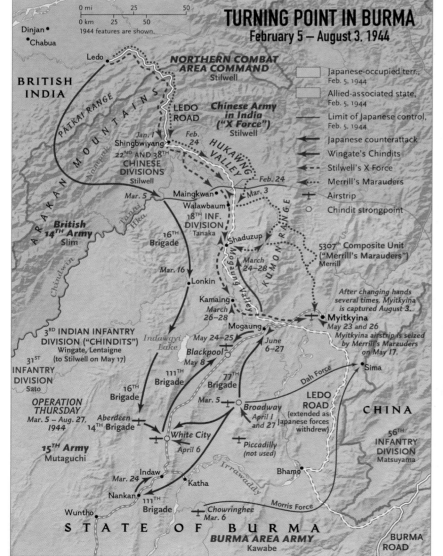

TURNING POINT IN BURMA
February 5 – August 3, 1944

1944 features are shown.

Japanese-occupied terr., Feb. 5, 1944

Allied-associated state, Feb. 5, 1944

Limit of Japanese control, Feb. 5, 1944

Japanese counterattack

Wingate's Chindits

Stilwell's X Force

Merrill's Marauders

Airstrip

Chindit strongpoint

NORTHERN COMBAT AREA COMMAND
Stilwell

LEDO ROAD

Chinese Army in India ("X Force")
Stilwell

22ND AND 38TH CHINESE DIVISIONS
Stilwell

British 14TH Army
Slim

18TH INF. DIVISION
Tanaka

16TH Brigade

5307th Composite Unit ("Merrill's Marauders")
Merrill

After changing hands several times, Myitkyina is captured August 3.

Myitkyina
May 23 and 26
Myitkyina airstrip is seized by Merrill's Marauders on May 17.

3RD INDIAN INFANTRY DIVISION ("CHINDITS")
Wingate, Lentaigne (to Stilwell on May 17)

31ST INFANTRY DIVISION
Sato

111TH Brigade

77TH Brigade

Dah Force

LEDO ROAD
(extended as Japanese forces withdrew)

OPERATION THURSDAY
Mar. 5 – Aug. 27, 1944

16TH Brigade

Broadway
April 1 and 27

CHINA

56TH INFANTRY DIVISION
Matsuyama

Aberdeen
14TH Brigade

White City
April 6

Piccadilly (not used)

15TH Army
Mutaguchi

111TH Brigade

Chowringhee
Mar. 6

Morris Force

STATE OF BURMA
BURMA AREA ARMY
Kawabe

BURMA ROAD

PATKAI RANGE
MOUNTAINS
HUKAWNG VALLEY
KUMON RANGE
ARAKAN
Mogaung Valley

British INDIA

Dinjan
Chabua
Ledo

Shingbwiyang
Jan. 1
Feb. 24

Maingkwan
Mar. 5
Walawbaum
Mar. 3
Feb. 24

Shaduzup
March 24-28

Mar. 16
Lonkin

Kamaing
March 26-28

Mogaung
May 24-25

Indawgyi Lake
Blackpool
May 8
June 6-27

Sima

Indaw
Mar. 24
Katha

Nankan
Wuntho

Bhamo

INVADING BURMA Chindits like the men above, aiding a wounded comrade, infiltrated Burma from India by air and ground in early 1944, as shown on the map at left, and severed Japanese supply lines while Merrill's Marauders and Chinese troops of Stilwell's X Force descended on Myitkyina. After seizing the air base outside that town in May, Stilwell besieged Myitkyina, which fell in August.

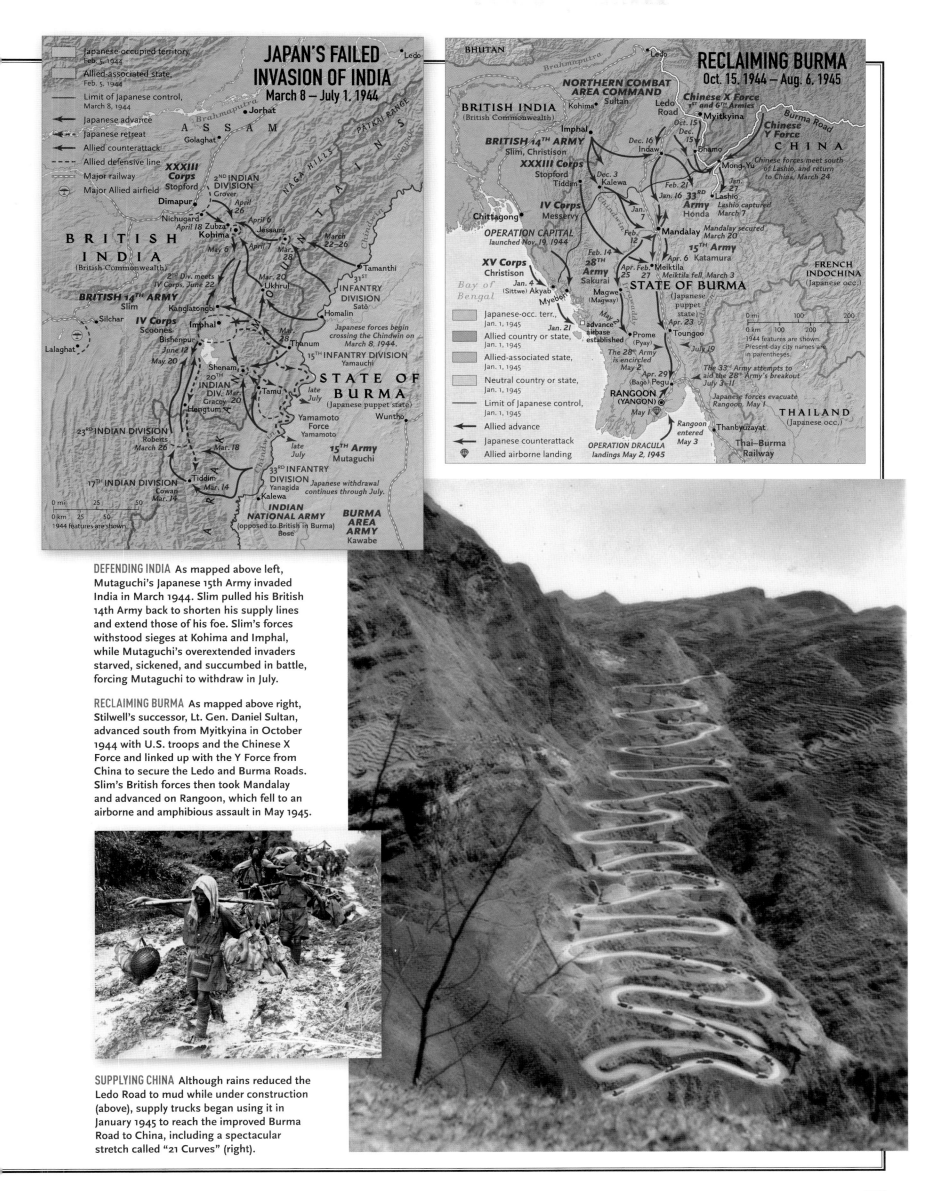

JAPAN'S FAILED INVASION OF INDIA
March 8 – July 1, 1944

- Japanese-occupied territory, Feb. 5, 1944
- Allied-associated state, Feb. 5, 1944
- → Limit of Japanese control, March 8, 1944
- → Japanese advance
- ⇠ Japanese retreat
- ⇢ Allied counterattack
- - - Allied defensive line
- ⊦⊦ Major railway
- ⊕ Major Allied airfield

BHUTAN
Brahmaputra
Ledo
ASSAM
Jorhat
NAGA HILLS
PATKAI RANGE
Golaghat
XXXIII Corps Stopford
2ND INDIAN DIVISION Grover
Dimapur
April 26
Nichugard
April 18 Zubza
April 6
Kohima
Jessami
May 6
April
Mar. 28
March 22–26
Ukhrul
Mar. 20
Tamanthi
31ST INFANTRY DIVISION Satô
BRITISH INDIA (British Commonwealth)
2nd Div. meets IV Corps, June 22
Homalin
BRITISH 14TH ARMY Slim
Silchar
Kanglatongbi
IV Corps Scoones
Bishenpur
Imphal
Mar. 28
June 12
Thanum
May 20
15TH INFANTRY DIVISION Yamauchi
Lalaghat
Japanese forces begin crossing the Chindwin on March 8, 1944.
Shenam
20TH INDIAN DIV. Mar. 20 Gracey
Tamu
STATE OF BURMA (Japanese puppet state)
Hengtum
late July
Yamamoto Force Yamamoto
Wuntho
Mar. 18
late July
15TH Army Mutaguchi
23RD INDIAN DIVISION Roberts March 26
Tiddim Mar. 14
33RD INFANTRY DIVISION Yanagida
17TH INDIAN DIVISION Cowan Mar. 14
Kalewa
Japanese withdrawal continues through July.
INDIAN NATIONAL ARMY (opposed to British in Burma) Bose
BURMA AREA ARMY Kawabe

0 mi 25 50
0 km 25 50
1944 features are shown.

RECLAIMING BURMA
Oct. 15, 1944 – Aug. 6, 1945

BHUTAN
Brahmaputra
Ledo
NORTHERN COMBAT AREA COMMAND
BRITISH INDIA (British Commonwealth)
Kohima Sultan
Ledo Road
Chinese X Force 1ST and 6TH Armies
Oct. 15
Myitkyina
Burma Road
Imphal
BRITISH 14TH ARMY Slim, Christison
Dec. 16
Indaw
Dec. 15
Bhamo
Chinese Y Force
CHINA
XXXIII Corps Stopford
Dec. 3 Kalewa
Tiddim
Feb. 21
Mong-Yu
Chinese forces meet south of Lashio, and return to China, March 24
Jan. 16
Jan. 7
33RD Army Honda
Jan. 27
Chittagong
Lashio
Lashio captured March 7
OPERATION CAPITAL launched Nov. 19, 1944
IV Corps Messervy
Feb. 2
Mandalay
Mandalay secured March 20
XV Corps Christison
Feb. 14
Feb. 12
15TH Army Katamura
Apr. 6
Bay of Bengal
Jan. 4 (Sittwe) Akyab
28TH Army Sakurai
Apr. Feb. 25 27
Meiktila
Meiktila fell, March 3
FRENCH INDOCHINA (Japanese occ.)
Myebon
Magwe (Magway)
STATE OF BURMA (Japanese puppet state)
Jan. 21
advance airbase established
May 1
Prome (Pyay)
Apr. 23 Toungoo
July 19
- Japanese-occ. terr., Jan. 1, 1945
- Allied country or state, Jan. 1, 1945
- Allied-associated state, Jan. 1, 1945
- Neutral country or state, Jan. 1, 1945
- Limit of Japanese control, Jan. 1, 1945
- → Allied advance
- → Japanese counterattack
- ◈ Allied airborne landing

The 28th Army is encircled May 2
Apr. 29 (Bago) Pegu
RANGOON (YANGON) May 1
Rangoon entered May 3
Thanbyuzayat
Thai–Burma Railway
THAILAND (Japanese occ.)
OPERATION DRACULA landings May 2, 1945

0 mi 100 200
0 km 100 200

The 33rd Army attempts to aid the 28th Army's breakout July 3–11
Japanese forces evacuate Rangoon, May 1

1944 features are shown. Present-day city names are in parentheses.

DEFENDING INDIA As mapped above left, Mutaguchi's Japanese 15th Army invaded India in March 1944. Slim pulled his British 14th Army back to shorten his supply lines and extend those of his foe. Slim's forces withstood sieges at Kohima and Imphal, while Mutaguchi's overextended invaders starved, sickened, and succumbed in battle, forcing Mutaguchi to withdraw in July.

RECLAIMING BURMA As mapped above right, Stilwell's successor, Lt. Gen. Daniel Sultan, advanced south from Myitkyina in October 1944 with U.S. troops and the Chinese X Force and linked up with the Y Force from China to secure the Ledo and Burma Roads. Slim's British forces then took Mandalay and advanced on Rangoon, which fell to an airborne and amphibious assault in May 1945.

SUPPLYING CHINA Although rains reduced the Ledo Road to mud while under construction (above), supply trucks began using it in January 1945 to reach the improved Burma Road to China, including a spectacular stretch called "21 Curves" (right).

RETURN TO THE
PHILIPPINES
INVASIONS AND DELIVERANCE

CHRONOLOGY

OCTOBER 20, 1944 MacArthur's troops land on Leyte in the Philippines.

OCTOBER 23–26, 1944 The U.S. Third and Seventh Fleets inflict a crushing defeat on the Japanese Navy in the Battle of Leyte Gulf.

JANUARY 9, 1945 Several American divisions land on the main Philippine island of Luzon, MacArthur's ultimate objective.

FEBRUARY 3, 1945 U.S. troops enter Manila, where they will battle Japanese troops holding out in the city's walled historic district, Intramuros.

MARCH 3, 1945 MacArthur's forces take Manila, but their efforts to secure Luzon and other Philippine islands will continue into the summer.

MacArthur's original plan to liberate the Philippines called for his forces to advance step-by-step from the island of Mindanao in the south to the main island of Luzon and the capital Manila in the north. In September 1944, he decided to bypass Mindanao and land on Leyte, closer to Luzon. Leyte, he wrote, "was to be the anvil against which I hoped to hammer the Japanese into submission in the central Philippines—the springboard from which I could proceed to the conquest of Luzon, for the final assault against Japan itself." More than 100,000 troops would invade Leyte on the first day, a huge logistical challenge that involved coordinating shipments of men and equipment from numerous bases on New Guinea and other islands in transports escorted by warships (see planning map opposite). To supplement the modest Seventh Fleet, known as "MacArthur's Navy," Admiral Nimitz assigned Halsey's powerful Third Fleet to guard Leyte Gulf, through which invasion forces and any Japanese warships menacing them would pass.

On October 20, 1944, four divisions of Lt. Gen. Walter Krueger's Sixth Army landed on Leyte's east coast (inset map opposite). They faced little opposition initially because Japanese troops had withdrawn inland. But their beachhead was not secure until U.S. naval forces defeated the Japanese fleet decisively in Leyte Gulf the following week. Progress was fitful thereafter as Krueger's troops captured airstrips on the east coast but met with fierce resistance at "Breakneck Ridge," a treacherous pass in the north along the highway to Ormoc on the west coast, where Japanese reinforcements from Luzon were landing. Not until late December—after a desperate Japanese airborne attack on the American-held airstrips was repulsed and an amphibious assault by Krueger's 77th Infantry Division secured Ormoc—could MacArthur declare victory and target Luzon. ∎

LEYTE LANDING On October 20, 1944, troops form a human chain to unload cargo from a U.S. Coast Guard–manned LST (landing ship tank), which landed troops and supplies as well as tanks at Leyte. MacArthur waded ashore that same day in a dramatic gesture caught on camera (top) and proclaimed by radio: "People of the Philippines, I have returned."

INVASION PATHS As mapped at right, four U.S. divisions landed on Leyte on October 20. The 24th Infantry and First Cavalry Divisions advanced along the north coast and battled Japanese troops at Breakneck Ridge. Meanwhile, the Seventh Infantry Division crossed the mountains to the west coast, where the 77th Infantry Division landed in December and took Ormoc, cutting off enemy reinforcements and sealing the American victory.

CONVOY ROUTES This top secret map plots the movements of transports and warships that would depart far-flung American bases in the southwest Pacific and form a convoy to Leyte. Transports and destroyer escorts (DE) at places far from Leyte, like Bougainville, would leave first, followed by those at ports closer to Leyte, like Hollandia on New Guinea. The ships would rendezvous southeast of the Philippines with two destroyer escorts and two escort aircraft carriers (CVE) from Kossol Roads (a base on Palau) that would accompany the convoy to Leyte.

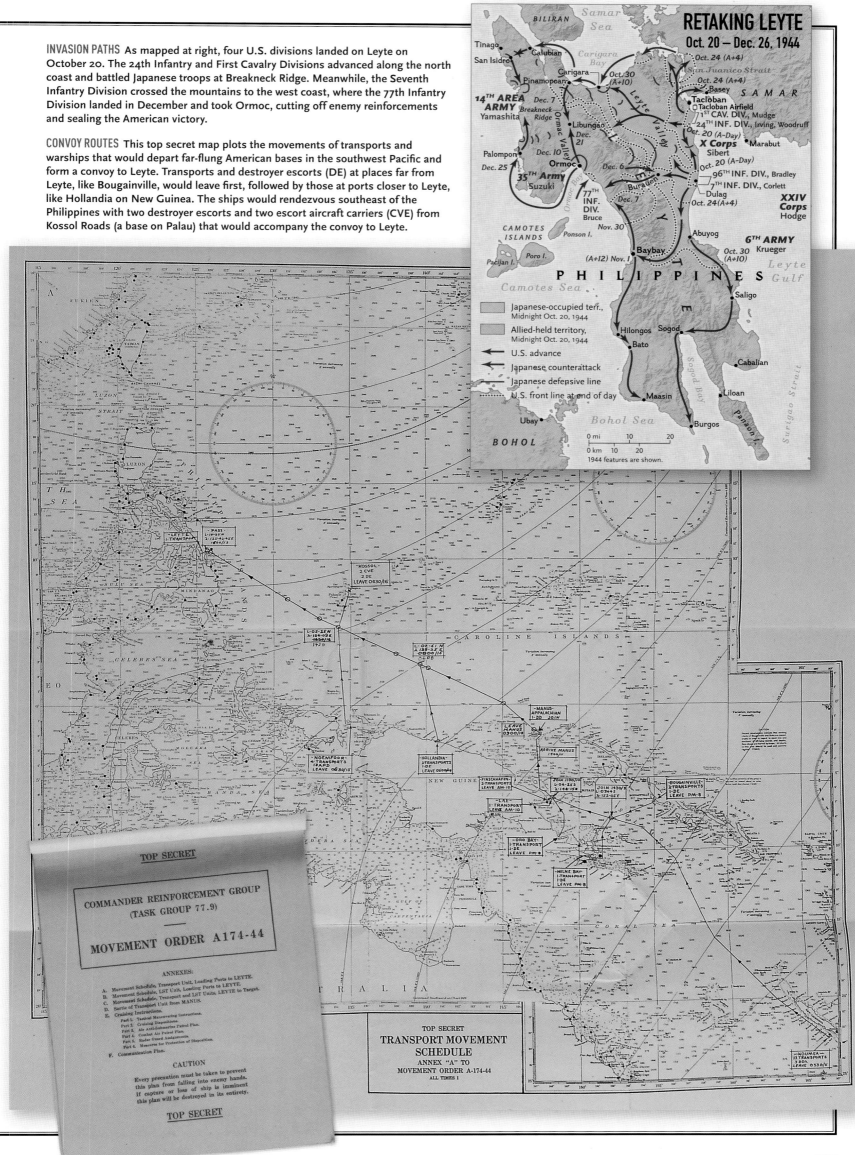

RETAKING LEYTE
Oct. 20 – Dec. 26, 1944

Japanese-occupied terr., Midnight Oct. 20, 1944
Allied-held territory, Midnight Oct. 20, 1944
→ U.S. advance
→ Japanese counterattack
···· Japanese defensive line
······ U.S. front line at end of day

0 mi 10 20
0 km 10 20
1944 features are shown.

TOP SECRET

COMMANDER REINFORCEMENT GROUP
(TASK GROUP 77.9)

MOVEMENT ORDER A174-44

ANNEXES:

A. Movement Schedule, Transport Unit, Loading Ports to LEYTE.
B. Movement Schedule, LST Unit, Loading Ports to LEYTE.
C. Movement Schedule, Transport and LST Units, LEYTE to Target.
D. Sortie of Transport Unit from MANUS.
E. Cruising Instructions.
   Part 1. Tactical Maneuvering Instructions.
   Part 2. Cruising Dispositions.
   Part 3. Air Anti-Submarine Patrol Plan.
   Part 4. Combat Air Patrol Plan.
   Part 5. Radar Guard Assignments.
   Part 6. Measures for Protection of Disposition.
F. Communication Plan.

CAUTION

Every precaution must be taken to prevent this plan from falling into enemy hands. If capture or loss of ship is imminent this plan will be destroyed in its entirety.

TOP SECRET

TOP SECRET
TRANSPORT MOVEMENT SCHEDULE
ANNEX "A" TO
MOVEMENT ORDER A-174-44
ALL TIMES I

LAST HURRAH FOR JAPAN'S NAVY

As their fleet lost strength, Japanese admirals resolved to risk what remained in battle to halt the American advance and save Japan. "Would it not be a shame to have the fleet intact while our nation perishes?" asked Vice Adm. Takeo Kurita, who was chosen by his commander in chief, Adm. Soemu Toyoda, to lead an all-out attack on U.S. naval forces shielding MacArthur's troops on Leyte. Kurita's Center Force would go after the Seventh Fleet (see map opposite). Vice Admiral Ozawa's Northern Force—whose surviving carriers had lost most of their planes and pilots in the Battle of the Philippine Sea—would serve as a decoy, luring Halsey's Third Fleet away from Leyte Gulf. Squadrons under Vice Admirals Shoji Nishimura and Kiyohide Shima would converge to form the Southern Force and support Kurita.

Toyoda's complex offensive soon faltered for lack of coordination. Nishimura entered Surigao Strait ahead of Shima on the night of October 24 and went down with his ship under a devastating bombardment directed by Vice Adm. Jesse Olden-dorf of the Seventh Fleet. Earlier that day, U.S. submarines had spotted Kurita's Center Force and alerted Halsey, who launched air strikes that doomed the superbattleship I.J.N. *Musashi* and damaged another behemoth, I.J.N. *Yamato*. On October 25, Kurita led what remained of his force through San Bernardino Strait. Meanwhile, Halsey went after Ozawa, leaving Rear Adm. Clifton Sprague near Leyte Gulf to hold off Kurita with destroyers and escort carriers—converted merchant ships designated CVE, which cynics said meant "combustible, vulnerable, and expendable." Heroic efforts by airmen on those carriers and by Sprague's outclassed destroyers saved the American beachheads on Leyte. Kurita then withdrew rather than risk annihilation by "Bull" Halsey, who was returning after his pilots sank the carrier *Zuikaku* (below) and other warships of Ozawa's force in a rout dubbed the "Battle of Bull's Run." That was the crowning blow in the Battle of Leyte Gulf, which shredded the Japanese Navy. The main threat to U.S. warships thereafter were suicide missions by kamikazes (opposite). ■

PARTING SALUTE Crewmen on the listing carrier *Zuikaku* offer a final banzai salute to their flag and emperor after being attacked by naval airmen of Halsey's fleet on October 25, 1944. In addition to the heavy carrier *Zuikaku*, three light Japanese carriers went down during the Battle of Leyte Gulf.

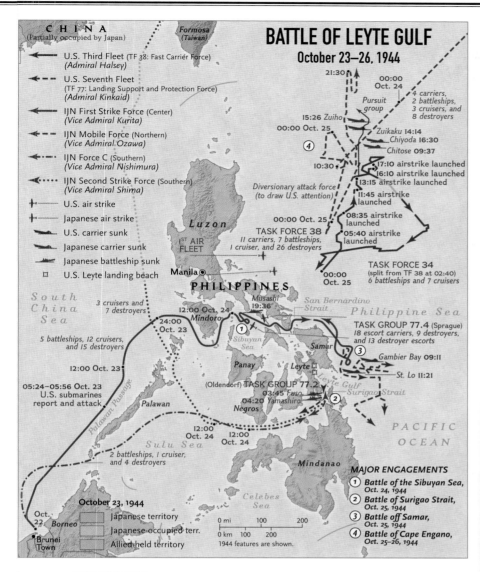

BATTLE OF LEYTE GULF
October 23–26, 1944

←—— U.S. Third Fleet (TF 38: Fast Carrier Force) (Admiral Halsey)

←- - - U.S. Seventh Fleet (TF 77: Landing Support and Protection Force) (Admiral Kinkaid)

←—— IJN First Strike Force (Center) (Vice Admiral Kurita)

←- - - IJN Mobile Force (Northern) (Vice Admiral Ozawa)

←—— IJN Force C (Southern) (Vice Admiral Nishimura)

←····· IJN Second Strike Force (Southern) (Vice Admiral Shima)

╬ U.S. air strike

╬ Japanese air strike

⬟ U.S. carrier sunk

⬟ Japanese carrier sunk

⬟ Japanese battleship sunk

▫ U.S. Leyte landing beach

CHINA (Partially occupied by Japan)

Formosa (Taiwan)

Luzon

1ST AIR FLEET

Manila

PHILIPPINES

South China Sea

3 cruisers and 7 destroyers

12:00 Oct. 24 — Mindoro

24:00 Oct. 23

5 battleships, 12 cruisers, and 15 destroyers

12:00 Oct. 23

05:24–05:56 Oct. 23 U.S. submarines report and attack

Palawan

12:00 Oct. 24

12:00 Oct. 24

2 battleships, 1 cruiser, and 4 destroyers

Negros

Panay

Sibuyan Sea

Sulu Sea

Mindanao

Celebes Sea

October 23, 1944

Oct. 22 *Borneo*

Brunei Town

	Japanese territory
	Japanese-occupied terr.
	Allied-held territory

0 mi   100   200
0 km   100   200
1944 features are shown.

21:30

00:00 Oct. 24

Pursuit group

4 carriers, 2 battleships, 3 cruisers, and 8 destroyers

15:26 *Zuiho*

00:00 Oct. 25

Zuikaku 14:14
Chiyoda 16:30
Chitose 09:37

10:30

17:10 airstrike launched
16:10 airstrike launched
13:15 airstrike launched
11:45 airstrike launched
08:35 airstrike launched
05:40 airstrike launched

Diversionary attack force (to draw U.S. attention)

00:00 Oct. 25

TASK FORCE 38
11 carriers, 7 battleships, 1 cruiser, and 26 destroyers

00:00 Oct. 25

TASK FORCE 34
(split from TF 38 at 02:40)
6 battleships and 7 cruisers

Musashi 19:36

San Bernardino Strait

Philippine Sea

TASK GROUP 77.4 (Sprague)
18 escort carriers, 9 destroyers, and 13 destroyer escorts

Samar

Gambier Bay 09:11

St. Lo 11:21

Leyte

(Oldendorf) **TASK GROUP 77.2**

03:45 *Fuso*

04:20 *Yamashiro*

Leyte Gulf

Surigao Strait

PACIFIC OCEAN

MAJOR ENGAGEMENTS
① **Battle of the Sibuyan Sea,** Oct. 24, 1944
② **Battle of Surigao Strait,** Oct. 25, 1944
③ **Battle off Samar,** Oct. 25, 1944
④ **Battle of Cape Engano,** Oct. 25–26, 1944

DECISIVE BATTLE As mapped above, Kurita's Center Force, Shima and Nishimura's Southern Force, and Ozawa's Northern Force remained divided and were soundly defeated around Leyte Gulf by Halsey's Third Fleet and by Seventh Fleet forces under Oldendorf and Sprague. The outcome devastated the Japanese Navy.

SUICIDE MISSIONS Attacks by kamikaze pilots like those at left, saluting their commander before take-off, began during the Battle of Leyte Gulf and continued afterward. On November 25, 1944, kamikazes hit the carrier U.S.S. *Intrepid,* which was stationed off Leyte to support MacArthur's forces. Fires on board were contained (above), but 69 men died and were buried at sea (top).

ADVANCING TO LUZON AND MANILA

Unlike earlier campaigns in which MacArthur made big gains without paying a steep price, the struggle for Luzon and Manila proved costly for all concerned. Kamikaze attacks on the invasion fleet damaged more than 20 ships and killed hundreds on board. On January 9, 1945, after Gen. Tomoyuki Yamashita withdrew most Japanese forces inland, nearly 70,000 U.S. troops landed safely along Lingayen Gulf (see map below), but they soon met with concerted opposition at Clark Field and did not take that air base until month's end. Another 40,000 Americans landed at San Antonio on the west coast and were caught under lethal fire at Zig-Zag Pass by enemy gunners who held fast on high ground until they were bombed and burned out with napalm. At Corregidor, Japanese troops trapped in caves that served earlier in the war as MacArthur's headquarters committed suicide by triggering a huge explosion that also killed some Americans.

Prodded by MacArthur, men of the First Cavalry Division entered Manila on February 3 and freed starving Allied prisoners held at Santo Tomás University. Most of Yamashita's troops had abandoned Manila, but naval forces under Rear Adm. Sanji Iwabuchi clung to the Intramuros, the walled inner city, and terrorized the populace by killing civilians. Many other inhabitants died in fires or under bombardment in war-torn Manila. By the time Japanese resistance was crushed in March, nearly 100,000 civilians had perished there and MacArthur had suffered more than 30,000 casualties on Luzon. His efforts to secure the Philippines continued into the summer, by which time the American advance on Japan had bypassed that country. Like the Allied invasion of Italy, the Philippines campaign did not lead directly to victory but nullified enemy forces that might have prolonged the war. More than 300,000 Japanese troops died fighting there, roughly 15 percent of the total lost by Japan in combat. ∎

ROAD TO MANILA As mapped above, the Luzon invasion fleet (inset) landed I Corps and XIV Corps of Krueger's Sixth Army at Lingayen Bay on January 9, XI Corps of Eichelberger's Eighth Army at San Antonio on January 29, and other forces in and around Manila Bay, where paratroopers helped capture Corregidor in February. MacArthur's troops took Manila in March after a month-long siege but did not secure all of Luzon from Yamashita's forces until summer.

FREED IN MANILA Among those liberated by U.S. troops who entered Manila in early February 1945 were Americans Lee Rogers (far left) and John Todd (near left), emaciated after three years of harsh confinement at Santo Tomás University, where the Japanese held civilians from Allied countries. In late February, American soldiers freed the women pictured below, held hostage by Japanese troops in a church in Manila's walled inner city, the Intramuros. Many men held captive separately were killed by Japanese soldiers incensed by the support Americans received from Filipino guerrillas and civilians, who trusted that the United States would soon fulfill its pledge to grant their country independence.

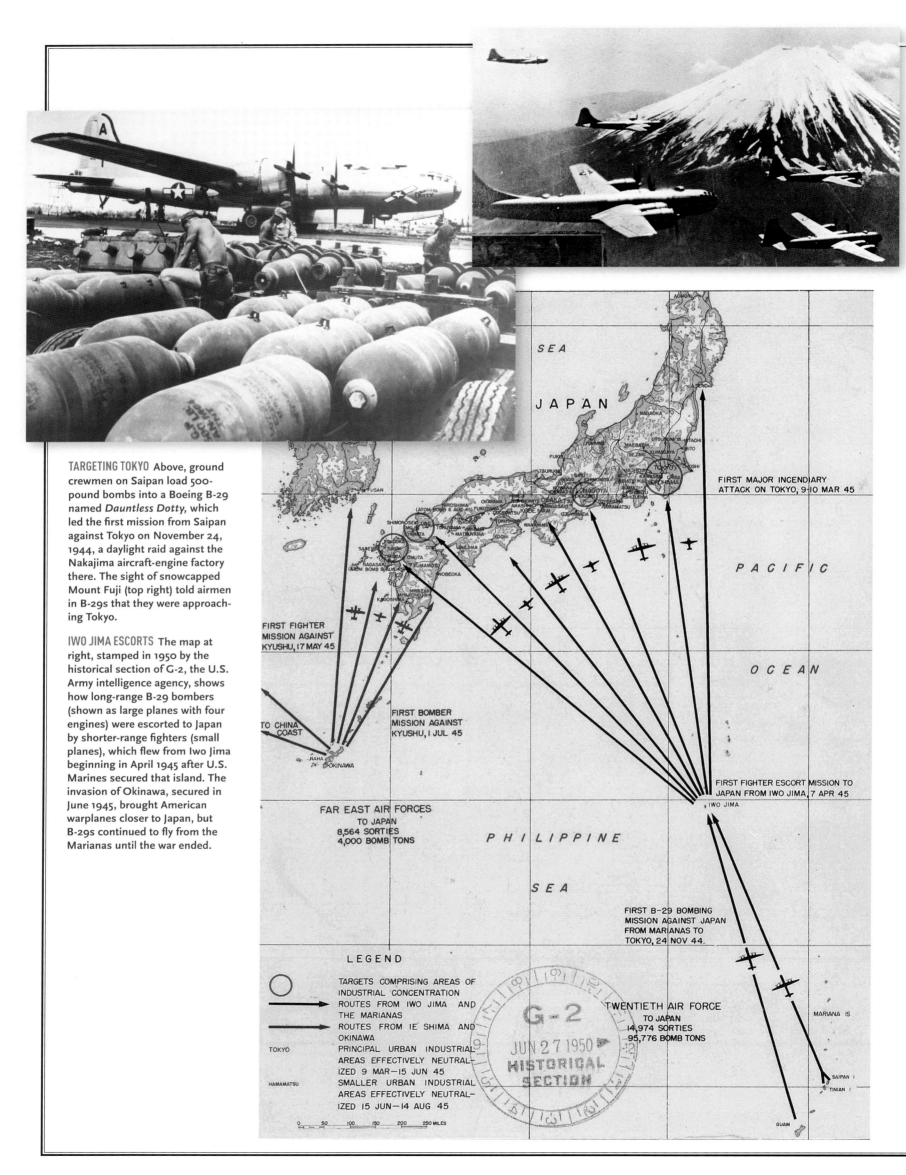

TARGETING TOKYO Above, ground crewmen on Saipan load 500-pound bombs into a Boeing B-29 named *Dauntless Dotty*, which led the first mission from Saipan against Tokyo on November 24, 1944, a daylight raid against the Nakajima aircraft-engine factory there. The sight of snowcapped Mount Fuji (top right) told airmen in B-29s that they were approaching Tokyo.

IWO JIMA ESCORTS The map at right, stamped in 1950 by the historical section of G-2, the U.S. Army intelligence agency, shows how long-range B-29 bombers (shown as large planes with four engines) were escorted to Japan by shorter-range fighters (small planes), which flew from Iwo Jima beginning in April 1945 after U.S. Marines secured that island. The invasion of Okinawa, secured in June 1945, brought American warplanes closer to Japan, but B-29s continued to fly from the Marianas until the war ended.

FIRST MAJOR INCENDIARY ATTACK ON TOKYO, 9-10 MAR 45

FIRST FIGHTER MISSION AGAINST KYUSHU, 17 MAY 45

FIRST BOMBER MISSION AGAINST KYUSHU, I JUL 45

TO CHINA COAST

FIRST FIGHTER ESCORT MISSION TO JAPAN FROM IWO JIMA, 7 APR 45

FAR EAST AIR FORCES TO JAPAN 8,564 SORTIES 4,000 BOMB TONS

FIRST B-29 BOMBING MISSION AGAINST JAPAN FROM MARIANAS TO TOKYO, 24 NOV 44.

TWENTIETH AIR FORCE TO JAPAN 14,974 SORTIES 95,776 BOMB TONS

G-2 JUN 27 1950 HISTORICAL SECTION

LEGEND

○ TARGETS COMPRISING AREAS OF INDUSTRIAL CONCENTRATION

→ ROUTES FROM IWO JIMA AND THE MARIANAS

→ ROUTES FROM IE SHIMA AND OKINAWA

TOKYO PRINCIPAL URBAN INDUSTRIAL AREAS EFFECTIVELY NEUTRALIZED 9 MAR—15 JUN 45

HAMAMATSU SMALLER URBAN INDUSTRIAL AREAS EFFECTIVELY NEUTRALIZED 15 JUN—14 AUG 45

0   50   100   150   200   250 MILES

SEA

JAPAN

PACIFIC

OCEAN

PHILIPPINE

SEA

MARIANA IS

SAIPAN I

TINIAN I

GUAM

CLOSING IN
—ON JAPAN—
FROM IWO JIMA TO HIROSHIMA

Assigned in January 1945 to take charge of the 21st Bomber Command, which targeted Japan from bases on Saipan, Tinian, and Guam in long-range B-29s, Maj. Gen. Curtis LeMay noted that those big bombers had not yet "made much of a splash in the war." Flying at 30,000 feet, above the range of antiaircraft guns, they were buffeted by the jet stream, seldom bombed with much precision, and remained vulnerable to enemy fighters, which sometimes shot them down or rammed them in suicide attacks. Applying tactics used against Germany, LeMay planned to fire-bomb Tokyo and other Japanese cities at night from lower altitude. Worries that airmen might "get the holy hell shot out of us," as one of them put it, failed to deter the hard-driving general. But he urged the Navy and Marine Corps to proceed with a perilous invasion of Iwo Jima to seize enemy air bases there, which could then

be used to provide B-29s with fighter escorts (see map opposite).

The landings on Iwo Jima in February and the fire-bombings that began in March marked the final phase of the Pacific war, during which that brutal struggle became even crueler and deadlier. Neither the inferno that killed more than 80,000 people in Tokyo on the night of March 9 nor subsequent fire-bombings that scorched large areas (mapped below) and left millions homeless induced Japan to surrender. Plans to invade that nation proceeded, beginning in April with a costly assault on Okinawa, the staging area for an attack on Japan's home islands. The bloodbath at Okinawa foretold huge casualties if U.S. troops had to fight their way to Tokyo. Deliverance for those Americans and defeat for their foes came in August after two blinding nuclear blasts devastated Hiroshima and Nagasaki, bringing an end to the carnage. ■

CHRONOLOGY

FEBRUARY 19, 1945 U.S. Marines land on Iwo Jima.

MARCH 9–10, 1945 B-29s fire-bomb Tokyo, devastating the Japanese capital.

APRIL 1, 1945 American forces invade Okinawa, incurring desperate Japanese opposition on land and at sea.

JULY 26, 1945 Allied leaders issue the Potsdam Declaration, threatening Japan with destruction unless it surrenders unconditionally.

AUGUST 6 AND 9, 1945 Atomic bombs are dropped on Hiroshima and Nagasaki.

AUGUST 15, 1945 Emperor Hirohito yields to the Potsdam Declaration.

SEPTEMBER 2, 1945 Japan formally surrenders.

BOMBING OF JAPAN'S CITIES

KOBE · OSAKA · Osaka Bay · 0 mi 6 · 0 km 6

TOKYO · Tokyo Harbor · 0 mi 6 · 0 km 6 · KAWASAKI · YOKOHAMA · Tokyo Bay

NAGOYA · 0 mi 3 · 0 km 3 · Ise Bay

Area of severe fire damage
Highly populated area
Railway

BURNED OUT A photo taken from a B-29 shows Toyama, Japan, consumed by fire during a bombing raid on the night of August 1, 1945. By then, most of Japan's major cities had been fire-bombed, including those mapped above with burned-out areas in red—Tokyo and nearby Kawasaki and Yokohama (left), Osaka and nearby Kobe (upper right), and Nagoya (lower right).

MAPPING IWO JIMA

Planning for the American invasion of Iwo Jima began several months in advance. The top secret map opposite, produced in October 1944, was based on aerial reconnaissance that enabled photo interpreters to locate Japanese defenses such as antiaircraft batteries. As indicated by the map, Lt. Gen. Tadamichi Kuribayashi was intent on defending Iwo Jima in depth rather than going all-out to stop Americans as they landed. Many defensive installations on the map were marked as "unidentified" or as "covered artillery emplacements" because Kuribayashi's men were digging into soft volcanic rock, hardening their positions with concrete, and camouflaging them.

Despite such signs of deep enemy defenses, U.S. Navy planners hoped that sustained preliminary air and naval bombardments would allow Marines to capture Iwo Jima within a matter of days. A planning map (below left) for "Dog Day," or D-Day, reflects that optimistic outlook, showing ambitious objectives for invasion forces at the end of that first day (O-1) and the second day (O-2). As stated on the map, the Marines would be preceded by underwater demolition teams that would clear paths through reefs for landing craft while "covered by air and naval bombardment." When disguised Japanese coastal batteries answered that covering fire, U.S. Navy gunners drew a bead on them and put them out of action. But many fortified Japanese artillery and machine-gun posts withstood preliminary bombardment and were not easily silenced in the furious battle that followed. Lines on a relief map of Iwo Jima (below right) chart the painfully slow progress of the Marines, who landed on February 19, 1945, and soon came under lethal fire from nearby Mount Suribachi. It took Marines several days to fight their way up that peak—atop which they raised their flag on the 23rd (inset)—and more than a month to secure the island and its airfields at a cost of some 30,000 casualties.

Kuribayashi's men heeded his order to resist to the end, making their position their tomb. He hoped their sacrifice would delay "enemy air raids on Tokyo." By the time he committed suicide on Iwo Jima in late March, however, much of Tokyo had been incinerated. ∎

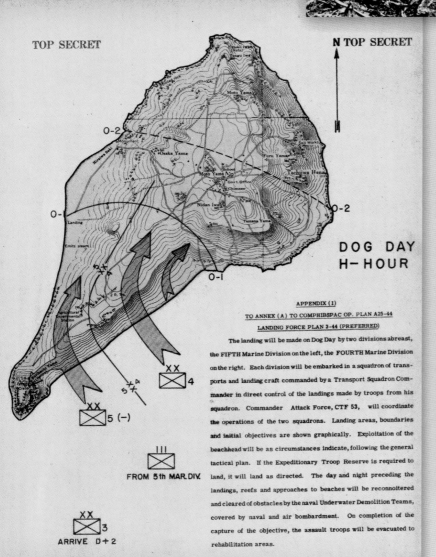

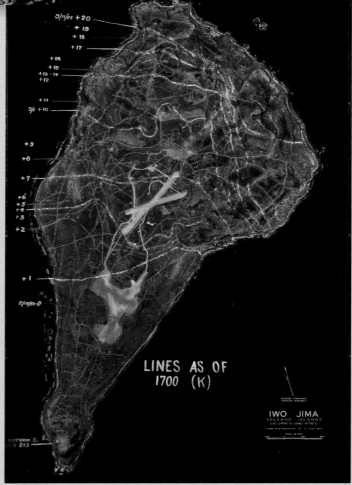

BEFORE AND AFTER The pre-invasion map at left shows landing zones for the Fourth and Fifth Marine Divisions—to be followed by the Third Marine Division—and objectives for the first and second days. The relief map above, on which lines were drawn daily with chalk, shows their actual progress on Iwo Jima, slowed by deep Japanese defenses.

HARD TARGETS A topographical reconnaissance map ordered by Maj. Gen. Harry Schmidt, the Marine commander on Iwo Jima, shows Mount Suribachi at lower left near landing zones coded Red, Yellow, and Blue as well as Japanese defensive positions and airfields, which would be seized for American use. The blue grid denotes artillery target squares, and red annotations mark enemy troop activity. Some Japanese defenders on Iwo Jima held out in caves and were blasted with explosives (right).

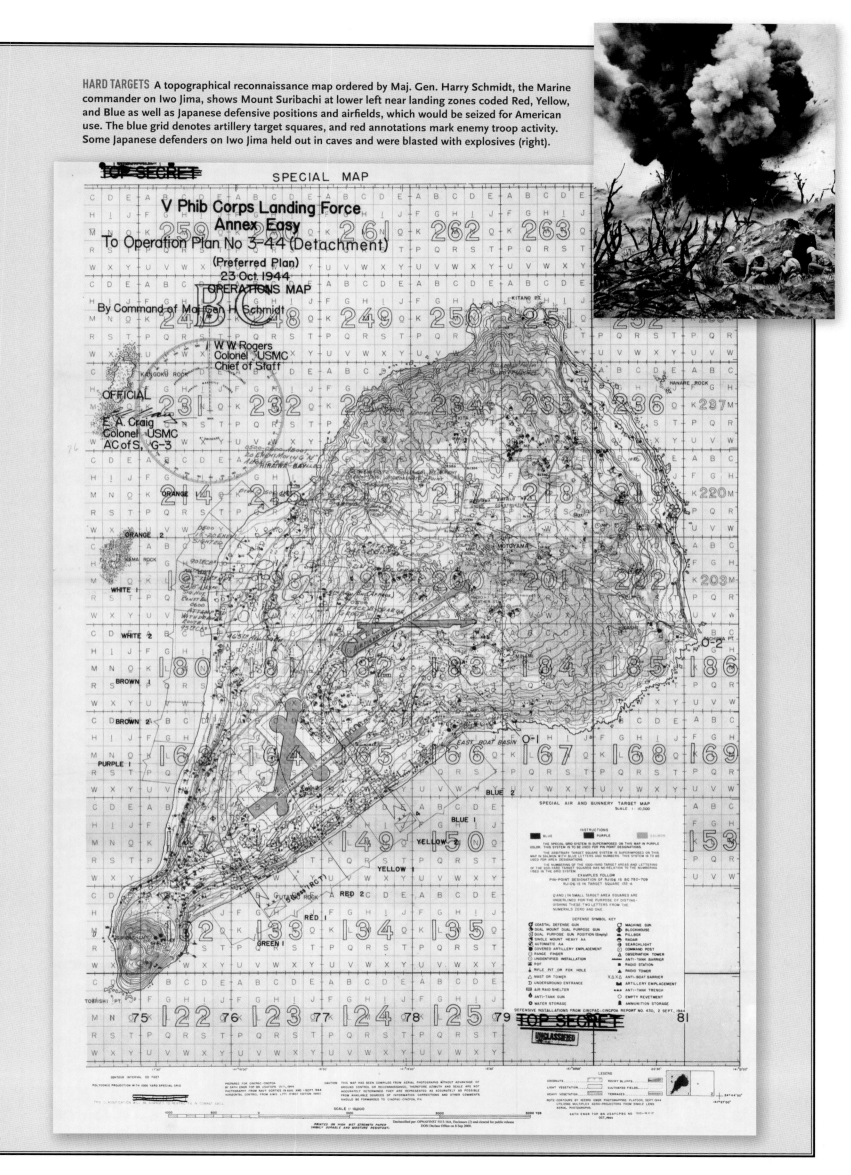

OKINAWA: ORDEAL BY LAND AND SEA

The struggle for Okinawa offered a grim preview of what lay ahead if U.S. forces invaded Japan. Many of Okinawa's 450,000 inhabitants were conscripted to help fortify and defend the island. Including Okinawans and troops of his 32nd Army, Lt. Gen. Mitsuru Ushijima had more than 100,000 men at hand. His defensive lines crossed narrow parts of the island in the south (see map below), where ridges laced with caves and tunnels offered his troops cover. Headquartered at Shuri Castle in Okinawa's capital, Naha, Ushijima allowed the U.S. 10th Army under Lt. Gen. Simon Bolivar Buckner, Jr., which included three Marine divisions, to land uncontested north of Shuri on April 1, 1945, and awaited assault on his formidable defenses.

Aware that Okinawa might be used to invade their home islands, the Japanese launched suicide attacks on the Fifth Fleet's task forces, shielding Buckner's offensive. The superbattleship I.J.N. *Yamato*, sent with other remnants of the Japanese Navy to "fight gloriously to the death," was sunk by carrier-based warplanes before it could enter battle. More dangerous were frequent Japanese air strikes, many of them kamikaze attacks. As charted on the U.S. Navy map opposite, most planes were shot down before they struck targets. But kamikazes sank nearly 30 American ships and killed or wounded thousands of sailors, including over 600 crewmen aboard the carrier U.S.S. *Bunker Hill*, flagship of Vice Adm. Marc Mitscher, which survived an attack that cratered its flight deck.

The land battle for Okinawa began in earnest in mid-April. Outnumbered nearly two to one, Ushijima's troops fought tenaciously against the oncoming Americans, who had to claw their way up muddy slopes strewn with dead bodies. As one Marine recalled, it was like being "flung into hell's own cesspool." The struggle might have lasted longer had entrenched Japanese units not launched costly attacks to no avail. In late May, Ushijima withdrew from Shuri Castle to his last line of defense. Buckner—the son of a Confederate general who had surrendered unconditionally to Ulysses Grant—dropped a message by air urging Ushijima to surrender, but like many of his officers he chose instead to commit suicide. Buckner was killed by Japanese shellfire on June 18 as the battle drew to a close. Victory cost Americans more than 50,000 casualties on land and at sea. At least 150,000 Japanese troops and Okinawans died, including many civilians. Judging by those figures, invading Japan threatened to be horrendous for both sides. ∎

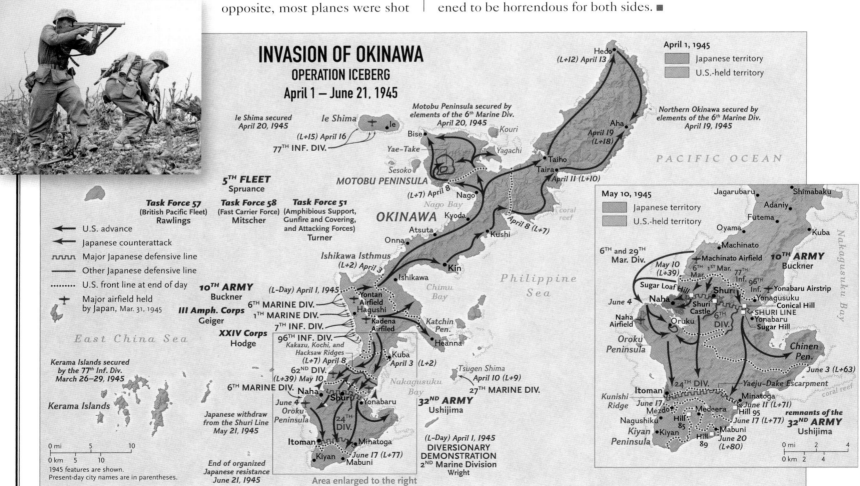

INVASION OF OKINAWA
OPERATION ICEBERG
April 1 – June 21, 1945

April 1, 1945
☐ Japanese territory
☐ U.S.-held territory

Hedo (L+12) April 13

Ie Shima secured April 20, 1945
Ie Shima
(L+15) April 16
77TH INF. DIV.

Motobu Peninsula secured by elements of the 6th Marine Div. April 20, 1945
Kouri

Northern Okinawa secured by elements of the 6th Marine Div. April 19, 1945

Aha
April 19 (L+18)

PACIFIC OCEAN

5TH FLEET Spruance

Bise
Yae-Take
Sesoko
MOTOBU PENINSULA
Yagachi
Taiho
Taira
April 11 (L+10)

Task Force 57 (British Pacific Fleet) Rawlings
Task Force 58 (Fast Carrier Force) Mitscher
Task Force 51 (Amphibious Support, Gunfire and Covering, and Attacking Forces) Turner

(L+7) April 8
Nago
Nago Bay
OKINAWA
Kyoda
April 8 (L+7)
coral reef

◄— U.S. advance
◄— Japanese counterattack
〰〰 Major Japanese defensive line
——— Other Japanese defensive line
········· U.S. front line at end of day
✠ Major airfield held by Japan, Mar. 31, 1945

Onna
Atsuta
Kushi

Ishikawa Isthmus (L+2) April 3

May 10, 1945
☐ Japanese territory
☐ U.S.-held territory

Jagarubaru
Shimabaku
Adaniy
Futema
Oyama
Kuba
Machinato

10TH ARMY Buckner
III Amph. Corps Geiger
XXIV Corps Hodge

(L-Day) April 1, 1945
6TH MARINE DIV.
1ST MARINE DIV.
7TH INF. DIV.
96TH INF. DIV.
Kakazu, Kochi, and Hacksaw Ridges (L+7) April 8
62ND DIV. (L+39) May 10
6TH MARINE DIV.

Ishikawa
Kin
Yontan Airfield
Hagushi
Kadena Airfield
Chimu Bay

Philippine Sea

6TH and 29TH Mar. Div.
May 10 (L+39)
Machinato Airfield
10TH ARMY Buckner
6TH 1ST Mar. 77TH Inf.
Mar. 96TH Inf.
Sugar Loaf Hill
Yonabaru Airstrip
Shuri
Yonagusuku
Conical Hill
June 4
Naha
Shuri Castle
6TH DIV.
SHURI LINE
Yonabaru
Sugar Hill

East China Sea

Kerama Islands secured by the 77th Inf. Div. March 26-29, 1945

Kerama Islands

Naha Airfield
Oruku
Oroku Peninsula

Chinen Pen.

June 3 (L+63)

24TH DIV.

Kunishi Ridge
Itoman
Minatoga
June 11 (L+71)
Yaeju-Dake Escarpment
Mezado
June 17
Medeera
Hill 95
June 11 (L+77)
remnants of the 32ND ARMY Ushijima
Nagushiku
Hill 85
Mabuni
June 20 (L+80)
Kiyan Peninsula
Kiyan
Hill 89

0 mi 2 4
0 km 2 4

Katchin Pen.
Heanna
Nakagusuku Bay
Kuba April 3 (L+2)

Tsugen Shima April 10 (L+9)
27TH MARINE DIV.

32ND ARMY Ushijima

Naha
Shuri
Yonabaru
June 4
Oruku
Oroku Peninsula
24TH DIV.
Itoman
Minatoga
June 17 (L+77)
Kiyan
Mabuni

Japanese withdraw from the Shuri Line May 21, 1945

End of organized Japanese resistance June 21, 1945

(L-Day) April 1, 1945
DIVERSIONARY DEMONSTRATION
2ND Marine Division Wright

0 mi 5 10
0 km 5 10
1945 features are shown. Present-day city names are in parentheses.

Area enlarged to the right

EMBATTLED ISLAND As charted above, Marines feigned a landing on Okinawa's south coast on April 1, 1945, while the actual invasion took place on the west coast by Marine and infantry divisions of Buckner's 10th Army. His forces had to overcome two defensive lines before Ushijima's troops withdrew southward from Shuri to their last line of defense (inset map) and were defeated in June by Americans advancing across blasted terrain (inset photo).

PRAYING FOR DELIVERANCE The injured soldier above, clenching his hands as he awaits evacuation, was one of nearly 40,000 Americans wounded or killed on Okinawa. The U.S. Navy suffered more than 10,000 casualties off Okinawa as a result of kamikaze attacks on ships like the aircraft carrier *Bunker Hill* (right) and regular air strikes that often coincided with those suicide missions.

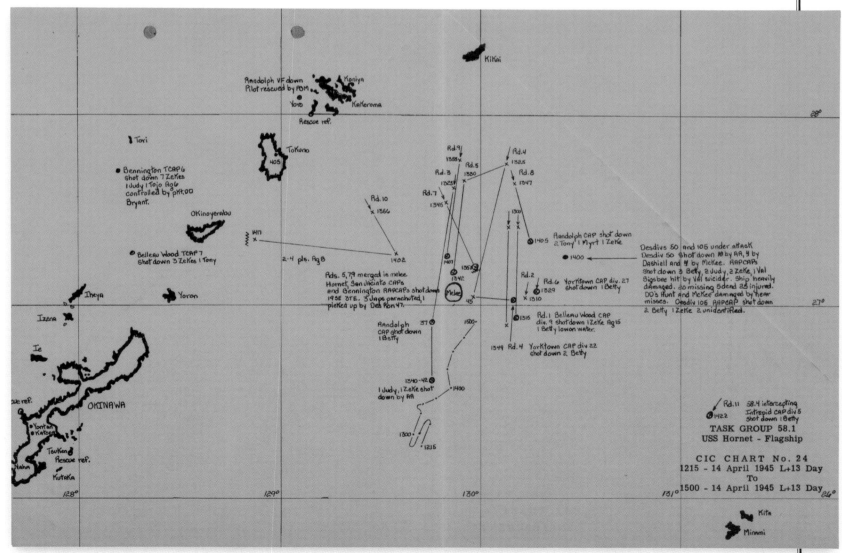

AIR RAIDS Flights by kamikazes and other pilots against Task Force 58 off Okinawa on April 14 are listed on a U.S. Navy chart in the order that radar detected them, beginning with Rd. 1 at 1300 hours, intercepted by a combat air patrol (CAP) from the carrier U.S.S. *Belleau Wood.* Many planes, including Zekes (Mitsubishi fighters), Bettys (Mitsubishi bombers), Judys (Yokosuka bombers), Vals (Aichi dive-bombers), Tonys (Kawasaki fighters), and Tojos (Nakajima fighters), were downed by U.S. fighters or antiaircraft (AA) fire. But a Val kamikaze hit one ship in the task force, causing 60 casualties.

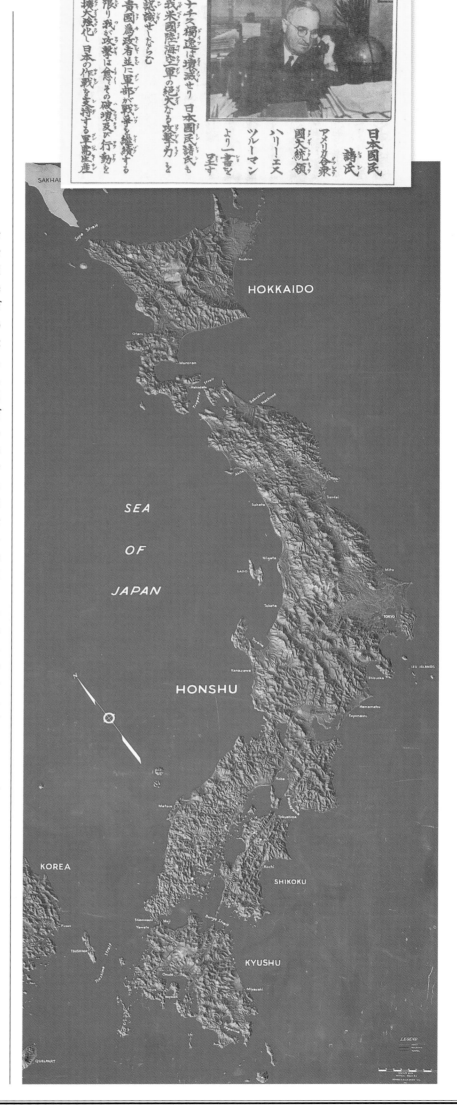

SECRET PLANS TO DEFEAT JAPAN

The death of President Roosevelt on April 12, 1945, shortly before Germany was defeated, left his successor, Harry S. Truman, responsible for defeating Japan. Not until after taking the oath of office was Truman told that the United States was secretly developing atomic bombs of enormous power. They had not been tested, and there was no assurance that using them would vanquish Japan, which had not yielded after the ruinous fire-bombing of Tokyo and other cities. Truman was also informed of the secret plan to invade Japan, designated Operation Downfall. That massive offensive, aimed first at the island of Kyushu and ultimately at the main island of Honshu (see map opposite), would involve several million soldiers, sailors, and airmen. The Japanese did not know how the invasion would unfold, but they planned to fight to the death by using some 10,000 remaining aircraft for kamikaze attacks on American forces and enlisting all male civilians from 15 to 60 and all women from 17 to 40 as home guards, armed with firearms or bamboo spears. Based on steep casualties at Iwo Jima and Okinawa, it was estimated that as many as one million Americans and several times as many Japanese might be killed or wounded before the struggle ended.

Meeting with the Joint Chiefs on June 18, Truman approved an invasion of Kyushu in late 1945 but put off a decision to invade Honshu. As commander in chief, he felt obligated to defeat Japan while minimizing American casualties, and he was ready to use nuclear weapons to that end. Soon after arriving at Potsdam, Germany, in mid-July to confer with Allied leaders, Truman learned that an atomic bomb had been successfully tested in the New Mexico desert. He informed Stalin that the United States had developed a "new weapon of unusual destructive force," which might be used against Japan. Stalin had already been informed of the bomb by Soviet spies and was preparing to join the war in Asia by invading Japanese-occupied Manchuria. On July 26, Allied leaders issued the Potsdam Declaration, calling on Japan to surrender unconditionally or face "prompt and utter destruction." Truman included in the declaration a pledge to remove Allied occupation forces from Japan once a "peacefully inclined and responsible government" was established there. But he rejected language that would have allowed Emperor Hirohito, Japan's commander in chief, to remain in power as a constitutional monarch. Japanese leaders refused to yield, triggering their nation's downfall. ∎

PRIME TARGETS A plaster map prepared by the OSS to give commanders targeting Japan an in-depth view of the terrain highlights major cities in red such as Tokyo, Nagoya, and Osaka, all of which had been heavily fire-bombed by the time nuclear weapons were perfected in 1945. The leaflet at top, dropped over Japan after Truman became president, stated that unconditional surrender did not mean "obliteration of the Japanese people or bondage."

DYING FOR JAPAN At left, a Mitsubishi "Zeke" warplane delivers a glancing blow to the battleship U.S.S. *Missouri,* killing the pilot during a kamikaze attack off Okinawa on April 11, 1945, one day before Truman succeeded Roosevelt. The determination of many Japanese to die fighting rather than yield to the United States led Truman to use nuclear weapons in an effort to preclude an invasion that threatened appalling casualties.

LAST RESORT In Operation Downfall (mapped below), the combined forces of General MacArthur and Admiral Nimitz would attack Japan in two stages—Operation Olympic, an invasion of Kyushu and neighboring Shikoku by some 750,000 troops, and Operation Coronet, an even larger assault on Honshu. Desperate resistance expected from five Japanese armies plus home guards and kamikazes made this America's last resort for achieving victory.

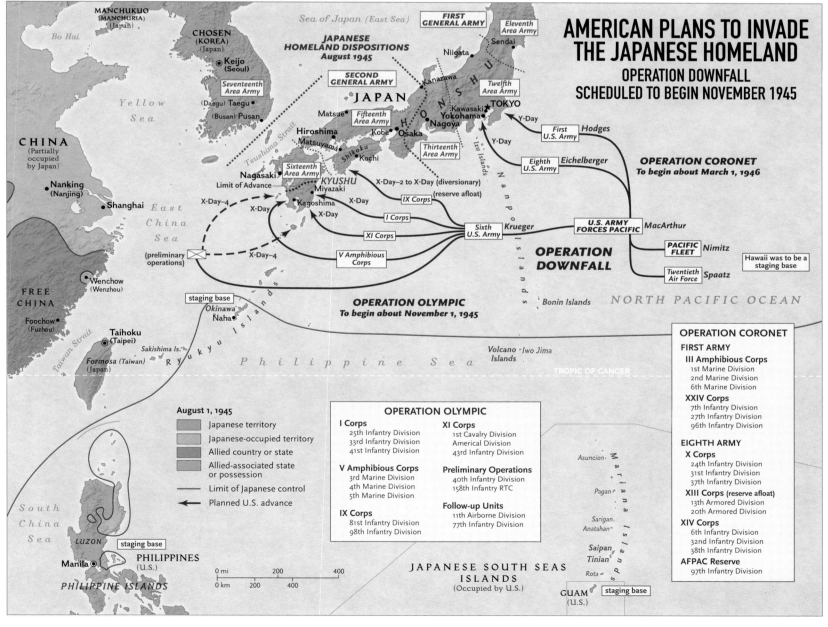

AMERICAN PLANS TO INVADE THE JAPANESE HOMELAND
OPERATION DOWNFALL
SCHEDULED TO BEGIN NOVEMBER 1945

OPERATION CORONET
To begin about March 1, 1946

OPERATION OLYMPIC
To begin about November 1, 1945

OPERATION DOWNFALL

Hawaii was to be a staging base

August 1, 1945
- Japanese territory
- Japanese-occupied territory
- Allied country or state
- Allied-associated state or possession
- — Limit of Japanese control
- → Planned U.S. advance

OPERATION OLYMPIC

I Corps
25th Infantry Division
33rd Infantry Division
41st Infantry Division

V Amphibious Corps
3rd Marine Division
4th Marine Division
5th Marine Division

IX Corps
81st Infantry Division
98th Infantry Division

XI Corps
1st Cavalry Division
Americal Division
43rd Infantry Division

Preliminary Operations
40th Infantry Division
158th Infantry RTC

Follow-up Units
11th Airborne Division
77th Infantry Division

OPERATION CORONET

FIRST ARMY

III Amphibious Corps
1st Marine Division
2nd Marine Division
6th Marine Division

XXIV Corps
7th Infantry Division
27th Infantry Division
96th Infantry Division

EIGHTH ARMY

X Corps
24th Infantry Division
31st Infantry Division
37th Infantry Division

XIII Corps (reserve afloat)
13th Armored Division
20th Armored Division

XIV Corps
6th Infantry Division
32nd Infantry Division
38th Infantry Division

AFPAC Reserve
97th Infantry Division

BOMBING OF
HIROSHIMA AND
NAGASAKI
August 6 and 9, 1945

FATEFUL FLIGHTS As charted above, the B-29 that bombed Hiroshima on August 6 flew straight there from Tinian and back. The flight on August 9 passed over the primary target, Kokura, where visibility was poor, then bombed Nagasaki and refueled on Okinawa.

H-HOUR The blast that shattered Hiroshima (below) stopped the clock shown here at 8:16 A.M. and produced a mushroom cloud (right) that pilot Tibbets described as "terrible and incredibly tall."

HIROSHIMA AND NAGASAKI

Five Japanese cities were spared strategic bombing in early 1945 to serve as possible targets for nuclear weapons—Niigata, Kyoto, Hiroshima, Kokura, and Nagasaki (see map at left). Secretary of War Henry Stimson then ruled out bombing Kyoto, the historical heart of Japan. Hiroshima was the primary target when Col. Paul Tibbets and crew took off from Tinian before dawn on August 6, 1945, in a B-29 carrying an atomic bomb fueled with uranium-235. At daybreak, a weather plane reported clear skies over Hiroshima and Tibbets received the go-ahead. At 8:16 A.M., the bomb detonated, destroying much of the city and killing more than 100,000 people directly, a death toll that later increased as those sickened by radiation perished.

In the early hours of August 9, Soviet troops invaded Manchuria. Around the same time, a B-29 piloted by Maj. Charles Sweeney left Tinian carrying a bomb fueled with plutonium-239. The primary target was Kokura, site of a major arsenal, but smoke obscured the aiming point there. Running low on fuel, Sweeney decided to strike Nagasaki and refuel on Okinawa. Cloud cover prevented the bomb from being dropped precisely, but it killed 40,000 people and doomed many others to sickness and death. On August 15, Hirohito announced that Japan would yield to prevent its "ultimate collapse and obliteration." Japanese representatives formally surrendered on September 2 aboard the battleship *Missouri*, targeted by a kamikaze earlier that year. A catastrophic world war that claimed the lives of more than 20 million combatants and at least 30 million civilians was over. "The next war might destroy the world," wrote Gen. George Marshall. "It must not come." ∎

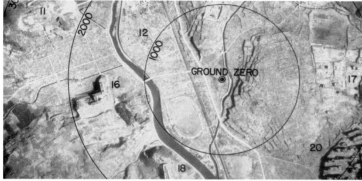

GROUND ZERO As documented by the two photos above, taken before and after an atomic bomb exploded above a stadium in Nagasaki on August 9, little was left standing within a few thousand yards of ground zero. People close to the blast, which produced the mushroom cloud pictured below, were vaporized. Others farther from ground zero, like the victims at right, suffered burns and other injuries that often proved fatal.

To create an innovative book like *Atlas of World War II*, you need a team of talented people with a passion for excellence. When Lisa Thomas, publisher and editorial director of National Geographic Books, asked me to produce a new kind of World War II atlas, I immediately thought of Kenneth Rendell, founder and director of The International Museum of World War II. Ken was quick to see the power of combining rare wartime maps in his comprehensive collection with authoritative new National Geographic maps and graciously opened his museum to us and invited me to comb through its exhibits and archives. With the help of Paul Cook, I selected over 150 maps and artifacts that became the foundation of the atlas, including those featured in Ken's foreword to this book.

Other museums and collections provided additional wartime maps to enhance the atlas. Tim Nenninger and Richard Peuser at the National Archives directed me to secret OSS maps from Burma. Toni Hiley and Robert Byer at the CIA Museum helped locate OSS plaster relief maps and a collection of tools used by OSS cartographers during the war. Claude Berube and Sondra Duplantis at the United States Naval Academy Museum helped me obtain rare wartime maps of naval warfare at Midway, Tarawa, and Okinawa and the secret D-Day Invasion maps on the front and rear endpapers of this book. Other remarkable maps came from the Library of Congress, the Imperial War Museum, and the United States Holocaust Memorial Museum.

To tell the epic story of the war through maps, I worked with a gifted team of long-time creative collaborators. Author Stephen Hyslop helped me develop a plan for the atlas that covered the war's causes, campaigns, and major battles in five coherent chapters and wrote interpretive text that wove the maps and the crucial events they portrayed into a compelling narrative. National Geographic cartographer Gregory Ugiansky created 100 definitive new maps using meticulous research and advanced digital mapping techniques. Military historian Harris Andrews helped refine those maps and reviewed the text, keeping us focused on the essence of complicated historical events. Art director Carol Farrar Norton designed layouts that gracefully combined maps with artifacts and documentary photographs. Researcher Uliana Bazar acquired hundreds of high-resolution image files for publication and found several rare Russian military maps that augment this book.

Finally, I want to thank Sharyn Kagan for her love and support and for all she has done to keep Kagan & Associates running smoothly. My family—Sharyn, Josh, Lisa, Lewis, and Julius—have always been a source of strength, inspiration, and creativity.

—Neil Kagan, *Editor*

ADDITIONAL READING

Atkinson, Rick. *An Army at Dawn: The War in North Africa, 1942–1943*. New York: Henry Holt, 2002.

——. *The Day of Battle: The War in Sicily and Italy, 1943–1944*. New York: Henry Holt, 2007.

——. *The Guns at Last Light: The War in Western Europe, 1944–1945*. New York: Henry Holt, 2013.

Beevor, Antony. *The Second World War*. New York: Little, Brown, 2012.

Chasseaud, Peter. *Mapping the Second World War*. New York: Chartwell Books, 2016.

Costello, John. *The Pacific War, 1941–1945*. New York: Harper Perennial, 2009.

Evans, Richard J. *The Third Reich at War*. New York: Penguin Books, 2009.

Faulkner, Marcus. *War at Sea: A Naval Atlas, 1939–1945*. Annapolis, Md.: Naval Institute Press, 2012.

Griess, Thomas E., ed. *West Point Atlas for the Second World War: Asia and the Pacific*. Garden City Park, N.Y.: Square One Publishers, 2002.

——. *West Point Atlas for the Second World War: Europe and the Mediterranean*. Garden City Park, N.Y.: Square One Publishers, 2002.

Keegan, John. *The Second World War*. New York: Penguin Books, 1990.

——. *Atlas of World War II*. New York: HarperCollins Publishers, 2006.

Kershaw, Ian. *Fateful Choices: Ten Decisions That Changed the World, 1940–1941*. New York: Penguin Press, 2007.

Kirchubel, Robert. *Atlas of the Eastern Front, 1941–45*. Oxford, U.K.: Osprey Publishing, 2016.

Messenger, Charles. *The Chronological Atlas of World War Two*. New York: Macmillan Publishing, 1989.

Natkiel, Richard, and Robin L. Sommer. *Atlas of World War II*. New York: The Military Press, 1985.

Swanston, Alexander, and Malcolm Swanston. *The Historical Atlas of World War II*. New York: Chartwell Books, 2014.

Time-Life Books, eds. *The Third Reich*. 21 vols. Alexandria, Va.: Time-Life Books, 1988–1991.

——. *World War II*. 39 vols. Alexandria, Va.: Time-Life Books, 1976–1983.

Toland, John. *The Rising Sun: The Decline and Fall of the Japanese Empire, 1936–1945*. New York: Modern Library, 2003.

United States Military Academy, Department of History, About Our Atlases (links to maps for WWII European Theater and WWII Asian/Pacific Theater): www.westpoint.edu/history/sitepages/our atlases.aspx.

ILLUSTRATIONS CREDITS

Cover: (Map), Kenneth W. Rendell, The International Museum of World War II; (Photo), U.S. Navy/National Archives/The LIFE Picture Collection/Getty.
Back cover: (UP LE), Keystone/Getty; (LO LE), NG Maps; (UP RT), Kenneth W. Rendell, The International Museum of World War II; (LO RT), U.S. National Archives, #80-G-413988, photo by Joe Rosenthal. Spine, W. Eugene Smith/The LIFE Picture Collection/Getty. Endsheets, Courtesy of U.S. Naval Academy Museum.

1, Underwood Archives/Getty; 2-3, Hulton Archive/Getty; 4-5, Kenneth W. Rendell, The International Museum of World War II; 8-9 (ALL), Kenneth W. Rendell, The International Museum of World War II; 10 (UP), ullstein bild/ullstein bild via Getty; 10 (CTR and LO), Kenneth W. Rendell, The International Museum of World War II; 11 (UP), Three Lions/Getty; 11 (LO), Kenneth W. Rendell, The International Museum of World War II; 12 (UP), Kenneth W. Rendell, The International Museum of World War II; 12 (LO), Louis R. Lowery/U.S. Marine Corps/The LIFE Picture Collection/Getty; 13, Kenneth W. Rendell, The International Museum of World War II; 14 (BOTH), Durham County Record Office, U.K.; 15 (ALL EXCEPT PHOTO), Kenneth W. Rendell, The International Museum of World War II; 15 (PHOTO), Durham County Record Office, U.K.; 16-17, ullstein bild/ullstein bild via Getty; 18 (UP), Kenneth W. Rendell, The International Museum of World War II; 18 (LO), Bettmann/Getty; 19 (UP LE), Kenneth W. Rendell, The International Museum of World War II; 19 (UP CTR), Bundesarchiv Bild; 19 (UP RT), United States Holocaust Memorial Museum Collection, Gift of Denise Kopecky; 19 (LO LE), Acme News Pictures Inc./National Geographic Creative; 19 (LO RT), Laski Diffusion/Getty; 20 (UP), Topical Press Agency/Getty; 20 (LO), Paul Popper/Popperfoto/Getty; 21 (UP), Hilary Jane Morgan/Getty; 21 (LO), Bettmann/Getty; 22 (UP), Hulton-Deutsch Collection/CORBIS/Corbis via Getty; 22 (LO), Imagno/Getty; 23 (LE), Hulton-Deutsch/Hulton-Deutsch Collection/Corbis via Getty; 23 (RT), Universal History Archive/UIG via Getty; 24 (TOP THREE), United States Holocaust Memorial Museum, courtesy of Stephen Glick; 24 (UP), Universal History Archive/UIG via Getty; 24 (CTR LE), Kenneth W. Rendell, The International Museum of World War II; 24 (CTR RT), United States Holocaust Memorial Museum, courtesy of Hans Pauli; 24 (LO LE and LO RT), Kenneth W. Rendell, The International Museum of World War II; 25 (UP), Kenneth W. Rendell, The International Museum of World War II; 25 (LO), The Print Collector/Print Collector/Getty; 26, Keystone/Getty; 27 (UP), Universal History Archive/UIG via Getty; 27 (LO), Kenneth W. Rendell, The International Museum of World War II; 28, Bettmann/Getty; 29 (UP), AP Photo; 29 (LO), ullstein bild; 30 (UP), Popperfoto/Getty; 30 (LO), Hulton-Deutsch Collection/CORBIS/Corbis via Getty; 31, Fox Photos/Getty; 32, ullstein bild/ullstein bild via Getty; 33 (LE), Courtesy Imperial War Museum, Neg. #4756; 33 (RT), ullstein bild/ullstein bild via Getty; 34 (LE), Galerie Bilderwelt/Getty; 34 (RT), Courtesy Imperial War Museum, Neg. #4778; 35, ullstein bild/ullstein bild via Getty; 36, Courtesy Imperial War Museum, Neg. #4394; 37, akg-images; 38 (UP), Kenneth W. Rendell, The International Museum of World War II; 38 (LO LE), Bert Hardy/Keystone/Getty; 38 (CTR RT and LO RT), Kenneth W. Rendell, The International Museum of World War II; 39 (UP), Topical Press/Getty; 39 (LO), Universal History Archive/UIG via Getty; 40 (UP), Universal History Archive/UIG via Getty; 40 (LO), akg-images/The Image Works; 41, Bettmann/Getty; 42 (UP), Kenneth W. Rendell, The International Museum of World War II; 42 (LO), Keystone/Getty; 43, Kenneth W. Rendell, The International Museum of World War II; 44, SeM/UIG via Getty; 45 (UP LE), Keystone/Getty; 45 (UP RT), AP Photo; 45 (LO), Kenneth W. Rendell, The International Museum of World War II; 46 (UP), German Air Force photographer/ IWM via Getty; 46 (LO), Acme News Pictures Inc./NG Archives; 46-7, Kenneth W. Rendell, The International Museum of World War II; 47, CORBIS/Corbis via Getty; 48, Courtesy Imperial War Museum, Neg. #LBY_046093_1; 48-9, Courtesy Imperial War Museum, Neg. #011929_J_1; 49 (UP LE), Popperfoto/Getty; 49 (UP RT), Kenneth W. Rendell, The International Museum of World War II; 49 (LO), Daily Mirror/Mirrorpix/Mirrorpix via Getty; 50 (UP), Topical Press Agency/Getty; 50 (LO), Popperfoto/Getty; 51, The National Archives/SSPL/Getty; 52 (BOTH), ullstein bild/ullstein bild via Getty; 53, Jung/ullstein bild via Getty; 54 (LE), Bettmann/Getty; 54 (RT), ullstein bild/ullstein bild via Getty; 55, ullstein bild/ullstein bild via Getty; 56-7 (ALL), Kenneth W. Rendell, The International Museum of World War II; 58 (UP), Universal History Archive/UIG via Getty; 58 (LO), AP Photo/File; 59, Roger Viollet/Getty; 60 (LE), Yad Vashem Photo Archive, 4613_584; 60 (UP RT), Galerie Bilderwelt/Getty; 60 (LO RT), United States Holocaust Memorial Museum, courtesy of Instytut Pamieci Narodowej; 61 (UP LE), United States Holocaust Memorial Museum, courtesy of National Archives and Records Administration, College Park, MD; 61 (UP RT), United States Holocaust Memorial Museum, courtesy of Sharon Paquette; 61 (LO), akg-images/Pictures From History; 62, Sovfoto/UIG via Getty; 63 (UP), RIA Novosti/The Image Works; 63 (CTR), WWII Aerial Photos and Maps, www.wwii-photos-maps.com; 63 (LO), TASS via Getty; 64, Uncredited/AP/REX/Shutterstock; 64-5, Kenneth W. Rendell, The International Museum of World War II; 65, Sovfoto/UIG via Getty; 66-7, Bettmann/Getty; 68 (UP), Keystone/Hulton Archive/Getty; 68 (LO), Official U.S. Navy Photo/U.S. National Archives; 69 (UP LE), Courtesy of the family of Alexandra Braciejowski, daughter of the artist, Arthur Szyk; 69 (UP RT), Kenneth W. Rendell, The International Museum of World War II; 69 (LO LE), Official U.S. Navy Photo/U.S. National Archives; 69 (LO RT), Ralph Morse/The LIFE Picture Collection/Getty; 70, Keystone-France/Gamma-Keystone via Getty; 70-1, Kenneth W. Rendell, The International Museum of World War II; 71 (UP), Imagno/Getty; 71 (LO), Popperfoto/Getty; 72 (PHOTO), Universal History Archive/UIG via Getty; 72-3 (MAPS), Stanford University Libraries; 74 (UP), Universal History Archive/UIG via Getty; 74 (LO), ullstein bild/ullstein bild via Getty; 75 (UP), AP Photo; 75 (LO), AP Photo/H.S. Wong; 76, Wolfgang Weber/ullstein bild via Getty; 77 (UP), Library of Congress Prints and Photographs Division, 2002724144; 77 (LO), Nationaal Museum van Wereldculturen. Coll. no.TM-10013732 (https://creativecommons.org/licenses/by-sa/4.0/legalcode); 79, Kenneth W. Rendell, The International Museum of World War II; 80 (UP), U.S. National Archives; 80 (LO), From Reports of General MacArthur, Vol. II, part 1 (Department of the Army, 1966), p. 69; 80-1, Kenneth W. Rendell, The International Museum of World War II; 81, U.S. Naval History and Heritage Command Photograph; 82, From Reports of General MacArthur, Vol. II, part 1 (Department of the Army, 1966), p. 69; 83, U.S. National Archives; 84 (UP LE and UP RT), Henry Groskinsky/The LIFE Images Collection/Getty; 84 (LO LE), U.S. National Archives; 84 (LO RT), Bettmann/Getty; 85 (UP LE), Henry Groskinsky/The LIFE Images Collection/Getty; 85 (UP RT), Official U.S. Navy Photo/U.S. National Archives; 85 (CTR LE), Franklin D. Roosevelt Library/U.S. National Archives; 85 (CTR RT), Kenneth W. Rendell, The International Museum of World War II; 85 (LO LE and LO CTR), Kenneth W. Rendell, The International Museum of World War II; 85 (LO RT), Official U.S. Navy Photo/U.S. National Archives; 86, ullstein bild/ullstein bild via Getty; 87, U.S. Signal Corps/The LIFE Picture Collection/Getty; 88 (LE), Keystone/Getty; 88 (RT), Kenneth W. Rendell, The International Museum of World War II; 89 (BOTH), U.S. National Archives; 90 (LE), U.S. Naval History and Heritage Command Photograph; 90 (RT), Official U.S. Navy Photo/U.S. National Archives; 91, Universal History Archive/UIG via Getty; 92 (UP), Dorothea Lange/Library of Congress Prints and Photographs Division, LC-USZ62-23602; 92 (LO), Japanese American National Museum (Gift of A. Iwata, 97.194.4); 93 (UP), Kenneth W. Rendell, The International Museum of World War II; 93 (CTR LE), Toyo Miyatake; 93 (CTR RT), Terry Heffernan/California State University, Sacramento/Japanese American Archival Collection Library; 93 (LO), Dorothea Lange/U.S. National Archives; 94, Official U.S. Navy Photo/U.S. National Archives; 96-7 (ALL), Official U.S. Navy Photo/U.S. National Archives; 98, U.S. Air Force Photograph; 98-9, Image Courtesy of U.S. Naval Academy Museum; 99 (BOTH), Image Courtesy of U.S. Naval Academy Museum; 100 (LE), Official U.S. Navy Photo/U.S. National Archives; 100 (RT), Keystone/Getty; 102 (BOTH), Kenneth W. Rendell, The International Museum of World War II; 103 (UP), Time Life Pictures/U.S. Marine Corps/The LIFE Picture Collection/Getty; 103 (CTR and LO), Kenneth W. Rendell, The International Museum of World War II; 104 (UP), U.S. Naval History and Heritage Command Photograph; 104 (LO), Hulton Archive/Getty; 105, Official U.S. Navy Photo/U.S. National Archives; 106 (UP), National Geographic Archives; 106 (LO), Hulton-Deutsch Collection/CORBIS/Corbis via Getty; 106-107, NG Maps; 108, George Silk/The LIFE Picture Collection/Getty; 110, ullstein bild/ullstein bild via Getty; 111 (BOTH), Kenneth W. Rendell, The International Museum of World War II; 112-13, ullstein bild/ullstein bild via Getty; 114 (UP), U.S. National Archives; 114 (LO), U.S. Air Force, courtesy Fold3.com; 115 (UP LE and UP RT), Kenneth W. Rendell, The International Museum of World War II; 115 (LO LE), TASS via Getty; 115 (LO RT), Kenneth W. Rendell, The International Museum of World War II; 116 (BOTH), Kenneth W. Rendell, The International Museum of World War II; 117 (UP), Mondadori Portfolio via Getty; 117 (LO), Roger Viollet/Getty; 118 (UP), Courtesy Imperial War Museum, Neg. #HU 047954; 118 (LO), Courtesy Imperial War Museum, Neg. #HU 047953; 119 (LE), Universal History Archive/UIG via Getty; 119 (RT), U.S. Air Force; 120 (BOTH), ullstein bild/ullstein bild via Getty; 120-21, Kenneth W. Rendell, The International Museum of World War II; 122 (LE), ullstein bild/ullstein bild via Getty; 122 (CTR), Hulton-Deutsch Collection/CORBIS/Corbis via Getty; 122 (RT), akg-images; 123, Bettmann/Getty; 124 (ALL EXCEPT PHOTO), Kenneth W. Rendell, The International Museum of World War II; 124 (PHOTO), ullstein bild via Getty; 125 (ALL), Kenneth W. Rendell, The International Museum of World War II; 126 (UP), AP Photo; 126 (LO LE and LO RT), Kenneth W. Rendell, The International Museum of World War II; 127 (UP LE), U.S. National Archives; 127 (UP CTR), U.S. Navy/Museum of Science and Industry, Chicago/Getty; 127 (UP RT), U.S. National Archives; 127 (CTR and LO), ullstein bild/ullstein bild via Getty; 128 (UP LE), Peter Hore; 128 (UP RT), The National Archives of the U.K.; 128 (LO), Peter Hore; 129 (UP LE), Rebecca Hale/National Geographic Staff (photo), National Cryptologic Museum (artifact); 129 (UP RT), Trinity Mirror Publishing Limited; 129 (CTR), David Pike; 129 (LO), Kenneth W. Rendell, The International Museum of World War II; 130, AP Photo; 131, Hulton Archive/Getty; 132, Universal History Archive/UIG via Getty; 132-3, U.S. National Archives; 134-5, U.S. National Archives; 135, ullstein bild/ullstein bild via Getty; 136 (LE), U.S. National Archives; 136 (RT), Kenneth W. Rendell, The International Museum of World War II; 137 (UP LE), Courtesy Imperial War Museum, Neg. #W 1846776; 137 (UP RT), Courtesy Imperial War Museum, Neg. #4102; 137 (LO), AFP/Getty; 138 (UP), Kenneth W. Rendell, The International Museum of World War II; 138 (LO), Lt. F A Hudson/IWM via Getty; 139, Time Life Pictures/U.S. Army/The LIFE Picture Collection/Getty; 140, Keystone/Getty; 140-41, Kenneth W. Rendell, The International Museum of World War II; 141, Keystone/Getty; 142, Daily Mirror/Crown/Mirrorpix/Mirrorpix via Getty; 142-3, Kenneth W. Rendell, The International Museum of World War II; 143, Popperfoto/Getty; 144 (UP), Popperfoto/Getty; 144 (LO), U.S. National Archives; 144-5, Kenneth W. Rendell, The International Museum of World War II; 145, U.S. National Archives; 146 (UP), ullstein bild/ullstein bild via Getty; 146 (LO), CORBIS/Corbis via Getty; 148-9, Kenneth W. Rendell, The International Museum of World War II; 149, SeM/UIG via Getty; 150, Kenneth W. Rendell, The International Museum of World War II; 151 (UP), Mondadori Portfolio via Getty; 151 (LO), Kenneth W. Rendell, The International Museum of World War II; 152, U.S. Air Force Photo, courtesy Fold3.com; 153, Mondadori Portfolio via Getty; 154 (LE), Trinity Mirror/Mirrorpix/Alamy Stock Photo; 154 (RT), Kenneth W. Rendell, The International Museum of World War II; 155 (UP LE), Keystone/Getty; 155 (UP RT and LO), Kenneth W. Rendell, The International Museum of World War II; 156-7 (ALL), Kenneth W. Rendell, The International Museum of World War II; 158-9 (ALL), Kenneth W. Rendell, The International Museum of World War II; 160 (UP), Courtesy Imperial War Museum, Neg. #4909; 160 (LO), Courtesy Imperial War Museum, Neg. #4914; 161 (UP), akg-images/ullstein bild; 161 (LO), Walter Hahn, Dresden/The Image Works; 162 (UP), CIA Imaging and Publishing Services, CIA Museum; 162 (CTR LE), From the American Geographical Society Library, University of Wisconsin Milwaukee Libraries; 162 (CTR RT and LO), CIA Imaging and Publishing Services, CIA Museum; 163 (ALL), CIA Imaging and Publishing Services, CIA Museum; 164, TASS via Getty; 165 (UP), Arthur Grimm/ullstein bild via Getty; 165 (LO), Slava Katamidze Collection/Getty; 166-7, WWII Aerial Photos and Maps, www.wwii-photos-maps.com; 167, Sovfoto/UIG via Getty; 168, Roger Viollet/Getty; 168-9, Kenneth W. Rendell, The International Museum of World War II; 169, Keystone/Hulton Archive/Getty; 170, Sovfoto/UIG via Getty; 171 (UP), Art Media/Print Collector/Getty; 171 (LO), TASS via Getty; 172 (UP), akg-images/ullstein bild; 172 (LO), United States Holocaust Memorial Museum, courtesy of National Archives and Records Administration, College Park, MD; 173, United States Holocaust Memorial Museum, courtesy of Leopold Page Photographic Collection; 174-5, U.S. Coast Guard Collection/U.S. National Archives; 176 (UP), Kenneth W. Rendell, The International Museum of World War II; 176 (LO), CORBIS/Corbis via Getty; 177 (UP), U.S. National Archives; 177 (CTR), Kenneth W. Rendell, The International Museum of World War II; 177 (LO LE), Popperfoto/Getty; 177 (LO RT), Kenneth W. Rendell, The International Museum of World War II; 178 (UP), Kenneth W. Rendell, The International Museum of World War II; 178 (LO), Popperfoto/Getty; 179, Prisma by Dukas Presseagentur GmbH/Alamy Stock Photo; 180 (UP LE), Roger Viollet/Getty; 180 (UP RT), Kenneth W. Rendell, The International Museum of World War II; 180 (LO LE), Library of Congress, Geography and Map Division, ct002437a; 180 (LO RT), U.S. National Archives; 181 (UP LE), Kenneth W. Rendell, The International Museum of World War II; 181 (UP CTR LE), Courtesy Imperial War Museum, Neg. #HU 06606; 181 (UP CTR), The National Archives of the UK; 181 (UP CTR RT), The National Archives of the UK; 181 (UP RT), Courtesy Gerry Czerniawski; 181 (CTR), PhotoQuest/Getty; 181 (LO), Kenneth W. Rendell, The International Museum of World War II; 182, © Robert Capa © International Center of Photography/Magnum Photos; 182-3, Collection of Joseph P. Vaghi, Jr.; 184, U.S. Coast Guard Collection/U.S. National Archives; 185 (LE), U.S. National Archives; 185 (RT), Hulton-Deutsch Collection/CORBIS/Corbis via Getty; 186 (UP), Kenneth W. Rendell, The International Museum of World War II; 186 (CTR LE), U.S. National Archives; 186 (CTR RT), Kenneth W. Rendell, The International Museum of World War II; 186 (LO LE), CIA Imaging and Publishing Services, CIA Museum (photo), courtesy Lorna Catling (passport); 186 (LO RT), U.S. Army Center of Military History; 187 (UP LE), U.S. National Archives; 187 (UP RT), Kenneth W. Rendell, The International Museum of World War II; 187 (CTR LE), Kenneth W. Rendell, The International Museum of World War II; 187 (CTR RT), Three Lions/Getty; 187 (LO LE and LO RT), Kenneth W. Rendell, The International Museum of World War II; 188, Bettmann/Getty; 188-9, ullstein bild/ullstein bild via Getty; 189, CORBIS/Corbis via Getty; 190, Popperfoto/Getty; 191 (UP), Kenneth W. Rendell, The International Museum of World War II; 191 (LO), Heritage-Images/Keystone Archives/akg-images; 192, Library of Congress, Geography and Map Division, 2004629122; 192-3, Bob Landry/The LIFE Images Collection/Getty Images; 193 (LE), Robert Doisneau/Gamma-Rapho/Getty; 193 (RT), Serge De Sazo/Gamma-Rapho via Getty; 194 (UP LE), Bundesarchiv Bild; 194 (UP RT), Mr Walton/IWM via Getty; 194 (LO), Kenneth W. Rendell, The International Museum of World War II; 195 (LE), Fox Photos/Getty; 195 (RT), Popperfoto/Getty; 196 (LE), U.S. National Archives; 196 (CTR), U.S. Army; 196 (RT), PhotoQuest/Getty; 197 (UP LE), Library of Congress, Geography and Map Division, 2004630231; 197 (UP RT), akg-images; 197 (LO), AFP/Getty; 198 (UP LE), U.S. National Archives; 198 (UP RT), Time Life Pictures/U.S. Army/The LIFE Picture Collection/Getty; 198 (LO), CORBIS/Corbis via Getty; 199 (UP), Library of Congress, Geography and Map Division, 2004630298; 199 (LO LE), Library of Congress, Geography and Map Division, 2004630304; 199 (LO CTR), Library of Congress, Geography and Map Division, 2004630318; 199 (LO RT), Library of Congress, Geography and Map Division, 2004630334; 200, U.S. National Archives; 201 (UP), CORBIS/Corbis via Getty; 201 (LO), Library of Congress, Geography and Map Division, 2004631921; 202, Courtesy Friends of Popski's Private Army; 202-203, CIA Imaging and Publishing Services, CIA Museum; 204, Victor Temin/Slava Katamidze Collection/Getty; 204-5, TASS via Getty; 207 (UP), AP Photo/U.S. Army; 207 (LO), Fred Ramage/Keystone/Getty; 208, Ivan Shagin/Getty; 209 (UP), © Khaldei/Voller Ernst/akg-images; 209 (CTR), William Vandivert/The LIFE Picture Collection/Getty; 209 (LO), WWII Aerial Photos and Maps, www.wwii-photos-maps.com; 210 (UP LE), akg-images/ullstein bild; 210 (UP RT and LO), U.S. National Archives; 211 (UP), United States Holocaust Memorial Museum, courtesy of Muzeum Niepodleglosci; 211 (LO), United States Holocaust Memorial Museum, courtesy of National Archives and Records Administration, College Park, MD; 212-13, Official U.S. Navy Photo/U.S. National Archives; 214 (UP), U.S. Navy/The LIFE Picture Collection/Getty; 214 (LO LE), Apic/Getty; 214 (LO RT), U.S. National Archives; 215 (UP LE), U.S. Marine Corps/The LIFE Picture Collection/Getty; 215 (UP RT), W. Eugene Smith/The LIFE Picture Collection/Getty; 215 (LO LE), Everett Collection Historical/Alamy Stock Photo; 215 (LO RT), Photo by Uliana Bazar/Library of Congress Prints & Photographs Division, 0068a-7s; 216, Bettmann/Getty; 217, Hulton Archive/Getty; 218 (UP), Image Courtesy of U.S. Naval Academy Museum; 218 (CTR), U.S. Marine Corps, Official Photograph; 218 (LO), Image Courtesy of U.S. Naval Academy Museum; 219, ullstein bild/ullstein bild via Getty; 220, Bettmann/Getty; 221, U.S. Coast Guard/Getty; 222 (UP), Owens Archive; 222 (LO), Kenneth W. Rendell, The International Museum of World War II; 223, Kenneth W. Rendell, The International Museum of World War II; 224, U.S. Navy/Interim Archives/Getty; 225, U.S. Navy/The LIFE Picture Collection/Getty; 226 (LE), CORBIS/Corbis via Getty; 226 (RT), Bettmann/Getty; 228, U.S. National Archives; 228-9, Image Courtesy of U.S. Naval Academy Museum; 229, U.S. National Archives; 230 (UP), © Don Troiani/Bridgeman Images; 230 (LO), U.S. National Archives; 231, William Vandivert/The LIFE Picture Collection/Getty; 232 (UP LE), CIA Imaging and Publishing Services, CIA Museum; 232 (UP RT), From Behind Japanese Lines (Rand McNally & Co., 1979), opposite p. 123; 232 (CTR), Keystone/Hulton Archive/Getty; 232 (LO LE and LO RT), U.S. National Archives; 233 (ALL), U.S. National Archives; 234, William Vandivert/The LIFE Picture Collection/Getty; 235 (LE), GRANGER—All rights reserved; 235 (RT), U.S. National Archives; 236 (UP), MacArthur Returns Leaflet For The Philippines/Private Collection/Photo © Don Troiani/Bridgeman Images; 236 (LO), U.S. National Archives; 237 (BOTH), Kenneth W. Rendell, The International Museum of World War II; 238, U.S. Naval History and Heritage Command Photograph; 239 (UP and CTR), CORBIS/Corbis via Getty; 239 (LO), The Asahi Shimbun via Getty; 240, U.S. National Archives; 241 (UP), Carl Mydans/The LIFE Picture Collection/Getty; 241 (LO), U.S. Army/The LIFE Picture Collection/Getty; 242 (UP LE), Keystone-France/Gamma-Keystone via Getty; 242 (UP RT), Bettmann/Getty; 242 (LO), U.S. National Archives; 243, Time Life Pictures/U.S. Air Force/The LIFE Picture Collection/Getty; 244 (UP), U.S. National Archives; 244 (LO LE and LO RT), Kenneth W. Rendell, The International Museum of World War II; 245 (UP), W. Eugene Smith/The LIFE Picture Collection/Getty; 245 (LO), U.S. Army Center of Military History; 246, Bettmann/Getty; 247 (UP LE), W. Eugene Smith/The LIFE Picture Collection/Getty; 247 (UP RT), Roger Viollet/Getty; 247 (LO), Image Courtesy of U.S. Naval Academy Museum; 248, CIA Imaging and Publishing Services, CIA Museum; 249, W. Eugene Smith/The LIFE Picture Collection/Getty; 250 (UP LE), Universal History Archive/UIG via Getty; 250 (UP RT), Brian Brake/Science Source; 250 (LO), Keystone/Getty; 251 (UP LE), MPI/Getty; 251 (UP RT), ADN-Bildarchiv/ullstein bild via Getty; 251 (LO), Prisma by Dukas Presseagentur GmbH/Alamy Stock Photo.

Boldface indicates illustrations.

A

Aachen, Germany 177, 196, 197, **197**
Abe, Hiroaki 104, 105
Adachi, Hatazo 220
Admiralty Islands 215, 220, **220**, 223
Aerial reconnaissance 154, **154**, 160, 162, **163**
Akagi, I.J.N. 80, 96, 97
Alam el Halfa, Egypt 134, 135
Albania, Italian occupation of 19
Aleutian Islands 69, 214
Alexander, Harold 134
Alexandria, Egypt 10, **10**, 11
Algeria 115, **138**, 139
Antonescu, Ion 205
Antwerp, Belgium 177, 195, 196, 197
Anzio, Italy 115, 149, **150**, 151, **151**, 159
Ardennes region, Belgium-Frsance 35, 35, 198, **198**, 200
see also Bulge, Battle of the
Arizona, U.S.S. 82, 83, 84, **85**
Arnhem, Netherlands 196
Arnim, Hans-Jürgen von 139
Atlantic, Battle of the (1942–1943) 122–129
"American Shooting Season" **126–127**, 126–127
Enigma machines 122, 128–129, **128–129**
introduction 114, 122
maps 123, 124–125, 126
U-boat charts and instruments 124–125, **124–125**
Atlantic Wall 116, 157, 178, 179
Atomic bombs *see* Nuclear weapons
Attu, Aleutian Islands 69, 214
Auchinleck, Claude 132, 134
Auschwitz concentration camp 173, 176, 210, **210**, 211
Austin, Marshall 225
Austria, German annexation of 18, 19, 26, 27

B

B-17 bombers 115, **152**, 153, 189
B-24 Liberators **2–3**, 153, 186, 189
B-25B Mitchell bombers 90, **90**
B-29 bombers 214, 215, **215**, 227, **242**, 243, 250
Badoglio, Pietro 146
Baku, Soviet Union 115, 164, 165, 166
Balkans, war in **52**, 52–55, **53**, **54**, **55**, 156
Balme, David **128**, 129
Barber, Rex **111**
Bastogne, France 198, **198**, 199
Bataan Death March 88–89, **89**
Bayerlein, Fritz 189
Belarus 61, 204, 205
Belgium 18, **34**, 35, 38, 119
Belgrade, Yugoslavia 19, 53
Berlin, Germany
Allied bombing raids 44, 115, 160–161
fall of 177, 207, 208–209, **208–209**
maps 160, 206, 209
postwar division 176, 206, 207
Bernard, Lyle **144**
Betio, Tarawa Atoll 218, 219, **219**
Binder, R. R. 102
Birkenau extermination camp **210**, 210–211
Bismarck Sea, Battle of the (1943) 69
Blaskowitz, Johannes 29
Bletchley Park, Britain 122, 129, 134
Blind, Georges **116**
Blitz *see* Britain, Battle of
Bloody Ridge, Battle of (1942) 69, 100, 101
Bocage (fields with hedgerows) 184, **185**, 189
Bock, Fedor von 29, 35, 58, 166
Bohemia and Moravia, Protectorate of 116
Bougainville **1**, 69, 101, 110, 111, 214, 216
Bradley, Omar
Berlin, Germany 207
Italian campaign 141, 144
from Normandy to the Rhine 177, 188, 189, 196, 197, 200, 201
Operation Overlord **178**, 185
West Wall, pursuit to 196, 197, 200
Britain *see* Great Britain
Britain, Battle of 42–51
bombing victim **19**
British intelligence report **48**
dogfights 44, **45**
Germany, bombing of 50, **50**
home guard **49**
London, bombing of 19, 44, 46, **46**, 47, **47**
maps 43, 45, 46–47, 48–49
Operation Sea Lion 12, 44, 48
RAF pilots-in-training **42**
Brown, Tommy 129
Broz, Josip (Marshal Tito) 177, 204
Brugioni, Dino 211
Brussels, Belgium 177, 197
Buchanan, Charles 140
Buchenwald concentration camp 211

C

Bückeburg, Germany 25
Buckner, Simon Bolivar, Jr. 246
Budapest, Hungary 176, 205
Bulgaria 19, 53, 177, 204, 205
Bulge, Battle of the 11, **11**, 176, 177, 198–199, **199**
Bulldog, H.M.S. 128, 129
Buna-Gona, Battle of (1943) 69, 108, 109
Bunker Hill, U.S.S. 246, **247**
Burma
as British colony 76, **76**
fight to reclaim 214, 215, 234–235, **234–235**
Japanese invasion 69, 79, 86, **86**, 87, 215, 230
maps 232, 234, 235
see also China-Burma-India theater
Butaritari, Makin Atoll, Gilbert Islands 218, 219
Byron D. Benson (oil tanker) **127**

C

Caen, France 176–177, 184, 185
Calais, France 176, 178–180, **179**, 184
California, U.S.S. 84
Callaghan, Daniel 104, 105
Capa, Robert 182
Carlson, Evans 106, **106**
Caroline Islands 69, 215, 217
Cassino, Italy 115, 148–149, **149**
Cavalla, U.S.S. 229
Cham, Germany 155
Chamberlain, Neville 26, 27, 42
Chambois, France **189**
Chennault, Claire 214, 230, 234
Cherbourg, France 176, 184, 185
Chiang Kai-shek 74, 75, 86, 230
China
Japanese occupation 68, **68**, 69, 70, 72, **74–75**, 74–75, 230
western imperialism 76
China-Burma-India theater 214, 230–235, **231**, **232**, **234–235**
Chindits (Indian commandos) 230, 234, **234**
Choltitz, Dietrich von 192
Chuikov, Vasily 168, 209
Chungking, China 74, **74**
Churchill, Winston
in air-raid helmet 43
Allied bombing raids 153, 161
Battle of Britain 48
Berlin, Germany 206
doubts about Stalin 207
Dunkirk evacuation 38
French Vichy poster **115**
Italian campaign 140
North African campaign 114, 132, 134, 139
Operation Dragoon 191
RAF bombing force 50
SOE 116
Tehran Conference (1943) 115
on truth in wartime 180
U-boats, fear of 122
U.S. entry into war 82
victory, resolve concerning 42, 113, 114
Yalta Conference 176, 207
Clark, Mark Wayne 115, 146, 149, 151
Coastwatchers 69, 100
Colditz Castle, Germany **14**, 15, **15**
Cologne, Germany 160, 161, 201
Comet Line 114, 118, 119
Concentration and extermination camps
Auschwitz 173, 176, 210, **210**, 211
Birkenau **210**, 210–211
Buchenwald 211
Dachau 211
"Final Solution" 114, 172–173, **172–173**
gas chambers 115
inmates working on V-2 missiles 195
Kristallnacht internees 19
Treblinka 115
see also Holocaust
Coral Sea, Battle of the (1942) 69, 94, **94**, 95, 108
Corregidor, Philippines 69, **88**, 240
Coventry, England 50
Crete (island), Greece 19, 53–55, **54**, **55**
Crimea 19, **115**, 164, 165
Curl, Vincent 214, 232
Cyclops (British freighter) 126
Czechoslovakia
emergence 21
escape map 156
German occupation of 18, 19, 26, **26**
resistance movement 115, 116, 177

D

D-Day
Allied casualties 176, 182
invasion map 180
landing force *174–175*, 178, **182**
map 182–183
mapmaking 12, 14
plans for 178

reconnaissance maps endpapers
see also Normandy, Allied invasion
Dachau concentration camp 211
Daladier, Édouard 26
Darlan, Jean 115, 139
Davis, Benjamin, Jr. 158, **158**
De Gaulle, Charles 36, 114, 192
Declaration of the United Nations 114
Denmark, German invasion 18, 32, 33
Dewey, George 68
DeWitt, John 92
Dieppe Raid (1942) **112–113**, 115, **120**, 120–121
Dönitz, Karl **124**
Atlantic, war in 122, 124, 126, 225
Atlantic, withdrawal from 114, 129
as Reich chancellor 177
surrender 177, 208
Donovan, William 233
Doodlebugs *see* V-1 guided missiles
Doolittle, James 69, 90, **90**
Doolittle Raid 69, 90, **90**, 91, **91**
Doorman, Karel 86
Douglas bombers 97, **97**, **222**
Dresden, Germany **161**, 177
Dumais, Lucien 120
Dutch East Indies 68, 76, **77**, 79, 86, 87
Dykers, Thomas 225

E

Eaker, Ira 153, 158
Eastern Solomons, Battle of the (1942) 69, 104, **105**
Egypt 114, 131, 134
Eichelberger, Robert 108, 240
Eifler, Carl 214, 232, **232**
Eisenhower, Dwight D.
Berlin, Germany 177, 206
Bulge, Battle of the 198
Italian campaign 140
Operation Dragoon 191
Operation Overlord 176, 178, **178**, 182
Operation Torch 138, 139, **139**
Paris, liberation of 192
West Wall, pursuit to 196, 200
El Agheila, Libya 114, 130, 131
El Alamein, Battles of (1942) 114, 115, 130, 133–137, **135**, **136**, **137**
England *see* Great Britain
Enigma cipher machines 115, 122, 128–129, **128–129**, 134
Eniwetok, Marshall Islands 215, 217
Enola Gay (B-29) **215**, 250
Enterprise, U.S.S.
commander 90
Kwajalein 68
Midway, Battle of 96, 97, 99
reconnaissance 218
Solomons Islands 104, 105, **105**
warplanes, delivery of 82
Escape maps **9**, 14, 15, 156–157
Esso oil company, war maps 12
Estonia 18, 30, 61
Ethiopia, Italian invasion 19, 22, **22**
Extermination camps *see* Concentration and extermination camps

F

Falaise, France 177, **188–189**, 189
Fasson, Anthony 129, **129**
Finland 18, 19, 28, 30, **30**, 31, **31**, 177
Fitch, Alva 89
Fitch, Aubrey 94
Fletcher, Frank 94, 96
Flying Tigers 230, **230**
Foch, Ferdinand 40
France
alliances 21
Allied bombing raids 153
declaration of war 28
fall of 18, 40, **40**, 41
German invasion 18, 35–36, **37**, 38, 40, 41
map of escape routes 118
Panzer Corps, map of 36
postwar occupation of Germany 206
Vichy government 18, 40, 115, **115**, 116
see also French resistance
Franco, Francisco 19, 20, 22, **23**, 117
French resistance 114, **116**, 116–119, **117**, **118–119**, 119, 186–187, **186–187**, 192, 193
Freyberg, Bernard 54, 55
Fuchida, Mitsuo 82

G

Garby-Czerniawski, Roman **181**
Gavin, James 141
George, David Lloyd 20
Germany
Allied bombing raids 50, **51**, 114, **152–153**, 152–153, 160–161, **161**

destruction of 204–211
forced labor 116
maps 28, 117, 156–157, 206
postwar divisions 176, 206, 207
prelude to war 20, 28
Tripartite Pact 19, 68, 69, **69**
unconditional surrender 177, 208
World War I 20
see also Hitler, Adolf; specific campaigns
Gilbert Islands 214, 216, 218–219, **218–219**
Goebbels, Joseph 19, **19**, 177
Gordon, Nathan Green 223
Göring, Hermann 38, **44**, 46, 144
Grazier, Colin 129, **129**
Great Britain
Declaration of the United Nations 114
declaration of war 28
Far East, colonies in 76, 86
Germany, postwar occupation of 206, 207
Washington Naval Treaty (1922) 69
see also specific campaigns
Greece 19, 52, **52**, 53, 156, 177
Grosvenor, Gilbert 106
Guadalcanal
coastwatchers 69
Japanese casualties **69**, **103**
land battle 11, 69, 100, **100**
maps 101, 102, 103, 105
naval battle 69, 101, 104, 105, **105**
Operation I-Go 111
relics 102, **102**, 103
Yamamoto's death 12, 69, 110–111
Guam 67, 69, 82, 214, 215, 217, 227
Guderian, Heinz 36, 40, 41, 58, 62
Guérisse, Albert-Marie (Patrick O'Leary) 118, 119, 120
Gustav Line (Winter Line) 115, 146, 147, 148–149, 151

H

HA-19 (Japanese mini-submarine) 84, **84**
Haile Selassie, Emperor (Ethiopia) 22
Halder, Franz 48, 58
Hall, Virginia 186, **186**
Halsey, William "Bull"
Guadalcanal 100, 104
Leyte, Philippines 236, 238, 239
Operation Cartwheel 214, 216, 217
Pearl Harbor, vengeance for 90
Hamaguchi, Osachi 70
Hamburg, Germany 115, 161
Hardegan, Reinhard 124, 126
Harris, Arthur 153, 155, 161
Hata, Shunroku 76
Hawaii 68, 92
see also Pearl Harbor
Henderson, Lofton 100
Henry Stimson 250
Heydrich, Reinhard 60, 114, 115, 116, 172, **172**
Hill, Louis 158
Himmler, Heinrich 25, 60, **172**, 211
Hirohito, Emperor (Japan) 70, **71**
assumption of power 69, 70
China, invasion of 70, 74
postwar fate 248
Saipan, importance of 227
surrender 215, **215**, 250
war against U.S., authorization for 69, 80
war against U.S., efforts to avoid 79
Hiroshima, Japan 215, 243, 250, **250**
Hiryu, I.J.N. 96, 97, **98**, 99
Hite, Robert **91**
Hitler, Adolf
assassination attempt 177, 189
background 18
Britain, Battle of 42, 44, 48, 50
Bulge, Battle of the 176, 198, 199
Dunkirk and 36, 38
France, fall of 40, **40**
Franco and 117
Führerbunker, Berlin 208, **209**
German loss of faith in 161
Holocaust 60, 172
Italian campaign 146
Kharkov, Second Battle of 166
Kursk, Battle of 171
"Last Appeal to Reason" 42, **42**
Mussolini and 146
nonaggression pact (1939) 28
Normandy invasion and 178, 180, 188, 189
North African campaign 131, 132, 137, 139
Operation Barbarossa 12, 19, 30, 53, 54, 57, 58, 62, 64, 164, 166, 172
Operation Sea Lion 18, 19, 48
Paris, France and 192
Poland, invasion of 28, 172
prelude to war 20, 21, 22, 26
racial dogma 25

rallies 25, **25**
rise to power 19
Soviet Union, invasion by 205
Stalingrad offensive 115, 168
suicide 177, 208, 209
as Teutonic Knight **18**
U.S., declaration of war on 19
V-1 guided missiles 195
World War I 20
Hitler Youth **24**, 25
Hodges, Courtney 189
Hoepner, Erich 62
Holocaust
by bullets 60–61, **60–61**
"Final Solution" 114, 172–173, **172–173**
maps 61, 173
see also Concentration and extermination
camps
Homosexuals 172
Hong Kong, Japanese invasion 67, 69, 82
Honshu (island), Japan 248, 249
Hoover, J. Edgar 92
Horii, Tomitaro 108
Hornet, U.S.S. 69, 90, **90**, 96, 97, 99, 104
Hoth, Hermann 36, 40, 41, 58, 170, 171
Hungary 19, 28, 53, 176, 204, 205
Hunger Plan 60
Hürtgen Forest 11, 177, 197

I

Ichiki, Kiyono 102, 103
I.G. Farben 210, **210**, 211
Iizuka, Tokuji 80
Ilu, Battle of the (1942) 102, **103**
India 76, 86, 234, 235
see also China-Burma-India theater
Indochina 69, 76, 79
Intelligence maps 162–163, **162–163**
Intrepid, U.S.S. 239, 239
Iron Bottom Sound, Solomon Islands 104, **104**,
105
Italian campaign (1943–1944) 140–151
Allied advances **146**, 146–147
Anzio to Rome 150–151, **150–151**
British landings 142–143, **142–143**
introduction 114, 140
long haul **202**, 202–203
maps 140–145, 147–149, 151, 202–203
Monte Cassino 148–149, **149**
Patton's race 144–145, **144–145**
Tuskegee Airmen 158, 159
Italy
Ethiopia, invasion of 19, 22, **22**
liberation 202
prelude to war 20
surrender 115
Tripartite Pact 19, 68, 69, **69**
Iwabuchi, Sanji 240
Iwo Jima
Allied invasion 12, **12**, 13, 214, 215, 243, 244,
245
mapping 244–245
Tokyo bombing raids from 242

J

Japan
acoustic devices **71**
Allied drive to 216–217, **216–217**
Allied secret plan 248–249
China, invasion and occupation of 68, **68**, 69,
70, 72, 74–75, **74–75**, 230
China-Burma-India theater 234, 235
defeat of 212–251
First Sino-Japanese War 68
imperialism 72–73, 76, 77
Indochina, conquest of 79
isolationism 68
Korea, annexation of 69
militarized culture 71
offensive 78–89
prelude to war 70–77
Russo-Japanese War 68
submarine fleet 225
surrender 215, **215**
Tripartite Pact 19, 68, 69, **69**
war plans 79
Washington Naval Treaty (1922) 69
see also specific campaigns
Japanese Americans, internment of 68, **92–93**,
92–93
Java Sea, Battle of the (1941) 68, 86
Jedburgh teams 186, **186**
Jews, German assault against
Kristallnacht 18, 19
Nazi racial dogma **24**, 25
Star of David emblem **19**
see also Concentration and extermination
camps; Holocaust
Jongh, Andrée "Dédée" de 114, 118, **118**, 119
Juneau, U.S.S. 104, **104**

K

Kachin warriors 214, 230, 232, **232**, **233**, 234
Kaga, I.J.N. 96, 97
Kamikaze attacks 214, **214**, **239**, 240, 246, 247,
248, **249**
Kasai, Tom and Ruth **93**
Kasserine Pass, Battle of (1943) 114
Kelly, Richard **202**
Kenney, George 215, 216, 220, 222, 223
Kent, England 194, 195
Kesselring, Albert 142, 144, 146
Kharkov, Ukraine 114–115, 164, 165, 166–167, **167**
Khrushchev, Nikita 166
Kiev, Ukraine 19, 115, 171
King, Ernest 214, 216
Kingman, Howard 213
Kinkaid, Thomas 220
Kleist, Ewald von 36, 41
Kluge, Günther von 29, 189
Koga, Mineichi 215
Köln, Germany *see* Cologne, Germany
Kondo, Nobutake 104, 105
Konev, Ivan 171, 208
Königsberg, East Prussia **204–205**
Kristallnacht 18, 19
Krueger, Walter 236, 240
Küchler, Georg von 29
Kumm, Otto 64
Kunming, China 215, 230, **230**
Kuribayashi, Tadamichi 214, 244
Kurita, Takeo 238, 239
Kursk, Battle of (1943) 114, 115, **170–171**,
170–171
Kursk, Ukraine 114, 164
Kusaka, Ryunosuke 229
Kwajalein, Marshall Islands 68, 90, 215, 217
Kyushu (island), Japan 215, 248, 249

L

Lane, Earl **159**
Lanphier, Thomas, Jr. 12, 111, 111
"Last Appeal to Reason" (Hitler) 42, **42**
Lattre de Tassigny, Jean de 190
Latvia 18, 30, 61
Lawton, Henry **77**
Layton, Edwin 90, 111
League of Nations 18, 20, 69, 70
Lee, Willis 104, 105
Leeb, Wilhelm Ritter von 35, 58
LeMay, Curtis 243
Lenin, Vladimir 18, 21, 30
Leningrad, Soviet Union 19, **56**, 58, **59**, 115, 164,
171
Lexington, U.S.S. 82, 90, 94, **94**, 95, 96, 229
Leyte, Philippines 214, 215, **236**, 236–239, **238**,
239
Libya **130**, 131, 132, **132**
Lindbergh, Charles 19
Liscome Bay, U.S.S. 216
List, Wilhelm 29
Lithuania 18, 30, 61
Livorno, Italy 155, **155**
Lockwood, Charles 225
London, England 11, 44, 46, **46**, 47, **47**, 195, **195**
Low Countries, German invasion 18, 34–35
Lübeck, Germany 114, 161
Lucas, John 151
Luxembourg, German invasion 18, 35
Luzon, Philippines 88, 215, 240
Lviv, Poland-Ukraine 60

M

MacArthur, Douglas
Japan, drive against 214, 216, 217, **217**, 249
New Guinea 100, 101, 108, 214, 215, 216, 217,
220–221, 222
Papua 100, 101, 108
Philippines 69, 88, 89, 217, 220, 225
Philippines, return to 214, 215, **236**, 236–242
Maginot Line 35, **40**, 41
Makin Atoll, Gilbert Islands **212–213**, 214, 216,
217, 218, 219
Malaya
as British colony 76
Japanese attack 67, 68, 69, 79, 82, 86, 87
Manchuria (Manchukuo) 68, 69, 70, **72**, 215, 250
Manhattan Project 68, 214
Manila, Philippines 215, 240, **241**
Mannerheim, Carl Gustaf 30
Mannheim, Germany 50, **161**
Manstein, Erich von 171
Mao Zedong 74, 75
Maquis (resistance fighters) 116, **117**, 186, **186**,
187
Mariana Islands
Allied bombing raids from 214, 215, **242**, 250
Allied invasion 214, 215, **215**, 217, 225, 226–
227, **226–227**
Japanese invasion 67, 69, 82, 214

Marseille, France 116, 119, 190, 191
Marshall, George 114, 140, 191, 250
Marshall Islands 68, 69, 90, 215, 217
Matsuoka, Yosuke 68
Mauldin, Bill 202
McAuliffe, Anthony 198
Meiji, Emperor (Japan) 68, 70
Merrill, Frank 230
Merrill's Marauders 230, 234
Messerschmitt aircraft **10**, 42, 44, **45**, 159
Messina, Italy 144, 145
MI9 (British agency) 118, 119, 120, 157
Michael I, King (Romania) 205
Midway, Battle of (1942) **68**, **96–97**, 96–99
maps 97, 98
secret report 99, **99**
U.S. victory 69, 96, 97
Yamamoto's plan 81, 90, 94, 96
Mikawa, Gunichi 104
Mikuma, I.J.N. 97, **97**
Minneapolis, U.S.S. **212–213**
Minsk, Belarus 19, 176, 205
Missouri, U.S.S. 215, **249**, 250
Mitchell, John 111
Mitscher, Marc **90**, 215, 229, 246
Model, Walther 164, 170, 171, 200, 201
Monte Cassino, Italy 115, 148–149, **149**, 159
Montgomery, Bernard "Monty"
Antwerp, Belgium 177, 196, 197
Brussels, Belgium 177, 197
Italian campaign 115, 141, 142, 144, 145, 146
from Normandy to the Rhine 176–177, 188,
189, 196, 197, 200, 201
North African campaign 115, 134, 135, **136**,
137, 139
Operation Goodwood 176–177
Operation Market Garden 196, 200
Operation Overlord 178, **178**, 180, 184, 185
West Wall, pursuit to 200
Morgan, Frederick 178
Morocco 115, 138, 139
Mortain, France 177, 188, 189
Moscow, Soviet Union 12, 19, **57**, 58, 62–63,
62–63, 164
Moulin, Jean 114, 116
Mulberries (artificial harbors) 184
Munich, Germany 50
Mussolini, Benito **22**
arrest 114, 115, 146
execution 177, 202
fall from power 145, 146
as German puppet 115, 146, **146**
prelude to war 20, 22, 26
support for 18
Mutaguchi, Renya 215, 234, 235
Myitkyina, Burma 215, 231, 232, 233, 234

N

Nagasaki, Japan 215, 243, 250, **251**
Nagumo, Chuichi 80, 81, 96, 97
Nanking, China 69, 74, **75**
Nautilus, U.S.S. 218, 219, 225
Netherlands 18, 35, 76, **119**, 177
New Britain *see* Rabaul, New Britain
New Georgia 101, 216
New Guinea
Allied invasion 100, 101, 108, 214, 215, 216,
217, **220–221**, 220–223, **222**
Japanese invasion 68, 87
maps 109, 221, 222, 223
POW execution **214**
survival charts 222, 223
New Ireland 223
Neyer, Avraham **172**
Nijmegen, Netherlands 196, 200
Nimitz, Chester
Coral Sea, Battle of the 94
Guadalcanal 100, 106, **106**
Japan, drive against 214, 216, 217, **217**, 249
Midway, Battle of 68, 96, 99
Pacific Fleet command 68, 90
Philippines 215, 236
Yamamoto's death 111
Nishimura, Shoji 238, 239
Normandy, Allied invasion 178–187
beachhead expansion 184–185, **184–185**
D-Day **174–175**, 176, 178, **182**, 182–183,
184
deception campaign 178, 180–181, **180–181**,
184
French resistance and 186–187, **186–187**
introduction 12, 14, 178–179, **178–179**
maps 179–183, 185, 187, endpapers
Operation Cobra 177, 184, 189
planning 178, **178**, 179
postponement 115, 176, 182
North African campaign 130–139
British commandos 131
El Alamein 114, 115, 130, 133–137, **135**, **136**,
137

introduction 114, 131
maps 130–139
Operation Torch 138–139, **138–139**
prisoners of war **130**, 131
Rommel's big push **132**, 132–133
Tuskegee Airmen 158, 159
Norway **16–17**, 18, **32**, 32–33, **33**
Nuclear weapons 68, 214, 215, 243, 248, 250, **250**,
251
Nuremberg, Germany **25**, 61

O

Office of Strategic Services (OSS)
authorization 115, 162
China-Burma-India theater 214, 230, **232**,
232–233
escape maps and gear 157
French resistance and **117**, 186
Italy, agents in **202**
maps 157, 162–163, 187, 202–203, 233, 248
Okinawa 214, 214, 215, 242, 243, 246–247,
246–247
Oklahoma, U.S.S. **81**, 82, 83
Oldendorf, Jesse 238, 239
O'Leary, Patrick 118, 119, 120
Omaha Beach **174–175**, 180, **182**, 182–183, 184,
184, endpapers
Operation Anvil *see* Operation Dragoon
Operation Bagration 176, 204–205
Operation Barbarossa 56–65
authorization for 19
Baku 115, 164, 165, 166
carnage in the "meat-grinder" 64, **64**, **65**
Hitler's resolve 30, 62, 64
Holocaust 60–61, **60–61**
invasion **58**, 58–59, **59**
maps 59, 63, 64–65
Moscow 12, **57**, 58, 62–63, **62–63**, 164
plans for 53, 56, **56–57**
postponement 54
Soviet resolve 30, 58, 62, 164, **165**
Soviet resurgence 164–171
Operation Blue 164, 165
Operation Bodyguard 178, 180–181, **180–181**,
184
Operation Cartwheel 214, 216, 217
Operation Citadel 171
Operation Cobra 177, 184, 189
Operation Coronet 249
Operation Downfall 248, 249
Operation Dragoon 177, 190–191, **190–191**
Operation Drumbeat 114, 122, 125, 126, **127**
Operation Dynamo 38, 39
Operation Goodwood 176–177
Operation Heydrich 115, **172**
Operation Husky *see* Sicily, Allied invasion
Operation I-Go 110, 111
Operation Market Garden 177, 196, 196, 200
Operation Olympic 249
Operation Overlord *see* Normandy, Allied
invasion
Operation Sea Lion 12, 18, 19, 44, 48–49
Operation Supercharge 137
Operation Torch 138–139, **138–139**
Operation Uranus 168
Operation Vengeance 110–111
Oradour-sur-Glane, France 176, 186
OSS *see* Office of Strategic Services
Ozawa, Jisaburo 227, 228, 229, 238, 239

P

P-47 Thunderbolts 158, **159**
P-51 Mustangs **114**, 115, 153, **158**
Palermo, Italy 144, 145
Papua 69, 87, 100, 108, **108**, 109, 111
Paris, France 18, 40, **40**, 177, 192–193, **192–193**
Patch, Alexander 190
Patton, George
Bulge, Battle of the 198
Italian campaign 138, 141, **144**, 144–145
from Normandy to the Rhine 177, 188,
189
Operation Bodyguard 180, **180**, 181
Operation Torch 138, 139, **139**
reprimand and reassignment 146
West Wall, pursuit to 196, 197, 200
Paulus, Friedrich 114, 166, 168
Pearl Harbor, cryptanalysts 111
Pearl Harbor, Japanese attack on
car plate **69**
go-ahead for 79
Japanese forces 80, **80**
maps 80–81, 82, 83, 84, 85
relics 84, **84**, **85**
surprise attack 68, 69, 82
U.S. wreckage **66–67**, **81**, 82, 83, 83
Peenemünde, Germany 195
Peers, William 233
Percival, Arthur 86
Perry, Matthew 68

Pétain, Philippe 18, 40
Petard, H.M.S. 129
Philippine Sea, Battle of the 215, **228–229**, 228–229
Philippines
  Allied invasion 217, 220, 225
  Bataan Death March 89, **89**
  Corregidor 69, **88**, 240
  Japanese invasion 67, 69, 79, 82, 87, 215
  Leyte 214, 215, **236**, 236–239, **238**, **239**
  Luzon 88, 215, 240
  MacArthur's evacuation from 69
  MacArthur's return 214, 215, **236**, 236–242
  maps 88
  Spanish-American War 68, 76, **77**
Playing cards, maps on **9**
Ploesti, Romania **2–3**, 115, 153, 205
Poirier, Robert 211
Poland
  escape map 156
  German invasion 18, **18**, 19, 28, **28**, 29, **29**, 172
  Holocaust 60, **60**, **61**, 172, **172**
  postwar 206
  resistance movement 116
  Soviet occupation 28, 204, **204**, 205
  World War I 21
Popov, Dusko **181**
Potsdam Conference 206, 215, 248
Prisoners of war
  atrocities against 60
  Bataan Death March 89, **89**
  in concentration camps 172
  Doolittle Raid 90, 91, **91**
  escape maps and gear 14, 15, 156–157, **157**
  escapes **14**, **15**
  executions of **214**
  Falaise, France 188–189
  North Africa **130**, 131
  Philippines 89, **89**, 240, **241**
  release to resume fighting 149
Propaganda maps 11
Pujol Garcia, Juan 180, **181**

Q

Quincy, U.S.S. **104**
Quisling, Vidkun 32

R

Rabaul, New Britain
  Allied air strikes 101, 214, 216, 217
  Japanese control 68, 100, 101, 103, 110, **110**, 111
Radio **19**, **117**, 186, **187**
Raeder, Erich 48
Rangoon, Burma 69, 215, 235
Reconnaissance photography 154, **154**
Redfin, U.S.S. 225, 229
Reichenau, Walter von 29, 60
Reinhardt, Georg Hans 36
Remagen, Germany 177, 200
Resistance movements **116**, 116–119
  Czechoslovakia 115, 116, 177
  prisoners of war, assistance to 157, **157**
  Yugoslavia 157, **157**
  see also French resistance
Reynaud, Paul 40
Rhine River 176, 177, **200**, 200–201
Ritchie, Neil 132, 134
Rochefort, Joseph 90
Rogers, Lee **241**
Rol-Tanguy, Henri 192
Roma 172
Romania 19, 28, 53, 177, 204, 205
Rome, Italy 18, 115, 151, **151**, 154–155, 176, 202
Rommel, Erwin
  France, tank warfare in 36, 40
  maps 132–135
  Normandy invasion and 178, 179, **179**, 182

North African campaign 10, 114, 115, 130–135, 132, 137, 139
  on stopping the enemy 175, 182
  suicide 177, 189
Roosevelt, Franklin D.
  death 215, 248
  declaration of war 82
  as international good neighbor 19
  Italian campaign 140
  Japan, embargo against 69
  Japan, war against 214, **217**
  Japanese Americans, internment of 68, 92
  Manhattan Project 68
  North African campaign 139
  OSS, authorization of 115, 162
  Pearl Harbor attack and 79, 84
  Philippines campaign 215
  Tehran Conference (1943) 115
  Two-Ocean Navy Act 69
  unconditional surrender, call for 114
  victory, resolve concerning 113
  Yalta Conference 176, 207
Roosevelt, Theodore 68
Ruhr region, Germany 177, 196, 200, 201
Rundstedt, Gerd von 29, 35, 36, 58, 178, 189
Russia (post-revolution) *see* Soviet Union
Russia (pre-revolution) 12, 18, **19**, 20, 22
Russo-Japanese War 68
Rzhev, Soviet Union 64

S

Saint-Lô, France 177, 184, **185**, 188, 189
Saipan, Mariana Islands 214, 215, **215**, 217, **226**, 226–227, **242**
Salerno, Italy 115, 146, **146**, 147
Sangamon, U.S.S. **214**
Santa Cruz Islands, Battle of the (1942) 69
Saratoga, U.S.S. 90
Savo Island, Battle of (1942) 69, 104, **104**
Schmidt, Harry 245
Sergueiew, Nathalie "Lily" **181**
Sevastopol, Crimea 115, 164, 165
Shanghai, China 69, 70, 72, 74, **74**, **75**
Shaw, U.S.S. **66–67**
Shelburne Line 118, 119, 120
Shikoku (island), Japan 249
Shima, Kiyohide 238, 239
Shoho, I.J.N. 94, 95
Shokaku, I.J.N. 94, 95, 229
Sicily, Allied invasion 140, 140–145, **141**
  British landings 142–143, **142–143**
  chronology 115
  introduction 114
  maps 4–5, 140–145
  Patton's race 144–145, **144–145**
Siegfried Line *see* West Wall
Sims, U.S.S. 94, 95
Singapore 68, 86
Slaughter, Bob 182
Slim, William 234, 235
SOE (Special Operations Executive) 115, 116, **117**, 186
Solomon Islands
  Allied advance 214, 216, 217
  Japanese invasion 68, 87
  maps 101, 104, 105, 110
  naval battles 69, 104–105, **104–105**
  Operation Vengeance 110
  Tulagi 69, 94, 95, 100
Sorge, Richard 56, 62
Soryu, I.J.N. 96, 97
Soviet Union
  Berlin, Battle of (1945) 208, **208**, 209
  Declaration of the United Nations 114
  Finland, invasion of 18, 28, 30, **30**, 31, **31**
  formation of 20
  Germany, invasion of 198, 205
  Germany, postwar occupation of 206, 207
  Holocaust 61

North Central Europe, operations in 204
OSS intelligence maps 162
Poland, occupation of 28
  resurgence 164–171
South Central Europe, operations in 204
Spanish Civil War 22
sphere of influence 28
  see also Russia; *specific campaigns*
Spanish-American War (1898) 68, 76
Spanish Civil War 19, 20, 22, 23
Special Operations Executive *see* SOE
Speer, Albert 40
Spencer, U.S.C.G.C. **114**
Sprague, Clifton 238, 239
Spruance, Raymond 96, 214, 215, 227, 229
Stalin, Joseph **30**
  atomic bomb and 215, 248
  Berlin, fall of 177, 208
  Bessarabia, control of 53
  Eastern Europe, annexation of 205
  German invasion of Russia 18, 30, 56, 58, 62, 64
  nonaggression pact (1939) 28
  rise to power 18
  secrecy 56
  Soviet resurgence 166, 168
  Spanish Civil War 22
  Tehran Conference (1943) 115
  Winter War (1939–1940) 177
  Yalta Conference 176, 207
Stalingrad, Soviet Union 115, 164, 165, 166, 168–169, **168–169**
Stilwell, Joseph 86, **87**, 214, 215, 230, 232, 234
Student, Kurt 54, 55
Stuka dive-bombers **18**, **29**, 35
Stumme, Georg 137
Submarine warfare 224–225, **224–225**
  see also U-boats
Sudetenland 19, 26, 27, **27**
Sullivan brothers 104, **104**
Sultan, Daniel 235
Supermarine Spitfires 42, 44, 154, **194**
Suribachi, Mount, Iwo Jima **12**, 244, **244**
Sweeney, Charles 250

T

Tanaka, Raizo 104, 105
Tarawa Atoll 213, 214, **215**, 216, **216**, 217, 218, **218**, 219, **219**
Tehran Conference (1943) 115
Tenaru, Battle of the (1942) 102, **103**
Thailand, Japanese invasion 69, 82, 87
Tibbets, Paul 215, **215**, 250
Timoshenko, Semyon 30, 31, 62, 166
Tinian, Mariana Islands 214, 215, **215**, 217, 227, 250
Tito, Marshal 177, 204
Tobruk, Libya 115, 130, 131, 132, 133, 134
Todd, John 241
Tojo, Hideki 79
Tokyo, Japan
  Allied drive to 216–217, **216–217**
  bombing of 69, 90, **90**, 214, 215, 227, **242**, 243
Toulon, France 190, 191
Toyama, Japan **243**
Toyoda, Soemu 238
Treblinka extermination camp 115
Tripartite Pact 19, 68, 69, **69**
Truk, Caroline Islands 215, 217
Truman, Harry S. 215, 248, 249
Truscott, Lucian 151, 190, 191
Tulagi, Solomon Islands 69, 94, 95, 100
Tunisia 114, 139, 140
Tuskegee Airmen 158–159, **158–159**

U

U-boats
  in American waters 11, 115

Atlantic, Battle of the 114, **122**, 122–129, **123**, **127**, **128**
  attacks on **114**, 128
  charts and instruments 124–125, **124–125**
  Mediterranean Sea 132
  torpedoes **122**, 125, **125**, **126**
Ukraine 21, **56**, **57**, 58, 60, **60**
United Kingdom *see* Great Britain
United States
  Declaration of the United Nations 114
  Germany, postwar occupation of 206, 207
  segregated forces **115**, 158
  Spanish-American War 76, **77**
  Washington Naval Treaty (1922) 69
  see also specific campaigns
Ushijima, Mitsuru 246

V

V-1 guided missiles 176, 194, **194**, 195
V-2 ballistic missiles 177, 195, **195**
Vaghi, Joseph 182
Vandegrift, Alexander 102, 106
Versailles, Treaty of (1919) 18, 20, 32
Vichy government 18, 40, 115, **115**, 116
Vienna, Austria 177, 206
Vietinghoff, Heinrich von 202
Vladivostok, Soviet Union 72, 73, 91
Voronezh, Soviet Union 164, 166
Vraciu, Alexander **229**

W

Wake Island, Japanese attack on 67, 69, 82
Wannsee Conference 114
Warsaw, Poland 18, 176, 177, 205
Warsaw Ghetto, Poland 114, 115, 172, **172**, 173, **173**
Warspite, H.M.S. **140**
Washington Naval Treaty (1922) 69
West Virginia, U.S.S. 83, **83**
West Wall (Siegfried Line) 11, 196–197, 200
Weygand, Maxime 40
Wingate, Orde 230, 234
Winter Line (Gustav Line) 115, 146, 147, 148–149, 151
Winter War (1939–1940) 30, **30**, 31, **31**, 177
Women's Auxiliary Air Force (WAAF) **8**
World War I 18, 20, **20**, 21, **21**, 40

Y

Yalta Conference 176, 207
Yamakaze, I.J.N. **224**, 225
Yamamoto, Isoroku
  background 68
  with Combined Fleet officers **79**
  Coral Sea, Battle of the 94
  death 12, 69, 110–111
  Midway, Battle of 81, 90, 94, 96
  Operation I-Go 110, 111
  Pearl Harbor, attack on 68, 79, 80, 82
  U.S. intelligence on 90
Yamashita, Tomoyuki 240
Yamato, I.J.N. 238, 246
Yorktown, U.S.S.
  Coral Sea, Battle of the 94, 95
  Midway, Battle of **68**, 69, 96, **96**, 97, 98, 99
  in Pacific Fleet 90
Yoshikawa, Takeo 80
Yugoslavia 19, 21, 52, **52**, 53, **53**, 157, **157**, 177, 204

Z

Zhing Htaw Naw (Kachin chief) 232
Zhukov, Georgi 62, **63**, 64, 208
Zuikaku, I.J.N. 94, 95, 238, **238**
Zyklon-B **115**, 173

Since 1888, the National Geographic Society has funded more than 13,000 research, exploration, and preservation projects around the world. National Geographic Partners distributes a portion of the funds it receives from your purchase to National Geographic Society to support programs including the conservation of animals and their habitats.

National Geographic Partners
1145 17th Street NW
Washington, DC 20036-4688 USA

Get closer to National Geographic explorers and photographers, and connect with our global community. Join us today at nationalgeographic.com/join

For rights or permissions inquiries, please contact National Geographic Books Subsidiary Rights: bookrights@natgeo.com

ISBN: 978-1-4262-1971-9

Printed in Malaysia

20/IVM/2

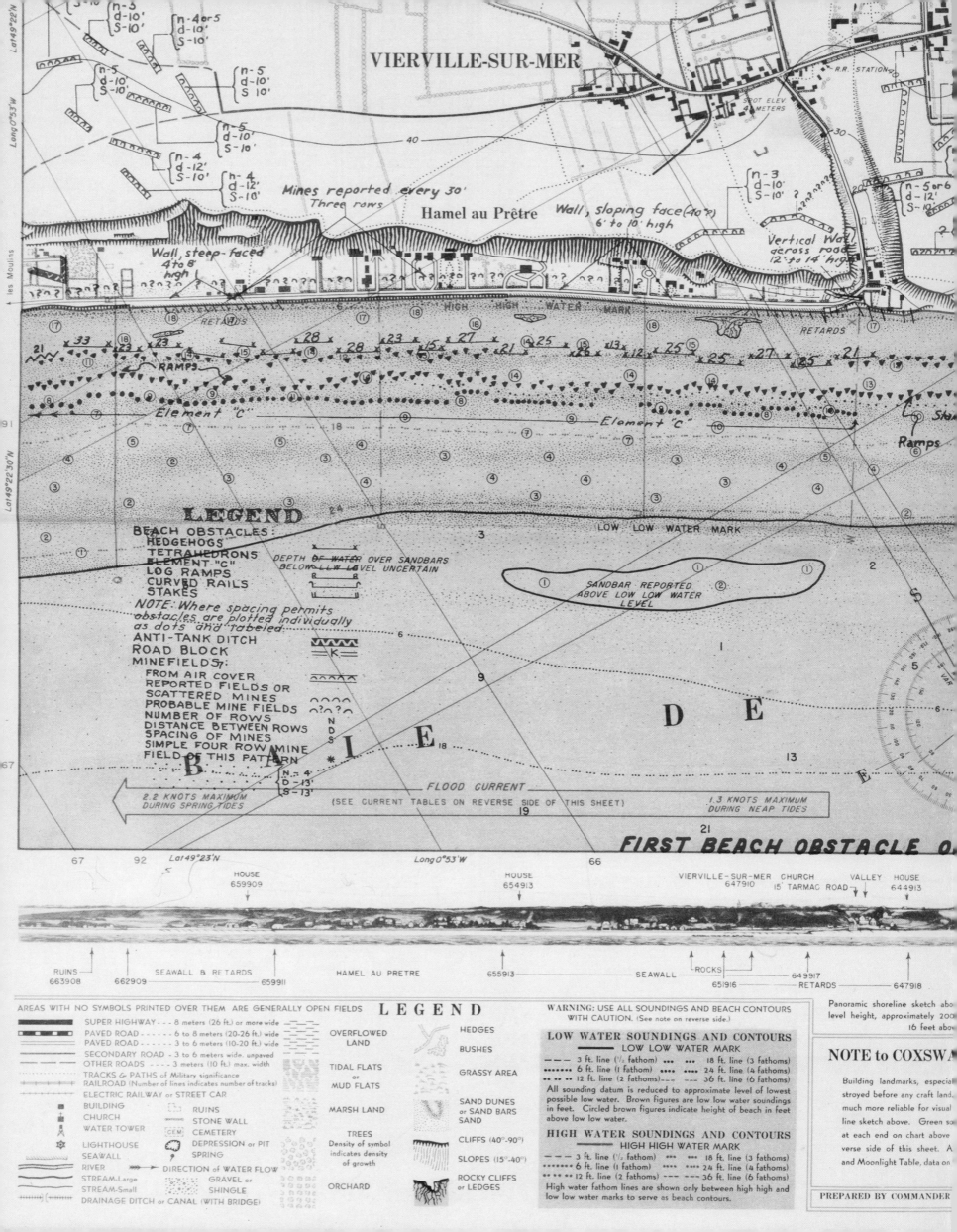